A DIFFERENT VISION

Since the civil rights movement of the 1960s, public discourse on race relations has tended to focus on political and social inequality rather than the economic impact of racism. *A Different Vision: Race and Public Policy* redresses this imbalance.

A Different Vision brings together for the first time, the ideas, philosophies and interpretations of North America's leading African American economists. Presented in two volumes, each of the thirty-five chapters focuses on various aspects of the social and economic experiences of African Americans, past and present. The volumes thus present a unique perspective on the most important contemporary economic issues. **Volume 2** includes:

- an analysis of urban poverty;
- discussion of aspects of racial inequality and public policy, including affirmative action and self-help solutions;
- an examination of the theory and method which underlie public policy;
- studies of the impact of racism on the socio-economic status of African Americans; and
- an accessible approach which is free of technical jargon.

Volume 1, *African American Economic Thought,* assesses the contribution and influence of major African American economic philosophies and economists, and provides a detailed discussion of the economics of race and gender.

The authors' findings clearly illustrate that African American economists do indeed have "a different vision." These volumes demonstrate that the impact of racial inequality is immense and race is an important variable in every sphere of American life. By investigating its various dimensions, the authors arrive at a common conclusion – race matters.

Thomas D. Boston is Professor of Economics at Georgia Institute of Technology. He is editor of *The Review of Black Political Economy.* He previously served as a Senior Economist to the Joint Economic Committee of Congress and was President of the National Economic Association. He has lectured and published widely on issues of race and economics.

A DIFFERENT VISION

Race and Public Policy,
Volume 2

Edited by Thomas D. Boston

London and New York

First published 1997
by Routledge
11 New Fetter Lane, London EC4P 4EE

Simultaneously published in the USA and Canada
by Routledge
29 West 35th Street, New York, NY 10001

Typeset in Garamond by
Pure Tech India Ltd, Pondicherry
Printed and bound in Great Britain by Clays Ltd, St. Ives PLC

British Library Cataloguing in Publication Data
A catalogue record for this book is available from the British Library

Library of Congress Cataloging in Publication Data
A catalogue record for this book has been requested

ISBN 0–415–09591–3 (hbk)
ISBN 0–415–12716–5 (pbk)

To Catherine Laverne Ross
My Best Friend, Closest Colleague, and Wife

CONTENTS

Part III Theory and method

ILLUSTRATIONS

FIGURES

TABLES

CONTRIBUTORS

Richard America
Adjunct Lecturer
School of Business Administration
Georgetown University
Georgetown, Virginia

Bernard E. Anderson
Assistant Secretary of Labor
U.S. Department of Labor
Washington, DC

Ronald Bailey
Professor of African American Studies
South Carolina State University
Orangeburg, South Carolina

Willie J. Belton, Jr.
Associate Professor of Economics
School of Economics
Georgia Institute of Technology
Atlanta, Georgia

Thomas D. Boston
Professor of Economics
School of Economics
Georgia Institute of Technology
Atlanta, Georgia

Andrew F. Brimmer
Economic & Financial Consultant
Wilmear D. Barrett Professor of Economics
University of Massachusetts at Amherst
Amherst, Massachusetts

Juanita F. Carter
Assistant Dean / Undergraduate Programs
Assistant Professor / Finance Department
School of Business
Clark Atlanta University
Atlanta, Georgia

Robert Cherry
Professor of Economics
Brooklyn College
of the City of New York
New York, New York

Augustin K. Fosu
Professor of Economics
Oakland University
Rochester, Michigan

John W. Handy
Professor of Economics
Morehouse College
Atlanta, Georgia

C. Michael Henry
Economist
Institute for Social & Policy Studies
Yale University
New Haven, Connecticut

Edward D. Irons
Dean Emeritus
School of Business
Clark Atlanta University
Atlanta, Georgia

James H. Johnson, Jr.
E Maynard Adams Professor of Business, Geography & Sociology
Frank Hawkins Kenan Institute of Private Enterprise
The University of North Carolina at Chapel Hill
Chapel Hill, North Carolina

Wilhelmina A. Leigh
Senior Research Associate
Joint Center for Political and Economic Studies
Washington, DC

Patrick L. Mason
Associate Professor
Department of African Studies
Wayne State University
Detroit, Michigan

Ronald B. Mincy
Program Officer
Ford Foundation
New York, New York

Juliet E. K. Walker
Professor
Department of History
University of Illinois at Urbana
Champaign, Illinois

Warren C. Whatley
Associate Professor of Economics and of
Afro American and African Studies
Associate Dean of Graduate Studies
University of Michigan – Ann Arbor
Ann Arbor, Michigan

Stephanie Y. Wilson
Group Vice President
Art Associates Inc.
Bethesda, Maryland

PREFACE

These two volumes are designed to fill a major void in our knowledge of the African American economic experience. The chapters contained herein represent the thinking of some of America's most distinguished scholars on the topic. We have entitled the book, *A Different Vision*. As you read the various essays, you will see that the idea of a "different vision" is more than just a title. Indeed, these authors have a different set of scholarly priorities and interpretations that are grounded in the dissimilar life experiences and life chances of African Americans.

Each author was given the freedom to write on any aspect of the African American economic experience, but was asked to write in a style that is accessible to a wide audience. The contributions cover several well defined areas. These include economic philosophy and history, the political economy of race and gender, the history of African American economic thought, public policy and racial inequality, and economic method. They are organized into two volumes. Volume 1 is subtitled "African American Economic Thought" and Volume 2 is subtitled "Race and Public Policy".

This enormous undertaking has stretched over quite a long period of time. During this period, each author has graciously given of his or her time not only in developing the essays, but also in responding to editor's queries and even serving as reviewers of companion essays. This unusual level of commitment reflects the dedication of each author to the successful completion of this project.

To add a finishing touch to *A Different Vision*, we asked Atlanta artist Michael Ellison to illustrate the jacket covers of each volume. His two panel subtractive woodblock color prints, entitled "Everyday Life", capture the essence of contemporary urban black life. The background symbols and visual imagery he employs are haunting reminders of the past and present racial barriers.

We thank all contributors for their generosity. We thank the following individuals for serving as reviewers: Robert S. Browne, Robert Cherry, William Darity, Jr., Julian Ellison, Augustin K. Fosu, Herbert M. Hunter, Wilhelmina A. Leigh, Margaret C. Simms, and Stephanie Y. Wilson. Each made invaluable comments on various chapters of the two volumes. Graduate assistant Paula Stevens also provided extremely helpful editorial assistance.

This is the second time that I have had the opportunity of undertaking a project with Routledge and on each occasion, the experience has been very pleasurable. The editors have provided tremendous support and great optimism throughout. In particular, we thank Alan Jarvis, Alison Kirk and Ann King.

We hope the essays contained herein are useful to all individuals interested in learning more about the African American economic experience. Of course, a project such as this, no matter how ambitious, cannot cover all relevant areas. In this regard, we chose to sacrifice empirical and theoretical contributions for others focusing on philosophy, history, and public policy. In this way, the subject can be digested by a broader audience of readers.

Finally, we sincerely hope this project is worthy of the efforts of so many fine contributors. We thank you all.

Thomas D. Boston

1

PREAMBLE

The economic cost of discrimination against black Americans*

Andrew F. Brimmer

* * *

ANDREW FELTON BRIMMER

Dr. Andrew Felton Brimmer is President of a Washington, DC-based economic and financial consulting firm, and he serves simultaneously as Wilmer D. Barrett Professor of Economics at the University of Massachusetts-Amherst. He is also Chairman of the Presidentially-appointed Financial Control Board which oversees the fiscal affairs of the District of Columbia.

Brimmer was born in 1926 in Newellton, Louisiana, a small town located in the northeast section of the State a few miles from the Mississippi River. His family had been long-time cotton farmers who were forced off the land as the boll weevil devastated the crops.

After graduating from the local, racially segregated high school, Brimmer joined an older sister and her family in Bremerton, Washington, in 1944. During the day, he worked as an electrician's helper in the Bremerton Navy Yard where war-damaged ships were repaired. At night, he continued his education at the equivalent of a community college. He was drafted into the US Army in May 1945, and served through November 1946. Ten months of that service was in Hawaii.

In January 1947, Brimmer enrolled in the University of Washington, Seattle. He completed his undergraduate work in three years. He first studied journalism; but, half way through, he switched his major to economics earning a BA in March 1950. He continued in the field and was awarded an MA in the summer of 1951. Brimmer won a Fulbright grant for the academic year 1951–52, which enabled him to study at the Universities of Delhi and Bombay in India. Between September 1952 and June 1955 he was enrolled in the doctoral program at Harvard University. He received his PhD in economics in March 1957, with a dissertation entitled "Monetary Policy, Interest Rates, and the Investment Behavior of Life Insurance Companies."

From June 1955 through August 1958, Brimmer was an economist at the Federal Reserve Bank of New York. During three and a half months of that period, he

* Reprinted, with permission, from *Economic Perspectives on Affirmative Action*, edited by Margaret Simms (Washington, DC: Joint Center for Political and Economic Studies, 1995).

served on a three-man mission to Sudan to help that country establish its central bank. He taught economics at Michigan State University from 1958to1961. He taught money and banking and macroeconomics at the Wharton School, University of Pennsylvania, during 1961–63. On leave of absence from the University, he served as Deputy Assistant Secretary and Assistant Secretary for Economic Affairs in the US Department of Commerce, from May 1963 until early March 1966. From March 9 of that year Brimmer began a fourteen-year term as a member of the Board of Governors of the Federal Reserve System – having been appointed by President Lyndon Johnson. He served for eight and a half years. He resigned in August 1974 to return to Harvard University, where he was appointed Thomas Henry Carroll Visiting Professor in the Harvard Business School. He held that position during the period 1974–76. In 1976 he established his consulting firm.

Brimmer is a Director of a number of major corporations – including Bank of America and the Du Pont Company. He has published extensively, and is the author of several books and many articles in economic and financial journals – with the main concentrations in banking and monetary policy, international finance, and the economic status of black Americans. Brimmer states that the economic research of which he is most proud is the Testimony he prepared when he was in the US Department of Commerce which demonstrated the burden of racial segregation on interstate commerce. The US Supreme Court cited it extensively in its unanimous opinion upholding the Public Accommodations Section of the Civil Rights Act of 1964.

Brimmer has been honored a number of times by the economics profession. He was the Richard T. Ely Lecturer of the American Economic Association in 1981, and he was Distinguished Lecturer on Economics in Government of the Association (joint with the Society of Government Economists) in 1988. He was Vice President of the AEA in 1989. He served as Westerfield Lecturer of the National Economics Association in 1990. He was President of the Eastern Economics Association in 1991–92, and he was elected a Fellow in 1993. He was President Elect (1996) of the North American Economics and Finance Association.

* * *

The disparate treatment of blacks cost the American economy about $241 billion in 1993. This figure is equal to roughly 3.8 per cent of that year's gross domestic product (GDP). While part of the loss can be attributed to the lag in blacks' educational achievement, the bulk of the shortfall appears to be related to continued discrimination, which limits their access to higher-paying jobs. Furthermore, over the last quarter-century, the relative cost of discrimination seems to have risen. And, given the slow rate at which blacks are being absorbed into managerial, professional, and technical positions, the income deficit they face – and the corresponding economic cost to the nation – will probably narrow very little in the years ahead.

ECONOMIC IMPACT OF RACIAL DISCRIMINATION

The earliest assessment of the economic cost of discrimination against nonwhites in the United States was prepared by the President's Council of Economic Advisers (CEA) in 1962.[1] The CEA estimated the cost at approximately $17.8 billion, or 3.2 per cent of gross national product (GNP) – which totaled $554.9 billion in that year. (Note that GNP, the value of total production of goods and services measured at market prices, was the official measure of economic activity in use in 1962.)

In 1965, when I was assistant secretary of commerce, at my request the US Bureau of the Census made estimates of the cost of discrimination against nonwhites for the years 1949 through 1963. The Census Bureau's estimating procedure was more comprehensive than that employed earlier by the CEA. The Census Bureau's estimates sought to account for the economic losses originating from two sources: inefficiencies in the use of the labor force arising from failure to use fully the *existing* education, skills, and experience of the population, and failure to develop fully *potential* education, skills, and experience. The losses were described in terms of the gains that might accrue to GNP if discrimination were eliminated – or had been eliminated in the past. However, the Census Bureau recognized that, because the legacy of past discrimination affects the contemporary occupational, geographic, and capital structures as well as the education, training, and skills of the nonwhite labor force, the gains would accrue only over time as the labor force is upgraded and the economy adjusts.

Based on the Census Bureau's analysis described above, I estimated that discrimination against nonwhites cost about $20.1 billion in lost GNP in 1963, equal to 3.5 per cent of that year's total GNP of $583.9 billion. Roughly $11.1 billion (1.9 per cent of GNP) reflected the failure to use fully nonwhites' existing skills, and $9.0 billion (1.6 per cent of GNP) arose from the failure to improve and fully use their educational achievement.[2]

Applying the Census Bureau's technique as used in 1965, I have recently updated the estimates for the economic cost of discrimination against blacks. The detailed results for four years (1967, 1973, 1979, and 1993) are shown in Appendix Tables 1.A1 and 1.A2.

TRENDS IN THE ECONOMIC COST OF DISCRIMINATION

The figures show that, over the last twenty-five years or so, the American economy has been losing between 1.5 per cent and 2.2 per cent of GDP because racial discrimination against blacks limits the full use of their existing educational attainment. In 1967, this loss amounted to 1.5 per cent of GDP or $12.1 billion (Table 1.1). Another 1.4 per cent ($11.1 billion) of GDP was lost because of the failure to *improve* and fully utilize blacks' educational level. In combination, lost GDP amounted to $23.2 billion, equal to 2.9 per cent of the 1967 total of $814.3 billion. By 1993, the shortfall in GDP due to the failure to use blacks' existing education amounted to $137.5 billion (2.2 per cent of GDP). Failure to improve their

Table 1.1 Economic cost of discrimination against blacks, 1967–93 (estimated loss of Gross Domestic Product, $ billion)

Year	Gross Domestic Product	Gain from full use of present education		Gain from full use of improved education		Total gain from full use of present and improved education	
		Amount	*Percentage*	*Amount*	*Percentage*	*Amount*	*Percentage*
1967	814.30	12.10	1.49	11.10	1.36	23.20	2.85
1973	1,349.80	22.90	1.70	19.40	1.43	42.30	3.13
1979	2,488.60	45.80	1.84	38.20	1.53	84.00	3.38
1993	6,374.00	137.00	2.15	103.90	1.63	240.90	3.79

Source: Prepared by Brimmer & Company, Inc. Data for GDP from the US Department of Commerce, Bureau of Economic Analysis. Percentage increases in compensation and other income estimated by Brimmer & Company, Inc., based on data from the US Department of Commerce, Bureau of the Census

education cost $103.9 billion (1.6 per cent). The aggregate loss was estimated at $240.9 billion – 3.8 per cent of GDP.

The statistics in Table 1.1 enable one to apportion the loss in GDP between contemporary discrimination against blacks (failure to use fully their existing education) and the legacy of past discrimination (failure to improve their education). The figures suggest that, while no dramatic shifts have occurred over the last two and a half decades, the proportion of the loss that can be attributed to current discrimination has risen slightly. The latter component varied from 52.2 per cent in 1967, to 54.31 per cent in 1973, to 54.44 per cent in 1979, and to 56.87 per cent in 1993.

FACTORS CONTRIBUTING TO THE COST OF RACIAL DISCRIMINATION

A number of interwoven factors lie behind the loss of GDP from racial discrimination. In the first instance, discrimination has historically restricted many blacks to working in positions in which they could not fully utilize their qualifications. For example, for many years, the US Postal Service employed thousands of black men with college degrees in mathematics, chemistry, and other sciences who could not find jobs in the private sector. There were numerous cases where blacks with BA and MA degrees in business administration worked as warehouse and stockroom clerks – while their white counterparts held managerial jobs in areas such as banking, insurance, and real estate. Even today, despite the lessening of restrictions because of equal opportunity laws and the spread of affirmative action practices in industry, many blacks are still concentrated in positions which do not make full use of their talents. If racial discrimination were to be eliminated, blacks could migrate more freely from low to high productivity occupations where their contribution to total production would be increased. The result would be a gain in the nation's total output of goods and services.

Furthermore, a more rational use of the labor force most likely would require increased investment in the stock of capital. Plant and equipment outlays would rise – further boosting the gain in output. Thus, capital as well as labor incomes would be enhanced.

Self-employed entrepreneurs (particularly blacks) would have greater access to markets – and thus, become more efficient – in the absence of racial discrimination. In response, their incomes would rise to reflect their higher productivity. This is another source of the gain in GDP resulting from the elimination of racial discrimination.

LONG-TERM OUTLOOK

There appears to be little likelihood that the economic cost of racial discrimination will diminish appreciably over the current decade. While overt acts of discrimination in industry will almost certainly continue to decline, institutional or systemic discrimination will nevertheless persist due to the legacy of previous discrimination. Consequently, blacks' educational levels will remain well below those of whites, and they will continue to be underrepresented in the higher-paying positions and overrepresented in those at the low end of the occupational scale. The net result will be a continuation of large deficits in blacks' employment and income. The latter will continue to be translated directly into a sizeable loss in GDP.

The significant gap between blacks' educational attainment and that of the nation at large can be seen in Table 1.2. The figures compare the distribution of black workers by years of school completed with the corresponding distribution of all workers in 1990. It will be noted that, while blacks represented 10.15 per cent of total employment, they accounted for 13.29 per cent of workers with less than a high school education. At the

Table 1.2 Distribution of total and black workers, by years of school completed, 1990 (thousands)

	All workers		*Black workers*		
Years of school	*Number*	*Percentage distribution*	*Number*	*Percentage distribution*	*Percentage of all workers*
Less than High School	17,922	15.20	2,381	19.90	13.29
High School	46,340	39.30	5,157	43.10	11.13
1–3 Years of college	25,353	21.50	2,669	22.30	10.53
4 Years of college or more	28,299	24.00	1,759	14.70	6.22
Total	117,914	100.00	11,966	100.00	10.15

Source: Prepared by Brimmer & Company, Inc. Data from *Monthly Labor Review*, November 1991

high school level, they represented 11.13 per cent of the total. The black proportion was 10.53 per cent among workers with one to three years of college, and 6.22 per cent among those with four or more years of college. Expressed differently, in 1990, 45.5 per cent of all workers had at least some college education compared with 37.0 per cent of all black workers. The weighted average number of years of schooling for all workers combined was 13.29. The corresponding weighted average for blacks was 12.66 years. This meant that the typical black worker's average level of education lagged about 4.75 per cent behind that of all workers. Although the differential will probably narrow somewhat, it most likely will not be closed any time soon.

In a similar vein, blacks will continue to hold a disproportionately small share of the high-ranking occupations. The occupational profiles of blacks and all employees in 1990 are shown in Table 1.3. A projection by the US Bureau of Labor Statistics (BLS) for all workers for the year 2005 is also shown – along with Brimmer & Company's estimate for blacks in the same year.

Several features stand out: While blacks represented 10.0 per cent of total occupational employment in 1990, they fell progressively short of that proportion as one moved up the occupational scale. At the opposite end of the spectrum, their actual shares were 1.5 to 1.7 times their proportion of total employment. By the year 2005, BLS projections suggest that blacks' overall occupational profile will probably have changed only moderately. They will then hold about 11.1 per cent of all jobs. Using this benchmark, blacks will have raised their already above-par share of administrative and clerical positions, and they will be near parity with respect to technical and related jobs. They will also have narrowed slightly the gaps between parity and their actual holdings of managerial and professional occupations. Nevertheless, blacks will still be overrepresented in jobs at the foot of the occupational ladder.

The foregoing black employment and occupational disparities translate into large and persistent deficits in blacks' share of money income. The scope of these disparities is shown in Table 1.4. The statistics describe estimates and projections of the US population, civilian labor force, employment, and money income, by race, for the years 1991, 1992, 1993, and 2000. It will be noted that, in each year, blacks' labor force share, employment share, and income share all fall short of their share of the total population. Moreover, in each case, the size of the gap is projected to narrow only slightly over the remainder of this decade.

The magnitude of the disparity in blacks' money income can be seen in Table 1.5. For example, it is estimated that in 1993 blacks received $300.7 billion in money income, equal to 7.6 per cent of total money income received. This amount represented a sizeable deficit in the income of the black community – no matter what benchmark is used to measure parity. If

Table 1.3 Occupational distribution of employment, by race, 1990 and projection to 2005 (thousands)

	All workers				Black workers					
	1990		*2005*		*1990*			*2005*		
Occupation	*Number*	*Percentage distribution*	*Number*	*Percentage distribution*	*Number*	*Percentage distribution*	*Percentage of all workers*	*Number*	*Percentage distribution*	*Percentage of all workers*
Executive, Administrative, Managerial	12,451	10.2	15,866	10.8	747	5.9	6.0	1,269	7.8	8.0
Professional specialty	15,800	12.9	20,907	14.2	1,106	8.8	7.0	1,882	11.5	9.0
Technicians and related	4,204	3.4	5,754	3.9	378	3.0	9.0	604	3.7	10.5
Marketing and Sales	14,088	11.5	17,489	11.9	845	6.7	6.0	1,259	7.7	7.2
Administrative Support, including Clerical	21,951	17.9	24,835	16.9	2,415	19.2	11.0	3,186	19.5	12.8
Service occupations	19,204	15.7	24,806	16.9	3,265	26.0	17.0	3,857	23.6	16.0
Agricultural, Forestry, Fisheries	3,506	2.9	3,665	2.5	210	1.7	6.0	201	1.2	5.5
Precision production and Craft	14,124	11.5	15,909	10.8	1,130	9.0	8.0	1,511	9.2	9.5
Operators, Fabricators, and Laborers	17,245	14.1	17,961	12.2	2,587	20.6	15.0	2,571	15.8	14.3
All Occupations	122,573	100.0	147,191	100.0	12,573	100.0	10.0	16,340	100.0	11.1

Source: Estimates for blacks prepared by Brimmer & Company, Inc. Data from *Monthly Labor Review*, November 1991

Table 1.4 Estimates and projections of the US population, civilian labor force, employment, and money income, by race, 1991–2000 (numbers in thousands, money income in $ million)

	1991		*1992*		*1993*		*2000*	
Population	*Number*	*Percentage*	*Number*	*Percentage*	*Number*	*Percentage*	*Number*	*Percentage*
White	210,899	83.63	212,648	83.42	214,778	82.78	224,574	81.72
Black	31,164	12.36	31,673	12.42	32,137	12.62	35,525	12.93
Other race	10,114	4.01	10,601	4.16	11,012	4.27	14,696	5.35
Total	252,177	100.00	254,922	100.00	257,927	100.00	274,815	100.00
Civilian labor force								
White	107,486	85.78	108,776	85.65	109,222	85.33	120,374	84.83
Black	13,542	10.81	13,780	10.85	14,080	11.00	15,893	11.20
Other race	4,275	3.41	4,444	3.50	4,698	3.67	5,633	3.97
Total	125,303	100.00	127,000	100.00	128,000	100.00	141,900	100.00
Employment								
White	101,039	85.45	101,583	86.38	102,789	86.16	114,568	85.69
Black	11,863	10.15	11,960	10.17	12,192	10.22	13,985	10.46
Other race	3,975	3.40	4,057	3.45	4,319	3.62	5,147	3.85
Total	116,877	100.00	117,600	100.00	119,300	100.00	133,700	100.00
Money income								
White	3,228,041	88.98	3,347,468	89.00	3,517,240	88.90	5,055,765	88.30
Black	277,552	7.65	284,347	7.56	300,686	7.60	455,191	7.95
Other race	122,367	3.37	129,385	3.44	138,474	3.50	214,712	3.75
Total	3,627,960	100.00	3,761,200	100.00	3,956,400	100.00	5,725,668	100.00

Source: Estimates by Brimmer & Company, Inc. Data from US Department of Commerce, Bureau of the Census, and US Department of Labor, Bureau of Labor Statistics

Table 1.5 Black money income deficit, 1993 and projection to 2000 ($ million)

Benchmark	*1993*				*2000*				*Deficits as percentage of GDP*	
	Percentage share of total income	*Amount of income*	*Deficit*		*Percentage share of total income*	*Amount of income*	*Deficit*			
			Amount	*Percentage*			*Amount*	*Percentage*	*1993*	*2000*
Gross Domestic Product		6,374,000				8,942,000				
Money income:										
Total		3,956,400				5,725,668				
Black income										
Actual	7.60	300,686			7.95	455,191				
Parity										
Population	12.46	492,967	−192,281	−39.10	12.93	740,329	−285,138	−38.52	−3.02	−3.19
Civilian Labor Force	11.00	435,204	−134,518	−30.91	11.20	641,275	−186,084	−29.02	−2.11	−2.08
Employment	10.22	404,344	−103,658	−25.64	10.46	590,905	−135,714	−22.97	−1.63	−1.52

Source: Prepared by Brimmer & Company, Inc. Data from Table 1.4

blacks' share of population is used as the yardstick, the shortfall was $192.3 billion, or 39.1 per cent. Using their share of the civilian labor force, the income gap was $134.5 billion, or 30.9 per cent; by share of employment, it was $103.7 billion, or 25.6 per cent.

It is estimated that, in the year 2000, blacks' income may amount to $455.2 billion. This figure would represent 7.95 per cent of the total. Again, if blacks' share of population is taken as parity, the income deficit would amount to $285.1 billion, equal to 38.52 per cent. Using blacks' civilian labor force share as parity, the deficit would be $186.1 billion (29.02 per cent), while using their employment share would produce a deficit of $135.6 billion, equal to 22.97 per cent.

It should also be noted that all of the projected deficits in the year 2000 would be essentially unchanged in percentage terms compared with what they were in 1993.

The black income deficits also represent losses in GDP over and above those discussed earlier, because the income loss reduces consumption. As shown in Table 1.5, using blacks' population share as the parity benchmark, the income deficit was equal to 3.02 per cent of GDP in 1993. With the labor force share as benchmark, it was 2.11 per cent; and for employment, it was 1.63 per cent. By the year 2000, these three parity measures are projected to yield income deficits equal to 3.19 per cent, 2.08 per cent, and 1.52 per cent of GDP, respectively.

Again, it will be noted that black income deficits in relation to GDP remain essentially unchanged over the remainder of this decade. Thus, the economic cost of racial discrimination will continue as a major burden on the American economy.

CONCLUDING OBSERVATIONS

The analysis presented here has shown that, while blacks' educational attainment continues to fall short of that for the population as a whole, many blacks also continue to be employed in jobs well below what their actual education and skills would justify. To a considerable extent, these disparities mirror the effects of past – and present – racial discrimination.

The failure to use fully blacks' existing educational attainments – compounded by the failure to improve their educational levels – results in a sizeable shortfall in the money incomes earned by blacks. The income deficits can be translated into losses in GDP. Since the mid-1960s, these losses have represented between 3 per cent and 4 per cent of GDP. Thus, they provide a rough indication of the cost to the nation of discrimination against blacks.

Looking ahead, there is little reason to expect this cost to be diminished very much by the unaided operation of the labor market. Consequently, there is a continuing need for investment to improve blacks' education and skills. There is also a continuing need for vigorous affirmative action programs to eradicate the lingering racial discrimination in American industry.

APPENDIX: TECHNIQUE FOR ESTIMATING THE COST OF RACIAL DISCRIMINATION

The first step in gauging the magnitude of the loss in Gross Domestic Product (GDP) because of discrimination against blacks was to estimate the gain that would occur if their present educational achievement were fully used. The question to be answered was: What would be the gain in GDP if blacks, with a given level of education, had the same average earnings as whites in the jobs which blacks actually hold? To make this estimate, data from the US Census Bureau's *Current Population Reports* on "Money Income" were used.

Initially, for each age-sex-education group, the mean earnings of blacks were multiplied by the number of persons in each category and the results summed to produce the amount of money income received by blacks in a given year. This level was expressed as the *Base Case*.

Next, for each of the same age-sex-education categories, the mean earnings of blacks were changed to equal the mean earnings of whites. The multiplication and summation steps described above were repeated. These calculations produced *Adjusted Case I: Full Use of Present Education*. The resulting percentage increases in earnings for the years 1967, 1973, 1979, and 1993 are shown in Appendix Table 1.A1, Column (1).

In the second step, an estimate was made of the gain in income that might result if blacks' educational levels could be improved to the point where they equaled the levels achieved by whites and if blacks had the same mean earnings as whites at the same level of education. These calculations produced the percentage increases expressed as *Adjusted Case II: Full Use of Improved Education*, shown in Appendix Table 1.A.1, Column (2).

The results of Adjusted Case I and Adjusted Case II were combined to produce *Adjusted Case III: Total Gain From Full Use of Improved Education (II) and Present Education (I)*, shown in Appendix Table 1.A.1, Column (3).

In the third step, the percentage increases in earnings were used to estimate gains in GDP. These are shown in Appendix Table 1.A2.

Initially, the wages and salaries component of GDP (including supplements) was raised by the percentage increases in total earnings brought over from Appendix Table 1.A.1. The resulting gain in wages and salaries for Adjusted Case I is shown in Appendix Table 1.A.2, Column (4). Next, the remaining component of GDP (equal to GDP minus the wages composition of employees) was derived. Column (6) for Case I shows the gain. Finally, the resulting combined increases in GDP for Case I are shown in

Column (8). The same procedure was used to estimate the increase in GDP that might occur from full use of improved educational achievement by blacks – Adjusted Case II. The corresponding gains in this case are presented in Columns (10), (12), and (14).

The potential gain in GDP from the full use of blacks' present educational achievement and the full use of their improved education is shown in Case III, Columns (16), (18), and (20).

Table 1.A1 Gains in earnings from full use of present and potential educational achievement of blacks in the United States, 1967–93 (percentage)

Year	*Adjusted Case I Full use of present education*	*Adjusted Case II Full use of improved education*	*Adjusted Case III Total gain from full use of improved education (II) and present education (I)*
1967	1.88	1.72	3.60
1973	2.12	1.80	3.92
1979	2.30	1.92	4.22
1993	2.70	2.04	4.74

Source: Estimates prepared by Brimmer & Company, Inc. Data from US Department of Commerce, Bureau of the Census

NOTES

1 See Council of Economic Advisers, Press Release issued 25 September 1962.
2 See Andrew F. Brimmer, "The Negro in the American Economy."

REFERENCES

Brimmer, Andrew F. (1966) "The Negro in the American Economy," Chapter 5 in *The American Negro Reference Book*, edited by John P. Davis, Englewood Cliffs, NJ: Prentice Hall.

Council of Economic Advisors (1962). Press release dated 25 September.

Monthly Labor Review (1991) vol. 114, no. 11.

US Department of Commerce, Bureau of the Census, 1993. "Money Income of Households, Families, and Persons in the United States: 1992," *Current Population Reports*, Series P–60, Washington, DC: US Government Printing Office.

US Department of Commerce, Bureau of the Census, 1993. "Population Projections of the United States, by Age, Sex, Race, and Hispanic Origin: 1993 to 2050," *Current Population Reports*, Series P25–1104 (November), Washington, DC: US Government Printing Office.

Table 1.A2 Estimated gain in Gross Domestic Product from full use of present and potential educational achievement of blacks in the United States, 1967–93 ($ billion)

		Base levels		Adjusted Case I Full use of present education					
	GDP	Comp. of employees	Other income	Increase in comp. of employees		Increase in other income		Total increase in GDP	
Year	amount (1)	amount (2)	amount (3)	amount (4)	percentage (5)	amount (6)	percentage (7)	amount (8)	percentage (9)
1967	814.3	475.5	338.8	8.9	1.88	3.2	0.94	12.1	1.49
1973	1,349.8	812.8	537.0	17.2	2.12	5.7	1.06	22.9	1.70
1979	2,488.6	1,496.4	992.2	34.4	2.30	11.4	1.15	45.8	1.84
1993	6,374.0	3,781.1	2,592.9	102.1	2.70	35.0	1.35	137.1	2.15

	Adjusted Case II Full use of improved education						Adjusted Case III Total gain from full use of improved education (II) and present education (I)					
Year	Increase in comp. of employees		Increase in other income		Total increase in GDP		Increase in comp. of employees		Increase in other income		Total increase in GDP	
	amount (10)	percentage (11)	amount (12)	percentage (13)	amount (14)	percentage (15)	amount (16)	percentage (17)	amount (18)	percentage (19)	amount (20)	percentage (21)
1967	8.2	1.72	2.9	0.86	11.1	1.36	17.1	3.60	6.1	1.80	23.2	2.85
1973	14.6	1.80	4.8	0.90	19.4	1.43	31.8	3.91	10.5	1.96	42.3	3.13
1979	28.7	1.92	9.5	0.96	38.2	1.53	63.1	4.22	20.9	2.11	84.0	3.38
1993	77.1	2.04	26.4	1.02	103.5	1.62	179.2	4.74	61.5	2.37	240.7	3.78

Source: Prepared by Brimmer & Company, Inc. Data for GDP from the US Department of Commerce, Bureau of Economic Analysis. Percentage increases in compensation and other income estimated by Brimmer & Company, Inc., based on data from the US Department of Commerce, Bureau of the Census

Part I

POVERTY, INEQUALITY AND PUBLIC POLICY

2

MYRDAL'S CUMULATIVE HYPOTHESIS

Its antecedents and its contemporary applications

Robert Cherry

It is now fifty years since Gunnar Myrdal's study *The American Dilemma* (1944) was first published. It was a pivotal study in changing public attitudes towards racism and racial inequality. He was hopeful that informed public policies would help society overcome these problems. Rather than representing a historic relic, this paper will argue that his work continues to provide a foundation for some of the current liberal perspectives on the persistence of racial economic inequality. In particular, this paper will highlight one aspect of Myrdal's work: his culture-of-poverty explanation for the persistence of racial inequality. Embedded in his cumulative hypothesis, this explanation focused on the role of behavioral traits in the persistence of black poverty. According to Isabell Sawhill (1988: 1109), the culture-of-poverty thesis contends that

> the poor, or at least a subset of them, are different from the nonpoor in terms of their attitudes, values, or aspirations and that these personality traits produce behaviors that mire them in long-term poverty. A softer version of this hypothesis is that attitudes and behaviors, whatever their origins, change only slowly in response to greater opportunities, and thereby contribute to the persistence of poverty.

Myrdal did not invent the culture-of-poverty thesis, and this paper will identify some of the early presentations of this thesis. We will find that these earlier presentations focused on European immigrant groups. Myrdal was the first economist, however, to use this thesis to explain the persistence of racial inequality. After Myrdal, behavioral explanations for the persistence of racial inequality have had their defenders and detractors. This paper will identify three prominent liberal social scientists whose work continues to incorporate culture-of-poverty aspects of Myrdal's pathbreaking work.

ROBERT CHERRY

RACIAL THOUGHT IN THE EARLY ECONOMICS PROFESSION

During the first part of the twentieth century, racial theories supporting the belief in Nordic superiority developed and thrived in the United States. These theories buttressed anti-immigration responses to the increasing labor unrest of that period. General Amasa Walker, one of the founders of the American Economics Association (AEA) maintained that the immigrants of the 1880s and 1890s were inferior. He stated,

> [They] are beaten men and beaten races; representing the worst failures in the struggle for existence. Centuries are against them, as centuries are on the side of those who formerly came to us. They have none of the ideas and aptitudes which would fit them readily and easily to take up the problems of self-care and self-government, such as belong to those who are descended from the tribes that met under the oak tree of old Germany to make laws and choose a chieftain.
> (1896: 828)

Many other leading economists were vocal in their racial beliefs at the turn of the century. For example, Richard T. Ely (1891: 402) felt that the "most general statement possible is that the causes of poverty are hereditary and environmental, producing weak physical, mental and moral constitutions." To support his thesis, Ely (1891: 403–5) cited the cases of the "Jukes and the Tribe of Ismael." These family histories, which were thought to demonstrate how individual genealogy explains intergenerational poverty, were often cited by supporters of eugenics measures. These attitudes were also reflected in the content of American economics journals.[1]

Within the movement for immigration restriction economists were quite influential. Mark Haller (1963: 74) considered Irving Fisher to be the most influential spokesman for the Eugenics Movement: Thomas N. Carver, Henry P. Fairchild, and Prescott Hall were active members of the Immigration Restriction League; John R. Commons was a member of the National Civic Federation; and Jeremiah Jenks and W. J. Lauck were the principal investigators for the US Immigration Commission. An important concern of all of these economists was the racial composition of recent immigrants. Let us now describe the various positions held by economists.[2]

The genetic racial position

This position argued that the recent immigrants, were of inferior genetic stock, thus reducing the quality of racial strains in America. These immigrants allegedly had hereditary criminal traits, as well as inferior intelligence. Hence, these economists urged immediate immigration restrictions as part of a general eugenics program. Economists of note who supported this position were Prescott Hall. Frank A. Fetter, and Irving Fisher. Hall claimed,

> The class of persons, other than the state officials, who are becoming interested in immigration matters, consists of medical men and the medical society. These men come in direct contact with the evil results of the immigration of people of poor racial stock. The studies made under the auspices of the Eugenics Record Office show how much damage bad racial strains can do.
>
> (1913: 753)

His book, *Immigration and Its Effects*, was considered by individuals of similar views, such as Fetter (1916: 353), to be the outstanding scientific work in this area. Fetter was also a vocal advocate of eugenics measures. He believed,

> The ignorant, the improvident and the feebleminded are contributing far more than their quota to the next generation... Unless effective means are found to check the degeneration of the race, the noontide of humanity's greatness is nigh, if not passed... Great changes in thought are impending, and these will include the elimination of the unfit ...and the conscious improvement of the race. Under the touch of the new science of eugenics, many of our most perplexing problems would disappear, making possible the better democracy which we are just beginning to seek.
>
> (1907: 91)

In his early writings Fetter (1904: 179–80) had thought that "education and native talent are in a degree interchangeable," but by 1915 he discounted any effects of education. At that point Fetter (1915: 419) stated, "Few thoughtful persons now hold the view that the race can be improved biologically, rapidly if at all, or by the process of education of individuals." Finally, Fetter (1918: 234) claimed that labor unrest was the result of the changing racial composition of the working class toward groups which had no appreciation of democratic institutions.

Irving Fisher believed an individual's rate of time preference played a critical role in determining economic inequality. He reasoned,

> The effect will be, for society as a whole, that those individuals who have an abnormally low appreciation of the future and its needs will gradually part with the most durable instruments, and that they will gravitate into the hands of those who have the opposite trait. By this transfer an inequality in the distribution of capital is gradually effected and this inequality once achieved tends to perpetuate itself.
>
> (1907: 232)

Fisher then posited that racial theory indicated which groups are present-oriented and hence poor. He (1907: 292) said, "Among communities and people noted for lack of foresight and for negligence with respect to the future are China, India, Java, the negro communities of the southern states, the peasant communities of Russia, and the North and South American Indians."

Fisher (1907: 298–9) initially felt that environmental factors and "the influence of training" were also great. Like Fetter, however, he came to believe that only genetic factors were significant in explaining social and mental characteristics. By 1911 Fisher (1911: 476) saw the problem in the United States as one of "race suicide" and indicated approvingly that a "method of attaining the contrary result – namely reproducing from the best and suppressing reproduction from the worst – has been suggested by the late Sir Francis Galton of England, under the name of 'eugenics'."

While vice president of the Race Betterment Foundation, Fisher [1916: 710–11] recommended that "by a policy of restricting immigration by excluding those unfit to become American citizens . . . we shall help solve some of our problems, including that of the distribution of wealth." He (Fisher and Fisk 1915: 299–300) suggested that "the 80,000 prisoners supported in the United States are recruited not evenly from the general population, but mainly from certain family breeds." To correct this, Fisher (Fisher and Fisk 1915: 324) recommended the "segregation of defectives so that they may not mingle their family traits with those of sound lines . . . [and] sterilization of certain groups of hopeless defectives."[3]

Environmental position

The environmental position was held by many of the Progressives, including Jencks and Lauck. These Progressives argued that continued immigration would lead to a lowering of native workers' wages. Indeed, Hall criticized the US Immigration Commission for saying little about heredity and nothing about eugenics. He said,

> The instincts and habits which cause a low standard of living, willingness to underbid native labor, and migratory habits are matters of race and inheritance. One can not imagine the Baltic races being willing to live as do many of our recent immigrants, no matter how poor they might be.
>
> (1912: 676)

Fisher (1921: 226) also voiced this same criticism: "The core of the problem of immigration is one of race and eugenics, despite the fact that in the eighteen volumes of the report of the Immigration Commission scarcely any attention is given to this aspect of the immigration problem."

Environmentalists did not focus on racial differences because, unlike the genetic racialists, they had a hopeful view of acculturating the southern and eastern European immigrants who had already entered the United States. They were hopeful because most Progressives believed that the racial inferiority of immigrants was primarily due to cultural and social factors. While they did not dispute the "fact" that genetic differences were present, most Progressives felt that cultural changes could effectively offset these deficiencies. The most influential economist among Progressives was John R. Commons who agreed that there were genetic differences between Nordic and non-Nordic European immigrants. He said,

> The North Italian is an educated, skilled artisan, coming from a manufacturing section and largely from the cities. He is teutonic in blood and appearances. The South Italian is an illiterate peasant from the great landed estates, with wages one-third his northern compatriot. He descends with less mixture from the ancient (nonteutonic) inhabitants of Italy.
>
> (1920: 78)

Commons (1920: 213) believed, however, that the problem of southern and eastern European immigrants was one of primitiveness of civilization and that "all children of all races of the temperate zone are eligible to the highest American civilization."

Commons's union strategy was interwoven with his racial and nativist notions.[4] He (1920: 220) believed that unions were instrumental to the assimilation of the new immigrants:

> The influence of schools, churches, settlements, and farming communities applied more to the children of immigrants than to the parents. The immigrants themselves are too old for Americanization, especially when they speak a non-English language. To them the labor-union is at present the strongest Americanizing force.

Commons (1919: 108) considered the union shop particularly important in helping develop democratic values in the eastern and southern European immigrants:

> When this particular shop scheme was started, many of the workers were newly arrived immigrants, acquainted only with the despotism of Austria, Hungary, Russia... Many were what is known as Bolsheviks... Many were successful agitators, hostile to employers as a class. In the course of time their employers were astonished with the changes that came over them.

ATTITUDES CONCERNING AFRICAN AMERICANS

Genetic racialists, like Walker (1891), had little fear that the extremely inferior "black race would overwhelm civilization." Their position was supported by Frederick Hoffman's "Race Traits and Tendencies of the American Negro" which was a widely circulated publication of the AEA. Hoffman (1896: 95) believed that the high incidence among American Negroes of diseases, such as tuberculosis and syphilis, would lead to their extinction. Better health conditions would not help:

> It is not the conditions of life but the race traits and tendencies that we find the causes of excessive mortality. So long as these tendencies are persisted in, so long as immorality and vice are a habit of life of the vast majority of the colored population, the effect will be to increase mortality by hereditary transmission of weak constitutions and to lower still further the rate of natural increase until the births fall below the deaths, and gradual extinction results.

This position was reinforced by the 1902 AEA publication. "The Negro in Africa and America." by Joseph Tillinghast. Tillinghast blamed the social and economic difficulties faced by African Americans on their African heredity, for this resulted in a race lacking in industry, energy, and foresight. Like Hoffman, Tillinghast foresaw the elimination of the inferior black race as it was forced into greater competition with whites.

That those who took a genetic racial position on non-Nordic Europeans should have a similar view of African Americans is not surprising. What is noteworthy, is that many Progressives, including John R. Commons and Walter Willcox, who had an environmental position with respect to the newer immigrants, took a genetic racial position with respect to African Americans.

John R. Commons

Commons held open little possibility that African Americans as a group could attain equality with Americans of European descent.[5] Commons did not believe that social institutions could overcome the genetic inferiority of African Americans. Only crossbreeding would allow African Americans to rise up to the standards of European Americans. Commons (1904: 222) stated, "Amalgamation is their door to assimilation. Frederick Douglass, Booker Washington, Professor Du Bois are an honor to any race, but they are mulattoes." Like Fisher, Commons accepted the notion that an African American is so present oriented that he is notorious for his improvidence:

> His neglect of his horse, his mule, his machinery, his eagerness to spend his earnings on finery, his reckless purchase of watermelons, chickens and garden stuff when he might easily grow them on his own patch of ground, these and many other incidents of improvidence explain the constant dependence of the Negro upon his employer and creditor.
>
> (Quoted in Ramstad and Starkey, 1992)

Commons believed that unions were necessary to protect workers from competing against themselves, thus lowering the wages for all workers. Since African Americans were docile and uncompetitive, unions were unnecessary. Indeed, Commons (1920: 136) claimed that the tropical climate produced a race which was so "indolent and fickle" that "some form of compulsion" was necessary if it were to adopt the industrious life. While he was careful not to exclude individual African Americans from equality, Commons predicted that the race was doomed once it had entered into competition with European Americans after emancipation. Echoing the thoughts of Tillinghast and Hoffman, Commons believed that African Americans were ill-prepared for freedom. Commenting on the failure of education and democracy to uplift southern blacks, Commons (1920: 3–4) claimed. "[T]he fearful collapse of the experiment is now recognized…as something that was inevitable [given] the nature of the race at that stage of development."

Walter Willcox[6]

With respect to African Americans, Willcox was the most influential economist. He was instrumental in the decision of the AEA to publish both the Hoffman and Tillinghast articles; in 1900 he handpicked the members of the AEA Committee to Investigate the Condition of the Negro; and shaped the census data on African Americans gathered in his capacity as statistician for the Census Bureau from 1899 to 1931. Willcox sympathized with the higher aspirations of African Americans, was a regular contributor to many black institutions, and found white racism distasteful. Willcox did not completely rule out the possibility that environmental factors might explain a substantial portion. He even suggested that African Americans could approach equality if they were raised by whites until they were twenty-one years old. He believed, however, that African Americans were inferior primarily due to genetic deficits. Willcox wrote, "My own tendency is to believe that a large part, perhaps the large part of the difference between the two races is due to racial heredity" (quoted in Aldrich 1979: 4).

Similar to Commons, he believed that the Negro was deficient and "what the Negroes need most of all to learn are those habits of obedience, industry, self-restraint, and sexual morality, the lack of which is now gradually undermining the race and may prove its destruction." Like Commons, he too believed that slavery had protected African Americans and with emancipation they were unable to compete. Like Tillinghast and Hoffman, Willcox predicted that they would suffer extinction due to disease, vice, crime, and discouragement brought on by their own inability to compete in the economic struggle for existence.

Willcox's (1908) work on Negro criminality became a source of scientific support for Southern oppression of blacks. In particular, Mississippi governor James Vardaman cited Willcox's work to support his view that suffrage and education should be withheld from African Americans. As Aldrich notes,

> Although objecting to Vardaman's shrillness and his conclusion that education and suffrage for blacks should be restricted, Willcox agreed with his basic premise that [Negro] crime partly stemmed from racial characteristics. This and several other incidents such as his introduction to Tillinghast's work and the role which he played in the Census Bureaus decision not to collect lynching statistics... alienate[d] black leaders such as [Roscoe] Bruce [of Tuskegee], Du Bois, and others, as they accurately came to perceive that Willcox was in fact providing scientific support for the emerging Southern caste system.
>
> (1979: 11)

EMERGENCE OF A CULTURE OF POVERTY THESIS

While the genetic racial view was widely held during the first quarter of the twentieth century, eventually the culture-of-poverty thesis became the major explanation for the alleged inferiority of African Americans. This section will summarize the views of a number of social scientists who had important roles in shifting professional attitudes.

Booker T. Washington

Booker T. Washington was an early exponent of a culture-of-poverty thesis with respect to African Americans. He (1902: 26) rejected the genetic racial position noting that the "Negro is behind the white man because he has not had the same chances, and not from any inherent difference in his nature or desires." Washington did, however, believe that African Americans were culturally inferior to whites. He (1970: 74) contrasted the "semi-barbarous" African race with the white race having attained "the highest civilization that the world knows." Washington (1970: 16) believed that the African culture was at a lower stage of development than European society. Washington said

> The natives have never been educated by contact with the white man in the same way as has been true of the American Negro.... their ambitions have never been awakened, their wants have not been increased, and they work perhaps two days out of the week and are in idleness during the remaining portion of time.... How different in the Southern part of the United States where we have eight million of black people!... these people have not by any means reached perfection but they have advanced on the whole much beyond the condition of the South Africans.
>
> (1970: 59–60)

To explain why African Americans were the most advanced blacks in the world, Washington (1970: 16) believed we must admit that "the Negro did gain certain benefits from slavery." Through slavery, African Americans gained self-discipline and future-oriented values. While slavery improved blacks, they still were not the equal of whites at the time of emancipation. As a result, Washington (1963: 58–61) considered the Reconstruction era to be an inappropriate preparation for an "ignorant and inexperienced" black population. Reconstruction, by offering blacks preferential treatment increased their present-orientedness by enabling them to begin "at the top instead of at the bottom;" to seek "a seat in Congress . . . [rather] than real estate or industrial skill." While recognizing the importance of legal rights, Washington claimed that "it is vastly more important that we be prepared for the exercise of these privileges."

Washington's and Commons's views on black inferiority differ substantially. Commons claimed individual African Americans gain equality with Nordics only by crossbreeding while Washington (1970: 13) claimed it was due to the "Negro imitating the best" of the white man's culture. Whereas Commons considered the failure of Reconstruction preordained since African Americans were unable to compete against whites, Washington believed that the failure stemmed from a wrong set of policies.

Edward A. Ross and Louis Wirth

Another important building block of the culture of poverty thesis was the sociological thesis that the transition to an urban culture creates disorganization among those who migrate from rural areas. Interestingly, this thesis was first developed to explain the alleged inferiority of Polish-Russian Jewish immigrants by liberal sociologists Edward A. Ross and Louis Wirth. During the early twentieth century, these Jews had all of the social disorganization found in other immigrant groups. Jewish criminal activity was widespread resulting in public outcries. The desertion of families became such a large problem that the *Jewish Daily Forward* routinely ran a "Gallery of Missing Husbands" to assist women in locating their errant husbands.[7]

Wirth completed his dissertation on Jewish immigrants in 1927. He believed that the newer Jewish immigrants from eastern Europe were culturally inferior to earlier German-Jewish immigrants. He stated,

> While the Jews of the east lived in large part in rural communities, in a village world, those of the west were predominantly a city people in touch with the centers of trade and . . . with the pulsating intellectual life of the world. While the Jews of the Rhine cities were associating with men of thought and of affairs, their brethren in Russia were dealing with peasants and an uncultured, decadent nobility. While the

> Jewries of the west were already seething with modernistic religious, political, and social movements, those of the east were still steeped in mysticism and medieval ritual. While the western Jews were moving along with the tide of progress, those of the east were still sharing the backwardness and isolation of the gentile world of villages and peasants.
>
> (1956: 267)

There were two ways in which these allegedly deficient qualities of eastern European Jews led to their social disorganization. On the one hand, city life created conflict with traditional relationships. In rural societies social interactions are limited and characterized by long term, stable relationships. In contrast, Wirth (1956: 120) emphasized that the "segmental character and utilitarian accent of interpersonal relations in the city find their institutional expression in the proliferation of specialized tasks." The need to judge the limits and choices of social relationships according to Wirth (1956: 123) "may be regarded as prerequisites for rationality and which lead toward the secularization of life." Thus, Wirth (1956: 128) believed that the urban mode of life is associated with "a substitution of secondary for primary contacts, the weakening of bonds of kinship, and the declining significance of the family, the disappearance of the neighborhood, and the undermining of the traditional basis of social solidarity."

Wirth (1956: 130) considered this mode of life to be difficult for individuals so that "personal disorganization, mental breakdown, suicide, delinquency, crime, corruption, and disorder might be expected under these circumstances to be more prevalent in the urban than in the rural communities." This would be the case for groups, like eastern European Jews who he (1956: 268) claimed "were still clinging to the old bonds that exclusion and oppression had fashioned."

Like Wirth, Edward Ross also believed cultural deficiencies explained the antisocial behavior of Jewish immigrants from eastern Europe. Writing at the time of the First World War, Ross focused on the criminal behavior of this immigrant group and believed it was a product of the oppression they faced:

> The truth seems to be that the lower class of Jews of eastern Europe reach here moral cripples, their souls warped and dwarfed by iron circumstance. The experience of Russian repression laws made them haters of government and corrupters of the police. Life amid a bigoted and hostile population has left them aloof and thick-skinned. A tribal spirit intensified by social isolation prompts them to rush to the rescue of the caught rascal of their own race.... When now they use their Old World shove and wile and lie in a society like ours... they rapidly push up into a position of prosperous parasitism, leaving scorn and curses in their wake.
>
> (1972: 68–9)

Similar to Commons's views, Ross believed that once these immigrants experience the fairness of society these traits would wane:

> Gradually, however, it dawns upon this twisted soul that there is no need to be weasel or hedgehog. He finds himself in a new game, the rules of which are made by all the players. He himself is a part of the state that is weakened by his law-breaking, a member of the profession that is degraded by sharp practices. So smirk and cringe and trick presently fall away from him and he stands erect.
>
> (1972: 69)

Like Wirth, Ross believed that the immigration process had separated Jews from stabilizing institutions. While eventually this would lead to a more rationalist secular individual the undermining of old world institutions made things worse in the short run. Ross noted,

> Enveloped in the husks of medievalism, the religion of many a Jew perishes in the American environment. The immigrant who loses his religion is worse than the religionless American because his early standards are dropped along with his faith. With his clear brain sharpened in the American school, the egoistic, conscienceless young Jew constitutes a menace.
>
> (1972: 71)

Ross lamented that too few Jews had adopted the socialist ethics of Jewish labor leaders to replace their lost religious orthodoxy.

Wirth's views on the impact of urbanism on eastern European Jewish immigrants became more generalized into a thesis which was applied to all rural migration. In particular, it became a basis for explaining the rise in crime rates and the breakdown of traditional families as African Americans migrated to urban areas. This became a staple of culture-of-poverty theories which developed in the post-Second World War era.

Gunnar Myrdal

In *American Dilemma*, Myrdal (1944: 208) noted "the low standards of efficiency, reliability, ambition, and morals actually displayed by the average Negro." Unlike the earlier Progressives, however, Myrdal (1944: 149) rejected genetic explanations. For Myrdal (1944: 928–9), cultural deficits were the predominant explanation:

> American Negro culture is not something independent of general American culture. It is a distorted development, or a pathological condition, of the general American culture.... [Its] characteristic traits are mainly forms of social pathologies which, for the most part, are created by caste pressures.

For example, Myrdal (1944: 595) attributed African American laziness to the paternalistic attitude of upper-class white employers, which tended "to diminish the Negroes' formal responsibilities." Moreover, as a result of the lower expectations, Myrdal (1944: 643) claimed that Negro youth "is not expected to make good in the same way as white youth. And if he is not extraordinary, he will not expect it himself and will not really put his shoulder to the wheel." In general, Myrdal (1944: 645) argued that these social pathologies could be rectified through education which would "diffuse middle class norms to the uneducated and crude Southern 'folk Negroes,' emerging out of the backwardness of slavery."

When discussing Negro criminality, Myrdal's beliefs closely paralleled the views of Wirth and Ross. Like Ross, Myrdal (1944: 959) suggested that racism induces African Americans to have less respect for laws: "life becomes cheap and crime not so reprehensible." According to Myrdal (1944: 763), this hostility to whites promoted the "shielding of Negro criminals and suspects." Like Wirth, Myrdal pointed to the social disorganization caused by the urbanization process:

> Social disorganization is generally at a low level among Southern Negroes, but disorganization only reaches its extreme when Negroes migrate to cities and to the North. The controls of the rural community are removed; and the ignorant Negro does not know how to adjust to a radically new type of life. Like the European immigrant, he comes to the slums of the Northern cities and learns the criminal ways already widely practiced in such areas.... With uncertain sex mores and a great deal of family disorganization, Negroes are more likely to act with motives of sexual jealousy. The over-crowdedness of the home and the lack of recreational facilities augment the effect of all these disorganizing and crime-breeding influences.
>
> (1944: 977–8)

Myrdal also found more family disorganization among blacks than whites:

> Perhaps the best indirect index of family stability that is available is that of illegitimacy.... For the United States as a whole... Negroes have about eight times as much illegitimacy as native whites and about sixteen times as much illegitimacy as the foreign-born whites.... Broken families were 30 percent of all Negro families, but only 20 percent among native whites, despite the greater concentration of Negroes in rural-farm areas where broken families are least frequent.[8]
>
> (1944: 933)

Myrdal (1944: 932) thought that family disorganization among African Americans was not only a legacy of slavery but also "poverty and ignorance were... obstacles to acculturation."

Finally, Myrdal seemed to accept the views of Booker T. Washington that African civilization was backward when compared to European culture. When discussing the attempt by some historians to find greatness in African culture, Myrdal stated,

> In spite of all scholarly pretenses and accomplishments, this movement is basically an expression of the Negro protest. Its avowed purpose is to enhance self-respect and race-respect among Negroes by substituting a belief in race achievements for the traditional belief in race inferiority.... Propagandist activities go on side by side with scholarly ones.... In one phase of their activities, Negro historians have the support of some white scientists. This is in the field of African culture... One white anthropologist, Melvin J. Herskovits, has recently rendered yeoman service to the Negro History propagandists. He has not only made excellent field studies of certain African and West Indian Negro groups, but has written a book to glorify African culture generally and to show how it has survived in the American Negro community.
>
> (1944: 752–3)

Condemning ethnic cheerleading, Myrdal (1944: 754) rejected the "double standard" created when "some lesser Negro poets and actors are getting applause because they are Negroes rather than because they have outranked the whites in free competition." In defense of the goal of a universalistic culture, Myrdal (1944: 754) feared "the 'parallel civilization' theory... that Negroes should retain 'their own' cultural heritage and not lose it for the general American culture."

CONTEMPORARY CULTURE OF POVERTY VIEWS

During the 1960s, it appeared as if an emphasis on behavioral traits would no longer provide the foundations for theories of poverty and inequality. When Daniel Moynihan (1965) updated Myrdal's discussion of the African American family, he was subject to severe criticism. His culture-of-poverty thesis was characterized as a "blaming-the-victim" ideology and seemed to fall into disrepute.[9] With the modest effectiveness of liberal policies, however, many social scientists began incorporating behavioral explanations into their analysis. The concept of the underclass highlights the way dysfunctional behavioral traits can identify a subset of the poor.

While various culture-of-poverty theses may have gained a new life, its appeal to economists remains rather limited. Labor economists continue to focus their inquiry on testing the relationship between human capital variables and earnings. In recent years, the economics profession had tended to reject discrimination and find that income inequality is primarily a result of a lack of human capital. But even when human capital differences are emphasized, most labor economists refrain from hypothesizing the source of this inequality. They rarely engage in tests to determine whether human capital inequality is due to behavioral traits – the culture-of-poverty thesis – or other external factors. Thus, they have generally not embraced culture-of-poverty explanations for the persistence of black poverty and racial earnings differentials.

While certainly not embracing culture-of-poverty explanations, there have been some notable liberal social scientists who have incorporated behavioral variables into the analysis. This section will briefly discuss three: Richard Freeman, Michael Piore, and William J. Wilson. Their work not only points to the resilience of Myrdal's cumulative hypothesis, but also to the distinction between Sawhill's soft and hard culture-of-poverty explanations.

Richard Freeman

During the early 1970s, Richard Freeman's work (1973) provided the most important evidence that civil rights legislation substantially reduced racial income inequality. He (Bound and Freeman 1989) continues to believe demand-side factors dominate explanations of the ebbs and flows of national measures of racial income inequality. While Freeman emphasizes demand-side variables when studying aggregate racial income inequalities, he is quite willing to incorporate culture-of-poverty variables when studying black–white differences among young males. Indeed, numerous articles in his most recent edited work on inner city black youth employment problems promote culture-of-poverty (behavioral) explanations. For example, Kip Viscusi (1986) contends that black, inner city youth find criminal activities an acceptable alternative to legal employment. Similarly, Harry Holzer (1986: 52) suggests that "outside income generated by illegal activities (and other sources) for young blacks with low skill levels may be an important source of their relatively high reservation wage." Even the one article (Culp and Dunson 1986) which documents the persistent racist nature of employment practices rejects emphasizing anti-discrimination legislation.

In his own work on black youth employment difficulties, Freeman also explores explanations derived from the culture-of-poverty thesis. For example, he (1986) claims that there is a positive correlation between church attendance and productive time (school, work, or household activities) and, more generally, that family environment plays a significant role in determining the productive activity of young black males.

Michael Piore

Piore is another liberal economist who emphasizes the role of behavioral traits in determining employment possibilities. He argues that due to discrimination many of the those who possess the proper behavioral traits for decent jobs are forced into low-wage secondary labor markets. However, Piore suggests that once individuals enter the environment of the secondary labor market they adopt culture-of-poverty values:

> Even individuals who are forced into the secondary sector initially by discrimination tend, over time, to develop the traits predominant among secondary workers. Thus, for example, by working in a world where employment is intermittent and erratic, one tends to lose habits of regularity and punctualiry.... Illegitimate activity also tends to follow the intermittent work pattern prevalent in secondary employment, and the attractions of such activity, as well as life patterns and role models it presents to those not themselves involved but associating with people who are, foster behavioral traits antagonistic to primary employment.
>
> (1977: 95)

This culture-of-poverty thesis is quite similar to the one presented by Myrdal. Both presume that dysfunctional behavior is the primary reason why most individuals end up in the secondary market and their behavior adversely affects even those individuals who initially possess the proper behavioral requirements. Most importantly, both Piore's and Myrdal's models suggest that virtually all individuals who have worked in the secondary labor market for any length of time no longer have the ability to function effectively in the primary job markets. Thus, even if discrimination would be eliminated, it would have little impact on the employment situation of African Americans who currently work in secondary labor markets.

William Julius Wilson

The implication that the ending of labor market discrimination would have little impact on African Americans is highlighted by William J. Wilson in his work *The Truly Disadvantaged*. Wilson (1987) emphasizes the debilitating pathologies present in inner city African American communities. These pathological problems are exemplified by the explosion of female-headed households, teenage out-of-wedlock pregnancies and violent criminal behavior. While Wilson blames past racial discrimination and the lack of male employment for providing an environment in which these dysfunctional behaviors are nurtured, he criticizes those who blind themselves to the massive internal inadequacies present within African American communities. In contrast, he quotes, approvingly, culture-of-poverty theorists James Q. Wilson, Richard Nathan and Glen Loury. Wilson (1987: 129) considers Kenneth Clark, Daniel Moynihan and Lee Rainwater visionaries who were unfairly attacked during the 1970s for correctly perceiving that "self-perpetuating pathologies" were becoming rampant within poor

African American communities. Not surprisingly, *Commentary* reviewer Lawrence Mead (1988: 48) writes, "Wilson is brutally realistic in describing the ghetto . . . He describes bluntly how crime and illegitimacy have escalated in the inner city. He calls liberals squeamish for refusing to admit such problems."

Wilson updates Myrdal's cumulative process by which past discrimination induces African Americans to maintain feelings of inferiority and adapt in ways which are dysfunctional – ways which are reinforced by the structural black unemployment created by the loss of inner city manufacturing employment. Wilson rejects claims that contemporary discrimination is responsible for the problems faced by poor blacks. Indeed, Wilson suggests that the *lessening* of discrimination – by allowing upwardly mobile blacks to leave the inner city – has increased the social isolation of low-income blacks from middle-class role models. Without role models and community institutions provided by these more affluent African Americans, the vicious cycle of poverty grows, and pathological behaviors are intensified.

None of these social scientists should be considered culture-of-poverty theorists. They do not believe that dysfunctional behavior is the primary impediment to advancement. In addition, they believe that external factors are responsible for the development of these attributes. Freeman, Piore, and Wilson believe, however, that dysfunctional attitudes and behaviors change only slowly in response to greater opportunities and, thus, their views are consistent with Sawhill's soft definition of a culture-of-poverty thesis.

CONCLUSIONS

This chapters identifies some of the intellectual antecedents of Myrdal's cumulative hypothesis. This thesis accepts the notion that groups may develop pathological behavior, but focuses on external forces including racism and poverty rather than on internal predispositions. During the first part of this century most liberal economists applied this culture-of-poverty thesis to European immigrants. Liberals rejected the notion that economic differences between immigrants and native American workers reflected genetic differences. For Commons, these immigrants had developed dysfunctional behavior because of the undemocratic environments of eastern and southern Europe. For Ross and Wirth, environmental factors helped explain the distinction between Russian and German Jewry.

While they focused on environmental factors when explaining differences between immigrant and native workers, liberals generally continued to accept genetic explanations for the differences between whites and blacks. Unlike Booker T. Washington, liberals were not yet prepared to hold out hope that with proper institutional changes, black Americans would be capable of attaining economic equality with white Americans. It was Myrdal's work which signaled a change in liberal attitudes. Once the same culture-of-poverty thesis was used to explain black–white differences, it opened the door to a vision of racial economic equality.[12]

Myrdal's cumulative process claimed that racism and poverty reinforced dysfunctional behavior within the black population. These black attitudes and actions would only reinforce racism and institutional barriers which would perpetuate racial economic inequality. Myrdal hoped that government policies could reverse the process by providing role models and rising aspirations which would undermine the dysfunctional culture in which many poor blacks were mired.

This chapter has found that at least some liberal social scientists continue to incorporate important aspects of Myrdal's cumulative hypothesis into their analysis. Dysfunctional behavioral traits play a role in the analysis of inner city black poverty presented by Richard Freeman and his associates. Michael Piore points to the dynamics of secondary labor markets as a reinforcing mechanism. Finally, William J. Wilson finds that the elimination of middle-class role models and the institutions they provide may be an important factor in explaining the dysfunctional behavioral traits increasingly associated with poor inner city blacks.

APPENDIX: TEENAGE OUT-OF-WEDLOCK BIRTHS

In the last decade, there has been increasing notoriety given to the alleged explosion of births to unwed African American teenagers.[10] Explanations which emphasize pathological behavior are rampant. Virtually all commentators approve government policies which will implicitly coerce young African American women to avoid motherhood. Whereas liberals emphasize abortions, conservatives emphasize the implantation of birth control devices and welfare penalties.[11]

Recently, researchers have demonstrated that the large number of out-of-wedlock births to poor African American teenagers may be quite rational. Elaine McCrate (1990) studied a group of young women. She found that high school completion rates for African American women who had children before they were eighteen years old were 40 per cent lower than the rate for those who did not. This differential was less than the 77 per cent differential found in the white community. McCrate reasoned that within African American communities, substantial support from extended families reduces costs to young mothers who wish to attend school. Without these support networks, young white mothers find it more costly to attend school so that their educational attainment is much lower than the educational attainment of white women who delay motherhood.

Most importantly, McCrate found that African American women had a lower rate of financial return from delaying motherhood than white women. Delaying motherhood only raised African American wage rates by 9 per cent where it raised white wage rates almost 30 per cent. McCrate contends that with such low payoffs, it is quite rational for young African American women to have higher birth rates than young white women.

There are also health factors which make it quite rational for African American women to avoid delaying motherhood. Within the middle-class white population, health care advances have increased the viability of pregnancies for older women. In contrast, without decent health care available, poor African American women have a marked increase in pregnancy complications during young adulthood. These health problems make it even more rational for poor African American women to have children while they are still healthy.

Another study by Arline Geronimus and Sanders Korenman (1991) suggests that McCrate's findings may overstate the educational and wage benefits poor African American teenagers gain from delayed motherhood. These researchers also found that women who delayed motherhood were more likely to graduate high school and had higher incomes than those who had children as teenagers. However, factors other than delayed motherhood could explain these differences. For example, the group that had children as teenagers came from poorer socio-economic backgrounds than the group that delayed motherhood. They found that when adjustments were made for these factors, delaying motherhood had virtually no impact on educational attainment and income.

Geronimus and Korenman were able to adjust for these other factors in a very precise manner. Their sample included sisters. These researchers found no difference in the likelihood of attaining high school degrees and no income differences between women who had children as teenagers and their sisters who delayed motherhood. Thus, there are few economic benefits for poor African American teenage women to delay motherhood and substantial health reasons not to.

These findings suggest that childbearing differences between poor African American women and middle-class women are not due to differences in attitudes or motivation; both groups react rationally to the benefits and costs they face. Labelling the behavior of young African American women as pathological is racist, and recommendations to implement coercive birth control policies or aggressively promoting abortions should be condemned in the strongest possible manner.

Delayed motherhood is a function of the economic benefits from advanced education available to women and the health services provided to mothers. If poor African American women faced less job discrimination and were provided decent health care, they too would find it rational to delay motherhood. We should change the deplorable conditions young African American women face rather than demeaning their rational responses. Public policies should treat these women with dignity and improve their situation directly rather than "blaming the victim."

NOTES

1 For details on journal publications, see Cherry (1976, 1980).

2 This section will summarize the two most prominent viewpoints: the genetic and the environmental racialist positions. Both of these groups considered immigrants to be inferior but different as to the source of that inferiority. There was a a third group that completely rejected the notion of inferiority. Since this group was not as influential and not relevant for the issues at hand, they will be ignored. For a summary of these views, see Cherry (1976).

3 For a discussion of the relationship of Fisher's racial thought and his economics, see Mark Aldrich (1975).

4 In his analysis of the anti-Chinese movement in California in the 1880s. Commons (1918: 252–3) contended. "The anti-Chinese agitation in California, culminating as it did in the Exclusion Law of 1882, was doubtless the most important single factor in the history of American labor, for without it the entire country might have been overrun by Mongolian labor and the labor movement might have become a conflict of races instead of one of classes."

5 For a detailed discussion of Commons's views on blacks, see Aldrich (1985) and Ramstad and Starkey (1992).

6 This section follows the material found in Aldrich (1979).

7 For a further discussion of the Jewish immigrant experience, see Steinberg (1981).

8 When standardized for location – rural farm, rural nonfarm, urban – African American broken families were twice the rate of white broken families.

9 Among the important books condemning the Moynihan Report see William Ryan (1971), Charles Valentine (1968), and Herbert Gutman (1976).

10 In fact, fertility rates for young African American women fell substantially between 1965 and 1985. For a discussion on how to evaluate changing fertility rates see McLanahan (1985).

11 Wisconsin and New Jersey have passed legislation penalizing welfare mothers who have additional children. Others are considering paying welfare mothers money if they accept the Norville birth control implant.

12 Myrdal selected Wirth as his white social science critic. For the full relationship between Wirth and Myrdal, see Southern (1987).

REFERENCES

Aldrich, Mark (1975) "Capital Theory and Racism," *Review of Radical Political Economy* 7 (Fall): 33–42.

——(1979) "Progressive Economists and Scientific Racism: Walter Willcox and Black Americans, 1895–1910," *Phylon* 40 (March): 1–14.

——(1985) "The Backward Races and the American Social Order." Mimeo.

Bound, John and Richard Freeman (1989) "Black Economic Progress: Erosion of the Post-1965 Gains in the 1980s?" In *The Question of Discrimination*, ed. by Steven Shulman and William Darity, Jr, 32–49. Middleton, CT: Wesleyan Univ. Press.

Cherry, Robert (1976) "Racial Thought and the Early Economics Profession," *Rev. Soc. Econ.* 33(Oct): 147–62.

——(1980) "Biology, Sociology, and Economics," *Rev. Soc. Econ.* 37(Oct): 140–51.

Commons, John R. (1904) "Amalgamation and Assimilation," *The Chatauquan* 39(April): 217–27.

——(1918) *History of Labor Movements in the United States*, New York: Macmillan.

——(1919) *Industrial Goodwill*, New York: Macmillan.
——(1920) *Races and Immigrants in America*, New York: Macmillan.
Culp, Jerome and Bruce Dunson (1986) "Brothers of a Different Color: A Preliminary Look at Employment Treatment of White and Black Youth." In *The Black Youth Employment Crisis*, ed. by Richard Freeman and Harry Holzer, 233–60. Chicago: Univ. of Chicago Press.
Ely, Richard T. (1891) "Pauperism and Poverty," *North Atlantic Review* 152: 393–404.
Fetter, Frank A. (1904) *Principles of Economics*, New York: Macmillan.
——(1907) "Discussant," *AEA Publications*, Third Series 8: 92–4.
——(1915) *Economic Principles*, New York: Macmillan.
——(1916) *Modern Economic Principles*, New York: Macmillan.
——(1918) "Discussant," *American Economics Review* 8: 234–5.
Fisher, Irving (1907) *The Rate of Interest*, New York: Macmillan.
——(1911) *Elementary Principles of Economics*, New York: Macmillan.
——(1916) "Some Impending National Problems," *Journal of Political Economy* 24: 691–711.
——(1921) "Impending Problems of Eugenics," *Scientific Monthly* 13(September): 214–31.
Fisher, Irving and E. Fisk (1915) *How to Live*, New York.
Freeman, Richard (1973) "Changes in the Labor Market for Black Americans, 1958–72," *Brookings Papers* (Summer): 67–131.
——(1986) "Who Escapes? The Relation of Churchgoing and Other Background Factors to the Socioeconomic Performance of Black Youths." In *The Black Youth Employment Crisis*, ed. by Richard Freeman and Harry Holzer, 353–76. Chicago: Univ. of Chicago Press.
Geronimus, Arline and Sanders Korenman (1991) "The Socioeconomic Consequences of Teen Childbearing Reconsidered," *Quarterly Journal of Economics*.
Gutman, Herbert (1976) *The Black Family in Slavery and Freedom, 1750–1925*, New York: Pantheon.
Hall, Prescott (1908) *Immigration and Its Effects*, New York.
——(1912) "Review." *American Economics Review*, 2: 672–6.
——(1913) "Immigration and Immigration Restrictions," *J. of Pol. Econ.*, 21: 735–51.
Haller, Mark (1963) *Eugenics*, New Brunswick, NJ: Rutgers University Press.
Hoffman, Frederick (1896) "Race Traits and Tendencies in the American Negro," *AEA Publications*, First Series 9: 1–329.
Holzer, Harry (1986) "Black Youth Nonemployment: Duration and Search." In *The Black Youth Employment Crisis*, ed. by Richard Freeman and Harry Holzer, 23–70. Univ. of Chicago Press.
Jencks J.W. and W.J. Lauck (1911) "Economic Aspects of Immigration," *Pol. Science Quarterly*, 26: 615–42.
McCrate, Elaine (1990) "Returns to Education and Teenage Childbearing," *Review of Black Political Economy*.
McLanahan, Sara (1985) "Charles Murray and the Family." In *Losing Ground: A Critique*, ed. by Sara McLanahan *et al.*, 1–7. Madison, WI: Institute for Research on Poverty, Univ. of Wisc.
Mead, Lawrence (1988) "The New Welfare Debate," *Commentary* 85: 44–52.
Moynihan, Daniel P. (1965) *The Negro Family: The Case for National Action*, Washington, DC: Office of Policy Planning and Research, US Department of Labor.
Myrdal, Gunnar (1944) *An American Dilemma*, 2 Vols. New York: Harper & Row.
Piore, Michael (1977) "The Dual Labor Market." In *Problems in Political Economy*, ed. by David Gordon, 91–5. Lexington, MA: D.C. Heath.

Ramstad, Yngve and James Starkey (1992) "The Racial Theories of John R. Commons." Mimeo.

Ross, Edward A. (1972 [1916]) "The Old World in the New." In *Kike!*, ed. by Michael Selzer, 63–76. New York: World Publishing.

Ryan, William (1971) *Blaming the Victim*, New York: Random House.

Sawhil, Isabel (1988) "Poverty in the US: Why is it so Persistent?," *Journal Econ Lit.* 26: 1098–1115.

Southern, David (1987) *Gunnar Myrdal and Black–White Relations*, Baton Range: Louisiana State University Press.

Steinberg, Stephen (1981) *The Ethnic Myth*, New York: Antheum.

Tillinghast, John (1902) "The Negro in Africa and America," *AEA Publications*, 3rd Series 3: 401–638.

Valentine, Charles (1968) *Culture and Poverty*, Chicago: Univ. of Chicago Press.

Visarsi, Kip (1986) "Market Incentives for Criminal Behavior." In *The Black Youth Employment Crisis*, ed. by Richard Freeman and Harry Holzer, 301–46. Chicago: University of Chicago Press.

Walker, Francis A. (1891) "The Colored Race in the United States," *Forum* 11: 501–9.

——(1896) "Restriction on Immigration," *Atlantic Monthly* 25: 822–9.

Washington, Booker T. (1902) *The Future of the American Negro*, New York.

——(1963 [1903]) *Up From Slavery*, Garden City, NY: Doubleday.

——(1970 [1907]) *The Negro in the South*, New York: Carol Publishing.

Willcox, Walter (1908) "Negro Criminality." In *Studies in the American Race Problem*, ed. by Alfred Stone and Walter Willcox, 443–75. New York: Macmillan.

Wilson, William J. (1987) *The Truly Disadvantaged*, Chicago: University of Chicago Press.

Wirth, Louis (1956) *Community Life and Social Policy.* Chicago: University of Chicago Press.

3

GHETTO POVERTY

Black problem or harbinger of things to come?*

Ronald B. Mincy

During the 1980s, researchers and policy analysts emphasized the increasing concentration of poverty, labor force detachment, and related social problems among blacks in our nation's largest cities (Clark and Nathan 1982; Gottschalk and Danziger 1986; Kaus 1986; Wilson 1987; Reischauer, 1987; Hughes, 1989). Using terms like *under class,*** *ghetto poverty*, and *impacted ghetto*, several books and articles gave detailed descriptions of black neighborhoods with high rates of poverty, welfare dependency, male joblessness, crime and drug abuse, high school drop-out, and out-of-wedlock childbearing among adults and teenagers (Glasgow 1980; Auletta 1982, Lehman, 1986; Wilson, 1987).

Not until the Los Angeles riots in 1992, however, were commitments to address these problems echoed among policymakers and political leaders, and even these belated commitments were short-lived. After a brief flirtation with a bill that would have provided summer jobs for inner city youth and enterprise zones, the new, national urban agenda quickly vanished. Given mainstream concerns about the deficit, health care costs, a sluggish economy, and lagging US productivity, how could an agenda focused so narrowly on the needs of the black inner city poor be sustained?

Perhaps this narrow focus on inner city blacks is precisely the problem. Wilson (1987), the leading theorist of the under class, pointed to macrostructural changes as the principal cause and called for race-blind policies as the cure. Nevertheless, his attempts (and those of others) to measure the phenomenon focused on low-skilled blacks in large northeast and north

* This chapter is a product of the Underclass Research Project. Partial funding for this paper was provided by the Rockefeller Foundation. The author wishes to thank Isabel Sawhill, Sheldon Danziger, and James Smith for their comments on earlier drafts. I also wish to thank Mitch Tobin and Susan Wiener for their research assistance.

Opinions expressed are those of the author and should not be attributed to the Urban Institute or its sponsors.

** For reasons elaborated in this chapter I use the expression under class for the noun (and therefore under-class as the corresponding adjective) by analogy with working class etc.

central metropolitan areas. This empirical strategy obscures the connection between macro-structural changes and non-black, non-urban concerns. Unless this connection is made, however, the public and policymakers will continue to view black-urban and mainstream concerns as competing, and therefore, efforts to reverse the effects of macro-structural changes on low-skilled populations will be politically unsustainable.

Empirical studies of the size and growth of Wilson's concern leave unanswered questions about the race and ethnic composition of underclass and poverty neighborhoods.[1] Studies agree that blacks are over-represented, but vary widely in estimates of how many whites and members of other ethnic groups were involved. For example, the earliest studies of concentrated, or ghetto poverty, assumed or concluded that only minorities are involved (Clark and Nathan 1982; Gottschalk and Danziger 1986; Kaus 1986; Wilson 1987; Bane and Jargowsky 1988). This conclusion may have been the result of focusing on larger metropolitan areas, where blacks and Puerto Ricans concentrate. Ricketts and Sawhill (1988), who studied the spatial concentration of social problems (under-class neighborhoods), found that whites were a significant minority, but they did not distinguish between Hispanic whites and non-Hispanic whites. This raises the question, "How would disaggregation of the Hispanic population affect our understanding of the racial and ethnic composition of under-class neighborhoods?"

Uncertainty about the racial and ethnic composition of the under-class and poverty neighborhoods leaves theoretical and policy questions unanswered. Theoretical questions arise because of the emphasis on macro-structural changes. For example, Why did the adverse effects of these changes fall so disproportionately on inner city minorities? Policy questions arise from criticisms of studies that focus on social problems other than poverty, narrowly defined as income below the government poverty standard. Several observers claim that these studies have a chilling effect on social policy because they blame poor minority members for their problems (Gans 1990; Wilson, 1991). Would the same chilling effect exist if the under-class phenomenon affected low-skilled members of all racial and ethnic groups, including whites?

Mincy (1988) examined the racial and ethnic composition of under-class and extreme poverty neighborhoods in 1980, separating Hispanics, non-Hispanic blacks (from now on, blacks), and non-Hispanic whites (from now on, whites). There were two important findings. First, the racial and ethnic compositions of under-class and extreme poverty neighborhoods were remarkably similar. Neighborhoods with non-Hispanic white majorities represented about a fifth of all under-class and extreme poverty neighborhoods and about a fifth of the population living in each type of neighborhood was non-Hispanic white. Second, unlike neighborhoods with black and (probably) Puerto Rican majorities, white under-class and extreme poverty neighborhoods were concentrated in smaller metropolitan and non-metropolitan areas.

Now that the 1990 Census data are available, a new round of estimates of Wilson's concern is underway. In my view researchers and policy analysts are again ignoring what is taking place among non-blacks in smaller metropolitan and non-metropolitan areas.[2] Therefore, this chapter analyzes changes in the under-class and extreme poverty neighborhood populations in the 1980s in non-metropolitan areas and in small, middle-sized, and large metropolitan areas. The results amplify the findings of Mincy and Wiener (forthcoming) concerning the divergence of under-class and extreme poverty neighborhood population in the 1980s. They show that while the under-class neighborhood population changed little in the 1980s, the extreme poverty area population nearly doubled. This chapter shows that two-thirds of the growth occurred in non-black extreme poverty neighborhoods. The growth of the population in white extreme poverty neighborhoods was three times the growth in black extreme poverty neighborhoods, so that now white extreme poverty and the under class are problems of the same order of magnitude.

To begin, the chapter explains my choice of terms, before reviewing the rationale for studying the spatial concentration of poverty and examining the potential effects of this criterion on estimates of the racial and ethnic composition of the under class. This review shows that studies focused on larger metropolitan areas could bias estimates of the racial/ethnic composition of under-class and extreme poverty neighborhoods. Second, the chapter reviews hypotheses about the emergence and growth of under-class and extreme poverty neighborhoods that anticipate the racial and ethnic composition of these neighborhoods. Third, the chapter discusses the data used to analyze the racial and ethnic composition of these neighborhoods and presents the results of the analysis. Finally, the chapter offers policy conclusions, based on a clearer understanding of the racial, ethnic, and size-of-place in under-class and extreme poverty neighborhoods.

TERMINOLOGY

Though precise definitions of terms are given below, some discussion at the outset will avoid unnecessary confusion. The controversy surrounding Moynihan (1965) left a legacy for research on black Americans that persists even today. The effects of this controversy are evident in the list of terms used by empirical researchers to identify the population or neighborhood on which they focus. Researchers choose terms to distinguish their work from (or relate their work to) prior work, to avoid charges of racism and victim blaming, and to avoid unflattering characterizations of the population in question. For all these reasons, the remainder of this chapter uses the terms under class and extreme poverty wherever possible.

Under-class neighborhoods are census tracts in which non-mainstream behaviors are commonplace (Ricketts and Sawhill 1988). Unfortunately, behavior is a very ambiguous word, especially in interdisciplinary work. Some readers assume that behavior reflects primarily or exclusively the culture, attitudes, or preferences that individuals bring to decision making. This is a trap I wish to avoid. Instead, this chapter uses the term *under-class* neighborhood to remind readers of familiar class distinctions emphasizing earnings, employment or occupational status, as well as the social context which people maintain for themselves and for family members. For example, upper-class neighborhoods are places where the typical resident is at the top of occupational and earnings hierarchies. Successful entrepreneurs, corporate and political leaders, and high earning members of other professions (e.g., doctors and lawyers) reside in these neighborhoods. By analogy, under-class neighborhoods are places where the typical residents are at the opposite extremes of occupational and earnings hierarchies. These people have trouble entering and remaining in the labor force, and they derive much of their income from informal, illegal, or irregular employment, or from public assistance (Van Haitsma 1989 and Mincy forthcoming).

In recent years, *ghetto* has become synonymous with a distressed black, urban neighborhood. For example, impacted ghettos are black-majority neighborhoods (in the largest metropolitan areas) in which non-mainstream behaviors are commonplace (Hughes 1989). Concentrated poverty and ghetto poverty neighborhoods are census tracts in which the black poverty rate is at least 40 per cent (Jargowsky and Bane 1990). However, this chapter is not just about poor black neighborhoods in large metropolitan areas. Therefore, I avoid the term ghetto. Instead, this chapter uses the term *extreme poverty* neighborhood, which is a census tract (in a non-metropolitan area or a metropolitan area of any size) in which the poverty rate (of all residents) is at least 40 per cent.

RATIONALE FOR STUDYING THE SPATIAL CONCENTRATION OF POVERTY

According to Wilson (1987), two developments are responsible for the growth of poverty and social problems in inner city neighborhoods. First, macro-structural changes in urban economics reduced the demand for low-skilled workers, which led to the growth in urban joblessness, and thus increased inner-city poverty. Second, the increasing concentration of poverty in inner-city neighborhoods produced an increase in social problems. Wilson argues that government policies such as the Fair Housing Act and equal employment opportunity legislation favored better-educated blacks. This promoted out migration of working and middle-class blacks from once stable, economically integrated, but racially segregated, neighborhoods. Thus, out-migration of advantaged blacks resulted in the increasing concentration of inner-city poverty and social problems.

Outmigration is an important aspect of Wilson's hypothesis of underclass formation. He asserts that when located in the same neighborhoods where less-advantaged blacks lived, middle and working-class blacks provided valuable community resources that stabilized inner city neighborhoods. These included: 1 role models of upward mobility for the children of poorer blacks; 2 networks leading to mainstream jobs for poorer blacks; 3 resources for maintaining neighborhood institutions (e.g., churches, local businesses); 4 social sanctions against criminal behavior; and 5 mainstream patterns of schooling and family formation.

Once working and middle-class blacks left inner city neighborhoods, these resources were no longer available. This destabilized black, inner city neighborhoods. The result, according to Wilson, was the growing isolation of poor black neighborhoods from mainstream society and an increase in social problems in the isolated neighborhoods (e.g., crime, joblessness, welfare dependency, single parenting, and dropping out of high school). Increasing concentrations of poverty caused an increase in social problems through what Wilson calls "concentration effects."

To support his thesis of the under class Wilson amassed data on poverty and other social problems from several disparate sources. He frequently presented tabulations from published sources, disaggregated by race, ethnicity, and metropolitan area residence. He made the strongest case for growth in the spatial concentration of poverty for the largest five and the largest fifty cities. Together these data supported two propositions about changes during the 1970s and early 1980s. First, spatial concentration of poverty increased dramatically over the period, and the increase among blacks dominated increases among other race and ethnic groups. Second, social problems also grew most dramatically among blacks.

Extensions of Wilson's analysis offered the earliest comprehensive measures of the under class (Gottschalk and Danziger 1986; Nathan 1986; Bane and Jargowsky 1988). Most of these studies used published census data on the poor population in poor neighborhoods (i.e., the concentrated poverty neighborhood population) in large cities and examined blacks and Hispanics only. Some studies focused on neighborhoods with poverty rates of 20 per cent or more (poverty neighborhoods), others focused on neighborhoods with poverty rates of 40 per cent or more (extreme poverty neighborhoods).

These studies supported the idea that the under class was almost exclusively a minority problem. Table 3.1 shows typical results for the racial and ethnic composition of the poor in poverty and extreme poverty neighborhoods, using published data for the 100 largest cities.[3] Blacks were 57 per cent of the poor in poverty neighborhoods, Hispanics were 23 per cent, and whites were 17 per cent (column 2). Minority shares of the poor living in extreme poverty neighborhoods were even larger. Blacks were 68 per cent of this population, Hispanics were 21 per cent, and whites were just 10 per cent (column 5).

Table 3.1 The distribution of poor persons living in poverty areas in the hundred largest central cities, by racial/ethnic group and type of poverty area, 1980

	Poor persons in poverty areas			*Poor persons in extreme poverty areas*		
Racial/ethnic group	*Number poor*	*Percentage of all poor in these areas*	*Percentage of racial/ ethnic group in these areas*	*Number poor*	*Percentage of all poor in these areas*	*Percentage of racial/ethnic group in these areas*
Non-Hispanic black	2,971,409	57	37	1,248,151	68	51
Non-Hispanic white	902,278	17	23	175,178	10	39
Hispanic	1,168,567	23	37	383,355	21	52
Other	148,860	3	n.a.	27,700	2	n.a.
Total	5,191,114	100	34	1,834,384	100	50

Source: US Bureau of the Census, "1980 Census of the Population, vol. 2: Poverty Areas in Large Cities," Subject Reports PC80-2-8D, Table 1 (Washington, DC: US Government Printing Office, 1985)
Note: a This column should be interpreted as: 37 per cent of Non-Hispanic black persons in poverty areas are poor

Location patterns, which vary considerably by race and ethnicity, partly account for these results. For example, Table 3.2 shows (for 1980) the fraction of the US population living anywhere in the 100 largest cities and the fractions of the US poverty population living anywhere, in poverty neighborhoods, and in extreme poverty neighborhoods in these same cities. For purposes of discussion, divide the fractions in the table for each

Table 3.2 The percentage distribution of the total population and the poverty population in the hundred largest central cities, by race and type of poverty area, 1980

	Percentage of US population living in 100 largest central cities	*Percentage of US poverty population living in 100 largest central cities*		
Racial/ethnic group	*All areas of city*	*All areas of city*	*Poverty areas*	*Extreme poverty areas*[a]
Non-Hispanic black	47	48	40	17
Non-Hispanic white	15	17	6	1
Hispanic	41	47	35	11
Other	33	33	17	3
TOTAL	21	30	19	7

Sources: US Bureau of the Census, "1980 Census of Population, vol. 1: General Social and Economic Characteristics," US Summary PC80–1–C1 (Washington, DC: US Government Printing Office, 1983) Tables 74, 75, 96, 171. US Bureau of the Census, "1980 Census of the Population, vol. 2: Poverty Areas in Large Cities," Subject Reports PC80–2–8D (Washington, DC: US Government Printing Office, 1985) Table 1
Note: a This column should be interpreted as: 17 per cent of poor blacks live in extreme poverty areas in the 100 largest central cities

minority group by the fractions for whites. The results are the relative propensities of minorities to live in large cities.[4]

Minorities were two to three times as likely to live anywhere in these cities. Further, blacks had higher relative propensities to live in these cities than Hispanics. Finally, as neighborhood poverty rates declined, the relative propensities of poor minorities to live in these cities increased. Thus, poor blacks were 6.6 times as likely as poor whites to live in poverty neighborhoods in these 100 cities. Poor blacks were 17.0 times as likely as poor whites to live in extreme poverty neighborhoods in these cities.

Very different hypotheses could account for these location patterns. Historically, minorities may have preferred large cities because these cities held better job prospects for low-skilled workers. More recently, the decline in demand for such workers in large cities may have increased their poverty rates. But if sources of public assistance are more readily available in larger cities, these groups would be more likely to remain (Kasarda 1993). Segregation is another possible explanation. Segregation in low-income housing markets in smaller cities may restrict poor minorities to larger cities. Finally, Hispanics may concentrate in large cities because these cities are close to the points at which they, or their parents, entered the country.

Thus, spatial criteria affect the racial and ethnic composition of the under class. Poor whites are less likely than poor minorities to live in poverty or extreme poverty neighborhoods in the 100 largest cities. Therefore, a more racially and ethnically diverse under class might emerge if studies: 1 used some criteria other than the poverty rate to define an under-class neighborhood; and 2 included data from small, middle size, and large places.

THEORY AND THE RACIAL/ETHNIC COMPOSITION OF THE UNDER CLASS

Do theoretical considerations also give us reason to expect more racial and ethnic diversity than studies of large cities show? Most of the conceptual literature tries to explain the emergence of a black under class. Studies rarely consider the possibility that non-blacks are in the under class. Therefore, to answer our question, we must reinterpret the conceptual literature.

Values, attitudes, and migration determine the racial and ethnic composition of the under class in the conceptual literature. For example, Lehman (1986, 1991) argues that the least successful blacks in northern cities were descendants of recent immigrants to cities who brought values and attitudes that differed from those of longer term, urban residents (whites). This explanation implies that the under class is almost exclusively black. The remaining explanations emphasize structural economic change, migration, and government policy and do not assume that values and attitudes are transported through migration or that values and attitudes vary by race or ethnicity. Instead, if values and attitudes play a role at all, this role may be as either cause or effect.

Lehman's explanation of the emergence of the under class has implications for blacks only. Blacks are descendants of immigrants with values and attitudes shaped by share-cropping and employment discrimination in rural southern towns after slavery. Through share-cropping, blacks learned to accept economic dependence upon whites. Through employment discrimination, black men became accustomed to a life of "hustling," rather than stable employment. With very unstable incomes, these men rarely supported their families consistently. So unstable common-law marriages, matriarchal families, and male non-participation in the labor force developed into accepted patterns in lower-class black communities. When blacks migrated north they brought these attitudes with them. In the present generation, these attitudes are manifest in social problems such as welfare dependency, female-headed households, and male labor force detachment.

Other explanations need not apply strictly to blacks. Recall that Wilson's explanation rests on two key ideas. First, macro-structural changes reduced the demand for low-wage labor in urban neighborhoods, leaving low-skilled blacks in these neighborhoods jobless and poor. Second, out-migration of middle and working-class blacks isolated low-skilled blacks from mainstream role models and other resources.

These ideas seem plausible, but not for blacks exclusively. Low-skilled members of other racial and ethnic groups were not immune to macro-structural changes. These changes also reduced employment and real wages among low-skilled whites and Hispanics (Lichter 1988; Berlin and Sum 1988; Juhn, Murphy, and Pierce 1989, Blackburn, Bloom, and Freeman 1990; O'Hare and Curry-White 1992). Wilson's second argument seems to apply strictly to blacks, but this argument receives mixed support from the data. The Fair Housing Act of 1970 released a flood of middle and working-class blacks who wanted to leave ghetto neighborhoods. Similar phenomena did not come into play for non-blacks. But, at the end of the decade, poor and non-poor blacks were no more spatially isolated from one another than poor and non-poor members of other racial and ethnic groups (Massey and Eggers, 1990). If poor whites and Hispanics were also isolated from upwardly mobile members of their racial and ethnic group, why didn't their neighborhoods destabilize? Why didn't social isolation from mainstream role models and resources produce some increase in labor force detachment among these groups?

Government policies play a key role in conservative explanations of emergence of the under class (Murray 1984; Mead 1986). For example, Mead argues that the War on Poverty provided Aid to Families with Dependent Families (AFDC) benefits and other assistance to the poor, but these programs did not impose social obligations (e.g., work, finishing high school, and delaying parenthood until one can support children). So these programs encouraged the social problems associated with the under class.

While minorities furnish their main examples, Murray and Mead do not assume that values and attitudes regarding work and welfare vary by race and ethnicity. Therefore, their explanations should apply to low-skilled members of other racial and ethnic groups, who presumably also find government programs attractive alternatives to work at low wages.

Finally, one might argue that migration prevented the emergence of an under class among low-skilled non-blacks. Then why did migration not prevent the formation of an under class among low-skilled blacks? Kasarda (1993) argues that in the metropolitan areas hardest hit by structural change, low-skilled blacks found substitutes for the income, goods, and services formerly derived from employment. The major substitutes – welfare, public housing, and employment in the underground economy – removed the pressure for jobless blacks to migrate to other neighborhoods where the demand for low-skilled workers remained high. But were displaced members of other racial and ethnic groups more likely than displaced blacks to migrate?[5] Were they less likely than displaced blacks to depend on welfare, public housing, and the underground economy? These questions remain unanswered.

RATIONALE FOR STUDYING SPATIAL CONCENTRATION OF SOCIAL PROBLEMS

Wilson (1987) also provided the rationale for studying the spatial concentration of social problems. His definition of the under class emphasized a heterogeneous grouping of families and individuals. Although members of this grouping had distinct social problems, they lived and interacted in the same troubled neighborhoods, which helped to isolate them from the mainstream.

Ricketts and Sawhill (1988) designed a measure of under-class neighborhoods to reflect this definition. According to Ricketts and Sawhill (from now on R/S), an under-class neighborhood is a census tract with above average rates of the following four social problems: 1 male detachment from the labor force; 2 households receiving public assistance; 3 households headed by females with children; and 4 dropping out of high school among teenagers. This definition used the areal unit of observation in census tract data. This allowed R/S to study a heterogeneous group of families and individuals that exhibited distinct social problems, but lived and interacted in the same neighborhood.

Conceptually, everyone who lives in an under-class neighborhood is in the under-class-neighborhood population, whether or not they exhibit the social problems used as under-class-neighborhood criteria. Some observers object that this stigmatizes people because of their residence. Neither

Wilson nor R/S intended to stigmatize. Instead, they used inclusive conceptual and empirical constructs meant to center attention on concentration effects.

For example, a boy who grows up in a neighborhood where a large fraction of the men rarely work, or look for work, may eventually accept this outcome as the norm for adult males. When a girl sees that women head a large fraction of the neighborhood families and support these families by AFDC, she may foresee this outcome for the family she might someday form. Finally, children growing up in neighborhoods where a large fraction of the teenagers – including their older brothers and sisters – fail to complete high school, may themselves expect to become high school drop-outs. Such concentration effects receive mixed support in the quantitative literature, partly because it is hard to separate the effects of family background from the effects of neighborhood characteristics, but stronger support exists in the qualitative literature.[6] If such concentration effects are important, the focus of study and policy should not only include those who already exhibit social problems, but should extend to those who are at risk for developing social problems. People at risk live in neighborhoods where social problems are commonplace. The inclusive constructs proposed by Wilson and R/S meet this objective.

The R/S study has three other features that merit close attention. First, its definition is very restrictive. A census tract cannot become an under-class neighborhood unless the incidence of each social problem is at least one standard deviation above the mean for all tracted neighborhoods. Such values coincided for 880 neighborhoods in the R/S study. These neighborhoods included 2.5 million people. Second, R/S assess the incidence of social problems in a neighborhood through comparisons with means for all tracted neighborhoods, not means for each metropolitan area. The mean for all tracted neighborhoods more closely resembles norms that prevail throughout society, while the mean for a particular metropolitan area could vary considerably from social norms. This would make standards for including neighborhoods in the under class vary from one metropolitan area to another (Ricketts and Mincy 1990). Third, because R/S use all tracted neighborhoods, there should be no large metropolitan area bias in their results.

R/S disaggregated the under-class-neighborhood population into three racial and ethnic groups: blacks, whites, and Hispanics who did not report their race as white. They found that blacks represented 59 per cent of the under-class-neighborhood population, whites represented 28 per cent, and Hispanics represented 10 per cent. The R/S estimate of the white share of the under-class-neighborhood population is much higher than estimates based on the spatial concentration of poverty in the 100 largest cities. This leads one to ask what the white share of the under-class-neighborhood population would be, if Hispanic whites and non-Hispanic whites were tabulated separately.

This introduces a second rationale for studying the spatial concentration of social problems by race and ethnicity. Jargowsky and Bane (1990) and Jargowsky (1993) studied the poor in poverty neighborhoods and the social conditions of all people in such neighborhoods. Thus, their study uses both exclusive and inclusive constructs, though they reject the term *under class* in favor of *ghetto poverty.* Both studies omitted whites from discussions of the level of ghetto poverty because the earlier study revealed three findings for 1980: 1 few whites live in poor neighborhoods; 2 white ghetto poverty is constant across regions and cities; and 3 whites who live in neighborhoods with poverty rates exceeding 20 per cent appear to be either college students or Hispanics. The third observation suggests that the concentration of poverty among whites is some kind of anomaly, unworthy of policy attention.[7]

Spatial concentrations of the social problems that Wilson and R/S emphasize are not subject to this interpretation. Concentrations of idle teenagers, idle adult males, and female-headed families that depend upon welfare, reveal a serious and undeniable social problem. This heterogeneous grouping of troubled families and individuals cannot be mistaken for a population that postpones employment to invest in schooling. Further, if we are careful to distinguish between racial and ethnic groups, the data can tell us if the problem belongs to minorities exclusively.

RECONCILING THE ESTIMATES: DATA AND METHODS

To reconcile and update estimates of the racial and ethnic composition of residents of under-class and extreme poverty neighborhoods, we make four adjustments to previous work. First, we include small, medium, and large metropolitan areas in the sample to adjust for differential location patterns by race, ethnicity, and size-of-place neighborhood. Second, we disaggregate race and ethnicity into mutually exclusive groups: 1 persons of Hispanic origin (Hispanic); 2 non-Hispanic black; 3 non-Hispanic white; and 4 other. Third, we make both spatial measures inclusive by including all persons living in under-class neighborhoods or all persons living in extreme poverty neighborhoods. In this way, both measures reflect concentration effects, and we avoid confusing results for non-Hispanic whites with results for non-Hispanic members of other racial groups. Fourth, we include data for 1990.

Finally, to be clear, this chapter measures under-class neighborhoods in the same way that R/S measured under-class neighborhoods. I change the term to emphasize why I believe the four R/S criteria are important. I think Van Haitsma (1989) is correct: detachment from the labor force and earnings are the principal problems of the under class. This is why the term under class fits neatly with terms such as upper, middle, and lower class, which emphasize employment (or, occupational) status and earnings. The first R/S criterion measures labor force detachment (for males) directly. The second criterion measures income from public assistance. The other two criteria measure barriers to labor force attachment.

The data come from the Urban Institute Under Class Data Base (UDB), which includes tabulations from over 34,000 tracts in the 1970 Census, 42,000 tracts in the 1980 Census and 61,000 tracts in the 1990 Census. These tabulations include demographic characteristics and social problem indicators for each tract. Although UDB includes three decades, we use only the 1980 and 1990 data, because these two decades have comparable definitions of Hispanic.[8]

The source of these tabulations is the 1980 and 1990 Censuses of Population, Summary Tape File 3A. These files contain aggregate counts of people with different characteristics in each census tract. The major advantage of these data is that they are very large and contain very detailed information about small geographic neighborhoods (census tracts) that are the statistical equivalents of neighborhoods. On average each census tract includes 4,000 persons. The unit of observation for this data file is a census tract – the census analog for the neighborhood – not a person. This unit of observation is the same used by R/S and is well suited for Wilson's inclusive under class concept.

The data have three disadvantages. First, the 1980 STF3-A files covered only tracted neighborhoods, 99 per cent of which were inside metropolitan areas. In 1990, the Census Bureau established Block Numbering Areas (BNAs) in small statistical subdivisions of non-metropolitan counties, where local census statistical committees had not established census tracts. Therefore, one cannot observe concentrations of poverty and labor force detachment in non-metropolitan neighborhoods in 1980, but these are observable in 1990. Consequently, our results should underestimate the under-class and extreme poverty neighborhood populations in 1980, but not in 1990. Second, the data are aggregate cross-tabulations of characteristics chosen by the Census Bureau, which means that one cannot specify certain subgroups or social problems as precisely as one might like. In particular, one cannot distinguish many of the social and economic characteristics of the poor who live in extreme poverty neighborhoods from the social and economic characteristics of the non-poor who live in those neighborhoods. Third, because many of the poorest households in low-income and minority communities are not counted, the data tend to underestimate the level of poverty, labor force detachment, and other variables measured in the sample (long form) questionnaire (Brownrigg 1993).

FINDINGS

Size-of-place has an important effect on the racial and ethnic composition of residents of under-class and extreme poverty neighborhoods. This effect is apparent when we look at the distribution of racial and ethnic groups across neighborhoods in metropolitan areas of different sizes. It is also apparent when we look at black, white, and Hispanic neighborhoods across metropolitan areas of different sizes. These results show that residents of the under-class and extreme poverty neighborhoods are of all racial and ethnic groups and that focusing on large cities hides white residents of these neighborhoods.

Population by type of neighborhood

The racial and ethnic composition of under-class and extreme poverty neighborhoods was remarkably similar in 1980, but by 1990 the two populations began to diverge.[9] Blacks represented 58 to 59 per cent of the people in under-class and extreme poverty neighborhoods, whites represented 20 to 21 per cent, and Hispanics represented 19 per cent (Table 3.3a). After including small, medium, and large metropolitan areas, blacks and Hispanics were still overrepresented in these neighborhoods, but clearly this was not exclusively a minority problem.

Table 3.3a The racial/ethnic distribution of the population in under-class neighborhoods and extreme poverty neighborhoods, 1980 and 1990

Racial/ethnic group	*Under-class neighborhoods Percentage distribution 1980*	*Under-class neighborhoods Percentage distribution 1990*	*Extreme poverty neighborhoods Percentage distribution 1980*	*Extreme poverty neighborhoods Percentage distribution 1990*
Non-Hispanic Black	58	57	59	47
Non-Hispanic White	21	20	20	26
Hispanic	19	20	19	22
Other	2	3	2	5
TOTAL	100	100	100	100

Source: Urban Institute calculations based on 1980 and 1990 Census data

The 1990 data make this very clear, at least for extreme poverty neighborhoods. Mincy and Wiener (forthcoming) show that while there was virtually no change in the growth, regional, or racial/ethnic composition of the under-class neighborhood population in the 1980s, the extreme poverty neighborhood population nearly doubled and there were significant shifts among regions and racial/ethnic groups. The fourth column of Table 3.3a, which reproduces their results, shows that the black share of the extreme poverty neighborhood population declined by ten percentage points and the white share rose by six percentage points.

Further disaggregating these results by size-of-place underscores the multiracial and multiethnic character of the populations in under-class and extreme poverty neighborhoods (Tables 3.3b and 3.3c). In 1980, blacks represented more than half of the people in under-class neighborhoods, no matter what the size of the metropolitan area. Whites were the next largest demographic group, except in under-class neighborhoods located in metropolitan areas with 5 million people or more. Hispanics represented the smallest of the three major racial/ethnic groups, except in these largest metropolitan areas.

Table 3.3b Distribution of under-class neighborhood residents, by metropolitan-area size and racial/ethnic group, 1980 and 1990

Metropolitan-area size and racial/ethnic majority	*Population percentage 1980*	*1990*
5 to 10 million		
Non-Hispanic black	52	61
Non-Hispanic white	9	6
Hispanic	37	31
Other	2	2
Total	100	100
2 million to 4,999,999		
Non-Hispanic black	69	64
Non-Hispanic white	21	21
Hispanic	9	12
Other	2	3
Total	100	100
1 million to 1,999,999		
Non-Hispanic black	58	51
Non-Hispanic white	22	27
Hispanic	18	19
Other	2	4
Total	100	100
380,000 to 999,999		
Non-Hispanic black	54	52
Non-Hispanic white	28	28
Hispanic	16	16
Other	2	3
Total	100	100
Less than 380,000		
Non-Hispanic black	54	48
Non-Hispanic white	37	37
Hispanic	7	12
Other	2	2
Total	100	100
Not in an SMSA		
Non-Hispanic black	58	37
Non-Hispanic white	25	46
Hispanic	2	6
Other	15	11
Total	100	100

Table 3.3c Distribution of extreme poverty neighborhood residents, by metropolitan-area size and racial/ethnic group, 1980 and 1990

Metropolitan-area size and racial/ethnic majority	*Population percentage 1980*	*1990*
5 to 10 million		
Non-Hispanic black	59	52
Non-Hispanic white	7	9
Hispanic	33	36
Other	1	3
Total	100	100
2 million to 4,999,999		
Non-Hispanic black	76	62
Non-Hispanic white	16	20
Hispanic	6	14
Other	2	4
Total	100	100
1 million to 1,999,999		
Non-Hispanic black	62	56
Non-Hispanic white	18	21
Hispanic	18	20
Other	2	3
Total	100	100
380,000 to 999,999		
Non-Hispanic black	62	46
Non-Hispanic white	24	23
Hispanic	11	27
Other	3	4
Total	100	100
Less than 380,000		
Non-Hispanic black	40	35
Non-Hispanic white	35	41
Hispanic	24	21
Other	1	3
Total	100	100
Not in an SMSA		
Non-Hispanic black	50	34
Non-Hispanic white	30	41
Hispanic	6	11
Other	14	14
Total	100	100

Source: Urban Institute calculations based on 1980 and 1990 Census data

Close examination of these data suggests that size-of-place was almost as important as race in explaining the racial and ethnic composition of the population in under-class neighborhoods. In metropolitan areas with five million people or more – Chicago, New York, and Los Angeles – blacks represented 52 per cent of the people in under-class neighborhoods (Table 3.3b) and 59 per cent of the people in extreme poverty neighborhoods (Table 3.3c). Hispanics represented 37 per cent of the people in under-class neighborhoods and 33 per cent of the people in extreme poverty neighborhoods. Whites represented 9 per cent of the people in under-class neighborhoods and 7 per cent of the people in extreme poverty neighborhoods in these large metropolitan areas.

The racial and ethnic composition of the population in under-class neighborhoods changes in smaller places. For example, in (1980) metropolitan areas with two to five million people (e.g., Boston, Baltimore, Detroit, Houston, Oakland–San Francisco, and Sacramento), the Hispanic share of the population in under-class neighborhoods fell sharply, and the black and white shares rose. Then as the size of the metropolitan area fell, the black share of population in under-class neighborhoods also fell, but the white and Hispanic shares rose. There were few Hispanics in non-metropolitan areas, so whites represented 25 per cent of the people in under-class neighborhoods and 30 per cent of extreme poverty neighborhoods in non-metropolitan areas. These data show that if observers looked beyond Chicago, New York, and Los Angeles, they would find that under-class neighborhoods are most likely to be populated by blacks, then whites, then Hispanics.

By 1990, the inverse relationship between the size of the metropolitan area and the black share of the under-class neighborhood population increases. In fact, the black share of the under-class neighborhood population increases, only in metropolitan areas with between five and ten million people. The black share of the extreme poverty neighborhood population declines for all metropolitan areas. In metropolitan areas with between 380,000 and one-million people, the shift of the extreme poverty neighborhood population is from blacks to Hispanics. In all other metropolitan area sizes, the shift is from blacks to whites.

Racial/ethnic majority neighborhoods

Although the foregoing results suggest that the under-class and extreme poverty neighborhoods have multiracial and multiethnic populations, inclusive definitions still leave room for skepticism. Observers wedded to the conventional wisdom that under-class and extreme poverty neighborhoods are minority problems might suspect that the whites in these neighborhoods were simply residents of neighborhoods in which troubled blacks and Hispanics made up most of the population. To test this hypothesis, we disaggregate neighborhoods into categories depending upon which racial/

ethnic group represented most of the population. These categories represent census tracts in which either black, white, or Hispanic people constituted more than 51 per cent of the population. We refer to neighborhoods where whites, blacks, or Hispanics are in the majority as white, black, or Hispanic neighborhoods, respectively.

Disaggregating neighborhoods by the race and ethnic majority of the population produces little change in our picture of racial/ethnic composition (Table 3.4a). In 1980, blacks were in the majority in 59 per cent of the under-class neighborhoods and 60 per cent of the extreme poverty neighborhoods. These neighborhoods included 58 per cent of all people living in under-class neighborhoods and 61 per cent of all people living in extreme poverty neighborhoods. There were more under-class and extreme poverty neighborhoods with white majorities than Hispanic majorities, although these neighborhoods contained roughly equal shares of all people living in under-class or extreme poverty neighborhoods. Between 1980 and 1990, the proportion of under-class neighborhoods with black majorities changed little, but there were substantial reductions in the proportion of extreme poverty neighborhoods with black majorities and in the proportion of the extreme poverty neighborhood population living in these neighborhoods.

Neither are the findings of the previous section changed when we disaggregate these results by size-of-place (Tables 3.4b and 3.4c). In 1980, black under-class neighborhoods represented half or more of all under-class neighborhoods, no matter what the size of the metropolitan area. Hispanic neighborhoods represented the second largest share of under-class neighborhoods only in the largest metropolitan areas. Black neighborhoods represented the overwhelming majority of under-class neighborhoods in metropolitan areas with two to five million people. Then as the size of the metropolitan area declined, the black share of under-class neighborhoods also declined, but the white share rose. Between 1980 and 1990, the black share of under-class neighborhoods and the share of the under-class neighborhood population residing in black under-class neighborhoods rose only in metropolitan areas with five to ten million people. The same

Table 3.4a Distribution of under-class and extreme poverty areas, by racial/ethnic majority and resident population, 1980 and 1990

	Ricketts/Sawhill percentage				*Extreme poverty percentage*			
	Tracts		*Population*		*Tracts*		*Population*	
Racial/ethnic group	*1980*	*1990*	*1980*	*1990*	*1980*	*1990*	*1980*	*1990*
Non-Hispanic black	59	61	58	57	60	52	61	48
Non-Hispanic white	19	18	16	16	19	23	16	22
Hispanic	15	13	17	17	16	16	18	21
Other	7	9	9	10	6	9	6	9
Total	100	100	100	100	100	100	100	100

Source: Urban Institute calculations based on 1980 and 1990 Census data

Table 3.4b Distribution of under-class tracts, by racial/ethnic majority and size of metropolitan area, 1980 and 1990

Metropolitan-area size and racial/ethnic majority	*Tracts* Proportion of this racial/ethnic majority within metropolitan-area size		*Population* Proportion of population in metropolitan-area size that is this racial/ethnic majority	
	1980	*1990*	*1980*	*1990*
5 to 10 million				
Non-Hispanic black	0.50	0.67	0.47	0.61
Non-Hispanic white	0.03	0.01	0.02	0.01
Hispanic	0.38	0.24	0.38	0.29
Other	0.09	0.08	0.13	0.09
Total	1.0	1.0	1.0	1.0
2 million to 4,999,999				
Non-Hispanic black	0.73	0.66	0.74	0.65
Non-Hispanic white	0.19	0.19	0.16	0.17
Hispanic	0.03	0.06	0.05	0.08
Other	0.05	0.10	0.05	0.10
Total	1.0	1.0	1.0	1.0
1 million to 1,999,999				
Non-Hispanic black	0.61	0.55	0.60	0.49
Non-Hispanic white	0.21	0.24	0.16	0.24
Hispanic	0.10	0.13	0.13	0.16
Other	0.08	0.08	0.12	0.11
Total	1.0	1.0	1.0	1.0
380,000 to 999,999				
Non-Hispanic black	0.57	0.57	0.56	0.50
Non-Hispanic white	0.26	0.23	0.26	0.24
Hispanic	0.11	0.10	0.12	0.15
Other	0.07	0.11	0.06	0.11
Total	1.0	1.0	1.0	1.0
Less than 380,000				
Non-Hispanic black	0.54	0.51	0.57	0.50
Non-Hispanic white	0.38	0.37	0.35	0.35
Hispanic	0.02	0.04	0.02	0.06
Other	0.06	0.08	0.06	0.09
Total	1.0	1.0	1.0	1.0
Not in an SMSA				
Non-Hispanic black	0.64	0.44	0.69	0.43
Non-Hispanic white	0.29	0.38	0.15	0.34
Hispanic	0.00	0.02	0.00	0.04
Other	0.07	0.17	0.15	0.19
Total	1.0	1.0	1.0	1.0

Source: Urban Institute calculations based on 1980 and 1990 Census data

patterns prevailed in extreme poverty neighborhoods, with two exceptions. In 1980, black neighborhoods represented a somewhat larger share of

Table 3.4c Distribution of extreme poverty tracts, by racial/ethnic majority and size of metropolitan area, 1980 and 1990

Metropolitan-area size and racial/ethnic majority	*Tracts* Proportion of this racial/ethnic majority within metropolitan-area size		*Population* Proportion of population in metropolitan-area size that is this racial/ethnic majority	
	1980	*1990*	*1980*	*1990*
5 to 10 million				
Non-Hispanic black	0.54	0.53	0.57	0.48
Non-Hispanic white	0.06	0.07	0.03	0.05
Hispanic	0.33	0.32	0.32	0.38
Other	0.07	0.08	0.08	0.09
Total	1.0	1.0	1.0	1.0
2 million to 4,999,999				
Non-Hispanic black	0.76	0.65	0.81	0.64
Non-Hispanic white	0.17	0.18	0.11	0.16
Hispanic	0.04	0.08	0.04	0.12
Other	0.03	0.09	0.04	0.08
Total	1.0	1.0	1.0	1.0
1 million to 1,999,999				
Non-Hispanic black	0.62	0.60	0.65	0.57
Non-Hispanic white	0.20	0.18	0.13	0.15
Hispanic	0.11	0.12	0.09	0.19
Other	0.06	0.10	0.05	0.10
Total	1.0	1.0	1.0	1.0
380,000 to 999,999				
Non-Hispanic black	0.63	0.54	0.66	0.47
Non-Hispanic white	0.22	0.21	0.21	0.18
Hispanic	0.09	0.16	0.09	0.26
Other	0.06	0.08	0.05	0.09
Total	1.0	1.0	1.0	1.0
Less than 380,000				
Non-Hispanic black	0.46	0.42	0.41	0.36
Non-Hispanic white	0.34	0.41	0.33	0.41
Hispanic	0.17	0.13	0.23	0.19
Other	0.04	0.04	0.03	0.04
Total	1.0	1.0	1.0	1.0
Not in an SMSA				
Non-Hispanic black	0.58	0.39	0.56	0.40
Non-Hispanic white	0.23	0.35	0.22	0.33
Hispanic	0.07	0.11	0.05	0.11
Other	0.12	0.15	0.17	0.15
Total	1.0	1.0	1.0	1.0

Source: Urban Institute calculations based on 1980 and 1990 Census data

extreme poverty neighborhoods, and between 1980 and 1990 this share fell in non-metropolitan areas (Table 3.4b).

Values could explain these patterns, but not only in the way Lehman (1986) hypothesizes. According to Lehman, the share-cropper system cultivated dependency among blacks, which is now manifested as welfare dependence and labor force detachment. The data in Tables 3.1 through 3.4 are consistent with this hypothesis, because blacks are over-represented in under-class areas. However, the data also suggest an alternative hypothesis, namely that values about work and dependency are constant across racial and ethnic groups; however, there are important cross-race and cross-ethnic group differences in poverty rates (Massey 1990) and in preferences for large places, which translate into differences in employment opportunities. Minorities are more likely to be poor than whites, and they may be more likely than whites to prefer large metropolitan areas. Furthermore, the large metropolitan areas in which blacks concentrated experienced reductions in employment opportunities for low- and high-skilled black workers in the 1970s and 1980s (Bound and Freeman 1990). On the other hand, poverty rates among whites could have increased because of less severe reductions in the demand for low-skilled workers in smaller metropolitan and non-metropolitan areas and because of the decline in real wages of low-skilled workers in general. As a result, there were significant increases in white extreme poverty, especially in the non-metropolitan areas and smaller metropolitan areas where whites concentrate.

Tables 3.5 and 3.6 show most clearly how a focus on large metropolitan areas distorts the picture of the race and ethnic composition of under-class and extreme poverty neighborhoods. These tables show how black, white, and Hispanic under-class and extreme poverty neighborhoods were distributed by size-of-place in 1980 and 1990. In 1980, metropolitan areas with five million or more people contained 66 per cent of the Hispanic under-class neighborhoods and 54 per cent of the Hispanic extreme poverty neighborhoods. Puerto Ricans, the Hispanic group least likely to derive income from work, concentrate in these metropolitan areas (Tienda and Jenson, 1988). These same metropolitan areas contained 22 per cent of the black under-class neighborhoods and 24 per cent of the black extreme poverty neighborhoods. But these metropolitan areas contained only 4 per cent of the white under-class neighborhoods and 8 per cent of the white extreme poverty neighborhoods. Media and scholarly accounts focusing on these metropolitan areas would conclude that under-class and extreme poverty neighborhoods are almost exclusively minority problems.

Adding metropolitan areas with between two and five million people greatly increases the number of under-class and extreme poverty neighborhoods with black and white majorities. Metropolitan areas with over two million people contained almost half the black under-class and extreme poverty neighborhoods. These metropolitan areas also contained almost one-quarter of the white under-class and extreme poverty neighborhoods. Adding metropolitan areas with between two and five million people

Table 3.5 Distribution of under-class neighborhoods, by racial/ethnic majority and size of metropolitan area, 1980 and 1990

Racial/ethnic majority and city size	*Tracts* Proportion of all under-class tracts of this racial/ethnic majority *1980*	*1990*	*Population* Proportion of total population in under-class tracts of this racial/ethnic majority *1980*	*1990*
Non-Hispanic black				
5 to 10 million	0.22	0.34	0.23	0.38
2 million to 4,999,999	0.26	0.28	0.29	0.28
1 million to 1,999,999	0.18	0.12	0.17	0.09
380,000 to 999,999	0.20	0.12	0.17	0.12
Less than 380,000	0.13	0.10	0.12	0.09
Not in an SMSA	0.02	0.04	0.02	0.04
Total	1.0	1.0	1.0	1.0
Non-Hispanic white				
5 to 10 million	0.04	0.02	0.04	0.02
2 million to 4,999,999	0.20	0.27	0.23	0.27
1 million to 1,999,999	0.18	0.17	0.16	0.16
380,000 to 999,999	0.27	0.17	0.29	0.21
Less than 380,000	0.28	0.25	0.27	0.23
Not in an SMSA	0.02	0.11	0.01	0.11
Total	1.0	1.0	1.0	1.0
Hispanic				
5 to 10 million	0.66	0.60	0.66	0.62
2 million to 4,999,999	0.05	0.11	0.07	0.11
1 million to 1,999,999	0.12	0.13	0.12	0.10
380,000 to 999,999	0.16	0.10	0.13	0.12
Less than 380,000	0.02	0.04	0.02	0.03
Not in an SMSA	0.00	0.01	0.00	0.01
Total	1.0	1.0	1.0	1.0

Source: Urban Institute calculations based on 1980 A990 Census data

produces little change in the shares of Hispanic under-class and extreme poverty neighborhoods.

Finally, non-metropolitan areas and small and medium size metropolitan areas – those with less than one million people – contained most (76 per cent) of the white under-class and extreme poverty neighborhoods.

The 1990 data show some changes in these size-of-place patterns by racial and ethnic group and type of neighborhood. Metropolitan areas with two million or more people contained 62 per cent of the black under-class neighborhoods and 30 per cent of the white under-class neighborhoods in 1990 (Table 3.5). Most of the growth of black neighborhoods between 1980 and 1990 occurred in the largest metropolitan areas, while the growth of the white under-class neighborhoods took place in metropolitan areas with between two and five million people. There was little change in the

Table 3.6 Distribution of extreme poverty neighborhoods, by racial/ethnic majority and size of metropolitan area, 1980 and 1990

Racial/ethnic majority and city size	*Tracts* Proportion of all extreme poverty tracts of this racial/ethnic majority		*Population* Proportion of total population in extreme poverty tracts of this racial/ethnic majority	
	1980	*1990*	*1980*	*1990*
Non-Hispanic black				
5 to 10 million	0.24	0.20	0.25	0.20
2 million to 4,999,999	0.22	0.24	0.23	0.23
1 million to 1,999,999	0.16	0.13	0.16	0.12
380,000 to 999,999	0.21	0.17	0.19	0.17
Less than 380,000	0.14	0.14	0.14	0.13
Not in an SMSA	0.03	0.12	0.03	0.16
Total	1.0	1.0	1.0	1.0
Non-Hispanic white				
5 to 10 million	0.08	0.06	0.06	0.05
2 million to 4,999,999	0.15	0.15	0.12	0.13
1 million to 1,999,999	0.17	0.09	0.12	0.07
380,000 to 999,999	0.23	0.15	0.23	0.14
Less than 380,000	0.32	0.30	0.41	0.33
Not in an SMSA	0.04	0.25	0.05	0.29
Total	1.0	1.0	1.0	1.0
Hispanic				
5 to 10 million	0.54	0.39	0.49	0.35
2 million to 4,999,999	0.04	0.11	0.04	0.10
1 million to 1,999,999	0.11	0.08	0.12	0.09
380,000 to 999,999	0.11	0.16	0.09	0.21
Less than 380,000	0.19	0.14	0.25	0.15
Not in an SMSA	0.01	0.11	0.01	0.10
Total	1.0	1.0	1.0	1.0

Source: Urban Institute calculations based on 1980 and 1990 Census data

proportion of black and white extreme poverty neighborhoods in metropolitan areas of more than two million people (Table 3.6) and little change in the distribution of Hispanic under-class or extreme poverty neighborhoods by size-of-place.

Since the 1990 data include BNAs, one would expect to observe non-metropolitan under-class and extreme poverty areas that were hidden in the 1980 data. This occurs for extreme poverty neighborhoods with black, Hispanic, and, especially, white majorities and for under-class neighborhoods with white majorities.

Focusing on the total population living in under-class and extreme poverty neighborhoods also highlights black and Hispanic neighborhoods in larger places (Table 3.5, column 3). Of persons living in black under-class neighborhoods in 1980, 52 per cent lived in metropolitan areas with two million or more people; 34 per cent lived in metropolitan areas of 380,000 to 1,999,999; and 14 per cent lived in smaller places.[10] Table 3.6 shows that 48 per cent of the people living in black extreme poverty neighborhoods in 1980, lived in metropolitan areas of more than two million, 35 per cent lived in middle-sized metropolitan areas, and 17 per cent lived in smaller places.

The large, metropolitan area concentration of the population living in Hispanic under-class neighborhoods is even more striking. Metropolitan areas with two million or more people contained 73 per cent of persons living in Hispanic under-class neighborhoods; another 25 per cent of this population lived in middle-sized metropolitan areas; and only 2 per cent lived in the smallest places. Table 3.6 also shows that metropolitan areas with two million or more people contained 53 per cent of the population living in Hispanic extreme poverty neighborhoods; middle-sized metropolitan areas contained 21 per cent; and smaller places contained 26 per cent.

Again, non-metropolitan areas and small- and middle-sized places contained a disproportionate share of the population living in white under-class neighborhoods. Metropolitan areas with two million or more people contained 27 per cent of this population while middle-sized metropolitan areas contained 45 per cent and smaller places contained the remaining 28 per cent. Data for the population living in white extreme poverty neighborhoods show 18 per cent living in the largest metropolitan areas, 35 per cent in middle-sized metropolitan areas, and 46 per cent in smaller places.

The shifts by race, ethnicity and neighborhood type are reflected in population shifts as well. For example, in 1980, 52 per cent of the people living in black-majority under-class neighborhoods lived in metropolitan areas with two million people or more. By 1990, 66 per cent of the people living in black majority under-class areas lived in these large metropolitan areas.

Thus, two features could account for the popular perception that under-class and extreme poverty neighborhoods are minority problems: 1 the number of such neighborhoods with white majorities and the size of the population living in these neighborhoods; and 2 the distribution of such neighborhoods by race, ethnicity, and size of place. About a fifth of all under-class and extreme poverty neighborhoods are white-majority neighborhoods (Table 3.4a). In 1980, 423,000 people lived in white under-class neighborhoods and 2.2 million people lived in white extreme poverty neighborhoods. Further, small- and medium-sized metropolitan areas – those with less than one million people – contained most such neighborhoods and most people living in such neighborhoods. Second, most metropolitan areas in the United States had less than one million people. Put differently, there are only a few white under-class and extreme poverty neighborhoods and these neighborhoods are in small and medium sized places all around the country. By contrast there are many minority under-

Table 3.7 Number, population, and population density of under-class and and extreme poverty neighborhoods, by racial/ethnic majority of neighborhood, 1980–90

	Under-class neighborhoods								
	Neighborhoods			*Population*			*Population density*		
Racial/ethnic group	*1980*	*1990*	*Percentage change*	*1980*	*1990*	*Percentage change*	*1980*	*1990*	*Percentage change*
Non-Hispanic black	517	562	9	1,447,931	1,536,160	6	2,801	2,733	−2
Non-Hispanic white	171	165	−4	398,901	423,002	6	2,333	2,564	10
Hispanic	129	116	−10	414,592	448,752	8	3,214	3,869	20
Other	63	85	35	222,252	274,290	23	3,528	3,227	−9
Total	880	928	5	2,483,676	2,682,204	8	2,822	2,890	2
	Extreme poverty neighborhoods								
	Neighborhoods			*Population*			*Population density*		
Racial/ethnic group	*1980*	*1990*	*Percentage change*	*1980*	*1990*	*Percentage change*	*1980*	*1990*	*Percentage change*
Non-Hispanic black	1111	1,780	60	3,358,550	4,987,592	49	3,023	2,802	−7
Non-Hispanic white	349	785	125	880,991	2,243,196	155	2,524	2,858	13
Hispanic	297	542	82	991,627	2,208,843	123	3,339	4,075	22
Other	104	310	198	309,859	954,323	208	2,979	3,078	3
Total	1861	3,417	84	5,540,937	10,393,954	88	2,977	3,042	2

Source: Urban Institute calculations based on 1990 Census data

class and extreme poverty neighborhoods and these neighborhoods are in the largest, most visible places.

Nevertheless, the growth of white and other extreme poverty neighborhoods in the 1980s merits attention, even though this growth did not occur in the most visible places (Table 3.7). The change in the number of under-class neighborhoods varied by race and ethnicity, and there was modest growth in the under-class neighborhood population. However, extreme poverty neighborhoods and population nearly doubled, and most (66 per cent) of the growth occurred in non-black neighborhoods. In particular, the number of white (and other) extreme poverty neighborhoods more than doubled as did the populations of white, Hispanic, and other extreme poverty neighborhoods. Black extreme poverty neighborhoods were the only ones in which the population increased by less than a multiple of two and the only ones in which population density declined. Indeed, between 1980 and 1990, the population in white extreme poverty neighborhoods grew at two-thirds the rate of growth of the under-class neighborhood population between 1970 and 1980, so that the former population is now almost as large as the latter.[11]

Besides being located in metropolitan areas of different sizes, and experiencing different rates of growth in the 1980s, do white, black, and Hispanic under-class neighborhoods differ in other respects? In particular, are minorities who live in under-class and extreme poverty neighborhoods worse off than their white counterparts?

The data in Appendix Tables 3.A1 through 3.A4 suggest that they are not. When compared with white under-class and extreme poverty neighborhoods, black and Hispanic under-class and extreme neighborhoods generally have higher mean poverty rates and higher mean values of indicators of labor force detachment. But after adjusting for statistical variations, these differences are statistically insignificant (Appendix Tables 3.A1 through 3.A4, columns 1–6).[12] The most striking difference among these neighborhoods is that they are almost all black, all white, or all Hispanic. Two-thirds to four-fifths of the residents of these neighborhoods are members of the same race or ethnic group, though we required only a 51 per cent majority for disaggregation (Appendix Tables 3.A1 through 3.A4, columns 7–9).

SUMMARY AND CONCLUSION

Most studies of the concentration of poverty and joblessness center attention on minorities, especially blacks, in large cities, but the conceptual literature does not adequately justify this focus. This literature explains that structural changes in urban economies have disproportionately affected minorities, but these forces should have had some adverse effects on low-skilled members of all racial and ethnic groups. Thus, one suspects more racial and ethnic diversity than the earliest studies show. Nevertheless, new empirical studies of ghetto poverty and under-class neighborhoods continue to focus on blacks in large metropolitan areas. This chapter examines changes between 1980 and 1990 in the racial and ethnic composition of under-class and extreme poverty neighborhoods in non-metropolitan areas and in small, medium, and large metropolitan areas. The findings show that blacks are still the predominant population in both types of neighborhoods, but the similarity between neighborhood types ends there. Building on earlier findings, the results show that the near doubling of the extreme poverty neighborhood population was due in large part to the growth in non-black extreme poverty neighborhoods. Specifically, the growth of population in white extreme poverty neighborhoods was three times the growth in black extreme poverty neighborhoods. Since the under-class neighborhood population remained basically unchanged, this means that white extreme poverty and the under class are now problems of the same order of magnitude.

Despite these findings, the popular perception, that concentration of poverty and labor force detachment are black problems, could continue for two reasons. First, there are only a few under-class and extreme poverty neighborhoods with white majorities, compared with the number of such neighborhoods with black majorities. Second, white under-class and extreme poverty neighborhoods are concentrated in non-metropolitan areas and smaller metropolitan areas all around the country, while black under-class and extreme poverty areas are concentrated in the largest, most visible metropolitan areas.

Throwing the spotlight on large metropolitan areas has benefits for research and policy. Large metropolitan areas experienced the greatest increases in the spatial concentration of poverty and labor force detachment between 1970 and 1980. Large metropolitan areas also may have experienced the greatest losses in high paying jobs for low-skilled workers. These losses, which were not reversed in the 1980s, are important in explaining the growing spatial concentration of poverty and labor force detachment. Thus, research and policy targeted at large metropolitan areas may have greater immediate payoffs.

But putting the spotlight on large metropolitan area has important costs. This large-metropolitan-area focus: 1 undermines the conceptual focus on economic changes that affected all low-skilled workers in the 1980s; 2 feeds the public's perception that concentrations of poverty and labor force detachment are black problems; and 3 undermines the call for non-race specific policies to help ameliorate the effects of these changes. The last two are the most serious costs.

Blacks will probably remain the largest single group in under-class and extreme poverty neighborhoods, but this chapter shows that other race and ethnic groups, including whites, are being drawn especially into the latter.

Ignoring the trend among non-blacks will leave the American public prepared to show no more foresight than we have shown about other problems that emerged among blacks and later became major national problems.

Labeling problems as black or inner city problems has been very unproductive in the past, because such labeling puts blacks on the defensive or generates inadequate or inconsistent public support for policies to ameliorate the problems. The growth in female-headed families, highlighted by the Moynihan Report in the 1960s, is a case in point. While the black community devoted its energy to explaining why the quarter of black families headed by women was a sign of its strength, uniqueness, and resilience, the problem reached crisis proportions among blacks. Meanwhile, the growth in female headed families (and the consequent feminization of poverty) has become a national problem, and there is growing consensus that the consequences for children are negative. So, we are busily re-inventing the welfare system to address poverty among the quarter of all US families headed by women. The drug problem, once thought to be confined primarily to blacks, is another case in point. Historically, the abuse and sale of illegal drugs has received inconsistent public attention. Now, the black community has lost hundreds of thousands of its members to drug-related AIDS, violence, dependency, and incarceration. Meanwhile, the drug problem also has become such a national problem – with billions of dollars lost to reduced productivity, absenteeism, health care costs, and accidents in public transportation – that we are heavily engaged in a national War on Drugs.

It could be that extreme poverty and labor force detachment among blacks in large metropolitan areas are also harbingers of things to come for all low-skilled Americans. If so, the ghetto poverty literature – through its silence on the emerging diversity of this problem by race, ethnicity, and size of place – will have helped to lull policymakers and the public into a false sense of security. The result will be complacency and inaction until these problems become much more visible among low-skilled whites and others. Then, the costs of fixing the problem will be much higher.

APPENDIX

Table 3.A1 Indicators of labor force detachment, poverty rates, and racial/ethnic distribution within under-class neighborhoods, by racial/ethnic majority, 1980

	Indicators of labor force detachment and poverty rates (as a percentage of tract population)						*Racial/ethnic group (average percentage of tract population)*		
Racial/ethnic majority	*Female-headed families*	*High school dropouts*	*Male non-labor force participants*	*Welfare recipient*	*Poor*	*Unemployed*	*Non-Hispanic white*	*Non-Hispanic black*	*Hispanic*
Non-Hispanic black									
Mean	0.65	0.37	0.59	0.36	0.46	0.19	0.10	0.84	0.06
Standard deviation	0.12	0.10	0.09	0.12	0.12	0.08	0.12	0.15	0.10
Non-Hispanic white									
Mean	0.51	0.47	0.54	0.27	0.36	0.16	0.73	0.16	0.08
Standard deviation	0.14	0.18	0.09	0.07	0.10	0.08	0.14	0.13	0.10
Hispanic									
Mean	0.56	0.39	0.57	0.40	0.50	0.15	0.12	0.19	0.67
Standard deviation	0.12	0.09	0.08	0.10	0.10	0.06	0.11	0.13	0.13
Other									
Mean	0.52	0.42	0.55	0.31	0.39	0.16	0.30	0.30	0.32
Standard deviation	0.11	0.15	0.09	0.07	0.11	0.07	0.15	0.15	0.14

Source: Urban Institute calculations based on 1990 Census data

Table 3.A2 Indicators of labor force detachment, poverty rates, and racial/ethnic distribution within extreme poverty neighborhoods, by racial/ethnic majority, 1980

	Indicators of labor force detachment and poverty rates (as a percentage of tract population)						*Racial/ethnic group (average percentage of tract population)*		
Racial/ethnic majority	*Female-headed families*	*High school dropouts*	*Male non-labor force participants*	*Welfare recipient*	*Poor*	*Unemployed*	*Non-Hispanic white*	*Non-Hispanic black*	*Hispanic*
Non-Hispanic black									
Mean	0.65	0.24	0.59	0.37	0.51	0.18	0.08	0.86	0.05
Standard deviation	0.15	0.14	0.11	0.13	0.10	0.09	0.11	0.14	0.09
Non-Hispanic white									
Mean	0.32	0.23	0.62	0.14	0.51	0.11	0.76	0.15	0.06
Standard deviation	0.30	0.28	0.16	0.15	0.12	0.09	0.15	0.14	0.09
Hispanic									
Mean	0.45	0.31	0.52	0.34	0.49	0.13	0.10	0.16	0.73
Standard deviation	0.20	0.14	0.11	0.14	0.08	0.06	0.11	0.14	0.16
Other									
Mean	0.47	0.32	0.57	0.30	0.49	0.16	0.26	0.29	0.28
Standard deviation	0.21	0.22	0.13	0.13	0.11	0.08	0.17	0.17	0.17

Source: Urban Institute calculations based on 1990 Census data

Table 3.A3 Indicators of labor force detachment, poverty rates, and racial/ethnic distribution within under-class neighborhoods, by racial/ethnic majority, 1990

	Indicators of labor force detachment and poverty rates (as a percentage of of tract population)						*Racial/ethnic group (average percentage of tract population)*		
Racial/ethnic majority	*Female-headed families*	*High school dropouts*	*Male non-labor force participants*	*Welfare recipient*	*Poor*	*Unemployed*	*Non-Hispanic white*	*Non-Hispanic black*	*Hispanic*
Non-Hispanic black									
Mean	0.71	0.36	0.62	0.36	0.50	0.23	0.08	0.85	0.06
Standard deviation	0.13	0.10	0.11	0.13	0.16	0.11	0.11	0.15	0.11
Non-Hispanic White									
Mean	0.53	0.42	0.55	0.29	0.40	0.18	0.72	0.16	0.09
Standard deviation	0.11	0.15	0.09	0.08	0.10	0.07	0.14	0.13	0.11
Hispanic									
Mean	0.57	0.37	0.55	0.39	0.48	0.20	0.11	0.18	0.68
Standard deviation	0.14	0.11	0.07	0.10	0.12	0.06	0.11	0.14	0.12
Other									
Mean	0.54	0.38	0.57	0.31	0.43	0.18	0.32	0.26	0.27
Standard deviation	0.11	0.12	0.08	0.09	0.11	0.08	0.16	0.16	0.16

Source: Urban Institute calculations based on 1990 Census data

Table 3.A4 Indicators of labor force detachment, poverty rates, and racial/ethnic distribution within extreme poverty neighborhoods, by racial/ethnic majority, 1990

	Indicators of labor force detachment and poverty rates (as a percentage of of tract population)						*Racial/ethnic group (average percentage of tract population)*		
Racial/ethnic majority	*Female-headed families*	*High school dropouts*	*Male non-labor force participants*	*Welfare recipient*	*Poor*	*Unemployed*	*Non-Hispanic white*	*Non-Hispanic black*	*Hispanic*
Non-Hispanic black									
Mean	0.69	0.20	0.61	0.34	0.53	0.23	0.11	0.84	0.04
Standard deviation	0.15	0.14	0.12	0.13	0.12	0.11	0.13	0.15	0.09
Non-Hispanic White									
Mean	0.38	0.18	0.58	0.17	0.53	0.14	0.77	0.13	0.05
Standard deviation	0.25	0.22	0.15	0.15	0.14	0.10	0.16	0.14	0.08
Hispanic									
Mean	0.44	0.24	0.52	0.29	0.51	0.17	0.10	0.11	0.77
Standard deviation	0.20	0.14	0.10	0.14	0.10	0.07	0.11	0.13	0.15
Other									
Mean	0.45	0.23	0.59	0.29	0.51	0.20	0.26	0.22	0.20
Standard deviation	0.19	0.18	0.13	0.14	0.11	0.10	0.17	0.19	0.18

Source: Urban Institute calculations based on 1990 Census data

NOTES

1 Two other (non-spatial) measures, persistent poverty and multiple problem populations, focus on the characteristics of individuals and households. These measures reveal nothing about sample respondents' neighbors, but concentration effects – the idea that neighbors affect the preferences of individuals – are central to Wilson's under class concept. For a review of the measurement literature see Ricketts (1992) and Mincy (forthcoming).

2 See Huang (1992), Kasarda (1993), and Jargowsky (1993), which focus exclusively on blacks or large metropolitan areas and, by contrast, Galster and Mincy (1993) and Mincy and Wiener (forthcoming), which sample from all race and ethnic groups, and from metropolitan areas of all sizes.

3 The source of these data is the 1980 Census of Population report (PC80 – entitled "Poverty Areas in Large Cities." This report includes data for the 100 largest central cities, which vary considerably by population size. Cities with over 1 million people constitute 30 per cent of this group. More than two-thirds of the cites in this group have less than 1 million people.

4 For example, Table 3.2 shows that 15 per cent of all non-Hispanic whites in the US lived in the 100 largest cities, while 41 per cent of all Hispanic whites lived in these cities. Dividing the latter by the former shows that Hispanic whites were 2.7 times as likely as non-Hispanic whites to live in the 100 largest cities. This is the meaning of relative propensity.

5 This is quite possible. Blacks in the 1970s were mostly second generation migrants to metropolitan areas in the North. As such, they were more likely to reject employment at low wages than low-skilled whites who had no recent parental migrant experience with which to compare, or Hispanics, who arrived more recently (Piore, 1979). Many working age blacks were just one or two generations removed from family members who migrated from the South. Therefore, they might be less likely to migrate South for employment than low-skilled whites or Hispanics who had no recent experience with Southern out-migration.

6 See Mayer and Jencks (1989) and Mincy (forthcoming) for recent reviews of the concentration effects literature.

7 Jargowsky and Bane (1990) do not make this explicit conclusion.

8 In the 1970 Census, the count of Hispanics was determined by observations of census enumerators, by the surname of respondents, or by residence in South America, which many respondents took to mean southern United States. In the 1980 and 1990 Census, the count of Hispanics was determined on the basis of respondent's answers to questions about family origin (i.e., Persons of Hispanic origin).

9 This is not a necessary result. The two spatial measures imply different numbers of tracts. For example, in 1980 there were 880 under-class neighborhoods and 1861 extreme poverty neighborhoods. Further, under-class neighborhoods were not entirely a subset of extreme poverty neighborhoods. About 60 per cent of the under-class neighborhoods were also extreme poverty neighborhoods. Since the number of extreme poverty neighborhoods in 1990 was three times the number of under-class neighborhoods, there is even more reason to think that residents of these two types of neighborhoods have different demographic characteristics.

10 Some people living in black under-class neighborhoods are not black.

11 In 1970 there were 204 under-class neighborhoods with a total population of 752,000. In 1980 there were 880 under-class neighborhoods with a total population of 2,484,000. Thus under-class neighborhoods grew by 331 per cent and the

under-class neighborhood population grew by 230 per cent (Ricketts and Mincy, 1990).

12 Assuming normality, tests of null hypotheses that mean values of social problem for minorities exceed mean values of social problem indicators for whites are rejected at the ninety-five per cent significant level.

REFERENCES

Auletta, Ken (1982) *The Underclass*, New York: Random House.

Bane, Mary Jo and Paul A. Jargowsky (1988) "Urban Poverty Areas: Basic Questions Concerning Prevalence, Growth and Dynamics." Center for Health and Human Resources Policy Discussion Paper Series, John F. Kennedy School of Government, Harvard University.

Berlin, Gordon and Andrew Sum (1988) "Toward A More Perfect Union: Basic Skills, Poor Families, and Our Economic Future." Ford Foundation, February.

Blackburn, McKinley L., David E. Bloom, and Richard B. Freeman (1990) "The Declining Economic Position of Less Skilled American Men," in Gary Burtless, (ed.), *A Future of Lousy Jobs?: The Changing Structure of US Wages*, Washington, DC: The Brookings Institution.

Bound, John and Richard B. Freeman (1990) "What Went Wrong? The Erosion of the Relative Earnings and Employment of Young Black Men in the 1980s." Mimeo, National Bureau of Economic Research, November.

Brownrigg, Leslie (1993) US Bureau of the Census Washington, DC. Telephone interview with author, 22 April.

Clark, Kenneth B. and Richard P. Nathan (1982) "The Urban Underclass," in *Critical Issues for National Policy: A Reconnaissance and Agenda for Further Study*, Washington, DC.: National Research Council, Committee on National Urban Policy, pp. 33–53.

Galster, George and Ronald B. Mincy (1993) "Understanding the Changing Fortunes of Metropolitan Neighborhoods, 1980–1990". Paper commissioned for the Fannie Mae Annual Housing Conference, 23 June, Washington, DC.

Gans, Herbert J. (1990) "Deconstructing the Underclass," *APA Journal*, 271, Summer.

Glasgow, Douglas G. (1980) *The Black Underclass*, San Francisco: Jossey Bass.

Gottschalk, Peter and Sheldon Danziger (1986) "Poverty and the Underclass." Testimony Before the Select Committee on Hunger, US Congress, August.

Huang, Qi (1992) "Growth of the Underclass in New York City." Paper presented to The International Conference on Applied Demography, September, Bowling Green, Ohio.

Hughes, Mark Alan (1989) "Misspeaking Truth to Power: A Geographical Perspective on the Underclass Fallacy," *Economic Geography*, 65: 187–207.

Jargowsky, Paul A. (1993) "Ghetto Poverty Among Blacks in the 1980's." Mimeo, School of Social Science, University of Texas, January.

Jargowsky, Paul A. and Mary Jo Bane (1990) "Neighborhood Poverty: Basic Questions," In Michael T. McGeary and Lawrence E. Lynn, Jr. (eds), *Concentrated Urban Poverty in America*, Washington, DC: National Academy Press.

Juhn, Chinhui, Kevin Murphy, and Brooks Pierce (1989) "Wage Inequality and the Rise in Returns to Skill." Paper presented to AEI Conference on *Wages in the 1980s*, Washington, DC.

Kasarda, John, D. 1993. "Inner-City Poverty and Economic Access," in Sommer, Jack and Donald A. Hicks (eds), *Rediscovering Urban America: Perspectives on the 1980s*, Washington, DC: US Department of Housing and Urban Development, Office of Policy Development and Research, January.

——"Jobs, Migration, and Emerging Urban Mismatches," in Michael G. H. McGeary and Laurence E. Lynn, Jr. (eds), *Urban Change and Poverty*, Washington, DC: National Academy Press.

Kaus, Mickey (1986) "The Work Ethic State," *The New Republic* (July): 22–33.

Lehman, Nicholas (1986) "The Origins of the Underclass," *The Atlantic* (June): 31–55, and (July): 54 – 68.

——(1991) *The Promised Land: The Great Black Migration and How it Changed America*, New York: Vintage Books.

Lichter, Daniel T. (1988) "Racial Differences in Underemployment in American Cities," *American Journal of Sociology* 93(4): 771–92, (January).

Massey, D. (1990) "American Apartheid: Segregation And The Making Of The Underclass," *American Journal of Sociology* 96: 329–57.

Massey, D. and M. Eggers (1990) "The Ecology Of Inequality: Minorities And The Concentration Of Poverty, 1970–1980," *American Journal of Sociology* 95: 1153–88.

Mayer, S. and C. Jencks (1989) "Growing Up In Poor Neighborhoods: How Much Does It Matter?" *Science* 243: 1441–5.

Mead, Lawrence M. (1986) *Beyond Entitlement: The Social Obligations of Citizenship*, New York: The Free Press.

Mincy, Ronald B. (1988) "Is There a White Underclass?" Mimeo, The Urban Institute.

——(forthcoming). "The Underclass: Concept, Controversy, and Evidence," in S. Danziger, D. Weinburg, and S. Sandefeur (eds), *Poverty and Public Policy: What Do We Know, What Can We Do?*, Cambridge: Harvard University Press.

Mincy, Ronald B. and Susan J. Wiener (forthcoming) "Under Class Growth in the 1980s: Changing Concept, Constant Reality." Mimeo, The Urban Institute.

Moynihan, Daniel (1965) *The Negro Family: The Case for National Action*, US Department of Labor, Office of Policy Planning and Research, Washington, DC: US Government Printing Office.

Murray, Charles (1984) *Losing Ground: American Social Policy 1950–1980*, New York: Basic Books.

Nathan, Richard P. (1986) "The Underclass: Will It Always Be With Us?" Paper prepared for symposium at the New School for Social Research, 14 November.

O'Hare, William P. and Brenda Curry-White (1992) "The Rural Underclass: Examination of Multiple-Problem Populations in Urban and Rural Settings." Mimeo, Population Reference Bureau, January.

Piore, Michael J. (1979) *Birds of Passage: Migrant Labor and Industrial Societies*, Cambridge, MA: Cambridge University Press.

Reischauer, Robert D. (1987) "Geographic Concentration of Poverty." Mimeo, The Brookings Institution.

Ricketts, Erol (1992) "The Nature and Dimensions of the Underclass," in Glaster, G. and Edward Hill (eds), *The Metropolis in Black and White: Place, Power, and Polarization*, New Jersey: Rutgers, The State University of New Jersey.

Ricketts, Erol and Ronald Mincy (1990) "Growth of the Underclass," *Journal of Human Resources*, 25(1), Winter.

Ricketts, Erol and Isabel V. Sawhill (1988) "Defining and Measuring the Underclass," *Journal of Policy Analysis and Management*, 7(2): 316–25, Winter.

Tienda, Marta and Leif Jenson (1988) "Poverty and Minorities: A Quarter-Century Profile of Color and Socioeconomic Disadvantage," in Tienda, Marta and Gary

Sandefur (eds), *Divided Opportunities: Minorities, Poverty and Social Policy*, New York: Plenum Press.

Van Haitsma, Martha (1989) "A Contextual Definition of the Underclass," *Focus*, 12: 1 (Spring and Summer): 27–31.

Wilson, William Julius (1987) *The Truly Disadvantaged*, Chicago: The University of Chicago Press.

——(1989) "The American Underclass: Inner-City Ghettos and the Norms of Citizenship." Paper presented as *The Godkin Lecture*, JFK School of Government, Harvard University, 26 April.

——(1991) "Studying Inner-City Social Dislocations: The Challenge of Public Agenda Research, 1990 Presidential Address," *American Sociological Review*, 56: (February): 1–14.

4

IS THERE A NEW BLACK POVERTY IN AMERICA?

Lessons from history

Warren C. Whatley

Is there a new black poverty in America? It has been argued that concentrated urban poverty among African Americans is a new kind of black poverty, the origins of which are found in the socio-economic restructuring of American cities that followed the Second World War. Is this true? In this chapter I present empirical evidence on the history of urban poverty and unemployment among African Americans that questions the claim that concentrated urban poverty among African Americans is new.[1]

THE NEW BLACK POVERTY

William Julius Wilson is the most eloquent proponent of the view that concentrated poverty among urbanized African Americans is new. In his book, *The Truly Disadvantaged* (1987), he describes the new black poverty as the concentrated urban poverty of inner-city neighborhoods that offers few economic and social opportunities to their inhabitants. In part, these neighborhoods were produced by "historical discrimination," primarily past racial discrimination in housing markets and in the provision of educational opportunities. But Wilson goes on to argue that today's black poverty is more than a legacy of historical discrimination. He argues that the economic stagnation of the 1970s and the 1980s, and the migration of industrial jobs to the suburbs have been particularly detrimental to these neighborhoods. In addition, the black middle classes that historically resided in these communities and buffered them from extreme deprivation during times of general economic stagnation, have recently escaped to the suburb, consigning those remaining behind to live in neighborhoods where struggle against poor life chances has become the community norm.

Empirical evidence abounds. The migration of manufacturing jobs to the suburbs is well documented, as is job mis-matching between suburb and city (e.g., Kasarda 1989; Rosenbaum and Popkin article in Jencks and Peterson 1991). Evidence that the less-educated are falling further and further behind economically is overwhelming (e.g., Murphy and Welch 1989, 1991, 1992; Bound and Johnson 1992; Backburn *et al.* 1990). The incidence of poverty is on the rise, and much of it is concentrated in our inner cities (e.g., Massey and Eggars 1990).

Douglas Massey (1991) shows how the intersection of residential segregation by race and by class generates pockets of concentrated urban poverty among African Americans. His stylized depiction of these findings illuminates several salient features of concentrated urban poverty that I will use to organize the remainder of this essay (see Massey 1991 for more details).

First, in 1970 the poverty rates among urban blacks were already twice the rates among whites. That is, relative economic deprivation among African Americans predates the economic stagnation of the 1970s and 1980s. Second, racial segregation makes a bad situation worse because African Americans are, on average, poorer than others. While residential segregation by class increased the poverty level of poor black communities by 12.5 percentage points in 1970 and by 15 percentage points in 1980, residential segregation by race increased it another 15 percentage points in 1970 and another 30 percentage points in 1980.

Third, residential segregation by race magnifies the effects of economic stagnation on the poverty rates of poor black communities. If the typical American city had been segregated by class but not by race, then the recession of the 1970s would have increased the poverty rate in poor black communities by only 5 percentage points. The imposition of racial segregation caused it to increase by 20 percentage points. Race and class segregation heaped much of the recession onto poor black communities.

Fourth, in 1980 the class dissimilarity among blacks was still significantly lower than the class dissimilarity among whites. While the black middle class did begin to escape the inner city during the 1970s, that alone can not explain the higher incidence of poverty in poor black communities (Massey and Eggers 1990). Most of it is explained by the persistence of racial segregation in housing patterns and how those patterns magnify the impact of economic recession on the poverty rates of poor black communities.

Most of the debate about the new black poverty has been dominated by the controversy over the underclass. Is the underclass a useful concept? What is the correlation between extremely concentrated poverty and the underclass, however defined? How can one measure neighboorhood effects when people choose which neighborhoods to live in? In the remainder of this essay I want to step back from the underclass controversy and address a more fundamental issue: Is concentrated poverty among African Americans new?

The facts of slavery are self-evident, but even following the emancipation of slavery most African Americans have lived in pockets of concentrated poverty.[2] To be sure, the rural South was very different from the urban North. But if it is the urbanity of today's black poverty that makes it a new black poverty then we need to know why. Is the important spatial dimension over-crowding, rather than the homogeniety of economic status? Is it poverty stripped of means of self-employment? Is it poverty in the midst of affluence?

In any case, the fundamental question remains: is concentrated *urban* poverty new? I will argue that it is not. Historical indices of neighborhood poverty levels do not exist, but I will argue from other existing evidence that: 1 urbanized African Americans have always experienced higher levels of poverty and unemployment than urbanized European Americans; and 2 today's patterns of residential segregation by class and by race were established before the Second World War.

By implication I also argue that "historical myopia" explains why recent *increases* in concentrated poverty among urbanized African Americans are interpreted as the rise of a *new kind* of poverty among African Americans. The decades that followed the Second World War were exceptionally prosperous times for African Americans, so it is not surprising that, when measured against these decades, the recent increase in concentrated poverty among urbanized African Americans looks like a new development. However, when measured against the economic situation of African Americans before the Second World War, the same increase in concentrated poverty looks like a return to prewar conditions. The exception is the economic prosperity of the postwar decades, not high levels of concentrated poverty.

RACIAL DIFFERENCE IN URBAN POVERTY RATES?

Rising wage-inequality and the new black poverty

There is no denying that American cities have deindustrialized since the Second World War. One effect of deindustrialization has been a reduction in the economic return to education among less-educated workers, and these are the workers who are most likely to be segregated by race and by class from the more educated segments of the population. Between 1973 and 1989, wage–age profiles for youngsters collapsed so much that a young high school graduate earned in 1989 no more than a high school drop-out earned in 1973 (Bound and Johnson 1992). Among blacks, the situation was even worse. Demand shifts away from manufacturing in the 1970s had only small effects on the wages and employment of most classes of workers, but demand shifts can explain from one-third to one-half of the employment decline for less-educated young black males (Bound and Holzer 1991). Much has been written about rising wage inequality since the early 1970s, where the less-educated have become relatively poorer and the better-educated have become relatively richer. Recent increases in the concentration of inner city poverty intersect with these developments. Does that mean there is a new black poverty among urbanized African Americans?

Viewed from a historical perspective, one would have to say that the jury is still out. The recent increase in wage inequality is often thought to be a reversal of a twentieth-century trend toward greater wage equality, reflecting recent reductions in the wage premia paid for education and skill. However, Claudia Goldin and Robert Margo (1992) argue that this view of the past may be wrong – that the recent increase in wage inequality may actually be a recovery from a "great compression" in relative wages that occurred between 1940 and 1970, and that it is more like a return to the pattern of wage inequality that existed before 1940 than a reversal of a twentieth-century trend.

If this is true, then it has serious implications for the claim that there is a new black poverty. Sure, black workers have suffered during the recent increase in wage inequality, but no more than they suffered before 1940. Prior to the First World War, black workers were excluded out-right from most industrial jobs in the North, being confined to low-paying and menial service jobs like janitors, personal servants and porters. After the First World War, some of them found better-paying jobs in the industrial sector, but they were primarily confined to low-paying, dirty, and disagreeable jobs that no other workers had to take. And until recently, a black worker holding a clerical or office job was so rare that it was considered unthinkable. Not until the Second World War did large numbers of black workers begin to secure the kinds of well-paying industrial jobs that have recently disappeared.

Rising unemployment and the new black poverty

Post-war deindustrialization may have caused disproportionately more unemployment among urban black workers. Aggregate unemployment data show that black and white unemployment rates were approximately equal before the Second World War, but after the war the aggregate unemployment rate among blacks approaches twice the unemployment rate among whites (see Table 4.1). Does this mean that a new postwar poverty among African Americans can be traced to new and higher levels of unemployment among urban black workers?

Not exactly. The aggregate unemployment rates for black and white workers were approximately equal before the Second World War because they were approximately equal in the rural south, where most African Americans lived. The situation in the urban North was very different. Take 1930 as an example (see Table 4.2). Although the rates of black and white unemployment were approximately equal in the South, in the East North Central the rate of unemployment among blacks was nearly twice the rate among whites. In the West North Central the rate among blacks was more than twice the rate among whites. More important, the rate of unemployment among northern black workers in 1930 is comparable to today's rate of unemployment among blacks (see Table 4.1).

Table 4.1 Racial differences in unemployment rates

Year	*White*	*Black*	*Ratio (Black/White)*
1890	4.41	4.07	0.92
1900	6.47	7.57	1.17
1930	6.59	6.07	0.92
1940	9.50	10.89	1.15
1950	4.9	9.0	1.84
1955	3.9	8.7	2.23
1960	5.0	10.2	2.04
1965	4.1	8.1	1.98
1970	4.5	8.2	1.82
1975	7.8	13.8	1.77
1980	6.3	13.1	2.08
1985	6.2	13.7	2.21
1990	4.7	10.1	2.15

Source: US Bureau of the Census

Table 4.2 Unemployment by race in 1930

	Unemployment rates					
	Males		*Females*		*All*	
Region	*White*	*Black*	*White*	*Black*	*White*	*Black*
USA	7.1	6.4	4.7	4.7	6.6	5.8
New England	9.1	12.9	6.6	8.4	8.5	11.4
Middle Atlantic	9.0	13.1	4.9	6.9	8.0	10.9
East North Central	8.8	17.0	4.7	10.2	8.0	15.0
West North Central	4.5	10.6	3.3	8.1	4.3	9.9
South Atlantic	4.3	4.4	3.8	4.4	4.2	4.4
East South Central	3.4	3.0	3.5	2.1	3.4	2.7
West South Central	4.5	4.6	3.4	4.1	4.4	4.4

	Ratio of B/W Unemployment rates		
Region	*Males*	*Females*	*All*
USA	0.91	1.00	0.89
New England	1.41	1.28	1.35
Middle Atlantic	1.46	1.41	1.36
East North Central	1.92	2.17	1.87
West North Central	2.37	2.45	2.30
South Atlantic	1.03	1.16	1.05
East South Central	0.89	0.58	0.79
West South Central	1.02	1.18	1.02

RESIDENTIAL SEGREGATION BY CLASS

Was urban poverty less concentrated before the Second World War? We do not have solid historical evidence on residential segregation by class. We are beginning to gather historical evidence on the characteristics of urban unemployment and job stability, and this evidence can help us address the issue of historical changes in residential segregation by class. Residential segregation by class is the outcome of location decisions based on expected income, so one should expect residential segregation by class to increase as labor force segmentation increases. The historical evidence suggests that the nineteenth-century labor force was not as segmented as today's labor force, with poverty periodically visiting most working-class families, and making it difficult for the poor to be residentially segregated from the larger working-class community. However, by the Second World War both labor force segmentation and residential segregation by class increased.

For example, in 1910 the monthly probability that an urban worker would become unemployed was 1.30 per cent. In 1977–9 (recent years of comparable overall unemployment) it was 0.95. In 1910, the monthly probability that an unemployed urban worker would find a job was 24.45 per cent. In 1977–9 it was only 19.33 per cent. Consequently, the average duration of a spell of unemployment was only 3.93 months in 1910, but was 5.17 months in 1977–9 (Margo 1990; Murphy and Topel 1987).

In addition, unemployment in the late nineteenth century was less correlated with the characteristics of individuals than it is today. Seasonal unemployment was greater because many firms reduced their labor forces during winter and summer months (Goldin and Engerman 1991). Most workers labored 10–11 hours a day, six days a week for fifty-two weeks of the year, so that many of the days lost to unemployment were actually respites from work (Goldin and Margo 1991). Wide-spread unemployment, for shorter durations, often due to seasonality in employment, illness, vacation, and the need to rest, suggests that idleness conferred less stigma in the late nineteenth century than it does today (Garraty 1978; Keyssar 1986).

Sometime around the turn of the century the American working class began to divide into segments of workers with significantly different expectations of job security and wages. Ford's famous Five Dollar Day occurred in 1914 Susan Carter and Elizabeth Savoca (1990) argue that as early as the 1890s the distribution of job tenures in San Francisco begin to look much like today's. William Sundstrom (1988) also finds evidence of internal job-ladders dating back to the 1890s. A more general study by Sanford Jacoby (1992) finds that the American working class was not vastly segmented until after the First World War. For our purposes, it is important to note that all of the evidence points to increasing labor force segmentation long before the Second World War.

The impact on residential segregation by class was reinforced by changes in transportation technology – like urban trolly systems and the automobile – that offered the better-paid segments of the labor force cheap transportation to the surburban housing developments that came to ring most American cities in the 1920s (Jackson 1985; Ward 1989).

RESIDENTIAL SEGREGATION BY RACE

Residential segregation by race proceeded alongside residential segregation by class. The classic study by Karl and Alma Taeuber (1965) shows that the racial residential patterns of today's northern cities were established sometime between the First World War and the Second World War, and most likely before the Great Depression. Countless studies have told the stories of black migrants who left the rural South during the First World War and the 1920s in search of the Promised Land in the North, only to find themselves increasingly segregated into large and growing urban ghettos.

Joe Trotter (in Katz 1993) and others have argued that the wartime increase in the size and spatial segregation of the northern black population brought a new race–class configuration to many northern cities that looks very much like Millian Julius Wilson's view of the socially-integrated black neighborhoods of old. Prior to the First World War, the small number of black residents in the North kept racial competition over jobs and space to a minimum, during which time elite blacks enjoyed an unprecedented degree of social acceptability. All of this changed when large numbers of poor black southerners began to arrive. The established black elites tried to distance themselves from these poor migrants because their presence heightened the kinds of racial antagonisms that threatened the elite's racial accord with the city's white population. In their place stepped a new race-conscious black middle class that viewed the black working poor as a basis for economic development and political empowerment rather than a source of embarrassment.

Is this the socially-integrated black community that Wilson speaks of? A black middle class whose livelihood rests on the political and economic development of black neighborhoods?[3] This possibility deserves much more attention than it has heretofore received. The important question is not whether the recent middle-class exodus from these neighborhoods has left behind a social space devoid of positive role models.[4] Rather, the important questions concern community development in the face of racial discrimination in capital markets. Redlining was widespread.[5] It made African Americans undesirable neighbors, and it depressed the value of the neighborhood's housing stock. What role did resident black capitalists play in all of this? When neighborhoods "tipped", which way did the wealth transfer flow? Did resident black capitalists help decide? Did this change after the Second World War? I find it curious that a controversy that has placed "neighborhood effects" on the national research agenda has not adequately addressed the question of racial discrimination in urban housing markets.

CONCLUSION

In this essay I have presented historical evidence that questions the claim that concentrated poverty among urbanized African Americans is new. It is well-known that urban black workers were poorer in the past than they are today, and that the income gap between urban black and white workers was wider in the past than it is today. What is perhaps less well-known is that: 1 today's level of unemployment among urban black men was reached as early as 1930; 2 the patterns of residential segregation by race and by class were probably established by 1930 as well; and 3 the narrowing of the black–white wage gap that occurred between 1940 and 1970 is explained as much by rich whites becoming less rich as it is by poor blacks becoming less poor.[6] When viewed from this perspective, the recent increase in wage inequality in America and the recent increase in concentrated poverty among African Americans are not so much signs of a reversal of black economic progress as they are signs of the end of an exceptional period of black–white economic convergence.[7]

NOTES

1 This essay began as a review of the book *The "Underclass" Debate: Views from History* (Katz 1993), a collection of essays commissioned by the Social Science Research Council to investigate the historical antecedents to today's inner-city poverty. While writing that review I was struck by the meager attention social scientists have given to the history of urban poverty in general, and especially to the history of urban poverty among African Americans. This essay builds on that review.

2 The Black Belt in the South (which is where the majority of America's black population resided before the Second World War) consisted of over 300 counties running from the Piedmont of North Carolina, through South Carolina, Georgia, Alabama and into the Mississippi River Delta regions of Louisiana, Mississippi and Arkansas. African Americans were often the majority of the population in these counties, sometimes reaching as high as 90 per cent of the residents. Within these counties there was further segregation along race and class lines, with black families located primarily in the countryside, laboring as share-croppers in expansive agricultural cities called plantations. These areas were extremely poor, reaching levels of poverty that surpass those of today's poorest inner city neighborhoods. Mark Stern reports a poverty rate of 82 per cent among southern black families in 1939 (in Katz (ed.) 1993).

3 Robin Kelley (in Katz 1993) and Thomas Jackson (in Katz 1993) argue that there was little racial solidarity between the middle classes and the poor during the Civil Rights Movement, and that the Movement never really addressed the problem of the poor at all, concentrating instead on the integration of the black middle class into the mainstream of American political and economic life.

4 That seems to me to be a contradiction in terms, for if the golden age was truly a period of integration among black classes then middle-class norms should have permeated the social fabric of all inhabitants of the space. At the very least, middle-class norms should have been stronger among the black poor than among other segments of the poor because the black poor had greater exposure to a middle class for a longer period of time. This – coupled with the fact that even today class segregation among blacks remains lower than class segregation among whites – makes it hard to argue that there is a new black poverty in America caused by the absence of middle-class norms and role models in the black community.

5 We know that after 1933 the federal government played a central role in institutionalizing statistical discrimination in mortgage lending practices when it rated black communities as high-risk "red" zones, to be avoided at all costs because federal credit guarantors believed that blacks "naturally" inhabited only those neighborhoods in decline (Bartelt in Katz 1993).

6 James Smith and Finis Welch estimate that between 1940 and 1970 the percentage of employed black men defined as "below the middle class" decreased from 76 per cent to 24 per cent, and reflects the economic gain of migration from the low-wage South, as well as improvements in educational and employment opportunities (Smith and Welch 1989).

7 I do not mean to imply that there is no difference between urban black poverty today and urban black poverty before Second World War, only that what is different cannot be explained by recent increases in black poverty or its concentration.

REFERENCES

Blackburn, McKinley L., David E. Bloom, and Richard B. Freeman, "An Era of Falling Earnings and Rising Inequality?" *Brookings Review* 9 (Winter 1990/91): 38–43.

Bound, John and Harry Holzer, "Industrial Shifts, Skill Level and the Labor Market for Whites and Blacks," NBER Working Paper no. 3715 (May 1991).

Bound, John and George Johnson, "Changes in the Structure of Wages in the 1980s: An Evaluation of Alternative Hypotheses," *American Economic Review* 82 (1992).

Carter, Susan and Elizabeth Savoca, "Labor Mobility and Lengthy Jobs in Nineteenth Century America," *Journal of Economic History* 50 (March 1990): 1–16.

Denby, Charles, *Indignant Heart: A Black Worker's Journal*, (Boston, 1978).

Frye, W., "Black In-Migration, White Flight and the Changing Economic Base of the City," *American Sociology Review* 44 (1979): 425–48.

Garraty, John, *Unemployment in History: Economic Thought and Public Policy* (New York: Harper Row, 1978)

Goldin, Claudia, *Understanding the Gender Gap* (New York: Oxford, 1990).

Goldin, Claudia and Stanley Engerman, "Seasonality in Nineteenth-Century Labor Markets," NBER-DAE Working Paper No. 20 (1991).

Goldin, Claudia and Robert Margo, "Downtime: Voluntary and Unvoluntary Unemployment of the Past and the Present," unpublished mimeo (1991).

Goldin, Claudia and Robert Margo, "The Great Compression: The Wage Structure at Mid-Century," *Quarterly Journal of Economics* (February 1992).

Jackson, Kenneth, *Crabgrass Frontier: The Suburbanization of the United States*, (New York: Oxford University Press, 1985).

Jacoby, Sanford and Sunil Sharma, "Employment Duration and Industrial Labor Mobility in the United States, 1880–1980," *Journal of Economic History* 52, 1 (March 1992): 161–79.

Jencks, Christopher and Paul E. Peterson (eds), *The Urban Underclass*, (Washington DC: The Brookings Institution, 1991).

Kasarda, John, "Urban Industrial Transition and the Underclass," *Annals of the American Academy of Political And Social Science* 501 (January 1989).

Katz, Michael, (ed.), *The "Underclass" Debate: Views From History*, (Princeton: Princeton University Press, 1993).

Keyssar, Alexander, *Out of Work: The First Century of Unemployment in Massachusetts*, (New York: Cambridge University Press, 1986).

Margo, Robert, "The Incidence and Duration of Unemployment: Some Long-Term Comparisons," *Economic Letters* 32 (1990): 217–20.

Massey, Douglas and M. Eggars, "The Ecology of Inequality: Minorities and the Concentration of Poverty, 1970–1980," *American Journal of Sociology* 95 (1990): 1153–88.

Massey, Douglas and N. Denton, "Suburbs and Segregation in United States Metropolitan Areas," *American Journal of Sociology* 94 (1988): 582–96.

Massey, Douglas, "American Apartheid: Segregation and the Making of the Underclass," *American Journal of Sociology* 96 (September 1991).

Murphy, Kevin M., and Robert Topel, "The Evolution of Employment in the United States: 1968–1985," in Stanley Fisher (ed.), *NBER Macroeconomics Annual* 1987 (Cambridge: MIT Press, 1987).

Murphy, Kevin M., and Finis Welch, "Wage Premiums for College Graduates: Recent Growth and Possible Explanations," *Education Researcher* 18 (May 1989): 17–20.

Murphy, Kevin M., and Finis Welch, "Wage Differentials in the 1980s: The Role of International Trade," *Economic Inquiry* (1991)

Murphy, Kevin M., and Finis Welch, "The Structure of Wages," *Quarterly Journal of Economics* (1992).

Smith, James and Finis Welch, "Black Economic Progress After Myrdal," *Journal of Economic Literature* 27 (June 1989): 519–64.

Stigler, George, *Domestic Servants in the United States, 1900–1940*, NBER Occasional Paper Number 24 (New York: NBER, 1946)

Sundstrom, William, "Internal Labor Markets Before World War 1: On the Job Training and Employee Promotion," *Exploration in Economic History* 25 (October 1988): 424–45.

Taeuber, Karl E. and Alma F. Taeuber, *Negroes in Cities: Residential Segregation and Neighborhood Change*, (Chicago: Aldine Publishing Company, 1965).

Ward, David, *Poverty, Ethnicity, and the American City, 1840–1925: Changing Conceptions of the Slum and the Ghetto*, (Cambridge: Cambridge University Press, 1989).

Whatley, Warren C., "African-American Strikebreaking From the Civil War to the New Deal," *Social Science History* (1993).

Whatley, Warren C. and Gavin Wright, "Getting Started in the Auto Industry: Black Workers at the Ford Motor Company, 1918–1947," unpublished mimeo, 1991.

Whatley, Warren C., and Thomas Maloney, "Making the Effort: The Racial Contours of the Detroit Area Labor Market, 1918–1947," unpublished mimeo, 1991.

Wilson, William Julius, *The Truly Disadvantaged: The Inner City, The Underclass and Public Policy*, (Chicago: University of Chicago Press, 1987).

Wolters, Raymond, *Negroes in the Great Depression: The Problem of Economic Recovery* (Westport: Greenwood Publishing, 1970).

Vedder, Richard and Lowell Galloway, "Racial Differences in Unemployment in the United States, 1890–1990," *Journal of Economic History* 52 (September 1992): 692–702.

5

A FRAMEWORK FOR ALLEVIATION OF INNER CITY POVERTY

*C. Michael Henry**

INTRODUCTION

This framework of poverty alleviation targets black and Hispanic poor. The inner city is its bailiwick. Our desideratum is economic self-sufficiency effected by employment and entrepreneurial strategies that spawn a viable inner city market. The employment strategy encompasses job readiness and skill endowment of inner city labor (for gainful employment). The objective here is to enlarge the effective supply of skilled labor, but this may not be a worthwhile strategy if there are socially contrived barriers to adequate employment opportunities for our target group. Demand for this labor is assured by an entrepreneurial strategy that entails transmission of entrepreneurial skills to *inner city entrepreneurs who employ this labor* (as well as other factor inputs) to supply goods and services to households and contractual services to public institutions. Skilled entrepreneurship in combination with adequate financial capital will generate gainful employment of labor that provides a standard of living which obviates public assistance. The strength of the market is assured by earnings which induce substantial household expenditures within the inner city as long as these goods are qualitatively adequate and their prices are competitive. Two markets are considered, the secondary inner city household market and a primary market for procurement contracts.

In what follows, we briefly review, over the past three decades, trends in quintile shares of income, inequality and poverty, proportions of blacks and Hispanics amongst the poor and their growing concentration in the inner city. Second, we present the framework and proffer reasons why it will effect alleviation of poverty.

* I should like to thank my colleague Michael Montias for his thoughtful comments on this chapter. All errors are my responsibility.

INCOME INEQUALITY, POVERTY AND INNER CITY POOR

Over the past three decades, mean and median family incomes, depicted in Table 5.1, grew at average annual rates of 1.4 per cent and 1.6 per cent, respectively. In 1960, the share of income received by the highest fifth of families was almost nine times that received by the lowest fifth, but in 1991, this relative share increased approximately tenfold. In short, average income of the lowest relative to the highest quintile of families declined (Danziger 1993). Furthermore, during this period, earnings of black relative to white family-heads declined. Indeed, according to Darity and Myers (1993), in 1976, the earnings ratio of black to white family-heads was 0.63, whereas in 1985, it was 0.59. This means that for every $100 earned by white family-heads in 1976, their black counterparts earned $63, which fell to $59 in 1985. The Gini coefficient presented below in Table 5.1 (column 7) corroborates the growth in inequality observed between 1960 and 1990. (Gini coefficients of zero and 1.0 indicate perfect equality and perfect inequality, respectively).

Table 5.1 The level and distribution of family income, 1960–91 (1990 dollars)

Year	*Median income*	*Mean income*	*Percentage distribution of aggregate income* Lowest fifth	*Highest fifth*	*Top five per cent*	*Gini coefficient*
1960	22,833	25,229	4.8	41.3	15.9	0.364
1970	31,226	35,147	5.4	40.9	15.6	0.353
1980	33,386	38,073	5.1	41.6	15.3	0.365
1990	35,353	42,652	4.6	44.3	17.4	0.396
1991	34,488	41,491	4.5	44.2	17.1	0.397

Source: Danziger 1993

During this period, labor market opportunities for less-skilled workers declined. But in the decade of the 1980s, employment grew faster (19 per cent) than the population subset (12 per cent) comprised of labor at least sixteen years old (Blank 1992). Thus, the economy absorbed a large increase in number of workers, yet demand for, and earnings of less-skilled labor declined. Actually, some less-skilled jobs were created during this period but they were really "bad jobs" in the sense that they paid low wages, and offered few non-wage benefits and opportunities for advancement. In short, it was mainly jobs for skilled labor which were created during the period. In addition, inflation adjusted wages of the less-skilled declined, especially with respect to new entrants to the labor force (Blackburn *et al.* 1991; (Bound and Johnson 1992; Murnane *et al.* 1993; Murphys and Welch 1991). This decline arose because demand for less-skilled labor fell faster than the number of these workers in the economy, effecting a downward pressure on wages. This fall in demand is related to urban economic and social restructuring (deindustrialization) brought about by increasing internationalization of the economy, technological change and decline in unionization (Bound *et al.* 1991; Freeman 1980; Murnane *et al.* 1993; Murphys and Welch 1991; Wilson 1987). The ill-effects of these changes were exacerbated by economic stagnation of the 1970s and 1980s. However, decline in earning opportunities for the poor was due not only to a shrinking availability of jobs but also to an increase in the number of female-headed households that significantly changed the household composition of poor families (Darity and Myers 1993). In these families, there is a relatively small likelihood of more than one family member employed full time, and, in addition, child care expenses may have to be incurred, increasing work-related expenditures. Furthermore, since women earn less than men, earnings of female-headed households are less than those of males. In fact, with respect to annual full time earnings, on the average, women earn roughly 70 per cent of that of men. Moreover, owing to decline in demand for, and real earnings of, less-skilled labor, incentives to work declined. Hence (with the exception of females), labor force participation among the less-skilled declined, of which, the steepest decline occurred among black males. In short, opportunities for the poor to earn their way out of poverty have been relatively limited, *a fortiori*, amongst black males. This, in part, explains the relative decline in earnings of the lowest quintile of families.

Subsequent to 1970, an increase in inequality led to a rise in the proportion of poor in the populace. Indeed, by the official measure of poverty, the impoverished subset of the populace declined from 22.2 per cent in 1960 to 11.1 per cent (its lowest level of decline) in 1973, after which it increased to 13.5 per cent in 1990 and to 14.2 per cent in 1991.

Regardless of deindustrialization, however, poverty and destitution have been a constant in the lives of the black residentiary of inner cities (Taeuber and Taeuber 1965). Massey (1991) has shown how existing patterns of residential segregation by race and class spawned urban poverty amongst blacks. This, we explain, in brief, with the aid of Table 5.2.

Assume a city with sixteen neighborhoods each equal in population density and having a population distribution of 25 per cent and 75 per cent black and white, respectively. Further, assume poverty rates (in 1970) of 20 per cent and 10 per cent for blacks and whites, respectively. These are representative of rates in the major cities [Massey and Eggars 1990 where, for example, in Chicago, poverty rates (in 1970) for blacks and whites were 20 per cent and 10 per cent, respectively, and in New York, 21 per cent and 10 per cent, respectively.

In a world free of segregation, each neighborhood would have a population distribution of 25 per cent and 75 per cent for black and white, respectively, and a poverty rate of 12.5 per cent, given by the weighted sum of poverty rates for black and white in the city as a whole (see the

Table 5.2 Characteristics of poor black neighborhoods

Characteristics	*No segregation* 1970	*No segregation* 1980	*Class segregation* 1970	*Class segregation* 1980	*Class and racial segregation* 1970	*Class and racial segregation* 1980
Neighborhood poverty level	0.125	0.150	0.250	0.300	0.400	0.600
Median household income	18,826	17,488	13,020	11,235	8,160	4,523
Percentage of families on public assistance	11.5	13.4	21.1	24.6	36.1	51.0
Percentage of families with female heads	11.7	13.2	19.2	22.2	33.5	45.5
Percentage of houses boarded-up	1.7	2.0	3.5	4.3	7.5	10.5
Major crime rate (per 1,000 persons)	47.9	49.9	57.8	61.8	68.3	84.2
Childhood death rate (0–4)	12.2	12.5	13.9	14.5	19.8	22.5
High school drop-out rate	9.9	10.4	12.4	13.5	14.6	18.6

Source: Massey 1991

entry in row 1, column 1). In addition, assume the poverty rate for blacks increased from 20 per cent to 30 per cent between 1970 and 1980 while that for whites remained unchanged. This rate distribution mirrors actual rates observed in the major cities. For example, during the decade of the 1970s, the rate for blacks in Chicago increased from 20 per cent to 28.3 per cent, and in New York, it increased from 21.4 per cent to 29.6 per cent, whereas rates for whites in both cities remained invariant. This decadal rise effected an increase in the neighborhood poverty rate from 12.5 per cent (1970) to 15 per cent (1980) for blacks as well as whites (row 1, column 2).

Now assume segregation by class exists in each neighborhood, where class gradation is defined in terms of income i.e. a neighborhood social hierarchy based primarily on difference in income. Thus, the shape of the class structure in each neighborhood is virtually identical to the shape of the income distribution. Class segregation means that poor blacks and poor whites are excluded from the upper hierarchy. This segregation, in effect, doubles the poverty rate because the poor are now concentrated in one area (see row 1, columns 3 and 4).

Finally, assume segregation by both class and race obtains (in each neighborhood) where the latter indicates complete separation, in which case blacks, representing 25 per cent of the populace, are prohibited from inhabiting more than 25 per cent of the neighborhoods of the city. This segregation increases poverty rates in black neighborhoods to 40 per cent and 60 per cent, in 1970 and 1980, respectively (row 1, columns 5 and 6, Table 5.2). In poor white neighborhoods, however, the rate increased by 20 per cent in both 1970 and 1980.

Other entries in columns 5 and 6 of the body of the table summarize inimical effects of race and class segregation. For example, segregation *vis-à-vis* the segregation-free case reduces median household income by some 43 per cent in 1970, and by 26 per cent in 1980. Segregation also adversely affects the crime rate and the percentage of families receiving public assistance, increasing the former by some 20 per cent in 1970 and by 34 per cent in 1980, and the latter, by some 25 per cent in 1970 and by 38 per cent in 1980. Superimposed on ill-effects of segregation by race and class are further adverse effects of deindustrialization on crime rates and the population proportion receiving public assistance. In short, deindustrialization was bad for what ails the economic well-being of blacks, i.e. it was deleterious to their psychological and socio-economic health (Kasarda 1989).

Subsequent to manumission, most blacks lived in concentrated poverty. They represented a significant portion of denizens in the Black Belt of the south comprised of some 300 counties. Within these counties, there was segregation by class and race, but blacks were domiciled mainly in rural areas, where they worked as sharecroppers. Indeed, according to Stern (in Katz 1993), poverty levels in these communities were extremely high, affecting some 82 per cent of black families in 1939, thus exceeding poverty rates in present-day inner cities.

Actually, the fall in demand for labor effected by deindustrialization explains about 33 to 50 per cent of decline in demand for less-skilled black labor which, as noted by Darity and Myers (1993), gave rise to greater wage inequality. But black labor had suffered effects of wage inequality prior to 1940, when they were excluded from most industrial jobs in the north where they were given Hobson's choice of low paying menial jobs and other dirty jobs which others had the option to deem unacceptable (Whatley 1992). Hence, the period between 1940 and 1970 was really a temporary aberration (Goldin and Margo 1992). Prior to the Second World War, aggregate data, given in Table 5.3, show black and white labor having approximately equal unemployment rates. But when these data are disaggregated, the unemployment rate among blacks in the northeast exceeds twice that for whites. Subsequent to the war, however, aggregate data indicate rates for blacks that were twice that for whites.

The patterns of residential segregation by race and class in cities of the north originated in the interwar (the First and Second World Wars) period. Southern blacks who migrated to the north during the World War First and in the 1920s were segregated into large and growing urban ghettos from which they were unable to escape. Indeed, the high wage policies of the New Deal era militated against expansion of employment opportunities for blacks. And the Civil Rights Movement of subsequent decades never really addressed problems of impoverished blacks. The focus of the movement was integration of the black middle class into mainstream political and social life and not escape of the black poor from penury. Furthermore, the difficulties of

Table 5.3 Racial differences in unemployment rates in the United States, 1890–1990

	Unemployment rate (percentage)			*Nonwhite–white unemployment rate ratio*
Year	*White*	*Nonwhite*	*Difference*	
1890	4.41	4.07	−0.34	0.92 to 1
1900	6.47	7.57	1.10	1.17 to 1
1930	6.59	6.07	−0.52	0.92 to 1
1940[1]	9.50[1]	10.89[1]	1.39	1.15 to 1
1950	4.90	9.0	4.10	1.84 to 1
1955	3.9	8.7	4.8	2.23 to 1
1960	5.0	10.2	5.2	2.04 to 1
1965	4.1	8.1	4.0	1.98 to 1
1970	4.5	8.2	3.7	1.82 to 1
1975	7.8	13.8	6.0	1.77 to 1
1980	6.3	13.1	6.8	2.08 to 1
1985	6.2	13.7	7.5	2.21 to 1
1990	4.7	10.1	5.4	2.15 to 1

Source: Whatley 1992
Note: 1 Counting government emergency workers as employed; counting them as unemployed increases white unemployment to 14.15 per cent, nonwhite unemployment to 16.87 per cent and the nonwhite–white unemployment ratio to 1.19

the impoverished were exacerbated by the Federal government after 1933, when, as noted by Barlett (in Katz 1993), it institutionalized the practice of statistical discrimination in the mortgage market, by rating black neighborhoods as high risk "red" zones to be avoided, because Federal credit guarantors considered these as declining neighborhoods (Birnbaum and Weston 1974; Jackman and Jackman 1980; Whatley 1992). This effectively depressed the value of residential homes and other property in the neighborhood and made it difficult for blacks to accumulate wealth through home ownership (Terrel 1971).

Table 5.4 depicts present-day racial composition of the poor. In 1990, whites constituted about two-thirds of the poor, while blacks and Hispanics represented about 29 per cent and 18 per cent, respectively. (These percentages do not add up to 100 per cent owing to differing definitions of race over the years. (See note following Table 5.4). However, about 32 per cent and 28 per cent of blacks and Hispanics, respectively, are poor but, in contrast, only about 11 per cent of whites are poor. Within the poor subset, the proportion of blacks remained relatively constant (at about 30 per cent) between 1960 and 1990 whereas Hispanics increased from 9 per cent (1970) to 18 per cent (1990). Furthermore, the proportion of the poor residing in metropolitan areas increased from 44 per cent in 1960 to 73 per cent in 1990, and in central cities, the residentiary poor increased from 27 per cent to 42 per cent. The poor are therefore concentrated in metropolitan

Table 5.4 Profile of the poverty population

	Percentage of the poor population				*Percentage poor*			
	1960	*1970*	*1980*	*1990*	*1960*	*1970*	*1980*	*1990*
All persons	100	100	100	100	22.2	12.6	13.0	13.5
Race								
White	71.0	68.5	67.3	66.5	17.8	9.9	10.2	10.7
Black[1]	29.0	30.0	29.3	29.3	55.9	33.5	32.5	31.9
Asian or Pacific	na	na	na	2.6	na	na	na	12.2
Hispanic	na	8.5	11.9	17.9	na	24.3	25.7	28.1
In metropolitan areas	43.9	52.4	61.6	73.0	15.3	10.2	11.9	12.7
In central city	26.9	32.0	36.4	42.4	18.3	14.3	17.2	19.0
In suburbs	17.0	20.4	25.2	30.5	12.2	7.1	8.2	8.7
Outside metropolitan areas	56.1	47.6	38.4	27.0	33.2	17.0	15.4	16.3

Source: Danziger 1993
Note: 1 In 1960, blacks included other races, whereas, throughout the three decades, Hispanics may be of any race

areas where blacks constitute a relatively large proportion of inner city poor.

In short, poverty due to race and class segregation was exacerbated by the lack of opportunities for remunerative and meaningful employment (Myrdal 1962). Indeed, this poverty may be characterized as multiple-deprivation (Darity and Myers 1993; Henry 1992); that is, deprivation of gainful employment, adequate health-care, education, housing, clothing, food, etc. Despite its multiple dimensions, however, it may be measured by income and thus, its alleviation may be effected by establishment of a significant circular flow of inner city income through formation of a community economic base to foster socio-economic development.

THE FRAMEWORK FOR POVERTY ALLEVIATION

To reverse the widespread immiserization in inner cities, we propose a framework that will help to generate a significant and stable circular flow of income in a community of which a significant portion of its residents is subject to a color bar. Hence, the first step in alleviation is creation of productive activities in the community that effect direct inflows of resources which will induce expenditure and establishment of additional viable productive activities (within the community). In this framework, activities which engender resource inflows are fundamental to alleviation since they give rise to earnings that induce strong local consumer demand as well as establishment of enterprises to satisfy this demand. In this respect, two significant barriers must be considered: 1 racial barriers; and 2 skill barriers. These barriers may be causally linked in the sense that the former effects the latter. However, the latter may be overcome by endowing inner city labor with skills specific to activities undertaken. But racial barriers are enduring and problematic (Myrdal 1962). Thus, the resource inflow is effected by awarding procurement contracts to developed inner city entrepreneurs. In this respect, we presume that government, especially at the Federal level, will not create racial barriers to prevent development of this subset of the citizenry. In short, given the significance of resource inflows, in order to avoid this barrier – encountered regularly in the private sector by our target group – long term contracts between inner city entrepreneurs and the government may be deemed necessary to generate significant and stable inflows (Cadogan *et al.* 1994; Prager 1993). Such contracts are fundamental to diffusion of labor market opportunities to inner cities to foster socio-economic development.

Our conceptual scheme for socio-economic development is meant to increase opportunities for inner city denizens by establishment of two sectors: a *basic* and a *nonbasic sector* (Tiebout 1962). In the basic sector, entrepreneurs earn a return from provision of contractual services to public institutions – Federal, State and local. (Private institutions are not excluded from this framework but, at this point, focus is on public institutions). The nonbasic sector is adaptive. Initially, it arises, primarily to satisfy household demand induced by income earned in the basic sector but subsequently, it satisfies demand induced by earnings from basic as well as nonbasic activities. To be viable, the latter activity must supply qualitatively adequate goods and services, at competitive prices, to inner city households.

Necessary conditions for efficient supply of goods to households and services to institutions are: a developed inner city entrepreneurship; skilled inner city labor; and availability of adequate financial loan capital to entrepreneurs. Skill endowment of labor comprises: 1 general training for job readiness, which involves development of behavioral traits (discipline, punctuality etc.) appropriate to gainful employment; and 2 acquisition of skills specific to sectoral activities. Entrepreneurial development encompasses endowment of organizational, managerial and technical skills specific to enterprises satisfying institutional and household demand. This will require provision of managerial, organizational and technical courses to inner city entrepreneurs. The specific content of courses may be determined by a survey of inner city entrepreneurs, data from which will be analyzed to uncover entrepreneurial and other requisite skills in which they are deficient. Subsequent to course completion, a five-year entrepreneurial extension service will be established to give counsel and guidance to entrepreneurs engaged in sectoral activities. In this framework, successful course completion is the principal prerequisite to ownership of a sponsored enterprise (an enterprise formally included in the basic or nonbasic sector), eligibility for financial loan capital and participation in the extension program. Gainful employment of labor by entrepreneurs to supply goods and services will establish a circular flow of income and enhance the standard of living of the community.

Latterly, a relatively effective approach to development of minority entrepreneurship was undertaken by an alliance of public agencies, including the Port Authority of New York and New Jersey, and private firms – The Regional Alliance for Small Contractors. According to Bates (1993), this Alliance is a nonprofit endeavor initiated in response to formidable barriers to participation in construction (in the New York–New Jersey subregion) by enterprises owned by minorities and women. The Alliance provides technical assistance, loan programs and information on business opportunities to enhance participation of these contractors in the construction industry. Technical assistance, termed "Managing Growth," encompasses practical classroom instruction to enable contractors to compete successfully for larger contracts from the Port Authority. Instruction is given at the basic, intermediate and advanced levels in courses such as: bidding strategies; contract law; contract administration; construction management; financial management etc. Table 5.5 gives a list of courses taught in the Spring and Autumn of 1992. These courses, offered for a fee of $75, are taken by minority and nonminority (male and female) contractors who receive a certificate on completion of course-work. In 1992, more than 700 contractors received certificates including 118 white males and 436 of minority origin of which 279 and 101 were black and Hispanic, respectively. Courses are taught by executives of member-firms of the Alliance and infrequently, by procurement officers of public agencies.

In addition, the Alliance sponsors studies on which it makes policy recommendations on a wide range of issues including transformation of procurement policies and practices, especially with respect to facilitating access to bonding and bank loans etc. for minority contractors.

The efficacy of the Managing Growth (MG) or technical assistance program has been remarkable (Bates 1993). It effected significant increase in the dollar volume of contracts awarded to minority proprietors who successfully completed courses relative to a control group of minority nonMG contractors. For example, in 1991, a sample of twenty-seven minority MG contractors was awarded $1.48 million in prime contracts and $1.64 million in subcontracts (as Port Authority contractors), whereas the control group (thirty contractors) won no prime contracts and received $0.82 million in subcontracts. Furthermore, in 1992, a sample of twenty-seven MG minority contractors won $5.20 million in contracts, of which $1.56 million were prime contracts and $3.64 million subcontracts, while the control group won only $0.41 million, of which $75,000 were prime contracts and $335,000 were subcontracts. In short, between 1991 and 1992, awards to MG contractors increased some 67 per cent as a result of successful completion of courses and fraternization between minority

Table 5.5 Managing growth courses offered in 1992[a]

Spring Semester

1 Basic construction business techniques
(Turner Construction Company)
2 Construction management – Principles and practice
(HRH Construction Corporation)
3 Contracting with New York City DGS and other NYC agencies
(NYC Department of General Services)
4 Financial strategies for the growing contractor
(Mitchell/Titus and Deloitte & Touche)
5 Hands-on computer training
(Praxis, Inc.)
6 Managing projects between $10,000 and $1 million
(Tishman Construction Corporation of NY)

Fall Semester

1 Construction contract law
(Shea & Gold)
2 Contract administration
(Port Authority, Dormitory Authority, NYC School Construction Authority)
3 Estimating
(Projex, Inc., McQuilkin & Associates)
4 Financial management II (Computerized accounting systems)
(Deloitte & Touche)
5 Understanding your company's financial statements
(Gary Kahn & Co.)
6 Hands-on computer training (Introduction)
(Praxis, Inc.)
7 Hands-on computer training II (Intermediate)
(Praxis, Inc.)
8 OSHA and your responsibilities – understanding safety
(Lehrer McGovern Bovis, Inc.)

Source: Bates 1993
Note: a Private firms or public agencies, executives of which are course instructors, are noted in parenthesis below the course listed

contractors and executives (mentors) of member-firms (of the Alliance) which, in the past and presently, have bid successfully for large Port Authority contracts, a growing proportion of which they now subcontract to certified (MG) minority contractors. This Alliance thus offers a carefully thought-out program which, over time, can effect significant increase in the number of viable minority entrepreneurs.

At this point, we address determination of the vector of viable nonbasic activities i.e. profitable activities serving the inner city. This is obtained from an inner city household expenditure survey for analysis of household expenditure patterns (Bates 1989; Prais and Houthakker 1971) to determine commodities and commodity groups that may be profitably supplied, over time, at competitive prices, to households with different characteristics (age composition, education of head of household, etc.) and income levels.

To achieve socio-economic development, therefore, the inner city economy must be bifurcated into a *nonbasic sector* that satisfies household demand and a *basic sector* that supplies services to public institutions. Implicit in this division is a causal link. The basic sector is considered the prime mover of the economy; indeed, it determines the economic health of the community (Tiebout 1957; 1960); hence, the importance of the role of government in creation of this sector and provision of financial loan capital to entrepreneurs to undertake these activities. Two points should be noted in regard to basic activities. First, the basic sector may only supply services for which demand is cyclically stable and for which production is relatively labor intensive. Cyclical stability implies that inner city basic income and employment are not subject to extreme swings (Tobin 1992). In short, the policy objective must be a mix of basic activities that are not highly sensitive to cyclical fluctuations. Increasing the employment of minorities has implications for countercyclical policy, macro and monetary, particularly with respect to downward adjustment of the unemployment target (back to an aggregate unemployment rate of 5 per cent or less) of policy makers. Second, basic activities serve a market whose level, to inner city entrepreneurs, is set by political decisions. Given the assumption that policy-makers are favorably disposed to long term contractual arrangements between government (or quasi public agencies) and inner city entrepreneurs, the dollar volume of basic activities is determined by the effective skill capacity of entrepreneurs and labor, and the availability of financial capital to entrepreneurs. The larger the dollar volume of basic activities, the greater the inducement to establish nonbasic activities, and the larger are 1 the proportion of basic sector labor income spent on goods and services, and 2 the proportion of the wage bill in total costs of nonbasic activities, the larger is the nonbasic sector.

By way of example, assume inner city entrepreneurs secure annual service contracts of $20,000,000, of which 60 per cent pay wages and salaries (net of taxes) to inner city labor. This $12,000,000 represents annual household income (from the basic sector). In addition, assume households spend fifty cents of every dollar of income (propensity to consume) on goods and services supplied by the nonbasic sector. That is, households spend $6,000,000 of income *locally* on goods and services generating internal (inner city) sales revenue of $6,000,000. Furthermore, assume every dollar of sales revenue creates seventy cents of income (local income created per dollar of sales) in the nonbasic sector. That is, $4,200,000 of sales revenue pays wages and salaries to inner city labor (employed in the nonbasic sector) and, given the propensity to consume, households spend $2,100,000 of this income on goods and services (supplied internally), of which seventy per cent or $1,470,000 pays wages and salaries to inner city labor.

This process of *internal income generation* will continue until annual inner city income increases by approximately $18,461,538 as a result of external injection of $12,000,000 of basic sector income. It is important to note, however, that this income will be created, *if and only if*, inner city entrepreneurs are developed and are provided with adequate financial capital, and inner city labor is skilled for gainful employment by entrepreneurs, and profitable household (inner city) markets are identified.

Internally generated income may be increased by raising the dollar volume of basic activities [Pfouts and Curtis 1957; 1958], everything else constant. Endogenous increases in income may also arise by increase in local income created per dollar of sales, or by increase in the propensity to consume goods supplied locally, or by both. From the above example, if the propensity to consume were to increase from 0.5 to 0.65 and local income created per dollar of sales increased from 0.7 to 0.8, then the multiplier for exogenous increase in basic income increases from 1.54 to 2.1. That is, income increases by $2 for a dollar increase in exogenous expenditure as a result of increase in these parameters. Moreover, a larger increase per dollar change in exogenous expenditure may obtain if, in addition to the propensity to consume, the model were expanded to include propensities to invest in local business, human capital, local housing etc. The income stream swells as more dollars change hands locally. Prior to establishment of viable nonbasic activities, the dollars flow to enterprises outside the community. Thus, a policy which induces greater consumption of goods supplied locally will augment income created per dollar of sales and make for a more self-sufficient (with respect to government transfers) inner city community.

It is important to note, however, that the foregoing effects may not obtain in the absence of a basic sector (Tiebout 1956; 1957; 1960). Thus current efforts by the New York city based Local Initiatives Support Corporation (LISC), a nonprofit organization founded by the Ford Foundation, to establish retail shopping centers and like enterprises in inner cities (with contributions of $24 million from ten major corporations) cannot be an effective means for the poor to earn their way out of poverty. Inner city residents cannot prosper by taking in each other's washing, i.e. there must be a net inflow of funds to stimulate and support secondary activities. But retail shopping centers and similar enterprises are secondary activities which do not spawn viable markets in the absence of basic activities (Bates 1989; US Commission on Minority Business Development 1992). Actually, this LISC initiative is equivalent to establishing shopping centers in a community after closure of the military base on which it was totally dependent for resource inflow (which induced secondary activities). Clearly, owing to weak consumer demand arising from fall in income subsequent to the base closure, establishment of a retail shopping center would be an unthinkable investment. Furthermore, as a result of inadequate consumer demand, derived demand for labor will be weak, wage opportunities limited, and the ensuing result is an unacceptable level of unemployment. Thus, the present endeavor by LISC to establish these centers and similar enterprises will effect neither significant nor enduring increases in inner city employment. Consequently, the proportion of resident poor will at least remain the same. In short, such inner city enterprises will not have the capacity to supply qualitatively adequate, and price competitive goods and services, unless they are provided with large government subventions. But such subventions are a drain on the public purse because, over time, they will not spawn opportunities that provide economic self-sufficiency of the community.

As noted in the foregoing, basic sector activities effect net inflows of resources (Tiebout 1962). If a large proportion of labor in the inner city were gainfully employed beyond its boundary and annual earnings provided significant net inflows, this would be the equivalent of basic sector activity. But alas, presently, such equivalence does not obtain owing to barriers noted above. Thus, inner city serving activities are, in the main, nonviable and therefore fail (Bates 1989; Holsey 1938). This nonviability is due, in part, to anaemic market demand and lack of business know-how coupled with inadequacy of financial capital (Bates 1991; UN Commission on Minority Business Development 1992). According to recent findings (Bates 1992), black-owned enterprises enjoying some degree of success serve markets (outside the inner city) made up of white and nonwhite clientele (but disproportionately white). For example, mean sales ($52,308) of black enterprises with predominantly minority clientele are approximately 51 per cent less than mean sales ($102,207) of black enterprises with mixed clientele (Bates 1992). But the number of the latter enterprises is statistically insignificant.

SOME ISSUES IN BRIEF

A pittance of financial capital, skill deficiencies, lack of business know-how and experience, and minority exclusion from the "old boy's network" have led to some corrupt practices in regard to procurement contracts earmarked for minority enterprises. One case in point is that of cash-strapped black entrepreneurs who engage in "joint ventures" with well-heeled white entrepreneurs (or those with access to financial institutions for loan capital). But minority members of these ventures are often referred to pejoratively as "fronts" because, invariably, they are involved in thinly veiled attempts by their white counterparts to usurp procurement contracts reserved for minority entrepreneurs. In essence, minority members of these ventures are paid for their participation since the enterprise functions *de facto* as a single proprietorship owned by the white "partner." Other cases involving outright bribery include the Wedtech Corporation, the executives of which formed a front corporation that bribed Washington officials to award them lucrative contracts from a minority loan program (Cadogan *et al.* 1994). Thus, in a recent Wall Street Roper Poll of 472 black entrepreneurs (*Wall*

Street Journal 1992), about 44 per cent stated that "securing state and local government business is a major problem, despite the widespread policy of purposely steering a portion of public contracts to minority-owned firms." Indeed, about two thirds of these respondents indicated that "despite reams of publicity in the past ten years, government programs to promote minority business development haven't improved, and may actually have gotten worse." Hence, given the importance of the basic sector to this framework, in addition to development of inner city entrepreneurship and a skilled labor force, an *effective mechanism* must be put in place to assure that procurement contracts intended for minorities are not steered to others (Heckman and Brook 1989). This insidious steering subverts public policy and leaves minority entrepreneurs and indeed, the community as a whole, permanently depressed economically; and, over time, creates conditions conducive to conduct which "compels" policy makers to the "popular solution" of building more prisons.

If the playing field is adjudged uneven in the sense that black entrepreneurs are awarded either a negligible number of contracts or contracts insignificant in dollar value relative to their white counterparts, and if this unevenness is due to lack of entrepreneurial skills and experience and inadequate access to loan capital, then endowment of entrepreneurial and labor skills, and entrepreneurial access to loan capital will level the playing field. Thus, there will be no need for set asides. If, however, the uneven playing field is due to enduring socially contrived barriers that prevent award of contracts of significant dollar value to blacks, notwithstanding their entrepreneurial skills and experience, then a set aside program as well as an enforcement mechanism will be necessary if procurement contracts are to serve as the pivotal source of development of the inner city.

Implementation of this framework is eminently worthwhile. It has several advantages and its costs are not exorbitant; in fact, the cost of not undertaking it can be very high. One of its principal advantages, in addition to poverty alleviation, is the effectiveness with which it will reduce the gap in wealth between blacks and whites through development of black entrepreneurship (Blau and Graham 1990; Smith and Welch 1986; Soltow 1972; Terrel 1971). This development will reduce differences in inherited wealth between blacks and whites, for example, differences in *inter vivos* transfers for defrayment of costs of college education, downpayment on a house or a share in the family business etc. Indeed, intergenerational transfer of household wealth can only be made if there is wealth in the family to transfer, hence the relatively large wealth-gap observed between blacks and whites. Second, black enterprises employ primarily black labor. Recent research evidence shows that 74 per cent of black businesses employ a work force comprised of at least 75 per cent blacks (Bates 1992). Thus, entrepreneurial development in the inner city will augment employment of black labor enhancing their prospects for long term employment and provide blacks with opportunities for advancement (Bates and Dunkam 1991). Third, this framework addresses elements of both demand and supply. The demand side relates to decomposition of demand for goods and services supplied by inner city entrepreneurs. The supply side deals with the nature of the inner city economic environment. This, for example, has to do with availability of adequate finance for entrepreneurs, and development of inner city entrepreneurship as well as a skilled labor force. Fourth, the analysis may be cast in terms of income, employment or sales. Albeit, sales are problematic since in effect they double count. That is, the volume of recorded sales is lower if producers sell directly to retailers than if they sell to wholesalers who, in turn, sell to retailers. This shortcoming may be avoided if value-added (roughly, sales less cost of materials purchased from other enterprises) were used. Nonetheless, consider a sales tax. Given its rate and coverage, the revenue depends on local sales. Hence, use of sales as a unit of measurement provides a basis for forecasting sales volume, and in turn, tax revenues. And if income is the unit of measurement, this makes possible a forecast of the yield (local) of an income tax. Such forecasts would be a boon to city (as well as state and Federal) planners in regard to public expenditures in the urban community.

In addition, implementation remedies labor market and related problems peculiar to minorities (Bates 1992; Darity *et al.* 1992). The effectiveness of the two large scale job placement and training programs, the Job Training Partnership Act (1982) and its predecessor, the Comprehensive Employment and Training Act (1973), designed to remedy labor market problems of minorities has, so far, been limited, in terms of significant impact on labor market participation or earnings levels of minorities (Simms 1989). This is due, in part, to discrimination in hiring practices by white employers (Blinder 1973; Braddock *et al.* 1987; Myers 1993). In short, the capacity of the private sector to absorb minorities, whether skilled or unskilled, on an equal footing (earnings, etc.) with whites is limited. This absorptive capacity is enhanced, in part, through development of black entrepreneurship. Indeed, implementation changes the composition of the inner city labor force in terms of skilled relative to unskilled labor as well as the occupational structure of the labor force in terms of entrepreneurs relative to labor. However, it may leave untouched impoverished subsets of the community with potentially only tenuous attachment to the labor force. Such subsets include the disabled (*not* the handicapped), aged, unemployable etc. whose albatross is poverty as well as incapacitating disabilities.

A number of questions have been addressed in regard to this framework. To begin with, one question often raised, apropos of black entrepreneurship, has to do with the signal success of self-employed Asian immigrants relative to prevalent failure of self-employed blacks (Bates 1992). In point of fact, however, self-employed Asians, especially Koreans, are often highly educated, prosperous, and invest heavily in their business enterprise. Black businessmen, on the other hand, invariably lack requisite educational credentials and possess a paucity of financial capital both of which explain, in part, widespread failure of black enterprise (Bates 1987; Holsey 1938; Light 1979). Clearly, racial differences in wealth distribution and educational credentials significantly inform disparities in successful self-employment between blacks and Asians, as well as between blacks and whites.

A second question has to do with reliance on procurement contracts to minority entrepreneurs as the mainstay of the basic sector which is critical to the economic health of the community. Some are apprehensive of this reliance owing to uncertainties associated with contracts earmarked for minorities. Minorities are denied opportunities for adequate schooling, skill acquisition, jobs, business experience etc., and these very deficiencies are used to deny them significant awards of procurement contracts. This is a vicious circle. But these contracts can give the basic sector that mix of activities which are not subject to cyclical swings in income and employment. More than three decades ago, a similar response was voiced in the initial stage of Martin Luther King's struggle against racial injustice. Had he heeded those "warnings," the civil rights struggle would not have achieved the progress, albeit small, in which he was instrumental. Hence, it seems that the question to be addressed should concern measures to be taken to put an end to the systematic exclusion of minorities from meaningful participation in the market for procurement contracts (Prager 1993). What are the costs to minorities and indeed society as a whole if an end is not put to this unjust state of affairs? In the absence of heroic efforts on the part of progressive thinking citizens, or implementation of progressive social policy, minorities will continue to be systematically excluded from significant participation in the economic affairs of the nation. Albeit, our framework does not necessarily imply a reliance on set aside programs. Set asides are necessary when the playing field cannot be levelled over a period of, say, at most five years, after entrepreneurs have been endowed with skills requisite to successful bidding for procurement contracts. The objective of the Regional Alliance for Small Contractors, noted above, represents a small step, through skill endowment, to expand the effective range of entrepreneurial activities by minorities in the economic life of the nation. The Alliance does not necessarily require set asides. Nonetheless, we should add that work is still in progress to determine if a statistically significant difference exists between the dollar volume of prime contracts and subcontracts awarded to minority and nonminority (male and female) contractors who successfully completed courses offered by the Alliance.

Some analysts have suggested use of casual empiricism in lieu of systematic surveys of: 1 inner city household expenditure for determination of profitable commodity and commodity groups, over time; and 2 inner city entrepreneurs for determination of deficiencies of entrepreneurial and other skills requisite to viable enterprise. This attitude of "we already know what the problems are" has serious limitations. It is interesting to know that a viable enterprise will normally undertake market surveys before endeavoring to expand supply of its product to new markets, whether it be Coca Cola, Pepsi-Cola or whatever. Then, why should minority enterprises not formally take these measures to achieve their objectives? Indeed, it would be most instructive to have these surveys to avoid duplication of errors of the past, when in the 1960s SBA made loans to minority businessmen who lacked business know-how and experience and turned the program into an abysmal failure (Bates 1973; Price Waterhouse 1992). In mobilizing the human and financial resources of the inner city for its long term development, entrepreneurial and labor skills must be combined with the complementary factor, adequate financial capital, to supply goods and services in a buoyant market (Bates 1990). If any one of these factors is weak, the enterprise will not be viable. To be sure, given the complementarity of these factors, it behooves us to ensure market viability, developed entrepreneurs and skilled labor (Betes 1989; 1990). In the absence of the formal inquiries included in this framework, we will continue to demonstrate an enormous incapacity to design a program that will permit the impoverished residentiary of the inner city to work their way out of poverty and make a productive contribution to national product.

Another question with respect to this framework concerns demographic changes in the inner city as its residents grow prosperous over time. That is, if residential preferences of high and middle income families change, they may relocate to the suburbs. This will cause decline in local consumer demand and thus shrinkage of the nonbasic sector. But this scenario assumes that as income rises other aspects of the inner city environment will not change in like manner. For example, life styles of the residentiary, property values, the quality of schools and other inner city institutions will all be enhanced, over time, with growth of the fortunes of the community. These are all factors that foster immigration (pull factors) to, rather than emigration (push factors) from the inner city. Moreover, from the historical record, we have learned that the rate at which blacks are absorbed into relatively prosperous white suburbs is extremely low (Jackman and Jackman 1980). In general, people do not normally leave a growing and prosperous community where they are relatively happy to relocate to areas where their welcome is, at best, uncertain.

Finally, implementation of this framework will provide an environment in which blacks and Hispanics are unfettered by pure and statistical discrimination, and discrimination arising from an urge to satisfy a penchant for discrimination by others. Moreover, such an environment is conducive to growth of self-confidence amongst minority youth as they observe large numbers of blacks and Hispanics in highly remunerative responsible positions. In this environment, recompense for diligence, hard work and enterprise is based on merit and not on capricious criteria such as race, pigmentation of skin etc. Furthermore, the range of minority professionals who serve as positive role models for inner city youth enlarges significantly beyond sports and entertainment personalities. As knowledge and skills gain ascendancy in the ethos of the community and indeed, in the hierarchy of values of inner city youth, the quality and dedication of inner city students is transformed. Learning in school becomes a worthwhile endeavor. This makes increased expenditures for education the compelling policy option rather than construction of more prisons. Indeed, this environment provides incentives that make it possible to realize the creative potential of inner city youth for betterment of the community as well as the nation as a whole.

SELECTED REFERENCES

Bates, Timothy, (1973), "An Econometric Analysis of Lending to Black Businessmen," *Review of Economics and Statistics* (56).

——(1981), "Black Entrepreneurship and Government Programs," *Journal of Contempory Studies* (4).

——(1987), "Self Employed Minorities: Traits and Trends," *Social Science Quarterly* (68).

——(1989), "Small Business Viability in the Urban Ghetto," *Journal of Regional Science* (29) 4.

——(1990), "Entrepreneurial Human Capital and Small Business Longevity," *Review of Economics and Statistics* (62) 4.

——(1991), "Financial Capital Structure and Small Business Viability," in *Advances in Small Business Finance*, Rassoul Yazdipour (ed.) (Kluver Academic Publishers).

——(1992), An Analysis of Korean-Owned Small Business Startups with Comparisons to African American and Nonminority-owned Firms" (unpublished Paper).

——(1993), *Case Studies of State Minority Business Assistance Programs*, The Council of State Community Development Agencies. US Department of Commerce: Minority Business Development Agency (September).

——and Constance R. Dunkam, (1991), "Facilitating Upward Mobility Through Small Business Ownership," paper presented at the Urban Opportunity Program, Airlie House, Virginia.

Birnbaum, Howard and Rafael Weston, (1974), "Home Ownership and the Wealth Position of Black and White Americans," *Review of Income and Wealth* (20).

Blackburn, McKinley L., David E. Bloom and Richard Freeman (1991), "An Era of Falling Earnings and Rising Inequality?" *Brookings Review.*

Blank, M. Rebecca (1992), "The Employment Strategy: Public Policies to Increase Work and Earnings," paper presented at the Institute for Research on Poverty Conference, University of Wisconsin–Madison, 28–30 May.

Blau, Francine D., and John W. Graham, (1990), "Black–White Differences in Wealth and Asset Composition," *Quarterly Journal of Economics*.

Blinder, Alan S., (1973), "Wage Discrimination: Reduced Form and Structural Estimates", *Journal of Human Resources* (7).

Bound, John and George Johnson, (1992), "Changes in the Structure of Wages in the 1980's: An Evaluation of Alternative Hypotheses," *American Economic Review* (82).

Bound, John and Harry Holzer, (1991), "Industrial Shifts, Skill Level and The Labor Market for Whites and Blacks," NBER Working Paper No. 3715.

Braddock, Jomills Henry, Jr. and J. M. McPartland, (1987), "How Minorities Continue to be Excluded from Equal Employment Opportunities: Research on Labor Market and Institutional Barriers," *Journal of Social Issues* (43), 1.

Cadogan, Godfrey *et al.*, (1994), "A Retrospective on the *City of Richmond* v. *J. A. Croson Co.*, 109S. Ct. 706 (1989): Are Government Transfers Needed for Women and Minority Owned Firms?" paper presented at the Morehouse Research Institute's Sixth Annual Conference (April).

Danziger, Shelton H., (1993), "The Historical Record: Trends in Family Income, Inequality and Poverty," paper presented to the ISPS Seminar on Inner City Poverty, 28 April.

Darity, William A., Jr. and Samuel L. Myers (1992), "The Problem of Racial Inequality," paper presented at the American Economic Association Meetings, Boston, MA, 1993.

——(1993), "Racial Earnings Inequality and Family Structure," paper Presented at the Western Economics Association Meetings, Lake Tahoe, Nevada, 21–24 June.

Freeman, Richard B., (1980), "Black Economic Progress Post-1964: Who Gained and Why?," in *Studies in Labor Markets*, Sherwin Rosen (ed.) (Chicago: University of Chicago Press).

Friedly, Philip, (1965), "A Note on the Retail Trade Multiplier and Residential Mobility," *Journal of Regional Science* (6).

Goldin, Claudia and Robert Margo, (1992), "The Great Compression: The Wage Structure at Mid-Century," *Quarterly Journal of Economics*.

Heckman, James J., and Brook S. Payner, (1989), "Determining the Impact of Federal Antidiscrimination Policy on the Economic Status of Blacks; A Study of South Carolina," *American Economic Review* (79).

Henry, C. Michael, (1992) "Toward Alleviation of Inner City Poverty: A Conceptual Framework," prepared for the ISPS Faculty Seminar on Inner City Poverty, Yale University.

Hildebrand, George H., and Arthur Mace, Jr., (1950), "The Employment Multiplier in an Expanding Industrial Market: Los Angeles, 1940–47," *Review of Economics and Statistics* (22).

Holsey, Albon, (1938), "Seventy-Five Years of Negro Business," *The Crisis* (45).

Jackman, Mary R. and Robert W. Jackman, (1980), "Racial Inequalities in Home Ownership," *Social Forces* (57).

Jackson, Thomas, (1993) in Katz (1993) *op. cit.*

Jaynes, Gerald and Robin Williams (eds), (1989), *A Common Destiny: Blacks and American Society*, (Washington, DC: National Academy Press).

Jencks, Christopher and Peter E. Peterson (eds), (1991), *The Urban Underclass*, (Washington, DC: The Brookings Institution).

Johnson, Charles S., (1930), *The Negro in American Civilization: A Study of Negro Life and Race Relations in the Light of Social Research*, (New York: Henry Holt).

Kain, John F. and John M. Quigley, (1972), "Housing Market Discrimination, Home Ownership and Savings Behavior," *American Economic Review* (72).

Kasarda, John, (1989), "Urban Industrial Transition and the Underclass," *Annals of the American Academy of Political and Social Science*.

Katz, Michael (ed.), (1993), *The Underclass Debate: Views from History*, (Princeton: Princeton University Press).

Kelley, Robin, (1993) in Katz *op. cit.*

Light, Ivan (1979), "Disadvantaged Minorities in Self Employment," *International Journal of Comparative Sociology* (20).

Massey, Douglas, (1991), "American Apartheid: Segregation and the Making of the Underclass," *American Journal of Sociology* (96).

——and M. Eggars, (1990), "The Ecology of Inequality: Minorities and the Concentration of Poverty 1970–80," *American Journal of Sociology* (95).

McClaughry, John, (1969), "Black Ownership and National Politics," in *Black Economic Development*, G. Douglas Pugh and William F. Haddard (eds) (Englewood Cliffs, NJ: Prentice Hall).

Murnane, Richard, Frank Levy *et al.* (1993) "The Growing Importance of Cognitive Skills in Wage Determination," paper presented to the ISPS Faculty Seminar on Inner City Poverty (March).

Murphy, Kevin and R. Topel, (1987), "The Evolution of Employment in the United States: 1968–85," in Stanley Fisher (ed.) *NBER Macroeconomics Annual*, (Cambridge, MA: MIT Press).

Murphy, Kevin and Finis Welsh (1989), "Wage Premiums for College Graduates: Recent Growth and Possible Explanations," *Education Researcher* (18).

——(1991), "Wage Differentials in the 1980's: The Role of International Trade" in *Workers and their Wages: Changing Patterns in the US*, Marvin Kosters (ed.) (Washington, DC: American Enterprise Institute).

—— (1992), "The Structure of Wages," *Quarterly Journal of Economics*.

Myers, Samuel L., (1993), "Remedies for Racial Inequality," paper presented at the Working Conference on Current Research on Inequality, University of North Carolina at Chapel Hill, (19–21 June).

Myrdal, Gunnar, (1962), *An American Dilemma*, (New York: Harper and Row).

Oakland, William, F. T. Sparrow, and H. L. Stettler III, (1971), "Ghetto Multipliers: A Case Study of Hough," *Journal of Regional Science*, (11), 2.

——(1971), "The Economic Implications of Area-Oriented Anti-Poverty Programs," *Journal of Regional Science* (11).

Pfouts, W. R., and Earle Curtis, (1957), An Empirical Testing of the Economic Base Theory," *Journal of the American Institute of Planners* (2).

——(1958), "Limitations of the Economic Base Analysis," *Social Forces* (26).

Prager, Jonas, (1993), "Contracting Out Government Services: Lessons from the Private Sector," Research Report # 93–12, C.V. Starr Center for Applied Economics, New York University.

Prais, S. J., and H. S. Houthakker, (1971), *The Analysis of Family Budgets*, (Cambridge: Cambridge University Press).

Price Waterhouse, (1992), *Evaluation of the Small Business Administration's 7(a) Guaranteed Business Loan Program,* (Price Waterhouse).

Simms, Margaret, (1989), "The Effectiveness of Government Programs," The Joint Center for Political Studies, (unpublished paper).

Smith, James and Finis Welch, (1986), *Closing the Gap: Forty Years of Economic Progress for Blacks*, (Santa Monica: Rand Corporation).

——(1989), "Black Economic Progress after Myrdal," *Journal of Economic Literature* (27).

Soltow, Lee, (1972), "A Century of Personal Wealth Accumulation," in *The Economics of Black America*, H. G. Vatter and T. Palm (eds). (New York: Harcourt Brace & Jovanovich).

Taeuber, Karl E., and Alma F. Taeuber, (1965), *Negroes in Cities: Residential Segregation and Neighborhood Change*, (Chicago: Aldine Publishing Co.).

Terrel, Henry S., (1971), "Wealth Accumulation of Black and White Families: The Empirical Evidence," *Journal of Finance* (26).

Tiebout, Charles M., (1956), "The Urban Economic Base Reconsidered," *Land Economics* (32).

——(1957), "Input-Output and Foreign Trade Multiplier Models in Urban Research," *Journal of the American Institute of Planners* (13).

—— (1960), "Community Income Multipliers: A Population Growth Model," *Journal of Regional Science* (2).

—— (1962), *The Community Economic Base Study*, Supplementary Paper No. 16 (New York: Committee for Economic Development).

Tobin, James, (1992), "Poverty in Relation to Macroeconomic Trends, Cycles and Policies," paper presented at the Institute for Research on Poverty Conference, University of Wisconsin–Madison.

United States Commission on Minority Business Development, (1992), *Final Report on Historically Underutilized Businesses*.

Vedder, Richard and Lowell Galloway, (1992), "Racial Differences in Unemployment in the United States 1890–1990," *Journal of Economic History* (52).

Wall Street Journal, (1992), Special Edition, 3 April.

Whatley, Warren C., (1992), "Is There a New Black Poverty?" (unpublished paper).

Wilson, William Julius, (1987), *The Truly Disadvantaged: The Inner City, the Underclass and Public Policy*, (Chicago: University of Chicago Press).

6

ARE THE CHICKENS COMING HOME TO ROOST?

Strategic investment in youth up-front or debilitating cost at the rear

Juanita F. Carter and Edward D. Irons

INTRODUCTION AND PROBLEM STATEMENT

President Clinton has succeeded in fulfilling a campaign pledge to place 100,000 new policemen on the street in 1994. In addition to the increased law enforcement personnel, his new anti-crime bill calls for the construction of more jails and mandatory and longer jail sentences. State and local governments are following the same strategies as they vow to bring crime under control. The general public is largely in favor of increased incarceration to tame the rise in crime. The deployment of additional law enforcement personnel at all levels of government, the construction of the additional jails, together with the supporting cost of providing food, clothing and other services to care for inmates of correctional institutions are likely to cost ten or more billions of dollars annually. Although in the short run, this approach may assuage the fears of the public, in the long run this additional cost of the prison system superimposed upon the already burdensome cost of the Correctional System will add yet another financial burden on the American taxpayers and an additional drag on the American economy. And most importantly, it is our opinion that the current trend of crime will continue unabated.

In addition to the cost of crime, the cost of other social welfare programs (entitlements) has also increased exponentially. Included among these entitlement programs are Food Stamps, Aid to Dependent Children, unemployment compensation, housing assistance, and Medicaid and related programs. As can be seen in Table 6.1, in 1950 the cost of these social welfare programs for Federal, State and Local governments was $23.5 billions. By 1990, the cost had increased to slightly more than one thousand billion annually. Moreover, the cost as a percentage of Gross Domestic Product (GDP) has more than doubled, from 8 per cent in 1950 to just under 19 per cent in 1990. Significantly, these social costs rose four times as

Table 6.1 Social welfare spending under major public programs, 1950–90 ($ million)

	Federal expenditures		*State and Local expenditures*		*Federal, State, Local expenditures*	
Year	*Amount*	*Percentage of GDP*	*Amount*	*Percentage of GDP*	*Amount*	*Percentage of GDP*
1950	10,541.0	3.1	12,967.3	4.5	23,508.3	8.2
1960	24,956.0	4.9	27,336.6	5.3	52,293.2	10.2
1970	77,130.2	7.6	68,425.0	6.8	145,555.2	14.4
1975	166,884.2	10.5	122,288.8	7.7	289,173.0	18.2
1980	303,165.5	11.2	189,548.2	7.0	492,713.7	18.2
1985	450,785.8	11.2	281,458.9	7.0	732,244.7	18.1
1990	613,821.0	11.1	431,551.5	7.8	1,045,372.5	18.8

Source: Social Security Administration, Division of Statistics Analysis, "Public Social Welfare Expenditures, Fiscal Year 1990," *Social Security Bulletin*, vol. 56, no. 2, Summer 1993

fast as GDP. If these trends are extrapolated into the foreseeable future, it does not take the mind of a rocket scientist to envision what our national budget and our lives will be like.

There has, and will continue to be, a raging debate regarding the causes of these social problems and the concomitant cost associated with them. The analysis of the various positions regarding this issue is beyond the scope of this chapter. Instead, this chapter argues that the fundamental cause of these problems begins with labor force participation rates of the affected population, primarily minority youth, and effective, relevant education. The complexity of this issue raises the question of the relationship between employment and education; which comes first, the chicken or the egg? For example, citizens need a job and the associated income to pay for their education. Without a job, they (or their parents) cannot pay for an education. Without an education, they cannot get the job. These two variables are so intertwined that they resist definitive analysis. In this paper, we will treat these two variables together, giving each equal weight in the treatment of this issue.

In this regard, Figure 6.1 reveals that while black and white males 16–19 years of age participated in the labor force at about the same rate in 1960, 58 per cent and 56 per cent, respectively, by 1990 white youth had increased their participation rate to 60 per cent, in effect holding their own. However black youth's participation rate had fallen to 41 per cent, a relative decrease of 30 per cent. In other words, while black males participated at a slightly higher rate than white youth at the beginning of this period, by the end of this thirty year period, white youth participated at a rate 50 per cent higher than that of black youth.

A male child whose parents are not able financially to provide that child with comparable amenities to those of his peers, is likely to be unable to compete in that environment. He is likely to become withdrawn, lose

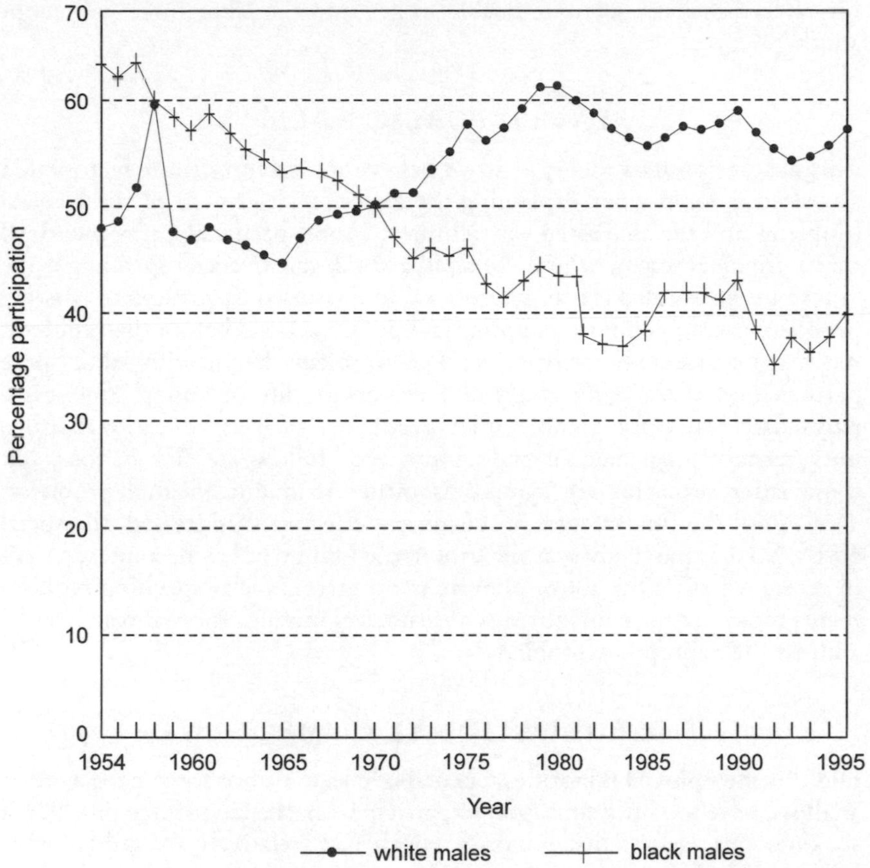

Figure 6.1 Labor force participation rates, black and white males – ages 16–19
Source: US Department of Labor, Bureau of Labor Statistics (Data, Charles Chinnis, 1996)

confidence in himself and finally drop out of school. Thus, the problem starts with his parents' inability to provide the proper support system necessary for that child to perform effectively in school and to interact with his school mates as peers.

Once the youth drops out of school, he will inevitably encounter difficulty securing employment and income that will pay him a living wage. After confronting repeated tries and rejections, he quits trying and seeks other less favorable alternatives, then becomes hopeless. It is at this period that he adopts the attitude; "If I can't get what I want one way, I'll get it another."

If we proceed under the assumption that work habits, life aspirations, life style and social behavior begin forming at this stage in life, the literature is replete with evidence that those who are productively employed adopt one life style, and those who are unable to get into the labor force will adopt another.

FLAWED PUBLIC POLICY

This chapter posits a theory that we believe underscores those factors that are often ignored when explaining the exponential growth of these social problems and the associated expenditures. More specifically, it is theorized that a principal reason behind the rapid growth rate in social spending is the failure by policy makers to incorporate long-run consequences of existing problems facing youth into appropriate policy actions before the problems reach the intractable costly stage. The problems begin with labor force participation at the early stages of the working life of young Americans, particularly minority youth. Other problems, such as educational drop-outs, teenage pregnancy, juvenile crime, etc., follow the lack of jobs, but these latter problems are symptoms rather than fundamental problems. Thus, until the fundamental problems are effectively addressed, the social cost will continue to grow at the exponential rate that has become apparent in recent years. If the above premise is on target, social spending requirements today are the consequences of historical misallocation of resources to address the appropriate problem.

THE EDUCATIONAL COMPONENT

Did the unemployed minorities, cited above in the labor force participation analysis, have too little education to participate in the labor force in 1990? If so, does this suggest that minority youth had (relatively to white Americans) more education in 1960 when they participated in the labor force at a higher rate than white youth? Where is the logic in such a conclusion? The evidence suggests that this cannot be true. There is considerable evidence that minority youth currently drop out of school at alarming rates. Do they drop out because they just do not want an education? Or were there environmental and circumstantial problems which they faced that led them to drop out? While the analysis of the dropout phenomenon is beyond the scope of this paper, we believe that drop-outs are a function of the students' inability to compete in the social environment in which they find themselves at school. We further believe that their inability to compete is economic based: they do not have the money to buy clothes like their peers, or buy lunch, etc., or their home does not afford the environment within which appropriate study habits are fostered or possible. At any rate, an examination of the educational progress of minority youth beginning with the 16–19 age cohort, may be instructive.

In this regard 16–19-year-old teenagers who failed to complete high school in the mid-1970s tend to be disproportionately represented among unemployed members of the labor force later in life. For instance, 16–19-year-old teenagers who were high school drop-outs in 1965–7 are less likely to have been enrolled in college in 1968–72, and are less likely to be members of the home-owning class when they are 30 to 34 years old. Instead, this group is likely to be disproportionately represented in the public dependency group as they move through later age groups rather than being tax paying self-supported citizens of society.

The thesis addressed in this chapter is that the secular rise in spending on entitlements is caused by under-allocation of resources to address the problem in its formative stage. Justification for added resources with which to address current problems usually focuses narrowly upon current benefits while ignoring long-run reduction in prospective social costs that could be avoided if appropriate resources were devoted to this purpose in the early stages. Thus, to arrive at the optimal level of current expenditures that could be appropriately devoted to solving these problems, one must quantify the inter-generational transmission of today's circumstances as they impact future activities and discount measured future cost back to the present. In short, the future costs of existing programs which are designed to address problems facing the youth population today, are severely inflated, given the misallocation of current program resources. Savings in terms of future cost of social programs must be discounted using future savings as well as current benefits. *In this chapter, social conditions facing 16–19-year-old teenagers in 1960 are quantified in terms of their effects as these teenagers age through life. Thus, this chapter takes a life cycle approach to developing possible solutions to address the crisis facing the young population in America.*

In an attempt to demonstrate how historical negligence of underlying conditions impacts future social welfare spending, this chapter focuses on educational attainment, labor force participation, crime, and poverty as they impact social welfare expenditures. An ideal continuum is posited that spans from the age of the 15-year-old youth to retirement. This ideal life cycle pattern is then compared to actual patterns to elicit influences regarding the extent to which the population in one period is likely to become participants in social programs as they age.

The generally accepted view is that 15–22 year-old youths should spend the majority of their time concentrating on attainment of an education to help them secure employment as adults. Upon completion of their formal education, they are expected to assume productive roles in the labor market, as gainfully employed citizens, form households, produce offspring and experience growth in income. This progression of events should enable them to accumulate the resources necessary to educate their children and provide funds for use in retirement. Expectations of the younger generation are probably not very different from those of their parents at similar ages. Having been reared in their parents' household, they aspire to become at least as well-off as their parents. With more education than the generation that came before them and greater access to opportunities, aspirations of today's youth can be expected to match or exceed those of their parents in terms of material well-being. Thus, one would expect the economic status of the population to improve from one generation to the next. That is, age-earning profile would be expected to shift upward over time as one generation improves in relation to its predecessors. While the current generation may not conform to this pattern, this profile has prevailed throughout the modern history of the country's populations.

Based upon the above scenario, a 15-year-old youth would be more likely to complete high school by age 18 than previous generations; complete college by the age of 22 and begin a work career at a higher initial wage than previous generations. One would expect the individual's employment status to be more stable, generating increased income over time, enabling such a person to retire with a financial condition well in excess of his/her parents'.

Table 6.2 shows the percentage of 15–17-, 18–19-, and 20–24-year -old black males and black females that can be considered on track. By on track, we mean the achievement of an educational level that would normally be expected by that age. As the table shows, there is a significant number of youth and young adults who were not moving along chronologically at a pace that offers promise for the future. In fact, as the cohorts move up in age, their relative educational achievement decreases. For instance, only 65.6 per cent of black males 15–17 years of age had completed the nine to eleven years of education that would be expected for that age group in 1991. By the time they reached the 20–24 cohort, only 16.4 per cent had completed at least two years of college, the educational level that was expected of that age group. For black females, the achievement levels were somewhat better with 74.3 per cent considered on track in the 15–17 age cohort.

Table 6.2 Actual vs expected level of educational attainment, 1982–91

	Black males (aged)			*Black females (aged)*		
Year	*15–17*	*18–19*	*20–24*	*15–17*	*18–19*	*20–24*
1982	69.3	44.2	19.7	75.2	58.8	22.7
1983	72.2	43.3	18.1	75.3	53.2	22.5
1984	69.1	45.0	16.2	74.8	55.7	23.3
1985	69.1	42.4	18.0	72.5	68.8	22.4
1986	66.1	50.4	20.7	75.7	63.0	27.4
1987	65.1	38.9	23.2	75.4	56.0	21.4
1988	68.5	40.5	20.7	73.4	56.6	22.0
1989	60.8	44.4	17.4	77.9	57.7	22.4
1990	62.6	41.6	18.9	76.9	55.3	21.4
1991	65.6	44.4	16.4	74.3	59.0	21.6

Source: US Department of Commerce, Bureau of the Census: *Educational Attainment in the United States*, p. 20 (various issues)

The complement of the percentage of youth that are considered on track represents the number that would be considered off track. Those figures suggest an alarming trend, as 83.6 per cent (100.0 – 16.4) of young black males and 78.4 per cent of black females had not completed the years of education that would have normally been expected of them based on their age cohort.

Programs designed to motivate young people to stay in school are all the more important for the foreseeable future, particularly given the changing job demands for the twenty-first century. Increasingly, the type of jobs that will be available will require more education than was true in the current century. In addition to the higher educational requirement of the new jobs being created in the future, Table 6.3 shows the value of education from an earnings point of view. In this regard, it can be seen by the income for the various labor force groups that college education increases the earning capacity by two thirds, with the exception of white men whose increase is 86 per cent.

Table 6.3 Income value of a college education (dollars)

Student group	*High School*	*College*	*Difference*
Black	18,620	30,910	12,290
White	22,370	37,490	15,120
Black women	16,960	28,130	11,170
White women	18,250	30,520	12,270
Black men	20,730	34,340	13,610
White men	26,790	43,690	16,900

Source: US Census Bureau, *Survey of Consumer Income*, 1993

Thus, the difference between the incomes of those with high school only and those with a college degree measures the value of college in per year earnings. Using the average cost of four years of college and earnings of employed persons over four years, the opportunity cost of college, and the life expectancy table, one computes the lifetime net benefits of college. It then becomes a simple calculation to compute the additional income earned by this segment of the population and the commensurate public welfare spending reduction. From the above analysis there is evidence that labor force participation rates and educational attainment are linked. And since the issue is education versus crime, it is significant that $25 billion was devoted to correctional cost in 1992. With the average daily number of inmates at 408,000, the annual cost of maintaining the average inmate in 1992 was $61,000. We could pay tuition, room and board for at least four students at a typical state school for a year for this amount.

Table 6.4 shows the consequences of educational attainment and labor force participation. Characteristics of recipients in 1988 are cross-classified

Table 6.4 Characteristics of participants in major public benefit programs, 1992

	Total Population Millions		*Medicaid*		*Housing Assistance*		*Food Stamps*		*AFDC*	
			Millions	*Percentage*	*Millions*	*Percentage*	*Millions*	*Percentage*	*Millions*	*Percentage*
US Pop	237.817[1]		21.615	9.1	11.555	4.9	21.918	9.2	12.347	5.2
White	200.936		13.115	6.5	6.337	3.2	12.702	6.3	4.921	3.4
Black	28.952		7.265	25.1	4.844	16.7	8.309	26.7	4.605	15.9
Hispanic	18.842		3.656	19.4	1.531	8.1	3.639	19.3	2.210	11.7
Age		%								
<18	63.318	26.6	10.304	16.3	4.536	7.2	10.888	17.2	7.050	11.1
18–64	147.192	61.9	8.746	5.9	5.450	3.7	9.564	6.5	5.141	3.5
65>	27.307	11.5	2.565	9.4	1.564	5.7	1.466	5.4	0.157	0.0
Gender										
Male	115.536	50.7	8.791	7.6	4.591	4.0	9.284	8.0	5.052	4.4
Female	112.281	40.3	12.825	10.5	6.964	5.7	12.634	10.3	7.295	6.0
Educational Attainment										
<4 yrs HS	41.047	23.5	6.432	15.7	3.325	8.1	6.143	15.0	2.690	6.6
HS grads	58.975	33.8	3.284	5.6	2.334	4.0	3.400	5.8	1.873	3.2
≤1 yr. col.	74.478	42.7	1.596	2.1	1.361	1.8	1.488	2.0	0.734	1.0
Employment and Labor force status										
Employed FT	91.937		1.183	1.3	1.983	2.2	1.848	2.0	0.589	0.6
Employed PT	20.901		0.873	4.2	0.616	2.9	918	4.4	0.448	2.1
Unemployed	5.321		1.098	20.6	0.634	11.9	1.493	28.1	0.895	16.8
Not in LF	56.340		8.157	14.5	3.787	6.7	6.677	12.0	3.366	6.0

Source: US Department of Commerce, Bureau of the Census, *Measuring the Effects of Benefits and Taxes on Income and Poverty*, p. 60 (selected years)

Note: 1 The sum of whites, blacks and hispanics exceeds total population because a high percentage (89%) of hispanics classify their race as white. They are included in both categories.

according to various social and economic conditions. Information presented in Table 6.4 permits an evaluation of the influence of racial, age, gender, educational attainment, employment and labor force status on the likelihood of participation in each of four major social welfare programs. The number of persons participating in the programs at any time during calendar year 1988 is shown along with the percentage of the population this group represents.

Food Stamps and Medicaid represent the most prevalent of the four major benefit programs. In 1988, 21.615 million, or 9.1 per cent of the US population, received Medicaid and 21.918 million, 9.2 per cent of the population, participated in the Food Stamp program. Participation in AFDC represented a smaller number of participants: 12.347 million, or 5.2 per cent of the population. Significantly, however, blacks are far more likely to participate in AFDC than the three other groups. Similarly, at 25.1 per cent, blacks are four times as likely to participate in Medicaid as whites and 29 per cent higher than Hispanics. As for Housing Assistance, at 16.7 per cent, blacks are five times more likely to participate as whites and twice as likely as Hispanics. This pattern prevails with respect to all benefit programs.

The consequences of low educational attainment, unstable employment, and labor force status on dependence upon public (governmental) support are also shown in Table 6.4. There is a clear, inverse relationship between the levels of educational attainment and dependency. For example, persons with less than four years of high school education, are thirteen times as likely to receive public assistance as those with one or more years of college – 6.3 per cent versus 0.5 per cent. Similarly, persons with less than four years of high school are five times as likely to receive Housing Assistance, and seven times as likely to receive Food Stamps and Aid to Dependent Children.

Finally, employment and labor force participation rates, predictably, have a dramatic impact upon the degree to which persons participate in Public Assistance Programs. In this regard, unemployed persons are 4.5 times as likely to participate in Public Assistance Programs as persons who are employed full-time. They are 16 times as likely to receive Medicaid, 5, 14, and 28 times as likely to participate in Housing, Food Stamps and Aid to Families with Dependent Children (AFDC), respectively.

SIMPLE ANALYTICAL ILLUSTRATIONS

The impact of changes in employment, education, and matrial status on the level of social welfare expenditures, C, are represented in the following equation:

$$C = C(x_1, x_2, x_3) \qquad 6.1$$

$$\Delta C = \frac{\Delta C}{\Delta x_1}\Delta x_1 + \frac{\Delta C}{\Delta x_2}\Delta x_2 + \frac{\Delta C}{\Delta x_3}\Delta x_3 \qquad 6.1a$$

where x_1 = number of people with specific levels of educational attainment
x_2 = number of people unemployed
x_3 = number of people with specific marital status (e.g., single women heads of households).

Changes in cost, ΔC, due to a change in the value of x_i $(i = 1, 2, 3)$, the effect of specific conditions on the level of social welfare expenditures can be evaluated. Thus dividing equation 6.1a by Δx_i yields:

$$\frac{\Delta C}{\Delta x_1} = \frac{\Delta C}{\Delta x_1}\frac{\Delta x_1}{\Delta x_1} + \frac{\Delta C}{\Delta x_2}\frac{\Delta x_2}{\Delta x_1} + \frac{\Delta C}{\Delta x_3}\frac{\Delta x_3}{\Delta x_1}$$

Since $\frac{\Delta x_2}{\Delta x_1} \neq 0$ and $\frac{\Delta x_3}{\Delta x_1} \neq 0$, $\frac{\Delta x_2}{\Delta x_1} \neq 0$ and $\frac{\Delta x_3}{\Delta x_1} \neq 0$, then the net effect of additional education on the level of social spending consists of the direct effect, $\frac{\Delta C}{\Delta x_1}$, and an indirect effect $\frac{\Delta C}{\Delta x_2}\frac{\Delta x_2}{\Delta x_1} + \frac{\Delta C}{\Delta x_3}\frac{\Delta x_3}{\Delta x_1}\frac{\Delta C}{\Delta x_2}\frac{\Delta x_2}{\Delta x_1} + \frac{\Delta C}{\Delta x_3}\frac{\Delta x_3}{\Delta x_1}$. However, additional education reduces the likelihood of unemployment and increases the likelihood of marriage. Thus, to account for the direct effect of changes in education on spending on social programs, the indirect effects must be isolated. That is:

$$\frac{\Delta C}{\Delta x_1} - \left(\frac{\Delta C}{\Delta x_2}\frac{\Delta x_2}{\Delta x_1} + \frac{\Delta C}{\Delta x_3}\frac{\Delta x_3}{\Delta x_1}\right) = \frac{\Delta C}{\Delta x_1}$$

$\frac{\Delta C}{\Delta x_1}$ can be approximated using information contained in Table 6.4.

The number of households drawing payments from the four primary public benefit programs and the associated dollar amount of such assistance are shown in Table 6.5. Participation and dollar amount of payments, cross-tabulated by level of both participation as well as the amount of benefit payments, decline with increases in education. For instance, 9 per cent of approximately 22 million households whose head of household has less than a high school education received AFDC and housing assistance, 15.6 per cent Food Stamps, and 21.8 per cent received payment under the Medicaid Program. These dependency burdens declined to 4.4 per cent for AFDC and Housing Assistance, to 6.7 per cent in Food Stamps and 8.9 per cent for Medicaid for the 53.4 million households whose head of household had completed high school. For those whose head had completed four years of college, participation declines to one per cent or below for AFDC, Food Stamps and Housing Assistance, and to 2.1 per cent for Medicaid.

The decline in need for support is perhaps even more evident in cost consequences. Over half of the $41.4 billion that was expended under these

Table 6.5 Number of households and amount of benefits received through selected public programs ($ millions and thousands of households)

	Households		*Less than High School*		*Completed High School*		*1–3 yrs College*		*Completed College*	
	Number	*Percentage*	*Number*	*Percentage*	*Number*	*Percentage*	*Number*	*Percentage*	*Number*	*Percentage*
Number of households	93,347	100	21,717	100	53,423	100	17,121	100	21,086	100
AFDC	4,062	4.4	1,963	9.0	1,469	4.4	508	3.0	122	0.6
Housing	4,085	4.4	1,987	9.1	1,466	4.4	424	2.5	208	1.0
Food Stamps	4,481	4.8	1,358	15.6	2,247	6.7	696	4.1	180	0.9
Medicaid	9,181	9.8	4,736	21.8	2,970	8.9	1,035	6.0	440	2.1
Dollar amounts	41,366	100	20,897.8	50.5	14,000.4	33.9	4,950.4	12.0	1,517.4	3.7
AFDC	14,373.5	100	7,439.8	51.8	4,716.9	32.8	1,840.9	12.8	375.8	2.6
Medicaid	11,559.8	100	5,403.8	46.8	3,970	34.4	1,522.5	13.2	662.6	5.7
Food Stamps	8,574.7	100	4,569.8	53.6	2,905.4	33.9	880.1	10.1	192.4	2.2
Housing	6,857.9	100	3,457.4	50.4	2,407.2	35.1	706.8	10.3	286.6	4.2

Source: US Department of Commerce, Bureau of the Census, *Measuring the Effects of Benefits and Takes on Income and Poverty* (1992)

programs in 1989 went to households whose head of household had not completed high school. Approximately one-third went to those households whose head of household had only completed high school.

The primary focus of this paper is the value, measured in terms of future savings associated with income maintenance programs, of keeping a youth in school. The present value of the future cost of entitlements that could be required for income maintenance programs provides a measure of the specific amount of initial investment that is warranted to be devoted to programs to keep a youth in school. Not only should the current level of expenditures be considered, more importantly, we would argue that such an approach to determining the necessary level of public investment is conservative. A more long-term view would justify more resources to such programs and less to corrections and incarcerations.

To illustrate the basic reasoning behind this approach, we offer a hypothetical example of a youth who is contemplating not finishing high school. The only public benefit program used in this exercise is the Food Stamps Program. Additional cost consequences associated with the individual qualifying for AFDC, Housing Assistance, and Medicaid are excluded, making the warranted, upfront investment conservative. The computations are presented in Table 6.6. The estimated value is computed assuming that high school is completed versus not completed, some college (1–3 years) is obtained versus only high school, and the incremental value of completing four years of college. The calculations are made using a discount factor of 5 per cent, and the annual stream of payment in Food Stamps is treated as an annuity.

The present value, PV, is given by equation 6.2.

$$PV = \frac{C}{r} - \frac{C}{r}\left[\frac{1}{(1+r)^t}\right] \qquad 6.2$$

where PV = Present Value of future costs of Food Stamps,
C = Annual costs of Food Stamps,
r = discount rate, and
PV = \$8,130.29.

Using this approach, the amount of funds that the future level of expenditures in Food Stamps warrants that society devotes is as much as \$9,561.36 annually in upfront investments in education to assure that a high school student who might drop out of high school completes high school. The value of Food Stamps savings declines sharply after the youth completes high school. For instance, only \$629.27 in Food Stamps savings is recognized as net returns for enabling youth to attain 1–3 years of college. This saving increases only slightly for 4 years of college, \$801.36.

Table 6.6 Hypothetical illustration of costs and savings on the Food Stamps Program

Education X_i	*Social Welfare C (thousands)*	*Expenditures* $\Delta C\$$	*Persons receiving Benefits N (thousands)*	ΔN	*Probability* $P(C\|x_i)$	$\Delta C/\Delta N$ (\$)	$P(C\|x_i)\Delta N$
< High School	4,596,830	–	1,358	–	0.156	3,385	\$528.06
High School	7,502,201	2,905,371	3,600	2,247	0.067	1,293	86.63
1–3 yrs College	8,382,297	880,096	4,301	696	0.041	1,264	51.82
4 yrs College	8,574,717	192,420	4,481	180	0.009	1,069	9.62

CONCLUSION

From the above analysis, it seems clear that if the exponential increase in social spending is to be ameliorated, effective ways must be found to keep minority youth in school. In addition, we must find effective ways to keep them in the labor force, and the appropriate reinvestment must be made to facilitate this process. This conclusion is neither new nor profound. However, unless public policy makers change the priority with which they attack these problems, the crime rate is likely to continue unabated. Moreover, the social fabric of our society may ultimately be in jeopardy.

Notwithstanding the magnitude of the current federal deficit and the political environment within America, sources of funds must be found to make appropriate investment toward the solution of these problems. We are among the first to suggest that the trade-off will not be easy. Policy makers who provided the direction that gave rise to the largest and most debilitating federal debt in history are likely to be the first to say that, "we cannot increase the deficit for any reason." We fully accept that there is risk in increasing the deficit. We believe, however, that the risk is manageable and worth taking.

If our proposal is on target – appropriate investment in keeping minority youth in school while at the same time investing in job creation and placement for this segment of the population – this action will reduce crime and othe social costs in the foreseeable future. As a consequence, any deficit incurred in this process would be offset by future savings on these social costs. The savings would comprise not only the reduction in social cost, but also an increase in personal income and the taxes that would accrue to the government. The decision, we believe, revolves around the questions, "do we pay (invest) now or do we pay later?"

For example, if we made a policy decision to reinvest in our crumbling infrastructure throughout the nation, we would be meeting two critically important needs, i.e. making our infrastructure safe again while providing productive (not make-work) jobs for people who might otherwise be on one or more public assistance programs. An increase in the deficit, however, would likely occur in the process in the early years. Sure there is risk associated with this strategy as set forth herein, but we would argue that there is an even greater risk in failure to invest, the upshot of which would be to continue escalation of crime and associated social costs.

7

GOVERNMENT INTERVENTION, ANTI-DISCRIMINATION POLICY, AND THE ECONOMIC STATUS OF AFRICAN AMERICANS

Bernard E. Anderson

INTRODUCTION

Equal job opportunity is central to the enjoyment of many benefits of American society. The opportunity to work provides the main source of income to support a family's standard of living, and to prepare for the future. The denial of employment because of race, sex, creed, national origin, or other factors unrelated to individual's productive potential is one of the most disgraceful practices possible in a nation committed to equal opportunity and economic justice.

The nation's struggle to live up to its high ideals as a land of opportunity is reflected in the continuing efforts to address the troublesome presence of race. W. E. B. Du Bois, the dean of black intellectuals, wrote shortly after the turn of the century that "the greatest issue of the 20th century is the problem of color line." History has shown the wisdom of Du Bois's judgment.

The struggle for equality began with the painful and destructive Civil War that culminated in the Emancipation Proclamation abolishing slavery. The struggle continued for the following century as the nation grappled with the legacy of slavery, expressed most vividly in the pervasive web of segregation. Race relations were characterized by a systematic denial of opportunity aimed at preserving second-class citizenship for black, Hispanic, and other racial minorities during the late nineteenth and the early twentieth centuries. The denial of the rights of women, also a prominent feature of the American experience during that time, was only partly relieved when women gained the right to vote during the 1920s.

Discrimination and the systematic exclusion of racial minorities and women from full participation in the economy became embedded in the attitudes, values, and behavior of virtually all institutions in American life. The labor market was replete with occupations in which the normal expectation was that no minorities or women would be employed. Job ceilings were imposed in occupations where minorities and women were permitted to work. America was widely heralded as the "land of opportunity," but that phrase was clearly understood to apply almost exclusively to white men.

The civil rights movement, often called America's second revolution, began to change the status quo by challenging the denial of basic rights and insisting upon the protection of equal opportunity. Beginning with the US Supreme Court's epochal decision in *Brown v Board of Education* (1954), the nation was forced to abandon its support of segregation and discrimination, and to begin to address the pervasive and stubborn barriers to full participation by minorities and women in American life. Institutions, attitudes, and behavior had to be changed in ways that allowed the previously excluded to make their contribution to society.

In 1961, affirmative action was adopted as public policy to assure the full participation of minorities and women in the job market. "Affirmative action" today has many meanings, but essentially, it defines a set of special measures that take race and gender into account when making decisions on hiring, promotion, and other aspects of employment. The consideration of such factors certainly is not new to the American experience. What is different about affirmative action, however, is that the use of personal characteristics is a device to assure equal job opportunity for the specially identified groups, rather than a weapon to exclude them.

Government intervention in the labor market is indispensable in the achievement of equal job opportunity. In the absence of government intervention, there are no "natural forces" that would lead automatically and inexorably toward the equalization of job opportunities for racial minorities and others.

But economic theory suggests that competition in the labor market will lead employers to hire and promote the most productive workers, without regard to race or gender, in pursuit of profit maximization. The theory, however, can accommodate discrimination. As Gary Becker observed in *The Economics of Discrimination*, employers might have a "taste for discrimination" that must be satisfied simultaneously while maximizing profits.[1] That means an employer who discriminates is willing to forego part of the monetary benefits of production that might be gained otherwise in order to indulge the "taste for discrimination."

Under these conditions, discrimination in the labor market might continue indefinitely if no countervailing force is introduced to eliminate it. The persistence of racial inequality in the labor market before the adoption of public policies to protect equal job opportunity demonstrates the failure of natural competitive forces to reduce discrimination.

STATUS OF RACIAL MINORITIES

The need for affirmative action is reflected in the continuing disparity between the economic status of minorities and others in the labor market. A brief summary of recent evidence on economic inequality might be instructive.

Black employment and income

In 1992, there were 13,891 thousand black workers in the civilian labor force; 11,933 thousand were employed and 1,958 thousand were unemployed. The total civilian labor force included 126,982 thousand workers, of whom 117,598 thousand were employed, and 9,384 thousand were unemployed. Thus, black workers accounted for 11.0 per cent of the labor force, 10.0 per cent of those employed, and 21.0 per cent of those unemployed.

The inability to find and keep work has long been a pervasive and persistent problem in the black community. The unemployment rate among black workers has been at, or above, 10 per cent for thirteen of the last twenty years, but has not reached that level among whites at any time during the postwar period.

Unemployment among black youth, higher than 20 per cent each year since the early 1960s, now stands close to 40 per cent.

Black workers in the economy are like the caboose on a train. When the train speeds up so does the caboose; and when the train slows down, the caboose does likewise. But in the normal course of events, the caboose remains far behind the engine. When the economy expands rapidly, black employment growth speeds up, but when an economic downturn occurs, black unemployment leads the downward spiral.

For example, during the 1981–2 recession, from July 1981 through December 1982, black employment dropped by 150,000 or 9.1 per cent, while total employment fell by 1.5 million, or 1.6 per cent. Similarly, during the recovery and expansion, the period from late 1982 through early 1986, black employment spurted ahead by 17.1 per cent, compared to employment growth of 9.9 per cent among workers generally. But the residue of past unemployment has accumulated over time, and as a result, the black unemployment rate was 1.89 times higher than that of others at the depth of 1981 – four years after continuous economic growth!

During the 1990–1 recession, total employment declined by 1,700 thousand, or 1.5 per cent, while black employment fell by 336 thousand, or 2.8 per cent. At the trough of the recession (the second quarter of 1991) the black unemployment rate reached 13.2 per cent, compared with 6.2 per cent among white workers. The recovery following the recession was much weaker than previous recoveries during the postwar period. In part for that reason, black unemployment has remained relatively high through 1993.

Persistent unemployment helps explain why black workers drop out of the labor market faster and earlier than other workers, and why they delay their market entry longer. The labor force participation rate, the most general measure of labor market activity, has sharply declined among black men since 1970. Dropping out of the labor force is most prevalent among the less educated and among workers eligible for social security and disability programs.

When employed, black workers are heavily concentrated in blue collar (36 per cent) and service jobs (23 per cent), but this occupational distribution has changed markedly over time. For example, only 13 per cent of employed black workers were in white collar jobs in 1960, but 29 per cent were so employed in 1980. Similarly, 15 per cent of black employees, mostly women, were private household workers in 1960, but twenty years later, only 3 per cent held such jobs. The growth in white collar employment largely reflects the entry of black women into clerical jobs, but black employment in professional, technical, and managerial jobs also grew faster than the black workforce.

Less change occurred in the industry location of black workers, but during the past two decades they increased their share of employment in manufacturing, professional and related services, and public administration. At the same time, they lost ground in construction, while holding their own in the trade and financial sectors.

The ability to find and keep a job significantly influences earnings and family income. Weekly earnings for employed black males are about 73 per cent of their white counterparts, while fully employed black women are near earnings parity with other women (about 95 per cent). But this comparison conceals some important differences in labor market experience among some segments of the black workforce. For example, black adult men are nearly twice as likely as white men to hold part-time jobs, and black women are about one third more likely than white women to work part-time. This work experience, coupled with the higher unemployment and lower labor force participation of black workers, depresses their income. Thus, in 1989, the median income of black families was $18,000, or about half the income of the average white family. Only when both husband and wife worked full-time, year round, did black family income approach that among white families (87.6 per cent). Work, not wealth, is the bedrock of the black middle class, and employment is the sine qua non of economic security.

Changes in the composition of black families reduced income gains in recent years. In the mid-1960s, about one-fourth of black families were headed by single women; today that ratio approaches one-half. Two thirds of such families are poor. If families headed by single women are excluded from comparison, the black community would show greater income gains compared with the white since 1965. But even then a significant gap in family income between the two groups would still exist.

THE RATIONALE FOR AFFIRMATIVE ACTION

The unequal economic status of minorities, women, and majority group men is not solely the result of current discrimination in the labor market, and would not disappear immediately if discrimination ceased to exist. Interpersonal differences in occupation status, income, and other measures of economic well-being reflect a broad range of personal characteristics including, but not limited to, personal preferences, age, education, attitudes, and values. Observed differences among groups in economic status also reflect the present effects of past discrimination against members of particular groups based on their race, sex, and other personal characteristics. Thus, although current acts of discrimination might be widely condemned as incompatible with contemporary American values, and punished because they are unlawful, the mere enforcement of laws against discriminatory behavior will not assure equal opportunity. Something more is required to secure and protect the rights of all persons to participate fully in the economy.

As president Lyndon B. Johnson said at the Howard University Commencement, Washington, DC, in 1965:

> You do not take a person who for years has been hobbled by chains, liberate him, bring him up to the starting line of a race and then say, "You are free to compete with all others," and still believe [that you are] being fair. It is not enough just to open the gates of opportunity. All of our citizens must have the ability to walk through those gates. This is the next and more profound stage of the battle for civil rights...

Supreme Court Justice Harry Blackmun recognized the same imperative when he observed, "In order to get beyond racism we must first take account of race."

The use of racial gender identification for inclusionary rather than exclusionary purpose altered the nature of antidiscrimination policy. The rationale is that affirmative action helps make social goods and opportunities more equal and fair. Professor Richard Wasserstrom of the Department of Philosophy, University of California, Santa Cruz captured the essence of the problem when he observed,

> we are living in a society in which a person's race (and sex) is a socially significant and important characteristic. It affects both the way the individual looks at the world and the way the world looks at the

> individual. In our society, to be black is to be at a disadvantage in terms of virtually every conceivable measure of success or satisfaction – be it economic, political, or social. Viewed from the perspective of our social realities, race (and gender) in our world is taken into account in a certain way in the context of a specific set of institutional arrangements and a specific ideology which together create and maintain a system of objectionable, oppressive institutions and unwarranted beliefs and attitudes towards those who are (racial minority and female) and in favor of those who are (white and male).[2]

Affirmative action is aimed at the entrenched attitudes, behavior, and institutional arrangements that perpetuate the denial of equal opportunity to minorities and women. It is based on the reality that in the absence of conscious, deliberate efforts to assure equal opportunity, the legacy of past discrimination will be reinforced by contemporary actions. The expectation is that by pursuing the special measures of affirmative action temporarily, attitudes, values, and behavior will change in ways that redress the balance against population groups previously excluded from full participation in the job market.

IMPLEMENTING AFFIRMATIVE ACTION

When President John F. Kennedy issued Executive Order 10925, reauthorizing the Federal government's program to assure nondiscrimination in employment among government contractors, he built upon the record established by his three immediate predecessors. Beginning with President Franklin D. Roosevelt's Fair Employment Practices Commission, three successive agencies attempted to prohibit discriminatory practices in firms doing business with the federal government before Kennedy created the President Committee for Equal Opportunity (PCEEO). The experience of the previous agencies was not good, however, and President Kennedy's civil rights advisers recommended a more proactive policy aimed at the root of continuing discrimination.[3]

Indeed, the need for a stronger program than that implemented before 1960 was signaled in the final report of President Eisenhower's Committee on Government Contracts, chaired by then Vice President Richard M. Nixon. The Committee Report concluded:

> Overt discrimination in the sense that an employer actually refuses to hire solely because of race, religion – is not as prevalent as is generally believed. To a greater degree, *the indifference of employers to establishing a positive policy* of non-discrimination hinders qualified applicants and employees from being hired and promoted on the basis of equality.
>
> The direct result of such indifference is that schools, training institutions, recruitment and referral sources follow the pattern set by

> industry. Employment sources do not normally supply job applicants regardless of race, color, religion, or national origin *unless asked to do so by employers.*
>
> (Final Report, Committee on Government Contracts, Office of the President, Government Printing Office, 1960)

Executive Order 10925 introduced affirmative action as the device to get at institutional racism or institutional sexism – patterns of past discrimination built into institutional systems – described in the Nixon Committee's report. Affirmative action was a term drawn from the field of labor management relations, where employers found guilty of unfair labor practices regarding employee attempts to organize could be required to take steps to assure a work environment free of threats against future employee organizing activities. As interpreted at that time, the affirmative action requirement for government contractors meant special recruitment and pre-employment assessment policies aimed at producing more equal opportunity for available jobs.

The prototype for an affirmative action program was the agreement signed by the Lockheed aircraft company in 1961, after a complaint against its employment practices was filed with PCEEO by the National Association for the Advancement of Colored People. The company agreed to take special efforts to recruit and employ black workers in both white and blue collar jobs. Most importantly for future policy implementation, the company also agreed to record, and submit to the committee periodic reports on the number of employees hired, by race, sex, and occupational group.

A number of firms signed similar agreements, called Plans for Progress, and proceeded to alter their hiring policies in order to increase black employment. The voluntary program, however, eclipsed the Executive Order's enforcement activity aimed at non-signatory employers. Still, the special efforts seemed to produce modest gains. The 103 Plans for Progress companies increased the percentage of black employees from 5.1 per cent to 5.7 per cent within the first two years. That represented a gain of 40,938 of the companies' 341,734 vacancies – more than double the representation of black workers among those hired before Plans for Progress.

Toward goals and timetables

When Title VII of the Civil Rights Act of 1964 was passed, the administration of the federal government's antidiscrimination contractor program was reorganized. The President's Committee on Equal Employment Opportunity was abolished, and its responsibilities were transferred to the US Department of Labor's Division of Labor Standards. A new Agency, the Office of Federal Contract Compliance (OFCC), was created to enforce the new Executive Order 11246.

The new Office proceeded to develop regulations and procedures to assure equal job opportunity among government contractors. But the special problems with minority employment in the construction industry persisted with increased difficulty. Such problems were exacerbated by frequent demonstrations by civil rights activists in local communities where government supported construction proceeded with virtually all-white workers in all-black neighborhoods. In an effort to generate greater responsiveness by construction contractors toward equal employment, OFCC introduced the requirement for employment goals and timetables as a device for measuring compliance with the Executive Order.

The goals and timetables were part of the Philadelphia Plan, an agreement with contractors performing federally assisted construction in that city. The plan stated explicitly that the goals were not to be considered quotas, but were guideposts for measuring the contractor's progress toward equal opportunity. The maximum requirement of the government's program was a good faith effort to achieve the goals. There was no requirement to hire the unqualified, or to discriminate against non-minorities. What was important was the process employers used to integrate their workforce. If an employer failed to meet the goals and timetables, the response of the government typically was to investigate the efforts used to achieve the goals. Although OFCC retained ultimate authority to withdraw a contract, or refuse to award a future contract to an employer in noncompliance, that sanction was not applied until a decade later when Secretary of Labor, Ray Marshall withdrew a contract from a trucking company.

Goals and timetables were quickly introduced into contracts in non-construction industries, and were expanded to cover women under Revised order number 4 issued in 1971. This enforcement device sparked widespread and vociferous opposition. Some critics refused to concede that goals and timetables were not synonymous with quotas, despite clear statements to the contrary in both the Executive Order and its implementing regulations.

One line of attack against goals and timetables focuses on the attempt to compare the employment of minorities and women in various occupations to the presence of such groups in the local population. Thomas Sowell, for example, argues that to elevate employment and population parity to a legitimate public policy goal is to make statistical variance a federal offense.[4] He further observes that in no nation, at no time has there ever been parity between the number of persons of various racial, ethnic, or religious groups in the population, and their presence in all occupations, industries, and other classifications of employment. To suggest that statistical parity should be the goal of equal opportunity, according to their criticism, is to make goals synonymous with quotas, despite protestation to the contrary.

But another critic of affirmative action, Glenm Loury formerly of the Kennedy School of Government, Harvard, suggests that numerical information on racial and sexual employment practices can be useful in identifying firms that might warrant closer scrutiny for possible illegal discrimination.[5] Recognizing the limitations of a pure "color blind" position as the foundation of EEO enforcement, Loury concedes the value in comparing an employer's complement of minorities and women with their presence in the labor market.

But Loury is loathe to adopt goals and timetables as a device for hiring or promoting members of the legally protected groups, except in a finding of discrimination. In his view, to use goals and timetables except as a remedy against discrimination is to confer benefits on some minorities and women who are not entitled to such rewards. His view, then, is similar to Sowell's in rejecting the notion that statistical disparity between a group's employment and population representation is a legitimate basis for setting goals to achieve equal opportunity.

While critics continue to debate whether goals are in fact quotas, employers have adopted the affirmative action device as a regular part of their personnel practices. The Du Pont Corporation, for example, sets internal hiring and promotion goals higher than those suggested by OFCC. The rationale for that practice is that the Company pursues management by objectives and considers goals and timetables for equal job opportunity simply a useful tool for measuring the results of affirmative action policy.

To be effective, however, the implementation of affirmative action, including the skillful use of goals and timetables, requires strong support from the chief executive and careful staff training and technical assistance. What seems apparent is that in the wake of increased criticism of goals and timetables by senior officials of the federal government, including the Attorney General, the Chairman of the US Commission on Civil Rights, and others, during the 1980s, some business firms abandoned their focus on numerical measures of compliance with anti-discrimination policies. Others, especially large firms, continue to adhere to goals and timetables, but many have integrated EEO objectives into regular human resource development strategies. The result is a widespread perception that affirmative action is less important today than before – a perception reinforced by the virtual silence of senior corporate executives on the importance of equal job opportunity and affirmative action. According to Christine Kramer, Director, Affirmative Action Planning at CBS,

> There is no question in my mind, having been in the field for 15 years, that affirmative action has changed significantly. One of the things that I find most frustrating is that [some] larger companies continue to use entry level hiring as a cop-out for meeting their obligations under the Executive Order Program. A lot of us tried to begin to institutionalize affirmative action with a long-range goal of doing ourselves out of jobs so that there wouldn't be a need for such a function, and that

worked in a lot of companies, even in specific divisions and parts of companies. But I do see that changing.

(House Committee on Education and Labor, Report on Affirmative Action, 1987)

Affirmative action under Title VII

Title VII of the Civil Rights Act of 1964, as amended, confers on the US Equal Employment Opportunity Commission the authority to investigate charges of discrimination. The Act gave the federal courts broad power to issue orders once unlawful employment practices were found. Affirmative action was among the remedies the courts were authorized to require. This provision of Title VII has spawned a number of judicial orders with major provisions allocating job opportunities to minorities and women.[6] Courts have ordered unions to grant membership to minority group applicants, ordered employers to hire or promote equal numbers of minority and non-minority employees up to a certain percentage of the workforce, and ordered public and private employers to adopt special recruitment and testing policies designed to assure opportunities for minorities and women to compete for jobs. These requirements have been upheld by the US Supreme Court.[7]

Armed with the authority approved by Courts, EEOC adopted "creative rulemaking" during the 1970s to establish affirmative action procedures in employee selection. Affirmative action was also negotiated with employers who signed consent decrees. Among the most extensive uses of such practices were the provisions included in the consent decrees signed by AT&T, General Motors, and the US Steel Company.

Attempts by EEOC to go beyond an exclusive focus in the investigation of individual complaints to a broader assault on discrimination included the creation of a national program division targeted at several major multi-plant companies, such as IBM and Sears & Roebuck, in an attempt to achieve major gains in minority and female employment, with limited staff resources at EEOC. The assumption was that economies of scale would be achieved by focusing major staff resources on a few large employers, in an attempt to "presure" them voluntarily to strengthen their affirmative action policies. EEOC's strategy, however, was not entirely successful. Sears & Roebuck challenged EEOC's charge of discrimination and launched a long, costly legal battle against the agency. The case was finally settled in 1984, very much in Sears' favor. Similarly, IBM proved that its policies and practices on EEO were among the most progressive in the nation, and as a result, withstood the EEOC charges without any significant change in its affirmative action program.

Today, EEOC no longer plays a pioneering role in defining creative ways to implement affirmative action. During the 1980s the Commission's leadership was philosophically opposed to the use of goals and timetables, and sought alternative enforcement measures. But in the wake of the US Supreme Court's Summer 1986 trilogy of cases upholding the use of numerical preferences under certain conditions, EEOC announced that goals and timetables would again be approved in consent decrees and settlement agreements.

Non-government affirmative action efforts

An important feature of the current scene is the action of private, voluntary organizations to use community based support to persuade public and private employers to adopt affirmative action measures beneficial to minorities and women. Such actions often include a threat to withhold purchasing power from specific companies that refuse to adopt policies and programs to expand minority employment and in other ways broaden their support for minority economic well-being. Prominent among efforts of this type were the selective patronage campaigns launched by the Rev. Leon H. Sullivan and 400 ministers in Philadelphia during the early 1960s, the consumer boycotts initiated by Operation PUSH in Chicago and other cities during the 1970s, and the "reciprocal trade" agreements negotiated by the NAACP with several major entertainment and public utility firms.

Similar affirmative action goals have been pursued through the political process, most often in cities where minorities and women have organized to bring pressure on local governments to increase employment among members of the "protected" groups and expand government purchase of goods and services sold by minority and female businesses.

Private, voluntary efforts in pursuit of affirmative action are important for several reasons. First, they often require target employers to go beyond the goals agreed upon by government agencies as a part of an approved affirmative action plan. Employers have little choice in altering their position in response to a serious threat of losing an important consumer market or serious damage to the firm's public image. Second, the actions of voluntary community organizations can disturb the competitive position of firms in the labor market. Two firms in the same labor market might have very different product market characteristics, and thus be subject to different consumer group pressures. Such differences can well disturb the prospects for affirmative action progress in some firms which, while not the object of consumer group pressure, might have an unfavorable record on the employment of minorities and women.

Fred Rasheed, former Director of Economic Development of the NAACP, considers such voluntary efforts a critical supplement to affirmative action plans. According to Rasheed, "... companies will respond better to the black community when the profit margin is at stake. It is in the self interest of the black consumer to spend his dollars where he can work, and with firms willing to return something to the black community." (Interview with Fred Rasheed, Director of Economic Development, NAACP, February 1986.)

Similarly, the Rev. Jessie Jackson, President of PUSH, considers the "consumer covenants" agreed to by his organization and target companies a form of trade reciprocity in which a *quid pro quo* is reached between target firms and black purchasers. Such agreements, however, are self-enforcing and have no legal standing. Their effectiveness depends on the sincerity of the target firm's management and its determination to follow through on the commitments made to the community. In that sense, such agreements differ little from government approved affirmative action plans. In both cases, management desire to see results from affirmative action is critical to success.

Apprenticeship outreach

Another voluntary effort aimed at an affirmative action goal was the apprenticeship outreach strategy developed in the construction industry. Outreach programs worked in the supply side, in contrast to the Philadelphia Plan which focused exclusively on generating a demand for minority construction workers. Outreach programs, conducted mainly by the National Urban League, the Recruitment and Training Program, and the Negro Trade Union Leadership Council during the 1970s, recruited potential minority group apprentices and helped strengthen their basic skills and knowledge of the craft so they would have a better chance to pass the apprenticeship entry exams. Such programs worked closely with the trade union movement strong funding support from the US Department of Labor.

But Herbert Hill of the University of Wisconsin, and former Labor Director of the NAACP, argued that discrimination in the construction industry was too deep-seated to yield to voluntary measures like the outreach programs.[8] The judicial docket is replete with cases in which building trades unions have been found guilty of discrimination against minorities and women. Indeed, one of the recent US Supreme Court decisions on affirmative action involved a craft union that lost the case largely because of its long-standing discrimination against black workers, and its refusal to adopt and implement an affirmative action plan.[9]

It is difficult to compare the effectiveness of enforcement measures, like the Philadelphia Plan, with voluntary outreach efforts in bringing equal job opportunity into the construction industry. Undoubtedly both played a role in generating change reflected in the larger numbers of minorities and women now working in the industry. But the limited growth in construction industry employment during the 1970s, and the deeply entrenched traditions affecting entry into the field, even now, make the construction industry one of the most serious challenges for affirmative action.

IMPACT OF AFFIRMATIVE ACTION

One of the most contentious issues concerning affirmative action is its impact both on the groups that historically suffered from discrimination, and on other groups whose employment expectations are inevitably affected by the disturbance of the status quo when equal opportunity is introduced. Efforts to widen job opportunities for minorities and women have sparked staunch resistance in many quarters, often fueled by anecdotes about "reverse discrimination." The impact of affirmative action on nonminority men, and even on the intended beneficiaries of the policies themselves has been discussed frequently in the scholarly literature, and in the public debate over affirmative action policy.

Professor William J. Wilson, a sociologist at the University of Chicago, gained wide attention when his 1978 book, *The Declining Significance of Race*, argued that affirmative action had benefited only the least disadvantaged segments of the black community.[10] In his view, embellished and reiterated numerous times in frequent debate, the economic and social conditions confronting persistently poor minorities will not yield to a strategy like affirmative action which, by its nature, benefits only those who have marketable skills, but have been denied job opportunity only because of discrimination.

Similarly, Professor Thomas Sowell has criticized civil rights leaders for supporting affirmative action without realizing that, in his view, such measures hurt the disadvantaged.[11] His position is based on the observation that affirmative action programs seem to concentrate on jobs above the minimum wage, and benefit minorities and women with better than average levels of education and labor market experience. Sowell believes the widening gap in personal income within the black community is evidence that affirmative action is biased toward the more advantaged groups. He argues that the occupational gains achieved by minorities and women during the 1970s resulted from factors such as economic growth, strong labor demand, and improved educational attainment among minority group youth, rather than civil rights legislation and affirmative action policy.

Professor Glenn C. Loury goes a step beyond Wilson and Sowell's criticism by suggesting that affirmative action generates a "self-reinforcing cycle of negative expectation."[12] He thinks minorities and women hired or promoted in an environment of affirmative action develop doubts about their ability to compete effectively on their own. According to Loury, they will doubt their competence to perform in an open system based strictly on merit, and equally important, will be viewed by others as less capable because they gained their position through preferential treatment. Such negative attitudes feed on themselves and make it difficult for minorities and women to ever be accepted on equal terms.

There is enough anecdotal evidence to lend some credence to these criticisms of affirmative action, but the full story is considerably more complicated. As a device to protect equal job opportunity, affirmative action is aimed at discriminatory behavior, and must take as given, prevailing economic and labor force conditions. Neither the origin nor history of affirmative action suggests that it ever was intended to address problems of structural unemployment, which accounts for much of the gap in unemployment between minorities and others. The fact that the black youth unemployment rate continues to exceed, by several times, that of white youth and adults; that an increasing proportion of black families are headed by single women, many of whom are poor; and that nearly one third of all black families continue to live in poverty says less about the impact of affirmative action policy than the ineffectiveness of many other social and economic policies aimed at such problems. Especially important in this connection, is that efforts to achieve full employment and to reduce poverty are central to the reduction of economic inequality.

As for self-doubts among minorities and women who benefit from affirmative action, the extent of such attitudes is not clear. There is little evidence from surveys of employees in large organizations to support the view that minorities and women feel in any way inferior because of affirmative action.[13] In fact, the reverse might be so because of the common educational experience in college and graduate school now shared by many minorities, women, and white males. By competing on equal terms in the classroom, members of such groups acquire knowledge and confidence about themselves and their relationship with others that should be transferred to the corporate office. Moreover, since affirmative action was introduced, performance assessment has been strengthened in many firms, and as a result, a more objective view of relative success on the job is now available. Good performance evaluation should minimize the tendency of either minorities, women, or nonminorities to question whether an individual's productive contribution is based on merit or on preferential treatment.

Aggregate measures of impact

The bulk of the statistical evidence supports the conclusion that the labor market position of minorities improved more rapidly since 1971 than might have been expected from earlier trends, general business conditions, or relative educational attainment of minorities. But female earnings have not increased significantly relative to males. Whether such stability at a time of rising female labor force participation would have been predicted by pre-

1970 experience has not been carefully studied.[14] To discern the impact of affirmative action on the observed trends, the effects of OFCC and EEOC must be measured. Such research, while not conclusive, suggests that OFFC has been a factor leading toward higher levels of employment of minorities than might have occurred without the agency, but that EEOC's impact is more difficult to measure.

Statistical studies of the impact of affirmative action often suffer from the lack of careful specification of precisely what in the operation of OFCC or EEOC would produce higher levels of employment for minorities and women than otherwise might exist. But if the burden of proof is lowered to a level more commensurate with limitations imposed by incomplete data, more positive results of affirmative action emerge.

For example, a study by Finis Welch and James Smith, two Rand Corporation economists thought to be unsympathic to affirmative action, concluded that "affirmative action has resulted in a radical reshuffling of black jobs in the labor force." They found that affirmative action shifted black male employment toward EEOC covered firms and industries, and that it resulted in an increase in the representation of black male workers in managerial and professional jobs in such firms. As a result, the authors wrote that "there has been a short-lived, but significant, positive effect on ages of younger black workers," and "the main beneficiaries of affirmative action – in terms of income – have been young, college educated blacks."[15]

An unreleased study conducted by OFCC in 1984 concluded that companies subject to Executive Order 11246 from 1974–80 showed more favorable employment gains for minorities and women than nonfederal contractors who, presumably, were obligated only to adhere to nondiscrimi nation – a less effective device for assuring equal job opportunity.[16] Specifically, the 77,000 companies reviewed had over 20 million employees. During the six year period, minority employment increased 20.1 per cent compared to total employment growth of 12.3 per cent. Female employment grew 8.2 per cent compared with total employment growth of 2.2 per cent during the same time period. Moreover, the federal contractors had a smaller proportion of minority and female employees in lower-paying jobs than noncontractors, and contractors showed significantly faster growth of minorities and women into managerial jobs.

Professor Jonathan Leonard of the University of California, Berkeley conducted one of the best conceived and thorough studies of the impact of Executive Order and Title VII on minority and female employment.[17] He concluded that while the OFCC program helped black workers, its impact on non-black minorities and women was less conclusive. He also found that class action litigation under Title VII had a relatively greater impact than affirmative action on black employment. Leonard's data, like the OFCC study, showed the greatest gains have been in the higher paying managerial, professional, and craft occupations, although gains were recorded across a wide range of fields. Significant gains were noted among black bus drivers and computer operators, as well as attorneys and psychologists.

A study conducted by the Bureau of National Affairs found that among 114 employers in a cross-section of US industry, women had achieved at least first-level management in almost nine out of ten firms, and executive positions in about half of the responding companies.[18] Female gains exceeded similar progress among minority employees. Similarly, in 1986 the Korn/Ferry executive search firm conducted a seven year follow-up study of senior-level executives in a broad range of industries. The results showed that of more than 1,300 respondents, 2 per cent of the senior executives were women, a ratio that, while low, was still several times the level observed in 1979. But there was little representation of minorities in senior positions, (less than one per cent), a status unchanged over a seven year period. Minorities, however, showed improved representation in middle management. The Korn/Ferry study suggests that despite government efforts to promote affirmative action, the impact on the race and sex composition of the executive suite has been minimal.

Individual company results

The impact of affirmative action on employment might be best observed by looking at the experience of specific companies. For example, in 1973, AT&T entered into a six-year consent decree with the EEOC to correct previous discriminatory employment practices.[19] Since that time, the company has registered significant goals in minority and female employment, as shown in the Table 7.1.

Table 7.1 Percentage of employees in AT&T occupations

Occupations of Minorities	*1972*	*1982*
Minorities in management	4.6	13.1
Women in management	33.3	39.6
Minorities in craft jobs	8.4	14.0
Women in crafts	2.8	12.3
Males in clerical jobs	4.1	11.4

These gains were the direct result of the Company's revised employee recruitment, selection, and assessment procedures adopted under the consent decree. There is no explanation, other than affirmative action, for these gains and no other company in the public utility industries can match AT&T's record of minority and female employment over the ten year period.

Impact of affirmative action: the public sector

Executive Order 10925, issued in 1961, established a policy of affirmative action for federal agencies, and gave the President's Committee on Equal Employment Opportunity the responsibility to monitor the plans and progress of such agencies in employing minorities and women. Title VII of the Civil Rights Act of 1964 transferred to The Civil Service Commission the responsibility for administering the federal EEO programs, but until the passage of the Equal Employment Opportunity Act of 1972, excluded state and local governments.

Under Title VI of the Civil Rights Act, federal agencies that provided financial assistance to state and local governments in the form of loans, grants, guarantees, and revenue sharing were required to assure that such funds were used in a nondiscriminatory way. This policy led federal agencies to adopt affirmative action requirements for state and local governments.

By 1970, however, about two dozen states and localities had adopted their own anti-discrimination policies and had created agencies to enforce such requirements. Some of the strongest agencies, including those in Connecticut and Michigan, and the cities of New York and Philadelphia, had extensive monitoring and investigatory powers which allowed them not only to correct individual cases of discrimination, but also to promote affirmative action in state and local employment.

A survey conducted by the US Commission on Civil rights in 1967, and another survey conducted by the National Civil Service League, showed low participation of minority group employees in state and local agencies, especially those with no service functions dealing with the poor and disadvantaged. The worst records were found in police and fire departments which employed virtually no minorities or women. Widespread use of discriminatory selection and promotion methods, unnecessary educational and experience requirements, and selective announcements of hiring and promotion opportunities were among the major barriers to equal opportunity. Precedent - setting court cases challenging such practices affecting protective service workers in Boston, Philadelphia, and Memphis have set new standards now applied by many communities throughout the nation.

Affirmative action in the cities

During the past decade, affirmative action has been embraced by many city governments. The extent of such efforts was revealed in a survey of 121 cities conducted by US Conference of Mayors in Summer 1986.[20] The following are some of the major findings of the survey:

- More than nine of every ten survey cities voluntarily adopted their affirmative action plan. In seven cities, plans were adopted following a court-approved settlement, and in four cities, the plan was imposed by court order. In eighteen cities, there were court findings of past discrimination.

- Affirmative action programs set or improved recruitment standards and procedures in 41 per cent of the cities, hiring and promotion standards in almost all cities, and employee performance reviews in about two-thirds of the cities.
- Respondents reported that affirmative action contributed to increased employee job satisfaction.

The Conference of Mayors' survey did not include trends in the profile of city government employment, but other studies shed light on that of equal opportunity. An analysis of data from 1,224 cities with populations of more than 10,000 showed that in 1985, 306 cities employed no black workers, 427 cities had less than one per cent, and 540 cities had less than 2 per cent black employees in official/administrative, professional, and protective service jobs.[21] Many of the cities were located in areas with black labor pools.

State and local employment

An earlier study, based on analysis of EEOC data, showed that in 1980, minority group men accounted for 11.2 per cent, and minority group women 9.8 per cent, of all full-time state and local government employees. White women comprised 31.2 per cent of all state and local workforce. Between 1973 and 1980 there was considerable improvement for women in all but para-professional and clerical jobs where they heavily represented substantial gains in protective services and skilled craft jobs, and more moderate gains in all other occupational categories.

Much more of the improvement in the number and occupational distribution of minority and female employees in state and local governments occurred through new hires. Moreover, the improvement seemed concentrated during the years of the late 1970s, suggesting that the adoption and refinement of affirmative action plans began to pay off for local governments at that time.

Equal employment, through affirmative action, has been advanced substantially by black elected officials. Since gaining office at the local level, city council members and other officials have placed greater emphasis on expanding job opportunities for minorities. Many municipal and state jobs are covered by civil service, but with the heightened visibility of black elected officials, more minorities have entered the pool of candidates applying for civil service jobs, and more have been successful in meeting the qualifying requirements. This is especially so in the fields of education, social welfare services, and protective services. The current racial/gender composition of middle management in municipal public service reflects the impact of enhanced political power on public employer hiring policy.

SUMMARY

The success of affirmative action, in the end, must be determined by numerical changes in the employment and occupational status of minorities and women. Affirmative action policy is predicated upon the assumption that current employment systems must be modified in ways that assure a fair and equal chance for groups previously excluded from employment to compete on equal footing with others who have long enjoyed artificial advantages in the labor market. In the absence of race and gender-specific measures designed to assure equal job opportunity, the present effects of past discrimination would perpetuate job inequality.

The available research, while often flawed methodologically, or limited by incomplete data, supports the conclusion that affirmative action plans, when well-designed and conscientiously implemented, have contributed to an improvement in the employment status of minorities and women. There is no persuasive alternative explanation for the obvious change in employment during the past decade in which many minorities and women have entered occupational fields from which previously they were systematically excluded. Yet, as indicated in the evidence discussed above, affirmative action has not been a panacea. Current labor market realities still find minorities and women in a substantially less favorable position, overall, than white males. This situation is not the sole product of overt discrimination, a practice that has undoubtedly changed over the past two decades, and affirmative action alone will not solve all the remaining problems. But there is no basis for concluding that affirmative action has no legitimate role to play today in the multi-part assault on the remaining vestiges of inequality in American economic life.

NOTES

1 Gary Becker, *The Economics of Discrimination* (Chicago, University of California Press, 1956).
2 Richard Wasserstrom, "A justification of Preferential Treatment Programs," Conference Report prepared for the Rockefeller Foundation, November 1983.
3 James E. Jones, Jr., "The Origins of Affirmative Action," *Iowa Law Review*, May 1985.
4 Thomas Sowell, *Civil Rights Rhetoric or Reality*?, (New York: Morrow Company, 1984).
5 Glenn C. Loury, "Equal Opportunity: Reality, Achievable Goal, or Elusive Dream?," unpublished paper prepared for Symposium for Senior Corporate Officers on EEO, New York, 11 December 1985.
6 Jones, *op. cit*, pp. 28–9.

7 Bureau of National Affairs, *Affirmative Action Today: A Legal and Practical Analysis* (Washington, DC: BNA, 1986, pp. 23–88).
8 Herbert Hill, "Race, Ethnicity, and Organized Labor: The Opposition to Affirmative Action," *Journal of Intergroup Relations*, pp. 31–82.
9 *Local 28 Sheet Metal Workers* v *EEOC*, 41 FEP Cases 107 (2 July 1986).
10 William J. Wilson, *The Declining Significance of Race* (Chicago: University of Chicago Press, 1978).
11 Thomas Sowell, *op. cit.*, p. 53.
12 Glenn C. Loury, "Comments on Affirmative Action," paper presented before the 7th Annual Judicial Conference of the District of Columbia Circuit, 19 May 1986.
13 John Fernandez, *Survival in the Corporate Fishbowl: Making It Into Middle and Upper Management*, (Massachusetts: Lexington Press, 1987).
14 Janice F. Madden, "The Persistence of Pay Differentials," Working Paper, University of Pennsylvania, Department of Regional Studies, 1986.
15 James P. Smith and Finis R. Welch, "Closing the Gap: Forty Years of Economic Progress for Blacks," *Rand Corporation Report*, 1986.
16 Employment Standards Administration, US Department of Labor, "Employment Patterns of Minorities and Women in Federal Contractor and Noncontractor Establishments, 1974–1980: A Report of OFCCP" (1984).
17 Jonathan S. Leonard, "The Impact of Affirmative Action on Employment," paper commissioned for the Study Group on Affirmative Action, June, 1987.
18 Bureau of National Affairs, "EEO Policies and Programs, Personnel Policies Forum Survey No. 141," Washington, DC, 1986.
19 Bernard E. Anderson, "Black Employment in the Telephone Industry," in Phyllis A Wallace, *Equal Opportunity and the AT&T Case*, (Cambridge, MA: MIT Press, 1974); and John A. Larson, *The Impact of the AT&T–EEO Consent Decree* (Philadelphia: Industrial Research Unit, University of Pennsylvania, 1979).
20 US Conference of Mayors, "Affirmative Action Programs in City Governments: A 121 City Survey," Washington, DC, September 1986.
21 Bureau of National Affairs, *op. cit.*, pp. 99.

8

IN THE MATTER OF RACE AND HOUSING

*Wilhelmina A. Leigh**

INTRODUCTION

The complete title for this chapter is, "In the Matter of Race and Housing – How Are Black Americans Served by the Federal Low-Rent Public Housing (LRPH) Program?" To answer this question, program enrollment data and findings from court cases are used to reveal the way in which the LRPH program serves black Americans.

Although race is not an eligibility criterion for federally subsidized rental housing programs, income is, and, in general, black Americans have lower incomes than white Americans. Thus, large proportions of the black population in many localities are eligible for federal housing assistance. At the same time, some of the white families eligible for federal housing assistance are unwilling to live near households of other racial groups, and the residents of many neighborhoods are able to successfully thwart efforts to build federally subsidized units nearby. These conflicts have shaped the terms of operation and the conditions of participation by black Americans in federally assisted housing programs.

Why was the LRPH program chosen as the focus for an examination of the interaction of race and federally assisted housing? The LRPH program was chosen for three major reasons. First, established in 1937, the LRPH program is the oldest extant federal housing assistance program. Because of its seniority, when people think of federally assisted housing, although they may not know the full name of this program, they think of the LRPH program. Second, when people think of this form of federally assisted housing, most commonly known as "the projects," they also think of households headed by females who are members of minority groups. Finally, in recent years, the LRPH program has confronted the challenges of tenant ownership and "vouchering out," two concepts that may change the program's role as a major source of federally assisted housing.

* This chapter represents the views of the author and does not necessarily reflect the views of her employer, The Joint Center for Political and Economic Studies, or her employer's sponsors.

This chapter begins with a brief discussion of how economists usually analyze the influence of race in the housing market and why this mode of analysis is of limited usefulness for answering the central question of this chapter. The next section describes federal housing assistance, in general, and the LRPH program, in particular. Then, enrollment data for the LRPH program are presented, followed by a discussion of the program experience of blacks as reflected by selected court cases. Finally, the shortcomings of the analysis are noted, along with a summary of findings and conclusions.

ECONOMIC ANALYSIS OF RACE AND HOUSING

Economists define housing – a dual consumption and investment good – as a bundle of characteristics, which are consumed jointly. A *characteristic* is defined as an objectively measurable, utility-affecting attribute of a model – such things as the number of rooms in a house, or the racial mix of the neighborhood. A *model* is a distinct, homogeneous, marketable, tied bundle of characteristics – such as a row house in a predominantly white neighborhood. A *good*, such as housing, is a set of models with a common set of characteristics, although the characteristics could be in different amounts per model.

Thus, "the housing bundle" includes such things as the location of the dwelling, with its associated environmental amenities, and its access to employment and services. The condition of the dwelling, the quality of the neighborhood, the characteristics of neighbors, the opportunities for income from investment in the housing, and the household's local support network also are characteristics of the bundle.

Hedonic regression analysis, a commonly used economic technique, is based on the belief that goods can be disaggregated into sets of basic characteristics and that the characteristics of a particular good, rather than the good itself, are arguments of a consumer's utility function.[1] Utility maximization subject to a budget constraint yields parameters for both the demand and the hedonic regression equations associated with housing. Variables such as race of neighbors (i.e., number of blacks, or percentage of blacks, or change in the number or percentage of blacks) or proximity to housing occupied by blacks or members of other minority groups are commonly included when hedonic regression analyses are used to estimate the impact on housing prices of a variety of characteristics.

Although hedonic regression analysis is widely used to assess the impact of the race of one's neighbors (among other characteristics) on the price of housing, the technique will be of limited value in helping to evaluate how blacks are served by the federal LRPH program. The factors underlying the supply, demand, and prices for LRPH render the market for this form of housing sufficiently different from the private housing market that the standard tools of the trade do not provide much information. The supply of LRPH units is determined primarily by the funding appropriated by Congress. The characteristics or amenities of these units are determined by federal regulations, rather than by the preferences of the consuming households. Because too little money is appropriated to assist all households who qualify, demand exceeds supply in most places at most times. Finally, prices (or rents) are determined as a fraction of household adjusted income, rather than being determined by a market-linked process.[2]

A likely use of hedonic regression analysis with federally assisted housing often is thwarted by the lack of data. Hedonic regression analysis and other tools could be (and have been) applied to explore the impact of the location of subsidized housing on nearby property values.[3] Data on the racial composition of projects often is incomplete, however, so the impact of race cannot always be separated from the impact of the presence of assisted housing on the value of nearby properties.

Thus, the investigation of how well black Americans are served by the federal LRPH program in this chapter is undertaken without the standard tools of the economist's trade. Program enrollment data and selected court cases are used for the analysis, instead.

FEDERAL HOUSING ASSISTANCE

Equal opportunity in housing

One of the seven major goals of federal housing policy is to provide equal opportunity in housing.[4] Equal opportunity in housing means the ability of households of all racial and ethnic groups to move into any neighborhood of their choice constrained only by whether they have the income to purchase or rent there. The Civil Rights Act of 1866 first codified this goal, when it guaranteed to all citizens in every state and territory the same right as is enjoyed by white citizens to inherit, purchase, lease, sell, hold, and convey real and personal property. The 1964 and 1968 Civil Rights Acts reaffirmed this goal. Title VI of the 1964 Civil Rights Act (hereafter, Title VI) prohibits racial discrimination in all programs that receive federal funding, while Title VIII of the 1968 Civil Rights Act (hereafter, Title VIII) prohibits discrimination in housing on the basis of race, color, religion, and national origin. The US Department of Housing and Urban Development (HUD) administers Title VIII by investigating complaints of housing discrimination and attempting to resolve them with conciliation. Also under Title VIII, the Justice Department is able to bring suits against parties believed to violate the statute. The 1974 Housing and Community Development Act added sex to the list of protected statuses.

The Fair Housing Amendments Act of 1988 (P.L. 100–430) expands the protected classes to include families with children and the handicapped. This Act also authorizes the Secretary of HUD to file complaints with administrative law judges on behalf of complainants who contact the agency. This new authority complements the authority of the Justice Department to file suits for violation of the nation's fair housing legislation.

HUD has tried to achieve equal opportunity in access to federally subsidized housing by three major means – enforcing fair housing and antidiscrimination laws, choosing sites for housing projects to enhance the racial integration of neighborhoods, and providing vouchers for rental housing.[5] The success of these efforts has been limited. Court challenges to the operation of federally subsidized housing programs have helped somewhat to foster the goal of equal opportunity within these programs, and some of these court cases are discussed later in the paper.

Eligibility for assistance

Since the 1930s, the federal government has intervened in the housing market to help meet the needs of households whose incomes were so low as to render their demand ineffective for procuring housing that met minimal standards of safety and adequacy. A specific housing policy goal – to ensure the availability of adequate and affordable housing, especially to low-income households – works toward this end. John Maynard Keynes provided theoretical support for government intervention to lessen poverty on the grounds that only activist but carefully calculated "government demand" could counteract deficiencies in aggregate demand.[6]

Also during the 1930s, because of the private sector's failure to house most Americans adequately, President Hoover convened the President's Committee on Home Building and Home Ownership to explore ways to use the housing sector to stimulate the economy. This Committee isolated "Negro housing" as a topic of inquiry, due to evidence that the units occupied by "Negroes" were undermaintained, overpriced, and crowded.[7] The Hoover Committee also found that "Negroes" paid a higher percentage of income for shelter than other population subgroups.

The most common rubric for income eligibility for housing assistance programs is some fraction of the median income for the metropolitan statistical area (MSA) in which a locality is located. Thus, federal rental assistance programs are open to households whose incomes are a certain percentage of their area's median income. Although eligibility for federal rental housing programs is based on income, these programs are not entitlements – that is, all the households with qualifying incomes do not receive assistance. In fact, in 1993, only 37 per cent of all eligible renter households with incomes below the poverty line throughout the nation received some form of housing subsidy.[8] Households accepted into most of these programs pay 30 per cent of income toward rent.

Because the income distribution of blacks has lower ranges and a lower median than that of whites, blacks tend to dominate the pools of households eligible for federal rental housing assistance. In 1992, black median household income was about $18,700 while white median household income was about $32,400.[9]

Low-rent public housing program

The low-rent public housing (LRPH) program, established by the US Housing Act of 1937, provides reduced-rent publicly owned dwellings for lower-income families and for elderly, handicapped, or displaced individuals.[10] The federal government finances both the construction and operation of these projects, which are administered by local housing agencies (LHAs).[11] The LHAs select tenants and compile waiting lists of households for the LRPH program and also are responsible for the maintenance and management of projects. The LRPH program currently shelters approximately 1.4 million households and provides about one-fifth of all federal housing assistance.[12]

Since 1937, the calculation of tenant rents for LRPH has changed in ways that have affected the populations served. Between 1937 and 1949, the eligible tenant population was defined as those of the lowest income group able to pay the rents required for LRPH to be financially self-sufficient. Thus, rents were related to production and operating costs. In 1949, eligibility was redefined to target those whose net incomes at the time of admission to the housing did not exceed five times the rents of their units.[13] Because the process of setting the rent levels was thus detached from the assessment of funds needed to operate the units, the LHAs faced shortfalls in operating expenses, which they tried to meet by raising rents. Later, to limit rent increases, the Brooke–Cranston Amendment of 1969 established 25 per cent of adjusted tenant income as the maximum tenant payment toward rent. The 1981 Omnibus Budget Reconciliation Act increased the maximum tenant rent payment to 30 per cent of adjusted tenant income – effective immediately for new tenants and by 1986 for current tenants, using 1 per cent annual increments.[14] Thus, the calculation of rents for LRPH has been completely disconnected from the costs associated with producing and operating this housing.

The adjusted tenant income currently used as a base for rent calculations results from subtracting several items from gross tenant income. These items are: $550 per dependent; $400 for an elderly family; medical expenses in excess of 3 per cent of annual income per family; child care expenses essential to the ability of an adult to work; 10 per cent of earned family income; and any payment by a family member to someone in another household for child support or alimony (subject to a limit).[15]

Although tenant ownership has long been an option for the residents of LRPH, since the mid-1980s, the Department of HUD has encouraged tenant ownership as a logical next step beyond tenant management of

LRPH projects and as a vehicle for the economic empowerment of low-income households.[16] The HOPE program, authorized by the Cranston–Gonzalez National Affordable Housing Act of 1990 (P.L. 101–625), codifies the more recent federal policy initiative for tenant ownership not only of LRPH but also of a variety of other types of both single- and multi-family housing owned by HUD. Under HOPE, program funds can be used to transfer ownership of the following types of properties to their low-income tenants: Public and Indian housing; HUD-owned or -held multi-family properties; and one-to-four family properties owned or held by HUD, by the Department of Veterans Affairs, by the Farmers Home Administration, and the Resolution Trust Corporation.[17]

These federal policies and programs, pushed largely during the Bush presidency by then HUD Secretary Kemp, find supporters among unlikely allies – those who would like to continue the federal retrenchment from an active role in federal housing assistance and the tenant groups that have been able to meet program regulations and therefore have been funded under these initiatives. A notable example is provided by the Kenilworth–Parkside LRPH project in Washington, DC, where units were renovated at $130,000 each (close to the 1988 median house price in the DC–MD–VA metropolitan area of $139,000), and the complex was sold to the resident management corporation for $1.[18] Expensive experiments such as this are unlikely to be replicated throughout the nation, at least not as long as the current budget woes prevail. They serve primarily to give windfall bonanzas to current tenants and to limit the supply of units available to low-income persons in the future. Thus, funding and the existence of suitable properties and able tenant groups have hindered the ability of HUD to achieve its desired revolution in tenant empowerment through the LRPH program.

Since the concept of tenant ownership was put forth as a vehicle for empowerment of low-income residents, other reform proposals for HUD and for the LRPH program have come forth during the 104th session of Congress. These proposals have ranged from abolishing HUD altogether to establishing block grants for all housing assistance to "vouchering out" the LRPH program.[19] Vouchering out LRPH would involve giving all current tenants vouchers that could be used to rent their current units or any other units within the jurisdiction of their housing authorities. Questions about the impact of this proposal on the financial viability of LRPH developments and about the ability of "hard to house" families to search for units within their localities remain unanswered.

PROGRAM ENROLLMENT DATA

Prior to 1970, tenant data for LRPH were sparse. A 1961 report by the US Commission on Civil Rights estimated that during the 1940s, blacks occupied 25 to 35 per cent of LRPH units. In 1960, when 65 per cent of the projects that provided occupancy data indicated that they were completely segregated by race, blacks occupied approximately 47 per cent of all units. In 1965, blacks occupied 49 per cent of the units; in 1970, they occupied half.[20]

These estimates are generally consistent with later figures prepared by HUD. In 1974, black households occupied 44 per cent of the units in public housing, and white households occupied 49 per cent of the units. By 1977, approximately 57 per cent of the residents of LRPH were minorities, and black Americans were 47 per cent of all residents. The proportion of minority residents was greater in central cities, where 65 per cent of the occupied public housing is located. In central cities, blacks occupied 71 per cent of the non-elderly public housing units.[21] In 1981, the percentages of blacks and whites served by the program were roughly the same – with 46 per cent of the households black and 45 per cent of the households white. In 1993, 52 per cent of all resident households were headed by blacks, and 34 per cent were headed by non-Hispanic whites.[22]

Data based on 90 per cent of the mid-size and 40 per cent of the large PHAs reporting as of 1 July 1991 reveal participation rates by race that vary by type of household served.[23] For example, 36 per cent of elderly households were black, while 52 per cent were white. Among handicapped households, the proportions were reversed – blacks were 53 per cent, and whites were 34 per cent. The majority of family households in LRPH are black, too. As of June 1993, 64 per cent of these households were black, while only 20 per cent were white.[24]

Relative to program eligibility, all federally subsidized rental housing programs, including LRPH, serve blacks more than whites. In 1989, 57 per cent of all income-eligible renters – that is, households with incomes below 50 per cent of area median income (excluding single non-elderly households) – were whites, and 26 per cent were blacks. Out of all housing subsidy recipients, however, whites were slightly under-represented at 48 per cent, while blacks were over-represented at 37 per cent.[25]

Elderly families are overserved by LRPH (and also by other federal rental subsidy programs). Elderly households are 33 per cent of all income-eligible renters but are 45 per cent of the tenants in LRPH.[26]

THE PROGRAM EXPERIENCE OF BLACKS

Because of the lack of comprehensive data on the nature of program participation, court cases filed by aggrieved parties, usually against localities, LHAs, or HUD, were used as the major sources of this information. An effort was made to provide a broad array of cases throughout the history of the LRPH program.

A catalogue of court findings may either overestimate or underestimate the extent of the conditions noted. Overestimation would result if the conditions about which the cases were filed existed only in the jurisdictions or under the LHAs named as defendants. Underestimation would result if many more instances of these conditions exist than have come to light through cases filed or judicial decisions rendered. If numerous similar cases were settled out of court, the cases tried could be merely the tip of the iceberg. The following fact – that some localities never have established LHAs, expressly to avoid having to provide federally assisted housing, and that citizens may not have filed suits to protest this – also would not be reflected in findings from the cases cited below.

Major issues in court challenges to the LRPH program that shed light on the nature of program participation for blacks include:

- exclusion of minorities from program participation;
- prohibiting or delaying construction of projects;
- impact of site selection on concentrations of minorities in the central cities; and
- discrimination and segregation by race among projects due to tenant selection policies.

Each of these issues is discussed below.

Exclusion

As the participation data suggest, minorities no longer are excluded from LRPH. Historically, though, the story is different. In 1953, a suit was filed in Toledo, Ohio, to gain access to public housing projects for minorities. In *Vann* v. *Toledo Metropolitan Housing Authority*, 1953, OH (113 F. Supp. 210), the District Court of Ohio ruled that a municipality charged with managing LRPH projects erected with public funds could not exclude persons of the "colored race." Such exclusion violated the 14th Amendment to the Constitution.

A similar case, *Detroit Housing Commission* v. *Lewis*, 1955, MI (226 F. 2d 180), was decided in Michigan in 1955. The 6th Circuit Court decided that enforced racial segregation by LHAs constituted state action in violation of the equal protection clause of the 14th amendment.

Prohibiting or delaying construction

In three cases, one each in North Carolina, Pennsylvania, and Virginia, the federal courts found that prohibiting or delaying construction of LRPH violates various civil rights statutes. In the Philadelphia case – *Resident Advisory Board* v. *Rizzo*, 1977, PA (564 F. 2d 126) – the court found that actions of the Philadelphia Housing Authority and the Redevelopment Authority of Philadelphia to terminate a low-income housing project

(Whitman Park Townhouse Project) had a racially discriminatory impact. The court rendered this finding even though it also noted that the two defendants had not acted with discriminatory intent.

In Greenville City, VA, and Clarkston, NC, federal courts held that localities had vetoed plans for LRPH for racially discriminatory reasons. In *Atkins* v. *Robinson*, 1982, VA (545 F. Supp. 852), the court found that the veto by the county board of supervisors of a proposed LRPH project violated the Civil Rights Act of 1866. In rendering its decision in *Smith* v. *Town of Clarkston*, 1982, NC (682 F. 2d 1055), the court noted that statements opposing subsidized housing need not be of a racial character to be viewed as racially motivated within the context of a need for assisted housing in the area.

Site selection

In eight court cases in places as varied as Illinois, Louisiana, New Jersey, New York, Pennsylvania, and Texas, LHAs and HUD have been found culpable for selecting sites for LRPH in ways that perpetuate racial segregation. In two cases filed by the late Dorothy Gautreaux in Chicago, the court found HUD at fault for approving sites and funding projects to maintain the racial segregation already existing within the system of public housing. (The cases are *Gautreaux* v. *Romney*, 1971, IL (448 F. 2d 731) and *Hills* v. *Gautreaux*, 1976, IL (425 US 284).)

In the Louisiana case, *Hicks* v. *Weaver*, 1969, LA (302 F. Supp. 619), the court found that HUD's behavior in selecting sites for public housing to maintain complete segregation of the races violated not only Title VI but also the 14th Amendment of the US Constitution. In the Pennsylvania case (*Rowe* v. *Pittsgrove Twp.*, 1977, PA (379 A. 2d 497)) and the Texas case (*Blackshear Residents Organization* v. *Housing Authority of the City of Austin*, 1972, TX (347 F. Supp. 1138)), the defendant localities also were found to violate Title VI and the 14th amendment with their rules for selecting sites for LRPH.

HUD and the LHAs are allowed to site LRPH in areas of racial concentration when they have weighed all relevant factors, and the need for housing over-rides the concern about racial concentration. In two cases, one each in New York and Pennsylvania, the federal courts decided that Title VIII does not preclude HUD from constructing housing in areas of racial concentration, but it does preclude HUD from funding construction *only* in areas of racial concentration. (See *Jones* v. *Tully*, 1974, NY (378 F. Supp. 286) and *Croskey Street Concerned Citizens* v. *Romney*, 1971, PA (335 F. Supp. 1251).) In *King* v. *Harris*, 1979, NY (464 F. Supp. 827), however, HUD was enjoined from funding lower-income housing projects in areas with concentrations of minority and low-income residents, because the agency had not satisfied the criteria for doing so.

Tenant selection policies

Racially discriminatory tenant selection policies have been challenged in several well-known cases. In addition, other cases are still pending, and compliance with court orders is being negotiated.

In two cases, *Young* v. *Pierce*, 1982 and 1985, TX (544 F. Supp. 1010) and (628 F. Supp. 1037), HUD and certain local housing agencies in thirty-six counties in the eastern part of Texas were found to have intentionally discriminated by selecting and assigning tenants to maintain racially segregated projects. A court-ordered reassignment of tenants was part of the remedy in this case. The decision in the case *Taylor* v. *City of Millington*, 1973, TN (476 F. 2d 599, 600) was a predecessor of the *Young* v. *Pierce* cases. In the *Taylor* case, the court ordered not only remedial steps for the existing segregation of tenants by race but also changes in future tenant assignment plans.

In yet another Gautreaux case – *Gautreaux* v. *Chicago Housing Authority*, 1969, IL (296 F. Supp 907) – "Negro" tenants were found to be entitled to relief against the use of racial quotas for certain of the family projects operated by that authority. A similar Pennsylvania case also overturned the use of an integration quota for the occupants of LRPH. (See *Burney* v. *Housing Authority of the City of Beaver*, 1982, PA (551 F. Supp. 746).) The court found that the plan, imposed as the result of a consent decree entered into with the state human relations commission, denied access to a government benefit because of race. The plan operated so that tenants of the non-preferred race in each of the five geographic districts affected might never be offered units.

Court orders have helped to foster tenant selection plans to reduce racial segregation in LRPH in both Ohio and Massachusetts. In December 1987, the court upheld a race-conscious affirmative action plan that had been adopted by the Lucas Metropolitan Housing Authority to desegregate LRPH in Toledo, Ohio. The race-conscious plan had been adopted as a result of the court decree in the case *Jaimes* v. *Toledo Metropolitan Housing Authority*, 1985, OH (758 F. 2d 1086 and C.A. 6 Ohio).[27]

Since being cited in October 1987 by the HUD Boston regional office for violating fair housing laws with its tenant placement process, the Boston Housing Authority (BHA) has been trying to develop a plan acceptable to HUD that would work toward desegregating its projects.[28] Although 52 per cent of BHA project residents are white and 42 per cent are minorities, in each BHA project, about 90 per cent of the residents are of the same race.

SHORTCOMINGS OF THE ANALYSIS

This analysis has two major shortcomings. First, the data on program participation by race are incomplete. Although HUD is updating its records on tenant characteristics, the most recent available data are based on subsets of the universe of tenants in LRPH. Once the updated data are made available on an annual basis, as mandated, describing the participation by race in the federal LRPH program will be easier than it is now.[29] Second, due to the lack of more comprehensive data, the nature of program participation for blacks is assessed using a selection of court cases. As mentioned in the discussion of these cases, the summary of selected court findings either may overstate or understate the prevalence of certain conditions.

SUMMARY

How are black Americans served by the federal LRPH program? The standard economist's tool, hedonic regression analysis, does little to help answer this question. Instead, enrollment data by race and the resolution of selected court cases are examined. Although available data on participation by race are sparse, the most recent data indicate that disproportionately large numbers of blacks – relative both to the pool of eligible black households and to the proportion of white households assisted – live in LRPH. Data on the quality and conditions of participation for black households taken from court cases may paint a biased picture, although the nature of the bias is unknown.

One thing that has made it difficult to assess how black Americans are housed in the federal LRPH program is the fact that race is not a policy variable or selection criterion for subsidized housing. The justifications for the provision of federally assisted housing are to meet the needs of households whose incomes are so low as to render their demand insufficient to procure housing that meets minimal standards of safety and adequacy and to provide equal opportunity in housing. Even given these justifications, expectations for program participation by race are unclear. For instance, would we expect equal proportions of blacks and whites among program participants, or would we expect the proportion of blacks served out of the universe of all eligible blacks to equal the proportion of whites served out of the universe of all eligible whites? Or would we expect the proportions of whites and blacks served by the LRPH program to be unequal (with blacks overserved) in order to redress past inequities in program participation?

Another question to ask is, although we find blacks disproportionately represented in LRPH, do we find them under-represented in other federally assisted housing programs? Racial differences between the pool of eligible households and the pool of participating households in the subprograms of Section 8, currently the largest federal housing assistance program although it was not established until 1974, provide an affirmative answer to this question.[30] In the early years, HUD estimates that 23 per cent of the participants in the Section 8 existing-housing and Moderate-Rehabilitation programs were black households, while 67 per cent were white households. A 1981 study by Abt Associates based on Section 8 projects in sixteen metropolitan areas found the rate of black participation in the Section 8 new construction program to be slightly less than their corresponding estimated proportion of the income-eligible population.[31] Among black elderly households, 14 per cent were eligible but only 8 per cent participated. Among black non-elderly families, although 25 per cent were eligible, 24 per cent participated. In 1989, blacks were 40 per cent and whites 57 per cent of Section 8 certificate and voucher recipients, although the shares that blacks and whites were of income-eligible renters in that year were 28 per cent and 67 per cent, respectively.[32]

The Section 8 new construction program serves white households more than blacks or Hispanics. Although 58 per cent of all income-eligible renters in the early years of this program were whites, 67 per cent of all households served by this Section 8 subprogram were white.[33] In addition, the Abt study found that 22 per cent of the Section 8 new construction projects sampled had no nonwhite tenants, while an additional 35 per cent had less than 10 per cent nonwhite tenants.[34]

This under-representation is aided and abetted by the fact that most of the privately owned but federally assisted housing (such as Section 8 new construction and substantial rehabilitation) is located outside of the central cities of metropolitan areas, the places where minorities are most likely to dominate the populations and from which minorities are able to relocate less frequently than are whites. Only 43 per cent of Section 8 new construction and substantial rehabilitation projects are located in central cities, while 65 per cent of the occupied LRPH units are found there.

Turning now to the court cases involving the LRPH program, segregation has been the basis for most of them.[35] The remedy mandated often has been some system of relocating current tenants or assigning future tenants that would work toward racial integration in the subsidized housing stock. The fact that suits continue to be filed reflects the ongoing but evolving dilemma related to black Americans as beneficiaries in the LRPH program.

CONCLUSIONS

What can we conclude from all this? Black Americans are the dominant tenants of a form of federally assisted housing that may be removed from the federal inventory by the selling of projects to their current tenants or through deterioration associated with vouchering out proposals. If this is achieved through either means, the supply of units available for income-eligible households – disproportionately blacks – in the future will be diminished.

Most of the new federal housing assistance money is provided under the Section 8 program, in many forms of which the representation of blacks is disproportionately low. Two solutions to the potential future problem are – to expand the participation of income-eligible blacks in programs other than LRPH and to increase the incomes of blacks so they no longer dominate the pools of households eligible for federal housing assistance.

Relying on programs other than LRPH could have the additional side effect of lessening the residential segregation, which seems to plague LRPH. The Section 8 programs, for example, allow households to locate in non-central city neighborhoods on scattered sites. To the extent that lower-income households are willing and able to choose units dispersed throughout metropolitan areas – rather than concentrated in central cities – segregation of lower-income households will diminish. The Gautreaux cases cited above were filed against segregation engendered by the siting of LRPH projects. The court-ordered remedy is a program using Section 8 certificates and vouchers to enable families to relocate from Chicago's South Side to its suburbs.[36]

The composition of applicant pools has been another major deterrent to eliminating segregation in many localities. In many places the applicant pool is dominated by members of minority groups, because their incomes are generally lower than the incomes of households of other racial groups and because income, unlike race, *is* a selection criterion for federal housing programs.[37] For local situations such as this, racial integration of federally assisted housing is unlikely to be achieved.

Since the lower incomes of blacks cause them to be the dominant tenants of LRPH in many localities, another way to lessen the segregation (by income) so often associated with this would be to increase the incomes of blacks. This could lessen the proportion of blacks and, thereby, increase the proportion of whites as applicants and enrollees in LRPH. Skill enhancement and job training programs to improve the incomes of black households exist, but to date have not been adequate to move enough black households out of poverty to reduce their shares of the applicant pools for, and of the program participants in, LRPH.[38] Recent modifications to the welfare program which emphasize job training could help the black LRPH residents among the 1.9 million low-income renters (or the 38 per cent of all subsidized households) who receive both housing assistance and income assistance.[39] Using housing assistance along with job training as a package for welfare recipients and other residents of LRPH could help address the problem of poverty that, along with racial discrimination in the housing markets of this nation, limits housing options for black Americans.

NOTES

1 For a discussion of hedonic regression analysis see: R. Edmonds (1984), Z. Griliches (1971), and S. Rosen (1974).

2 See details on rent calculation in the section entitled "Low-rent public housing Program."

3 For example, see Guy *et al.* (1985).

4 See R. J. Struyk and J. A. Tuccillo (1983). The other six goals are to: ensure the availability of adequate and affordable housing, especially to low-income households; increase residential construction and reduce cyclical instability in the construction industry; increase the availability of mortage credit; encourage homeownership; provide housing to persons with special needs, such as age or disability; and encourage neighborhood preservation and revitalization.

5 See C. T. Koebel (1984:1).

6 See R. Farley (1980: 20).

7 See J. M. Gries and J. Ford (1932).

8 See E. B. Lazere (1995: 4).

9 See US Department of Commerce, Bureau of the Census (1994: Table No. 706).

10 Lower-income households have incomes less than or equal to 80 per cent of the median incomes in their metropolitan areas.

11 Public housing authorities (PHAs) are a type of LHA. The generic label for local agencies that operate federal housing programs is LHA, although the PHA is the most commonly encountered such agency.

12 See US Department of Housing and Urban Development, Office of the Assistant Secretary for Fair Housing and Equal Opportunity (1995: 54).

13 This change affected the financial viability of LRPH and led to the federal government providing not only construction financing but also operating subsidies. Operating subsidies were first provided in 1961.

14 Although 30 per cent of adjusted household income is the usual tenant contribution, income-eligible tenants pay for rent the greater of: 30 per cent of adjusted family income, 10 per cent of monthly gross (unadjusted) income, or the shelter allowance from welfare assistance payments. Ten per cent of a household's unadjusted monthly income generally is the minimum payment required of all participants.

15 The limit (as a deductible from gross income) for child support or alimony payments for someone outside of the household is the lesser of (a) the legal limit, or (b) $550 for each individual for whom the payment is made.

16 Section 5(h) of the 1937 Housing Act states that a public housing authority may sell a Lower Income Housing project to its lower-income tenants on such terms and conditions as the agency may determine, without affecting the commitment of the Secretary of Housing and Urban Development to pay annual contributions for this project.

17 In order for a transfer of property ownership to take place under the HOPE program, there must be a sufficient supply of affordable rental units of the type targeted under each subprogram so that implementation of the program will not appreciably reduce the number of such rental units available to households eligible for residency in these units.

18 Over $35 million has been spent to renovate this complex, which translates into about $130,000 per unit. See R. Guskind and C.F. Steinbach (1991: 799–800).

19 Proposals to kill HUD are discussed in *Housing Affairs Letter* 95–02 (13 January 1995): 1–2. Proposals to establish block grants for housing assistance are discussed in *Housing Affairs Letter* 95–38 (22 September 1995): 1–2. Proposals for "vouchering out" the LRPH program are discussed in the following issues of *Housing Affairs Letter*: 95–14 (7 April, 1995): 1–2; 95–15 (14 April 1995): 1–2; 95–21 (26 May 1995): 2–3; and 95–27 (7 July 1995) 1–2.

20 See US Department of Housing and Urban Development, Office of the General Counsel (1985: 145–8).

21 *ibid.*, p. 80.

22 An additional 11 per cent of the households resident in LRPH were Hispanic whites. See Goering *et al.* (1994: 18).

23 US Department of Housing and Urban Development, Office of Fair Housing and Equal Opportunity (1991: 5).

24 See J. Goering *et al.* (1994: 20).

25 *ibid.*, p. 11.

26 See US Department of Housing and Urban Development, Office of the General Counsel (1985: 144).

27 See *Housing and Development Reporter* 15, No. 30 (14 December 1987): 554.

28 *Housing Affairs Letter* 88–9 (26 February 1988): 8 and *Housing Affairs Letter* 88–17 (22 April 1988): 3.

29 The 1987 Housing and Community Development Act mandates the Secretary of HUD to include in the annual report of the department characteristics of families assisted under the following programs: low-rent public housing, Section 8 rental assistance, and Section 202 (direct loans for housing for the elderly and handicapped). The characteristics to be reported include: family size, specifying the number of children; amount and sources of family income; age, race, and sex of family members; and whether the family head (or the spouse of such a person) is a member of the armed forces. (See Subtitle B, Section 166, Part 3, of Title I (Housing Assistance) of the Housing and Community Development Act of 1987.)

In addition, the 1987 Housing and Community Development Act requires both the Secretary of HUD and the Secretary of Agriculture to collect at least annually, data to enable the Congress to assess compliance with the federal fair housing laws (Title VI and Title VIII). Data are to be collected – on a building by building basis if necessary – on the racial and ethnic characteristics of persons eligible for, assisted by, or otherwise benefiting under each community development, housing assistance, and mortgage and loan insurance and guarantee program administered by the two Secretaries. (See Subtitle C, Section 562 of Title V (Community Development and Miscellaneous Programs) of the 1987 Housing and Community Development Act.)

30 In all the Section 8 subprograms – the major subprograms are new construction, substantial rehabilitation, moderate rehabilitation, existing-housing, and vouchers – HUD makes payments to cover the gap between a rent level that the agency estimates and the rental payments made by assisted tenants, who are low-income and very-low-income households. Rental assistance payments on behalf of lower-income tenants go either directly to owners of newly developed or rebuilt housing or through LHAs to owners of existing dwellings. The minimum tenant rental payment in Section 8 is 30 per cent of adjusted income, and the income adjustments are the same as in the LRPH program. The authority to fund units under the new construction and substantial rehabilitation subprograms has been repealed, however, except in conjunction with housing for the elderly and handicapped.

31 See US Department of Housing and Urban Development, Office of the General Counsel (1985: 108). See also Abt Associates Inc. (1981: S–6).

32 See C. Casey (1992: 5).

33 See US Department of Housing and Urban Development, Office of the General Counsel (1985: 144).

34 See J.O. Calmore (1986: 132).

35 The Congressional intent of federal fair housing laws – whether to merely limit segregation or whether to actively encourage integration – has been debated in numerous court cases. Although the legislation explicitly forbids market discri-

mination, it does not explicitly advocate integration. In a 1979 private market case (*Gladstone Realtors* v. *Village of Bellwood*, 99 S. Ct. 1601, 441 US 91, 60 L. Ed. 2d 66 (Illinois, 1979)), the Illinois court decided that it was the intent of federal fair housing laws to find racial steering a bar to integration and therefore antithetical to one of the goals of this legislation – integration.

36 Since its inception in 1977, Gautreaux program has helped 4,500 families or about 20,000 individuals to relocate to decent affordable housing throughout the Chicago metropolitan area. See *Housing Affairs Letter* 92–16 (17 April 1992): 1–3.

37 As of 1992, over 33 per cent of black Americans were below the poverty line. This third of the black population corresponds to 10.6 million people, out of the total of nearly 36.9 million people of all races who live in poverty. Black median household income was 58 per cent (nearly three-fifths) of white median household income in 1992. See US Department of Commerce, Bureau of the Census (1994: Table Nos. 706 and 730).

38 Programs to enhance the employability of lower-income households and that could ultimately remove them from the pool of income-eligible households for federally subsidized rental housing are operated by the Department of Labor, the Department of Health and Human Services, and the Department of Housing and Urban Development. Examples include the Job Training Partnership (JTPA) program, the Work Incentive (WIN) Program, the Community Work Experience Program (CWEP, better known as Workfare), and Project Self-Sufficiency.

39 See E. B. Lazere (1995: 19) and The Congress of the United States, Congressional Budget Office (1994: 34).

REFERENCES

Abt Associates, Inc. (1981) *Participation and Benefits in the Urban Section 8 Program: New Construction and Existing Housing*, Washington, DC: US Department of Housing and Urban Development.

Calmore, J. O. (1986) "National Housing Policies and Black America: Trends, Issues and Implications," in *The State of Black America 1986*, New York: The National Urban League.

Casey, C. (1992) *Characteristics of HUD-Assisted Renters and Their Units in 1989*, Washington, DC: US Department of Housing Urban Development.

The Congress of the United States, Congressional Budget Office, (1994) *The Challenges Facing Federal Rental Assistance Programs*, Washington, DC: Congressional Budget Office.

Edmonds, R. (1984) "A Theoretical Basis for Hedonic Regression," *AREUEA Journal* 12: 72–85.

Farley, R., (1980) "Theoretical Foundations for Government Subsidies to Low-Income People," *The Review of Black Political Economy* 11: 18–43.

Goering, J., Kamely, A., and Richardson, T. (1994) *The Location and Racial Composition of Public Housing in the United States*, Washington, DC: US Department of Housing and Urban Development.

Gries, J. M. and Ford, J. (eds 1932) *Report on the President's Conference on Home Building and Home Ownership: Negro Housing*, vol. VI, Washington, DC: National Capital Press.

Griliches, Z. (1971) "Introduction: Hedonic Price Indexes Revisited," in Z. Griliches (ed.) *Price Indexes and Quality Change: Studies in New Methods of Measurement*, Cambridge, MA: Harvard University Press.

Guskind, R. and Steinbach, C. F. (1991) "Sales Resistance," *The National Journal* 23: 798–803.

Guy, D. C., Hysom, J. L., and Ruth, S. R. (1985) "The Effect of Subsidized Housing on Values of Adjacent Housing," *AREUEA Journal* 13(4): 378–87.

Housing Affairs Letter (selected issues), Silver Spring, MD: CD Publications.

Housing and Development Reporter (selected issues), Boston, MA: Warren, Gorham & Lamont, Inc.

Koebel, C. T. (1984) "The Effects of Housing Assistance on Integration: Evidence from the Section 8 Existing Housing Program in Jefferson County, Kentucky," paper presented at the Mid-Year Meeting of the American Real Estate and Urban Economics Association, Washington, DC.

Lazere, E. B. (1995) *In Short Supply: The Growing Affordable Housing Gap*, Washington, DC: Center on Budget and Policy Priorities.

Rosen, S. (1974) "Hedonic Prices and Implicit Markets: Product Differentiation in Pure Competition," *Journal of Political Economy* 82: 34–55.

Struyk, R. J. and Tuccillo, J. A. (1983) "Defining the Federal Role in Housing: Back to Basics," *Journal of Urban Economics* 14: 206–23.

US Department of Commerce, Bureau of the Census (1994) *1994 Statistical Abstract of the United States*, Washington, DC: Government Printing Office.

US Department of Housing and Urban Development, Office of Fair Housing and Equal Opportunity (1991) *1990 Annual Report to Congress: Who Benefits? Civil Rights Data on HUD Program Applicants and Beneficiaries*, Washington, DC: US Department of Housing and Urban Development.

US Department of Housing and Urban Development, Office of Fair Housing and Equal Opportunity (1995) *1993 Consolidated Annual Report to Congress on Fair Housing Programs*, Washington, DC: US Department of Housing and Urban Development.

US Department of Housing and Urban Development, Office of the General Counsel (1985) "Subsidized Housing and Race," in US Congress, House, Committee on Banking, Finance and Urban Affairs, Subcommittee on Housing and Community Development, *Discrimination in Federally Assisted Housing Programs*, 99th Cong., 1st sess., Part I, Serial No. 99–83: 145–8.

9

THE THEORY OF RESTITUTION

The African American case

Richard America

SUMMARY AND RECOMMENDATIONS

Whenever there are chronic grievances – between nations, races, or other large social groups – a fundamental issue is invariably the sense that one party has perpetrated unremedied historic economic injustices. The Theory of Restitution is based on the intuition that it is possible:

- to reconstruct historic economic relations;.
- to specify "fair" standards – prices, wages, terms of trade, interest rates, return on investment – that were violated, usually by force;
- to audit the historic pattern of transactions between the groups, and compare the actual with the "fair" standard;
- to then estimate the deviation from "fairness;"
- to designate that result as unjust enrichment, and estimate its present value and distribution; and
- then to draw policy implications that will usually be in the form of lump sum or other redistributive income and wealth transfers, in-kind subsidies, or investments in real and human capital.

For over 370 years, income and wealth have been coercively diverted from Africans and African Americans to the benefit of Europeans and European Americans. This was primarily done through slavery and then discrimination in education, housing, and labor and capital markets.

It is possible now to reconstruct that history in some detail. And it is possible to develop theory and method to measure the magnitude of the income and wealth transfers, and to estimate their present value and distribution.

These unjust enrichments were not dissipated. They were transferred intergenerationally, and are currently enjoyed by whites in the top 30 per cent of the income and wealth distribution.

Since the processes that produced the benefits are now widely regarded as wrong, illegal and illegitimate – violating current standards of fairness – the benefits that have been produced are unjust. They should, therefore, be returned to those who were harmed or to their descendants collectively.

So there is a case for restitution. And the debt – which amounts, by some estimates, at $5 to 10 trillion – can be paid through adjustments in tax and budget policies over the next forty years. The debt should be paid primarily through investments in human capital, housing, and business formation.

THE PROBLEM

Many of the other contributions in this volume have exhaustively reviewed the economics of poverty. And they have chronicled the disparities by race in economic life. The inequalities are well known. And the basic reasons for continuing chronic economic distress, among a large minority of African Americans, have been thoroughly analyzed. But the descriptions and analyses have not produced behavior changes or innovative policies sufficient to eliminate the phenomenon of gross disparities in income and wealth by race. It is possible that the real problem is still not properly specified.

The race problem can be accurately defined this way. It is, for all practical purposes, the coerced and manipulated diversion of income and wealth from blacks to whites. That is the problem in a nutshell. Racism is a social mechanism that justifies, and helps make possible a wide range of decisions. These occur in education, housing, finance, employment and training. And they make possible and reinforce the wrongful accumulation of wealth by the beneficiaries of racism as a class. So racism, whatever else it might also be, is an instrument for creating and maintaining economic dominance and unjust economic relationships. It has persisted because, among other reasons, it is beneficial to many people.

Solving the primary American social problem – the race problem – is, therefore, a matter of making racism less attractive economically. Part of the solution is to retrieve some or all of the wrongful benefits that racism has produced for the white majority, and to intervene in markets and educational processes so they do not generate further benefits.

But the focus should be keenly on the benefit side – the benefits accruing to white Americans from continuing racial discrimination against blacks. For too long, we have focused simply on the costs of racism. And that way of looking at the problem is one reason relatively little progress has been made against intransigent, chronic economic underperformance and persistent poverty.

DISCUSSION

For generations the idea has persisted that whites owe blacks money. It has never been a mainstream idea. It has never had strong adherents in high places. It has never had strong theoretical or practical support among economists and policy analysts. Nonetheless, the idea has enough intuitive power that it never completely went away.

The idea that forty acres and a mule had somehow been promised after emancipation – rather than simply proposed – has endured. And that notion has kept alive the feeling that there really is something to the idea that even such a vast amorphous injustice as racial exclusion, exploitation and discrimination in many forms, and in many markets, can lead to a kind of debt. This obligation has also been felt but not articulated by many whites. And it seems to underlie many acts of altruism, "compassion" and charity. Some whites have gone further and said they acknowledge some kind of moral debt. But few have gone all the way to this idea: that the past produced tangible benefits to the white majority; these were accumulated, compounded and bequeathed, and today there is a measurable, unjust enrichment that should be surrendered and transferred back in some orderly, democratically agreed - upon way.

But that is the most obvious policy implication of the concept of restitution. The word used here is restitution rather than reparations. Reparations has inflammatory connotations. And it's associated commonly with the aftermath and consequence of military victory and defeat. Losers in war pay reparations, under duress. That's not what we have in mind. Instead, the concept is that justice and morality are operating broadly. And these are not compatible with holding in perpetuity benefits derived from past immoral and wrongful systemic transactions and processes. So, at the end of the twentieth century, Americans have the opportunity to look at their history collectively. They can acknowledge that much wealth has been built by methods that cannot stand scrutiny by today's standards. They may have been acceptable at the time. But moral people cannot accept the fruits of wrongful actions that were committed in their behalf – as posterity – by their collective if not direct biological ancestors.

Boris Bittker's 1972 book, *The Case for Black Reparations,* (Random House: New York) examined these questions thoroughly and successfully. He dealt with all the common objections – that raising these issues now so late in the game is ex post facto, and that we don't mete out justice that way under our system. On the contrary, he said, there is ample precedent for finding retroactive guilt, and correcting it, if practicable.

Guilt, incidentally, in the emotional sense, is not the point. That's another common objection. "Why try to play on guilt?" No. The point is that a careful examination leads to a finding of guilt. But it doesn't matter whether culprits feel emotional guilt or not. They are guilty in any event. So restitution, when all is said and done, depends on a large majority of Americans concluding that the distribution of income and wealth, by race, cannot be justified. It's based on wrongful acts. It implies an obligation to make restitution. And the key is to find ways that are politically feasible and practical in the actual circumstances.

BACKGROUND AND HISTORY

Slavery produced benefits for over 200 years. Agricultural slavery was primary. But many Americans only think of slavery in terms of agricultural commodity production. In fact, slavery generated great benefits in other ways as well. Slaves were used in manufacturing, services, and in activities that today would be called municipal or state government, running transportation, utility and emergency services. Also vitally important, slaves cleared land, and built infrstructure – roads, dams, levees, canals, railroads, and bridges.

Without this labor, it can be argued, the nation would not have expanded West as it did. Indeed, it is possible, and perhaps probable, that the United States would never have become a continental nation. It likely would not have been able to complete the Louisiana Purchase, nor gain the territories that became the Southwest and West coast states so vital to twentieth-century growth. The US could well have ended, territorially, at about the Mississippi River, and never emerged as a world power. The point is not to speculate on counterfactual history. But the crucial role of slave labor in creating the basis for expansion and total continental development is worth underlining.

Slave-produced goods and services benefitted most whites indirectly and passively. This happened through the process of human capital formation. Slaves made it possible for many whites to go into more rewarding occupations, gain increased skills, and generate greater lifetime earnings for themselves and their descendants. In these indirect and passive ways, slavery produced enormous benefits beyond those usually considered that flowed directly from production.

DISCRIMINATION

Similarly after slavery, exclusion and discrimination allowed millions of Americans and immigrants to enter occupations with greater prospects. In these ways, racism generated income and wealth that flows to present day recipients. That is an important reality. It should not be minimized.

Theodore Hershberg, at the University of Pennsylvania, has studied immigration. He found that successful, accomplished black tradespeople and skilled operators were displaced by immigrants. So it is not simply a matter of black entrance being blocked. Black earnings were established, and then forcibly discontinued by private practice, and by conscious, active, wrongful interventionist public policy.

Discrimination continued through the mid-twentieth century. And, in the past 100 years it produced far greater benefits than those piled up during the preceding 270 years because of the far greater population and size of the economy. So the most significant sources of unjust enrichments have fairly recent origins, notwithstanding the dramatic effects of compound interest on the earlier, longer stream of coercively, interracially diverted income.

PROCESSES

Exploitation, exclusion and discrimination were mechanisms that produced unjust enrichment. Exploitation is a loaded term. It carries great emotional baggage with the general public even when used in a technical sense. Here it simply refers to super benefits over and above "normal" returns on investment, or above a unit of labor's marginal productivity.

Exclusion refers to what is usually known as occupational discrimination, in which whites occupied jobs that otherwise, in a freely competitive market, would have been occupied by blacks of equal ability and training, exerting equal effort.

Discrimination refers to three other phenomena in addition to occupational discrimination.

- First, employment discrimination is commonly seen in the last hired, first fired practice. Blacks and whites of equal endowments experience different lengths of employment in similar economic cycles.
- Second, wage discrimination refers to whites and blacks, equally endowed, receiving different wages for the same occupational and skill contribution.
- Third, there are other forms of discrimination, as outlined by Lester Thurow in *Generating Inequality* (Basic Books 1975). These include capital, housing, medical/health, and other subtle twentieth-century practices.

RESULT

All these differential practices produce a diversion of benefits by race. All of them made whites better off relative to blacks, in the aggregate, than they otherwise would have been in a society, and in markets, using free and openly competitive selection processes.

The total consequence of all these direct and indirect, active and passive methods of diverting income and wealth interracially resulted in a massive unjust enrichment that can be measured, and that is enjoyed even to the present. The important objective is to refine the theory, locate and organize data, and create an econometric technique that can shed light on the processes' quantitative impact.

MEASUREMENT

There have been estimates; they have been preliminary and illustrative, not final and conclusive. In *The Wealth of Races*, (R. F. America (ed.),

Greenwood 1990), Marketti, Neal, Chachere and Udinsky, and Swinton applied contrasting methods over differing time periods. There is room for much more work of this kind. The National Association for the Advancement of Colored People, The National Urban League, the Joint Center for Political and Economic Studies and other civil rights groups should systematically engage in this task. And government organizations like the Bureau of Labor Statistics, Federal Reserve Board, Congressional Budget Office, Office of Management and Budget, General Accounting Office, House Ways and Means Committee, House and Senate Budget Committees, Joint Economic Committee should, as well.

Finally, the National Bureau of Economic Research, Brookings Institution, American Enterprise Institute, Progressive Policy Institute, Upjohn Institute, Urban Institute, Center for Budget and Policy Priorities, Economic Policy Institute, Committee on Economic Development, and other think tanks and research centers should also make it a priority to track this issue. They should produce measurements of the unjust enrichment over the entire period, 1619–1992, and they should track the annual consequences of discrimination, both costs and benefits.

Indeed, someone should create and produce an annual discrimination index. This would give readings on the economic consequences of discrimination much the same as readings on prices, corporate securities, employment, interest rates, output, and other important aggregate and sectoral activities. This quantification of harmful behavior, would help reduce it. That is, the announcement of monthly, quarterly and annual results would tend to shed light on discrimination as never before. The victims have always known, intuitively, that they've been hurt. But they've not had any idea by how much.

The beneficiaries don't seem to realize that they are beneficiaries. The information will be salutary for all concerned although it might produce grumbling among technicians who will quibble over technique and method. But that will be healthy. It will sharpen the analyses. And it will focus policy discussion on constructive alternatives.

POLICY IMPLICATIONS

That leads to the so what question? What difference will this information make? What practical value will Restitution Theory have?

Reasonable minds may differ. One school of thought says: "there is this debt, and civil rights groups and their friends should militantly demand that it be paid." How do they want it paid? Some say, lump sum cash – so much per individual. Others say, in government programs – invest in a Domestic Marshall Plan of some kind.

A second school of thought says, "demanding payment will be counterproductive." In reply, argue that the US is suffering prolonged economic stagnation for complex reasons. And one major reason is there is this historic imbalance caused by past injustices. If we look carefully, we see that economic underperformance is caused in part by the alienation of millions of people who believe they are victims of injustice, and so they withhold their best efforts in response.

The argument goes on that getting the entire country back on the healthy track requires that all lagging sectors receive overdue attention. They should be targets of investment, especially in human capital. This argument says: "demands will not work, but logic will." If there is restitution to be paid, most voters will come to accept, acknowledge, and respond if they see paying it as in their best interests collectively.

So it is fundamentally a moral issue. But it's also a practical matter. Restitution probably only stands a chance of gaining wide practical acceptance if it's presented in the context of the overall management of the economy and its long-term health. Thus, it may, in fact, gain broad support if it's understood as a matter of general social importance. Here are ways it can be paid.

AFFIRMATIVE ACTION

Restitution should be approached as a matter of broad income and wealth redistribution from Haves to Have Nots, and especially, though not only, from white Haves to black Have Nots. Affirmative action is essentially about income and wealth redistribution. But it hasn't been discussed that way. It has not been debated explicitly as a means of changing income and wealth distributions. It has been muddled. Discussion is based on the mistaken concept that restitution is intended to help "make up for past discrimination." That's the wrong formulation. And that's a major reason the concept is so confused in the public mind.

The correct rationale is, we want to correct a current not a past injustice. The current injustice is that the top 30 per cent of the income distribution, overwhelmingly white, enjoys this $5 to 10 trillion unjust enrichment at the expense of blacks. And the remedy includes affirmative action which will shift occupation, wage and employment distributions from whites in favor of blacks.

Putting it bluntly, this way will not produce an immediate, enthusiastic embrace. But it will put the matter properly on the table. Then the discussion can be rational and focused on the real problem and its solutions. No more evasion, euphemism, half truths and half measures. Affirmative action should be pursued because it is a good way to pay restitution. But it should also have a sunset. It should end in a limited time, say, two generations. That way it is recognized as not an open ended process. It will be expected to even the playing field, and then it should no longer be needed.

SET ASIDES

Business programs that provide entry to previously exclusionary markets are frequently attacked as unfair to white businesses. Those who make that argument generally, though not always, know better. They are dissembling. But the feelings among many disappointed white businesses are real and have political force. The programs should be explicitly seen and presented as paying restitution. That will produce angry reactions too, at the outset. But when passions subside, there will be a clean reason to redistribute opportunities interracially, which is what set asides should do. They, too should have a sunset provision. Two generations should be long enough to produce a large group of competitive African American businesses able to compete in most sectors at small, medium and large scale.

OTHER PREFERENCES

Other kinds of preference programs should also be clearly labeled as justified as ways to pay restitution. Housing mortgages, employment and training, scholarships, and so on all are justified as make-whole remedies. They are, or should be, intended to put African Americans, collectively, in their Rightful Place. That means they will be helped to raise their income and wealth to levels they would have achieved but for the wrongful interference of discriminatory practices that favored and benefited whites. This concept of Rightful Place should be asserted confidently, because that is essentially what is being sought. Let it be clear.

INCOME AND WEALTH REDISTRIBUTION

The quintiles now receive earned income roughly in the proportions shown in Table 9.1.

Table 9.1 Current income distribution in the US, by quintile

Quintile		*Percentage of total income received*
Top	20	44
Next	20	28
Third	20	14
Fourth	20	9
Fifth	20	5

In a fair world they would probably receive shares more or less as shown in Table 9.2.

Table 9.2 Income distribution in the US if it were more fairly shared, by quintile

Quintile		*Percentage of total income received*
Top	20	30
Next	20	25
Third	20	20
Fourth	20	15
Fifth	20	10

This would still provide ample incentives to the Haves to produce and take risks. But the effects of past injustice and gross exclusion, exploitation and domination would be greatly reduced. This kind of distribution is one objective of a program of restitution. The poor would still be poor, but the disparities would not be nearly so overwhelming, formidable and wrongful. Restitution thus helps create incentives for full participation by 20 to 40 per cent of the population now underused, under-represented, underappreciated, and who, importantly, unjustly enrich those at the top.

CONCLUSION: THE THEORY OF RESTITUTION

This entire discussion can be incorporated into a concept statement: systemic economic arrangements often are imposed by dominant social groups on less powerful ones. Invariably, these patterns of transactions produce costs for the latter and benefits for the former.

Economic injustices, sustained over time, produce cumulative benefits. These can be measured. When they are, the results can then be introduced into public policy discussion for the purpose of acknowledging the transgressions, admitting the consequences, and accepting the fact that remedies are proper, feasible and just.

So Restitution Theory offers a basis for correcting the lopsided results of distortions in markets characterized by coercion, exclusion and discrimination. And it raises the prospect that the simple fact of illuminating economic relationships this way will, in and of itself, tend to reduce the offending behavior. That is because a major reason the injustices were perpetrated in the first place, and then perpetuated, was that a veil of ignorance rested over the phenomena. Restitution Theory lifts that veil, And that in itself will make it harder in the future for economic injustices to become systemic. That is because they rely on the fact that their magnitude is not understood. Once that is discovered, in most cases, political and social forces will be mobilized to stop the practices and to retrieve the unjust enrichments that have been produced.

10

DONOR POLICIES IN AFRICA

A review of the past, a look to the future

Stephanie Y. Wilson

In the 1980s African governments, confronted with severe external shocks, significant macroeconomic imbalances, structural distortions, and rapid economic deterioration, were forced to take remedial actions. These included comprehensive structural adjustment programs that focused on macroeconomic stabilization, trade liberalization, and financial sector reforms.

Since 1980 the major emphasis of donor policy in Africa has been aimed at actively reforming economic policies throughout the region. During this period, more than $28 billion have been committed in policy-based assistance to thirty-six countries of Sub-Saharan Africa ($14 billion to thirty-five countries by the IMF, $6.8 billion by the World Bank, and at least $6 billion by other donors). Also, between 1985 and 1989, the United States Agency for International Development (USAID) funded twenty-seven separate policy reform programs in twenty-two different African countries at a total cost of $760 million. In addition, USAID used PL480 Title I and II Food for Peace Programs, and Food for Progress Programs to support policy reforms in agriculture in seven countries (Wolgin 1990).

The ostensible reason for donor insistence on extensive reform of African economic policies (structural adjustment programs) is to promote the development of African countries. The underlying assumption of the need for such donor policies has been the persistence of African economic policies and institutions that have encouraged government production over private production, import substitution over export promotion, urban development over rural development, consumption over investment, and debt over saving (Wolgin 1990). In short, it is strongly perceived that the major cause of Africa's lack of development was tied to ill-conceived country policies that thwarted any hope of long-term economic recovery, despite infusions of donor aid.

BACKGROUND

In 1949 Dean Acheson, the US secretary of state, stated that the objective of development assistance is "to show other people how to meet their own needs, not attempt to meet those needs ourselves." Somewhere between 1949 and the present, the original concept was lost. In 1963 President Kennedy's Foreign Aid Message stressed that a major aid objective should be to reduce and ultimately eliminate US assistance by enabling nations to stand on their own as rapidly as possible. Kennedy stated that "Our goal is not an arbitrary cut off date but the earliest possible 'takeoff' date – the date when their economies will have been launched with sufficient momentum to enable them to become self-supporting" (Woods 1989).

All too often, however, dependency seems to have won over development. In the 1960s, when the number of newly independent African countries increased, the desirability of assisting these countries to reach their "take off" point was clear. However, only a handful of countries that began receiving donor assistance in the 1950s and 1960s has ever graduated from dependent status.

Another trend is also apparent over this time period. Since 1950 the United States has experienced an influx of increasingly diverse "new Americans." Before the Second World War, 90 per cent of all immigrants came from Europe. The first year in which there were more immigrants from Latin America and Asia than from Western Europe was 1964. Today, about 90 per cent of all immigrants come from developing countries. If current trends continue, US citizens descended from European immigrants will be a minority by the year 2010 (Woods 1989). This concept of the "global village" has both forged a much stronger appreciation of the problems and issues of developing countries by Westerners, and created tensions within the donor communities as to the directions and extent of future development assistance. It will be interesting to see the extent to which US support of the newly independent countries (NICs) of Eastern Europe reduces the flow of resources to the southern hemisphere, a trend that does not bode well for Africa.

Some scholars have claimed that US policies toward Africa since the early 1960s have merely been the result of the idiosyncrasies of each administration. Others stated that the lack of a clear and consistent posture toward Africa originated during the Kennedy and Johnson administrations. Still others assert that donor policies were misguided in the past due to their emphasis on donor considerations rather than African development. The last two assertions will be examined below in more detail.

EARLY US POLICIES TOWARD AFRICA

Neither the Kennedy nor Johnson administrations adjusted to the rapidly changing circumstances in central and southern Africa. Instead, contrary to the Kennedy administration's early statements that it would allow the region to be free of undue outside influence – referred to as "Africa for Africans" – the administration relied largely on the Western European states to monitor and suggest policy toward the region. The Johnson administration assigned a low priority to African issues as Vietnam became the main focal point of its foreign policy.

Also, both administrations often equated the emerging nationalism of the Southern African region with Eastern European bloc influences. Consequently their policies toward the region – Mozambique and Angola in particular – failed to challenge prevailing political arrangements in a forceful manner, thus contributing to Marxist-leaning movements obtaining power during the Ford administration.

American foreign policy toward Africa could be described as having two underlying misconceptions. The first misconception was that donors understood the pace and nature of change in the region. Under this scenario, US policy makers often exaggerated the ability of donors to dictate change. The second misconception was that US policy makers understood the character of political movements in the region. These misconceptions became pronounced toward the end of the Kennedy administration (Dickson 1993).

Subsequent administrations unfortunately continued their predecessors' shortcomings. For example, in 1974 the Nixon administration was unprepared when a right wing Portuguese government collapsed and Angola and Mozambique moved aggressively toward independence. The Ford administration, which assumed office in 1974, was unable to understand the complex issues of the region, thus ignoring the possibility of a Marxist-dominated southern Africa. The Carter administration, during its tenure from 1977 to 1981, rejected economic sanctions against South Africa, thereby not lending strong support to Carter's stated anti-apartheid position. Instead Carter lent support to Britain and France, who favored diplomatic means to alter South Africa's conduct. The Reagan and Bush administrations did not feel that Sub-Saharan Africa was of strategic importance.

Scholars who agree with the above insterpretation of the evolution of US policy toward Africa argue that the need for an active and coherent donor policy toward Africa remains.

DONOR OBJECTIVES

While economic development is often stated as the primary goal of economic assistance, some scholars argue that donors in fact provide such assistance in pursuit of a wide variety of objectives. First, the donor or the recipient or both may obtain political, security, or other non-economic benefits. US assistance to Israel and Egypt serves as an example of such aid, as does French aid to francophone Africa. Second, the donor may obtain specific economic benefit through aid tying to the purchase of donor country goods and services although this may reduce the real value of such aid to the recipient, especially when higher-quality and/or lower-priced goods and services can be obtained elsewhere. In some cases superior services can be acquired more cheaply in the recipient's local or regional markets, and some authors speculate that aid tying imposes a cost of 15 to 20 per cent of the total aid provided to the recipient. Third, the recipients may perceive that they are benefiting because the volume of aid that donors are willing to extend in pursuing non-development objectives is higher than the amount they would have been willing to provide if the economic development of the recipient country and the improved allocation of resources were the donors' primary or sole objective (Krueger *et al.* 1989).

The pursuit of non-development objectives through aid can have serious negative effects on the way in which the aid is spent and the ultimate impact of the aid dispensed. Examples of donor interest superseding recipient development considerations are the Cold War aid allocations made by the United States and the trade tie interest in the French and British aid allocations to their former colonies. Likewise aid to countries with market importance to Japan's exporters was a strategic consideration for much of Japanese assistance.

Given the above donor considerations, the projects undertaken may not represent the highest development needs of the country. For example, access to imports of strategic minerals from Zaire has often been mentioned in USAID congressional testimony as one of the reasons US assistance is provided. Considerations of Zaire's lack of willingness to undertake needed economic and political reforms would otherwise have surely dictated alternative allocations (Krueger *et al.* 1989).

It is difficult to determine what the appropriate level of aid assistance would be if it were allocated solely with the objective of furthering the development of a country. It seems clear, however, that there is likely to be an offset between the level of aid given with non-developmental consideration and the effectiveness of such aid in promoting development. In fact aid based on non-developmental considerations may compromise a country's economic objectives entirely.

MORE CURRENT DONOR POLICY CONSIDERATIONS

Although the discussion of the "correct" path for African development has been ongoing since the time of Ghana's independence in 1957, the issues surrounding the debate crystallized around two documents in the early 1980s, each of which purported to identify the proper direction for Africa's development. In 1981 the World Bank issued the report, *Accelerating Development in Sub-Saharan Africa* (commonly called the Berg Report because its principal author was Elliot Berg). In 1980 the Economic Commission for Africa (ECA) and the Organization of African Unity (OAU) issued the *Lagos Plan of Action for the Development of Africa 1980–2000*. This report was commonly called the Lagos Plan of Action

(LPA), since the heads-of-state session that produced the document was held in Lagos.

There was a basic conflict between the two documents. The LPA called for the African nations to rally around a program of mutual support and development, self-reliance, and economic integration. The LPA was tied strongly to the concept of a New International Economic Order, which attempted to address the Western biases in international trading and financial practices such as the operations of multinational corporations. The dependence of the African economies on the dictates of the West were cited as the primary cause for Africa's economic situation.

The Berg Report, by contract, placed the major blame for Africa's economic deterioration on improper policies pursued by many African countries and offered prescriptions that were in many cases politically difficult for African leadership to implement. The report suggested overall policy reform in Africa and long-term program assistance versus short-term sector-specific project lending.

A comparison of the two documents was difficult given the divergence of issues covered in each and the varying levels of detail in the coverage of certain critical issues where the two reports did overlap. The major problem with the LPA document was that while it states a goal for Africa, it neither gives a listing of development priorities for the region, nor gives any plan of how to attain the stated goals. The primary theme of the LPA is one of self-reliance for Africa through the maximum use of the region's resources. Alternatively, the Berg Report stresses the need for a market-oriented approach and encourages African countries to support an outward looking or externally oriented export-led approach (Browne 1985).

The debate that stemmed from these two documents served as a catalyst for the next set of donor policies toward Africa. The next section will discuss the actual donor policies undertaken since the early to mid-1980s and will show the evolution in the thinking of the donors and the recipients about the correct path for African development given the "lessons learned." Subsequent sections will review the impact of current donor policies in Africa overall and in selected African countries. The final section will discuss proposals for the future of donor policies in Africa.

CURRENT DONOR POLICIES AND LESSONS LEARNED

The 1991 World Bank Annual Report states that the overall centerpiece of the Bank's work remains poverty reduction. The Bank suggests a two-part approach: "The first part encourages broadly based economic growth through productive use of the poor's most abundant asset – their labor. The second part requires investment in social services – especially basic education and health, family planning and nutrition – to improve living conditions and increase the capacity of the poor to respond to income earning opportunities arising from economic growth" (World Bank 1992).

The above stated policy adequately captures the current thinking on donor policy for most bilateral and multilateral institutions. The evolution of donor thinking was based largely on the Berg report, the LPA, and some lessons learned over the past decade about sustainable economic development, policy formation, and the impact of such policies on development.

Prior to 1980 the World Bank used project lending, which usually carried conditions to which the borrower had to agree. Such conditions were tied to the sector or the subsector for which the project was intended. Although some of the project loans also included policy changes, such changes were generally viewed as facilitating the success of the project undertaken.

Three important steps were involved in the 1980s Structural Adjustment Loans (SALs). The first was the use of program lending instead of project lending. Program lending is given as general support of a deficit balance of payments. Second, SALs combined program lending with policy reform conditions. Third, conditions were broadened from a sectoral or subsectoral level to the national economic level.

The SALs were developed in response to the problems associated with project lending. The first of these problems was the lengthy project cycle, which started with a project idea through an average of two years of project preparation to appraisal, negotiation of terms and conditions, implementation, and finally evaluation five years after implementation had begun.

A second problem associated with project lending was called the fungibility problem. Such a problem exists when the aid money is actually financing some other unidentified project of which the donor is unaware and which the recipient country would have undertaken anyway, even if it had not received the aid. In Sub-Saharan Africa this particular problem did not apply strongly because aid played such a large part in financing investment and imports.

A third set of problems concerned the general economic environment. Sub-Saharan Africa was finding it increasingly difficult to operate projects successfully given the poor performance of the economy overall. This is especially true with regard to the harnessing of domestic resources to complement the aid received from donors. Also, given the poor economic situation, local government counterpart funds were often not available. In addition, when economic policy is not well ordered the ability to change policies to adjust to external shocks becomes extremely difficult.

A fourth issue in project lending consisted of the inability of such loans to assist in long-term program lending, which was viewed as the approach that was necessary to persuade recipient governments to undertake often difficult economic and political reforms. Long-term program lending was likewise viewed as a necessary condition for improving the poverty impact of lending. The World Bank wanted to offer loans that were large enough to matter at the highest level in host country governments and were economy wide in scope and conditionality. Thus the SAL was initiated (Mosley 1991; *The Economist* 1991).

There remained, however, the issue of donor coordination. Prior to the onset of the SALs it had been agreed that the International Monetary Fund (IMF) would take the lead on exchange rates and restrictive trade systems, adjustments for balance of payment disequilibria, and stabilization programs. The World Bank was to take the lead on development programs including project evaluation and definition of development priorities. Financial institutions, capital markets, domestic savings, and domestic and foreign debt were overlapping responsibilities of the Fund and the Bank.

The introduction of the SALs made coordination between the two institutions more strained than usual and it was decided that the SALs would only be introduced in countries where the IMF stabilization program already existed. Soon, however, a problem arose in coordinating the Bank and Fund conditionalities, which work quite differently. The Fund's conditions are quantified and precise and are measured by macroeconomic performance indicators that are already in place. Failure to meet these conditions results in the termination of any further lending. In contrast, the Bank's conditions range from quantified to very qualitative, and compliance is not always easy to judge and is often negotiable. Therefore the Bank decided that in some cases for the most distressed countries it needed to decouple IMF and Bank lending and allow itself the flexibility to add new forms of conditions. Therefore in 1984 the Structural Adjustment Loan was replaced by the Sectoral Adjustment Loan (SECAL) as the major vehicle of adjustment lending after the Bank detected design flaws in the structure of the SALs (Mosley 1991).

The World Bank's attempt to use the SALs to influence top policy makers proved unsuccessful in several important ways. First, it was seen that one group of countries receptive to SALs was that which already had basic economic organizations conducive to growth. Second, another group of countries who found it difficult to change discontinued their use of SALs. In brief the countries least in need of the policy reform conditions accepted SALs most readily and those that needed such reform the most participated very little. The Bank's willingness to "buy" policy reform with SAL money tended to place policy reform in a context of bargaining. In this context those countries with the weakest bargaining strength were most likely to accept the conditions of the loans. Conditions for policy reform therefore tended to be disproportionately placed on countries that needed balance of payment support money. Such countries were not necessarily the countries that most needed policy reform, although in some cases, such as in Ghana, the two needs did coexist.

In addition, SALs were overambitious in the breadth and number of conditions imposed on the recipient country. The average SAL had conditions in ten of the possible nineteen policy reform areas and a particular SAL could have as many as 100 separate conditions (Mosley 1991). This large number of conditions created an administrative overload on the borrowing country, which in many cases already had a weak administrative structure, and caused confusion in the mind of the borrower about the importance of each condition. Likewise more conditions meant more monitoring tasks for the donors.

In the second half of the 1980s there were three developments in the design of structural adjustment lending. The first was the movement toward SECALs and away from SALs. The second was increased use of tranching, which allowed loans to be broken down into more achievable activities, each of which had the release of money dependent on the completion of the earlier task. The third was the front loading of conditionality, that is, the requirement that certain conditions be met prior to the release of any part of the loan (Mosley 1991).

Other innovations that occurred as a result of the lessons learned from the SAL experience included better Bank and Fund coordination. In 1989 two important documents were produced. The first was the Policy Framework Paper, which set out a joint understanding of the economic situation of the borrowing country and the policies necessary for successful stabilization and adjustment. This document allowed the Bank, the Fund, and the recipient country to all agree on the terms of the loan together, thus reducing the possibility of conflicting interpretations during the administration of the loan. The outline of a development plan was agreed to and projections about future policies were given. A second innovation was the establishment by the Fund of a Structural Adjustment Facility (SAF), which allowed the Fund to extend its medium-term lending but on a concessional basis. The Fund also created the Enhanced Structural Adjustment Facility (ESAF) for poor indebted countries pursuing stabilization policies. Agreement on a Policy Framework Paper was a prerequisite for access to this facility.

At this juncture another important question arose: Has the Bank/Fund cross-conditionality become too strong?

It was at this time that the concept of special program assistance arose. It was felt in the development community that the rigorous requirements of the conditions were better suited to middle income countries such as those in Asia where infrastructure and financial institutions already existed.

The most pervasive criticism of structural adjustment was that expenditure for health and education would contract drastically during adjustment. While more recent evidence indicates that countries are just as likely to expand the share of their budgets going to social services during adjustment as to contract such expenditures, this perception remains (Sahn 1992).

Other criticisms, which have been refuted by recent studies, were that food prices would increase rapidly and cause a food crisis for the poor and that massive de-industrialization would occur (Jaeger 1992; Stein 1992).

The donor community attempted to mitigate the overwhelming impression of the recipient countries, especially among the low-income and highly indebted countries of Sub-Saharan Africa, that enforcement of structural adjustment meant further erosion of the living condition of their populations, and little or no return for their reforms. Themes such as "adjustment with equity" and "adjustment with a human face" began to emerge. The donor community was anxious to show the results of the first phase of special program assistance (SPA) and launch a second phase.

Recommendations to improve the quality of SPA support were adopted. These included the phasing out by all SPA recipients by 1993 of their import and exchange controls and assistance in reinforcing their market-oriented reforms; elimination of the SPAs' tight administrative control over country import programs; fully untying by SPA donors of their import support programs; regular consultations with each recipient country; and, provision of specific technical assistance programs to strengthen public procurement, banking practices, customs administration, and foreign exchange operations. The key to the success of the program was that development efforts could be made more effective through "joint action."

The second phase of the special program of assistance (SPA II) began in October 1990 when eighteen donors pledged to cofinance and coordinate financing to support adjustment programs in the low-income, highly indebted countries of Sub-Saharan Africa. Other features of the program are adjustment lending, adjustment credits, access to resources from the Fund's adjustment facilities, and debt relief, including forgiveness of concessional loans and rescheduling of nonconcessional debt on softer terms. It is estimated that as much as 85 per cent of SPA assistance will be broadly untied (World Bank 1992).

The expansion and strengthening of these programs and others as well were cited as necessary to Africa's development. Long-term development strategies, it was argued, should be people-centered, human-resource centered, and meet basic needs.

The World Bank study, *Sub-Saharan Africa: From Crisis to Sustained Growth*, became a basic document for a high-level donors conference in 1991. Under the auspices of the Dutch government cochaired by Quett Masire, President of Botswana. The meeting was attended by most of the finance and planning ministers of Sub-Saharan Africa and the ministers in charge of aid to Africa from donor countries.

As a result of the conference and the linkages forged among the various donor communities and the African countries, various recent donor policies have emerged. Among them: the United Nations Development Program (UNDP) has made funding available to support national country efforts to carry out long-term perspective country studies; a three-year training and research program is being prepared at two national institutions, one in Benin and one in Senegal; two management teams of experts are being set up, one in Abidjan and one in Harare. The donors are also facilitating closer regional integration, one of the expressed wishes of the Lagos Plan of Action. The Bank is working with the Economic Community of West African States on a study of trade, is working closely with the Southern African Development Coordination Conference (SADCC), and is also providing technical assistance to the Conference. Recognizing the need to build up African institutional capacity the Bank, along with UNDP and the African Development Bank, established the African Capacity Building Initiative (ACBI) in 1991. The ACBI provides grants to strengthen public policy and develop management programs. Fellowships are available to local scholars, and local consulting firms and professional associations are receiving support to facilitate ties with the private sector (World Bank 1992).

The strengthening of local capacity will allow African nations to rely more on one another and less on outside technical assistance from the West. In recent years such assistance has been the subject of increasing criticism due to its lack of identifiable transfers of technology to local countries and counterparts (Berg 1993).

During the 1980s the Agency for International Development (A.I.D.) actively pursued its own Africa program strategy. While the overall goals of A.I.D.'s donor strategy were consistent with and supportive of the Bank's, A.I.D.'s institutional characteristics make its assistance distinctly different. First, A.I.D. has a comparative advantage over the Bank: its numerous resident overseas missions allow it to work more collaboratively with local governments. Second, unlike other bilateral donors, A.I.D. has considerable economic expertise and can provide substantive advice on the reform process. Also, unlike the Bank and the Fund, A.I.D.'s programs are limited to sectoral reform, and A.I.D. seldom engages in broad-based macroeconomic adjustment activities. The hallmark of A.I.D. policy reforms, according to one of the agency's leading economists, is the way they integrate resources – dollars, food assistance, local currencies, studies, training, and technical assistance – to help African governments implement reform programs they have already decided to undertake. The World Bank programs may be seen as "horizontal cuts across the broader parts of the economy, while A.I.D.'s more modest efforts are frequently vertical cuts going deeper into one specific sector" (Wolgin 1990).

About 85 per cent of A.I.D.'s reform programs have been in four categories: agricultural market liberalization, fertilizer market liberalization, trade and industrial policy, and social service restructuring. A.I.D.-supported adjustment programs in Africa have been a very successful part of the A.I.D. portfolio. It is believed that between two-thirds and three-quarters of these programs are clear successes. The programs have been credited with reducing waste through privatization efforts and technology improvement and allowing access to foreign exchange to many poor countries in Africa. Together with the World Bank and other donors, A.I.D. is embarking on a major effort to upgrade the economic management and analytic skills of both the public and private sectors through the African Capacity Building Initiative.

A.I.D. has had its share of problems, however, many of which have come under scrutiny in the past several years. As A.I.D. has become far more complex over the years the demands of Congress on country missions have imposed more of a focus on Washington politics and less on country needs. Also, the increasing administrative burden imposed by Congress requires more attention within A.I.D. on complying with new objectives and regulations. In addition, the absence of a clear political constituency for long-term foreign assistance has left A.I.D. vulnerable to numerous US policy shifts. While detractors can point to a number of failures, A.I.D.'s record of performance of adjustment support programs in Africa has been "better than we hoped when we started out, particularly given the nature of the problem" (Wolgin 1990).

IMPACTS OF CURRENT DONOR POLICIES ON AFRICA

Overall, studies of the impact of earlier structural adjustment programs (SALs) show that the implementation of structural adjustment programs was almost always favorable to export growth and to the external account. The influence of structural adjustment programs on aggregate investment is almost everywhere negative, and their influence on national income and on financial flows from overseas is on balance neutral. SALs were shown overall not to be as helpful to the economic performance of countries as the Bank had hoped (Mosley 1991).

During the first phase of SPA (1988–90), however, donors were able to demonstrate that a recipient country's domestic policy reform coupled with adequate financial assistance from bilateral donors and international agencies substantially improved economic performance. The donors pointed to three indicators of success. The first is growth in the Gross Domestic Product (GDP) of 4 per cent on average during the past three years, up from 1 per cent in 1980 to 1984, and almost double the growth rate in non-SPA African countries. The second is that countries that received SPAs experienced growth in export volumes at a pace 50 per cent above GDP growth. And third, SPA countries showed growth in the volume of investment at a pace three to four times faster than GDP. This strong economic performance contrasts sharply with that of African countries outside of the SPA (World Bank 1992).

An assessment of the overall economic impact of development assistance should be at both the microeconomic and macroeconomic levels. At the microeconomic level the contribution of aid can be assessed by examining the rate of return of individual activities. There have been a number of studies that use this approach, especially at the project level. For the most part, with the exception of several "white elephant" stories that have plagued development circles, these evaluations have shown that average rates of return on multilateral assistance projects have been rather high (Krueger *et al.* 1989). Past empirical analyses show that projects financed by the International Bank for Reconstruction and Development (IBRD) from 1960 to 1980 yielded a simple average rate of return of 17 per cent. Other multilateral agencies have had similar experiences with their projects (Krueger *et al.* 1989).

Less is known about projects financed by bilateral donors. About 30 per cent of such assistance consisted of non-project aid, and there have been fewer evaluations of rates of return by these donors. There are clear shortcomings in using the rate of return on a project as an indicator of a project's link to economic development. For example, the rate usually does not take into account externalities, which may have important effects on overall development, and most projects do not substantially affect behavior in the rest of the economy (Krueger *et al.* 1989).

Aid can affect macroeconomic growth in several ways. If aid allows countries to save and in turn such savings are channeled to domestic investment they have the potential to stimulate growth. Second, foreign aid provides access to import of goods and services. Often, however, the link of aid to economic growth in the recipient country is inconclusive, and depends on the proportion of aid relative to other macroeconomic aggregates (Krueger *et al.* 1989). One study showed, in a cross country specification, that no significant statistical relationship existed between GNP growth and aid as a percentage of GNP. There was little improvement in the results when various subgroups of developing countries or various subperiods were used (Mosley 1991). At best, the impact of aid on macroeconomic growth is argued by most to be positive, but modest. In general whether a country takes advantage of the potential that aid offers is a function of a country's own economic policies and is best examined in a single country context. Below, cases studies of four African countries – Mauritius, Ghana, Nigeria, and Malawi – are offered as examples of the impact of aid on the economic well-being of a country (Wilson 1990; Wolgin 1990).

Mauritius

The economic problems of Mauritius in the 1960s resemble those that face many African countries today. Mauritius' prospects were bleak: the population was growing at about 2.5 per cent per year, while per capita income was barely rising, rates of saving and investment were low, and exports were based exclusively on sugar. However, Mauritius has transformed its economic outlook by the sustained pursuit of sound macroeconomic and population policies. Incentives were provided to overseas manufacturing firms to locate their labor-intensive activities in the country and to convert imported raw materials into finished goods for export. Exports now comprise 63 per cent of GDP, and the economy has diminished its reliance on sugar. Investment and saving represent 20 per cent of GDP. Urban population growth has declined through favorable agricultural pricing policy. Emphasis on human resource development, including a successful population control program, has reduced the population growth rate to 1 per cent per year and extended average life expectancy to 68 years. Enrollment rates are almost 100 per cent for primary school and 50 per cent for secondary. These results hold promise for the rest of Africa.

Ghana

At independence, Ghana was the leading gold producer in West Africa, with an output of 1 billion ounces per year. Production dropped steadily for two decades, reaching a low of 277,000 ounces in 1983 as a result of currency overvaluation, numerous barriers to private investment, and insufficient funds for public investment in the gold mining sector. Realizing that the country has the potential to exceed its past production peak, the government has made the expansion of gold production a key objective of its economic recovery program.

The strategy has been to encourage investment in the mining sector by reforming the policy environment. In 1986, the government introduced a new coherent mining code, taxation rules, and a regulatory framework to attract private investors. A minerals commission now negotiates leases and exploration permits according to well-defined procedures.

These measures are supported by macroeconomic reforms that include a significant exchange rate adjustment. Foreign capital and technical expertise have been attracted. The approach is paying off, 1989 production figures showed a 50 per cent increase over the 1983 low point. The government also has forged strong partnerships with several private sector mining firms. In the mid-1980s the country opened its first new gold mine in forty years. This sector-specific approach appears promising. Ghanaians realize, however, that their country still has many problems to resolve (Wilson 1990).

In Ghana, the 6 per cent per year growth of recent years slowed to about 4 per cent, partly reflecting stagnant agricultural output caused by bad weather and the adverse effect of higher oil prices. The commitment of the government and the donor community to the country's structural adjustment program, however, remains strong. Increased financing from concessional sources helped to reduce Ghana's debt-service ratio from 60 per cent in 1989 to 36 per cent in 1990. The foreign exchange markets were unified in April 1990; twenty-three state enterprises were either divested or liquidated; the banking system was restructured; and the government took steps to improve the business environment by reducing taxes on corporate income, capital gains, and dividends (World Bank 1992).

Nigeria

The Government of Nigeria has turned its adjustment program into a national campaign with a billboard that proclaims, "National Self-Reliance or Foreign Economic Slavery? The Choice is Ours." The purpose of Nigeria's three-year-old austerity program from 1986 to 1989 was to curtail what is widely perceived as excessive government spending. It was also aimed at decentralizing the economy, reducing dependence on oil, and allowing free market forces to dictate economic operations. These reforms resulted in an 80 per cent devaluation of the currency, as well as greater incentives and higher prices for farmers. Food production grew modestly, an important indicator considering that the country was a net importer of food during the oil boom.

However, the results of Nigeria's effort remain mixed. Unemployment is being fueled by industry and civil service layoffs and a steadily growing population. Real per capita annual income fell by 20 per cent to less than US$300 in 1988 and 1989. Moreover, the World Health Organization reported in 1989 that malnutrition was growing at an alarming rate in Nigeria.

The overall GDP growth rate increased from 4.9 per cent in 1989 to 5.0 per cent, led by an expansion of oil production during the Gulf crisis. Non-oil GDP rose by 4.5 per cent, resulting largely from growth in agriculture of around 4 per cent and an increase in services. Manufacturing is estimated to have recovered somewhat from stagnation in 1989 and is growing at around 2 per cent. The overall commitment of the current government to reforms remains strong, but weak implementation capacity and pressures from interest groups have caused occasional lapses. For the next few years, the challenge facing Nigeria's government is to sustain the reform process while adhering to sound fiscal and monetary policies during the period of transition to civilian rule (World Bank 1992).

Several lessons emerge from Nigeria's experience. Most important is the need for prudence in spending the proceeds from a boom, for governments have great trouble curtailing public spending when the prosperity ends. Adjusting the structure of an economy to reduce spending levels is also troublesome. These difficulties delayed Nigeria's response to the collapse of oil reserves and led to a buildup of foreign debt that the country could not service.

A second lesson is that devaluation can promote agricultural production. A third is that considerable time is needed for any economic adjustment to take effect. Finally, adjustment must be viewed as an ongoing process;

unless fiscal discipline is maintained, inflation can easily undermine the reforms, causing social unrest.

As a Nigerian economist stated in 1990, structural adjustment programs (SAPs) are viewed as either a sure prescription for economic health or a mocking acronym for the nation's long-suffering population. Nigeria's poor are experiencing "austerity fatigue" and many resent the tendency of donors to focus exclusively on the crisis of the moment, known in development circles as "reform myopia."

> Donor policies in the 1970s did, in fact, overemphasize sector investment, launching huge projects that proved to be unsustainable. Little attention was paid to the macroeconomic environment in which these ambitious projects would have to survive. Ironically, when the reality of the severe macroeconomic crisis became apparent in the 1980s, too much emphasis was placed on macroeconomic policy and too little on old and new investments, especially in infrastructure and human capital.
>
> How much to spend on social services at a time of soaring national debts and limited resources is a volatile question that divides economists and policymakers across Africa. Defenders of SAPs argue that reforms are needed to revitalize Africa's economies and make them more self-reliant. Detractors charge that the poor are bearing far too much of the burden of the austerity measures.
>
> (Paarlberg 1989)

The idea of structural adjustment, of course, is to liberate markets so that market-determined prices reflect opportunity costs and result in a pattern of resource allocation that promotes maximum output and an optimal rate of growth. While this simplistic analysis may seem straightforward, it is the subject of continuous controversy.

In his earlier writings, Nobel Laureate W. Arthur Lewis, like most development economists in the 1950s and 1960s, was sympathetic to inflationary finance as a means to mobilize resources and accelerate growth. However, by 1988 Lewis was articulating the new consensus that had emerged on the adverse effects of inflation:

> The principal lesson we have all learned, LDC (less developed countries) and MDC (more developed countries) alike, is that inflation is a terrible scourge. But how to avoid it in face of all the pressures is yet to be seen
>
> (Lewis 1988)

That is, inflation is not only the outcome of ill-informed policies, it is also the consequence of very real social pressures.

Maintaining a balance between government responsibilities and resources clearly requires a workable consensus on development priorities. However, developing countries face innate difficulties in making the necessary resource allocation decisions. The recognition that development needs to be viewed as a generalized process of capital accumulation, not only physical capital but also human and social capital, represents an important advance in our understanding of the development process.

Our ability to help build an "enabling environment" to sustain previously introduced reforms, encourage the proposal and adoption of additional reforms, and enhance human capital is the challenge of the 1990s that economists must address if Africa is to develop (Wilson 1990).

Malawi

In 1985, A.I.D. and the Government of Malawi agreed on a three-year, $15-million program to reduce fertilizer subsidies from 27 per cent to 12 per cent. This was not an easy decision for the government to make and implement. The most important economic and political issue in Malawi is food security, and the government was wary of any policy change that might threaten overall production of maize and force Malawi to become an importer of maize. The government was also concerned about the squeeze that an increase in fertilizer prices would put on agricultural incomes. In addition to reducing fertilizer subsidies, the program called for the gradual shift from low-analysis to high-analysis fertilizers (HAF), that is, fertilizers with more nutrients per kilogram.

The first two tranche releases went smoothly, with the subsidy reduced to 17 per cent and the shift to HAF effectively implemented. Indeed, 1986 was a year of bumper harvests. However, in 1987, a number of factors indicated to the government that the goal of food security might be threatened. First, the price of fertilizer increased due to higher purchase costs and to a substantial devaluation of the kwacha. Second, Mozambican refugees poured across the border into Malawi (as many as 30,000 per month) seeking safety from the fighting in Mozambique. These refugees were expected to increase the demand for food. Third, the quantity of maize marketed by smallholders through official channels fell markedly.

The government felt that it could not pass on to farmers the full increase in fertilizer costs under these circumstances, and the fertilizer subsidy rose to its original level of around 27 per cent. After long discussions between A.I.D. and the government, in which A.I.D. pointed out that the shortfall in maize marketing was more likely to be due to the decline in the price of maize relative to that of groundnuts and other crops than to any increase in fertilizer price, A.I.D. and the Government of Malawi agreed that the conditions for the release of the third tranche of $5,000,000 had not been met, and those monies were de-obligated.

The subsidy reduction objectives of the Fertilizer Subsidy Removal Program were not met. However, the shift to HAF exceeded expectations.

In 1985, about 50 per cent of the fertilizer nutrients were imported as HAF; by 1988, the amount increased to 72 per cent. This shift saved the economy about $5,000,000 in 1987–8, and more in each subsequent year. So even if the subsidy removal program has stalled, the shift to HAF has had benefits well in excess of the $10,000,000 cost of the program (Wolgin 1990).

PROPOSALS FOR FUTURE DONOR POLICIES

As the world enters the twenty-first century, the traditional donor reliance on project-oriented programs that are subject to the fluctuating agendas of the Western countries will become irrelevant. To be effective in the 1990s and beyond, development policy must increasingly be: catalytic, leveraging funds and resources from the private sector and international financial institutions as well as from traditional donors; aimed at country-specific targets of opportunity where returns are likely to be high and not impose grand themes across all developing countries, which vary considerably from one another; and better coordinated across donors and allow greater collaboration with recipient countries. It has been noted that countries that have allowed their populations wider economic, political, and social choices have performed better and have tended to be growth oriented. Long-term evaluations should not only use indicators such as GDP and per capita income but also include quality of life measures such as infant mortality and educational achievement (Woods 1989). Development policies in the future must include improvements in multilateral donor and bilateral donor policies, and strong participation by the donor community in supporting policy implementation. The donor community consists of non-governmental organizations (NGOs), private volunteer organizations (PVOs), multilaterals, bilaterals, community organizations, universities, contractors, individuals, and scholars interested in promoting the development process.

MULTILATERAL DONORS

Policy-based lending has been described as a weapon designed by the World Bank to "kill two birds with one stone." The first goal is the provision of quick disbursing finances to deal with crises, and the second is the demolition of the policies that it blames both for increasing the incidence of project and program failure and for the poor economic performance in Africa. One instrument with two widely divergent policy objectives is problematic. A trade-off inevitably arises and the Bank at best finds itself in tense negotiations with the country involved.

In the future, particularly in the poor countries, structural adjustment policies on which program lending is based should embrace areas where it is appropriate to expand the role of the state (e.g., expansion of infrastructure) as well as define measures to remove harmful state interventions. Also, an attempt should be made to phase in interventions on an experimental basis, for example, privatization of food crop marketing could initially begin in only one province, thus allowing other provinces to see the benefits of such policy reform. In addition, models designed by the Bank to stimulate scenarios of changes in policies should be given to scholars and policy makers in developing countries to allow them to view for themselves the results of their preferred policies. The Bank might also make better use of local data and tap more efficiently into bilateral donor information and local expertise.

Another suggestion is to extend the use of Policy Framework Papers for middle income countries that do not use SAF or ESAF funds to enhance coordination between the Fund and the Bank.

In general, the Bank needs to aggressively strike an appropriate balance between growth and equity objectives and between regional and national objectives; between short-term macropolicy adjustments and long-term capacity building; and between physical and human capital development. Such a balance can only be achieved through the provision of multifaceted and sustained external assistance and in the context of a genuine policy dialogue. Such efforts on the Bank's part are more likely to lead to consistent and sustained domestic support (Lele 1989; Helleiner 1992).

Issues that will need to be addressed in the future are: land reform, so that land is distributed equitably and the security of tenure is clarified through legislation, thus helping to promote sustainable production patterns; institution building to increase the likelihood of implementation of needed reforms; access to infrastructure and services in support of rural reforms; support of local nongovernmental organizations to assist in stimulating the process of change; and assistance in easing the debt burden including consideration of the UN Secretary General's recommendation to cancel all official bilateral debt and other semiofficial debt such as export credits (World Bank 1992).

Finally, since the IMF no longer acts as a supplier of conventional liquidity to low-income countries – rather it collaborates with the World Bank in the development of short- to medium-term (three-year) overall economic policy frameworks and supplies modest amounts of supportive highly concessional medium-term financing – it may be appropriate to reconsider the role of the Fund in providing financing to low-income countries.

One recommendation is to build a new contingency finance arrangement into longer-term financing programs for low-income countries created by the World Bank and other aid donors also allow the IMF to focus on a relatively smaller role as a source of technical assistance on monetary issues (Helleiner 1992).

BILATERAL DONORS

A.I.D. has been mandated under the Development Fund for Africa to seek out new ways to improve the coherence and effectiveness of US assistance to the region in renewing economic growth that is broad based, market oriented, and sustainable. To this extent the donor community should support A.I.D.'s efforts to concentrate resources in programs that are doing well and put A.I.D.'s resources to work in collaboration with those of other donors, both US and African, public and private, in order to expand their impact.

Given its unique capacity to serve countries through its local missions, A.I.D. should focus its attention on the needs of host countries and assist in the coordination of host country counterparts and other donors.

A.I.D. first of all needs to define its development priorities. A.I.D. cannot continue to have its funding jeopardized by not following the latest whims of Congress even when A.I.D.'s programs address a country's need. A.I.D. also cannot be "all things to all people," the agency needs to assess its comparative advantages and concentrate its efforts in those areas (Berg 1993). The following are areas that draw on A.I.D.'s unique capabilities and access to the field. The first is participation in the reform process through pushing for broader dialogue among all groups participating in the reforms. The second consists of building the competence of the technical base to increase a country's capacity to analyze and implement policy reforms; the third involves promotion of private sector participation in solving a country's problems; and the fourth consists of strengthening the capacity of non-governmental institutions to both analyze problems and assist in policy discussions (Lele 1989; Berg 1993). A.I.D. should also continue to explore health financing in developing countries, where it is the leader in the field, and to support implementation of reforms, especially in the agricultural sector, for which it has been recognized as successful.

Finally, A.I.D. should assist in the development of local databases that can be easily accessed to facilitate the participation of Africans in their own development. In this regard it is recommended that A.I.D. strengthen its collaboration with institutions such as the African Development Bank, which stated as its 1992 goal "improving the human resource capacity by providing fellowship support; strengthening selected institutions responsible for training personnel and conducting research and evaluation; and by supporting other training efforts" (African Development Bank 1992).

THE DONOR COMMUNITY

Among Africans, African Americans living in the United States enjoy the highest standard of living in the world and therefore share a responsibility with the donor community to promote African development. Unfortunately, the African American community has displayed negligible interest in international affairs. In 1976, for example, Robert S. Browne, founder of the Black Economic Research Center, in an attempt to cite examples of African American involvement in international affairs, had to refer all the way back to the involvement of W. E. B. Du Bois in African issues during the 1940s and 1950s, to Paul Robeson's efforts in the 1950s to prevent African Americans from participating in any conflict with Russia and its allies during the Korean War, and to opposition to US involvement in the Vietnam War by a few African American congressmen in the 1960s (Browne 1976).

Since that time more African Americans have become involved, and have assisted in shaping US donor policy in Africa. For example, Randell Robinson directs TransAfrica's efforts to establish equality for Blacks in South Africa, Andrew Young and Donald McHenry have served as US ambassador to the United Nations, the late congressman Mickey Leland promoted assistance to the poor of Somalia, and Clifton Wharton has been appointed one of President Clinton's representatives to the State Department.

Thus, African American involvement in international affairs has increased, and one would believe that the stage has been set for African American involvement in crafting donor policies for Africa. Unfortunately, however, there is not a consensus, even at the highest levels of the African American community, that participation in African affairs is necessary. As recently as April 1991, Benjamin Hooks, executive director of the NAACP, stated, "There is little black Americans could or should do directly to help foster or affect political change in Sub-Saharan Africa. I don't think it is our business to meddle in their affairs" (Ayittey 1992).

African Americans enjoy the highest standard of living of Africans in the world. And many Africans would say to African Americans "if you are not part of the solution then you are indeed part of the problem" (Browne 1976). African Americans have a responsibility to assist the US government in accepting changes in global relationships and to ensure that the United States not only articulates a correct policy but that it also implements it. It is important that the goals of equitable and sustainable development be pursued in Africa. In the face of the enormity and complexity of the issues confronting Africa the task may seem overwhelming. If African Americans are coming of age, it is imperative that they rise to the sober responsibility which that new status entails and actively join the donor community in promoting African development interests.

In conclusion, donor policies have greatly improved over the past several decades in response to the needs of African countries. An international consensus has emerged that is inclusive of Africans, local leaders, and all country donors. A joint action plan is needed to promote the economic development of Africa, and such a plan should include features that contribute to the long-term sustainability of economic reform. Among the indicators of program success must be measures of the quality of life and improvement in institutional capacity. There is a need for continuing research on the impacts of adjustment programs and a need for assistance in assessing cross country and inter-regional comparisons of lessons learned as the adjustment process continues.

Donor aid has evolved over the years from one in which the United States depended on guidance from Western Europe to establish its policies; to one where donor policy was project specific with numerous non-development considerations; to one that focused on program assistance with numerous and harsh conditions; and finally to one that views adjustment with equity as its main policy focus.

It is important that donor policy be both consistent and inclusive. Consistency is needed to ensure continuous support of the economic reforms that are initiated – reform is a long-term process. Inclusiveness is needed to ensure that such reforms are owned by Africans and sustained by Africans. Inclusiveness is also needed to allow the shifting demographic profile of the United States to play a part in drafting policy from a more connected point of view. That is the influence of persons from the developing countries in the development of donor policy will allow a more closely linked dialogue to occur. This inclusion should extend to the private sector, to local NGOs, and to the African American community, among others. With such sustained effort it is hoped that these countries will "take off" as Kennedy stated in 1963 and be launched with sufficient momentum to enable them to be self supporting. The challenge remains. We need to respond.

REFERENCES

African Development Bank, *African Development Report*, 1992.

Agency for International Development, *Development Assistance for Africa: The Development Fund for Africa (DFA) Action Plan*, Washington, DC, May 1989.

Agricultural Marketing Improvement Strategies Project (AMIS) of USAID, (Abt Associates Inc.: Washington, DC), 1992.

Ayittey, George B. N., *Africa Betrayed* (St. Martin's Press: New York), 1992.

Berg, Elliot J., *Rethinking Technical Cooperation: Reforms for Capacity Building in Africa* (United Nations Development Program: New York), 1993.

Browne, Robert S., *The Black Stake in Global Interdependence*, "The Review of Black Political Economy," Winter 1993 vol. 21, no. 3, pp. 121–34 (first appeared RBPE, vol. 5, no. 4, Summer 1976, pp. 408–19).

Browne, Robert S. and Robert J. Cummings, *The Lagos Plan of Action vs. The Berg Report* (Howard University: Washington, DC), 1985.

Center for Research on Economic Development, University of Michigan, *Economic Reform in Africa: Lessons from Current Experience*, Conference 7–9 September 1988, Nairobi, Kenya, December 1988.

Cheru, Fantu, "Structural Adjustment, Primary Resource Trade and Sustainable Development in Sub-Saharan Africa," *World Development*, vol. 20, no. 4, April 1992, pp. 497–512.

Dickson, David A., "US Foreign Policy Toward Southern and Central Africa: The Kennedy and Johnson Years," *Presidential Studies Quarterly*, vol. 23, no. 2, Spring 1993.

Harrigan, Jane, *Malawi*, in Paul Mosley, Jane Harrigan, and John Toye (eds), *AID and Power: The World Bank and Policy-based Lending, Volume 2 Case Studies*, pp. 201–69.

Helleiner, G. K., "The IMF, The World Bank and Africa's Adjustment and External Debt Problems: An Unofficial View," *World Development*, vol. 20, no. 6, June 1992, pp. 779–92.

Heller, Peter S., *et al.*, *Implications of Fund-Supported Adjustment Programs for Poverty: Experiences in Selected Countries* (IMF: Washington, DC), 1988.

Jaeger, William K., "The Causes of Africa's Food Crisis," *World Development*, vol. 20, no. 11, November 1992, pp. 1631–45.

Kirschten, Dick, "Rethinking Foreign Aid," *National Journal*, 27 February 1993, p. 541.

Krueger, Anne O., Constantine Michalopoulos, and Vernon W. Ruttan, *Aid and Development* (Johns Hopkins University Press: Baltimore, MD), 1989.

Kristjanson, *et al.*, *Export Crop Competitiveness: Strategies for Sub-Saharan Africa*, APAP Technical Report No. 109, Agency for International Development, July 1990.

Lele, Uma, *Agricultural Growth, Domestic Policies, the External Environment, and Assistance to Africa: Lessons of A Quarter Century*, MADIA Discussion Paper 1 (The World Bank: Washington, DC), 1989.

Lele, Uma, Robert E. Christiansen, and Kundhavi Kadiresan, *Fertilizer Policy in Africa: Lessons from Development Programs and Adjustment Lending, 1970–87*, MADIA Discussion Paper 5 (Washington, DC: The World Bank), 1989.

Lele, Uma, Nicolas Van de Walle, and Gbetibouo Mathurin, *Cotton in Africa: An Analysis of Differences in Performance*, MADIA Discussion Paper 7 (World Bank: Washington, DC), 1989.

Lele, Uma, *et al.*, *Aid to African Agriculture: Lessons from Two Decades of Donor Experience*, MADIA Symposium discussion draft (World Bank: Washington, DC), 1989.

Lewis, W. Arthur, *Reflections on Development*, The State Department Economics, Gustav Ranis and T. Paul Schultz, eds (Basil Blackwell: New York), pp. 13–23, 1988.

Mosley, Paul, *Kenya*, in Paul Mosley, Jane Harrigan, and John Toye (eds), *AID and Power: The World Bank and Policy-based Lending, Volume 2 Case Studies*, pp. 270–310, 1991.

Mosley, Paul, Jane Harrigan, and John Toye, *AID and Power: The World Bank and Policy-based Lending*, vol. 1 (Routledge: New York), 1991.

Paarlberg, Robert L., and Merilee S. Grindle, *The Changing Political Economy of Agricultural Policy Reform: Implications for Donors*, paper prepared for Agricultural Policy Analysis Project, A.I.D., October, 1989.

Sahn, David E., "Public Expenditures in Sub-Saharan Africa During a Period of Economic Reforms," *World Development*, vol. 20, no. 5, May 1992, pp. 673–93.

Serafini, Phil and Boubacar Sada Sy, *Agribusiness and Public Sector Collaboration in Agricultural Technology Development and Use in Mali; A Study of the Mechanization of Cotton Production*, for the Agricultural Marketing Improvement Strategy (AMIS) Project, USAID, Washington, DC, 1992.

Stein, Howard, "Deindustrialization, Adjustment, the World Bank and the IMF in Africa," *World Development*, vol. 20, no. 1, January 1992, pp. 83–96.

The Economist, "Sisters in the Wood: A Survey of the IMF and the World Bank," 12 October 1991.

The World Bank, *Annual Report 1991*, Washington, DC, 1992.

Wilson, Stephanie Y., *Africa the Development Challenge of the 1990s*, The Review of Black Political Economy, vol. 19, no. 2, Fall 1990.

Wolgin, Jerome M., *Fresh Start in Africa: A.I.D. and Structural Adjustment in Africa*, Agency for International Development, August 1990.

Woods, Alan, *Development and the National Interest: US Economic Assistance into the 21st Century* (US Agency for International Development: Washington, DC), 1989.

Woodward, David, *Factors Influencing the Success of Agricultural Parastatal Divestiture in Sub-Saharan Africa*, USAID AMIS Project (Deloitte & Touche: Washington, DC) January 1992.

Part II

HISTORICAL PERSPECTIVES ON RACE, ECONOMICS, AND SOCIAL TRANSFERMATION

11

THE EAST AFRICAN COAST DURING THE AGE OF EXPLORATION

Thomas D. Boston

In his monumental *History of Economic Analysis*, Joseph Schumpeter makes the observation that mercantilism was the age of "buccaneering imperialism" where trade was associated with the uninhibited exploitation of colonies, and with conditions permanently verging on war (1954: 339). During this era, economic warfare, Schumpeter adds, was part and parcel of the policy of international economic relations. The mercantilist system extended from about 1500 to 1800 and its origins are commonly associated with the "Age of Discovery". Several characteristics seem to be common to the era. These include the fact that: 1 power was vital for the acquisition of wealth; 2 wealth was associated with the accumulation of gold and silver; 3 a balance of trade surplus was thought to be crucial to national prosperity; 4 the trade surplus was pursued by promoting exports while limiting imports and by "selling dear and buying cheap"; and 5 mercantilism was viewed as a means of achieving national autarky and the expansion of state power.

Williams (1944) and Inikori (1992) view this era as giving rise to the trans-Atlantic slave trade, many of the financial institutions of capitalism, and indeed the industrial revolution itself. Without question, Spain and Portugal initiated the era of mercantilism. Because Spain expanded into the New World, we are generally more familiar with the impact of its activities. Yet by the time Columbus landed in the Americas, Portugal had already spent three quarters of a century making a slow and methodical circumnavigation of Africa. Still today, we know very little about the outcome of this development.

Portugal's most important objectives in circumnavigating Africa were to: 1 find a Muslim-free route to the wealthy states of the East; 2 monopolize the trade in gold that was produced in regions of Zimbabwe and exported at coastal towns of present day Mozambique; 3 combine this gold monopoly with seaborne supremacy so as to control all trade in the Indian Ocean; 4 establish an alliance with the Christian Kingdom of Ethiopia; and 5 spread the influence of Christianity throughout the region.

This analysis focuses on Portugal's activities on the East African coast and in the Indian Ocean at the turn of sixteenth century. During this period, Portugal was at the forefront of European mercantilism. While both Portugal and Spain sought hegemony over the Indian Ocean trade, a major area of world commerce, Portugal's military superiority forced Spain to sail west to get to India instead of allowing it to circle the Horn of Africa. The impact of Portugal's activities on economies bordering the East African coast and Indian Ocean is just beginning to receive the level of attention that mercantile activities in the Atlantic have always received in the past (Salim 1992; UNESCO Courier 1989; Pearson 1976; and Axelson 1973).

One of the most fascinating documants this author has ever read is the manuscript of an anonymous historian who lived on the East African coast, in the region now known as Tanzania, during the time of Da Gama's visit in 1498. The manuscript was written about 1520 and reads in part:

> During the reign of al-Fudail there came news from the land of Musambih [Mozambique] that men had come from the land of the Franks. They had three ships, and the name of their Captain was al-Mirati (Dom Vasco da Gama). After a few days there came word that ships had passed Kilwa and had gone on to Mafia.
>
> The lord of Mafia rejoiced, for he thought they were good and honest men. But those who knew the truth confirmed that they were corrupt and dishonest persons who had only come to spy out the land in order to seize it.... They gave them all they asked, water, food, firewood and everything else. And the Franks asked for a pilot to guide them to India, and after that back to their own land – God curse it!
>
> (Freeman-Grenville 1962a: 140–1)

By the tone of the manuscript, it is clear that Africans viewed with hostility the first arrival of the Portuguese. The manuscript's uniqueness is derived not only from the fact that it provides a first hand account of a momentous historical event, but it does so from an African perspective. In the same vein, the Portuguese motives for landing at Africa are specified in King Manuel's Royal Instructions to Dom Francisco de Almeida, dated 5 March 1505. His instructions direct a force of twenty-two ships and 2,500 men, including 1,500 soldiers to build a trade factory at Sofala, the main port for gold export in Mozambique. Further, he orders the capture and looting of Kilwa, the commercial center of the East African Coast. Following this, he directs this expedition to capture and loot Mombasa and Calicut, India, the center of trade in the Indian Ocean. Finally, he orders the establishment of a monopoly over commerce in the East by the establishment of a blockade over all strategic sea lanes in the Indian Ocean, the Red Sea and the Persian Gulf. His instructions read in part:

> We the King make known to you Dom Francisco d'Almeida our council that these are the instructions that we hold.... and command

> you to uphold and keep on this voyage upon which with the help of Our Lord we are sending you to India as captain-major of the fleet you are taking...
>
> Item, as you know it is on this voyage that we intend with the help of Our Lord to build the fortress of Sofala....
>
> You shall go along the river Sofala so peacefully and leisurely that it might seem you are but trading ships such as have called there before, and then you shall try to trade as best you may, taking out and displaying the merchandise for the purpose. And using this pretence you shall leap ashore there from your longboats and using such care and dexterity as you may, you shall forthwith take all the Moorish merchants who may be there from foreign parts and all the gold and merchandise you find upon them...
>
> And having landed [at Kilwa], you shall endeavor to take this place, ...For we are assured that the King as well as the merchants there have great riches, and we trust you to use good care to see that everything is saved, and whatever is seized shall be delivered to our factor aboard your nao as we ordered you to do in the exploit of Sofala.... King.
>
> (National Archives of Rhodesia and Nyasaland 1964: 181)

The analysis of this chapter examines the impact of these actions for the coastal economies of East Africa and on Indian Ocean trade. Admittedly, it is a preliminary investigation and many gaps remain to be filled. Yet based on this investigation, we offer the following hypotheses. First, Portuguese mercantilism arose because of the isolation of the country from the world's leading commercial centers and because of its own internal economic crises. Second, the coastal economies of Africa had achieved a level of economic and material development that compared favorably with the economies and cities of Portugal and Spain, as revealed in the diaries of Portuguese visitors. This level of development was achieved through their involvement in long distance trade which was fueled by the gold export from southern Africa. The disruption of this trade had a catastrophic effect on economic development along the coast. Finally, having gained control of Indian Ocean commerce through force, Portugal was unable to develop this into a peaceful economic monopoly because it lacked the level and character of domestic production that could meet the demands of Indian Ocean economies. This deficiency made Portugal rely more regularly on the use of force and usurpation and the kinds of policies that accelerated the economic decline of the region.

PURPOSE AND BACKGROUND

During the fifteenth century, world commerce was centered in a few geographic regions. Perhaps the largest and wealthiest was the Indian Ocean trading region, simply referred to in Europe as "the East". This area included the states along the East African coast up to Egypt, the states of the Arabian Peninsular, India, Southeast Asia, China and Japan. These economies were engaged in sea going commerce reaching from China to East Africa as far back as the eighth century. Chinese records indicate that trade between China and the East African coast was so abundant that in 1147 and 1219, it imposed import restrictions on East African commodities to reverse the drain on its currency (Freeman-Grenville 1962a: 37–8). A second important economic region was the Middle East which included the Ottoman Empire, parts of the Arabian Peninsula, and Persia. The Mediterranean, a third region, included Venice and Genoa and other important cities of Northern Italy, states of North Africa, and the Maghreb (Algeria, Lybia, Morrocco and Tunisia). This region was prominent because goods from the Indian Ocean, Middle East, North Africa, the Maghreb, and West Africa passed through it *en route* to Western Europe. Finally there was Western Europe whose prominent economies were Germany, France, and the Netherlands. During this period, however, Europe's attention was focused more on internal development than long distance trade. More importantly, centuries of religious hostility between the Christians of Europe and the Muslims of North Africa precluded the former from having a significant role in the commerce of North Africa, the Middle East, East Africa, or the Indian Ocean.

Western Europe had no direct contact with the East but Portugal and Spain sought to change this by finding a route that bypassed the hostile islamic states of the Maghreb and the Middle East.

HISTORICAL SETTING

By the mid-thirteen hundreds, most of Portugal was still uncultivated and poor, and the country was experiencing a severe balance of trade deficit. This deficit stemmed from a low demand for its exports in the rest of Europe and the Mediterranean. Its main exports were dried fish, honey, wax, leather, skins, wool, and some salt while its major imports were spices, sugar, silk woolen textiles, weapons, grains, and other household and luxury goods. The trade deficit so depleted Portugal's gold reserves that occasionally it had to cease minting gold coins (Marque 1973: 93). This low demand for Portuguese products occurred even in East Africa. In fact, when the Portuguese established their trading factory at Sofala in 1505, the gold trade went poorly because local merchants had no demand for their products. The diary of Pedro d'Anhaya, the Captain of the factory at Sofala notes that, "the gold trade did not progress favorably with the merchandise taken from the Kingdom [Portugal] . . . the negroes of Sofala did not care for it, as they wanted articles which the Moors procured from India, especially from Cambaya" (de Barros 1964: 277).

Portugal adjusted to this shortage of reserves by debasing its currency, that is by minting new coins with the same face value but containing less gold or silver. But this debasement caused hyper-inflation and created a monetary crisis. One mark of silver in 1325, weighing 230 grams, was equivalent to 19 Portuguese libras. In 1435, this same mark cost 25,000 libras. In the late 1300s a mark of gold was 250 libras. By 1433 it had risen to 251,000 libras (Axelson 1973: 128–34).

In the early fifteenth century the problem was so severe that domestic purchases were often made in foreign currencies or in kind because national coins were refused. This monetary crisis produced growing social discontent. By 1340, the aristocracy was being driven into ruin as revenues on agricultural production and real estate diminished. With the growing bankruptcy of the aristocracy, feudal stability broke down.

These developments were followed in 1348 by the plagues that ravaged Europe and wiped out nearly one third of Portugal's population. The diminished economic activity and trade resulting from the plagues, a chronic shortage of foreign exchange, the general poverty of serfs, price inflation, and unproductive lands combined to create a chaotic situation in Portugal. The nobility sought to resolve these problems by seeking wealth through the conquest of new lands outside the continent.

In contrast, by the fourteenth century the Indian Ocean trading region was among the wealthiest in the world. This vast region encompassed the countries that bordered on and traded directly in the Indian Ocean, Red Sea, Persian Gulf, Bay of Bengal, and other nearby waters. Prior to Portugal's circumnavigation of Africa, most of Europe's first hand information on this area came from the diaries of Marco Polo's travels.

To the farthest point west, this network started at Sofala, which is located on the coast of Mozambique just south of Beira. This city was the center for gold export in the Indian Ocean. Gold, usually denominated in Mithqals (1 = 0.1366 oz in 1502 along the East African coast), was the primary medium of international exchange and the Shona political states of present day Zimbabwe and central Mozambique mined it. During this period, there were three major Nations in this area: the Zimbabwe Nation which flourished from the twelve to the fifteen hundreds and produced the celebrated stone ruins at Great Zimbabwe; the Munhu Mutapa Kingdom which was pre-eminent from the fifteenth to the late nineteenth century; and the Torwa State which flourished between the late fifteenth and seventeenth centuries. Gold was exported at several cities on the Mozambican coast. Besides Sofala, others included Quelimani, Angoche, and Moçambique Island; the site of Vasco Da Gama's first landing in East Africa.

Gold export linked southern Africa and eastern Africa to the system of international trade in the Indian Ocean and this trade led to the emergence of a string of wealthy cities along the East African coast. The most important cities were Kilwa Kisiwani, Mafia, Zanzibar, and Pemba in present

Figure 11.1 Leading commercial centers at the turn of the sixteenth century

day Tanzania and Mombasa, Malindi and Pate in present day Kenya. Allen has estimated that between 1300 and 1700, eighty-seven important settlements existed on the East African coast (Allen 1981: 324), see Figure 11.1.

By the turn of the fourteenth century Kilwa Kisiwani was the wealthiest city in East Africa because of its monopoly of the gold trade at Sofala. This monopoly began in the eleventh century. In 1339 Pate invaded Kilwa and other coastal cities and exercised political control over the East African coast. Toward the end of the fourteenth century, Mombasa also challenged Kilwa's trade monopoly. But by the turn of the sixteenth century, when the Portuguese arrived, Kilwa once again had a firm monopoly over coastal trade. Yet, its government was weakened by succession fights within the ruling family and Kilwa, along with Mombasa, was engaged in political conflict with nearby Malindi. Farther down the coast, the inland Shona nations surrounding Sofala were fighting a civil war that, by 1500, had lasted for three quarters of a century. Portugal exploited these rivalries in attempting to gain a foothold in East Africa.

An elaborate system of taxes and duties were imposed by Kilwa to regulate trade along the East African Coast. This system was described in 1506 by Diogo de Alcacova in a letter to the King of Portugal. In addition to confirming the economic dominance of Kilwa, the letter implies that a merchant travelling from India or other foreign locations to trade for gold at Sofala would maximize profits by selling all commodities at northern coastal cities of East Africa, instead of going directly to Sofala. That is, the trade duty that Kilwa imposed on merchanise from foreign lands increased significantly as one traded closer geographically to Sofala. Merchants of northern cities in turn maximized profits by selling at cities to their immediate South instead of bypassing them and trading directly at Sofala, and so forth (de Alcacova 1964: 397–9). This system appears to have promoted more even economic development along the East African coast. Salim notes

> The material prosperity of the Coastal towns in 1500 was very impressive. The rulers lived in palaces and the elite in stone dwellings, many of which were multi-storied and built around central courtyards...The townsmen's high standard of living is reflected in the importation and use of such luxury items as damasks, silks, satins, copper objects, Chinese porcelains, Middle Eastern glass vessels and glass beads. Men from Kilwa were seen as far east as Malacca selling East African goods such as gold, ivory, copal and ambergris, and bringing back cottons, silks and satins.
>
> (Salim 1992: 754–5)

In AD 1331, Ibn Buttuta, the Moroccan traveler whose chronicles rival those of Marco Polo, visited Kilwa. He noted that "Kilwa is one of the most beautiful and well-constructed towns in the world. The whole of it is elegantly built" (Freeman-Grenville 1962b; 31). In 1500, Pedro Cabral noted that Kilwa "is a small island, near the mainland, and is a beautiful country. The houses are like those of Spain. In this land are rich merchants, and there is much gold and silver and musk and pearls. Those of the land wear clothes of fine cotton and of silk and many fine things, and they are black men" (Freeman-Grenville 1962b: 60). Another description comes from the 1505 diary of Francisco d'Almeida. As he was preparing to loot and sack the city he wrote "from our ships the fine houses, terraces, and minarets, with palms and trees in the orchards, made the city look so beautiful that our men were eager to land and overcome the pride of this barbarian [Amir Ibrahim ibn Sulaiman] who spent all that night in bringing into the island archers from the mainland" (de Barros 1964: 235–6).

North of modern day Kenya, the Indian Ocean network included Mogadishu and around the Gulf of Aden and opening into the Red Sea was the city of Zeila, behind which lay the Abyssinian Kingdom of Ethiopia. The Egyptian cities of Cairo and Alexandria were further outlets for this trading system which also included Jiddah, Mecca and Aden on the Arabian Peninsula. At the Gulf of Oman this network included the city of Muscat and along the Persian Gulf, the cities of Basra and Ormuz. From there trade stretched across the Arabian Sea to India, which was the commercial center of the region. The ancient cities involved on the Indian sub-continent were Diu and Cambay in the Kingdom of Gujarat, and Gao, Calicut, and Cochin in the Kingdom of Malabar. The trading network then extended to the city of Columbo in Ceylon (Sri Lanka) and across the Bay of Bengal to Pegu in Burma and to the Kingdom of Siam (Thailand). At the tip of Southeast Asia in Malaysia, the Port city of Malacca (Melaka) also participated along with the Island of Sumatra in Indonesia. Trade also reached up the South China Sea to the Chinese port cities of Macau and Canton. Finally, the network ended at the islands Marco Polo called Cipango (Japan).

From the Indian Ocean, network commodities reached Western Europe by passing up the Red Sea to Cairo and Alexandria and then on to the Italian cities of Venice and Genoa. Goods reached Eastern Europe by way of the Persian Gulf through Basra, Baghdad, and Trabriz in Persia. West African gold, mined in the empires of Ghana (200 to 1000 AD), Mali (mid-1200 to mid 1300 AD), and Songhai (late 1400 to late 1500 AD) reached Europe by way of trans-Saharan trade.

Southern Africa was primarily noted for its gold production. But in addition, it exported ivory and ebony. India exported smaller quantities of gold and ivory but large amounts of pearls, crystal, ebony, sugar, incense, silks, calico, and linen. Persia and Arabia exported horses while Ceylon exported cinnamon, pepper, pearls, rubies, sapphires, and other precious stones, brasilwood, and dyes. The countries of Southeast Asia exported a variety of spices including mace, nutmeg, and cloves, and China was renowned for its export of porcelain and other fine wares.

The isolation of Europe from this system stemmed from the half millennium of Muslim–Christian religious wars. By the time they ended for Portugal, during the middle of the thirteenth century, an Islamic cordon that was hostile to Christianity stretched from the Middle East clear across northern and western Africa and from Egypt down the East African coast to Sofala. In these regions, Christian traders were not welcome beyond the coast and were restricted to very small trade delegations at major cities of the Maghreb.

The Italian merchants of Genoa, Venice, Pisa, and Florence monopolized trade going to western Europe by way of the Mediterranean. This led to an immense accumulation of wealth in Italy and the appearance of the earliest capitalist institutions at Venice.

The information received on a Christian kingdom in East Africa named "Prester John" (Ethiopia) reinforced Portugal's desire to find a Muslim-free route to East Africa. Ethiopia sent embassies to Europe as far back as the twelfth century and Portugal hoped that it would be an ally in its conquest of the region.

The final impetus for exploration came during the 1400s when the Ottoman Turks overran Balkan Europe and captured the Christian stronghold of Constantinople (Istanbul). This threatened the trade routes between the Italian cities and Western Europe. Therefore, some Italian merchants migrated west to the Iberian Peninsula where they financed the development of the Portuguese shipping industry and the subsequent period of exploration (Davis 1973: 2, 9, 27).

THE PERIOD OF CONQUESTS AND EXPROPRIATION

Portuguese expansion began with the invasion and occupation of Ceuta, Morocco in 1415. This stimulated the depressed Portuguese economy and allowed it to resume minting gold coins in 1438. The success also attracted the wealth and participation of the king's younger son, Henry, who threw his support and wealth behind the expeditions. The Portuguese assimilated the more advanced navigational knowledge of Muslim societies of Northern Africa and refined and expanded this in special Portuguese schools. Portuguese shipping expeditions subjugated and occupied the Madeira Islands in 1420, reached Cape Bojadar in 1422 and occupied the Azores after 1430.

In the process, trade in sugar and slaves was found to be very profitable. Slaves were originally used in the cash crops of the islands and during subsequent decades were imported into Portugal and Europe to work as domestic servants. Likewise, the profitability of sugar led Portugal to shift Madeira's agriculture entirely to sugar production. This policy was so drastic that by 1448 the island had to import food for domestic consumption. Portugal instituted this same policy toward other islands including Sao Tome, which became the world's largest supplier of sugar in 1475.

In 1443, Nuno Tristao brought the first cargo of slaves to Portugal and sold them profitably. This attracted the attention of other European nations that rushed to join the trade. As a result, "Portugal was brought under the eye of Europe, ceasing to be a small poor, remote country of little account. Gold, pepper, ivory and slaves introduced the Portuguese to European markets that had not previously known them and drew the attention of wealthy outsiders to new opportunities that were opening beyond the bounds of Europe" (Davis 1973: 9).

In 1444, six ships sailed the West African coast in search of slaves. The next year twentysix ships were licensed by Prince Henry to make the journey. For two decades they exploited the Sierra Leone region for slaves and in the 1450s, an extensive slave market developed in Portugal, importing 1,000 slaves per year. This early slave trade was financed by Italian merchants at Lisbon and undertaken by Italian, Spanish, Portuguese, and French subjects.

In 1469 Portugal renewed its quest to find a route around Africa which Bartholomew Diaz accomplished in 1487. By this time, Spain had became a serious threat to Portugal's maritime plans. But the latter's military supremacy kept Spain out of West Africa and led Pope Alexander VI, in the 1491 Treaty of Alcacovas and 1493 Treaty of Tordesillas, to grant Portugal economic and political expansion rights in the south eastern Atlantic. By these agreements, Portugal and Spain divided the world along an imaginary line 370 leagues west of the Cape Verde Islands on the west coast of Africa. All new lands Spain discovered to the west of this meridian were to become its territories. Everything to the east was to be Portuguese (Garraty and Gray 1972: 623). Given Europe's limited knowledge of the world at the time, this treaty clearly favored Portugal.

In January of 1498, Vasco Da Gama landed at the coast of Mozambique. Sheik Zacoeja, the governor of Moçambique Island, welcomed Da Gama's ships, thinking they were from Turkey. A detailed account of the dialogue between the Sheik and Da Gama is given in de Castanheda (1964: 364–7). The Portuguese were accorded the hospitality typically reserved for visiting merchants. But not long afterwards, residents discovered that they were from "the Land of the Franks". This revelation caused the Portuguese and Mozambicans to become mutually suspicious. On one occasion, Da Gama's men fired upon residents they suspected of attempting an ambush. As a result, Zacoeja withdrew all assistance to the Portuguese and sent a messenger to Da Gama to express his displeasure. The Portuguese diary of this messenger indicates that the Sheik said:

> For when they [Mozambicans] wished to rejoice with them [Portuguese], according to the custom of the country, when they came to get water they attacked them, wounding and killing some of them, and had also sent one of his zambucos laden with much merchandise to

> the bottom, for which he [Da Gama] owes him amends . . . and that at a time when he had thought him and his people trustworthy and that they spoke the truth, but now he found they were vagabonds who went about robbing the sea ports.
>
> (de Barros 1964: 176–7)

Da Gama left a terrible impression on residents all along the East African coast. No doubt this antagonism was fueled by the hostility he encountered along the coast once it was discovered that he was a Christian; that information preceded him at every port. The Moçambican pilot, who Da Gama abducted and forced to guide him up the coast, intentionally steered the Portuguese past Kilwa and onto an embankment near Mombasa. The residents of Mombasa forced them out of their port and as a result Da Gama sought refuge at Malindi. Exploiting Malindi's rivalry with Mombasa, he proposed a military alliance to which Malindi agreed. It also provided the Portuguese with the services of Ibn Majid, the most distinguished Indian Ocean navigator of the day. Majid guided Da Gama to Calicut, India, which he reached in May of 1498.

That same month, Da Gama returned to Portugal having successfully opened a sea route to the East. He had departed Portugal with a bare cargo, but returned with one valued at 1,000,000 ducats (in 1502, 1 ducat = 0.10258 oz. of gold). The gold was so plentiful that it was fashioned into a silver-gilt monstrance which is today one of Lisbon's most treasured art pieces.

In 1500, the Portuguese bombarded an Egyptian fleet off the coast of Calicut and blockaded the outlet to the Red Sea in order to deny Egyptian and Arabian ships access to the Indian Ocean. Then on 24 July 1505 the Portuguese, backed by artillery support, stormed Kilwa. The inventory of the loot taken there is recorded in one of the Portuguese diaries and testifies to the wealth of the city. After Kilwa, they sacked, looted and burned Mombasa and then Calicut and detached five ships to loot vessels in the Indian Ocean. From East Africa to China, almost every city that did not submit to Portuguese hegemony was pillaged.

The Mamluks who governed Egypt were also affected by the blockade of strategic lanes in the Indian Ocean. Therefore, the Sultan organized an enormous fleet consisting of the combined navies of Egypt, Gujarat, and Calicut to challenge Portugal's naval supremacy. Ibn Iyas, the noted Cairo author who lived during this period, mentions these events in his six volume history of Egypt. He has this to say about the encounter with the Portuguese:

> Rabi II 911 (September 1505): The Sultan formed an expeditionary force to resist European incursions along the coast of India. A large number of soldiers were mobilized and the preparation of equipment was actively pursued.

> Cha'ban 914 (December 1508): It was learned that the army sent to India under the command of Amir Husayn had won a victory over the Europeans who were overrunning the Indian Ocean. A great quantity of booty had been taken…
>
> Safar 915 (June 1509): It was learned that the army in India, commanded by Husayn Moushrif, had suffered a crushing defeat. The Europeans had wiped it out and had plundered all its ships. The Sultan appeared extremely dismayed at the news.
>
> Year 920 (1514): No cargo was delivered at the port of Jeddah because of the European corsairs sailing the Indian Ocean. It had been at least six years since merchandise had been unloaded in the port of Jeddah. (UNESCO Courier 1989: 30–1)

The defeat of the Egyptians was Portugal's greatest naval victory of the century.

THE CHARACTER OF PORTUGUESE MERCANTILE CAPITALISM

The lack of demand for Portugal's domestically produced products made naval superiority and force key elements in maintaining its mercantile monopoly in the area. In other words, because it could not sell its domestically produced exports in the Indian Ocean, Portugal could not peacefully exploit its maritime monopoly as other countries had done in previous periods. Unlike England in the Atlantic trade, Portugal was thereby forced to rely upon unequal exchange, duties, taxes, the confiscation of cargoes, and looting to accumulate wealth. These "predatory" forms of mercantilism disrupted Indian Ocean commerce and led to the decline of many economies. Cities that did not acquiesce were bombarded, looted, and burned and puppet governments were often installed.

Equally disruptive was Portugal's policy of prohibiting Swahili and Muslim merchants, the traditional middlemen in the area, from trading in the region. All trade was to be conducted by the Portuguese or their agents and all ships had to obtain a pass or "cortez". The poor quality of Portugal's domestic production also forced it to adopt a mercantile strategy that centered on controlling Sofala's gold trade. The idea was to use this as foreign exchange to purchase commodities in the region.

To accomplish this, Portugal had to overcome the resistance of the Teve Kingdom in Mozambique which controlled the territories surrounding Sofala. At one point, between 1511 and 1538, this resistance was so great that the ruler of Teve imposed a trade blockade on the Portuguese factory at Sofala. It did so to deny its rival, the Mutapa Kingdom, commercial and military contact with the Portuguese and to force the latter to supply Teve with the arms it needed to sustain its war against the Mutapa. The ruling Sachiteve also mandated that Swahili merchants, instead of Portuguese merchants, be used as middlemen in trade between the interior and the coast (Boston 1992).

Except for a few towns along the Zambezi River, Portugal was unable to control the interior regions of Southern Africa during the sixteenth century and it failed completely to control the gold supply. These situations also led to the use of force. Barred from the interior, Portugal continually tried to interfer in the internal politics and wars of inland states from its coastal factory. These conflicts, along with declining productivity in the gold mines of the region, severely disrupted the flow of gold to the coast. Malowist (1992: 13) observes that the reduction in the supplies of gold to Sofala adversely affected the position of Kilwa, Mombasa, and Malindi.

Prior to the sixteenth century, long-distance trade played a central role in the economies of Africa, particularly the trans-Saharan trade and trade along the East African coast. This trade led to the rise of urban areas, linked towns with the countryside and encouraged an increase in domestic productivity (Diagne 1992: 34). But just as Portugal violently expelled Swahili and Muslim merchants from the East African coast and the Indian Ocean in the early sixteenth century, in 1592, Spain and Portugal expelled Jews and Muslim merchants from Tunis and Algiers. These acts led to the decline of these economies, and the decline of urban trading centers caused a similar decline in the rural economies, forcing production to center on local consumption rather than long distance trade. African economies were further disrupted by the developing slave trade. Diagne notes that after Portuguese intervention, ports of East Africa, the Maghrid and North Africa "lived mainly by piracy and on tributes and duties, rather than by trade or new industries" (Diagne 1992: 36).

The Indian Ocean trading zone, once among the world's leading commercial regions entered a spiral of economic decline from which it has not fully recovered five centuries later. The organization of trade in the East was supplanted by the ruthless mercantilism of the West.

Between 1517 and 1580, the Ottoman Turks ruled Egypt and attempted again to dislodge the Portuguese from the Indian Ocean and Red Sea. There were several engagements between the Portuguese and the Turks on the East African Coast, in the Indian Ocean, and Persian Gulf. These ended when the Turks were defeated at Mombasa in 1589.

Across the Atlantic Ocean, Spain's attempt to subjugate the Americas was even more brutal. Merchant capitalism was in full bloom and ultimately gave rise to the slave trade and system of slavery in the New World and the development of capitalist institutions in Europe. The East became subservient to the West and Africa once again supplied a vital ingredient in the new system of world trade – human chattel. In this new system, Africa exported the commodities that Europe demanded. From the West African

Islands of Madeira and Sao Tome, Europe demanded sugar. To accommodate this demand it transformed these economies, with the help of slave labor, into cash crop production. From the Shona states of Zimbabwe a booming trade in ivory developed. Finally, from West and Central Africa, Europe demanded human chattel to build the new world and satisfy its labor shortages at home. In 1517 Genoese merchants paid 25,000 ducats to the King of Spain for the rights to supply 4,000 African slaves annually to the West Indies. This transaction was the formal beginning of the triangular trade.

THE ACCUMULATION OF WEALTH

During the first half of the sixteenth century, Portugal was the wealthiest country in Europe. By 1518, overseas trade accounted for 68 per cent of its national revenues. Forced to debase its currency because of a gold shortage, Portugal now minted gold coins for propaganda purposes. Between 1504 and 1551 the outflow of gold from Portugal to the rest of the world in payment of the vast imports amounted annually to only 40,000 cruzados. Its average annual import of gold alone, during the first twenty years of this period, was 200,000 to 240,000 cruzados. Half of this came from the West African coast and the remainder from the East (Axelson 1973: 59). By 1515, the value of spices imported into Portugal amounted to one million cruzados annually. This was followed in importance by copper, 475,000 cruzados; gold, 240,000 cruzados; silver and sugar worth 250,000 cruzados; brazilwood, 50,000 cruzados; slaves, 30,000 cruzados; and dyestuffs, 10,000 cruzados. Consequently, in one year total imports amounted to at least 2,055,000 cruzados. At the same time, the total expenditure on imports amounted to only 1.9 per cent of total imports. The destiny of the state was clearly linked with mercantile capitalism (Marques 1973: 261), and the economic stability it created between 1489 and 1539 provided the beginning of a new era in Portugal.

> Trade with Africa brought Portugal great profit. According to J. Lucio De Azevedo's calculations, the Crown gains, which had amounted to some 60 million Portuguese reals in the 1480s, reached 200 million reals during the rule of King Manuel (1491–1521) and at least 279.5 million reals by 1534. This increase was undoubtedly achieved through profits from trade not only with India but also to a large extent with Africa. Moreover, the considerable inflow of African gold made it possible for John II and his successor, Manuel, to stabilize their silver coinage, to mint the cruzados – a high-value gold coin – and, more importantly, to expand the fleet and the state and colonial administration.
>
> (Malowist 1992: 3)

During the last quarter of the sixteenth century, each ship docking at the Tagus unloaded a million cruzados worth of goods of all variety. Lisbon had supplanted Venice and Genoa as the leading commercial port for Europe. But the chief profits did not remain in Portugal. Instead, they went to the foreign financiers who provided the capital investments for overseas enterprises. Profits were also usurped by corrupt Portuguese administrators stationed abroad. The foremost financiers of Europe, now the Germans and Netherlanders, became wealthy while the Portuguese Crown increasingly incurred the tremendous debt associated with financing its overseas army, factories, and growing colonial administration.

Researchers have not definitively established why Portugal failed to derive long-term economic benefits from its explorations, but some factors are obvious. Malowist (1992: 3) observes:

> Portugal might have been thought – in the early sixteenth century – to have entered upon a path of lasting economic and political expansion. However, its backward and sluggish socio-economic structure eventually prevented this from happening. Overseas expansion necessitated large financial outlay and the purchase of gold and slaves depended on supplying Africa with large quantities of iron, brass and copper goods, cheap textiles and some silver, foodstuffs and salt. These goods were not produced in Portugal but had to be bought from foreign visitors or in Bruges and, later, from the major European trade centres at that time.
>
> (Malowist 1992: 3)

CONCLUSION

The decline of the East African economies was caused by a clash of two different systems of economic trade. One was based on historically established patterns of long distance commerce wherein nations derived mutual benefits from this trade. Here, commercial activity was centered on coastal towns and these markets stimulated inland production and created a link between rural and urban economies. Prior to the Portuguese presence, the Indian Ocean had experienced wars and conflicts. However, these conflicts did not permanently disrupt the continuity of trade and commerce in the region.

Descriptions given by visitors regarding the level of development in coastal towns of East Africa indicate that it was equivalent to many places in Western Europe and other parts of the world. But a few decades after the arrival of the Portuguese, the East African economies were in a state of irreversible economic decline and dependency. Diagne has observed:

> The impact of the predatory economy on the countries of the Nile and the Indian Ocean was equally disastrous. The East African ports

> had been known for their trading activities since the eleventh century. Although not as important either in size or influence as the Western Sudanese and North African towns, they nevertheless formed the framework of a substantial urban commercial civilization in touch with Arabia, Persia, India, China and the Mediterranean. The Portuguese invasion set off the progressive ruin of this urban commercial complex.
>
> (Diagne 1992: 39)

This is a classic example of the "predatory economy". Here also was a clash of two radically different economic systems. The indigenous one had prospered for centuries and was based on long distance trade. But the newer, "predatory" system employed force and unequal exchange as primary ingredients. While the agents of Portugal became rich, one of the world's leading commercial regions entered a period of decline and underdevelopment. Speaking of Da Gama's return after his second voyage, Livermore notes that it crowned three-quarters of a century of endeavor and turned the course of European history. "The hold of the Sao Gabriel was stuffed with specimens of pepper, cloves, nutmeg, cinnamon and precious stones. Europe, poor, enterprising and resolute, was no longer separated by the hostile confraternity of Islam from the splendid despotism of the east." King Manuel became the wealthiest ruler in Europe and was called "Lord of the Navigation, Conquest and Commerce of Ethiopia, Arabia, Persia and India," and "King of the Spices" (Livermore 1976: 138, 142).

The fundamental causes of the decline of the East African economies have been identified above. To put in perspective the impact of the Portuguese presence on these East African economies we ask the following question: suppose England had been suddenly and forcibly cut off from the Atlantic trade, is it likely that it would have later become the center of the industrial revolution? Yet this is what mercantile capitalism did to the major economies of the Indian Ocean commercial system.

REFERENCES

Allen, James D. V., (1981) "Swahili Culture and the Nature of the East Coast Settlement", *International Journal of African Studies*, vol. 14, no. 2: 324.

Axelson, Eric, (1973) *Portuguese in South-east Africa 1488–1600*, (Johannesburg: C. Struik).

Boston, Thomas D., (1992) "Sixteenth Century Expansion and the Economic Decline of Africa", *The Review of Black Political Economy*, vol. 20, no. 4 (Spring): 5–38.

Davis, Ralph, (1973). *The Rise of the Atlantic Economies*, (Ithaca: Cornell University Press).

de Alcacova, Diogo, (1964) "Diogo de Alcacova to the King of Portugal, 20 November 1506", National Archives of Rhodesia and Nyasaland, *Documents of the Portuguese in Mozambique and Central Africa 1497–1840* vol. 1: 397–9.

de Barros, Joao, ([1901] 1964) "Da Asia", in G. Theal (ed.) *Records of South-Eastern Africa*, (Cape Town: C. Struik, PTY, Ltd., vol. 6).

de Castanheda, Fernao l., ([1901] 1964) "History of the Discovery and Conquest of India by the Portuguese", in G. Theal (ed.) *Records of South-Eastern Africa* (Cape Town: C. Struik PTY Ltd, vol. 5).

Diagne, P., (1992) "African Political, Economic and Social Structures During this Period", in B. A. Ogot (ed.) *General History of Africa*, vol. v, (Berkeley: University of California Press: 23–45).

Freeman-Grenville, G. S. P., (1962a) *The Medieval History of the Coast of Tanganyika*, (Berlin: Akademie-Verlag).

Freeman-Grenville, G. S. P., (1962b) "The Anonymous Narrative of the Voyage of Pedro Alveres Cabral", in *The East African Coast: Select Documents from the First to the Earlier Nineteenth Century*, (Oxford: Clarendon Press).

Garraty, J. and Gay P., (1972) *The Columbia History of the World*, (New York: Harper and Row).

Inikori, J. E., (1992) "Africa in World History: The Export Slave Trade from Africa and the Emergence of the Atlantic Economic Order", in B.A. Ogot (ed.) *General History of Africa*, vol. v. (Berkeley: University of California Press: 74–112).

Livermore, H. V., (1976) A New History of Portugal (London: Cambridge University Press).

Marque, A. H. De Oliveira, (1973) *History of Portugal*, 2 vols (New York: Columbia University Press).

Malowist, M., (1992) "The Struggle for International Trade and its Implications for Africa", in B. A. Ogot (ed.) *General History of Africa*, vol. v (Berkeley: University of California Press: 1–22).

National Archives of Rhodesia and Nyasaland, (1964) "Instructions to the Captain-Major, March 5, 1505", *Documents of the Portuguese in Mozambique and Central Africa, 1497–1840*, (Lisbon: NARN, vol. 1).

Pearson, M. N., (1976) *Merchants and Rulers in Gujarat*, (Berkeley: University of California Press).

Salim, A. I., (1992) "East Africa: The Coast", in B. Ogot (ed.) *General History of Africa*, vol. 5 (Berkeley: University of California Press).

Schumpeter, Joseph, (1954) *History of Economic Analysis* (New York: Oxford University Press).

UNESCO Courier, (1989) "Rivalry in the Red Sea; Portugal's Impact on the Fortunes of Mamluk Egypt," April 1989.

Williams, Eric (1944) *Capitalism and Slavery* (New York: Capricorn Books).

12

TRADE AND MARKETS IN PRECOLONIAL WEST AND WEST CENTRAL AFRICA

The cultural foundation of the African American business tradition

Juliet E. K. Walker

> Aiye l'oja, oja, l'aiye: "The world is a market, the market is the world,"
> – Yoruba proverb.[1]
> *Sika sene, biribara nsen bio*: – "There is nothing as important as wealth"
> – Asante proverb.[2]

For over three and a half centuries the European transatlantic slave trade and the large monoculture plantation enterprises in the Americas ranked first among the most highly profitable multinational businesses in the new global economy of the emerging modern world. With the rise of merchant capital and maritime innovations Europeans, Christians and Jews, Islamic world Arabs, white America and Africans, including the African-Europeans, were involved in the marketing and trade of slaves and other commodities in international markets.[3] The Gold Coast ranked third among several regions in West and West Central Africa in the number of Africans sold as slaves in the United States. The transatlantic slave trade, moreover, intensified wealth disparities not only between Europe and Africa but also among and within precolonial African states.[4]

Certainly, the marketing and trading activities of the African masses could not compare with that of the professional merchants, brokers, and traders, whose commercial operations extended to commodity exchanges in large regional and international markets. As for the merchants on the Gold Coast in precolonial Africa, according to Ray Kea in his study of that region: "Many of these persons had annual incomes in excess of 30,000 dambas worth of gold.... In contrast a significant section of the urban population earned less than 500 dambas a year." The ultimate goals of the professional merchants, traders, and brokers and the seriousness with which they pursued commercial activities, are perhaps revealed in the morning prayer of the professional merchants on the Gold Coast which, according to Kea was: "My God, give me rice, give me yams, give me gold and aggrey beads, give me slaves, give me wealth, grant that I be healthy."[5]

This precolonial African propensity for trade and marketing, this entrepreneurial spirit, if you will, existed in all sectors of the society and underscores the thesis of this analysis: that the commercial culture of precolonial West and West Central Africa that existed during the transatlantic slave trading era provided the cultural foundation for the African American business heritage. As I previously emphasized, "Historians now readily acknowledge African participation in the slave trade, with its highly specialized commercial economies, but they fail to consider that Africans brought to the New World had also lived and worked in that same political economy."[6] In point of fact, "human capital" factors were those which made Africans the most desired laborers in the plantation economies of the Americas: their forced enslavement represented the profitable capitalization of an unpaid labor force in the development of these new nations. While African expertise in agricultural production has been increasingly recognized in studies of African survivalists with some recognition also given to their propensity for local market trade activities and various degrees of craft specialization, the commercial ethos, the African economic rationality, which permeated West and West African societies has not been considered as a basis for establishing the African heritage of the Black American business tradition.

Consequently, with a research focus limited primarily to slave plantation labor, scholars of the African American economic experience have, for the most part, failed to expand the scope of their historic assessments to include discussions of the complexity of the precolonial African commercial culture that existed during the transatlantic slave trading era. Indeed, in their analysis of African American economic life, most scholars would argue that an African American business culture, much less an African heritage inclusive of a commercial tradition, does not exist.[7] Certainly, African American business history has remained on the periphery of research agendas for scholars of the black experience in the United States.[8] Yet, even those existing historical studies, which document the economic activities pursued by antebellum free blacks have not been subjected to serious scholarly scrutiny.[9]

Certainly, confronted by repressive proscriptive legislation and racist constraints, which would seemingly preclude any chance of profitable economic activity, the potential for achieving any economic success by blacks during the age of slavery would appear unlikely. In that an African cultural propensity for commercial activity in trade and marketing survived, the agency of African American slaves and their descendants in contributing to their own survival must not be discounted. Indeed, blacks, both slave and free, participated in the business community of preindustrial America, with the most successful achieving comparatively great wealth. See Table 12.1.

Table 12.1 Wealthholding of representative leading black entrepreneurs, 1820–65 (minimum property values, $100,000)

Name	*Location*	*Business activity*	*Assessed wealth (dollars)*
Leidesdorff, William	San Francisco	merchandising, real estate	1,500,000
Smith, Stephen	Columbia; Philadelphia, Pa.	lumber merchant, real estate	500,000
Soulie, Albin & Bernard	New Orleans	merchant broker, capitalists	500,000
Lacroix, François	New Orleans	tailor, real estate	300,000
Lacroix, Julien	New Orleans	grocer, real estate	250,000
Ricaud, widow, & son, Pierre	Iberville Parish	sugar planters	221,500
DuBuclet, August	Iberville Parish	sugar planter	206,400
Pottier, Honore	New Orleans	commission broker, in cotton	200,000
DuPuy, Edmond	New Orleans	capitalist	171,000
Reggio, Auguste and Octave	Plaquemines Parish	sugar planter, overseer	160,000
McCarty, Mme. Cecee	New Orleans	merchandising, money broker	155,000
DeCuir, Antoine	Pointe Coupee Parish	sugar planter	151,000
Logoaster, Erasme	New Orleans	landlord	150,000
Colvis, Julien and Dumas, Joseph	New Orleans	tailors	150,000
Metoyer, Augustin	Natchitoches Parish	cotton planter	140,958
Durnford, estate of Thomas	Plaquemines Parish	sugar planter	115,000
Metoyer, Jean Baptiste	Natchitoches Parish	cotton planter	112,761
Casenave, Pierre A. D.	New Orleans	commission broker, undertaker	100,000
Donato, Martin	St. Landry Parish	cotton planter	100,000
Forten, James	Philadelphia, Pa.	sailmaker	100,000
Spraulding, Washington	Louisville, Ky.	barber, real estate	100,000

Sources: William Leidesdorff: William A. Leidesdorff. Estate Papers, 1842–52. Leidesdorff Collection, Bancroft Library, University of California, Berkeley; Leidesdorff and Folsom court records. Bancroft Court Records, Bancroft Library: *People ex rel. Attorney General* v. *Joseph L. Folsom*, 5 Cal. Rep. 373 (1855); and *U.S.* v. *Exec. J. Folsom*, U.S. Superior Court, Dec. term 1863, cases 168 and 236. When Leidesdorff's estate was settled, the final sale of the property brought in $1,442,232.35.

Stephen Smith: Pennsylvania, vol. 132, p. 322. R. G. Dun & Co. Collection, Baker Liblrary, Harvard Business School, Boston, Mass.

Albin and Bernard Soulie: ibid., Louisiana, vol. 11, p. 30, entry for 19 March 1857: "Are rich, w. 500m."

François Lacroix: ibid., vol. 10, p. 392, entry for 15 June 1860: "wor $300m."

Julien A. Lacroix: ibid., vol. 11, p. 92, entry for 1 June 1854: "est. w. $250m."

Widow Ricaud & son Pierre: U.S. Bureau of the Census, "Population Schedules of the Eighth Census of the United States, 1860, Louisiana, Iberville Parish," National Archives and Records Service. Washington, D.C., manuscript microscopy M-653, reel 411.

August DuBuclet: ibid.

Honore Pottier: Louisiana, vol. 10, p. 526, R.C. Dun & Co. Collection, entry for 1 Oct. 1869:. "In business many yrs prior to war ... owns R. E. wor 100m total wor $200m."

Edmond DuPuy: U.S. Bureau of the Census, "Population Schedules of the Eighth Census of the United States, 1860, Louisiana, New Orleans," manuscript microcopy M-653, reel 420.

Auguste and Octave Reggio: ibid., Plaquemines Parish, manuscript microcopy M-653, reel 414.

Mme. Cecee McCarty: *Macarty et al.* v. *Mandeville*, 3 La. An. 239 (March 1848; p. 240, note: "She is in possession of a fortune which ... exceeds . . . $135,000."

Antoine DeCuir: U.S. Bureau of the Census, "Population Schedules of the Eighth Census of the United States, 1860, Louisiana, Pointe Coupée Parish," manuscript microcopy M-653, reel 414.

Erasme Legoaster: ibid., New Orleans, manuscript microcopy M-653, reel 420.

Julien Colvis and Joseph Dumas: Louisiana, vol. 9, p. 140, R. G. Dun & Co. Collection, entry for June 1849: "w in RE $150m." Also see ibid., vol. 12, p. 39, for entry on "Dumas Frères," which notes for 11 March 1871 that their father, Joseph Dumas, "is wor a 1/2 a million-$s."

Augustin Metoyer: compiled from Natchitoches Succession Records of Pierre Metoyer, no. 193: Dominique Metoyer, no. 375; Jean B. L. Metoyer, no. 362; Marie S. Metoyer, no. 373; Agnes Metoyer, no. 395; Natchitoches Parish Records, Office of the Clerk of the Court, Natchitoches, La.

Thomas Durnford: Estate, U.S. Bureau of the Census, "Population Schedules of the Eighth Census of the United States, 1860, Louisiana, Plaquemines Parish," manuscript microcopy M-653, reel 414.

Jean Baptiste Metoyer: Succession of Jean Baptiste Metoyer, Natchitoches Parish Succession Records, no. 362.

Pierre A. D. Casenave: Louisiana, vol. 10, p. 497, R. G. Dun & Co. Collection, entry for 1 June 1864: "w at least 100m."

Martin Donato: U.S. Bureau of the Census, "Population Schedules of the Eighth Census of the United States, 1860, Louisiana, St. Landry Parish," manuscript microcopy M-653, reel 424.

James Forten: Martin R. Delany, *The Condition, Elevation, Emigration and Destiny of the Colored People of the United States* (Philadelphia, Pa., 1852), 94–95; and notes 13 and 38 in the text of this article.

Washington Sprauldіng: U.S. Bureau of the Census, "Population Schedules of the Eighth Census of the United States, 1860, Kentucky, Jefferson County," manuscript microcopy M-653, reel 378. See also Henry Clay Weeden, *Weeden's History of the Colored People of Louisville* (Louisville, Ky., 1897), 57. Spraulding died in 1865

Juliet K. Walker: "Racism, Slavery, Free Enterprise: Black Entrepreneurship in the United States Before the Civil War," *Business History Review*, Autumn 1986: pp. 350–51.

The multiplicity and diversity of slave economic activities has not, until recently, been the subject of scholarly inquiry, although, black bondsmen comprised almost 90 per cent of the African population in the United States before 1865.[10] In particular, the extent and complexity of those commercial activities have been generally ignored in scholarly discussions on the economic activities of African Americans and few provide any discussion of African survivalisms as a basis for the origin of the African American business heritage in the United States.[11] The interest of Americanists in the study of African survivalisms has been limited primarily to identifying expressions of an African folk and material culture that survived in the New World, paced by the pioneering work of Melville Herskovits in his seminal study of African survivalisms.[12]

Even the more recent cultural studies which focus on Afrocentricity and the "Black Atlantic," i.e., the African Diaspora, fail to include the extent to which a precolonial African economic and commercial cultural tradition persisted in the Americas.[13] Simply put, in their formulations, most cultural studies of African America life and thought fail to consider the existing scholarship which details economic life in precolonial Africa during the transatlantic slave trade era. Specifically, the prevailing discourse in African diaspora cultural studies is limited to analysis of the history of ideas, generated primarily in the minds of a contemporary diaspora African intellectual elite, as opposed to being inclusive of the totality of the forces of an historic reality.

In the absence of any contextual analysis which gives consideration to the historic reality of the transculturation of the precolonial African economic ethos and commercial culture during the transatlantic slave trading era, these new cultural configurations of intellectual and ideological discourse, which attempt to explain who the black man/woman is today and why, fail to provide an analysis which considers the totality of the African cultural diaspora. As I argued previously in emphasizing the importance of the African heritage as the foundation of black American business: "While the acculturation process produced the Afro-American, it did not fully obliterate the heritage of individuation and family economy that existed in Africa, characterized by an entrepreneurial spirit based on the equality of men and women as free, independent producers with access to property for self-directed development in the production of goods and commodities for markets."[14] Certainly acculturation accounted, in part, for the form and structure of African American business activities in their development in the United States, but the initial and sustaining propensity for black business participation in this country can be found in the transculturation and survival of an African commercial culture. As Thomas Sowell emphasizes: "Cultures are not erased by crossing a political border, or even an ocean, nor do they necessarily disappear in later generations which adopt the language, dress, and outward life-style of a country."[15]

In the historic reality of American slavery, the necessity to survive the brutal reality of a repressive economic institution involved more than the development of an aesthetic slave ethos of resistance and an African Christian theology of liberation. These cultural expressions, of course, can never be discounted as providing a sustaining basis for the psychological survival of African Americans. Yet, slaves also contended with the institution by structuring economic activities to ameliorate the appalling impoverishment of their material life. A decision in an 1860 case from North Carolina, *Lea* v. *Brown*, not only provides a general summary of some economic activities of slaves, but also reveals the deep concern southerners had with the degree of economic success achieved by the slave.

On its face, the decision also underscores the extent to which slaves operated in a cash nexus, revealing that the economic activity of slaves was a recognized and even accepted part of the institution, but that the impetus for slave economic activity derived from the slave master. That point, will not be argued here. Suffice it to say that, while the economic activities of African American slaves reflected a compromise with their owners, the initiative emanated from the slaves as they manipulated the conditions of their unpaid labor activities to capitalize on the market conditions where they lived. Slaves not only responded to that market but in some instances even created a demand for the goods and services they could provide. Moreover, some slaves were able to develop enterprises that provided more than what the system deemed desirable for slave economic activities as the record shows in the following case:

> This court has... treated it as commendable, to adopt a system of rewards, by which a slave is allowed a half, or a whole day, every time "the crop is gone over," to work a patch of cotton, corn or watermellons [sic] and the like, and to sell the proceeds, so as to make a little money... indulge a fancy for "finery in dress," for which the African race is remarkable; but when it comes to an accumulation of $1500, the question is a very different one,... The privileges allowed a slave,... to enable him to acquire that amount of money, extra, must necessarily in some degree, run counter to the policy of the statutes by which slaves are... not allowed to hire or to have the use of their own time... calculated to make other slaves dissatisfied... not calculated to promote good morals...[16]

Interestingly, while the broad scope of African American business activity during the age of slavery has been generally ignored, the "moral economy" of the slave has been the subject of scholarly discussion, primarily within the context of crime, specifically slave appropriation of their owner's property for sale in underground markets. Scholarly analysis is generally limited to the societal values of the slaveowner with only limited consideration given to the a slave-constructed morality. From the slave's perspective, property expropriation in the form of foodstuffs reveal that the slave saw his moral obligations as: 1 survival of self, family, and community; 2 a means to augment their meagre food allotment; and 3 securing just compensation for the value of their unpaid labor.

The historic reality is that African American slave economic participation was not limited only to an underground economy, although most slave economic activities were illegal. From the Colonial Era to the Civil War, the economic activities of Africans in America, including both free blacks and slaves, in providing not only goods but also services, represented an integral part of the business community in America's preindustrial American economy. Those business activities transcend the limited parameters of "moral economy" discussions of slave economic activities. Indeed, they reflect to an even greater extent the cultural ethos of an eighteenth-century precolonial West and West Central Africa commercial heritage of trade and marketing that survived the transatlantic crossing.

Consequently, my purpose is to establish that African survivalisms of the commercial culture provided the foundation for the origin of the African American business tradition. My discussion, a synthetic review from the literature in African history, of the African commercial infrastructure is limited to only the most distinctive features of the trade and marketing activities in the six major slave-exporting regions in precolonial West and West Central Africa. Five of the regions are in West Africa: 1 Senegambia; 2 the Upper Guinea Coast, which includes both Sierra Leone and the Windward Coast; 3 the Gold Coast; 4 the Bight of Benin; and 5 the Bight of Biafra. The sixth region, Congo/Angola, is in West Central Africa.

The geographic reach of African trade, some 3,000 miles stretching southeast from the Senegal river on the northwest Guinea Coast, some 200 miles inland, to Angola, south of the Zaire [Congo] river, was an area comparable in size to the United States from the Atlantic to the Pacific oceans. There were instances, however, when the slave trade extended almost 500 miles inland from the African coastal belt to some 7,000 miles to the north of Senegal south to Mauritania along the coast of Mozambique. While Africans from the Sudan and even Central, East and Southern Africa were victims of the trade, their numbers were comparatively negligible relative to those from West and West Central Africa.

With more than six thousand ethnic groups identified in Africa, along with innumerable state and stateless societies, my assessments consequently will be limited to either representative states or leading ethnic groups in precolonial West and West Central Africa.[17] In those six regions, a network of trade routes and markets linked towns and villages not only in the highly centralized economies of the larger states, but also in the smaller village states. In addition to local and regional internal trade economies within the interior regions and cabotage along the Guinea coast, the exchange, barter, and sale of goods from producing areas to consumer zones in West and

West Central Africa encompassed three international trade zones. The trans-Saharan, trans-atlantic, and European markets eagerly and profitably absorbed West and West Central African export commodities. In these interconnected economies, commodity exchanges included ecologically-specific agricultural, animal and forest products and highly specialized craftware in addition to slaves.[18]

At the same time, commodity exchanges with the Islamicized Sudan, *Bilad al Sudan* [Arabic, meaning land of the blacks], were extensive, and the study of the economic life of the great Sudanic empires of Ghana, Mail, and Songhay from the eleventh through the sixteenth centuries is important. With procolonial West Africa, these were complementary economic trade regions, and commerce in the Sudan existed not in isolation from that of the Guinea coastal states, but as a part of an interconnected West African economic unit. As it was, European greed to secure sub-Saharan trade commodities from West Africa, thus avoiding Arab middle men costs, propelled their exploration of Guinea Coast Africa.

In his discussion of the economic history of Africa, Ralph Austen describes the degree to which trade connections along the upper Guinea Coast in both precontact and precolonial West Africa had been either established with Sudanic trans-Saharan markets or were integrated into the Sudanic commercial world. As he indicates, the Senegambia–Upper Guinea region was "a direct extension of the Western Sudanic savanna although somewhat distant from its main economic and political centre of the Middle Niger." The forest regions of the Gold Coast and the Bight of Benin, he adds were "strongly linked to the Sudanic economy but never fully assimilated to it." Of the remaining three zones, located east and south of the Niger River and its coastal delta, the Bight of Biafra, Gabon-Congo and Angola, Austen said that "Sudanic contacts disappear entirely."[19]

Consequently, the political economies of the Sudanic empires should not be referenced as a basis for establishing the commercial heritage of Africans in America or as a substitute for a direct and specific analysis of the internal political economies of the Guinea Coast states in West and West Central Africa during the transatlantic slave era. As Elliott P. Skinner emphasizes in his study of West and West Central African economic systems, with reference to its neglect in discussions of the Sudanic trade: "Scholars have known that such towns as Kano, Timbuktu and others had large markets, but they have too often considered the other areas of West Africa as an economic wasteland. What they have not realized is that the markets of the larger societies could not exist without those of the smaller ones."[20]

Consequently, as a basis to establish the African origin of the African American business heritage, this study proceeds to review trade and marketing activities in precolonial West and West Central Africa during the transatlantic slave trade era. With each region, the most distinctive features of their trade and marketing activities are emphasized. As Philip Curtin emphasizes in his study of economic changes in precolonial Africa, specifically Senegambia, the region where the transatlantic slave trade began: "Perhaps the most durable of all myths about precolonial Africa is the belief that it contained myriad, isolated economic units – 'subsistence economies,' where the village group if not each individual family actually produced all it consumed.[21] Examining the complexity of the commercial infrastructure and the material life that distinguished the economic world of the West African victim of the transatlantic slave trade proves otherwise.

SENEGAMBIAN TRADE

The Senegambia region, located in the extreme western part of the Sudan between the Senegal and Gambia rivers, includes modern Senegal, Gambia, Mauritania and the western part of Mali. The political structure in the Senegambia region during the transatlantic slave trade era, particularly from the late seventeenth century to the middle of the nineteenth century, was not inclusive of a single nation state, but rather somewhat distinct political entities were comprised of ethnically homogeneous populations. The dominant ethnic group included the Mende-speaking people, more commonly known as the Mandingo or Mandinka, although the Wolofs accounted for the largest of the ethnic groups in that trading zone in addition to the Fulani and the Serer. Before the seventeenth century, perhaps a third of all African victims of the Atlantic trade were shipped from Senegambian ports. Of Africans brought to the United States between 1690 and 1807, some 13.3 per cent of the total originated from Senegambia (see Table 12.2). By the eighteenth century, however, transatlantic slave trade exports from Senegambia gradually declined and several Africanists note, "that the only slave trade of consequence was *through* Sengambia, not *from* it."[22]

In precolonial Senegambia, trade and marketing were distinguished by the production of goods for both domestic and international markets, the use of currency for exchange, and commercial activities which included the participation of brokers and merchants. The Senegal and Gambia rivers provided the major trade transportation routes in the interregional trade from the Atlantic Coast to the interior. In addition to providing slaves for both the Arab and Atlantic markets, Senegambian commodities produced for trade included foodstuffs, cattle and cow-hides, cotton textiles, hides, beeswax, ivory, ostrich feathers, gum, salt, metals, including gold, iron, and copper. Ecologically specific products from Sengambia included cattle, horses, and gum from the northern region kola nuts from the south. The acadia tree was the source of gum, a high demand export not only in the growing European printing and textile industries, but also for pharmaceutical uses[23] (see Table 12.3).

Table 12.2 African geographic origins of American slaves, 1690–1807

African to from	*North America*[1]	*Total Percentages South Carolina 1733–1807*[2]	*Virginia 1710–1807*
Senegambia	13.3	19.5	14.9
Sierra Leone	5.5	6.8	5.3
Windward Coast	11.4	16.3	6.3
Gold Coast	15.9	13.3	16.0
Bight of Benin	4.3	1.6	*
Bight of Biafra	23.3	2.1	37.7
Angola/Congo	24.5	39.6	15.7
Mozambique/Madagascar	1.6	0.7	4.1
Unknown	0.2	–	–
	100.0	100.0	100.0

Source: 1 Curtin, *Atlantic Slave Trade*, p. 157; 2. Elizabeth Donnan, *Documents Illustrative of the History of the Slave Trade to America*, 4 vols (Carnegie Institution Publications No. 409, 1930–1935), 4: pp. 175–276, passim; Also, Michael B. Craton, "The African Background in Miller and Smith, eds. *Dictionary of Afro-American Slavery*, p. 12; Lovejoy, *Transformation in Slavery*, Melville J. Herskovits, *The Myth of the Negro Past*, pp. 46–53, and Ralph Austen, *African Economic History: Internal Development and External Dependency* (London: James Currey Ltd., 1987), p. 84.

Table 12.3 Senegambian exports to Europe, 1680–1830

Commodity	*Percentage of total exports 1680*	*1730*	*1780*	*1830*
Gold	5.0	7.0	0.2	3.0
Gum	8.0	9.4	11.0	71.8
Hides	8.5	–	–	8.1
Ivory	12.4	4.0	0.2	3.0
Slaves	55.3	64.3	86.5	1.9
Wax	10.8	14.5	1.1	9.9
Peanuts	–	–	–	2.6
Total	100.0	100.0	100.0	100.0

Source: Philip Curtin, *Economic Change in Precolonial Africa: Senegambia in the Era of the Slave Trade* (Madison: University of Wisconsin Press, 1975, pp. 336–7.

The regional and local trade, particularly in foodstuffs, was more extensive than the European trade, Curtin emphasizes, noting that: "Hundreds of tons of foodstuffs were marketed each year to supply incipient urban centers. Thousands of tons of foodstuffs were exchanged on the desert fringes, where both the value and quantity of the cereals exchanged for animal products were far greater than the gum trade that figures so largely in European accounts."[24] Caravans provided the means of transporting the commodities of the long-distance, overland interregional trade which extended westward from the Gambian or Senegal rivers to the Niger river bend as well as to the Atlantic coast.

Each caravan, "*coffle*" in Gambian English, had a leader, a saatigi (invariably a merchant) who initiated and organized the caravan. Village heads or state officials also initiated caravans, but unlike the merchants, seldom traveled with them. The saatigi profited when other merchants joined the caravan by providing services during the journey and assisting in the sale of goods at the market, charging a fee for his services. "In return for 20 to 30 per cent of the final sale price of the goods carried, the saatigi promised to see the owner and his goods through to the coast, to pay the duties and cost of provisions along the way, and to act as broker in dealing with the Europeans."[25] The large slave caravans often numbered from 600 to 800 slaves, usually with an equal number of guards, porters, wives, and officials.

The Senegambian saatigi comprised a very small class, most were Muslims, often clerics, but they were usually quite wealthy since they also traded in their own goods. Their trading practices extended back to the Sudanic empires of Ghana, Mali and Songhary. Over the centuries in precontact Sudanic West Africa, the Muslim merchant clerics established commercial centers not only throughout Senegambia but also along trade routes in West Africa. These trade centers became part of a trade diaspora network, known as jula communities, which in Senegal included primarily the Soinke and Jahaanke [Diakhanke] peoples, but were invariably multiethnic/racial in composition. Curtin described Diakhanke as "pioneers" of the overland east–west trade routes. And, in describing the efficiency of juula carvans and the importance of their trade network, Curtin attributes their commercial success, which lasted from 1600 to 1850, to "the accuracy, detail, and speed of commercial information," emphasizing that, "The assumption that African merchants simply wandered around until they found someone to buy their goods is part of the myth of a stagnant economy in precolonial Africa."[26]

Facilitating the transfer of commodities from seller to buyer required a monetized exchange media which included commodity money represented in Sengambia by cloth-currency, iron-bar currency, and cowries, each circulating in distinct, but often overlapping currency zones, and each with a recognized standard exchange rate. Increasingly, the circulation of silver dollars minted in France, in addition to other European currency, which circulated as a medium of exchange in Senegambia in the eighteenth century, forced a shift from bar prices and iron currency to coined metallic currency.[27]

Sengambian political authorities accumulated wealth from overland trade in several ways. First, they required payment for free passage of trade. The amount paid varied, based as it was on an assessed percentage of the value of goods in transit, usually, "one-tenth of all passing merchandise," or the equivalent in commodities currency or specie, gold or silver. Road tolls were also collected by the state, determined by the volume of trade, and ceremonial gifts to political authorities were required. European traders on the Atlantic coast were also subject to the same trade payments which were eventually formalized into treaties with explicit terms of payment in the form of customs duties for imports and ground rents, and with slave commodities, the coastal African states were paid indeminities for the return of escaped slaves. The political authorities in Senegambia, primarily non-Muslim, as were the precolonial Senegambian masses, regarded trade "as a convenient source of wealth and power," and consequently, "trade was controlled and taxed, while other special privileges, such as autonomy for merchant communities, were favors to be sold, not simply granted."[28]

Yet, it was their agricultural, rather than their trade expertise that made Senegambians invaluable as slaves in the Americas, notwithstanding that, as producers, they also participated in a commercial network that extended beyond their fields. Reviewing the multiethnic character of the population in Senegambia and their relation to commerce, Curtin notes that: "Neither Wolof, Sereer, nor Malinke of the lower Gambia had a strong commercial tradition." Still, production was for the market and the Senegambian political economy was tied to the trade diaspora from which their leaders profited.[29]

In two ways, then, in the Senegambian interior, from where many of the slave trade victims were taken, this population participated in the economy – as both producers and consumers. Most important, they lived in a commercial world distinguished by the Diakhanké business culture with its networks or trade diasporas. Thus, while most Senegambians were not professional traders, neither were they insulated from nor did they remain unaffected by the distinctive culture of the Diakhanké traders, which included "a combination of pacifism, avoidance of political power and wordly rule, devotion to Islamic teachings as a profession, and a similar devotion to commerce."[30]

The Diakhanké however were not the only African players in the Senegambian trade. By the eighteenth century, commercial activities on the Senegambian coast, usually the province of European traders and merchants, were relegated to Africans. Initially, these were the mixed race Afro-Portuguese or Luso-Africans, who traded on the Gambian river and who operated as brokers in the European trade. Some succeeded quite well, financially, in their business activities until the 1730s, which: "marked a peak of Afro-Portuguese wealth and power, and of prosperity for the Gambia trade as a whole."[31] By then, Senegambian coastal Africans began to usurp Afro-Europeans in Atlantic trade activities by assuming the duties of brokers. As the slave trade progressed, European reliance on the business acumen of West Africans increased. In discussing British withdrawal from their Senegambian coastal factory in the late eighteenth century, Curtin attributes it more to African commercial competence than to British defeat by the French in 1779, explaining: "the functions of broker age and bulking that the fort had once performed could now be done competently and at lower coast by a variety of African specialists."[32]

The expertise demonstrated by coastal Senegambians in trade and marketing cannot be attributed solely to their commercial relationships with the Europeans. Rather, similarities in trade practices had provided the initial basis for commercial relations which facilitated operation of the European-African international trade that had developed in Senegambia. It was the region where Europeans first established direct trade with West Africa and the extent to which they succeeded in trade in the Senegambian was based on the fact that they had capitalized on pre-existing African trade networks and business expertise.

UPPER GUINEA COAST TRADE

The precolonial Upper Guinea Coast, located southeast of Senegambia and west of Gold Coast Ghana, was a heavily forested region with numerous rivers. Today, it includes much of present-day Liberia, Sierra Leone, Guinea, and Guine–Bissau. As an historical region, the southeastern littoral of the Upper Guinea Coast was known as the Malaguetta [pepper], Grain, or Windward Coast. Except for Sierra Leone, there were few natural harbors that allowed docking by seafaring ships.

In his study of the Upper Guinea Coast, Walter Rodney emphasizes the extent to which new state formation took place in this region during the seventeenth and eighteenth centuries. Three kinds of states are identified. The commonly referred-to "stateless" society was organized communally without a coercive state superstructure and included the Dioala, Balante and Tenda peoples. At the opposite extreme were the "conquest states," which included the states of Malinke, Susu Serer, and Fulbe state of Futa Jallon. The most prevalent kind of political entity in the Upper Guinea Coastal Region, however, was the microstate, the "small and stratified" state, such as the Gola, Kissi, Bullom, Temne, Limba, and Sherbro states.

The principal ethnic groups in the Upper Guinea Coast Region were the Mankingas, Djolas, Papels Balantas, Beafadas, Djalonkes, Fulas, Susus, Limbas Temnes Kissis, Bullom, the Mende, or peripheral Mande. The Kru people, who lived on the coast near Ghana, however, were economically tied to the Upper Guinea Coast by their participation in the trade of that region, "sometimes acting as middlemen for the exchange of African and European goods, and sometimes trading on their own."[33]

Diversified commodity production, including mixed farming and livestock raising, took place on the Upper Guinea coast. However, rice cultivation was the principal agricultural activity. The Djolas specialized in wet [irrigated] rice cultivation and Rodney notes that a French official travelling through their territory in 1685 commented that "there was no house which did not have a rice nursery nearby, while along the river banks the landscape had been transformed in a pattern of causeways with rice plants appearing above the flooded fields."[34] The Balante, an ethnic group in Guinea Bissau, were also skilled in irrigated rice farming, "devising techniques, for drainage, desalination and flooding." Dry rice, communally cultivated, required clearing the forest by cutting and burning trees to prepare the ground for cultivation. After the seed was planted, fields were watered and weeded until harvesting. The process, known as itinerant rotation, took some nine months and was repeated again each year.[35]

Class and caste distinctions were more significant than state or ethnic tribal divisions in the Upper Guinea Coast region. Using the Papel people as an example, Rodney notes that seven distinct social classes existed with kings nobles and chiefs at the top ruling the mass of "plebians." Paramount in their access to and control of wealth was the landholding pattern that existed which, in one respect, was common to that of West and West Central Africa in that land could not be alienated to outsiders who had no ethnic affiliation to the state. Yet, unlike most states in precolonial Africa, Rodney emphasizes that among the Papel, "the regime of private property is firmly established."[36] Using their control of land as a base to wield political power, the Papel nobility appropriated the labor and commodity production of the masses in their wealth-seeking activities.

Rodney emphasizes that class distinctions were evident in the dress, ornamentation, housing and furnishings of the nobility. While the poor lived in houses with thatched roofs, the rich had homes made of brick and adobe, which were whitewashed, and built with special porches used for leisure and relaxation. Also, the homes of the nobility were tastefully decorated with well-made furniture. Moreover, among the Papel, Even control of communication was monpolized by the ruling classes of the Papel. A traveler in the Upper Guinea Coast in the late seventeenth century noted that only the nobility could own the *bombalon*, the telegraph drum, with a sounding range extending up to ten miles. Not only was the drum costly to produce, but "The messages were sent by specially trained players, and these had to be paid."[37]

The hierarchical social structure in the Upper Guinea Coast was also reflected in the organization of craftsmen into castes, "with the major crafts being the cloth workers, leather workers, and iron workers.)...[while] The *griots* or entertainers were held in relatively low social esteem....[and] "the lowest ranks comprised the farming population and the intrusive Fulani herdsmen."[38] The commercial and trading class was represented by the Dyula, a term also used in West Africa to mean a Mande-speaking itinerant trader. By the eighteenth century, however, the Fulani stood along with the Mande as the leading ethnic group in the Upper Guinea Coast. According to Rodney, the Fulani seized power and exerted control over the region by forging alliances with several Muslim ethnic groups – the Malinke, Susu, and Dyalonke – and also with the traders and craftsmen.[39]

The invasions of the Mane, a southern Mande-speaking people, from 1545 to 1606, profoundly affected all aspects of society in the Upper Guinea Coast, not only in the hierarchical structure, but also in warfare. By the early seventeenth century in Sierra Leone, the people in that area, in resisting the Manes, "had learnt to fight in formation, using squadrons of archers" and to use Mane entrenchments in their battle strategies, as well as Mane military strategies in planning encirclements and in breaking out of sieges.[40]

With its dominant Mande influence, the Upper Guinea Coast could be considered a culture zone and Rodney emphasizes: "The Mande nobility lived by an aristocratic militaristic ethnic, which of course precluded direct participation in production." He adds in discussing the royal princes – the nyancho – of Kabu, that: "It was unbefitting that a nyancho's hand should touch a hoe or that he should take up trade; and there was no other way for him to live except by taxes and plunder."[41]

The Manes also had an impact on the secret societies of Sierra Leone, particularly the powerful Poro society. The society was hierarchically organized, with the top people – "the inner council" – Serving as "the effective government in the chiefdoms." They assumed responsibilities for making state policies and expected full compliance under the laws which they made. In the early seventeenth century, the seriousness of the Poro society in carrying out its responsibilities resulted in the establishment of an educational institution, which Rodney refers to as the Poro "University". It was located near Cape Mount, and "Students spent four years there, during which time they were equipped to conserve the peace, and deal with homicides and revolts."[42] By the eighteenth century, some of the Afro-Europeans, particularly the leading traders who had established themselves as chiefs, gained membership and assumed leadership in the Poro Society.[43]

The Afro-European traders served primarily as middlemen, working as agents and brokers for the European trading companies. They also participated in local and regional trade along the rivers, including both slave and non-slave commodities, particularly rice, salt, and kola nuts.[44] Rodney notes the value placed on education by this Afro-European trader group, explaining that one European commented that the Afro-Europeans sought education so that they could learn to "read book to learn and be rogue so well as white man."[45] These were the mulattoes, Africans with Portuguese or English fathers and African mothers, and their descendants. They were described by one contemporary as mixed people who "call themselves Portingales, and some few of them seem the same; others of them are Molatoes, between black and white, but the most part as black as the natural inhabitants."[46]

In their commercial activities Rodney describes this group as being "dynamic as their Dyula counterparts." Mande influence, however, remained quite strong into the second half of the eighteenth century, particularly since "Islam made great inroads among the coastal ruling class..."[47] In Futa Djalon, political and military hegemony, along with educational opportunities, increased the receptivity of the ruling class to Islam. A European visitor in 1794, emphasized the economic advantage of converting to Islam stating: "Those who have been taught in their schools are succeeding to wealth and power in the neighboring countries, and carry with them a considerable proportion of that religion and laws."[48]

Through trade, both European and Islamic influences made an impact on the culture and material life in the Upper Guinea Coast; however, it was not only the coastal areas in the Upper Guinea region that were influenced by the European trade culture. Particularly during the eighteenth-century peak of the transatlantic slave trading era to Colonial America and with increased African participation in the slave trade, "the hinterland too had immensely strengthened ties with the Atlantic trading system, so that, paradoxically, even influences from the interior reflected contacts with Europeans."[49]

In the late eighteenth century, the Upper Guinea Coast, absorbed another population wave in the area of modern day Sierra Leone which continued well into the nineteenth century. In 1787, the African repatriation movement began with the settlement of some 300 New World Africans. Most had left North America with the British after the American Revolution and had settled in London but were forced out of the country. England had purchased a twenty mile strip from the Temne for their settlement. A high mortality rate and Temne attacks reduced their numbers, but in 1792, when Freetown was founded, some one thousand repatriates from Nova Scotia were settled in Sierra Leone. Then in 1800, five hundred African-Jamaicans, known as maroons, were also settled in Freetown. They were joined by other liberated Africans from various parts of West and West Central Africa. Eventually repatriates became known as Creoles and would exercise a decisive influence on trade in Sierra Leone as would the African-Americans who settled in Liberia in the nineteenth century.[50]

THE GOLD COAST

The Gold Coast, present-day Ghana, was the third largest exporter of slaves to the United States. Of the total number of Africans exiled to this country, 15.9 per cent were from this region. The Akan comprised the principal ethnic group, and Gold Coast boundaries were almost synonymous with Akan country.[51] Ivor Wilks states that the dominant theme that gives unity to the history of the Gold Coasts is "the successive emergence of ever larger state systems, transcending local 'tribal' particularism, establishing a structure of authority and maintaining a rule of law over increasingly wide areas, and, by the encouragement of production and trade, seeking to maximise economic benefits."[52] In the seventeenth century the Gold Coast expansionist states of Denkyira, Akyem, and Akwamu, had established political and economic hegemony over the western, central, and eastern sections of Akan country with the Ashanti gaining dominance in the eighteenth century.

Ray A. Kea, in his impressive study of the Gold Coast, provides one of the most extensive analyses of any of the West African and West Central African regions during the transatlantic slave trading era. According to Kea, by the beginning of the eighteenth century almost 25 per cent of the Gold Coast was urbanized, with towns having an average population of 4,000 in both the inland and coastal districts. The towns of Mankessim, Agona, and Great Accra "may have had between 10,000 and 20,000 inhabitants." The Accra state, before its conquest and depopulation, between 1677 and 1681, was believed to have had a population exceeding 120,000. Of the coastal towns, Elmina was the largest, growing from 3,000 in 1621, to 20,000 by 1682. Until 1702, epidemics and wars resulted in depopulation, but by 1709. Elmina emerged as "the most populous port on the coast."[53]

Kea estimates that most urban places covered one square mile, even in the forest states. Towns were divided into quarters or wards, averaging from two to seventy-seven in each and "a few places had as many as 177 wards." Invariably district capitals were larger. Kea cites the Akwamu capital of Nyanaose which until 1730, "was nine miles long and about half a mile wide..."

Urban life on the Gold Coast was shaped by the location of numerous inns, "dancing houses," prostitution, and what Kea describes as "occupational corporations or guilds-artisan guilds, military guilds, and merchant broker guilds." A large number of craftsmen were also present. For example, in the port town of Amanfro in the late seventeenth century, the most numerous craftsmen were blacksmiths and goldsmiths, along with "hat and cap makers, mat makers, carpenters, bark clothmakers, and ivory carvers and wood carvers."[54]

The distinguishing features of Gold Coast urban life, were "multi-functionality" and "socio-economic heterogeneity," with the existence of three social classes: 1 the governing classes; 2 free and bonded commoners; and 3 slaves. In the coastal towns the upper class and their retinue of servants comprised 30 per cent of the population. The poor but free commoners comprised from 10 to 40 per cent, a figure Kea based on "the rather extensive system of public relief which was used to maintain indigent individuals and families."[55] The rest were free and somewhat prosperous.

In state capitals, located five to twenty miles inland, the administrative upper class and their servants comprised some 60 per cent of the population with other occupational groups including, "free commoners such as craftsmen organized in guilds, day laborers, market hawkers, and the like." The income of the upper and middle classes in the state capitals was "derived from farms worked by slaves and peasant corvée labor."[56] In addition to the wealthy brokers and merchants, the coastal and subcoastal towns and

Table 12.4 Gold Coast town occupations in the seventeenth century

Day laborers	Masons
Carpenters	Brick-layers
Blacksmiths	Goldsmiths
Bricklayers	Coopers
Stone cutters	Hammock carriers
Potters	Mat makers
Hat and cap makers	Thatchers
Wood cutters	Fishermen
Canoe-men	Ferrymen
Pilots	Woodcutters
Charcoal burners	Limemakers
Common soldiers	Hawkers
Market sellers	Bead makers
Water carriers	Water sellers
Low-ranking priests	Priestesses
Astrologers	Diviners
Doctors	Professional grave diggers

Source: Compiled from, Ray A. Kea, *Settlement Trade and Politics in the Seventeenth-Century Gold Coast*, (Baltimore: Johns Hopkins University Press, 1982 pp. 41, 308–10)

villages of the Gold Coast included the common people who worked in a variety of occupations in the seventeenth centuries (see Table 12.4) These were all wage-earning urban occupations paid in dambas in gold.

"The development of urban wage labor was linked to the trading classes."[57] Skilled craftsmen had assistants and apprentices, while the unskilled workers increased their limited incomes by working several jobs. Slaves also worked in the above occupations but were not paid. When hired out, their wages were paid to their owners. Additionally, some people worked in mines and served as porters in the caravans as well as slave overseers on the Gold Coast in the seventeenth century.

Large towns and their hinterland villages and hamlets were tied together by markets and Kea notes that many settlements were "specialized craft villages inhabited by potters, smiths, leather workers, workers in ivory and wood, canoe builders…" Other places specialized in salt production or livestock raising. These specialized villages and hamlets cannot be considered agrarian; rather, "All of them were characterized by production for the market, and their existence was necessarily predicated on widespread peasant market production."[58] Farm commodities were obtained from farming communities in the outlying agricultural areas or were imported. Kea distinguishes between peasant marketing of surplus and craftsmen who were specifically commodity producers.[59] Kea's occupational listing for the coastal towns extends beyond those found in the interior towns.

Regional settlements of Gold Coast towns, villages and rural areas did not exist in isolation from one another. Within this structure existed a hierarchy of marketing centers. As Kea said in explaining the multifunctional character of Gold Coast markets: "The commercial hierarchy implies the existence of trading towns, marketing activities, and the collection and distribution of commodities, money merchant capital, and the like."[60] In the interior or interregional trade, the leading trading peoples of West Africa who traveled to the Asante hinterland were the: Hausa from the east, the Mossi from the north and the Mande–Dyula from the West; i.e. the Middle Niger. With these groups, Arhin emphasize that trade in the Gold Coast went beyond simple commodity exchanges: "It will be seen that trading in the Asante hinterland had, indeed, reached the commercial stage.... For the Hausa, Mande and Mossi caravan traders, trading meant more than expeditions to acquire objects of use: its object was profit."[61]

Yet, by the mid-eighteenth century, a prevailing European consensus regarding the commercial culture of the Gold Coast was already in circulation with the emphasis being that this region of Africa was undeveloped and that its people lacked the capacity for any economic activity other than unskilled agricultural labor. It was a view expressed in a 1763 pamphlet which said: "The Gold Coast, Popo and Whidah Negroes are born in a part of Africa which is very barren. [Used to hard work to survive] they live better in general in our plantations; and they are always ready, on arrival there, to go to the hard work necessary in planting and manufacturing the sugar cane."[62]

Obviously, this was not the case. Kea's analysis of the political economy of the Gold Coast, then, is particularly important for underscoring not only the complexity of the commercial culture that existed in precolonial West Africa, but also the extent to which plantation slavery in America represented severe material deprivations and loss of economic opportunity. Interestingly, too, the urban occupational distribution of Gold Coast Africans in the seventeenth century parallels that of urban slave activities in seventeenth- and eighteenth-century Colonial America; although, from popular historical accounts, the general impression is that only in America did Africans gain these skills.

Moreover, while gold and slaves distinguished the Gold Coast export and import commodity trade with the Europeans, as Daaku emphasizes in his discussion of precolonial Akan trading patterns: "The trade in gold, guns, and slaves, the principal items in the transatlantic trade with the Gold Coast (Ghana) had long been preceded by the trans-Saharan trade in gold, kola nuts, and salt."[63]

THE BIGHT OF BENIN

This region includes modern day Togo, the southern part of the People's Republic of Benin, (Dahomey until 1975), and Western Nigeria. In precolonial Africa, the Bight of Benin encompassed the region from the Volta River to the Benin River, which extends to the Lagos river. Europeans referred to the core of the region as the Slave Coast. Of Africans exiled to the Americas, almost 20 per cent, some two million, originated from the Bight of Benin. Of the total number of Africans exported to the United States, only 4.3 per cent, 500,000, originated from the Bight of Benin. Of the ethnic origins of slaves exported from Bight of Benin, the Aja, which included the Fon, represented the largest number followed by the Yoruba. Both groups, which share common cultural similarities in language, customs and political and economic systems, comprised 90 per cent of Africans sold from this region.[64]

In the eighteenth century, the principal nation in the Bight of Benin was Dahomey which from 1727 to 1892 extended 200 miles from north to south and one hundred miles from east to west. Oyo a Yoruba inland state, however, was also very powerful, even subduing Dahomey in securing tribute in goods, money and slaves. Oyo was the earliest of these kingdoms and it covered a greater area than did Benin or Dahomey.[65] Along with Dahomey, the kingdoms of Oyo and Benin comprised a culture zone, Yorubaland.[66]

By the late seventeenth century Dahomey, the principal state and the largest kingdom in the Bight of Benin had: "become populous, had developed sizeable states, and had an economic organization which can be characterized as including both familial and commodity exchange modes of production, with a mercantile system linking it to other economies."[67] In his discussion of the origin of the Dahomey economic structure, as it developed prior to and independent of European contact, Manning postulates its development with the familial mode of production – self-sufficient families producing mainly for themselves. The commodity exchange sector participated in the slave trade, by selling slaves and by buying slaves for integration into families.[68] While slave exportation dominated the eighteenth century Dahomean economy, agricultural production through the familial mode of production was the long-standing basis of the economy with farm commodities produced for home consumption and the market.[69]

Major field crops included maize, manioc, yams, millet, and beans. Crop rotation was practiced. Men did the heavy field work; women planted, weeded and harvested. Tree crops, coconuts, pineapples, and oranges, were also extensive. Poultry raising included chickens, ducks, and guinea fowl. Pigs, goats, sheep and cattle were raised, with extensive fishing on the coast. Agricultural surplus, led to a commodity exchange mode of production and the development of markets for the exchange or sale of surplus. Expansive trading activities eventually led to a commodity currency for as Manning explains in discussing the economy and trade and marketing patterns in precolonial Dahomey: "The producers were tied together through a network of local markets, and used cowries as currency. The local markets were tied to more distant regions through caravans on the land and through large canoes on the lagoons and along the coast."

The development of local markets also encouraged population concentration, while the necessity for coherence in trade and marketing practices encouraged the development of an authority accepted by participants in the economy to mediate trade practices. Eventually local markets, which served as exchange centers for two or three villages, were linked to long distance markets.[70] Trade in Dahomey took place along the coast and interior water routes or along major trade routes and Manning said: "roads, which were well-worn footpaths, were arranged in a conventional network used by caravans, with clear stopping points, provisions and markets along the way." Regional trade was greater in some areas than others, proceeding either north and south in the east and western parts of Dahomey but "the most heavily travelled route, however, was the east–west route of the coastal lagoons."[71]

With participation in the slave trade, as Manning notes in his discussion of Dahomey markets: "The mercantile system tied local markets to each other and to other West African and Trans-Atlantic markets."[72] Dahomey's wealth from trade was substantial, even into the early twentieth century. The efficiency of the familial and commodity modes of production was such that Manning emphasizes: "In sum, seventeenth-century society resembled nineteenth- or even twentieth-century society in many details."[73]

In the origin of its economy and patterns of trade and marketing, Manning subscribes to the "early growth" thesis, as opposed to the "late growth" thesis, which suggests that the structure of Dahomey's political economy took shape only after European contact.[74] Within the context of precontact trade, Manning posits that "Dahomey developed its economic and social system independent of European contact."[75] Ultimately European colonization, exploitative commodity appropriation and destructive societal transformations, forced a virtual collapse of Dahomey's agrarian sector: as Manning notes, "the Peoples Republic of Benin is now listed among the world's poorest nations, with a 1974 per capita income of $120."[76]

THE BIGHT OF BIAFRA

By 1740, the Bight of Biafra, which includes the Niger Delta (formerly the Oil Rivers), had became the major slave exporter to the Americas.[77] And, with 23.3 per cent of the total number of Africans exiled to the United States from the Bight of Biafra, this region ranked second in the forced displacement of Africans to this nation. The mid-eighteenth century marked the high point of the transatlantic slave trade and, as the preeminent Nigerian scholar Kenneth Onwuka Dike notes, Iboland in the Bight of Biafra "supplied the greater part of the slaves shipped to the New World from the bights of Benin and Biafra."[78] Rodney states other victims from the Bight of Biafra interior were taken from Ibibio country and the Cameroun highlands.[79]

The Niger Delta, the low country of the Nigerian coastal plain, an area some 270 miles along the Atlantic coast and 120 miles inland, today includes Eastern Nigeria and Cameroon. The region is divided in two sections, north and south, with a series of navigable waterways, "It was as navigable waterways that the rivers of the Niger Delta become so important in the economic history of modern Nigeria...[linking]... not only places in the Delta but towns and villages along the 2,600 miles of the Niger Valley."[80] Large riverboats and canoes were used to transport both slaves and food from the densely populated Ibo hinterland in the interior to the Atlantic coast. Slaves were brought to the coast from the hinterland on the major rivers and their tributaries that formed the delta of the Niger river and the mouth of the Cross River.

These were the commercial highways of the Niger Delta. And, just as the precontact trans-Saharan trade with the Arabs saw the rise of internationally known cities such as Timbuktu, Jenne, and Goa on the Niger Bend, in the Niger Delta the Atlantic slave trade marked the new "frontier of opportunity" for the Bight of Biafra. Dike emphasizes that the commercial development of Lagos, Accra, Dahomey, and the Delta states "must be attributed to the development of maritime commerce."[81] Still, in the Bight of Biafra, unlike other African slave-trading regions, European and American slave traders lived on their ships instead of at coastal forts or factories. Niger Delta coastal rulers in the Bight of Biafra allowed only for the construction of warehouses, on the coast, which were used as holding pens for the victims until ships were available for transatlantic transport; other than that exception Europeans "had no foothold on African territory."[82]

The "House" or "Canoe" System, a corporate commercial organizational structure that developed in the Niger Delta, expedited the movement of Africans from the interior of the Bight of Biafra to the coast for their sale to the white slave traders. In assessing the magnitude of its efficiency in meeting the demands of the transatlantic slave market, Curtin indicates that the Bight of Biafra "supplied far more slaves per mile of coast or square mile of economic hinterland than any other part of eighteenth-century Africa."[83] Warfare was not the primary method for securing slaves in the Niger Delta and Cross River regions of the Bight of Biafra for sale to the Europeans, rather "Raiding, kidnapping, judicial conviction, and religously-sanctioned enslavement were the main sources."[84]

Trade and commerce ranked foremost as the basis of state organization in the Bight of Biafra, and the political structure that existed in the eighteenth century facilitated the extensive slave trade that developed in that region. The political system that distinguished the Niger Delta was the city-state. Until the late seventeenth century, independent villages governed by a chief and council, consisting of kinship elders, represented the prominent form of political organization in the Bight of Biafra. The pre-European contact

Bight of Biafra village states, however, were not primitive, isolated, self-sufficient societies.

The volume of trade before contact with the Europeans in the Bight of Biafra encouraged the development of towns on the Niger Delta coast and the Cross river estuary for Curtin adds: "By 1500, one of the villages at the lower fringe of the Delta was reported to have a population of 2,000 people and an active commerce through the system of creeks and lagoons."[85] He makes the point that Oporto, Portugal's second largest city in 1500 had only 8,000 people. Walter Rodney, too, emphasizes the continuity of town development in the Niger Delta and notes that by the end of the eighteenth century city-states in this region of the Bight of Biafra were, "the end-products of an indigenous process which predated significant foreign involvement and which persisted in the era of the foreign trade."[86]

The western delta was the site of the early canoe-building industry. Salt-making was also a prominent industry on the Niger Delta and was a valuable commodity in the north–south land trade, which along with fish was traded for foodstuff and livestock produced in the agricultural hinterland.[87] As the Atlantic slave trade escalated, and in response to the virtually inexhaustible demands of the European and American slavers, the Niger Delta village-states in the Bight of Biafra reorganized their political structure, which Basil Davidson compares to the city-state system of ancient Greece explaining: "Some, like ancient Athens were Republic. Others, like Sparta, were monarchies."[88]

The city-states that established monarchies also established royal lineages which were based in major trading port towns, including Bonny, Nembe or Brass, and Kalabari or New Calabar.[89] Under each political system, notwithstanding, the socio-economic and political administrative structure was known as the "House System," which exceeded in organizational hierarchy the extended family kinship system. The commercial success of the "House System," particularly in meeting the demands of the Atlantic slave trade, accelerated the development of this distinctive form of business organization. "The House may be seen as a kind of cooperative trading company based not so much on kinship as on commercial association between the head of a dominant family, his relatives and trading assistants, and all their followers and slaves."[90]

The House System or "canoe houses" was not only a trading unit, but also the foundation of a military organization. Its strength was enhanced by acculturating and assimilating slaves, a process, which was "designed to turn a foreign slave into a member of his community and kin to all other members of the House." Newly acculturated members of a "House" joined in trading activities which were often associated with military expeditions. Alagoa, recounting the European slave trader John Barbot's description of the commercial expeditions of these trading canoes in the first half of the seventeenth century, emphasized that "They carried javelins and shields for defence, with twenty paddlers, and were capable of carrying seventy to eighty warriors."[91] Before the end of the seventeenth century, "cannon were to be mounted on trade canoes and the warriors supplied with firearms."[92] With the expansion of trade, the canoes were made even larger and carried well over a hundred people in addition to trade commodities.

The two most prominent Niger Delta city-states and also the principal slave-trading ports were the Ijo kingdoms of Kalabari (New Calabar) and Bonny, which was "Africa's greatest slave mart." Both had origins that date to the fourteenth century, and both provide spectacular examples of the commercial success of the House System. From the late seventeenth to the end of the nineteenth century, Bonny was ruled by the Royal House of Pepples. Under King Pepple/Perekule, the commercial success of the House System marked the era of his reign in the eighteenth century as the "golden age" in the Bonny oral tradition.[93] "Bonny had 3,000 residents on its tiny island site, with many more on plantations and trading colonies (some of which were larger than Bonny itself)."[94] The trading colonies established by the Kingdom of Bonny were located inland in the Bight of Biafra.

In the eighteenth century, the economic history of the Bight of Biafra was distinguished by interior, local and regional trade diasporas, commercial trade relations that existed between the Niger Delta coastal states, and trade with the Europeans and American slavers. While Bonny and Calabar controlled the coastal trade, there were two major interior trading systems which dominated in the Bight of Biafra: the Awka System and the Arochuku system. The Awka people in Ibo land, who were both agriculturalists and craftsmen, were long-distance traders who carried their goods from market to market. Some of them were also priests of the Agbala deity whose reputations in these areas gave them welcome access to regional markets and enhanced their success as tradesmen and craftsmen. "These capacities were useful in establishing markets for their wares and services as skilled craftsmen – blacksmiths and carvers, and as in land pedlars [sic] of luxury items, notably ivory and coral beads. . . . "[95]

The Aro Trade system was associated with the Arochuku people, and in his discussions of markets in Iboland, Ukwu emphasizes that it was "the most famous trading community in Iboland."[96] While their origins date back to the fourteenth century, unlike the Awka people they capitalized on the Atlantic slave trade to enhance their commercial operations. Dike emphasized that the Arochuka people supplied the greater part of the slaves shipped to the New World from the both the bights of Benin and Biafra.[97] Throughout the eighteenth century, the Arochuku people controlled trade in Iboland. Despite their economic influence, their commercial agenda did not include attempts to establish political hegemony over Iboland. Indeed the Aro homeland was itself politically segmented, including people of Akpa, Igbo, and Ibibio origin. Alagoa attributes the success of the Aro system to "the coincidence of the interests of all its members abroad and at home"[98]

The Arochuku people used every possible means and method to establish economic hegemony over the hinterland trade and emerged as the "economic dictators of the hinterland."[99] The supremacy in trade of the Arochuku people can be attributed to their oracle, their trade diasporas, and "a system of military alliances and the extensive use of mercenary soldiers."[100] Dike also notes that the town of Aro achieved trade dominance in the interior region of the Bight of Biafra in part because of its military strength whereby it: "exercised what amounted to a monopoly of trade up and down the Niger valley...The entire trade of the Niger was held up at will by her war-canoes armed with brass and iron cannon."[101]

Also, the Arochuku people planned and organized their trading expeditions by establishing trade diasporas which dominated the inland markets. At least ninety-eight trade diasporas identified as Arochuku were established in the seventeenth century. As part of their strategy to enhance the success of their trading operations, the Arochuku people claimed that the oracle Aro Chuku, who "was universally respected and feared throughout Iboland," resided in their territory, that they were divinely guided and protected by this oracle, and that their trade colonies were divinely ordained. As a result, according to Dike, the Arochuku "held a privileged position throughout the land, erecting what amounted to a theocratic state over eastern Nigeria." Dike compares Arochuku state-building to the Greeks whose colonization expeditions were: "largely directed by the priests of the Delphic Oracle."[102]

However, in their drive for commercial supremacy in the Bight of Biafra hinterland, the success of the Aro system can be attributed to more than divine protection. In their trade diasporas and at local and regional markets, the Arochuku people, in addition to their commercial activities, acted as spies, assessing the strength of their business competitors. Subsequently they used their wealth to hire mercenaries to expand their political and economic hegemony over Iboland. Perhaps the guiding philosophy that distinguishes the business culture of the Arochuku people can be seen in a proverb of the Igbo people of Southeast Nigeria. In a discussion entitled, "Manipulating His World," Victor Uchendu said: "If you ask the Igbo why he believes that the world should be manipulated, he will reply 'The world is a marketplace and it is subject to bargain.'"[103]

By the end of the eighteenth century, at least 75 per cent of slaves sold at Bonny came from the Aro hinterland. As Dike explains, "The Aros became the middlemen of the hinterland trade."[104]

The Arochuku also traded with the Efik state of Calabar on the Cross River, which consisted of four trading towns. Calabar was the slave distribution center east of the Niger Delta in the Bight of Biafra. The Ibibio represented the largest group in this area and, based on their language, their place of origin was "likely to be the Benue valley or from the Bantu regions of Central Africa."[105]

The Niger Delta states and the Efik states differed in their political social and economic structures. Small independent microstates, governed by a chief and council distinguished the Efik States at Old Calabar. Their common bond was the Egbo secret society which for all practical purposes provided the ultimate legislative, executive, and judicial functions for the Efik States. Davidson describes the political structure of the Efik State of Calibar as "rule by a commercial oligarchy."[106] Only the ruling classes were eligible for membership in the Egbo society because, "the nobility felt the need for a bond of union, a supreme authority for enforcing peace among equals and rivals, and for safeguarding the interest and privileges of the nobility." Dike adds that "It seemed especially designed to keep women, slaves, and the masses of the population in subjection."[107] Unlike the Niger Delta, slaves in the Efik states were not assimilated, according to Alagoa who said: "Slaves were not integrated into the lineage and political system. Mostly kept separate on farms, they had no hope whatever of attaining positions of political power or social leadership."[108]

Trade commodities produced in the Bight of Biafra were sold or exchanged at local, regional and international markets. In Iboland, there were four-day and eight-day markets where exchanges were made based on surplus and specialization. Certain interior towns specialized in specific craft manufacturing – iron-working, blacksmithing, woodcarving and pottery-making – while the coastal Niger Delta and Cross River states traded European goods, including guns, in the interregional exchange, controlled by the Awka and Aruchuku middlemen in the interior. Bitter competition existed among the Niger Delta states, particularly Bonny and New Calabar, for both access to, and control of, interior markets. By 1790 Bonny emerged as the most powerful state after destroying New Calabar which by the early nineteenth century had regained its independence.

Today, among the modern countries in the Bight of Biafra, Nigeria, with oil resources that could provide a source of capital for development, has the most advantageous chance for success in the neocolonial world. Moreover, the Nigerian propensity for trade and marketing is known worldwide, although not always in a favorable light. In a 1993 trip to Hong Kong, several people mentioned to me that scarcely a week goes by in which some business "scam" by Nigerians is not reported in the newspapers of that British colony.

ANGOLA–CONGO

Combined, these two regions in West Central Africa sold some 100,000 or almost 24.5 per cent of the total African victims in the slave trade to the United States. In the transatlantic slave trade, as a whole, however, 40 per cent of all Africans brought to the New World, some 4,000,000 originated from West Central Africa, i.e., from Congo and Angola; and, in the eighteenth century alone over a million Africans were shipped from West Central Africa.[109] In the period from 1701–1810, Africans from Congo and Angola represented 41 per cent of the transatlantic slave trade victims, as compared to some 59 per cent from West Africa. In the United States, however, the great majority of Africans, some 73.5 per cent of the total slave imports during this period, were from West Africa.

Joseph Miller points to the extensive geographic region of West Central Africa, which he indicates is "larger than the United States east of the Mississippi River, and five times the territory of France."[110] In the early sixteenth century the Congo, located north of the Zaire [Congo] river, was referred to as Bakongo. Ndongo, located south and east of the Congo river was called Angola by the Portuguese. On the Atlantic coast, the region stretches almost one thousand miles south from Cape Lopez at the mouth of the Ogowe River, which flows just south of the Equator, to the Kunene river not far from the Kalahari Desert. Even into the eighteenth century, according to the French slave trader Degrandpre, when references were made to Angola it included "the whole country situated between Cape Lopez and Benguela."[111] Along the Atlantic coast, Congo extended some 460 miles, from Cape Lopez beyond the mouth of the Zaire river to Luanda Bay; whereas, Angola stretched south beyond the Zaire river, from the port of Ambriz south to the port of Benguela, a leading slave port.

From 1483 to the late sixteenth century, Portuguese settlement and influence in West Central Africa, its relative evangelical success, and the use of its armies in the interior, distinguished this region from the slave trading regions in precolonial West Africa. The Guinea states in West Africa controlled the slave trade in their respective regions by restricting the European presence to the coast. In West Central Africa, the slave trade was based on African-European collaboration and cupidity. As David Birmingham explains, for over a century the Portuguese insinuated themselves in the commercial structure of that region and he emphasizes: "This situation, in which profit was derived from a very small amount of capital and a rather larger amount of entrepreneurial skill, was often to be repeated in the heyday of the colonial period four hundred years later."[112]

During the seventeenth and eighteenth centuries, however, the Portuguese commercial challenge was successfully met not only by Angolan military resistance, but even more by sophisticated trade barriers. Birmingham credits the "commercial acumen" of West Central African entrepreneurs, who controlled the Angolan trade, with the failure of the Portuguese to break the African trade barriers and emphasizes that "These skills were probably rooted in a long tradition of growing trade specialization and showed themselves capable of adapting to changing economic conditions over several centuries."[113]

By the eighteenth century several major states in West Central Africa figured prominently in the transatlantic slave trade. In the Congo, the coastal kingdom of Loango, located north of the Zaire river, had emerged as the most important state in that region by the sixteenth century. Agriculture was the basis of its economy. However, trade and marketing, contributed to its development as the major state in the Congo in the seventeenth and eighteenth centuries. Its growth "must have been accompanied by considerable economic expansion and specialization."[114]

From the 1570s to 1650s, Ivory, palm cloth, redwood, animal skins, elephant tails and copper were exchanged for European cloth, rugs, mirrors, and beads. These goods were the principal commodities in the local and regional trade that existed before the Portuguese.[115] A 1591 description of the long-standing market at Buali, Loango's capital provided the following information: "there is a great market every day, and it doth begin at twelve of the clock. Here there is a great store of palm-cloths of sundry sorts, which is their merchandizes; and a great store of victuals, flesh, hens, wine, oil, and corn. Here is also very fine logwood, which they use to dye withall…and molangos [bracelets] of copper…."[116] Martin explains that in Loango, copper, in the form of jewelry, was a sign of wealth, that ivory was also used for making jewelry in addition to musical instruments and eating utensils, and that redwood was used for making dye and cosmetics. Palm cloth served as the principal medium of exchange.

Long-distance trade and craft specialization, coppersmiths, ivory carvers, redwood processers and raphia or palm cloth weavers accounted for the diversity of commodities sold in the Loango markets. The Vili also controlled the mining, smelting, and transport of copper sold in Loango. The Europeans consequently tapped into a highly organized complex commercial structure when they initiated trade in Loango. Moreover, as Martin emphasizes in discussing the business acumen of the Loango merchants and the trade network which existed when the Dutch began trading with the Vili "by 1642 the Vili traders had won a reputation among the Dutch as being skilled men of business who could always remain calm in a situation where there was a profit to be made."[117]

Trade with the Dutch began in the mid-seventeenth century and ivory was the principal commodity obtained from the Vili until the 1660s when Loango's trade in slaves with the Europeans escalated and eventually exceeded in volume previous trade items. Slave exports increased annually from 6,000 a year in the mid-1660s to some 14,000 a year a century later. From 1765 to 1790, slave exports averaged from 14,000 to 18,000 annually, accounting for a maximum of 360,000 in that twenty year period from the Loango Coast.

The Loango coast also included the kingdoms of Kakongo with Malemba as its principal port, and Ngogyo with Cabinda as its principal port, which by the mid-eighteenth century had supplanted Loango Bay, the principal port for Loango, as the leaders in the slave trade. According to Wallace, the veteran French slave trader of more than thirty years in the Congo,

Degrandpre, "suggests that the traders of Loango, Kakongo, and Ngoyo were both exploiting old trade-routes used in the copper and ivory trade in the sixteenth and seventeenth centuries, and also developing new trade routes."

By the eighteenth century, guns were the principal items of exchange for slaves in Loango in their trade with the Dutch, French, and the English. Wallace estimates that, with three guns exchanged for every slave an average of 50,000 guns entered Loango from the mideighteenth century on.[118]

Decline in the slave trade eventually destroyed the power of Loango and resulted in the loss of much of its territory, and changed its social, political and economic infrastructure. Wealth obtained from participation in the slave trade, as opposed to inherited position determined a state's and an individual's status. There were no limits to who could participate. The nobility entered the trade as merchants, and "common people found new opportunities open to those with business acumen. Even slaves were able to enrich themselves.... Technically, a man might remain a slave but he was protected by his new wealth."[119] Moreover, in the political arena, "new-type" politicians, whose wealth was obtained from the slave trade, used their power to claim authority along with the monarchy and the nobility. Reliance on the slave trade as the basis of the economy and political power eventually resulted in the disintegration of the Luango kingdom in the nineteenth century, a result, in part, of the American and British cessation of the transatlantic slave trade in 1807 and economic and political changes in Europe.

When the Portuguese made their initial forays in West Central Africa in the late fifteenth century, Loango was only one of several small coastal principalities in the Congo. The Kongo kingdom was ruled by the Nzinga dynasty. Portuguese interference in the political affairs of state and collusion with the enemies of the Nzinga, concomitant with subversive intrigues of the Catholic church, eventually lead to the virtual disintegration of the Kongo kingdom as a commercial power by the eighteenth century.[120]

In the Kongo kingdom, commercial exploitation was the primary goal of the Portuguese and was achieved by providing military assistance, while converting the ruling family to Catholicism. Much to their credit, the Kongo kings tried to oust the Portuguese, but they failed. King Alvaro III (1614–22) attempted, although unsuccessfully, to counter the western threat to his sovereignty by seeking technical assistance from Portugal and Spain, but "smiths, masons and craftsmen were all refus-ed lest he build strategic fortifications against Portuguese military intervention."[121] In the seventeenth century, Portuguese strategy to break the power and the influence of the Kongo kingdom included providing military aid to other West Central African states.

A complex economic system in the kingdom of the Kongo was in place before Portuguese instrusion, as seen in the market structure and in trading practices. Both local and regional trade took place and the merchants and traders exercised considerable business acumen in their commercial transactions. Consequently, when international trade with the Portuguese began it only "stimulated talents already well trained and commercial mechanisms already in effect."[122] In reference to a 1595 description of Kongo merchants and traders in *Historia do Reino do Congo* Balandier explains that the general consensus of European merchants was that "They give evidence of good judgment, particularly in business. They cheat astutely." Moreover, slaves figured prominently as participants in both local and regional trade. The rich and powerful owned slaves captured in war or obtained through purchase and assigned them to participate in the markets as merchants where, according to the same 1595 source, slaves would "buy and sell according to their master's orders." Slaves also organized the long distance trade caravans.[123]

While agriculture was the basis of the economy, and the people of the Kongo were skilled agriculturalists the commercial structure in trade and marketing was also strengthened by craft specialization, particularly ironmaking. Balandier emphasizes the extensive ironworking industry in the Kongo with its numerous blacksmith shops that produced various domestic pieces in addition to weapons. Copper mining and forging also existed. Other crafts included pottery, woodcarving, leathermaking, basketry, weaving, and textile art, one of the major industries in the Kongo.

Notwithstanding the complexity of their economy, Angolan intrusions, civil wars, internal disorders, and external mercenary attacks all contributed to Portuguese success in destroying the Kongo kingdom. In a series of wars which took place in the 1600s between Kongo and Angola, the Portuguese provided military assistance to Angola. They also hired the Jaga or Imbangala from the Ovimbundu highlands in the south of Angola as mercenaries to help defeat the Kongo kingdom and to destoy its dominance in the slave trade. Known for their cruelty, the "total war" tactics of the Jaga were feared throughout West Central Africa. By 1620, according to Curtin, "Jaga had come to mean 'savage, cannibal, inhuman barbarian.'"[124] In addition to using the Jaga as mercenaries, the Portuguese provided military assistance to dissident nobles and greedy in transigent merchants in the Kongo. After 1678, according to Fyfe, "the kingdom virtually disintegrated."[125]

By the eighteenth century, while the Vili people of Loango had gained control of the Congo slave trade, the Angolan capital of Luanda had emerged as the principal shipping point for slaves from West Central Africa. The extensiveness of the trade at Luanda and its complex commercial structure led Miller to describe Angola's capital as "virtually the only port on the entire coast that functioned entirely within the capitalist economy of the Atlantic."[126] In Angola, Luanda's importance as a slave port, however, declined in the eighteenth century when its hinterland came under control of Loango to the north and Benguela in the south.

Before Portuguese intrusion in Angola, salt, was perhaps the most important trade commodity the principal standard of currency, and it "probably formed the basis of an important commercial system."[127] It was also the principal trade commodity that initially attracted the Portuguese.

Export trade with the Portuguese and other Europeans, however, included beeswax, cattle hides, copper, camwood and other tropical commodities in exchange for European and Asian textiles, which constituted 50 per cent of Angolan imports. Alcohol, wine, brandy, gin, and Brazilian rum comprised 20 per cent of Angolan imports; guns and powder comprised another 10 per cent with the remaining imports consisting of miscellaneous items such as finished metal products.[128] In Angola, specialized markets existed and goods were exchanged either by barter or on a monetized basis. Eventually, slaves as commodities became the principal export in Angolan trade with the Europeans and contributed to the economic transformation and eventual decline of precolonial Angola.

In Angola, as in the Congo, the Portuguese achieved early success in the slave trade by violence. Wars of aggression resulted in the destruction of old states and the emergence of new political entitities that ensured their survival by participating in the slave trade. In the seventeenth century, the Angola Kingdom of Ndongo was virtually destroyed. Queen Nzinga, who came to power in 1623, unable to save her state from Portuguese aggression, retreated and founded the kingdom of Matamba. Despite her brilliance as a military tactician and her Machiavellian diplomacy, in her alliance with both the dreaded Jaga and the Dutch, Queen Nzinga failed to restore Ndongo's sovereignty. Using the slave trade as an economic base, she strengthened her kingdom, which by 1656 became an important commercial kingdom.

The Angolan slave trade was open to virtually anyone who could secure a slave for sale, usually in the area of his village. These were the petty traders. The extensive trade was carried out by the large merchant diasporas which moved with thousands of people, including slaves, porters, and guards.[129] Often, victims of the West Central African slave trade spent years in transit before reaching the Atlantic coast, while also experiencing several changes in ownership in addition to being sold in a variety of local and regional slave markets.[130] By the late seventeenth century, the centers of trade in the Congo and Angola moved east into the central African highlands interior.

By the end of the eighteenth century, the Lunda empire in the highlands had emerged as the most powerful state in Central Africa, peopled to a large extent by the Imbangala who had also been involved in the slave trade with the Portuguese since the seventeenth century. The strengths of Lunda's economy were agriculture, worked by serfs, its copper mines, and salt, which was the most important export product. The production of iron was significant not only for trade, but also for the status that was ascribed to those who produced it. In Lunda, trade operated on local, regional, and international levels with the slave trade being the most prominent from the sixteenth century on.

By the mid-seventeenth century, however, Portuguese commercial influence in the slave trade was limited in that they were driven out as direct participants in the trade and as Birmingham said: "beyond that the effects of overseas trade were transmitted by African enterprise."[131] By the eighteenth century, participation in the transatlantic slave trade led to the rise of a merchant class who, with their descendants, seized political power because of the wealth accumulated in the slave trade. "Their heirs eventually controlled a large enough proportion of the population to redefine political authority on the basis of commercial wealth and slave follower rather than on magico-ritual technique, agriculture, and tribute. The final product was a thoroughly bourgeois African polity constructed out of European credit and trading profits invested in human entourages."[132]

CONCLUSION

Even before the transatlantic slave trading era, the material life of precolonial Africans was shaped by the import of regional and international trade commodities. While participation in production and local and regional markets was the special province of the great mass of African men and women, access to international trade was generally limited to merchants and traders duly authorized by the ruling elites, particularly in the large state societies. Consequently, along with a diversity of occupations, even in small-scale African societies, trade and commerce were prevalent. "No matter what society is examined, the permanence of trade transcends the traditional contrast between states and stateless societies." Indeed, "The African continent has known two major phenomena: The mobility of its people and the volume of long-distance trade."[133]

Moreover, the extensive trade of Africans in Atlantic slave markets would have been impossible in "traditional" societies, that is, societies where commodity exchanges are limited to local or communal reciprocal or redistribution exchanges, or where low technology production exists only in the household as the only production unit. In his discussion of African trade and marketing activities, A. G. Hopkins, a foremost authority in the economic history of West Africa, emphasizes the complexity of those economies and cautions: "the economy of precolonial West Africa simply did not function in accordance with the principles which are supposed to characterise 'traditional' societies." Rather, Hopkins explains, the economic structure of precolonial West and West Central Africa must be understood within the context of the organizing principle of the market. "Indeed, the concept of a 'traditional' society is an ideal-type which is of questionable value in understanding reality."[134]

Despite the pervasiveness of trade and marketing in precolonial West and West Central Africa, which persisted in Colonial America, providing the basis for the development of black business activity, the most distinguishing feature in the history of the descendants of Africans in America has been a general perception that black people in this nation lack an historical and cultural tradition of business participation. From this perspective, the purported absence of a cultural heritage of enterprise and entrepreneurship has been used to account for the comparatively low business participation rates of African-Americans. Consequently the economic and business activities of African-Americans have been ignored in the scholarly literature. A reconstruction of the West and West Central African commercial culture thus provides a basis for the deconstruction of African diaspora cultural assessments to include this heritage.

APPENDIX: CONTEMPORARY THOUGHT

An analysis of the commercial culture, the marketing and trade operations that existed in precolonial West and West Central Africa during the transatlantic slave trading era requires examination by scholars of the African American experience in their discussions of African survivalisms and a diaspora cultural heritage. Today, almost five centuries after the African slave trade to the Americans began in 1501, popular assessments of the economic life of precolonial West and West Central Africa during the transatlantic slave trading era differ little from those stereotypes and misconceptions on the African heritage promulgated at the turn of this century.

The now infamous 1902 Tillinghast commentary is representative of serious historic distortions presented in the early twentieth century not only to academic communities but also to the general public as a basis for "justification for exploitation" of African resources during the early years of European colonization Most notable among his statements was one in which he said: "Previous to the appearance of Europeans, the extreme west coast of Africa was completely isolated from the outside world; its inhabitants lived in scattered villages buried in the forest, and remained in dense ignorance of any other desirable objects than the necessities of their own savage life." Only through European contact, Tillinghast asserts were Africans "moved to unwonted exertions," while also emphasizing that, "for ages the negroes were without such incitements to industry."[135]

Unfortunately, Tillinghast's assessments continue to underscore the premise of African American business history as indicated in a quite remarkable 1990 study that examines the history of African American property ownership. It was prefaced by a thesis which asserts that it was only with acculturation in the United States that African "slaves began to express their individuality through the acquisition of material wealth and property."[136] That such misconceptions still persist in the interpretation of the history of the African background of African Americans underscores the necessity for providing more than the simplistic, superficial analyses usually found in cursory examinations by American scholars of the commercial cultures of precolonial West and West African societies.

While assessing economic life in precolonial West and West Central Africa it is important to consider the extent to which parallels exist in present historical interpretations of the business tradition of both Africans and African Americans, especially within the context of Hopkins's 1973 analysis of the African domestic economy. Hopkins's study was approached from the perspective of countering many of the prevailing myths which view the African domestic economy as simply a subsistence economy, with limited entrepreneurial motivation stifled not only as he says "by the prevalence of anti-capitalist value system," but also by social and political institutional structures that prevented the accumulation of wealth. Hopkins decimates those myths, particularly the "Merrie Africa," and "Golden Age" myths, which insist that in precolonial West and West Central Africa, only limited productive efforts were made by Africans to enhance their material life. While a recognized surplus existed for trade and commodity exchanges, the prevailing assessment is that production of those commodities took place without organized effort or concentrated specialized labor. As Hopkins said, the general conclusion is that, since there was no need to work, an inordinate amount of leisure time was available for "interminable dancing and drumming."

The "Golden Age" and "Merrie Africa" myths persist to support what Hopkins calls the "True Whig interpretation of African history."[137] The basic premise of the Whig School posits that past events should be reconstructed to illuminate and account for, even to empower and legitimate, contemporary political administrations. In the instance of African history, the reality of past events is obscured as a basis to explain or rationalize their impact on the present. Or, more specifically, as Hopkins states, the Whig school proffers an historic formulation which shows: "the present states and rulers of West Africa as direct descendants of those of the precolonial era."[138]

Within this context, then, the Whig Interpretation of African history provides a basis for Africanists to rationalize the impoverishment of Africa today, but not on the grounds of the economic chaos resulting from decolonization or the exploitative forces of neocolonialism. Instead, the basic premise is that, since precolonial African rulers had no tradition in policy-making in the areas of economic planning and societal advancement, the absence of that heritage explains the "inability" of present heads of states to develop viable economic programs for the societal advances for their people.

Yet, in precolonial West and West Central Africa, economic planning centered on the existence of surplus that resulted from specialization of production at all levels: agricultural, the extractive industries, and craft manufacturing. It was the abundance of production which provided the basis of taxation and state surplus redistribution. For in precolonial African states "taxation appears as a form of internal exchange, in which the chief acted as a middleman distributing surplus productions within the group. The duty of the chief to provide for his people was widely recognized, and his political power was based on the proper fulfillment of this role." Furthermore, the existence of a communal surplus for redistribution meant that a minimum level of sustenance was provided for all. In late seventeenth-century Benin, the Dutch slave dealer William Bosman emphasized the absence of poverty. He indicates that the nobility provided charity to the poor, giving them work or even just maintenance: "so that here are no Beggars. And this necessary Care succeeds so well, that we do not see many remarkably poor amongst them."[139]

European destruction of customary African distribution practices concomitant with their appropriation of African surplus production, however, decimated colonial African economies. Within this context, "The decline of African rules with the advent of colonial rule can be ascribed to their dwindling incomes which inevitably led to waning political influence."[140] Moreover, the complexities of the economic structure of precolonial West and West African state systems is evident in the interest which those states had in trade. Invariably, fiscal policies of those states were based in part on expropriating profits from trade as seen in the collection of tolls on international trade commodities moving through the Yoruba state system in precolonial Nigeria. But the collection of tolls which took place in all Yoruba towns represented only one method of securing revenue. For as one historian notes: "Such tolls were an integral part of the economic basis of power. They were a major source of revenue, together with taxation, levies, judicial fees and fines, and death duties."[141] The toll system as well as other major sources of indigenous revenue collection was abolished under the British colonial administration, which provided a basis for them to secure the economic advantage in trade to the detriment of Nigeria.

African history, within the context of a Whig interpretation, thus ignores the prolonged and devastating effects of colonialism as the basis for contemporary African deprivation on all levels. Yet, interestingly, within the context of the Whig School of history, comparable and devastating assertions also find their parallels in the African American historic experience. The persistently low socio-economic status of African Americans is rationalized on the basis that blacks lack a historic tradition of economic initiative without much consideration given to either the pernicious effects of slavery and its continued impact in the national consciousness or to the lingering and destructive effects of racism.

In African American historiography, the Whig school of history is exemplified in the work of its most ardent practitioner, Ulrich B. Phillips. In his comments on the cultural background of black Americans, Phillips labels the African way of life as "savage" and far from "Idyllic," although he claims that food was to be had for "the plucking," and that "rainment is needless." Particularly, he insists that climate had an enervating effect on the intellectual capacity of Africans, explaining: "the climate not only discourages but prohibits mental effort of sustained character."[142] Literally, until the 1960s, when Phillips's commentary found reproof in subsequent analysis of precolonial African culture, mainstream American historiography incorporated, both explicitly and implicitly, Phillips's contention that the descendants of Africans in America lacked a cultural heritage that would enable them to succeed in American life. More specifically, within the constructs of prevailing assessments of African survivalisms there remains the persistent myth which insists that, since people of African descent have no tradition of business participation or entrepreneurship, their relative contemporary lack of business success cannot be attributed to the racist institutional infrastructure of white American business practices.

In the recent past, academics and policy makers have taken their cues more broadly from the 1963 study by Nathan Glazer and Daniel Moynihan. They attribute the comparative lack of African American business success to several principal factors found in the history of American race relations: that due to slavery, African Americans had no experience with money; because of their enslavement, African Americans were denied access to financial resources and consequent opportunities to develop skills in financial planning, business organization, and enterprise management; racism, prejudice, and discrimination, which continued after slavery ended, also found blacks locked out of both capital and consumer markets, which limited their access to financial resources, credit, and venture capital to develop businesses; blacks lacked not only markets, particularly in their own communities, but also racial/ethnic "clannishness" in support of their businesses; and "In the end, the most important factor is probably the failure of Negroes to develop a pattern of saving."[143]

Their assessments of slavery are incorrect because most slaves, even on plantations operated in a cash nexus. Their meager amount of cash, however, did not allow for savings. On the other hand, a substantial proportion of slaves who became free purchased their freedom, often saving for two decades or more to do so. Furthermore, after slavery, America's split labor market denied blacks access to full employment; for the majority who were employed, salaries at the lower end of the wage scale left blacks with barely enough to provide for the basic necessities of life much less sufficient residual funds to allow for savings.[144] Even more, at all levels – housing, food, clothing etc. – blacks pay at a much higher rate than whites: a phenomenon that has been referred to as the

"Black Tax." Denial of credit has also made it difficult for black businessmen not only to establish enterprises, but to provide, at competitive prices, the diversity of goods found in the businesses of their white competitors.

On the other hand, Glazier and Moynihan in their analysis ignored the opportunity structure developed by African Americans from the Colonial Period not only in the business activities of slaves and free blacks, but also in their organizing capacity seen in the founding of mutual aid societies which were the basis of black insurance and banks founded after the Civil War. No other minority ethnic group in America can compare in their efforts with that of blacks in the founding of black economic and social institutions.

Inevitably, however, there are those who view black entrepreneurial activity and business participation both in the United States and Africa as a contributing factor to the persistent economic underdevelopment of blacks in both Africa and the United States. What we have today, then, is an attack on the "moral economy" of the African and African American businessperson. Emphasizing the commentary of Chinweizu who denounces African capitalists, Manning Marable in his denunciation of African American capitalists said: "When Chinweizu writes bitterly, 'those whom Africa expected to liberate her from the yoke of Europe have instead chained her to that yoke, perhaps even more tightly, in exchange for crumbs of wealth and privilege,' a similar verdict must be levied against their American counterparts."[145]

In a society where wealth accumulation, which at this point begins with just getting a job, is based in part on educational excellence, young African Americans in search of self and identity find it difficult to reconcile their blackness within a cultural frame that seemingly rejects advancement in the economic mainstream. Presently, their formulations promote a culture of despair, for as an Ashanti proverb goes: "If any one invokes a fetish against you, saying, 'Let this man die,' he is not harming you as much as he would were he to say 'Let poverty lay hold on him.'" Ironically, the pursuit and achievement of academic excellence is viewed by many as a betrayal to the race, the very basis that provides the venue for the intellectual elite. In the United States, our intellectual elite should end their denouncement of wealth accumulation as only a "white man's thing," a pursuit they emphasize which stands in contradiction to that evidenced in the African cultural heritage.

And, in Africa, perhaps a beginning should be with OAU nations in encouraging bidding wars among competing multinational companies that sell or want to sell products in their respective countries, imposing sanctions and trade embargoes on those companies that refuse to share profits with them. Then, with both the multinational and the African companies, worker shareholding should be encouraged with share ownership included as part of the wage package. The OAU nations should also encourage the development and hiring of a mercenary army of western technocrats to operate in African nations on a "one-on-one" basis, each proceeding with his job while training an African counterpart to his/her position.

The OAU nations can encourage the development of a western consumer goods-producing infrastructure, allocating the production of specific consumer goods among each other, while tapping African continental markets for distribution and sales and demanding reciprocal trade relations with the advanced economies. Certainly, based on GNP per capita statistics compiled by the World Bank – some forty-five countries, including thirty in Africa with a GNP per capita of less than $500, most averaging less than $200 – aside from total and absolute impoverishment, there is not much that the OAU nations have to lose but everything to gain in a concerted African collective effort that benefits the continent as well as individual nation states. And, with the New South Africa, considerable attention must be given to its economic program of development.

In an increasingly global marketplace, Africans and African Americans cannot be left behind. A recent study by Joel Kotkin examines ethnicity and global business. In his *Tribes: How Race, Religion and Identity Determine Success in the New Global Economy*, Kotkin discusses how global "tribes," in which he includes the Anglo-Saxons, the Jews, Chinese, Indians, Japanese, as examples, use their race and ethnicity as a base for establishing business relationships. He concludes that ethnic groups, although dispersed globally, provide a basis not only for the creation, but also the continuity of business networks. With continuous exchanges of commercial information by "tribal" members dispersed throughout the world, the potential for expanded business and trade activities is enhanced as ethnic members constantly apprise each other of business activity and new technological developments in their respective nations.[146]

This has not yet become the case with African American and African businesspeople, compared to the other global "tribes." At the same time, for those black businesspeople in white corporate America, how does the issue of tribal affiliation relate to them? As African Americans, Peter Buxbaum notes in his review of Kotkin's study that they can make use of their African "tribal" affiliation:

> What can US exporters learn from Kotkin's study? The most important lesson: Use your own "tribal" affiliations and those of your employees and associates to penetrate new markets. If this contradicts your notions of American individualism and pluralism, remember that in a global economy ethnic affiliation will overshadow citizenship as a factor in individual identity. Let your company become a cosmopolis in its own right.[147]

Table 12.A1 African slave imports to the United States, 1620–1870

Years imported	*Numbers* Into USA	*Into Louisiana*	*Total*
1620–1700[1]	20,500		20,500
1701–1720[2]	19,800	1,200	21,000
1721–1740[2]	50,400	8,300	58,700
1741–1760[2]	100,400	8,500	108,900
Totals 1701–1760[2]	170,600	18,000	188.600
1761–1770[3]	62,668		62,668
1771–1780[3]	14,902		14,902
1781–1790[3]	55,750		55,750
1791–1800[3]	79,041		79,041
1801–1810[4]	114,090		114,090
Total 1761–1810[2]	326,451	10,200	336,651
1811–1870[2]	51,000		51,000
Total	568,551	28,200	596,751

Sources: 1. Robert W. Fogel and Stanley L. Engerman, *Time on the Cross: The Economics of American Negro Slavery* 2 vols (Boston: Little Brown and Company, 1974) 2: 30; 2. Philip D. Curtin, *The Atlantic Slave Trade: A Census* (Madison: University of Wisconsin Press, 1969), 140, 216 and 234; 3. Roger Anstey, "The Volume of the North American Slave Carrying Trade from Africa, 1761–1810," *Revue Francaise d'Histoire d'Outre-Mer* 62 (1975): 63, n. 75; 4. James A. Rawley, "Slave Trade, Atlantic," *Dictionary of Afro-American Slavery*, 678, for figure of 596,751. Also see, James A. Rawley, *The Trans-Atlantic Slave Trade: A History* (New York: Norton, 1981).

NOTES

1 Bernard I. Belasco, *The Entrepreneur As Culture Hero: Preadaptations in Nigerian Economic Development* (New York: Praeger Publishers, 1980, p. 21) said, "The pervasive market metaphor is one of the most durable strands within Yoruba oral tradition. It is an ancient usage which persists with contemporaneous force."

2 Ivor Wilks, *Asante in the Nineteenth Century: The Structure and Evolution of a Political Order* (London: Cambridge University Press, 1973, p. 673).

3 Ralph A. Austen, "The Uncomfortable Relationship: African Enslavement in the Common History of Blacks and Jews," *Tikkun: A Bimonthly Jewish Critique of Politics, Culture and Society* 9, 2 (March/April, 1994): 86 said: "We Jews, even liberal ones, who justifiably insist that the history of the Nazi Holocaust not be denied, can hardly urge African Americans to suppress the record of the slave trade and the involvement of our own ancestors in it." On Arab participation in the African slave trade see, Bernard Lewis, "The African Diaspora and the Civilization of Islam," in *The African Diaspora: Interpretative Essays*, Martin L. Kilson and Robert I. Rothberg (eds) (Cambridge, MA: Harvard University Press, 1976); Allan G. B. Fisher and Humphrey J. Fisher, *Slavery and Muslim Society in Africa: The Institution in Saharan and Sudanic Africa and the Trans-Saharan Trade* (Garden City, 1971); and, Ralph A. Austen, "The Trans-Saharan Slave Trade: A Tentative Thesis," in H. A. Gemery and J. S. Hogendorn (eds) *The Uncommon Market: Essays in the Economic History of the Atlantic Slave Trade*, (New York: Academic Press, 1974, pp. 23–76).

4 See Paul E. Lovejoy, "Atlantic Slave Trade Literature," *Journal of African History* 30 (1989): 365–73; E. Donnan, *Documents Illustrative of the History of the Slave Trade* to *America*, 4 vols (Washington DC: Carnegio Institution of Washington, 1930–35 and W. E. B. Du Bois, *The Suppression of the African Slave Trade to the U.S.A. 1638–1870* (New York, 1904). Walter Rodney, *How Europe Underdeveloped Africa* (Washington, D.C.: Howard University Press, 1974, p. 93). Rodney's thesis precipitated debate, finding increasing support in the 1980s. See, Paul E. Lovejoy, "The Impact of the Atlantic Slave Trade on Africa: A Review of the Literature," *Journal of African History* 30 (1989): 386–94, a rejection of David Eltis, *Economic Growth and the Ending of the Trans-Atlantic Slave Trade* (New York, 1987, p. 77), who claims that the slave trade "was not a critically important influence over the course of African history."

5 Ray A. Kea, *Settlements, Trade, and Polities in the Seventeenth-Century Gold Coast* (Baltimore: Johns Hopkins University Press, 1982, pp. 176–7).

6 Juliet E. K. Walker, "Racism, Slavery, Free Enterprise: Black Entrepreneurship in the United States before the Civil War," *Business History Review* 60 (Autumn 1986): 373.

7 Increasingly, publications of reference books document the African American business tradition. See, George H. Hill, *Black Business and Economics: A Selected Bibliography*, (New York: Garland Publishing, Inc., 1985); John N. Ingram and Lynne B. Feldman, *African-American Business Leaders: A Biographical Dictionary*, (Westport, CN: Greenwood Press, 1994); and Juliet E. K. Walker, *Encyclopedia of African American Business History*, (Westport, CN: Greenwood Press, forthcoming). On black business, slave and free, before the Civil War, Walker, "Racism, Slavery, Free Enterprise," *op. cit.*, provides extensive footnote bibliographic references on both primary and secondary sources. The R. G. Dun & Company [the predecessor to Dun and Bradstreet] Mercantile Credit Reports, Boston, Harvard University, Baker Business Library, provide information on the business worth of some antebellum black businesspeople and their capacity to assume debt.

8 For early general assessments on black business activity see Booker T. Washington, *The Negro in Business*, (Boston: Hertel, Jenkins and Company, 1907) and W. E. B. Du Bois, *Some Efforts Among Negroes for Their Own Social Betterment*, Atlanta University Publication No. 3 (Atlanta: Atlanta University Press, 1898). Also, J. H. Harmon, Jr., Arnett G. Lindsay, and Carter G. Woodson, *The Negro as a Businessman* (Washington: Association for the Study of Negro Life and History, 1929); Abram L. Harris, *The Negro As Capitalist: A Study of Banking and Business Among American Negroes*, (Philadelphia: American Academy of Political and Social Science, 1936; rep. ed. New York: Arno Press, 1968). More recently, John Sibley Butler, *Entrepreneurship and Self-Help Among Black Americans: A Reconsideration of Race and Economics*, (Albany: State University of New York, 1991).

9 Discussion of business activities by free blacks before the Civil War are included in, Ira Berlin, *Slaves Without Masters: The Free Negro in the Antebellum South* (New York: Pantheon Books, 1974): Leonard P. Curry, *The Free Black in Urban America, 1800–1850: The Shadow of the Dream*, (Chicago: University of Chicago Press, 1981); and Whittington Johnson, *The Promising Years, 1750–1830: The Emergence of Black Labor and Business*, (New York: Garland Publishing, Inc., 1993). Also, Juliet E. K. Walker, *Free Frank: A Black Pioneer on the Antebellum Frontier* (Lexington: University Press of Kentucky, 1983), on the entrepreneurial business activities of Free Frank McWorter (1777–1854), in Kentucky and Illinois, who purchased freedom for sixteen family members from slavery, including himself. For studies of black businesspeople who owned slaves for

commercial profit see Gary P. Mills, *The Forgotten People: Cane River's Creoles of Color* (Baton Rouge: Louisian State University Press, 1977); David O. Whitten. *Andrew Durnford: A Black Sugar Planter in Antebellum Louisiana* (Natchitoches, LA: 1981); Michael P. Johnson and James L. Roark, *Black Masters: A Free Family of Color in the Old South* (New York: Norton, 1984); Larry Koger, *Black Slaveowners: Free Black Slave Masters in South Carolina, 1790–1860*, (Jefferson, NC: McFarland & Company, 1985); Loren Schweninger, "Black-Owned Businesses in the South, 1790–1880," *Business History Review* 63 (Spring 1989): 22–60.

10 On slave business activities see, Philip D. Morgan, "Work and Culture: The Task System and the World of Lowcountry Blacks, 1700–1880," *William and Mary Quarterly* 39, 4 (October 1982): 563–99; Juliet E. K. Walker, "Pioneer Slave Entrepreneurship: Patterns, Processes, and Perspectives: The Case of the Slave Free Frank on the Kentucky Pennyroyal, 1795–1819," *Journal of Negro History* 68, 2 (Summer 1983): 289–308; Lawrence T. McDonnell, "Money Knows NO Master: Market Relations and the American Slave Community," in *Developing Dixie: Modernization in a Traditional Society*, Windred B. Moore, Jr., *et. al.* (eds) (Westport: CN: Greenwood Press, 1988, pp. 31–44); Betty Wood, "White Society" and the 'Informal' Slave Economies of Lowcountry Georgia, c. 1763–1830," *Slavery and Abolition* 11, 3 (December 1990): 313–331. Also, special issue, Ira Berlin and Philip Morgan (eds) "The Slaves Economy: Independent Production by Slaves in the Americas," *Slavery and Abolition* 12, 1 (May 1991): 1–27 and 131–208; Loren Schweninger, "The Underside of Slavery: The Internal Economy, Self-Hire, and Quasi-Freedom in Virginia," *Slavery and Abolition* 12, 2 (September 1991): 1–22. Also, Juliet E. K. Walker, "Slave Entreprepreneurs," *Dictionary of Afro-American Slavery*, Randall M. Miller and John David Smith (eds) (New York: Greenwood Press, 1988), 220–3. On slaves as managers and entrepreneurs, see Walker, "[Slave] Drivers," Walker. *Dictionary of Afro-American Slavery*, 196–8.

11 Presently, studies of the African American experience provide only a general survey of the West African background. In *Capitalism, Race, Entrepreneurship: The History of Black Business in America*, (New York: Twayne Publishers, forthcoming, chap. 1) Juliet E. K. Walker, examines the commercial culture in West and West Central Africa, as a basis to establish the African heritage of the Black American business tradition in its development in Colonial America.

12 Melville Herskovits, *The Myth of the Negro Past* (Boston: Beacon Press, 1941), the pioneering work in African survivalisms, provides one of the few, although brief, assessments on African economic survivals in his discussion on the African American mutual aid societies, which provided the basis for the origin of black insurance companies and banks. More recent studies focus primarily on language, religion artistic culture, music and folklore, with some emphasis on African survivalisms in agricultural labor. See, Joseph E. Holloway, (ed.) *Africanisms in American Culture* (Bloomington: Indiana University Press, 1991). Also, Roger D. Abrahams and John F. Szwed (eds) *After Africa* (New Haven: Yale University Press, 1983) and Vincent Bakpetu Thompson, "Euro-African Connection: Myth and Reality," in *The Making of the African Diaspora in the Americas 1441–1900* (Essex: Longman Group UK Limited, 1987). On survivalism in the material and folk culture, John M. Vlach, *The Afro-American Tradition in Decorative Arts* (Cleveland: Cleveland Museum of Art, 1978). African survivalisms in the Caribbean and South America are in greater evidence and the literature is much more extensive – see, Sidney W. Mintz and Richard Price, *An Anthropological Approach to the Afro-American Past: A Caribbean Perspective*

(Philadelphia: Institute for the Study of Human Issues, ISHI Occasional papers in Social Change, No. 2, 1976) and Sidney W. Mintz and Douglas G. Hall, *The Origin of the Jamaican Internal Marketing System*, Yale University Publications in Anthropology, No. 57 (New Haven, 1960). Also, Berlin and Morgan, (eds) "The Slaves Economy:" *Slavery and Abolition* 12, 1 (May 1991): 31–127.

13 See, Molefi K. Asante, *AfroCentricity: The Theory of Social Change* (Trenton, NJ: Africa World Press, 1980); M. K. Asante, *The AfroCentric Idea* (Philadelphia: Temple University Press, 1987). Asante and Kemet, *Afrocentricity and Knowledge* (Trenton, NJ: Africa World Press, 1990, rev. ed.,). Also, Paul Gilroy, *The Black Atlantic: Modernity and Double Consciousness* (Cambridge: Harvard University Press, 1993). Those studies fail to include the historic reality of the transculturation of the precolonial African economic ethos during the transatlantic slave trading era and its subsequent expression during the age of slavery within the context of the African American expression of "human capital" values and attitudes. Also see, Abdul Alkalimat, *Paradigms In Black Studies: Intellectual History, Cultural Meanings and Political Ideology* (Chicago: Twenty-First Century Books and Publications, 1990).

14 Walker, "Racism, Slavery, and Free Enterprise," p. 373. Slavery, however, did exist in Africa and slaves were involved in the commercial life of those societies – see, Suzanne Miers and I. Kopytoff (eds) *Slavery in Africa* (Madison: University of Wisconsin Press, 1977); Paul Lovejoy, *Transformations in Slavery: A History of Slavery in Africa*, (Cambridge: Cambridge University Press, 1983); F. Cooper, "The Problem of Slavery in African Studies," *Journal of African History* 20, 1 (1979): 103–25.

15. Thomas Sowell, *Race and Culture: A World View* (New York: Basic Books, 1994, p. 4).

16 Helen T. Catterall, (ed) *Judicial Cases Concerning American Slavery and the Negro*, 5 vols, (Washington, DC, Carnegie Institution, pp. 239–40).

17 George Peter Murdock, *Africa: Its Peoples and Their Culture History*, (New York: McGraw Hill Book Company, Inc., 1959 pp. 425–56), for listing of the more than 6,000 African ethnic groups. Also, Curtin, *Atlantic Slave Trade*, pp. 184–90 and 291–6, respectively, on European termino-logical imprecision of African ethnic groups during the era of slave trade and for "Koelle's Linguistic Inventory" of African languages.

18 For studies on African economic history see, Claude Meillassoux, (ed.) *The Development of Indigenous Trade and Markets in West Africa* (London: Oxford University Press, 1971); Richard Gray and David Birmingham, *Pre-Colonial African Trade: Essays on Trade in Central and Eastern African Before 1900*, (London: Oxford University Press, 1970); Robert W. July, *Precolonial Africa: An Economic and Social History*, (New York: Charles Scribner's Sons, 1975); J. F. Ade Ajayi and Michael Crowder, (eds) *History of West Africa*, 2 vols, (New York: Columbia University Press, 1972); Z. A. Konczacki and J. M. Konczacki (eds) *An Economic History of Tropical Africa: The Pre-Colonial Period*, vol. 1 (London: Frank Cass and Company Limited, 1977).

19 ibid., p. 83

20 Elliott P. Skinner, "West African Economic Systems," in *Peoples and Cultures of Africa: An Anthropological Reader*, Elliott P. Skinner, (ed.) (Garden City, NY: Doubleday/ Natural History Press, 1973, p. 205). Also, Paul E. Lovejoy, "The Internal Trade of West Africa Before 1800," in J. F. A. Ajayi, (ed.) *History of West Africa*, vol. 1 3rd edn (New York: Longman, Inc., 1985, pp. 648–90).

21 Philip Curtin, *Economic Change in Precolonial Africa: Senegambia in the Era of the Slave Trade*, (Madison: University of Wisconsin Press, 1975, pp. 336–7).

22 Philip Curtin, Steven Feierman, Leonard Thompson, and Jan Vansina, *African History*, (Boston: Little, Brown and Company, 1978, p. 231, noting, "The victims came from the far interior and were largely Mande in culture, captives taken during the rise and expansion of the Bambara states." Also Curtin, *Economic Change in Precolonia Africa*, p. xx, notes that Senegambia was a comparatively small and unimportant economic region, consisting of "a sufficiently homogeneous set of societies," as opposed to a single nation state.

23 Nehemia Levtzion, "North-west Africa: From the Maghreb to the Fringes of the Forest," in Richard Gray, ed. *The Cambridge History of Africa*, vol. 4 from c. 1600–1790 (London: Cambridge University Press, 1975, p. 221.)

24 Curtin, *Economic Change in Precolonial Africa*, p. 197.

25 ibid., p. 273.

26 Philip C. Curtin, "Pre-Colonial Trading Networks and Traders: The Diakhanke", in Claude Meillassoux (ed.) *The Development of Indigeneous Trade and Markets in West Africa* (London: Oxford University Press, 1971, p. 228). Also, Curtin, *Economic Change*, pp. 66–8 and 274.

27 Curtin, *Economic Change in Precolonial Africa*, pp. 197, 237–41, 264–5, and 270.

28 ibid., pp. 286–90.

29 ibid., p. 97

30 Curtin, "Pre-Colonial Trading Networks and Traders," p. 229.

31 Curtin, *Economic Change in Precolonial Africa*, p. 100.

32 ibid., p. 296.

33 Basil Davidson, *A History of West Africa to the Nineteenth Century*, (Garden City, NY: Doubleday & Company, 1966, p. 257); also, Walter Rodney, "The Guinea Coast", in J.D. Fage and Roland A. Oliver (eds), *The Cambridge History of Africa* vol. 4, (Cambridge: Cambridge University Press, 1975, p. 276) and Manning, *Slavery and African Life*, p. 135.

34 Walter Rodney, *A History of the Upper Guinea Coast, 1545 – 1800* (Oxford: Clarendon Press, 1970, pp. 20–5. Also, Kenneth Little, *The Mende of Sierra Leone*, (London: Routledge & Kegan Paul, 1951, pp. 78–82).

35 Rodney, *The Guinea Coast*, p. 290. See also Péter Woods.

36 Rodney, *Upper Guinea Coast*, p. 35.

37 ibid., pp. 36–7.

38 Rodney, *The Guinea Coast, p. 283. Also see, Curtin, Economic Change in Precolonial Africa,* pp. 31-2, for discussion of caste people who included craftsmen, blacksmiths, leather workers, woodworkers. He notes that, "While the free people everywhere thought of them as separate, they were not necessarily inferior."

39 Rodney, *The Guinea Coast*, p. 289. Alse, A. P. Kup, *Sierra Leone: A Concise History*, (New York: St. Martin's Press, 1975).

40 ibid., p. 61.

41 ibid., p. 282.

42 ibid., p. 68.

43 ibid., p. 221. Also see, Christopher Fyfe, *A History of Sierra Leone*, (London: Oxford University Press, 1962, p. 3.)

44 ibid., p. 21.

45 ibid., p. 221.

46 ibid., p. 200.

47 ibid., pp. 223 and 233.

48 ibid., p. 235. Also see, Lovejoy, *Transformations*, p. 48., "the coast near the Futa Jallon highlands was busy [exporting slaves] in the 1750s and 1760s."

49 Rodney, *Upper Guinea Coast*, p. 221 and 223.

50 Michael Banton, *West African City: A Study of Tribal Life in Freetown*, (London: Oxford University, 1957, pp. 3–5). Also see Lovejoy, *Transformations*, p. 48, who states that the "ports near where Monrovia and Freetown now stand handled some [slave] traffic at different times."
51 Rodney, *The Guinea Coast*, p. 296.
52 Ivor Wilks, "The Mossi and Akan States 1500–1800," in J. F. A. Ajayi and Michael Crowder, *History of West Africa*, vol. 1 (New York: Columbia University Press, 1972, p. 346).
53 Kea, *Settlements*, pp. 32–8; and, ibid., p. 11, where Kea states that, "certain districts were more urbanized and populous in the seventeenth century than they were in the late eighteenth or early nineteenth centuries."
54 ibid., p. 41.
55 ibid., p. 42.
56 ibid., p. 49.
57 ibid., pp. 254, 309–11.
58 ibid., p. 48.
59 ibid., p. 175.
60 ibid., p. 52.
61 Kwame Arhin, *West African Traders in Ghana in the Nineteenth and Twentieth Centuries*, (London, Longman, Inc., 1979, p. 2.)
62 "Considerations on the Present Peace, as far as it is relative to the Colonies and the African Trade" (London, 1763), II, p. 516.
63 Kwame Y. Daaku, "Trade and Trading Patterns of the Akan in the Eighteenth Centuries," in Meillassoux, *Development of Indigenous Trade*, p. 168. Lovejoy, *Transformations*, p. 57, on Gold Coast trade notes, "The Muslim factor was strong, providing commercial connections with the far interior, so that the Akan states were involved in continental trade on a scale that was at least equal to Oyo, Dahomey, and Benin and was perhaps even greater."
64 Patrick Manning, *Slavery, Colonialism and Economic Growth in Dahomey, 1640–1960*, (Cambridge: Cambridge University Press, 1982, p. 32). Also see, I. A. Akinjogbin, "The Expansion of Oyo and the Rise of Dahomey, 1600–1800," in J. F. A. Ajayi and Michael Crowder (eds). *History of West Africa*, vol. 1, p. 305.
65 J. D. Fage, *An Introduction to the History of West Africa*, (Cambridge: Cambridge University Press, 1959), p. 88.
66 Akinjogbin, "Expansion of Oyo," p. 305 and Rodney, *The Guinea Coast*, p. 226.
67 Manning, *Slavery, Colonialism*, p. 22. Also see, pp. 28–31 for ethnic origins of slave captives from Dahomey.
68 ibid., p. 10.
69 ibid., pp. 68–70.
70 ibid., pp. 24–7; Lombard, "The Kingdoms," p. 90.
71 ibid., p. 76.
72 ibid., p. 76.
73 ibid., p. 25.
74 ibid., pp. 22–4.
75 ibid., pp. 24–7.
76 Manning, *Slavery, Colonialism*, p. 22. p. 1.
77 Lovejoy, *Transformations*, p. 48. Also, G.I. Jones, *The Trading States of the Oil Rivers: A Study of Political Development in Eastern Nigeria*, (London: Oxford University Press, 1963).
78 Kenneth Onwuka Dike, *Trade and Politics in the Niger Delta: 1830–1885*, (London: Oxford University Press, 1959, p. 28).
79 Rodney, *The Guinea Coast*, p. 273.

80 Dike, *Trade and Politics*, p. 19; and, E. J. Alagoa, "The Niger Delta States and Their Neighbours, 1600–1800," in *History of West Africa*, Ajayi and Crowder, (eds) pp. 269–303.
81 Dike, *Trade and Politics*, p. 20.
82 ibid., p. 9. Also see Curtin *et al.*, *African History*, p. 244.
83 Curtin *et al.*, *African History*, p. 245.
84 Lovejoy, *Transformations*, p. 78.
85 Curtin *et al.*, *African History*, p. 244.
86 Rodney, *The Guinea Coast*, p. 265.
87 ibid., pp. 256–7.
88 Davidson, *History of West Africa*, p. 225.
89 Curtin *et al.*, *African History*, p. 246.
90 Davidson, *History of West Africa*, p. 127. Also see, Dike, *Trade and Politics*, p. 34 and Alagoa, "Niger Delta," pp. 280–1.
91 E. J. Alagoa, "The Niger Delta States and Their Neighbours, 1600–1800," in *History of West Africa*, Ajayi and Crowder, (eds) p. 293.
92 Alagoa, "Niger Delta," p. 295.
93 ibid., p. 287.
94 Rodney, *The Upper Guinea*, p. 260.
95 U. I. Ukwu, "Markets in Iboland," in *Markets in West Africa: Studies of markets and Trade Among the Yoruba and Ibo*, B. W. Hodder and U. I. Ukwu (New York: Africana Publishing Corporation, 1969, p. 132.
96 Ukwu, "Markets in Iboland," p. 132.
97 Dike, *Trade and Politics*, p. 28
98 Alagoa, "Niger Delta," p. 407.
99 Dike, *Trade and Politics*, p. 38.
100 Ukwu, "Markets in Iboland," p. 133.
101 Dike, *Trade and Politics*, pp. 26–7.
102 ibid., p. 38.
103 Victor C. Uchendu, *The Igbo of Southeast Nigeria* (New York: Holt, Rinehart and Winston, 1965, p. 15).
104 Dike, *Trade and Politics*, p. 28.
105 Alagoa, "Delta States," p. 410.
106 Davidson, *History of West Africa*, p. 225.
107 Dike, *Trade and Politics*, p. 33.
108 Alagoa, "Niger Delta," p. 410.
109 Joseph C. Miller, *Way of Death: Merchant Capitalism and the Angolan Slave Trade*, (Madison: The University of Wisconsin Press, 1988, p. 233.
110 ibid., p. 8.
111 Degrandpre, *Voyage to the Western Coast of Africa in the Years 1786 and 1787*, p. 1.
112 David Birmingham, "Early African Trade in Angola and its Hinterland," in *Pre-Colonial Trade*, Gray and Birmingham (eds) (London: Oxford University Press, 1970, p. 164).
113 ibid., p. 173.
114 Phillis Martin, "The Trade of Loango in the Seventeenth and Eighteenth Centuries," in *Pre-Colonial African Trade: Essays on Trade in Central and Eastern Africa before 1900*, Richard Gray and David Birmingham (eds) (London: Oxford University Press, 1970, p. 142).
115 J. Vansina, "Long-Distance Trade-Routes in Central Africa," in *An Economic History of Tropical Africa: The Pre-Colonial Period*, vol. 1, Z. A. Konczacki and J. M. Konczaki (eds) (London: Frank Cass and Company Limited, 1977, pp. 241– 2).

116 A. Battell, *The Strange Adventures of Andrew Battell in Angola and the Adjoining Regions*, E. Ravenstein (ed.) (London, 1901, pp. 43–4 in Martin, "Trade of Loango," p. 141.
117 Martin, "Trade of Loango," p. 144.
118 ibid., p. 153.
119 ibid., p. 158.
120 Rodney, *Upper Guinea Coast*, pp. 328–32.
121 ibid., p. 333.
122 Georges Balandier, *Daily Life in the Kingdom of the Kongo: From the Sixteenth to the Eighteenth Century*, trans. Helen Weaver (London: George Allen & Unwin Ltd, 1968, p. 133).
123 ibid., p. 133.
124 Curtin, p. 261 and Rodney, p. 355.
125 Christopher Fyfe, *A History of Sierra Leone*, (London: Oxford University Press, 1962, p. 70).
126 Miller, *Way of Death*, p. xix.
127 David Birmingham, "Early African Trade in Angola and its Hinterland," in *Pre-Colonial African Trade: Essays on Trade in Central and Eastern Africa before 1900*, Richard Gray and David Birmingham (eds) (London: Oxford University Press, 1970, p. 165)
128 Miller, *Way of Death*, p. 74.
129 ibid., pp. 173–6.
130 ibid., p. 224.
131 David Birmingham, "The Forest and the Savanna of Central Africa," in *The Cambridge History of Africa, from c. 1790 to c. 1870*, vol. 5, (Cambridge: Cambridge University Press, 1976, p. 230).
132 Miller, Way of Death pp. 184–5.
133 Catherine Coquery-Vidrovitch, "Recherches sur un mode de production africain," *La Pense's* 144 (1969): 61–78.
134 Anthony G. Hopkis, *An Economic History of West Africa*, (New York: Columbia University Press, 1973), p. 6.
135 Joseph A. Tillinghast, *The Negro in Africa and America* (New York, 1902, *Publication of the American Economic Assoc.*, 3rd series, vol. 3, 2 (May, 1902).
136 Loren Schweninger, *Black Property Owners in the South 1790–1915*, (Urbana: University of Illinois Press, 1990, p. 11).
137 Hopkins, *Economic History*, pp. 9–10.
138 ibid., p. 10; and Herbert Butterfield, *The Whig Interpretation of History* (New York: Scribner 1951).
139 Bosman, *Description of Guinea*, p. 439.
140 Lars Sundstrom, *The Exchange Economy of Pre-Colonial Tropical Africa* [published as *The Trade of Guinea* (Sweden, 1963)] (reprint edn London: C. Hurst & Company, 1974, p. 252).
141 Toyin Falola, "The Yoruba Toll System: Its Operation and Abolition," *Journal of African History* 30 (1989): 70.
142 Phillips, Ulrich, B. *American Negro Slavery*, (New York: D Appleton and Company, 1918, pp. 3,4,8).
143 Nathan Glazer and Daniel Patrick Moynihan. *Beyond the Melting Pot*, (Cambridge: Massachusetts Institutes Press, 1963, pp. 30, 33). For brief discussion refuting Moynihan's controversial *The Negro Family in America: The Case for National Action* (1965), which describes the contemporary black family as a "tangle of pathology," attributing this to the destruction of the black family during slavery: "The experience of slavery left as its most serious heritage a steady weakness in the Negro family, " see Herbert Gutman. *The Black Family*

in Slavery and Freedom 1750–1925 (New York Pantheon Books, 1976, pp. xvii–xix). In both instances, their historical misconceptions, the absence of a black heritage of business participation and a nuclear slave family were, based on the works of sociologists, especially E. Franklin Frazier, *The Negro in the United States* (New York: Macmillan, 1957). Moynihan failed to consider the complex economic and societal forces inherent in American slavery, specifically the profit motive that was "color-blind," even for black people aggressive enough to establish businesses, which before the Civil War included not only free blacks but also slaves. Both nuclear black families, slave and free, as well as black businessman slave and free, existed before the Civil War.

144 Edna Bonacich, "A Theory of Ethnic Antagonism: The Split Labor Market," *American Sociological Review* 37, 5 (October 1972): 547–9; and, "Advanced Capitalism and Black/White Race Relations in the United States: A Split Labor Maker Interpretation," 41,1 (February 1976): 34–51.

145 Manning Marable, *How Capitalism Underdeveloped Black America* (Boston: South End Press, 1983, pp. 135–6) from Chinweizu, *The World and the Rest of Us: White Predators, Black Slavers, and the African Elite* (New York: Vintage Press, 1975, p. 382). Also, Rodney, *How Europe Underdeveloped Africa*, p. 93.

146 Joel Kotkin, *Tribes: How Race, Religion and Identity Determine Success in the New Global Economy* (New York: Random House, 1993).

147 Peter A. Buxbaum, "Ethnic Affinities," *World Trade* 6, 4 (April 1993): 14.

13

"OUT OF SIGHT, OUT OF MIND"

The struggle of African American intellectuals against the invisibility of the slave[ry] trade in world economic history

Ronald Bailey

In a 1977 film called "The Deep," salvagers seek to recover Spanish treasure from a royal vessel which left Havana and sank off the coast of Bermuda in the 1700s. At one point, the crusty old captain tells his young fellow fortune-hunter:

> You know what they say about these waters. If the Jamaica pirates don't get ya, it'll be the cold embrace of the sea. And that's no lover's kiss. You know, every ship from the New World passed through these waters. They had to, taking porcelain from China, Japanese silk screens, ivory doo-dads from India, and all that Inca gold that Pizarro took out of Peru. Do you believe all of that, boy?[1]

Whether the "boy" believed it or not, the dialogue omitted the most important commodity to pass through the Caribbean waters. By the beginning of the eighteenth century, it is conservatively estimated that 631,000 Africans were transported to the Caribbean and Spanish America, with another 610,000 taken to Brazil. These "forced migrants" would work as slaves in the expanding plantation economy and the mines and represented the opening trickle which would turn into a veritable flood. The total number of Africans transported between 1700 and 1810 reached 3.2 million for the Caribbean, 927,000 for British and Spanish America, and 1.9 million for Brazil.[2]

The significance of the slave[ry] trade, as – I have labeled it – the slave trade and associated commerce and industrial activity, including shipbuilding, trade in slave-produced goods, and commerce with slave-based economies – should be all too apparent.[3] Until well into the nineteenth century, the Americas were more an extension of Africa than of Europe. Until 1820, for example, 8.4 million Africans as compared with 2.4 million Europeans "immigrated," most Africans involuntarily (Eltis 1983: 278). The triangular slave trade sent finished goods to Africa, slaves and gold to the Americas, and rice, tobacco, cotton and sugar to Europe. As trade goods, African peoples were the key element which helped fuel this commerce and led to great accumulations of wealth in England and in New England.

Moreover, slaves were unique trade goods when compared to other commodities – their labor-power could produce additional wealth. In 1860, 89 per cent of all of Great Britain's cotton imports was produced by slaves, as was all of the cotton consumed by the US textile industry, an amount which expanded by 125 per cent in each decade between 1830 and 1860. In addition, over 60 per cent of New England commerce revolved around commerce with the slave-based economies of the West Indies. Many of the great fortunes which financed the industrial revolution in England, and in New England – the Cabots, the Browns, the Lowells, and others – were garnered from the commerce of slaves, rum, molasses, and related commodities and industries (e.g., banking). And there were international ramifications as well: slave-produced cotton from the US South accounted for 58 per cent of the dollar value of all US exports in 1860 (Bailey 1992).

While novelists and scriptwriters, perhaps, can be tolerated or forgiven for ignoring the most valuable commodity to pass through the Caribbean waters in the 1700s, historians cannot. Black scholars and writers have been the most insistent voices that the role of Africans – as commodities which were traded and as workers whose labor was exploited – should not be excluded from the annals of world history. This article is a contribution in this venerable tradition.[4]

The focus of this article – the slave trade – is the period of transition between the African and the African American experience, one with great meaning for black life in the US, and for the history of the world.[5] I will focus first on the classical statement of the slave[ry] trade's significance as proposed by contemporaries of this trade – mercantilist theoreticians, businessmen, and policymakers. I will then summarize how this view has been echoed for generations in the writings of leading black scholars – African, Caribbean, and African American – who have explored such themes as Africa's link to world history and the relationship of the slave trade and slavery to the rise of industrial capitalism in Europe and the United States, concentrating on those scholars whose conclusions are based on their own pathbreaking research. I will conclude with how a more recent group of black scholars have responded to attempts over the past ten years to denigrate and dismiss the significance of the slave[ry] trade's contribution.

THE SLAVE TRADE IN THE WORLD OF HISTORY AND IN THE WORLD OF IDEAS

The key question I have posed to focus this discussion is this: Were Africa, the slave trade, and slavery-related commerce conventionally characterized as "the triangular trade" important to the development of commerce and industry in Europe, especially Britain, and the United States?[6] This issue has been discussed, and at times debated, among businessmen and scholars for over three hundred years. Contemporaries of the slave trade writing in the eighteenth century generally agreed with the businessman and mercantilist theorist Malachi Postlethwayt, whose view we might characterize as the conventional wisdom on the subject, widely echoed since his comment in 1745:

> But is it not notorious to the whole World, that the Business of **planting in our British colonies**, as well as the **French**, is carried on by the labour of **Negroes**, imported thither from **Africa**? Are we not indebted to those valuable people, the **Africans**, for our **Sugars, Tobaccoes, Rice, Rum** and all other imports into our colonies, from Africa, will not the Exportation of British manufactures among the Africans be in Proportion; they being paid for in such commodities only?
>
> (Postlethwayt 1745: 6)

This was an observation that Postlethwayt repeated several times in his writings. "The African trade," he said, "is the first principle and foundation of all the rest, the mainspring of the machine which set every wheel in motion ... the African trade is so very beneficial to Great Britain, so essentially necessary to the very being of her colonies, that without it neither could we flourish nor they long subsist...." (in Rees 1925: 142)

Joining in the chorus of praise were many other contemporaries of the slave trade, including those whom Eric Williams calls "the mercantilist intelligentsia ..., the leading mercantilists, Postlethwayt, Davenant, Gee, Sir Dalby Thomas, [and] Wood...." William Wood, for example, declared in 1718 that the slave trade was "the spring and parent from whence the others flow" (William Wood, A Survey of Trade, London, 1718, Part III, p. 178). It is not at all hard to discover why the mercantilist contemporaries of the slave trade were so glowing and enthusiastic in their endorsements. Mercantilism argued the advantages of increasing the national wealth in the form of precious metals through buying cheap and selling dear, resulting in a favorable "balance of trade." The slave[ry] trade, especially the triangular trade, was perfect in this regard (Darity 1982b).

But while the importance of this trade in humans was clear to the mercantilists and their contemporaries, the recognition of the slave[ry] trade's contribution to the world has had an interesting history, appearing to fade – sometimes quite precipitously – with each passing generation. And if there is a lesson in this, it is this one central point: what happened in *history* and what is recorded as "history" can be vastly different stories. It is for this reason that this volume which seeks to elaborate intellectual history – the history of ideas about economics and the economic history of the black experience – is to be applauded. This is what was promised by the Black Studies perspective in the late 1960s, and it remains no less a continuing challenge in the 1990s.

W. E. B. Du Bois's *The Suppression of the African Slave-Trade to the United States 1638–1870* is an important point of departure for this discussion.[7] Completed in 1896 and published as the first in a prestigious series of Harvard dissertations, the monograph is an exhaustive study of international, national, state, and local legislation intended "to limit and suppress the trade in slaves between Africa and these shores." Though his investigation is concerned primarily with political-legislative questions and does not systematically explore economic aspects of this legal activity, Du Bois does provide some insights into economic questions. He mentions the *Asiento* which gave England a thirty-year monopoly in supplying African slaves to Spanish colonies in the Americas, the profits to trading colonies from the slave trade, and the role of "property" in congressional debates and actions.

There is also a perceptive comment that "the history of slavery and the slave trade after 1820 must be read in light of the industrial revolution through which the civilized world passed in the first half of the nineteenth century" (Du Bois 1973: 151). He follows this comment with a list of inventions which revolutionized the manufacture of cotton in Europe and America between 1738 and 1830, "including Arkwright's [waterframe], Watt's [steam engine], Crompton's [mule], and Cartwright's [powerloom] epoch-making contrivances" (Du Bois 1973: 150), and which consequently intensified the exploitation of black slave labor in the production of this essential commodity.

In reference to New England, Du Bois points out that slave labor was not widely utilized because the climate and geography of the region precluded the extensive development of agriculture. Thus,

> the significance of New England in the African slave trade does not, therefore, lie in the fact that she early discountenanced the system of slavery and stopped importation, but rather in the fact that her citizens being the traders of the New World, early took part in the carrying trade and furnished slaves to the other colonies.
>
> (Du Bois 1973: 27)

Stressing the role of Massachusetts and of Rhode Island which later became "the clearing house for the slave trade of other colonies," Du Bois's account is similar to the now popularized "triangular trade" thesis. These analogies from geometry attempt to summarize the economic and geographic scope of the trade, especially its impact in facilitating the expansion of world trade.

> This trade formed a perfect circle. Owners of slavers carried slaves to South Carolina, and brought home naval stores for their shipbuilding as to the West Indies, and brought home molasses; or to other colo-

> nies, and brought home hogsheads to Africa for more slaves. Thus, the rum-distilling industry indicates to some extent the activity of New England in the slave-trade.
>
> (Du Bois 1973: 27)

In "An Apologia" to a new edition of *Suppression* in 1954, the noted black scholar is disturbed about his failure to use the works of Karl Marx because he "got the idea from his college training that his teachings already had been superseded" and consequently "gave little firsthand attention" to Marx's work. His failure to use Marxism in studying this important aspect of the black experience, according to Du Bois, "was important in my interpretation of the history of slavery and the slave-trade. For if the influence of economic motives on the actions of mankind ever had clear illustration it was in the modern history of the African race, and particularly in America. No real conception of this appears in my book" (Du Bois 1973: 29)

Instead, Du Bois says he relied on moral idealism in his analysis, wondering later "how could I or my advisers have neglected the classic work of Marx on the colonies as the source of primary capitalistic accumulation." Illustrating what idealism means in this context Du Bois says that he

> still saw slavery and the slave trade as chiefly the result of moral lassitude. I did not clearly see that the real difficulty rested in the willingness of a privileged class of Americans to get power and comfort at the expense of degrading a class of black slaves, by not paying them what their labor produced. I still seemed to miss the clear conclusion that slavery was more a matter of income than morals.
>
> (Du Bois 1973: xxxii)

Du Bois's summation of his insights after many years of additional study and struggle raises important issues regarding theory, method, and intellectual history in Afro-American Studies and in other academic disciplines.

> What I needed was to add to my terribly conscientious search into the facts of the slave-trade the clear concept of Marx on the class struggle for income and power, beneath which all considerations of morals were twisted or utterly crushed. Yet naturally it is too much to ask that I should have been as wise in 1896 as I think I am in 1954.
>
> (Du Bois 1973: xxxii[8])

Lorenzo Greene's largely unheralded *The Negro in Colonial New England* ranks in importance with the work of Du Bois on the African slave trade, but with an emphasis on the role of the slave[ry] trade in the United States. Greene's main thesis is that the slave trade occupied a central role in the New England economy:

> The effect of the slave trade was manifold. On the eve of the American Revolution it formed the very basis of the economic life of New

> England; about it revolved, and depended, most of her industries. The vast sugar, molasses and rum trade, shipbuilding, the distilleries, a great many of the fisheries, the employment of artisans and seamen, even agriculture – all are dependent on the slave traffic.
>
> (Greene 1942: 68)

He points out the specific role of the African slave trade in the development of a wealthy New England merchant class that was to play the leading role in the historical development of the United States.

> Slave merchants belonged to what was then known as the gentility. The names of many are famous in the annals of New England and others are intimately associated with the history of the United States. Many are honored with private and public offices of great trust, power, and responsibility. There was no stigma attached to trading in Negroes before the Revolution, for the slave trade was as honorable a vocation as lumbering or fishing. Wealthy slave merchants, like the industrial captains of the recent era, were successful men – the economic, political, and social leaders of their communities – and were regarded by their fellows as worthy of emulation.
>
> (Greene 1942: 57)

Greene follows this observation with a well-documented list of slave traders and a list of 162 slave-holding families – and it reads like a veritable "Who's Who in Colonial New England!"

Oliver Cromwell Cox was one of the few black scholars who attempted a systematic dissection of the capitalist system, though the economic crisis of the 1930s spurred a more radical critique among black scholars.[9] Cox's primary concern was "to analyze and characterize the significant economic and social phenomena of the capitalist system as they manifest themselves in its economic structure, its social matrix and its dynamics." He states that "the vital spark of early development, as we know, centered in New England and Boston was its nucleus. It was here, especially, that the native capitalist interests clashed with those of the mother country" (Cox 1964: 121). In *Capitalism as a System*, quoting David Macpherson Cox supports this assertion with a lengthy discussion of the commercial and industrial activity which centered in New England:

> In addition to the commerce supported by the produce of their fisheries..., a very profitable circuitous carrying trade which greatly enriched them and supplied most of the money which circulated among them..., building vessels, distilling rum, exchanging furs, and trading in Africa for slaves, gold dust, ivory, woods, wax and gums:
>
> (Cox 1964: 122)

Cox further pinpoints the importance of the slave trade and slavery to capitalist development in the US:

> Especially important was the vastly increased demand for tobacco, cotton, and sugar which could be produced in the South and sold abroad with greater facility than almost any product of the North.... Thus, the expansion of cotton and tobacco plantations in the South correlated with British colonial expansion. But the export of these products also stimulated the manufactures of New England and the agriculture of the Mid-west. In a very real sense, therefore, the American economy rested upon foreign commerce, of which slavery became a pivot.
>
> (Cox 1964: 124)

In addition to this very explicit statement on the importance of slavery and the slave trade to US capitalism, Cox also comments on the roots of slavery and racism in the economic relations of that epoch. His *Caste, Class, and Race* contains the most extensive discussion of his views on "the nexus between capitalism and race relations."

> Race antagonism is part and parcel of the class struggle, because it developed within the capitalist system as one of its fundamental traits. The interest behind racial antagonism is an exploitative interest – the peculiar type of economic exploitation characteristic of capitalist society.
>
> (Cox 1948: pp. lxii).

In studying Africa's relationship to Europe, black scholars have made clear statements about the role of the African slave trade and slavery in the development of industrial capitalism.[10] Wilson E. Williams's "Africa and the Rise of Capitalism" was one of the first efforts to seek an integrated understanding of: 1 the developmental process of capitalism in England; 2 its expansion into Africa and the Americas; and 3 the essential contribution made by African peoples to the growth of capitalism in Europe. Drawing heavily on the works of mercantilists and of Marx, he offers this sweeping conclusion, quoted at length because of its clarity and its general unavailability.

> The African trade was a very important factor in the growth of the capitalist economy in England. First, it furnished a considerable market for British manufactures, particularly textiles which exchanged for Africa's chief product, Negro slaves. We have noted, for example, the important role which Liverpool shipping played as a stimulus to Manchester manufacturing. Second, African gold was an important source of the medium of exchange which the rising capitalism of England demanded. Third, the great profits derived from the African trade, in spite of notorious losses, helped to build the large personal fortunes which eventually were turned from purely commercial to industrial employment. Finally, the African trade stimulated such

industries as shipbuilding, and thus was an important factor in bringing about England's supremacy in the overseas trade.

The West Indian plantation economy, forming the final and most important apex of the triangle, was also important in the development of English capitalism. The West Indies furnished, to some extent at least, an outlet for British manufactures. But, more important than this, the plantations were an important source of raw materials. From the exploitation of slave labor in the West Indian economy, large fortunes arose. Some of this wealth was transferred to the mother country, and eventually invested in industrial enterprise....

Without the Negro slave it is likely that neither the African trade nor the West Indian economy could have played an important part in the development of English capitalism; hence, it is unlikely that without the slave trade, English capitalism could have shown the phenomenal growth it did.

(Wilson Williams 1936: 39f)

In *Capitalism and Slavery*, the late Prime Minister of Trinidad popularized the "triangular trade" analogy as a description of the relationship between the enslavement of Africans and the rise of capitalism in Europe.

In this triangular trade England – France and Colonial America equally – supplied the exports and the ships; Africa the human merchandise; the plantations the colonial raw materials. The slave ship sailed from the home country with a cargo of manufactured goods. These were exchanged at a profit on the coast of Africa for Negroes, who were traded on the plantations, at another profit, in exchange for a cargo of colonial produce to be taken back to the home country. As the volume of trade increased, the triangular trade was supplemented, but never supplanted, by a direct trade between the home country and the West Indies, exchanging home manufactures directly for colonial produce.

The triangular trade thereby gave triple stimulus to British industry. Negroes were purchased with British manufactures; transported to the plantations, they produced sugar, cotton, indigo, molasses and other tropical products, the processing of which created new industries in England; while the maintenance of the Negroes and their owners on the plantations provided another market for British industry, New England agriculture and the Newfoundland fisheries. By 1750 there was hardly a trading or a manufacturing town in England which was not in some way connected with the triangular or direct colonial trade. The profits obtained provided one of the main streams of that accumulation of capital in England which financed the Industrial Revolution.

(Williams 1944: pp. 51, 52)

Eric Williams's detailed elaboration of the interconnections and interdependence of the many aspects of the economy at all three points of the triangular trade – England, Africa, and the Americas – makes *Capitalism and Slavery* the classic statement that it has remained. It is still central in a debate which has become "a historical perennial," a term which Woodman (1963) used in describing the closely related debate over the profitability of slavery. Eric Williams discusses the impact of the trade on shipping and shipbuilding, the growth of British seaport towns, and the variety of goods manufactured in Britain and sold during the trade – wool, cotton, sugar refining, rum distillation, pacotille (glass, beads, etc.), and metal products (guns, cuffs, etc.). He demonstrates how merchants and planters (dominating the West Indies but living as absentee landlords in Britain) used their profits not only to play a leading role in the economic and financial affairs of Britain, but also to act as a powerful political force shaping the decisions of the British parliament toward their overseas interests.

He also discusses the financing of the Industrial Revolution: He asks, "What men in the first three-quarters of the eighteenth century were better able to afford the ready capital than a West Indian sugar planter or a Liverpool slave trader?" He thereby links the triangular trade to banking (e.g., Barclays), insurance (e.g., Lloyd's), and to the development of heavy industry (e.g., the financing of Watt's steam engine). However, Eric Williams does not go so far as to claim that the triangular trade was alone responsible for financing British industrial capitalism, something that many current critics find it convenient to ignore:

> But it must not be inferred that the triangular trade was solely and entirely responsible for the economic development. The growth of the internal market in England, the ploughing-in of the profits from industry to generate capital and achieve still greater expansion, played a large part. But this industrial development, stimulated by mercantilism, later outgrew mercantilism and destroyed it.
>
> (Williams 1944: 7, 19)

There are other important points made in *Capitalism and Slavery* that should be noted. Williams's treatment of racism and its relationship to slavery parallels that of Oliver Cox:

> Slavery in the Caribbean has been too narrowly identified with the Negro. A racial twist has thereby been given to what is basically an economic phenomenon. Slavery was not born of racism; rather, racism was the consequence of slavery. Unfree labor in the New World was brown, white, black and yellow; Catholic, Protestant, and pagan.... The reason was economic, not racial; it has to do not with the color of the laborer, but with the cheapness of labor.
>
> (Williams 1944: 19)

Another key aspect of the analysis of *Capitalism and Slavery* is its emphasis on the role of economic forces in history and the importance of examining questions of morality and politics in light of these economic forces. Central to the objections of his most vociferous critics are Eric Williams's elaboration of two points in his conclusion: "1. The decisive forces in the period of history we have discussed are the developing economic forces;" and "2. The political and moral ideas of the age are to be examined in the very closest relation to the economic development" (pp. 210–11). These conclusions continue to propel *Capitalism and Slavery* to the very heart of historiographical debate in British and world history.[11]

Finally, C. L. R. James in *Black Jacobins: Toussaint L'Ouverture and the San Domingo Revolution* (1963) described how "the slave trade and slavery was the basis of the French Revolution," citing statistics on a triangular trade from Nantes in France to Guinea and on to the West Indies and involving a wide range of French commerce similar to Britain.

> Nearly all the industries which developed in France during eighteenth century had their origins in goods or commodities destined either for the coast of Guinea or for America. The capital of the slave trade fertilized them; though the bourgeoisie traded in other things than slaves, upon the success or failure of the traffic everything else depended.
>
> (James 1963: p. 48)

There is an important footnote here for a complete intellectual history of black economists and economic thinkers. Wilson E. Williams studied at Howard and wrote the MA thesis cited above under Abram Harris. Harris produced *The Black Worker* (with Spero) and *The Negro As Capitalist*, among other works. Williams's MA paper obviously took up Harris's observation in *The Negro As Capitalist* regarding the importance of the slave trade and slavery to British and American development, citing the mercantilist Postlethwayt.

> Africa supplied the Western world not only with labor, but with much of the gold that was necessary for a stable money economy in western European nations. In brief, the introduction of African labor into the British West Indies and the profits obtained from traffic in this labor and its products, as well as the exploitation of the African continent for gold, in the fifteenth and sixteenth centuries were fundamental to that accumulation of capital on the basis of which the English industrial system was raised in the eighteenth century. Similarly, in the United States the profits which the slave trade yielded to New England were an important factor in the growth of the shipping industry, and at the same time a source of surplus wealth for American industrialism.
>
> (Harris 1936: 1f)

Eric Williams, who taught at Howard, cites C. L. R. James's *Black Jacobins* as the source where the thesis advanced in *Capitalism and Slavery* was "stated clearly and concisely, and as far as I know, for the first time in English," despite the fact that Harris's book and Wilson Williams's thesis – which he also cites – were published in 1936 and 1938, respectively, and James's book did not appear until 1938. Eugene Holmes, in reviewing *The Negro as Capitalist* in *Science and Society*, points to Harris's failure to develop this theme (Holmes: 261).[12]

Some thirty years later, C. L. R. James returned to this theme, this time focusing on the intellectual history of the slave[ry] trade's story:

> The overwhelming majority of historians show a curious disinclination to deal with the seminal role played by the slave trade and slavery in the creation of what distinguished Western civilization from all other civilizations. As far back as 1847, Karl Marx states in very aggressive terms what modern civilization, and in particular the United States, owes to the enslavement of Black people from Africa. Karl Marx . . . made slavery the center of his comprehensive uncovering of the fires which stoked Western civilization:
>
> (James 1970)

Given what has been demonstrated regarding the writings of mercantilists who were contemporaries of the slave trade and of black scholars through the 1950s, this "curious disinclination" to which James refers is quite pronounced in recent decades. This casts serious doubt on the view that the further a society travels from an historical epoch, the clearer will be its historical re-creation of that period.[13]

RECENT ARGUMENTS AGAINST AND FOR THE SIGNIFICANCE OF THE SLAVE TRADE

The "history" of the slave[ry] trade's history is arguably one of the best examples that all of "history" is terribly socially constructed, and will reflect the ideas and ideals and, most importantly, the perceived interests of the races, nationalities, classes, and genders which construct it.

Thus it came to pass that what I have defined as the long-standing and conventional wisdom on the significance of the slave trade was challenged, and, if we take the words of the challengers, definitively repudiated. To quote the conclusion of the most widely cited proponent of this revision, Stanley Engerman:

> the aggregate contribution of slave trade profits to the financing of British capital formation in the eighteenth century could not be so large as to bear weight as *the*, or *a*, major contributing factor. Its role was positive in that there were some profits, and these might have led

to some new investment in industrial activities, but relative to total capital formation, this was of a relatively minor magnitude.

(Engerman 1972: 441)

Other scholars echoed Engerman. Anstey (1975) stated that "the most credible contribution of the slave trade profits to capital formation" is so low as to make it "sufficiently derisory [laughable] enough for the myth of the vital importance of the slave trade in financing the Industrial Revolution to be demolished." Another study concluded that most work to date seems to indicate that the profits of the slave trade, if any, were not abnormally large, and . . . that a relationship running from the slave trade to industrialization is dubious." Rawley (1981), Hughes (1983), Walvin (1983), McCusker and Menard (1985), and Reynolds (1993) all embraced Engerman's denial of the importance of the slave trade. Even scholars who once viewed the slave trade as significant were swayed by the arguments of Engerman and others that their assessment was incorrect. A most notable case is David Brion Davis (1975).

The importance of the Engerman article in subverting the conventional wisdom on the slave trade cannot be overemphasized. Explaining how such a wrong-headed view could become so popular is a task I have already undertaken (Bailey 1986). In essence, Engerman created an easily demolishable straw man. He deliberately chose to utilize a neo-classical model which denied the reality of "multiplier effects" which would have included, for example, the impact of the slave trade in stimulating shipbuilding and related industries. Though he acknowledges that this will yield vastly different results from the model used in *Capitalism and Slavery* and other works, he never asked if his model reflected the real world of a slave-trade based economy as described by the mercantilists. His footnoted caveats did not resonate with those who blindly followed his thinking as much as his misleading conclusions, since repudiated.[14]

In case I have left the impression that all black scholars agree on the significance of the slave[ry] trade to world history, let me illustrate that such is not the case with the work of Harvard sociologist Orlando Patterson. Patterson was very clear on the important role of the slave trade and the work of Eric Williams. He was equally clear in his rejection of recent cliometric studies of the same material:

> Cliometric studies of the Williams thesis are deficient and, indeed, downright spurious in an even more important way. By interpreting the Williams thesis in the narrowest terms possible, critics such as Roger Anstey have persuaded themselves that they have demolished the argument because they have shown that the contribution of the slave trade profits to capital formation was small (according to Anstey only 0.10 per cent). Such irrelevance is truly spectacular. Such views fail to take account of macro-sociological linkages in the development

> of Western society. Thus, if it can be proven that the development of Western industrial civilization depended on the resolution of certain critical contradictions, and that such resolutions depended on the development of plantation slavery, the Williams thesis admittedly elaborated, holds just as forcefully.
>
> (Patterson 1979: 250)

Patterson argues that the well-described crisis in Europe during the seventeenth century – commercial lapses, inflation, economic dislocations, plagues – was just such a crisis which was resolved with significant inputs from colonial slavery and the slave trade (p. 252).

In 1982, however, Patterson seems to shift gears in his widely acclaimed *Slavery and Social Death*:

> The late Eric Williams may have gone too far in his celebrated argument that the rise of capitalism itself could be largely accounted for by the enormous profits generated by the slave systems of the Americas. But no one now doubts that New World slavery was a key factor in the rise of the West European economies.
>
> (p. viii)

A clue to this shift is provided in his preface where he acknowledges "...many intellectual debts in the production of this work. One of the greatest is to Stanley Engerman, whose help and advice have been quite extraordinary" (p. xii).

It should come as no surprise, however, that the insistent voices of several African, Caribbean, and Afro-American scholars are found in the rising tide of commentary which has sought to reaffirm the conventional thesis that the slave[ry] trade was important to the economic rise of Europe and the United States. This body of scholarship, which has increased over the past ten years, has seriously challenged the challengers such as Engerman and others and hopefully signals a "paradigm shift" back to the position elaborated by Malachi Postlethwayt and his contemporaries, and by generations of black scholars and writers.[15] A brief review of these scholars follows, using the writings of Bailey, Inikori, and Darity as representative of a growing trend.

Bailey (1979, 1986, 1990, 1994) was one of the earliest responses to Engerman. His early work reviewed the historiography of the slave trade, and discussed the controversy over Eric Williams's *Capitalism and Slavery*. Using a sample of almost 4747 ships, including 122 slave ships carrying over 9000 slaves between 1718 and 1765 and other data, Bailey found a pattern of involvement by US merchants in the slave trade which was shaped by their dominant colonial status rather than moral considerations. British merchants with large ships controlled the more profitable routes, say between Africa and Charleston, South Carolina. But North American merchants played leading roles as slave traders on less lucrative routes such as those into Savannah.

Another contribution was Bailey's critique of the work of Stanley Engerman on the slave trade, one of the first published, which anticipated subsequent lines of discussion. Using assumptions more consistent with the "triangular trade" thesis, Bailey substituted profits from overseas commerce to the Caribbean instead of the slave-selling profits which Engerman preferred. He found that the profits from the Caribbean trade could have accounted for over 82 per cent of total capital formation in 1770, and could have yielded over four times the total amount of capital invested in British industry in this same year, very different from Engerman's dismissal of the slave trade's significance. Bailey concluded:

> Thus, for a source of capital sufficient to finance industrialization, and to support the expensive habits of the British ruling elites, we need look no further than the profits from the overseas trade to the Caribbean, of which the slave trade and related commerce was an indispensable prop.
>
> (Bailey 1986: 32)

Bailey also highlighted the impact of the slave trade on the shipping trade and the industrialization of textiles in New England. He elaborated an alternative approach to explaining the rise of industrialization by linking it to the impact of the slave trade on increasing trade and related commerce and expanding the production of commodities. Additionally, the slave trade increased the accumulation of capital which was used to finance industrial advances.

> The central thesis of this study is that the conduct of the slave trade by New England merchants and the entire colonial commerce to which the slave trade was inseparably linked made a large and essential contribution to the early development of the US capitalism and imperialism. First, it enabled colonial merchants to accumulate funds which were subsequently used to finance key aspects of the process of industrialization. Second, the expansion of commodity production to meet the increased demand for goods used in the "triangular slave trade" and related commerce caused a significant expansion of the productive capacity of the US economy and paved the way for rapid industrialization through increased division of labor, specialization, and improved technology.
>
> (Bailey 1979: 1)

This argument outlined much of the subsequent discussion in response to Engerman and others over the past ten years.

Bailey's work on the role of the slave[ry] trade in the rise of industrial capitalism in New England is his more significant work.

> New England's maritime trade and shipping laid the foundation for, raised the infrastructure of, and funded early industrial development. This was particularly the case for the cotton textile industry between 1815 and 1860. Maritime trade and shipping depended largely on the slave trade and on the slave-based economic system of the seventeenth, eighteenth, and nineteenth centuries. The early industries, such as shipbuilding and rum distilling, were directly tied to the slave trade and to maritime activities in general. These helped pave the way for the establishment of the textile industry, which, together with the production of cotton textile machinery, became the leading sector of US industrialization in the nineteenth century.... The contribution of the slave trade and New World slavery to the entire process is hard to exaggerate....[16]

Philip Curtin's (1969) *The Atlantic Slave Trade: A Census* spurred extensive debate. The book has been variously applauded and criticized. More important, Curtin's findings have been used by Engerman and others to discuss the issue of profitability. The debate continues to rage, largely as a result of the work of the Nigerian economic historian, Joseph E. Inikori. Inikori (1976a, 1976b) responded to the work of Curtin, Anstey, and others with three criticisms: the number of slaves exported was underestimated, the estimated prices paid for them were too high and their sale prices too low; and the value of raw materials returned in British ships was underestimated. All of this would have lowered the amount of profits calculated. In his book *Forced Migration: The Impact of the Export Slave Trade on African Societies* (1982), Inikori suggests an upward revision for Curtin's estimates: "The independent estimates made since my own assessment of Curtin's and Anstey's figures, and my own repeated re-examination of the subject, assure me that a 40 per cent upward adjustment of Curtin's global figure is quite reasonable" (p. 20).

Another assertion which sought to undermine the contribution of the slave trade was that by Bean and Thomas (1974) that the slave trade was characterized by a high degree of competition which prevented large monopoly profits; this was challenged by Inikori (1981). He presented evidence which showed that the top ten (of forty) firms in the 1790 Liverpool slave trade controlled almost 65 per cent of that trade, and that the London and Bristol trade was even more monopolized. This line of discussion is important because it is the basis for challenging certain theoretical assumptions of the paradigm which has been used to attack the slave trade's significance. It argues that we should trace the use of profits by the largest slave traders and not make a priori assumptions about the distribution of profits before such questions are studied concretely. Such an approach is also more effective than simply assessing the impact of slave trade profits on the aggregate of British national income and not the particular applications of leading merchants who may have helped finance industrialization.

In another important contribution, Inikori addresses the impact of the slave trade on economies outside Africa. His perspective is rooted in the theory of international trade and his conclusion is in the spirit of the early mercantilists:

> It is clear that the phenomenal expansion of world trade between 1451 and 1870, depended largely on the employment of African slaves in the exploitation of American resources, and that the development and growth of Western European and North American economies during this period were greatly influenced by the expanded world trade. This leads to the inference that the slave trade was a critical factor in the development of West European and North American economies in the period of this study.
>
> (Inikori 1979: 78–80)

Though he protested that linking him to the controversy over Williams's *Capitalism and Slavery* was "diversionary," Inikori's work represented an essential stance in the critique of those scholars who sought to downplay the slave trade's contribution as having largely been a "mythical" one. In another contribution, Inikori sought to demonstrate that the cotton textile industry in England developed as an "import substitution industry," replacing goods which had once been imported from India. A crisis was resolved by increasing exports of cotton textile for the slave trade in Africa and for the clothing of African slaves on New World plantations. Hence, "the revolution in cotton textile production in England owed a great deal to the slave trade from Africa and from African slavery in the New World" (Inikori 1992: 172).

Inikori's findings have been synthesized in his contribution to the *General History of Africa V: Africa from the Sixteenth to the Eighteenth Century* (1992), a significant publication with several articles related to this chapter. The articles ambitiously and successfully seek to explain Africa's place in world history, both its contribution to the rise of the Atlantic system which came to dominate the world, and Africa's own underdevelopment which is rooted in the same set of historical dynamics.

African American economist William Darity, Jr. has produced a rigorous and refreshing discussion of the triangular trade thesis. In a highly technical article, Darity seeks to test and defend what he calls "the Caribbean school thesis" – the work of C. L. R. James, Eric Williams, and Walter Rodney – that the slave trade boosted the economic development of Europe while simultaneously deepening the underdevelopment of Africa and the Caribbean. He applies a general equilibrium model to the triangular trade and concludes that even under the "least likely" case there is evidence to support the thesis, "in direct contrast to the prevailing orthodoxy" (Darity 1982a). In another article, Darity (1982b) argues that Williams's *Capitalism and*

Slavery should be understood in the context of explaining the role of the slave trade and plantation slavery in facilitating the economic policy of mercantilism in France and in Britain.

In another contribution, Darity assessed the implications of Inikori's argument that the slave trade was not perfectly competitive and his finding that Curtin, Anstey and others underestimated several factors which would lower the estimates of the trade's "profitability." Darity demonstrates that Inikori's revised figures can account for a profit rate of 30 per cent, a figure rejected by many scholars as too high and unsubstantiated with sound evidence. His conclusions regarding the triangular trade thesis are most intriguing and consistent with the discussion presented above.

> Williams' theory is more complex than the argument that profits from the slave trade were an important source of funds for industrial investment.... His theory really constitutes an analysis of the functional role that the slave trade and slavery played in implementing mercantilism in France and Britain.
>
> It was not profitability or profits from the slave trade that were essential in Williams' theory, but that the American colonies could not have been developed without slavery. Without the colonies, mercantilist development would have been crippled. Ironically, although the profitability controversy was precipitated by reaction to Williams' *Capitalism and Slavery*, the issue of profitability is of little relevance to the assessment of the theory.
>
> (Darity 1975: 702)

In fact, Darity argues that "...it is time to look at Williams' theory from the richer standpoint of mercantilist ideology and capitalist development. Indeed, the debate over the magnitude of the profits of the slave trade may be the 'diversion', and careful study of *Capitalism and Slavery* the main point" (p. 703).[17]

Another recent contribution links British industrialization to plantation economies, an argument which repudiates the views of several scholars who view the Caribbean as a drain on the resources of England (Darity 1992).

Beckles (1982), in an important historiographical commentary on the persistence of the controversy over *Capitalism and Slavery*, views the book as embodying three theses on: the origins of slavery; the contribution to industrialization; and the role of industrial capitalism in overthrowing slavery. Darity has made a contribution to the third element. In an article on the historiography of abolition, he summarized Williams's view that the slave trade and slavery in Britain, while called into existence by developing British industrial capitalism, was abolished by a mature industrial capitalism which no longer found their economic contribution as lucrative. This conclusion that abolition resulted from economic forces contradicted the long-standing view in British historiography that abolition was essentially a humanitarian undertaking (Darity 1988).

In his review of *Capitalism and Slavery* in 1945, Carter G. Woodson, known as the father of Negro History, said: "The book should make a strong appeal to those who now array themselves against the British Empire because of its present policy of grabbing all of the universe which it can find any excuse for taking over." Now, fifty years later, explorations of the slave trade and slavery, as historical roots of present-day exploitation and oppression of people of African descent, are as central to the discussion as they were when Woodson made his observation. And this is likely to remain the case, as the public policy debates and recent work of Inikori and Darity indicate.

Inikori was commissioned by the Government of the Federal Republic of Nigeria to examine the slave trade's relationship to the rise of the capitalist world economy as the "scientific basis of Africa's demand for reparations." Based on his research cited above, his conclusions are not surprising:

> From the evidence on the damage caused by the European slave trade to Africa's competitiveness within the capitalist world economy, and on the basis of the contribution of Africa to the development of capitalism in Western Europe and North America, it is clear that Africa's demand for reparations by Europe and North America can be based on a scientific analysis of the evidence. . . . Over and above the payment, Western Europe and North America should tender an apology to Africa and its people all over the world on the open floor of the United Nations.
>
> (Inikori 1991)

Indeed, Richard America's compilation *The Wealth of Races* (1990) contains even more astounding data. There, three economists calculated the 1983 value of incomes earned by African Americans and unjustly withheld by slaveholders up to 1860 at $1.4 trillion and between $2.1 and $4.7 trillion. Making this issue of reparations for the damage of the slave trade and slavery plausible is this fact: based on an agreement signed in Luxembourg between West Germany and the World Jewish Congress in 1952, the West German government has been paying reparations to victims of the Holocaust, an amount which has been estimated at $48 billion as of the 1980s. Reparations have also been paid by the US government to Japanese Americans for their "internment" in concentration camps during the Second World War and to Native Americans for lands illegally seized. William Darity (1990) puts forward this conclusion after reviewing the arguments in America's book:

> Those who now possess America's wealth, of course, will resist all calls for reparations, contending they are outrageous, despite ample precedents. They have the most to lose today and perhaps the most to fear from an unknown postreparations future. To overcome their resistance and to have reparations paid to black Americans – to let the forty acres and a mule – would require a revolutionary transformation of American society unto itself. Even then, would $1 trillion genuinely pay for the dark side of the heritage of blacks in America?

The other side of the coin to Darity's argument, of course, are the conditions faced by people of African descent, termed the "underdevelopment" of Africa by the late Walter Rodney, "persistent poverty" by the late George Beckford of Jamaica, and the growth of the "underclass" by a host of US scholars. Regardless of the terminology, the reality is clear: black people in Africa, the Caribbean, the United States and in other parts of the world bear a disproportionate share of the economic deprivation and social dislocation existing in those societies. That this burden is nowhere near commensurate with the historical contributions made by these peoples via the slave trade and slavery and other historical vehicles over the centuries is the central theme of the work of black scholars.

These facts speak to the continuing dynamics of race and class in America. It appears that Du Bois was right: the problem of the twentieth century will indeed be the problem of the color line. And it will be more. It should not surprise economists or those who will read a volume summarizing the economic thought of black scholars that Du Bois's admonition from 1954 (reprinted 1973) is likely to continue to be compelling: "What we need is to add to our terribly conscientious search into the facts of the slave-trade the clear concept of Marx on the class struggle for income and power, beneath which all considerations of morals were twisted or utterly crushed." Paraphrasing Du Bois, we should hope to become as wise in the twenty-first century as we should be from having lived through the twentieth and studied the lives of black people who have lived before.

The study of history, including the history of ideas, should provide as complete an understanding of what actually happened as possible. It should reveal a sense of the theoretical import of the historical events under examination – what it does to help us to explain about the particular issues under study, as well as all related and comparable circumstances. Finally, the study of history should also help reveal the present-day and future import and impact of understanding this historical event – what it does to help to explain and predict about where "history" and the consumers of historical knowledge are headed in the here and now, and beyond.

As to what actually happened in history, W. E. B. Du Bois put it clearly: "somebody in each era must make clear the facts with utter disregard to his own wish and desire and belief. What we have got to know, so far as possible, are the things that actually happened in the world." It is here that the glaring biases of much too much scholarship on the slave[ry] trade are all too obvious. How could so significant a story – with such powerful and far-reaching factual and theoretical implications – be left out of "history", or have had its significance so grossly distorted? It is in light of these omissions and distortions that the real import of Afro-American intellectual history on the subject becomes all the more profound.

In an unpublished essay, St. Clair Drake summed up the relationship of the rise of Black Studies to mainstream scholarship:

> The very use of the term Black Studies is by implication an indictment of American and Western European scholarship. It makes the bold assertion that what we have heretofore called "objective" intellectual activities were actually white studies in perspective and content; and that corrective bias, a shift in emphasis, is needed, even if something called "truth" is set as a goal. To use a technical sociological term, the present body of knowledge has an ideological element in it, and a counter-ideology is needed. Black Studies supply that counter-ideology.

An example from the sciences is appropriate. It is easy for us to understand how the Hubble telescope launched aboard a satellite in 1987 will gather "new science", and in the words of a NASA spokesperson, help us "rewrite the science textbooks." But it appears impossible for many scholars of history and culture to understand how new scholarship might correct intentional and unintentional biases, even on something as fundamental as the contributions of people of color to Western civilization.

The verdict from the most recent debates regarding our understanding of the history and relationship of slavery and the slave trade to the rise of capitalism is not yet in. But I am certain that the Africans who were the victims of this gruesome commerce, knowing what actually happened and upon reviewing the recent twenty-year record of scholarship on the slave trade's role in world history, would reach a conclusion similar to the eloquent words of Ralph Ellison (1952) in the opening paragraph of *The Invisible Man*:

> I am an invisible man.... I am invisible, understand, simply because people refuse to see me. Like the bodiless heads you see sometimes in the circus sideshows, it is as though I have been surrounded by mirrors of hard, distorting glass. When they approach me they see only my surroundings, themselves, or figments of their imagination – indeed, everything and anything except me.
>
> (Ellison 1952: 1)

It is this *invisibility* which has been the chief target of Afro-American intellectuals on the slave[ry] trade. And the increasing efforts to make issues of race and class invisible throughout the historical record and in contemporary intellectual and policy discussions will undoubtedly energize many such debates well into the twenty-first century.[18]

And in the spirit of academic excellence and social responsibility – the Black Studies' legacy of linking the intellectual to the practical struggle for social transformation – as we continue to understand the history of the slave trade and its role in spawning a continuing pattern of exploitation and oppressive inequities, black scholars and all scholars who review the evidence objectively must declare: "Never Again!"

NOTES

1 "The Deep" was based on a novel by Peter Benchley who co-wrote the screenplay with Peter Yates, the film's director. It was released in 1977 by Columbia Pictures/ECI and Casablanca Films, starring Nick Nolte and Eli Wallach.

2 I am here relying on Philip Curtin, *The Atlantic Slave Trade: A Census*, (Wisconsin, 1969, p. 269). For a criticism of these figures as being too low, see Inikori (1982), discussed below.

3 Flowing from my critique of the manner in which Engerman and others too narrowly constrict the triangular trade thesis to focus solely on the exchange of slave bodies as commodities, my use of the term slave[ry] trade is intended to counter this approach. In the spirit of Eric Williams's *Capitalism and Slavery* and other classic writings on the subject, it is the commerce in slave bodies, the trade of slave-produced commodities, the exchanges of goods with slave-based economies, and a variety of linked activities – banking, insurance, shipping and shipbuilding, to mention only a few – that comprise the extensive and complex network which came to be known as the triangular trade, a reality I hope I capture in calling it the slave[ry] trade.

4 There is a growing trend which gives serious attention to the historical moorings of contemporary Afro-American scholarship. See, for example, the following contributions: Darlene Clark Hine (ed.), *State of Afro-American History: Past, Present and Future*, (Baton Rouge: LSU, 1986); August Meier and Elliot Rudwick, *Black Historians and the Historical Profession, 1915–1980*, (Urbana: University of Illinois Press); Jacqueline Goggin, *Carter G. Woodson*, (Baton Rouge: LSU Press, 1993); William Darity, *Race, Radicalism and Reform: Selected Papers of Abram Harris*, (New Brunswick: Transaction Publications, 1989); Joyce Ladner, *The Death of White Sociology*, (New York: Random House, 1973). For a useful review of several subfields in Black Studies, copies might be located of an unpublished survey of course syllabi conducted by the Institute of the Black World and funded by FIPSE. One published contribution to this effort is Gerald McWorter and Ronald Bailey, "Black Studies Curriculum Development in the 1980s: Its Patterns and History," in *The Black Scholar* (March–April and November–December), 1984. Also important is Alkalimat, *Paradigms in Black Studies* (Chicago: Twenty First Century Books and Publications, 1991). David L. Lewis, *W. E. B. Du Bois: Biography of a Race, 1868–1919* (New York: Henry Holt, 1993) is most useful. In the field of literary studies see, for example, Maryemma Graham (ed), *How I Wrote Jubilee and Other Essays on Life and Literature* by Margaret Walker (New York: Feminist Press, 1990) and *On Being*

Female, Black, and Free: The Writings of Margaret Walker (University of Tennessee Press, forthcoming).

There is yet to be written a definitive synthesis of the practice of Afro-American scholarship and its meanings, responding, for example, to the provocative issues in E. F. Frazier's "The Failure of the Negro Intellectual.", *Negro Digest* (February, 1962).

5 I have deliberately confined my attention to the slave trade and closely related aspects of slavery. I have not taken up a full treatment of the debate over slavery. See Peter Paris, *Slavery: History and Historians* (New York: Harper and Row, 1989) for a review of the scholarship on the larger issue. Given the decision to award the 1993 Nobel Prize in economics to William Fogel and to Douglass C. North, for works which take up slavery in crucial ways, fuller and more critical reviews will hopefully be forthcoming.

6 See Ronald Bailey, "Africa, the Slave Trade, and Industrial Capitalism in Europe and the United States: A Historiographic Review," in *American History: A Bibliographic Review* (Volume II, 1986, pp. 1–92). Portions of this longer treatment have been used in developing the present paper. While the focus of this article is black intellectual history, contributions by white scholars to reiterating the significance of the slave trade – and to negating it – have also been important, and my bibliographic article covers the broader field of commentary.

7 I am reminded by Derrick Jackson, an African American columnist with *The Boston Globe*, that my conventional starting point in a discussion of black economic thought on the slave trade should perhaps not begin with Dr. W. E. B. Du Bois, or with the scholars who were formally trained in economics. On 4 July 1994, *The Boston Globe*, as is its custom, reprinted "The Declaration of Independence." His selection, drawn from Frederick Douglass, sharply reminded me of just how the parameters of discussion must be expanded if we are to understand Afro-American thought on the slave trade. Those Afro-American commentators who were close to the actual event and subject matter under discussion are sources of great clarity and understanding.

8 Du Bois is thus one of several black scholars who introduce the work of Karl Marx as a main source for commentary on the slave trade by nineteenth century observers. While Marx did not exhaustively investigate Africa and other third world societies firsthand, he placed the plunder of Africans and other people of color at the very foundations of modern capitalism. Marx's comments in *Poverty of Philosophy* (1847) and *Capital* (1867) are discussed in Bailey (1986, pp 10–11).

9 For a glimpse of the impact of the Depression on university-based black intellectuals, see, for example, two works on Ralph Bunche: Brian Urquhart, *Ralph Bunche: An American Life* (New York: W. W. Norton, 1993); and Benjamin Rivlin, *Ralph Bunche: The Man and His Times* (New York: Holmes and Meier, 1990), especially Charles Henry's "Civil Rights and National Security: The Case of Ralph Bunche," 50–68. See also William Darity, *Race, Radicalism and Reform: Selected Papers of Abram Harris* (New Brunswick: Transaction Publications), 1989.

10 In the more particular study of Africa's history, the path-breaking work of the late Walter Rodney provides much clarity. In addition to the general thesis expressed in the title of his most popular work, *How Europe Underdeveloped Africa* (1972), Rodney takes up the impact of the slave trade in his *A History of the Upper Guinea Coast, 1545 to 1800* (1970).

11 "Since the publication of *Capitalism and Slavery*, historical writing on the British West Indies has, to a large extent, involved a conscious confirmation or refutation of Williams's several theses." (Greene 1977: pp. 509–30). For a sampling of the manner in which Williams's *Capitalism and Slavery* continues to arouse the

passions of scholars see, for example, Barbara Solow, *British Capitalism and Caribbean Slavery: The Legacy of Eric Williams* (Cambridge: Cambridge University Press, 1987).

12 The importance of this is found in the historical significance of Howard University as a center for black intellectual and academic traditions, especially as a center for Pan-African interaction. E. Franklin Frazier (sociology), Ralph Bunche (political science), Doxey Wilkerson (education), James Porter (art), and Dorothy Porter Wesley (library) are a few of the scholars who were active at Howard in this period. The Joint Committee for National Recovery remains an essential case study in understanding the radicalization of black intellectuals in the 1930s. For contributions to this discussion, see Darity (1989).

13 This issue of shifting paradigms is at the core of the debate over Martin Bernal, *Black Athena: The Afro-Asiatic Roots of Classical Civilizations* (New Brunswick, NJ: Rutgers University Press) 1987–1991. See also Mary Lefkowitz, *Not Out of Africa: How Afro-Centrism Became an Excuse to Teach Myth as History.* (New York City: Basic Book, 1996).

14 While the repudiation has not been explicit – too few things are in too many sectors of the academy – it is a repudiation nonetheless. One fact of note is that Engerman has been associated with two conferences, one "honoring Eric Williams," and co-editor of two important volumes in which the preponderance of opinion found considerably more merit in the arguments of Eric Williams than he found in this 1972 essay: with Barbara Solow, *British Capitalism and Caribbean Slavery: The Legacy of Eric Williams* (Cambridge: Cambridge University Press, 1987); and with Joseph Inikori, *The Atlantic Slave Trade: Effects on Economics, Societies, and Peoples in Africa, the Americas, and Europe* (Durham: Duke University Press, 1992).

15 Again, this is not to imply that other non-black scholars have not made important contributions. By far the most detailed and useful account of the American slave trade is Jay Alan Coughtry's (1981) *The Notorious Triangle: Rhode Island and the Slave Trade 1700–1807.*

Economist Barbara Solow (1985), also using economic modelling, argues convincingly that the Williams thesis has been misconstrued by many critics. She sees substantial evidence that the slave trade and related commerce was "an engine of growth for the whole economy and in particular for the industrial sector."

While some scholars are thus shifting gears away from the conventional thesis advanced by the mercantalists and generations of scholars since then, and popularized by Eric Williams, Gavin Wright (1985) is among those finding a basis for renewed support.

16 So that an accurate intellectual history of the debate over the impact of the slave trade on industrial capitalism can someday be written, I must point to one of several interesting developments which seem motivated by something other than academic considerations. A conference was organized at Harvard in 1988 to take up this issue. My invitation to participate was extended informally, but did not materialize. I was later surprised to learn that David Richardson was invited to present a paper which was far removed from his usual emphasis on Africa and Great Britain. I was even more surprised when he failed to note in his paper that he had participated on a panel at the Joint Session of the American Economics Association/Economic History Association and the National Economics Association in New Orleans, LA. in December, 1986. I presented a paper "Africa, The Slave Trade, and the Rise of Industrial Capitalism in Europe and the United States," and shared materials with him. However, twenty years is simply too long

a gestation period for my book-length contribution to this debate, so I have no one to blame but myself if scholars who disagree with my views choose to ignore my work and not provide the reading public with full citations in the debate.

17 There is a growing body of Marxist scholarship which treats the role of the slave trade in the tradition of Karl Marx discussed above. Lloyd Hogan (1984) devotes considerable attention to "Atlantic slave operations as a major source of capital accumulation in Western Europe between 1450 and 1790." See also Cedric Robinson, *Black Marxism.* A useful starting point in this review is Abdul Alkalinat, *Paradigms in Black Studies* (Chicago: Twenty-first Century Books and Publications, 1993).

18 In fact, I would attribute the intense discussion over the slave trade (and slavery) and the rise of capitalism – this "historical perennial" – not mainly to a concern with history but in larger measure to a concern with how much of the present state of social and economic relations (e.g., racism, poverty, etc.) should be attributed to the long distant origins of these current realities.

McDonald (1979, 67) in reviewing the recent scholarship on the Williams thesis, linked *Capitalism and Slavery* to issues in the work of such writers as Daniel Moynihan and Gunnar Myrdal, saying Williams's book posed "a fundamental challenge to western historiographical tradition and western values."

The conservative swing in the United States has been well discussed, and its roots as a "backlash" in reaction to the black freedom movement and in response to the liberal agenda of the War on Poverty and other social programs is documented. Is it coincidental that the shift in interpretation of the slave trade's role occurred at the same time as conservative social and political winds gathered velocity? Just as black liberation activists and their supporters use the slave trade's "immense profitability" as a moral support in their demands for modern day justice, historians who minimize this profitability handle the moral issues differently.

REFERENCES

America Richard F., *The Wealth of Races: The Present Value of Benefits from Past Injustices* (New York, 1990). See also his *Paying the Social Debt: What White America Owes Black America* (Westport: Praeger, 1993).

Anstey, Roger, *The Atlantic Slave Trade and British Abolition 1760–1810*, Atlantic Highlands, NJ: Humanities Press, 1975.

Bailey, Ronald, "The Slave Trade and the Development of Capitalism in the United States: A Critical Reappraisal of Theory and Method in Afro-American Studies." PhD dissertation, Stanford University, 1979.

Bailey, Ronald, "Africa, the Slave Trade, and Industrial Capitalism in Europe and the United States: A Historiographic Review," *American History: A Bibliographic Review* (Volume II, 1986), pp. 1–91.

Bailey, Ronald "The Slave(ry) Trade and the Development of Capitalism in the United States: The Textile Industry in New England". *Social Science History*, Duke University Press, 14:3 (Fall 1990) pp. 373–414, in Inikori and Engerman, *The Atlantic Slave Trade: Effects on Economics, Societies, and Peoples in Africa, the Americas, and Europe*, Duke, 1992.

Bailey, Ronald, "The Other Side of Slavery: Black Labor, Cotton, and Textile Industrial in Great Britain and the United States," Agricultural History (68: 2), Spring 1994, 35–50.

Bean, Richard N. and Robert Thomas, "Fishers of Men: The Profits of the Slave Trade," *Journal of Economic History* 34 (1974): 885–914.

Beckford, George, *Persistent Poverty: Underdevelopment in Plantation Economies of the Third World*, London: Zed, 1983.

Beckles, Hilary, "Down but Not Out: Eric Williams' Capitalism and Slavery After Nearly Forty years of Criticism," *Bulletin of Eastern Caribbean Affairs* 8 (1982): 29–36.

Coughtry, Jay, *The Notorious Triangle: Rhode Island and the Slave Trade 1700–1807*, Philadelphia: Temple University Press, 1981.

Cox, Oliver Cromwell, *Class, Caste, and Race*, New York: Doubleday, 1948.

Cox, Oliver Cromwell, *Capitalism as a System*, New York: Monthly Review Press, 1964.

Curtin, Phillip, *The Atlantic Slave Trade: A Census*, Madison: University of Wisconsin Press, 1969.

Darity, William, Jr., "The Numbers Game and the Profitability of the British Trade in Slaves," *Journal of Economic History* 45 (1975): 693–703.

Darity, William, Jr. "A General Equilibrium Model of the Eighteenth Century Atlantic Slave Trade: A Least Likely Test," *Research in Economic History* 7 (1982a): 290–321.

Darity, William, Jr., "Mercantilism, Slavery, and the Industrial Revolution," *Research in Political Economy* 5 (1982b): 1–21.

Darity, William, Jr., "The Williams' Thesis Before Eric Williams," *Abolition and Slavery* 9:1 (May 1988): 29–41.

Darity, William, Jr., "Forty Acres and A Mule: Placing a Price Tag on Oppression," in Richard America (ed.), *The Wealth of Races*, pp.1–13, Westport: Greenwood, 1990.

Darity, William, Jr., "British Industry and the West Indies Plantations," in Joseph Inikori and Stanley Engerman, *The Atlantic Slave Trade: Effects on Economics, Societies, and Peoples in Aftica, the Americas, and Europe*, pp.247–82, (Durham: Duke, 1992).

Davis, David Brion, "Slavery and the Post-World War Historians," *Daedalus* 103 (1974): 1–16.

Davis, David Brion, *The Problem of Slavery in the Age of Revolution, 1770–1823*, Ithaca: Cornell University Press, 1975.

Du Bois, W. E. B., *Black Reconstruction in America*, New York: Antheneum, 1935.

Du Bois, W. E. B., *The Suppression of the African Slave Trade to the United States 1638–1870*. Millwood, New York: Kraus-Thomson, 1973. (Reprint of the 1954 edition published by Social Science Press.)

Ellison, Ralph, *Invisible Man*, New York: Random House, 1952.

Eltis, D., "Free and Coerced Transatlantic Migrations: Some Comparisons." American Historical Review 88 (1983): 278.

Engerman, Stanley L., "Slave Trade and British Capital Formation in the Eighteenth Century: A Comment on the William Thesis," *Journal of Business History* 46 (1972): 430–43.

Greene, Lorenzo Johnson, *The Negro in Colonial New England, 1620–1776*, New York: Columbia University, 1942.

Green, William, "Caribbean Historiography, 1600–1900: The Recent Tide." *Journal of Interdisciplinary Studies* 7 (1977): 509–30.

Harris, Abram L., *The Negro as Capitalist: A Study of Banking and Business Among American Negroes*, Philadelphia: American Academy of Political Science, 1936.

Hogan, Lloyd, *Principles of Black Political Economy*, Boston: Routledge and Kegan Paul, 1984.

Holmes, Eugene, review of Abraham Harris, "The Negro as Capitalist" in *Science and Society*, I (1936–1937): 261.

Hughes, Jonathan, *American Economic History*, Glenview, IL: Scott, Foresman and Company, 1983.

Inikori, Joseph and Stanley Engerman, *The Atlantic Slave Trade: Effects on Economics, Societies, and Peoples in Africa, the Americas, and Europe*, Durham: Duke, 1992.

Inikori, J. E., "Measuring the Atlantic Slave Trade: An Assessment of Curtin and Anstey," *Journal of African History* 17 (1976a): 197–223.

Inikori, J. E., "Measuring the Atlantic Slave Trade: A Rejoinder," *Journal of African History* 17 (1976b): 607–22.

Inikori, J. E., "The Slave Trade and the Atlantic Economies, 1451–1870," in UNESCO, *The African Slave Trade from the Fifteenth to the Nineteenth Century: Reports and Papers of the Meeting of Experts*, pp. 56–85, New York: Unipub, 1979.

Inikori, J. E., "Market Structure and the profits of the British African Trade in the Late Eighteenth Century," *Journal of Economic History* 41 (1981): 745–76.

Inikori, J. E., (ed.) *Forced Migration*, NY: Africana Publishing, 1982.

Inikori, J. E., "Market Structure and the profits of the British African Trade in Late Eighteenth Century: A Rejoinder." *Journal of Economic History* 43 (1983): 723–8.

Inikori, J. E., "The European Slave Trade to Africa. The Rise of the Capitalist World Economy, and the Relative Position of African Economies: An Examination of the Scientific Basis of Africa's Demand for Reparations," A Scientific Paper Commissioned by the Government of the Federal Republic of Nigeria (May 1991).

Inikori, J. E., "Africa in World History: the export slave trade from Africa and the emergence of the Atlantic economic order," in B. A. Ogot (ed.) *General History of Africa: Africa from the Sixteenth to the Eighteenth Century* (1992).

James, C. L. R., *Black Jacobins: Toussaint L'Ouverture and the Santo Domingo Revolution*, NY: Dial Press, 1963.

James, C. L. R., "The Atlantic Slave Trade and Slavery: Some Interpretations of Their Significance in the Development of the United States," in John A. Williams and Charles Harris (eds.), Amistad (New York, 1970).

McCusker, John J. and Russell R. Menard, *The Economy of British America, 1607–1789*, Chapel Hill: University of North Carolina Press, 1985.

McDonald, Roderick, "The Williams Thesis: A Comment on the State of Scholarship," *Caribbean Quarterly* 25 (1979): 63–8.

Marx, Karl, *Capital: A Critique of Capitalist Production*, New York: International Publishers, 1947.

Marx, Karl, *Poverty of Philosophy*, New York: International Publishers, 1963.

Ogot, B. A., (ed.) *General History of Africa V: Africa from the Sixteenth to the Eighteenth Century*. Berkeley: University of California Press, 1992.

Paris, Peter, *Slavery: History and Historians*. New York: Harper and Row, 1989.

Patterson, Orlando, "The Black Community: Is There a Future?," in Lipset, Seymour Martin (ed.), *The Third Century*, pp. 244–84, Stanford: Hoover Institution Press, 1979.

Patterson, Orlando, *Slavery and Social Death: A Comparative Study*, Cambridge: Harvard University Press, 1982.

Postlethwayt, Malachi, *The African Trade: The Great Pillar and Support of the British Plantation in America, by a British Merchant*, London: J. Robinson, 1745.

Rawley, James A., *The Transatlantic Slave Trade: A History*, New York: W. W. Norton & Company, 1981.

Rees, J.F., "The Phases of British Commercial Policy in the Eighteenth Century." *Economica* (June 1925): 142.

Reynolds, Edward, *Stand the Storm: A History of the Atlantic Slave Trade*, Chicago: I.R. Dee, 1993.

Robinson, Cedric, *Black Marxism: The Making of the Black Radical Tradition*, London: Zed, 1983.

Rodney, Walter, *A History of the Upper Guinea Coast, 1545 to 1800*, New York: Monthly Review Press, 1970.

Rodney, Walter, *How Europe Underdeveloped Africa*, Washington: Howard University Press, 1972.

Solow, Barbara L., "Caribbean Slavery and British Growth: The Eric Williams Hypothesis," *Journal of Development Economics* 17 (1985): 99–115.

Solow, Barbara, *British Capitalism and American Slavery: The Legacy of Eric Williams*, Cambridge: Cambridge University Press, 1987.

Spero, Sterling D. and Abraham L. Harris, *The Black Worker: The Negro and the Labor Movement*. New York: Atheneum, 1931.

Walvin, James, *Slavery and the Slave Trade*, Jackson: University Press of Mississippi, 1983.

Williams, Eric, *Capitalism and Slavery*, Chapel Hill: University of North Carolina Press, (1944): p. 19.

Williams, Wilson, "Africa and the Rise of Capitalism," Master's thesis, Howard University, 1936.

Woodman, Harold D., "The Profitability of Slavery: A Historical Perennial," *Journal of Southern History* 29 (1963): 1–24.

Wright, Gavin, (1985) "Capitalism and Slavery on the Islands: Lesson from the Mainland," in *Caribbean Slavery and British Capitalism*, Barbara L. Solow and Stanley L. Engerman, (eds), Cambridge: Cambridge University Press.

Wright, Richard, "12 Million Black Voices." In *Richard Wright Reader*, by Ellen Wright and Michel Fabre, 144–242. New York: Harper & Row, 1978.

Wood, William, A Survey of Trade, III: p.178, London, 1718.

14

PROMOTING BLACK ENTREPRENEURSHIP AND BUSINESS ENTERPRISE IN ANTEBELLUM AMERICA

The National Negro Convention, 1830–60

Juliet E. K. Walker

INTRODUCTION

Before the Civil War, twenty-two African Americans accumulated wealth ranging from $100,000 to $1.5 million.[1] They were entrepreneurs, whose profitable enterprises in antebellum America compare in rank and standing to the contemporary listing of America's Top 100 Black Businesses, *Black Enterprises*.[2] An established African American business class had emerged in post-Revolutionary War America. With almost 90 per cent of the black population in slavery and over 90 per cent of the free black population employed at menial labor, the black business class comprised but a small segment in the occupational distribution of the new nation's labor force. Yet, despite pervasive forces of racism and slavery, which limited the full participation of blacks in the pre-industrial mercantile economy of the American business community, the number of black business owners increased with each successive generation in the decades before the Civil War. By 1860, the proportion of black business owners, paradoxically, differed little from the proportion of black business owners in the post Civil Rights Era of late twentieth century America.[3]

Blacks, both slave and free, male and female, used "sweat equity" in their capacity as human capital to establish business enterprises in virtually all sectors of the American economy from the Colonial Era on. In addition to the illegal practice of slaves who hired their own time and established enterprises, an informal underground slave economy developed, primarily in the production and marketing of food-stuffs. These activities provided the initial basis for blacks to participate in the American economy.[4] Profits earned by slave businesspeople enabled some to purchase freedom. Once manumitted, most continued their business activities in enterprises initiated by them before their manumission. In some instances new enterprises were developed.[5]

African American business activity reflected entrepreneurial initiative, creativity, and expertise. However encouragement from the institutional antebellum black community, which provided support for their efforts, was also important. Prior to the Civil War, the National Negro Convention ranked foremost among the organizations founded by African Americans to promote black business participation. To underscore the significance of black business promotion before the Civil War, a review of the goals and activities of the National Negro Convention to promote black business provides the focus of this two-part study.[6]

In Part One, a summary review of the business goals of the National Negro Convention is provided. Because the origin of the National Negro Convention and its business promotional efforts were inextricably linked to black emigration activities and white colonization efforts, a brief discussion of the organization's position on emigration and colonization, especially in relation to Canada and Africa, is included. Simply put, in response to the devastatingly pernicious effects of their subordinate legal status and the tyranny of their economic oppression, it appeared to the National Negro Convention delegates that only two, although diametrically opposing alternatives, were available to African Americans to survive the structural violence inherent in America's racist slave society: either to leave the United States or to go into business.

There were black Americans who saw other alternatives to black survival in the United States, although most lacked the prominence and distinction of delegates to the National Negro Convention. Often, their voices were mute, but not that of the noted antebellum black activist Frances Ellen Watkins Harper. In 1859, while demanding an escalation in black abolitionist protest, Harper not only denounced what she perceived as the all-consuming drive by many leading antebellum blacks to accumulate wealth, she also indicted wealthy blacks for their failure to use their financial resources in the fight against slavery. She said:

> We have money among us, but how much of it is spent to bring deliverance to our captive brethren? Are our wealthiest men the most liberal sustainers of the Anti-slavery enterprise? Or, does the bare fact of their having money, really help mold public opinion and reverse its sentiments? Let us not defer all our noble opportunities till we get rich. And here I am not aiming to enlist a fanatical crusade against the desire for riches, but I do protest against chaining down the soul to the one idea of getting money [as a basis] for stepping into power or even gaining our rights in common with others.[7]

Ultimately, antebellum black business people, whether slave or free, were "captive capitalists," and within the context of Milton Friedman's historic analysis of the development of capitalism and the strides toward freedom, one can find, as he said: "economic arrangements that are fundamentally capitalist and political arrangements that are not free."[8] Thus, in Part Two, the major focal point of this analysis, my discussion centers on an examination of the business goals advocated for blacks by the National Negro Convention in each of the three decades before the Civil War, the 1830s, 1840s, and 1850s.

Presently, studies on antebellum black organizations, including the National Negro Convention Movement, limit their analyses to black social reform movements, abolitionism, and organizational pronouncements protesting the subordinate societal and legal status of free blacks. As Howard Bell emphasizes in his introduction to the records of the National Negro Convention: "During the entire era there was seldom a national conclave that did not preach the value of temperance, morality, education, economy and self-help."[9] Still, in those studies of the National Negro Convention, the economic issues confronting antebellum blacks, especially the "self-help" business promotion goals proposed by the Convention to address these issues have been studiously ignored.[10] Even the Convention's most consistent promotional effort, – the establishment of a manual trades school for African Americans – has not been emphasized as a basis for business training and development.

Moving beyond existing studies and their traditional focus on the goals of the National Negro Convention, a more expansive review of the minutes and proceedings of the organization provides a basis to establish the extent to which African Americans have an historical tradition of business promotion. This assessment expands the historiographical inquiry of a much-neglected area in the Black American experience and especially in Black Business history: the promotion of black entrepreneurship and business enterprise in antebellum America.

SECTION ONE

CONVENTION GOALS OVERVIEW

The records of the National Negro Convention, which met eleven times between 1830 and 1855 and once during the Civil War in 1864, are important as a basis for examining organized efforts by black leaders to promote African American economic freedom through the development of black entrepreneurship and business enterprise.[11] They are especially evidential as sources that document the extent to which business participation in the pre-Civil War economy was considered by many blacks as an important avenue for survival in a racist society decidedly hostile not only to their freedom but also to their economic advancement. Antebellum Black Americans recognized that the abolition of slavery and mitigation of oppressive and debilitating societal and legal constraints could not ensure that African Americans would be truly free. Without financial independence and economic security, real freedom for African Americans could not be achieved.

In their annual conventions from 1830–5, the Convention proceeded only indirectly in efforts to encourage black business development. This compares to their more deliberate and specific attempts made in this direction in the 1840s and 1850s. In promoting black entrepreneurship and business enterprise, the Convention proposed several areas for black business development. The establishment of a National Black Bank and investments by African Americans in government securities were encouraged as a basis for black capital formation. In conjunction with proposals that boycotts/sanctions be imposed on the purchase of slave produced commodities, recommendations were made to establish black producer and consumer cooperatives. Building international trade ties with blacks in the Caribbean was also encouraged, and Jewish success in business was held up as a model to underscore the importance of black business advancement.

The Convention placed special emphasis on the necessity for black parents to instill aspirations for business participation in their children. Specific roles in the promotion of business were assigned to black women as wives, mothers, and sisters. Proposals were also made for black businessmen to train the youth in business; these young entrepreneurs then would train the following generation. The Convention emphasized that, with percipient motivation and the development of pertinent business skills, even menial and often unskilled occupations could be transformed into sustaining enterprises. Through encouragement and support, industrious peddlers, draymen, and street vendors could realize profits which would enable them to become self-employed and proprietors of these enterprises.

Ironically, blacks who participated in business during the Age of American Slavery, especially those who developed enterprises in sectors of the economy regarded as "nigger work," particularly in the service and food industries, found they could survive with white competition, even in the South. Successful antebellum black businesspeople, North or South, used creative marketing strategies or developed incontestable skills in the production and delivery of goods and services they provided. Usually, those who satisfied an elite white clientele, especially in the South, found some protection from the threat of white business competitors.

Ultimately the success of all antebellum black businessmen, particularly those involved in enterprises that paralleled mainstream pre-industrial business activity, depended on shrewd business acumen. However, other factors occasionally contributed in ironic ways to this success. In the South, for example, the largest class of successful black businessmen were those engaged in agribusiness. Interestingly, some of the most successful were the slave-holding black owners of large cotton and sugar plantations. Another unusual case is that of Californian William Leidesdorff (1810–48). He passed as white, despite comments regarding his "swarthy complexion," and by 1848 he had amassed a fortune valued at $1.5 million.[12]

An example of more characteristic success – through shrewd business acumen – is that of Stephen Smith, known as "Black Steve". He was a Pennsylvanian lumber and coal merchant who had neither slave labor nor skin color to aid him in his success. Rather, he became the second wealthiest antebellum African American entrepreneur by developing creative management strategies while running his owner's lumber yard. He purchased his freedom with these profits and in 1865 he had accumulated wealth valued at $500,000.[13]

Consequently, the National Negro Convention could produce a record of African American business success. Certainly it did not push slaveholding as an area of black business development; and, Leidesdorff's passing for white, as a basis to achieve business success, could provide a role model for only a few African Americans. What the Convention could document in promoting black business participation was that participation provided the only area in antebellum American life where blacks, even slaves, could find some success.

OCCUPATIONS OF DELEGATES

An occupational cross-section and a veritable who's who of antebellum Black America distinguished the delegates who attended the National Negro Conventions, a surprising number of whom were businessmen, such as the lumber and coal merchant Stephen Smith and his business partner William Whipper.[14] Wealthy Chicago merchant tailor John Jones and leading New York caterer Thomas Downing were also delegates. In the 1840s and 1850s they were joined by a newly emerging and more militant group of younger blacks including: Martin Delany, a physician and leading business advocate, who flirted with the idea of emigration; Frederick Douglass, who opposed it; Reverend Henry Highland Garnett, perhaps the leading black nationalist of that era and an ardent supporter of emigration; John Mercer Langston, a lawyer; and Samuel Ringgold Ward and James McCune Smith, noted abolitionists. The black clergy was also represented by the esteemed Richard Allen, founder of the African Methodist Episcopal (AME) Church, who was also a businessman and first president-elect of the National Negro Convention.

While the first meeting of the National Negro Convention in 1830 attracted only forty male delegates who had been elected from various state and local organizations, the number at subsequent meetings increased to a high of 150 at the 1853 Convention. Most of the delegates to the National Negro Convention were also active in their respective state black conventions which afforded not only a degree of continuity and consensus among blacks in the promotion of the organization's goals, but also facilitated the communication of issues that were of national concern to antebellum African Americans. There was also interest in the Convention from the international black community.

At the 1832 Conference held in New York, the delegates were addressed by Reverend Mr. Harrison from Antigua. In offering support to the Convention he also provided information on the advances being made by blacks in the West Indies, indicating that there was: "great improvement in the religious, literary, and civil conditions" there. Following his presentation, convention members proposed a vote of thanks, underscoring the affinity of people of African descent in the diaspora for, as they said, they were all "children of the same persecuted family."[15]

By 1848, delegates to the National Negro Convention, as free blacks, considered that they had "arrived." They were sophisticated, articulate and self-congratulatory on their accomplishments, as indicated by the following remarks made in the Convention Address charting their progress: "Ten or twelve years ago, an educated colored man was regarded as a curiosity and the thought of a colored man as an author, editor, lawyer or doctor, had scarce been conceived – Such, thank Heaven, is no longer the case."[16] Slavery was also denounced with an unparalleled vengeance and delegates were reminded that as blacks, slave or free, they were "the most oppressed people in the world . . . [and] every one of us should be ashamed to consider himself free, while his brother is a slave."

Yet, the 1848 Convention was also rife with classism, evidenced by demeaning remarks made about blacks who worked in menial occupations considered degrading. Frederick Douglass attempted to amend the breach, reminding the delegates that he had been both a chimney sweep and wood sawyer. Notwithstanding, he called for a resolution in which the Convention would act to encourage blacks to "leave situations in which we are considered degraded, as soon as necessity ceases."[17] His position was endorsed in the Conference's "Address," where it was again emphasized that menial employment should not be considered degrading. Still, it was also noted that, since blacks had become so identified with menial employment, the conviction exists that "colored men are only fit for such employments." African Americans were advised that, to offset prejudice, when possible they should "cease from such employment" and use the trades as a basis to become business owners.[18]

A poll was taken on the occupations of the delegates at the 1848 Convention. It showed the delegates involved in the following enterprises: "Printers, Carpenters, Blacksmiths, Shoemakers, Engineer, Dentist, Gunsmiths, Editors, Tailors, Merchants, Wheelwrights, Painters, Farmers, Physicians, Plasterers, Masons, Students, Clergymen, Barbers and Hair Dressers, Laborers, Coopers, Livery Stable Keepers, Bath House Keepers, Grocery Keepers."[19] While most were tradesmen by profession, they were also independent businessmen who owned their own establishments. One can hardly imagine that in antebellum America, black workers would have been allotted time off to attend a three-day black convention which, including transportation time for many of the delegates, would have required more than a week's leave-of-absence.

While most black workers lacked the discretionary income to underwrite expenses associated with conference attendance, there were blacks with incomes that allowed them to live beyond self-sufficiency – an issue addressed at the Convention. In its 1848 "Address to the Colored People of the United States," the following statement was made advising black people not only to be discreet in their spending, but also to save their money to be used for the advancement of the race: "We beg and intreat [sic] you, to save your money – live economically, dispense with finery, and the gaieties which have rendered us proverbial, and save your money. Not for the senseless purpose of being better off than your neighbor, but that you may educate your children."[20]

While the goals of the Convention Movement were national in scope, delegates who attended the meetings were primarily from the northern states, particularly New York, Ohio, and Pennsylvania where the first Convention was held; although, blacks from Maryland, Delaware, Virginia, North Carolina, and Georgia were also in attendance. As Jane and William Pease explain in their discussion of the National Negro Convention Movement: "The function of the [national] conventions, as their structure implied, was not to grapple with the details of day-to-day issues, but rather to provide members of the black community with a sense of direction, to establish their priorities, and to coordinate their efforts."[21] In many ways the "Proceedings," which were published and distributed nation-wide to blacks and the white abolitionist communities, provided an antebellum "State of Black America," report similar to that published today by the National Urban League.

During the intervening years, when the National Negro convention did not meet, state black conventions and meetings of local organizations were held to advance its goals. Invariably, black leaders from these state conventions were also delegates to the National Negro Conventions. From 1840 to the Civil War, nine state conventions were held in New York and Ohio, three in California, two in Pennsylvania, Indiana, Illinois, Massachusetts and Connecticut, and one in New Jersey. Only one black state convention was held in the South; in 1859, the Maryland Free Colored People's Convention met in Baltimore.

While the last meeting of the National Negro Convention before the Civil War was held in 1855, two regional conferences took place in 1859. There was also a regional Convention held in Boston in 1859, the New England Colored Citizens Convention. Delegates from New York, New Jersey, Pennsylvania, Illinois, and Canada, however, attended in addition to those from all of the New England states except New Hampshire.

CONVENTION FOUNDING AND EMIGRATION

At the initial six consecutive meetings that took place from 1830 to 1835, the acquisition of land and commercial agricultural development were major areas of discussion by the Convention in the promotion of black economic self-sufficiency. These goals were a direct response not only to the agricultural base of the antebellum economy, they also mark the immediate concerns which prompted the founding of the National Negro Convention. In 1829, Cincinnati, attempting to block the settlement of new blacks in that city, embarked on a program of rigid enforcement of Ohio's 1807 Black Laws. Under duress, Cincinnati's black population was forced to register, show proof of their legal status as free blacks, post a $500 bond, or face expulsion from that state. Finally, a three day riot resulted and some 1,000 to 1,200 African Americans, virtually half of Cincinnati's entire black population, fled the city for Canada. Many were fugitive slaves, but even free blacks with papers left in fear of their lives. Cincinnati's black population in 1826 was 690; in 1829, 2,200; a year after the riot in 1830 only 1,090 blacks remained in the city.[22]

Racial violence was endemic in antebellum urban America. Threatened by the competition of blacks who worked for lower wages, various factions including native and immigrant laborers, businesspeople, and virulent proslavery forces resorted intermittently to pogrom-like violence to drive out the black populations. With Black Laws notoriously similar in both the North and South and with white racial violence undertaken with impunity, free blacks in antebellum urban America had a very real fear that Cincinnati's black expulsion program could establish precedent for other cities.[23]

An organized national response by free African Americans to the threat of expulsion was imperative, and prompted the founding of the National Negro Convention Movement by Hezekiah Grice of Baltimore. In April 1830, Grice sent a circular letter to leading antebellum blacks, urging them to convene for the purpose of presenting a national black platform on the issue of emigration, which he favored, "convinced of the hopelessness of contending against the oppressions in the United States." Grice's call for a national convention was a direct response to the 1829 Cincinnati riots.[24] With its initial meeting in Philadelphia in 1830, held at the Bethel AME Church, the Convention marked the first attempt by blacks to call for organized national protest against racial oppression in America.

The immediacy of their goals was clearly stated and prioritized in the official name of the organization: The American Society of Free Persons of Color, for Improving their Conditions in the United States; for Purchasing

Lands and for the Establishment of a Settlement in Upper Canada. At that initial meeting, the delegates denounced the Ohio Laws as racist and in violation of American constitutional principles, whereby blacks were subjected to "requisitions not exacted of the Whites, a course altogether incompatible with the principles of civil and religious liberty." At the same time, they also moved immediately to support the settlement activities of blacks who had emigrated to Canada.[25]

In the major speech presented at the 1830 convention entitled, "Address to the Free People of Color of the United States," four arguments explaining the Convention's support of Canadian settlement were presented: racism was absent in Canada; the language and culture were relatively the same; land was cheap; and industrious farmers could be successful. Delegates also proposed that the Convention be the catalyst for a national fundraising campaign to underwrite Canadian land purchases for the settlers. The emigration of blacks with construction skills was also promoted. "We would invite the mechanics from our large cities to embark in the enterprise; the advancement of architecture depending much on their exertions, as they must consequently take with them the arts and improvements of our well regulated communities." As noted in the 1830 Address, "It is to these we must look for the strength and spirit of our future prosperity." A general consensus reached by the delegates was that success of black Canadian settlements could advance the economic conditions of black Americans.[26]

CONVENTION FOUNDING AND COLONIZATION

On the other hand, at that initial meeting in 1830, the Convention voiced strong opposition to the American Colonization Society in its efforts to force the emigration of free blacks to Liberia, as well as its program advocating slave manumission only on the condition that the newly freed blacks would leave the United States. The position of the Convention was firmly and emphatically stated at the 1832 Convention. The greatest concern expressed at the 1832 Convention was that, if it went on record in support of black emigration, their actions could be construed by white America as a basis to justify and escalate the forces of white colonization. More important, as the proceedings show, delegates to the Convention feared that an endorsement of colonization would be seen as an indication that African Americans had "relinquished our claim to this being the land of our nativity."[27]

The position taken by the Convention was that it could not discourage individuals from emigrating. So, to counter the Liberian and Haiti relocation program supported by the American Colonization Society, the Convention endorsed and encouraged the settlement of blacks in the American West.[28] Moreover, at each convention, discussions of the various colonization schemes by whites in Africa was presented as evidence to show the nation's blacks that even in the Motherland they would not be free from white tyranny and oppression.

The Dutch and English colonization of South Africa was especially denounced in a report presented at the 1853 Convention. The report was prepared by Convention member, Reverend J.W.C. Pennington, an escaped slave. As a fugitive, he became active in the abolitionist and American Peace Movements. In the report, Pennington denounced both the American Colonization Society and the disastrous effect on Africa resulting from the colonization activities of the Dutch and the English explaining: "The influence of British *colonization* upon South Africa, and the interior and western coast, has been a curse to Africa; the whites there have nearly exterminated several tribes, to make room for themselves. They seized on the best lands, without paying the owners." As to Dutch Colonization, specific reference was made to the American Colonization Society: "Is that party aware that the Dutch Boors, the mortal haters of the Africans, have just established a Republic in Africa, with the avowed intention of incorporating into it, a large tract of the best inland?"[29]

Despite the catastrophic effects of white colonization in Africa, interest in emigration at the National Negro Convention escalated in the 1850s.[30] Yet, notwithstanding, the increasing militancy of the delegates, the general consensus was expressed at the 1853 Convention by Frederick Douglass. In an open letter addressed to Harriet Beecher Stowe read at the convention, Douglass said: "The truth is, dear Madam, we are here, and here we are likely to remain. Individuals emigrate – nations never."[31] Even up to the last Negro Convention held before the Civil War, the consensus was that the African American had invested too much in the making of America to write that investment off by emigrating.

SECTION TWO

CONVENTION BUSINESS GOALS, 1830s

African American interest in emigration and white colonization efforts remained persistent issues put forth for debate at the National Negro Conventions. Yet, the most pervasive theme articulated in the proceedings was the role of black business activities which they hoped would offset black interest in emigration and serve as a countermeasure to deflect the societal constraints inherent in the subordinate position of antebellum blacks. Business participation was also promoted by the convention as a strategy to undermine the economic base of slavery, and it was seen as a strategy to hit at the profits of northern businesses. Specifically, business activities, transformed into instruments of protest by blacks, as consumers, merchants, or producers, were central to those discussions.

At the 1833 convention, a recommendation was passed that delegates push for free labor produce consumer and marketing practices in their home states. In effect, black businesspeople would only sell, and black consumers would only buy those products that had not been produced from slave labor. The motion, as carried, stated: "the Convention recommend to the free people of colour in the United States, the formation of free labour produce Societies, wherever it may be practicable, and that each delegate use the utmost exertions in his private capacity, in recommending to coloured capitalists the establishment of stores on the principles above named."[32]

As a demonstration of the support that the Convention would provide for blacks who established Free Produce enterprises, the organization gave a unanimous commendation to Lydia White, who had established a "free labor store." This was followed by an announcement that stated: "all who feel an interest in promoting the cause of universal freedom, is [sic] cheerfully recommended to her store, No 42 Fourth-Street, in the city of Philadelphia."[33]

Interest in the Free Produce Movement was also demonstrated by the Convention in 1835 in its discussion of a new refining process, only recently developed in France, in which sugar was produced from beet. Again, using every opportunity to promote the boycott of slave-produced commodities and their derivatives, the Convention membership resolved: "That we recommend to our people the practicability of making an effort somewhere in this state [Pennsylvania], to produce sugar from that root, and if successful, to report to the next convention, the result of their efforts."[34]

Subsequent proceedings of the Convention fail to include information on whether any attempt was made to follow through on this proposal. That free blacks were encouraged to consider the production and consumption of beet sugar, as an alternative to slave-produced cane sugar, has significance: the recommendation reflected not only the Convention's efforts to undermine the profitability of plantation slavery, it was also inclusive of broader, although somewhat unspecified, programs to encourage black economic self-sufficiency.

In much the same way, the Convention moved to demonstrate against the societal constraints confronting them as free blacks. At the 1834 Convention, the delegates recommended a boycott against public transportation facilities and places of public accommodations that discriminated against them explaining: "To obviate all difficulty in travelling, *Resolved*, that our people be recommended to patronize those conveyances and establishments only, in which are granted us equal privileges for our money."[35]

Quite early in its history, the National Negro Convention had demonstrated an interest in the importance of capital investment by blacks. With the 1834 revision of its constitution, the organization specifically provided in Article IV that: "When the Treasury of the Convention shall contain a larger sum than five hundred dollars, it shall be invested in United States securities; the script for which to be held by the Conventional Board as Trustees of the convention."[36] More than an economic decision, the Convention's move to invest in United States securities announced, as much as their support for the nation's wars, that African Americans would never relinquish their claim to the rights, privileges, and benefits allowed American citizens.

Equally important, that presumption included the right to the exercise of economic freedom. Yet, until sufficient monies for investment by the masses of blacks could be generated, educational programs to facilitate the development of a broad class of black businessmen were the primary and more immediate means by which the National Negro Convention hoped that black financial independence could be achieved. Hence, the persistent interest in establishing a manual labor trade school was an important item on the agenda of the Conventions in the 1830s. The underlying purpose, always, was that the schools would provide the foundation for the development of a black business class. Indeed, in each of the eleven conventions held before the Civil War, the National Negro Convention emphasized that acquisition of skills in the "mechanic arts" would provide the basis for the formation of a substantial black business class.

It was not until the 1835 meeting that the convention formally addressed this issue in the report from its "Committee on the Exclusion of Colored Youths from Mechanical Employment." Despite expertise in areas of craft specialization, the committee emphasized the difficulties encountered by blacks in their efforts to establish business enterprises in the "mechanic arts." Based primarily on conditions in Pennsylvania, the committee indicated that the difficulties described in their report – racism and discrimination encountered by black craftsmen – applied generally to blacks in most states, especially in the North. As explained in that report:

> [T]here are several trades in this state accessible to colored youths, such as shoe makers, sail makers, carpenters, tailors & c. [but] they regret at the same time, to say, that after acquiring these arts, they are with few exceptions, excluded from any patronage, except that given to them by those with whom they acquire the trade, who are mostly colored men; consequently, the chance of pursuing their respective occupations, is very limited.[37]

The report also included information on crafts – described as these "lucrative arts." Easily translated into profitable enterprises, those were the very ones from which young blacks were "wholly excluded," such as jewellery, watch-making, and machining. From this report, the committee made three recommendations to combat "this great evil". The first, was "to enforce on the minds of their constituents the necessity of encouraging manual labour schools, where our youths may acquire the necessary arts, and afterwards become proprietors of establishments...." Then, once a business was established by a black artisan, that individual would assume the responsibility to "impart encouragement and instructions to others." Finally, the report included an appeal to white abolitionists, most of whom limited their activities to promoting the end of slavery, as opposed to advancing the economic condition of free blacks, "to take colored youths, and teach them their respective trades and encourage them in their pursuit."

Stephen Smith, a leading black businessman, who by the 1850s would be among the wealthiest blacks in the United States, was a member of the committee that drafted the 1835 report. The success of Smith's coal and lumber business reflected the importance of networking and mentorship as a basis for black business development and expansion. Smith not only provided employment for blacks as laborers and foremen in his lumber and coal yards, but also employed two blacks on his management team. Ulysses Vidal was his bookkeeper and accountant and William Whipper managed his Lancaster, Pennsylvanian business holdings. Both men became wealthy as a result of their business partnership with Smith.[38]

CONVENTION BUSINESS GOALS, 1840s

In its second decade, increasingly, specific emphasis was given to the promotion of black business by the National Negro Convention, as seen in the minutes and reports of the three conventions held in 1843, 1847, and 1848. At the 1843 Convention, one proposal recommended the employment of lecturers who would travel throughout the states and discourse on diverse topics that emphasized the importance of business participation. They would also encourage the formation of "associations for improvement in science and literature...and an application to the mechanic arts." Most important, the lecturers would stress that, business development through an "application to the mechanic arts," was singularly important for the uplift of the race as a whole.[39]

Proceeding from a black nationalist economic imperative, the 1843 "Committee Upon the Mechanic Arts," in making recommendations to promote business development emphasized: "the nearer the mechanical arts have been carried to perfection, the higher have the people risen in wealth and intellect." To reinforce the importance of business activities, the committee provided information to document that, "every country where proper attention is paid to education, the mechanics [i.e., businessmen] form a powerful and influential body." The committee stressed that unity of effort was needed in promoting black business participation: "Our duty to ourselves and our posterity should impell us into all those avenues which will influence and elevate our characters....Everything around us is on the move.... We again earnestly entreat our people to improve every opportunity in which they and their children can learn the mechanical arts."[40]

Racism stifled attempts by most free blacks to break into the mechanic arts, especially in the North. Consequently, notwithstanding the emphasis on black business development through the trades made by the National Negro Convention in the 1840s, the organization continued its promotion of agriculture as a viable road to wealth and independence, but only reluctantly. As a basis for business development, commercial agriculture was viewed as an exigent alternative enterprise. The emphasis placed on the commercialization of agriculture by the convention in the 1840s, nonetheless, signalled a change in direction from the previous decade. At the 1843 Convention, as announced in the "Report of the Committee of Agriculture" the new emphasis was that: "Farming... now has got to be a scientific business."

In its emphasis on the advantages of commercial agriculture as the road to wealth, the report presented by the committee provides an early lesson in agricultural economics in its formulation that wealth derived only from those commodities produced from the land. This is seen in the following commentary from that report:

> The soil alone possesses a real value – all other things have only a relative value: their value is to be computed from the amount of land they will purchase. Money and all other things are only creatures of exchange – representatives of a real value – that is, only a real value which can be made to serve the real purposes of life, the demands of our physical being; money and all other commodities are of real value, or are useless only, as they do, or do not answer this purpose; for this alone are they really wanted, and that which will directly serve this purpose, is not only really wealth, but the only wealth which is needed.... Money, ships, houses, merchandise, the professions, the mechanics arts, all these, however much to be appreciated in their proper use, are valueless, unless mother earth shall have first opened her hands, and supplied us of her bounty.[41]

The emphasis on commercial agriculture by that committee was problematic, however. In the 1840s, the National Negro Convention began a systematic review of the financial realities of business participation by blacks, particularly the difficulties encountered in acquiring venture capital. Comparative cost analyses of the venture capital required for the development of business enterprises versus commercial agriculture ventures were carefully formulated. As one analysis showed, a viable farm operation could be initiated at a sum of $300.00; whereas to establish a business enterprise, it was found: "that sum in money or in merchandise, commercial, or in most mechanical business, would be a capital insufficient from which to hope, even, for an ordinary living – in most cases, in most of the business operations, with a capital so small, despair would attend at every step."[42]

Since the Convention only reluctantly promoted commercial farming, the committee on agriculture found it necessary to emphasize that, as an enterprise, agricultural ventures had some consequential economic advantages, providing as such, the road to "respectability, wealth and financial independence." At the 1843 Convention, a report from the Carthagenia settlement established by blacks in Mercer County, Ohio was presented as an example of the rapidity by which African Americans could succeed in developing prosperous commercial agriculture enterprises. In six years, the settlement had become self-supporting through the purchase of several thousand acres of land. Over two hundred homes had been constructed in addition to a school, church, saw mill, and grist mill and, as the report also emphasized "to say nothing of some $10,000 which individuals of us have paid for our freedom."[43]

In its efforts to accentuate the financial successes achieved by blacks in agricultural settlements as opposed to the failures of urban life confronting blacks, the Committee emphasized that the Carthagenian settlers, former urban dwellers, had reported: "'We have found by experiment, that the same money which paid our rent and marketing in the city, will purchase new land and improve it in the country.'"[44] Information on other financially successful, black agricultural settlements in Ohio this was also presented in this report.

Also emphasized in that report was the expansion of civil rights attained by those settlers. Black children had the opportunity to attend school. Indeed, the Carthagenia children attended an integrated school (white children in the area of the settlement attended the school built by blacks for their children).

Moreover, in the minds of the Carthagenians, financial independence had increased their sense of responsibilities as American citizens. Included in that 1843 report was a statement made by them which said: "'We the colored people must become more valuable to the State. We must help it to raise a revenue and increase its wealth, by throwing our labor into profitable employment.'"[45]

While invidious comparisons were made in the 1843 report, which emphasized the economic disadvantages of urban life as opposed to agricultural life, the Committee on Agriculture nonetheless conceded that urban life had not defeated all blacks, particularly those who had accumulated capital for investment. In the promotion of black business, however, they used this opportunity to reprove those who failed to use their wealth to capitalize on its best investment advantage. Particularly, the low rate of interest returns on loans made by some, as an expression of business enterprise, was singled out as an example of poor capital management:

> Many of our people in the cities have money loaned at interest, and which netts [sic] them but 5 per cent, and themselves are, as they ever have been, following the dependent occupations peculiar to the same class in large cities,... when that money invested in a farm even in the new countries of the West, would yield at least 25 per cent from the commencement, and after a few years... [with improvements], it would be found to yield him many hundred per cent.[46]

To a great extent, the economic depression following the Panic of 1837 was a significant factor contributing to the Convention's emphasis on agriculture in the 1840s. With only limited employment options during periods of prosperity and business expansion, free blacks faced even greater obstacles in finding employment during periods of economic depression. Still, while strong promotional efforts were made in favor of farming as a viable commercial enterprise for blacks, the 1843 Committee on Agriculture acknowledged, somewhat reluctantly, that business participation in urban places was the preferable and more profitable economic activity.

Yet, racism precluded most African Americans from pursuing business opportunities: "We have not the capital to engage successfully in other business, which, with a large amount of capital, and fortune's smile might soon lead to wealth"[47] Denied access to venture capital because of racism, commercial agriculture seemed the only viable, economic alternative for blacks in their pursuit of economic freedom.

At the 1847 Convention, in a somewhat perfunctory report, the Committee on Agriculture expressed similar sentiments, even generating a degree of forced enthusiasm for the "virtues" of farming. The primary motivating force behind the 1847 agricultural report was the 140,000 acres of land in New York state that the white abolitionist Gerrit Smith had deeded to 3000 blacks. In that report, delegates to the Convention were urged to encourage the grantees "to take possession of these lands" and establish farm enterprises. The report emphasized that substantial financial returns could accrue to blacks with only a minimal investment in a commercial farm enterprise.

Still, there was a bitter acknowledgment that racism was the primary factor that limited the participation of blacks in the more favored non-agricultural business pursuits because of their limited access to venture capital as explained in the 1847 Committee of Agriculture report:

> The farmer's life is adapted to our pecuniary circumstances and conditions. To commence a business, in the business part of the country, which would yield, in ordinary cases, a competency, would require a capital much larger than any of us possess. But a few dollars, comparatively, will purchase a farm sufficiently large to afford a comfortable subsistence, at the outset... and at the same time be the

most productive investment that can be made of small sums of money.[48]

As before, the general tone of the Agricultural Committee Report was that only the necessity of economic exigencies impelled the National Negro Convention to promote commercial agriculture ventures. Clearly, urban business activities were regarded as the preferable way for African Americans to achieve financial security beyond economic self-sufficiency.

PROMOTING ECONOMIC PAN-AFRICANISM

Interest in developing and strengthening pan-African relationships and establishing trade ties in the West Indies had been expressed by the National Negro Convention at its 1831 meeting when discussion centered on the site for the location of the "College for the Education of Young Men of Colour." As the proceedings show, New Haven was considered the best site for this college: "The town of New-Haven carries on an extensive West India trade, and many of the wealthy coloured residents in the Islands, would, no doubt, send their sons there to be educated, and thus a fresh tie of friendship would be formed, which might be productive of much real good in the end."[49]

At the 1847 Convention, conference delegates were presented with a proposal that would further compel some members of the organization to reassess their views on black commercial agricultural ventures. A letter from the newly established Jamaica Hamic Association, proposing the establishment of trade relations between blacks in the United States and in the West Indies, indicated that agricultural commodities produced by African Americans would find a market beyond the United States. The Jamaica Hamic Association, a trade organization, was founded in response to a visit made by Reverend Pennington to that island. In the Convention's promotion of black business development and economic self-sufficiency, the possibility that international trade might prove profitable for black Americans seemed an enticing prospect.

A letter dated 28 April 1846 from the Kingston-based Jamaica Hamic Association, was included in the report presented to the 1847 Convention by its newly established "Committee on Commerce," of which Pennington was a member.[50] Read in its entirety, the letter was prefaced with a statement emphasizing the Black Diaspora noting: "By the mysterious providence of God, we find that captivity has dispersed our race far and wide." Unlike in the United States, however, slavery had ended in the West Indies in 1833. The letter then summarized the social, civil, and political advances made by black Jamaicans in their thirteen years of freedom contrasted with their limited economic gains. With surprisingly contemporary overtones the letter said: "In the jury box, in the magistracy, in the municipal corporations and the Legislature, we are rapidly filling our places. But in one respect our progress does not keep pace with our general advancement. In the Commerce of the country we have no proportionate share."

To emphasize the importance of international trade, the Jamaica Hamic Association letter included a summary of the importance of commerce in world history. The extent to which trade had contributed to the advancement of modern Europe was discussed, with particular emphasis on the economic advancement of Jews. The letter emphasized that "Commerce ever has been the great means by which the Jews... have been able to preserve their national existence." Nor did they fail to emphasize to African Americans that "America owes her present importance" to trade and commerce. For people of African descent, improvement in their economic position could be achieved, if inclusive of a Pan-African effort. As the letter explained: "if we would acquire any very great influence for good, we must join in the march of Commerce."

The Jamaica Hamic Association also emphasized that only through an international Pan-African joint effort in trade and commerce would white racism decline: "Unite the most repulsive of mankind in enlightened commercial intercourse, and their antagonism will be found to lose its edge, and the feelings of civility and politeness succeed to its place." To facilitate this goal, the Jamaica Hamic Association proposed the formation of a trade alliance with African Americans. In explaining their position, the Association said, "Now the relation existing between us and our brethern of North America, is one of mutual sympathy and co-operation in all that pertains to the general welfare of the race, and your co-operation with us, is in nothing more demanded than in *Commercial enterprise*."

In reviewing the economic advantages that would accrue to blacks through international trade, the Jamaica Association offered black Americans a "favored nation" trade status explaining: "In this island our people constitute emphatically the market, and in America abound those commodities which are in the greatest demand amongst us." Their position: African Americans should supply that market! The Association's proposal did not preclude the participation of whites; although, they castigated their so-called "white antislavery friends" who, despite their monumental humanitarian efforts to end slavery, remained reluctant to push for the economic advancement of free blacks.

Ultimately, slavery's demise in the United States, as expressed in the letter, would mark the beginning of economic progress for African Americans, which would prove beneficial to both groups by leading to "the elevation of our people, and engage them in Commerce throughout the wide range of our dispersion."[51] The initial response by the National Negro Convention to the Jamaica Trade Hamic Association was that a committee on West Indian Correspondence be appointed to examine the trade proposal, while maintaining communication with the Jamaicans.

PROMOTING BLACK BANKS

The 1847 National Negro Convention conference was exciting in yet another way. In addition to discussions calling for a National Black Press to provide for wider dissemination of a unified African American voice in the denouncement of slavery and the legal constraints imposed on free blacks, a recommendation was made at the 1847 Convention by the newly formed "Banks and Banking Institutions Committee" for the establishment of a national black bank. A national black bank would provide more than just an institution for the collective savings of blacks and an assertion of black financial self-sufficiency. Its establishment would represent a black economic nationalist statement that African Americans would no longer provide profit to support institutions that oppressed them, for as explained in the report: "a Banking Institution originating among the colored people of the U. States [is needed] because they at present contribute to their own degradation by investing capital in the hands of their '*enemies*'."[52]

Heated discussion surrounded the report. Arguments in opposition to a separate black bank reflected a persistent theme in the black historical experience that the promotion of segregated institutions by blacks would impede full integration into the mainstream of American life. According to this argument, a separate black bank would only reinforce distinctions between whites and blacks. Prominent abolitionist and early black historian William C. Nell, explaining why he could not support the proposal, stated that he "was opposed to establishing a Bank, Unless it be shown that the colored people cannot have the benefit of banks now in existence."[53] Henry Highland Garnett, an early pan-Africanist and one of the most radical members of the National Negro Convention also opposed the establishment of the bank.

After much acrimonious debate, the resolution was passed, with the convention obviously acceding to the persuasive argument of Thomas Van Rensselaer who supported a black bank but said its services should not be restricted by race. "'We should be willing to yield to the force of circumstances and establish a Bank for the purpose of our own elevation, though it should not be exclusive.'"[54] Only 10 per cent of the African American population were free and good banking practices would require accepting deposits from anyone.

Debate on the establishment of a black bank continued at the 1848 Convention and sentiments were expressed by some delegates that it was possible to assure economic success for blacks by working within the framework of the existing financial system and, as stated in the Convention's "Address to the Colored People of the United States," the consensus was: "Never refuse to act with a white society or institution because it is white, or a black one, because it is black; but act with all men without distinction of color.... We say avail yourselves of *white* institutions, not because they are white, but because they afford a more convenient means of improvement."[55]

Still, a prevailing Black nationalist sentiment existed at that convention that supported the establishment of a National black bank. And, in that same address, those remarks were followed by a plea urging blacks to become financially independent. "Understand this, that independence is an essential condition of respectability. To be dependent, is to be degraded." The ultimate goal for the African American, as stated in the 1848 address was: "It is plain that the equality which we aim to accomplish, can only be achieved by us, when we can do for others, just what others can do for us."[56]

Early on in the "Declaration of Sentiments," at the 1848 Convention, a resolution was passed which recommended that blacks obtain expertise in the "mechanical trade, farming, mercantile business, the learned professions, as well as the accumulation of wealth."[57] Considering that black wealth accumulation and financial self-sufficiency were the ultimate goals propelling the Convention's business promotion programs, doubtless the economic activities of black Americans would not preclude the establishment of a bank.

At the 1855, National Negro Convention, the last before the Civil War, a plan was proposed for a black financial institution, which, if successfully implemented, could have led to the establishment of a black bank. At that convention, in a report presented by the "Committee on Mechanical Branches among the Colored People of the Free States," it was recommended that "Trades Unions," more specifically credit unions or industrial banks, be established by blacks in various towns and cities. The proposal submitted recommended the following organizational structure for the establishment of an incipient credit union or industrial bank, but was referred to in the committee recommendations as:

> Co-partnerships, say from three to five in each business as the parties might prefer to engage; on the principle of divisions of labor and division of profits according to capability – looking to it that their financial man and bookkeeper be looked up to as an index of security – and let all the partners in the Union work to make the Capital pay if possible 25 per cent and keep on until the investment becomes a paying one: and thus show the fallaciousness of the 6 per cent idea of Savings Bank investments. A thousand dollars might in a judicious outlay in a lucrative business pay from 25 to 75 per cent.[58]

The plan proposed by the Committee included all of the features of a "rotating credit association," an informal banking system which provides venture capital on a rotating basis to members who make regular deposits.[59] In the United States this system was used by southern Chinese, Japanese, and West Indian immigrants to establish small businesses.[60] This was also the intent of the design proposed in the report presented to the 1855 Convention. In its conclusion the report explained how "co-partnerships" could provide venture capital for the development of black enterprise, noting: "The youth who has the spirit of accumulation, and is intelligent with figures and the Pen, having saved something as a beginning in life, ought like the whites buy goods and venture his turn in the stream of trade and business."

Doubtless, antebellum African Americans possessed the capital and incipient expertise to establish, support, and manage a National Black Bank.[61] Statistical evidence presented at the 1855 Convention also showed that blacks had the financial capacity, while limited, to support an independent financial institution, based on their deposits in white banks in their respective states, including: "the Six Hundred Thousand Dollars invested in Savings Banks in and around New York and its vicinity and also similar amounts around other cities."[62] Moreover, from the Colonial Period on, blacks had demonstrated a propensity for saving, beginning with the African Secret Burial Societies which expanded into the mutual aid and benevolent organizations founded by free blacks in the late eighteenth century. Their purpose was the pooling of monies deposited by members to assure the costs of funeral and burial expenses. The African Secret Burial Societies provided the foundation for the late eighteenth century development of the African American mutual aid self-help organizations, which increased in number before the Civil War.[63]

Consequently, antebellum blacks, including slaves who saved to purchase their freedom, had experience with saving not only in their own organizations, but also in white banking institutions including the National Negro Convention. At its founding in 1830, Article VI of the Convention constitution stipulated that the treasurer would be allowed to hold no more than $100.00 and that the remainder of "All monies above that sum shall be deposited in the United States Bank."[64]

Moreover, there were wealthy blacks who engaged in informal banking activities by loaning money. Some of the leading antebellum black entrepreneurs accumulated a substantial part of their wealth from the volume of business they developed and the earnings made from the low interest rates paid on the loans they made, not only to poor blacks, but particularly to white businessmen who did not want their temporary impecunious status known in the business community.[65]

Finally, emphasizing the necessity of establishing a National Black Bank, the 1855 Committee pointed to the value of business enterprises owned by blacks, apart from commercial farm ventures, in several states: Ohio, Illinois, and Michigan, $1,500,000; Massachusetts, Maine, Rhode Island, and Connecticut, $2,000,000; New York and Pennsylvania, $3,000,000.[66] Doubtless, these figures were an underestimate, because the Committee reported that California had only $200,000 in business; whereas, the proceedings of the 1856 California state convention stated that from 1850 to 1855, California's black population had accumulated wealth amounting to $2,375,000, with blacks in one county, alone, owning $300,000 in mining claims.[67]

CONVENTION AND BUSINESS EDUCATION

At each convention the promotion of economic advancement for African Americans was closely tied to educational advancement. In its initial efforts to promote black business participation, the major area of concern expressed by the National Negro Convention at its founding in 1830 was to promote training in the "mechanical arts," particularly: "in connection with the sciences, which . . . will eventually give us the standing and condition we desire."[68] At the 1831 Convention, the curriculum proposed for a manual labor school was broadened to include the liberal arts. It was also emphasized that limited financial circumstances would not be a basis for the exclusion of any prospective black student. The philosophy of black education advocated by the National Negro convention was that "the children of the poor may receive a regular classical education, as well as their more opulent brothers, and the charge will be so regulated as to put it within the reach of all."[69]

When the Convention met in 1835, the Committee on High Schools reported that six high schools and colleges accepted black youth.[70] By the 1850s, educational opportunities for black youth, i.e., admission to white colleges and universities, although still limited, had expanded. Consequently, at the two National Negro Conventions that met in 1853 and 1855, discussions on higher education centered on whether or not a black college was needed for providing a classical education for black youth or for training them in the professions. As Frederick Douglass said at the 1853 Convention, educational facilities were now accessible to train blacks as "*Ministers, Lawyers, doctors, Editors, Merchants & c,.*"[71]

The more pressing issue was what kind of higher education would best benefit black youth, considering the limited employment opportunities for college educated blacks juxtaposed against the cost of higher education. Douglass indicated in his 1853 speech to the convention that the masses of black families could neither afford those costs nor the income that would be lost to the family during the years that a young person attended a college. Black families might make those financial sacrifices, he noted, but emphasized that experience had shown it would be a futile effort at best. Simply put, Douglass said, there was no demand for black professionals. "White people will not employ them to the obvious embarrassment of their causes, and the blacks, taking their *cue* from the whites, have not sufficient confidence in their abilities to employ them."[72] Douglass also said that for lack of employment, many educated professional African Americans were forced to emigrate.

Even more critical, as Douglass indicated, Northern blacks were losing out on the unskilled menial labor jobs to whites. "In times past we have been the hewers of wood and the drawers of water for American society, and we once enjoyed a monopoly in menial employments, but this is no longer – even these employments are rapidly passing away out of our hands."[73] While agriculture offered economic opportunities, Douglass said that despite the poverty, hardship, and deprivation, blacks preferred urban life, facetiously commenting, "(perhaps the adage that misery loves company will explain)" this phenomenon: the antebellum African American preference for residing in cites as opposed to rural areas.

Until 1855, convention delegates pushed for the establishment of a manual training school or black college that would provide, through manual training in the crafts, a basis for blacks to develop business enterprises. In antebellum America, proficient craftsmen, including blacksmiths, carpenters, shoemakers, and cabinetmakers capitalized on their expertise and financial success by becoming shop keepers and business proprietors. In a pre-industrial market economy, craft skills were virtually the only available means for the production of many goods and services; and, for this reason, Douglass advocated the establishment of an industrial manual training school, despite the tremendous racist competition blacks faced in the trades/mechanic arts for as he explained:

> [P]rejudice against the free colored people in the United States has shown itself nowhere so invincible as among mechanics. The farmer and the professional man cherish no feeling so bitter as that cherished by these. The latter would starve us out of the country. At the moment, I can more easily get my son into a lawyer's office, to study law, than I can into a blacksmith's shop to blow the bellows, and to wield a sledge-hammer.[74]

Douglass's point was that a competitive market existed for the goods and services produced by the craftsman/mechanic, even those who were black. By owning their own business enterprises, blacks presented a competitive edge in their capacity to undercut the market by offering lower prices for the goods and services they could provide as "mechanics"/tradesmen. Consequently, Douglass's educational philosophy was shaped by the economic exigencies of historical circumstances which limited employment opportunities for antebellum free blacks not only in the professions, but even the unskilled menial occupations, especially in the North. It was within this context that Douglass asked the Convention to support the establishment of a manual labor training school.

> The argument in favor of an Industrial College, a College to be conducted by the best men, and the best workmen, which the

> mechanic arts can afford – a College where colored youth can be instructed to use their hands, as well as their heads – where they can be put in possession of the means of getting a living.... The fact is..., that colored men must learn trades – must find new employments, new modes of usefulness to society – or that they must decay under the pressing wants to which their condition is rapidly bringing them.... We must not only be able to *black* boots, but to *make* them.[75]

In many ways, the proposals of the National Negro Convention and particularly the educational philosophy expressed by Frederick Douglass presaged those of twentieth-century black leaders, particularly Booker T. Washington's emphasis on industrial training and William E. B. Du Bois's call for the liberal arts training of a "Talented Tenth." Reminiscent of Washington, who said in his infamous 1895 Atlanta "Compromise" Address: "It is at the bottom of life we must begin," Douglass said, perhaps based on his accomplishments, and those of the wealthy Stephen Smith and the Reverend James Pennington, all of whom were born slaves:

> Accustomed, as we have been, to the rougher and harder modes of living, and of gaining a livelihood, we cannot, and we ought not to hope that, in a single leap from our low condition, we can reach that of *Ministers, Lawyers, doctors, Editors, Merchants & c,*. These will, doubtless, be attained by us, but this will only be when we have patiently and laboriously, and I may add successfully, mastered and passed through the immediate graduations of agriculture and the mechanic arts."[76]

Of course, both Douglass and Washington were masterful politicians, who recognized that assertions of black capability proved threatening in a racist society. In both instances, each responded to the prospect of support from whites for black education; and, therefore were circumspect in their remarks, feeling that white support would be much more forthcoming for educational programs that did not prepare blacks to challenge the state of white supremacy. Douglass's proposal for a black manual school was incorporated into a letter to Harriet Beecher Stowe, a response to her query as to what whites could do to ameliorate the black condition. Douglass, unlike Washington, however, did not promote agriculture as the panacea for black economic independence.

At the 1853 Convention, few delegates could counter Douglass's proposal that argued the necessity for the establishment of a black manual labor training school. Particularly interesting is the contrast in the Convention's fundraising proposal for establishing a black manual labor school in 1853 with that proposed in 1831. In addition to relying on the goodwill of donors, the 1853 plan reflected the increasing sophistication of the delegates in applying principles of finance capitalism as a basis for raising money:

> We advise the issuing of joint stock under proper Directors, to the amount of $50,000 in shares of $10 each, or a less number of a larger amount, if considered advisable.... The sale of scholarships, at judicious rates, and the contributions of the liberal and the philanthropic, ought to give an additional $100,000 as an endowment, which sum properly invested, would be a guarantee, that the liabilities and expense of the Institution would be faithfully met.[77]

The implementation of that plan was given to the Committee on Manual Labor School of the new "National Council of the Colored People," an organization founded at the 1853 National Negro Convention, which under its constitution was given full authority to establish and run a Manual Labor School.[78] Yet, two years later, at the next and last National Negro Convention before the Civil War, the Convention withdrew its support for a black manual labor school; or more specifically, it presented several reasons for "discouraging the enterprise now under consideration."[79] Insufficient capital to provide a broad program in the mechanic arts, student inability to pay for tuition, length of time required for mastering a craft, and the time required for the collegiate courses, were among the reasons presented.

It was also argued that one school could not meet the needs of a large geographically dispersed black population. The ultimate reason for the Convention's rejection of the black manual labor school, paradoxically, predates the sociological jurisprudence rationale of the Brown decision argued a century later. "The Industrial School being necessarily (if not in theory, yet in fact) a complexional [i.e., separate and black] institution, must foster distinctions, and help to draw more definitely (so far as educational privileges are involved) those lines of demarkation, which we have labored and still are endeavoring to eradicate."[80] A letter published in the proceedings supported the consensus of the 1855 Convention in their objection to establishing a "complexional" school. It read:

> [Y]ou will see that I do not approve of separate colored schools, believing that education is the right of all, and that the only plan to lay the sure foundation of true Republicanism is, as far as practicable to educate male and female, white and colored, rich and poor, together, and so teach them that they are all human beings, united in a common brotherhood of universal love.[81]

CONVENTION BUSINESS GOALS, 1850s

At the two National Negro Conventions in the 1850s, a more direct and systematic program to encourage black business participation was developed. While the Convention in 1855 closed the doors to its support for a separate black manual labor training school, several resolutions were passed at both the 1853 and 1855 conventions, providing alternatives to the promotion of black business activity through participation in the "mechanics arts." As stated at the 1853 Convention proposals called for blacks to give "more permanent attention to business habits than heretofore, and the acquisition of mechanical branches."[82]

The program proposed in 1853 to promote greater interest and participation in business was also incorporated in the constitution of the newly formed National Council of the Colored People which was to be a permanent organization with its own office and staff. In many ways its activities predated the National Urban League founded in 1911.[83] Yet, the Council has the distinction of being the first national black organization specifically founded to promote black business and to advance the economic status of blacks through trade associations, employment offices, training programs and the use of statistical information to chart black economic and business progress, thus predating the National Negro Business League founded by Booker T. Washington in 1900. As stipulated in the Constitution of the National Council, the organization would promote black business activity.[84]

Also, resolutions were adopted at the 1853 National Negro Convention, with the emphasis on parental responsibilities and community involvement for the purpose of instilling good work habits and discipline in children and the desire to advance economically in society, particularly through the mechanical arts, and especially to "secure a more permanent attention to business habits than before." The black community's responsibility was to provide assistance in training the youth for employment and to provide employment for them through networking. One resolution also called for establishing an intelligence [employment] office "which shall register the names and places of business of such mechanic as are willing to employ colored youth; and also the names, age, residence, &c., of such youth as are desirous of learning trades." In addition, black men were advised to intensify their efforts to get into business and those with capital were urged to establish businesses.

> Resolved, That it is the duty of colored men, in any way connected with mechanical or business houses,... to use all fair and honorable means to secure for themselves business advantages, and especially to secure the admission of their children, or the children of others into mechanical establishments; and in every way practicable to use their influence to secure and extend business advantages and business connection to those now excluded from it.
>
> Resolved, That it is now expedient and necessary for those who have accumulated some means, to employ such means in some one or more

of the general avenues of business and profit, and to make for themselves a better business character than we now possess, and thus open and secure the way for the development of new business, and right business talent."[85]

At the 1855 Convention, the National Negro Convention expanded the scope of its black business promotion program, allocating some responsibilities to the newly formed National Council of the Colored People, while developing new strategies to increase black business participation including the following:

1 That black businessmen in the large cities hold conversational meetings in private homes to encourage business-mindedness among blacks, men, women and children.
2 As a means to encourage young black men to develop trades which can be translated into a business enterprise, each town would raise funds to be "loaned for a series of years sufficient to guarantee a hopeful success, provided the applicants can present the legitimate discharge of agreement of apprenticeship, and devotion to business, &c,."[86]

Discussion at the 1855 Convention, however, reveals that while there was strong and enthusiastic support for black business activity and participation in the mechanic arts, some people were not interested in entering the trades for themselves or their children. It was also acknowledged that there were blacks with money, but they were reticent about establishing a business. In one instance it was reported that "... several colored men who possess their thousands accumulated in California, are anxious to start in some business, but from well-grounded fear of success [failure], either do nothing here or return to California."[87]

Yet, the National Negro Convention could point to the progress made by blacks in business. At the 1853 Convention in the report from the Committee on the Importance of Colored Persons Engaging in Commercial Pursuits the following commentary was made: "we are awakening, especially throughout the less densely settled portion of the country, to active business relations; that we are beginning to become producers as well as consumers."[88] At the 1855 Convention it was reported that in Boston, black business participation was increasing, and it was noted that in "The past five years a spirit has been very active for real estate investments, both by individuals and land companies."[89]

BLACK WOMEN IN BUSINESS PARTICIPATION

In the programs proposed by the National Negro Convention in the 1850s to increase black business activity, the active participation of black women was encouraged. Until 1848, however, black women were not even admitted as delegates to the National Negro Convention; although, in 1832, a woman addressed the Convention, but the proceedings referred to her only as "a lady most friendly to the attainment of the rights of the people of color."[90] At the 1848 convention a black woman, Mrs. Sanford, addressed the convention on the issue of women's rights:

> 'True, we ask for the Elective Franchise; for the right of property in the marriage covenant, whether earned or bequeathed. True, we pray to cooperate in making the laws we obey; but it is not to domineer, dictate or assume.... And, to the delegates,... look not back, till you have justly secured *an unqualified citizenship of the United States, and those inalienable rights granted you by an impartial creator.*'[91]

It was also at the 1848 Convention that women were first admitted as delegates. The specific resolution, supported by Frederick Douglass, a leading proponent of women's rights read: "Whereas, we fully believe in the equality of the sexes, therefore, Resolved, That we hereby invite females hereafter to take part in our deliberations."[92] In 1855, Mary A. Shadd of Canada, a newspaper editor and publisher active in promoting Canadian emigration, and Elizabeth Armstrong from Pennsylvania were listed on the rolls as delegates to that Convention; although the proceedings show that Shadd's admission as a delegate was made at the 1855 Convention, where she was on record as being voted a corresponding member to the National Negro Convention.[93]

The way in which the National Negro Convention viewed the role of black women in business is seen in the recognition given the Lydia White Free Produce Store at the 1833 Convention. At the 1853 Convention, a Department of Industry for Women was established under the Committee On Manual Labor School. In that Committee's report, a statement was included from that department with recommendations for those areas which the Convention could support in promoting black business activity for women through manual labor training: "We are of opinion, that looms could be erected for the weaving of carriage and other trimmings; for bindings of various kinds; that the straw hat business in some of its branches, paper box making and similar occupation might from time to time be connected."[94]

Members of the Convention were quite aware of the business activities of black women, who comprised an important part of the antebellum black business community, some even achieving substantial wealth through their business activities. Still, not all women wanted to participate in business. At the Convention in 1855, it was proposed that those black women could participate in the more traditional roles of sisters, wives and mothers.

> 1 "That we recommend to our mothers and sisters to use every honorable means to secure for their sons and brothers places of profit

and trust in stores and other places of business, such as will throw a halo around this proscribed people, that shall in coming time reflect honor on those who have laid the corner stone to our platform of improvement."

2 That as black men, "We should get better access to the minds of our females. They could enter freely into the conversations, and correct ideas would finally be inculcated in the sentiments of wives and mothers as to the important part of the great duties which they are to perform in moulding the future character of our youth for improvement."

3 That as mothers it is: "to women on whom we must depend for our future leaders to inculcate a disposition for trades, agriculture, and such of the higher branches of business as are necessary to develop persistance."

4 That as Wives, they "will be prepared to introduce more of the element of the German and French character in social existence carried into our 'business relations,' of mutual assistance by council, clerkship, and physical labor."[95]

On review, the Convention's proposals on the role of black women in promoting black business activity perhaps reflected the black male perspective, even promotion of the "Cult of True Womanhood" that presumedly distinguished the antebellum American woman. Certainly, there was more than a degree of patronization evident in the proposals. While race limited the full expression of an American womanhood, it did not obviate a black feminist consciousness that distinguished the special character of her role as wife and mother, particularly in assuming those responsibilities that would enhance the economic position of black people. Still, the business promotion proposals advanced by the National Negro Convention, while generally applicable to black women interested in business, were not specific in addressing the immediate concerns of black women single heads of households, who too often had to develop enterprises to support themselves and their children.[96]

The 1855 Convention was the last before the Civil War. In October 1864, the National Negro Convention met again, for the last time but as the National Convention of Colored Men, with delegates from sixteen states and Washington, DC. For the first time, blacks from Florida, Louisiana, Mississippi, Missouri and Tennessee were in attendance. Two black women, Edmonia Highgate and Frances Ellen Watkins Harper addressed the Convention. The major areas of discussion at the 1864 convention were the progress of the war, violence from and the privileges of white immigrants, discrimination encountered by black soldiers in the Union Army, and the conditions of the freedmen. The prevailing concern at the last meeting of the National Negro Convention was: "Are we good enough to use bullets, and not good enough to use ballots?"[97]

CONCLUSION

Promoting slavery's demise and achieving civil and political rights for free blacks were paramount goals on the agenda of the National Negro Convention, and they provided a major focus of Convention business. Yet, always underlying demands for their rights as Americans was a concerted acknowledgment of the racial disparities in their socio-economic status. As a result, while nationalist pronouncements and denouncements of slavery pervaded the Convention's proceedings from its founding, discussions promoting black economic self-sufficiency were ubiquitous in the records of the organization throughout its existence.

Consequently, this assessment of the business promotion goals of the National Negro Convention expands the field of knowledge in African American business history. It documents the extent to which blacks have an historic tradition of promoting business development as well as the extent to which black Americans have recognized the importance of business activity. As stated at the 1853 Convention: "Through commerce, acquaintance and alliances are formed, and power secured."[98] At the same time, from a comparative historical perspective, the business goals proposed by the National Negro Convention seem contemporary in intent and focus. Many have been achieved. However, in many ways, the goals proposed by the Convention appear to have exceeded in scope many of the goals advanced by black Americans today in the promotion of black business.

Proceeding from yet another historic perspective, the study provides a basis to overturn a prevailing theory, propagated by the noted black sociologist E. Franklin Frazier, who attempted to explain what he perceived as the historic reason for the limited business participation and business failure of African Americans. In accounting for the comparatively poor performance of African Americans in business, Frazier said: "it appears from what we know of the social and cultural history of the Negro that it is the result largely of the lack of traditions in the field of business enterprise."[99] In moving beyond traditional assessments which emphasize financial limitations encountered by blacks in securing venture capital as the basis for the relatively poor performance of blacks in business, Frazier's mid-twentieth century thesis is used even today to obscure prevailing racist practices which continue to limit the full range of black business activity.

Analysis of the proceedings of the National Negro Convention reveals a persistent effort by African Americans to encourage business participation. This assessment, then, expands the historiographical inquiry of a much neglected area in the Black American experience, especially in Black Business history: the promotion of black entrepreneurship and business enterprise in antebellum America.[100] Interestingly, one of the last resolutions made at the 1855 National Negro Convention was the following: "Resolved, That we recommend the colored people to turn their attention to inter-state traffic and trade, and to commerce with foreign countries. Adopted."[101]

NOTES

1 Juliet E. K. Walker, "Racism, Slavery, Free Enterprise: Black Entrepreneurship Before the Civil War." *Business History Review* 60.3 (Autumn, 1986): 343–82. Wealth-holding sources of antebellum blacks documented from: R. G. Dun & Co. Collection, Baker Library. Harvard University Business School, Boston, MA.; US Bureau of the Census, "Population Schedules of the Seventh Census of the United States. 1850;" and, ibid., "Population Schedules of the Eighth Census of the United States, 1860," manuscript microcopy. National Archives and Records Services, Washington D.C.; municipal tax records; county deed records; wills and inventories of estates.

2 In 1974, *Black Enterprise* began its listing of the top 100 black businesses, published annually in the June issue, which also contains a listing of the leading black financial institutions.

3 See. Juliet E. K. Walker, "Prejudices, Profits, Privileges: Commentaries on 'Captive Capitalists,' Antebellum Black Entrepreneurs," in Edwin J. Perkins (ed.) *Essays in Economic and Business History* 8 (1990): 411–12, on calculations estimating the number of antebellum black business owners, a low figure of 5,000 in 1860 out of a free black population approximating 500,000; meaning, at least 1 per cent of that population were business owners compared to the approximate 1.3 per cent black owned businesses in 1982. See *Black Enterprise*, 18, 11 (June 1988): 95, which shows 339,239 black businesses in 1982, the most recent year census figures were available. With 26,683,000 black in 1980, the participation rate of black business owners then, would be 1.3 per cent, as compared to the 1860 1.0 minimum participation rate of antebellum free blacks, a figure not inclusive of slave "owned" and operated businesses.

4 On slave entrepreneurship and intrapreneurship (business managers) see, Juliet E. K. Walker, "Slave Entrepreneurship," and "Slave Drivers," in Randall G. Miller and John David Smith, *Dictionary of Afro-American Slavery* (Westport, CT: Greenwood Press, 1988, 196–8 and 220–2). Also, John Campbell, "As 'A Kind of Freeman'?: Slaves' Market-Related Activities in the South Carolina Upcountry, 1800–1860," in *Slavery and Abolition* 12, 1 (May 1991); Juliet E. K. Walker, "Pioneer Slave Entrepreneurship on the Antebellum Frontier," *Journal of Negro History* 68, 2 (Summer 1983): 289–308; Loren Schweninger, "A Slave Family in the Ante Bellum South," *Journal of Negro History* 60, 1 (January 1975); John Hebron Moore, "Simon Gray Riverman: A Slave Who Was Almost Free," *Mississippi Valley Historical Review* 49 (December 1962) 472–84; Clement Eaton, "Slave-Hiring in the Upper South: A Step toward Freedom," *Mississippi Valley Historical Review* 46 (1960): 663–78; Sumner Eliot Matison, "Manumission by Purchase," *Journal of Negro History* 33 (April 1948) 146–67; Herbert Aptheker, "Buying Freedom," in *To Be Free* (New York: International Publishers, 1945); John Hope Franklin, "Slaves Virtually Free in Ante-Bellum North Carolina," *Journal of Negro History*, 28 (1943): 284–310.

5 See Juliet E. K. Walker, *Free Frank: A Black Pioneer on the Antebellum Frontier* (Lexington: University Press of Kentucky, 1983). The slave Frank, Free Frank McWorter (1777–1854), set up a saltpeter manufactory in Kentucky during the War of 1812. Profits, after paying his owner to allow him to hire his time, enabled him to purchase his wife in 1817, himself in 1819, both for $800. Afterwards, Free Frank expanded his saltpeter manufactory, was a small land spec-

ulator and commercial farmer. He moved to Illinois in 1830 and in 1836 founded the town of New Philadelphia. Sixteen family members were purchased from slavery by Free Frank from his business profits.

6 Howard Holman Bell (ed.), *Minutes of the Proceedings of the National Negro Conventions, 1830–1864* (New York: Arno Press and the New York Times, 1969)

7 *The Anglo-African Magazine* 1, 5 (October 1859): 180. Also see, Margaret Hope Bacon, "'One Great Bundle of Humanity': Frances Ellen Watkins Harper (1825–1911)," *Pennsylvania Magazine of History and Biography* (January, 1989).

8 Milton Friedman, *Capitalism and Freedom* (Chicago, University of Chicago, 1962, p. 10). Also Walker, "Prejudices, Profits, Privileges," 400–1.

9 Bell. *Minutes*, i–ii.

10 See, Howard H. Bell. *A Survey of the Negro Convention Movement, 1830–1861* (New York, 1969). Also, William H. Pease and Jane H. Pease, "The Negro Convention Movement," in Nathan I. Huggins, Martin Kilson, and Daniel M. Fox (eds), *Key Issues in the Afro-American Experience* (New York, 1971. I: 191–209); Bella Gross, *Clarion Call: The History and Development of the Negro People's Convention Movement in the United States from 1817–1840* (New York, 1947); and Bella Gross, "The First National Negro Convention," *Journal of Negro History* 21 (October 1946): 120–38.

11 See Bell, *Minutes*. Included are "Proceedings" for 1830, including the Constitution; the next five meetings held 1831 to 1835, and the six subsequent meetings held in 1843, 1847, 1848, 1853, 1855, and 1864.

12 See: William A. Leidesdorff Estate Papers, 1842–52, Leidesdorff Collection. Bancroft Library, University of California. Berkeley; Leidesdorff and Folosm court records, Bancroft Court Records. Bancroft Library; *Peoples ex rel. Attorney General vs. Joseph L. Folsom*, 5 Cal Rep. 373 (1855): and *US vs. Exec. J. Folsom*, US Superior Court. Dec. term, cases 168 and 238. The final estate settlement, $1,442, 232.35.

13 On Smith, see the R. G. Dun & Company Mercantile Agency Credit Reports, Pennsylvania, vol. 132, p. 322, R. G. Dun & Co. for the following entries: "Sept 16/53 'Smith was formerly a slave to old "Ben Boude"... Good as the best worth $100m"; "July 18/57 King of the Darkies – worth $100m...."; "Apr. 1/65 Smith worth 500m$." Also, Walker, "Racism, Slavery, Free Enterprise," 353–4 and 360.

14 See US Bureau of the Census, "Population Schedules of the Ninth Census of the United States, 1870, New Jersey, Middlesex County, New Brunswick," manuscript microcopy M–753, reel 873, which documents Whipper's post-Civil War wealth at $108,000. Prior to the Civil War, Whipper, although wealthy, was worth less than $100,000.

15 Bell, *Minutes*, "Minutes and Proceedings of the Second Annual Convention For The Improvement of the Free People Of Color... Philadelphia, From the 4th to the 13th of June inclusive, 1832," 22.

16 Bell, *Minutes*, "Proceedings of the Colored National Convention, Cleveland, 1848," 18.

17 Bell, *Minutes*, "Proceedings of the Colored National Convention, Cleveland, 1848," 6. For success stories of prominent antebellum black entrepreneurs, most of whom were delegates to the National Negro Convention see, Martin R. Delany, *The Condition, Elevation, Emigration and Destiny of the Colored People of the United States* (Philadelphia, 1852; reprint, New York: Arno Press, 1968, 92–110). On Delany see, Nell Painter, "Martin Delany: Elitism and Black Nationalism," in *Black Leaders of the Nineteenth Century*, Leon Litwack and August Meier (eds) (Urbana: University of Illinois Press, 1988, 149–171).

18 Ibid., 19.

19 Bell, *Minutes*, "Proceedings of the Colored National Convention, Cleveland, 1848," 12.

20 Bell, *Minutes*, "Proceedings of the Colored National Convention, Cleveland, 1848," 20.

21 Pease and Pease, "Negro Convention Movement," 192.

22 Carter G. Woodson, "The Negroes of Cincinnati Prior to the Civil War," *Journal of Negro History* 1 (July 1916): 1–22.

23 See, Leonard P. Curry, *The Free Black in Urban America 1800–1850: The Shadow of the Dream*, (Chicago: University of Chicago Press, 1981).

24 "The First Colored Convention," *The Anglo-African*, 1, 10 (October, 1859), from interview with Hezekiah Grice and also comment, "At the present day, when colored conventions are almost as frequent as church-meetings, it is difficult to estimate the bold and daring spirit which inaugurated the Colored Convention of 1830." For reprint of this article see, Bell, *Minutes*, xi–xiv; and, "The Pioneer National Negro Organization," in Herbert Aptheker (ed.) *A Documentary History of the Negro People in the United States: From Colonial Times to the Civil War*, vol. 1 (New York: The Citadel Press, 1951, 98–102).

25 Bell, *Minutes*, "Constitution of the American Society of Free Persons of Colour.... Also The Proceedings of the Convention..., 1830," 9.

26 Bell, *Minutes*, "Constitution of the American Society of Free Persons of Colour.... Also The Proceedings of the Convention..., 1831," 10–11.

27 Bell, *Minutes*, "Minutes and Proceedings of the Second Annual Convention..., Philadelphia, From the 4th to the 13th of June inclusive, 1832," 10.

28 Bell, *Minutes*, "Minutes and Proceedings of the Third Annual Convention... Philadelphia, From the 3d to the 13th of June, inclusive, 1833," 27–8, where the following resolution was made: "That this Convention discourage, by every means in their power, the colonization of our people, anywhere beyond the limits of this continent; and those who may be obliged to exchange a cultivated region for a howling wilderness, we would recommend, to retire back into the western wilds, and fell the native forests of America, where the plough-share of prejudice has as yet been unable to penetrate the soil."

29 Bell, *Minutes*, "Proceedings of the Colored National Convention,... Rochester, July 6th, 7th and 8th, 1853," 49 and 55. Pennington received the degree of Doctor of Divinity from the University of Heidelberg. See, Carter G. Woodson, *The Negro in Our History*, (Washington, D.C.: 1928, 7–9). Also, J. W. C. Pennington, The Fugitive Blacksmith; or Events in the History of James W. C. Pennington (London, 1850). Also, Juliet E. K. Walker, *War, Peace and Structural Violence: Peace Activism and the African-American Historic Experience*, (Bloomington: Indiana University, Indiana Center on Global Change and World Peace, 1992, 12–13).

30 See Floyd J. Miller, *The Search for a Black Nationality: Black Emigration and Colonization 1787–1763*, (Urbana: University of Illinois Press, 1975, 93, 104–7). Also, Leon Litwack, *North of Slavery: The Negro in the Free States, 1790–1860*, (Chicago: University of Chicago, 1961) on black response to the 1850 Fugitive Slave Law, the anti-immigration laws passed by several northern states that made it illegal for blacks to settle in those states, and laws passed or proposed in several southern states that required free blacks in those states a choice of emigration or enslavement.

31 Bell, *Minutes*, "Proceedings of the Colored National Convention,... Rochester, July 6th, 7th and 8th, 1853," 36.

32 Bell, *Minutes*, "Minutes and Proceedings of the Third Annual Convention... Philadelphia, From the 3d to the 13th of June, inclusive, 1833," 30.

33 Bell, *Minutes*, "Minutes and Proceedings of the Third Annual Convention… Philadelphia, From the 3d to the 13th of June, inclusive, 1833," 30.

34 Bell, *Minutes*, "Minutes and Proceedings of the Fifth Annual Convention… Philadelphia, From the First to the Fifth of June, inclusive, 1835," 12.

35 Bell, *Minutes*, "Minutes and Proceedings of the Fourth Annual Convention… New York, From the 2d to the 12th of June, inclusive, 1834," 15.

36 Bell, *Minutes*, "Minutes and Proceedings of the Fourth Annual Convention… New York, From the 2d to the 12th of June, inclusive, 1834," 34.

37 Bell, *Minutes*, "Minutes and Proceedings of the Fifth Annual Convention… Philadelphia, From the First to the Fifth of June, Inclusive, 1835," 16.

38 Bell, *Minutes*, "Minutes and Proceedings of the Fifth Annual Convention… Philadelphia, From the First to the Fifth of June, Inclusive, 1835," 16. Also, William Frederic Wormer, "The Columbia Race Riots," *Lancaster County Historical Society* 26, 8 (Oct 1922): 177, on Smith's success in Columbia which resulted in a race riot by whites to force him out of business and out of town. Eventually Smith moved to Philadelphia.

39 Bell, *Minutes*, "Minutes of the National Convention of Colored Citizens: Held at Buffalo, on the 15th, 16th, 17th, 18th and 19th of August, 1843," 24 and 27.

40 Bell, *Minutes*, "Minutes of the National Convention of Colored Citizens: Held at Buffalo, on the 15th, 16th, 17th, 18th and 19th of August, 1843," 27.

41 Bell, *Minutes*, "Minutes of the National Convention of Colored Citizens: Held at Buffalo, on the 15th, 16th, 17th, 18th and 19th of August, 1843," 30–2.

42 Bell, *Minutes*, "Minutes of the National Convention of Colored Citizens: Held at Buffalo, on the 15th, 16th, 17th, 18th and 19th of August, 1843," 31.

43 Bell, *Minutes*, "Minutes of the National Convention of Colored Citizens: Held at Buffalo, on the 15th, 16th, 17th, 18th and 19th of August, 1843," 32–3.

44 Bell, *Minutes*, "Minutes of the National Convention of Colored Citizens: Held at Buffalo, on the 15th, 16th, 17th, 18th and 19th of August, 1843," 33.

45 Bell, *Minutes*, "Minutes of the National Convention of Colored Citizens: Held at Buffalo, on the 15th, 16th, 17th, 18th and 19th of August, 1843," 33.

46 Bell, *Minutes*, "Minutes of the National Convention of Colored Citizens: Held at Buffalo, on the 15th, 16th, 17th, 18th and 19th of August, 1843," 34–5.

47 Bell, *Minutes*, "Minutes of the National Convention of Colored Citizens: Held at Buffalo, on the 15th, 16th, 17th, 18th and 19th of August, 1843," 32.

48 Bell, *Minutes*, "Proceedings of the National Convention of Colored People, And Their Friends, Held In Troy, N.Y., on the 6th, 7th, 8th and 9th October, 1847," 28.

49 Bell, *Minutes*, "Minutes and Proceedings of the First Annual Convention of the People of Colour,… Philadelphia, From the Sixth to the Eleventh of June, Inclusive, 1831," 6.

50 Bell, *Minutes*, "Proceedings of the National Convention of Colored People, And Their Friends, Held In Troy, N.Y., on the 6th, 7th, 8th and 9th October, 1847," 21–5.

51 See, American Colonization Society, *Fifteenth Annual Report* (Washington, D.C., 1832), 43; Also, Luther Porter Jackson, *Free Negro Labor and Property Holding in Virginia, 1830–1860*, (New York: D. Appleton-Century Company, 1942, 144 and 148); and, Tom W. Schick, *Behold the Promised Land: A History of Afro-American Settler Society in Nineteenth-Century Liberia*, (Baltimore: Johns Hopkins University Press, 1977, 46 and 50), on the African-American Liberian/Baltimore based mercantile trading firm of Colston Waring and Francis Taylor, established in Monrovia in the mid-1820s. It specialized in the sale of "firearms, ale, and rum imported from Liverpool." In 1830, the firm had sales in the amount of $70,000. Also, Walker, *Capitalism, Race, Entrepreneurship*, on ante-

bellum African American international trade ventures, primarily with West Africa.

52 Bell, *Minutes*, "Proceedings of the National Convention of Colored People, Troy, N. Y., 1847," 14.

53 Bell, *Minutes*, "Proceedings of the National Convention of Colored People, Troy, N. Y., 1847," 15. See, Rhoda Golden Freeman, "The Free Negro in New York in the Era Before the Civil War," PhD dissertation, Columbia University, 1966, 274 and *Statistical Inquiry into the Condition of the People of Colour of Philadelphia*, which show that in 1837, free blacks in New York had $50,000–$80,000 on deposit and $200,000 on deposit in Philadelphia banks.

54 Bell, *Minutes*, "Proceedings of the National Convention of Colored People, Troy, N. Y., 1847," 15.

55 Bell, *Minutes*, "Proceedings of the Colored National Convention, Cleveland, 1848," 19.

56 Bell, *Minutes*, "Proceedings of the Colored National Convention, Cleveland, 1848," 19–20.

57 Bell, *Minutes*, "Proceedings of the Colored National Convention, Cleveland, 1848," 13.

58 Bell, *Minutes*, Proceedings of the Colored National Convention, Philadelphia, 1855," 19. In 1850 the American League of Colored Laborers proposed a plan to create a fund which would be used to provide venture capital to assist them in establishing and developing business enterprises. See, *New York Tribune*, 3 July 1850. Black activist and abolitionist Samuel Ringold Ward was president: Vice presidents were Lewis Woodson and Frederick Douglass, who very briefly in 1874 was President of the Freedmen's Bank. In California, however, blacks in 1859 founded the first African American banking institution, the Saving Fund and Land Association in San Francisco. Also, just before the Civil War, a financial organization was founded in New Orleans known as the Union Bank Society – see, William J. Trent, *Development of Negro Life Insurance Enterprise*, (Philadelphia: University of Pennsylvania Graduate School of Business, 1932, 8).

59 Shirley Ardener, "The Comparative Study of Rotating Credit Associations," *Journal of the Royal Anthropological Institute* 94, pt. 2 (1964): 201, who has defined this system as based on: "an association formed upon a core of participants who agree to make regular contributions to a fund which is given, in whole or in part, to each contributor in rotation."

60 See, Ivan H. Light, *Ethnic Enterprise in America: Business and Welfare Among Chinese, Japanese, and Blacks*, (Berkeley: University of California Press, 1972), 20–2, where Light reviews the literature; ibid. 30–44, discusses the Esusu, the West Indian rotating credit association and its West African origin: and concludes, ibid. 44, "that social conditions in the United States extirpated the esusu from the cultural repertoire of blacks in this country...." See K. Franklin Frazier.

61 Through the purchase of bank stock there were several instances before the Civil War of blacks who sat as official members on bank boards. See, Wormer, "Columbia Race Riots," 177, on Stephen Smith, who sat on the board of the Columbia Bank in the 1830s; noting that although he: "was the largest stockholder of his day in the Columbia bank; and, according to its rules, would have been president had it not been for his complexion. Being thus barred, he was given the privilege of naming the white man who became president in his stead." Also, Walker, *Capitalism, Race, Entrepreneurship*, on antebellum black banking activities.

62 Bell, *Minutes*, "Proceedings of the Colored National Convention, Philadelphia, 1855," 19.

63 The African Secret Burial Societies and mutual aid self-help organizations which, after the Civil War, along with fraternal organizations, provided the base for the financial institutional development of black banks and black insurance companies. On black insurance companies and banks see. J. H. Harmon, Jr., Arnett Lindsay, and Carter G. Woodson, *The Negro as a Businessman* (Washington, 1929. Repr., New York, Arno Press, 1969) and Abram L. Harris, *The Negro Capitalist: A Study of Banking and Business Among Negroes*, (Philadelphia, 1936; repr. New York: Arno Press, 1968).

64 Bell, *Minutes*, "Constitution...and Proceedings, Philadelphia, 1830," 7. Antebellum black organizations also purchased stock in white banks. See, *An Address Before the New York African Society for Mutual Relief in the African Zion Church*, 23 March 1815, being the Fifth Anniversary of Their Incorporation, 1815, 7, notes the organization had acquired $500.00 in bank stock by 1815. In South Carolina the 1835 estate of South Carolina barber Thomas Inglis included $19,303 in stock and bonds at the Mechanics Bank; see, South Carolina, Record of Wills of Charleston County, vol. 40, Book A, 1834–1839, 289–90. Also, Charleston Inventories, Appraisements & Sales vol. II 1834–1844 (Charleston County), 124, in Larry Koger, *Black Slaveowners: Free Black Slave Masters in South Carolina, 1790–1860*, (Jefferson, NC: McFarland & Company, Inc., 1985, 152). Abram L. Harris, *The Negro As Capitalist: A Study of Banking and Business Among American Negroes*, (Philadelphia: American Academy of Political and Social Science, 1936, 8), notes a Maryland black held stock in one of that state's banks, but indicates in the South, "special statutes and acts incorporating state banks prohibited Negroes from becoming stock-holders and depositors."

65 See, John Spencer Bassett, *Slavery in the State of North Carolina* Baltimore, (1899, 44–5), on slave-born John C. Stanley, "Barber Jack" of North Carolina, who both loaned money and discounted notes, using his wealth, $40,000 to purchase slaves, and "he made most of his money by discounting notes." In this enterprise, Stanley was a front for whites: "Certain white men of means who did not care to go openly into the business of sharp discounting took him for a partner and furnished the means." In discounting bank notes, antebellum blacks capitalized on the practice of state banks issuing their own notes at disparate rates and value. By giving favorable rates of exchange, many black informal bankers become quite wealthy. In this capacity they were known as: "'note shavers'," men "who would discount notes as banks do now, but presumably at a greater profit." See, Henry M. Minton, M.D., "Early History of Negroes in Business in Philadelphia," read Before the American Historical Society, March 1913, Moorland-Spingarn Research Center, Howard University, Washington, D.C., 17.

66 Bell, *Minutes*, "Proceedings of the Colored National Convention. Philadelphia. 1855." 19.

67 See. Rudolph M. Lapp. "The Negro in Gold Rush California." *Journal of Negro History* (April 1964). 96–8.

68 Bell, Constitution...and Proceedings, Philadelphia, 1830." 11.

69 Bell, *Minutes*, "Proceedings of the First Annual Convention, Philadelphia, 1831," 14. White abolitionists Arthur Tappan, Benjamin Lundy, and William Lloyd Garrison attended this convention for the purpose of addressing the body on the topic of education and "to submit a plan for establishing a College, for the education of Young Men of Colour." The Convention established a committee who proposed that the college should be established in New Haven, "and to be on the Manual Labour System, by which in connexion with a scientific education, they may also obtain a useful Mechanical or Agricultural profession." See

ibid., 5–6. The cost was $20,000: $1,000 would be donated by a white philanthropist if members of the Convention could raise $19,000 in one year. See, *Minutes*, 1833, reporting $1,000 raised and $10,000 donated.

70 Bell, *Minutes*, "Minutes of the Fifth Annual Convention, Philadelphia, 1835," 17.

71 Bell, *Minutes*, "Proceedings of the Colored National Convention. Rochester, 1853," 34.

72 Bell, *Minutes*, "Proceedings of the Colored National Convention, Rochester, 1853," 35. Even in the closing decade of the twentieth century, many black professionals, especially lawyers and trained MBAs are confronted with problems similar to their antebellum counterparts.

73 Bell, *Minutes*, "Proceedings of the Colored National Convention, Rochester, 1853," 37. Douglass was referring to the European immigrant, particularly in the North, who successfully competed with blacks in obtaining employment. Again, one can find parallels in the late twentieth century. New immigrants from Asia, the Middle East, Africa and the West Indies are securing employment in occupations in which African Americans had a monopoly and especially in owning businesses that provide goods and services to the black community.

74 Bell, *Minutes*, "Proceedings of the Colored National Convention, Rochester, 1853," 37.

75 Bell, *Minutes*, "Proceedings of the Colored National Convention, Rochester, 1853," 37.

76 Bell, *Minutes*, "Proceedings of the Colored National Convention, Rochester, 1853," 34.

77 Bell, *Minutes*, "Proceedings of the Colored National Convention, Rochester, 1853," 32.

78 Bell, *Minutes*, "Proceedings of the Colored National Convention, Rochester, 1853," 18.

79 Bell, *Minutes*, "Proceedings of the Colored National Convention, Philadelphia, 1855," 10.

80 Bell, *Minutes*, "Proceedings of the Colored National Convention, Philadelphia, 1855," 11.

81 Bell, *Minutes*, "Proceedings of the Colored National Convention, Philadelphia, 1855," 38.

82 Bell, *Minutes*, "Proceedings of the Colored National Convention, Rochester, 1853," 39.

83 Bell, *Minutes*, "Proceedings of the Colored National Convention, Rochester, 1853," 18–20, for the Constitution of the National Council of Colored People in which two of the fourteen articles specifically applied to the promotion of black business, including Article 5 which required the Council to: "report upon any avenues of business or trade which they deem inviting to colored capital, skill, or labor.... They shall receive for sale or exhibition, products of the skill and labor of colored people." Also see, *New York Tribune*, 16 April 1851. Also see, *Philadelphia North America and United States Gazette*, 11 April 1851 and *The Pennsylvanian*, 14 April 1851, for reports of an exhibition held by blacks in 1851, called the Colored American Institute for the Promotion of the Mechanic Arts and Science, where there was a display of the technological innovations and manufacturing contributions of African Americans.

84 See W. E. B. Du Bois, *The Negro in Business*, Atlanta University Publication, No. 4 (Atlanta: Atlanta University, 1899, 50), for the resolution proposed by Du Bois at the conference on blacks in business that he convened in 1898 for the organization of a national black business organization in which he called for: "The organization in every town and hamlet where colored people dwell, of Negro Business Men's Leagues, and the gradual federation from these of state

and national organizations." Also, C.C. Spaulding, "50 Years of Progress in Business," (Pittsburgh: Pittsburgh Courier, 1950, 1), on his discussion of that conference. Two years later, Booker T. Washington organized the National Negro Business League (NNBL) at a meeting held in Boston in 1900. See, Booker T. Washington, "The National Negro Business League," *World's Work*, 4 (October 1902), 271–5; Albon L. Holsey, "The National Negro Business League," in J. L. Nichols and Wiliam H. Grogman, *Progress of a Race: On the Remarkable Advancement of the American Negro*, (Naperville, Ill,: J. L. Nichols, 1920, 211–29); and, Louis R. Harlan, *Booker T. Washington: The Wizard of Tuskegee, 1901–1915*, (New York: Oxford University Press, 1983).

85 Bell, *Minutes*, "Proceedings of the Colored National Convention, Rochester, 1853," 39.

86 Bell, *Minutes*, "Proceedings of the Colored National Convention, Philadelphia, 1855," 17–18. The second proposal also reflects aspects of the "rotating credit association," only in this instance funds provided are from other individuals who pool their monies to underwrite business ventures for someone who has demonstrated a competence to succeed as a business owner.

87 Bell, *Minutes*, "Proceedings of the Colored National Convention, Philadelphia, 1855," 16.

88 Bell, *Minutes*, "Proceedings of the Colored National Convention, Rochester, 1853," 27.

89 Bell, *Minutes*, "Proceedings of the Colored National Convention, Philadelphia, 1855," 16.

90 Bell, *Minutes*, "Proceedings of the Colored National Convention, Philadelphia, 1832," 11.

91 Bell, *Minutes*, "Proceedings of the Colored National Convention, Cleveland, 1848," 11.

92 Bell, *Minutes*, "Proceedings of the Colored National Convention, Cleveland, 1848," 11–12, 17.

93 Bell, *Minutes*, "Proceedings of the Colored National Convention, Philadelphia, 1855," 10. The vote to admit Shadd as a corresponding member was "Yeas, 38 – Nays, 23." On Mary Shadd Cary (1823–93), considered the first black female lawyer, Howard University, 1870, see Jim Bearden and Linda Jean Butler, *Shadd: The Life and Times of Mary Ann Shadd*, (1971).

94 Bell, *Minutes*, "Proceedings of the Colored National Convention, Rochester, 1853," 32.

95 Bell, *Minutes*, "Proceedings of the Colored National Convention, Philadelphia, 1855," 18 and 29.

96 See Walker, "Antebellum Free Black Women Business Enterprises," in *Capitalism, Race and Entrepreneurship*. Also the comment by black woman activist Maria W. Stewart who in promoting the participation of black women in business said: "Do you ask, what can we do? Unite and build a store of your own. Fill one side with dry-goods and the other with groceries. Do you ask, where is the money? We have spent more than enough for nonsense to do what building we should want. We have never had an opportunity of displaying our talents; therefore the world thinks we know nothing." See, Maria W. Stewart (1803–79), Speech, Franklin Hall, Boston, 21 September 1832, in Dorothy Sterling (ed.) *We Are Your Sisters: Black Women in the Nineteenth Century*, (New York: W. W. Norton & Company, 1984, 154).

97 Bell, *Minutes*, "Proceedings of the National Convention of Colored Men,... - Syracuse, N. Y., October 4, 5, 6, and 7, 1864 With the Bill of Wrongs and Rights," 58.

98 Bell, *Minutes*, "Proceedings of the Colored National Convention, Rochester, 1853," 27, from "Report of Committee on the Importance of Colored Persons Engaging in Commercial Pursuits."

99 E. Franklin Frazier, *The Negro in the United States*, 2nd. edn., rev. (New York: Macmillan, 1957). Also, E. Franklin Frazier, *Black Bourgeoisie*, (Glencoe: The Free Press, 1957, 153–73), for what he describes as the "myth" of black business. Few studies have been undertaken on antebellum black businessmen or business activity, including only five monographs of antebellum black entrepreneurs. See, Edwin Adams Davis and William Ransom Hogan, *The Barber of Natchez*, (Baton Rouge: Louisiana State University Press, 1954); Gary B. Mills, *The Forgotten People of Color: Cane River's Creoles of Color*, (Baton Rouge: Louisiana State University Press, 1977); David O. Whitten, *Andrew Durnford: A Black Sugar Cane Planter in Antebellum Louisiana*, (Natchitoches: 1981): Juliet E. K. Walker, *Free Frank: A Black Pioneer on the Antebellum Frontier*, (Lexington: University Press of Kentucky, 1983); and, Michael P. Johnson and James L. Roark, *Black Masters: A Free Family of Color in the Old South*, (New York: W.W. Norton and Co. 1984). For regional studies which include discussion of business activities of antebellum free blacks see, Ira Berlin, *Slaves Without Masters: The Free Negro in the Antebellum South*, (New York: Pantheon Books, 1974); Leonard P. Curry, *The Free Black in Urban America, 1800–1850: The Shadow of the Dream*, (Chicago: University of Chicago Press, 1981); and, Loren Schweninger, *Black Property Owners in the South 1790–1915*, (Urbana: University of Illinois Press, 1990).

100 The initial study of African American business history was undertaken by blacks whose works seldom enter the mainstream of American scholarship, including, J. H. Harmon, Jr., Arnett G. Lindsay, and Carter G. Woodson, *The Negro As A Business Man*, (Washington, D.C.: Association for the Study of Negro Life and History, Inc., 1929; reprint, College Park, MD: McGrath Publishing Company, 1969) and Abram L. Harris, *The Negro As Capitalist: A Study of Banking and Business Among American Negroes*, (Philadelphia: American Academy of Political and Social Science, 1936; rep. ed. New York: Arno Press, 1968). Also, W. E. B. Du Bois, *Economic Co-Operation Among Negro Americans,* (Atlanta: Atlanta University, 1907). Two recent studies that make significant contributions in black business history are, John Sibley Butler, *Entrepreneurship and Self-Help Among Black Americans: A Reconsideration of Race and Economics*, (Albany: State University of New York Press, 1991) and John N. Ingham and Lynne B. Feldman, *African-American Business Leaders: A Biographical Dictionary* (Westport CT: Greenwood Press, 1994). Also, forthcoming, Walker, *Capitalism, Race, and Entrepreneurship*, the first comprehensive history of black business in America; George H. Hill, *Black Business and Economics: A Selected Bibliography*, (New York, 1985) and Juliet E. K. Walker (ed.) *Encyclopedia of African American Business History*, (Westport CT: Greenwood Press, forthcoming 1997).

101 Bell, *Minutes*, "Proceedings of the Colored National Convention, Philadelphia, 1855," 34.

Part III

THEORY AND METHOD

15

UNRAVELING THE PARADOX OF DEEPENING URBAN INEQUALITY

Theoretical underpinnings, research design, and preliminary findings from a multi-city study

James H. Johnson, Jr.

Following the Second World War, a number of social and economic indicators exhibited a trend toward greater equality in America. However, this trend ended abruptly in the early 1980s and the nation has now entered its second decade of increasing polarization along the economic dimensions of income, occupational prestige, and wealth accumulation (Michel 1991; Levy 1987; Harrison and Bluestone 1988; Oliver and Shapiro 1990). Perhaps the most visible manifestations of contemporary inequality are the growing incidence of poverty and the increasing geographic isolation of the poor from the mainstream of American society (Wilson 1987; Jargowsky and Bane 1991; Mincy and Ricketts 1990; Danziger, Sandefur, and Weinberg 1994). Recent studies indicate that, despite the implementation of anti-poverty, affirmative action, and a range of other anti-discrimination programs aimed at improving the quality of life of disadvantaged minorities during the 1960s and the 1970s, African Americans, in particular, remain disproportionately concentrated among the growing population of have-nots in American society (Ricketts and Sawhill 1988; Kasarda 1992; Hacker 1992; Orfield and Ashkinaze 1991; Jaynes and Williams 1989).

There are differences of opinion among social scientists and social policy analysts with respect to the forces responsible for the growing schisms between the haves and the have-nots in urban America. Conservative policy analysts attribute the high rates of joblessness and poverty to the combined effects of the growth of welfare benefits (Murray 1984) on the one hand, and to character deficiencies and deviant values of inner city residents, especially toward family (Loury 1985) and work (Mead 1992), on the other. Liberal and progressive scholars reject the views of these conservative policy analysts. They contend that contemporary urban inequality stems from fundamental changes in the basic structure of the US economy

(Wilson 1987), negative white attitudes that play a role in thwarting the social and economic aspirations of increasingly poor, non-white inner city minorities (Bobo and Kluegel 1991; Kirschenman and Neckerman 1991; (Feagin 1991), and enduring racial residential segregation (Massey and Denton 1992).

The discourse surrounding these competing perspectives has been lively and thought-provoking. However, the research on contemporary urban inequality suffers from several shortcomings. First, very little empirical evidence has been amassed to support the conservative perspectives (Ellwood and Summers 1988). Second, no consideration has been given to how the forces highlighted by liberal scholars interact to create and maintain inequality. Third, and perhaps most important, liberal and conservative policy analysts alike have failed to incorporate into their explanations of contemporary urban inequality the findings on growing class polarization in American society (Bluestone and Harrison 1982; Phillips 1990). These studies, as distinct from research on concentrated poverty and the underclass, identify the early 1980s as the historical turning point that signaled the end of the post-Second World War trend toward greater economic equality in America. Central to these accounts is the ascent of Ronald Reagan and the hegemony of conservative national politics (Johnson 1995; Grant and Johnson 1995).

In this chapter, I describe an interdisciplinary, primary data gathering initiative, The Multi-City Study of Urban Inequality (MCSUI), which is designed to advance our knowledge and understanding of the forces responsible for the growing schism between the haves and the have-nots in urban America over the past two decades. In the first half of the chapter, I highlight the study's research design and review the theoretical constructs that the MCSUI data will enable researchers to test. In the second half, I present the preliminary results of my initial exploratory analyses of the MCSUI data, which focus on the so-called cultural capital hypothesis. I conclude by discussing, briefly, the significance of both the MCSUI data gathering initiative and the specific exploratory analyses presented in this chapter.

BACKGROUND AND RESEARCH DESIGN

The MCSUI is the brainchild of an interdisciplinary team of research scholars – geographers, sociologists, economists, political scientists, and historians – representing fifteen different US colleges and universities. Funded principally by The Ford Foundation and the Russell Sage Foundation, the MCSUI is designed to broaden our knowledge and understanding of how three sets of forces – changing labor market dynamics, racial attitudes and polarization, and racial residential segregation – interact to foster contemporary urban inequality. To address issues in each of these domains, the MCSUI research team is engaged in a primary data gathering effort, involving linked household–employer surveys in four cities: Atlanta, Boston, Detroit, and Los Angeles.

In the area of *labor market dynamics* the MCSUI seeks to capture the "real world" experiences of workers and job seekers. The primary objective is to gather data that will broaden our understanding of the nature of labor market outcomes, that is, what determines labor force participation, extent of employment, unemployment and earnings.

Previous research has attempted to address these and related issues by surveying either employers (Braddock and McPartland 1987; Kirschenman and Neckerman 1991) or workers/job seekers (Freeman 1991; Osterman 1991; Marsden, Kalleberg, and Cook 1993). But recent studies suggest that both "demand-side" and "supply-side" forces influence labor market outcomes (Moss and Tilly 1991).

To assess the effects of influences on both sides of the labor market, the MCSUI utilizes a household survey to generate a sample of employers who, in turn, are interviewed over the telephone about their hiring and promotion practices as well as their perceptions and attitudes toward various race/ethnic groups in the labor market. In this way, researchers will be able to link the actual labor market experiences of individuals (i.e., the supply side) to the recruitment, hiring, and promotion practices of employers (i.e., the demand side).

Thus, in contrast to the Current Population Survey and other large scale surveys that contain a battery of questions pertaining to labor market outcomes, the MCSUI will gather more detailed information on the processes that surround entry into and exit from the labor market, including hiring, promotion, firing, and quits. And in contrast to most employer surveys, which typically generate their samples from sources like Dunn and Bradstreet that only list firms in the regulated economy, the MCSUI data will provide insights into the size and composition as well as the employment practices in the unregulated or informal sector of the economy, since the employer sample is generated from the supply-side rather than the demand-side.

The MCSUI will also gather primary data on *interethnic attitudes and beliefs*. Previous research typically focused on how the white majority feels about members of minority groups and on black–white relations (Schuman, Steeh, and Bobo 1988). Thus, we know comparatively little about how members of different minority groups feel about one another or, for that matter, how whites feel about minority groups other than blacks (Bobo and Kluegel 1991; Smith 1991). The linked household–employer surveys are designed to measure the attitudes, beliefs, and stereotypes that whites, blacks, Latinos, and Asians hold about one another. The paucity of research that exists on interethnic minority conflicts suggests that such beliefs may have a direct bearing on experiences in both the labor market and the housing market (Oliver and Johnson 1984; Johnson and Oliver 1989; Johnson and Farrell 1993).

In the area of *residential segregation*, the MCSUI builds upon and expands the types of questions included in the 1976 Detroit-Area Survey (DAS) of racial residential segregation conducted by Reynolds Farley and Howard Schuman of the University of Michigan. While the 1976 DAS focused solely on black–white residential segregation (Farley *et al.* 1978), data collected in two of the cities in the MCSUI (Los Angeles and Boston) will enable researchers to explore the issues of residential segregation in a multi-ethnic context.

At the same time, the Detroit and Atlanta data will afford the MCSUI research team and other interested scholars the opportunity to assess how and to what extent residential segregation continues to influence the structure of opportunity in black–white contexts. And in the case of Detroit, researchers also will be able to compare the results of the current study with those of the 1976 DAS (see Farley *et al.* 1994).

In contrast to other recent primary data gathering initiatives (e.g. the University of Chicago Urban Poverty and Family Life Project and the Boston Poverty Survey), the MCSUI is unique in its emphasis on inequality rather than poverty. Our goal is to complete a total of 8,600 interviews with a stratified random sample of adults living in households in both poor and non-poor neighborhoods in the four case study communities: 1200 in Detroit, 1600 in Atlanta, 1600 in Boston, and 4000 in Los Angeles (Table 15.1). In two of our case study communities (Detroit and Atlanta), the samples are stratified by race and poverty, and in the other two (Los Angeles and Boston) by ethnicity and poverty. By surveying Asians, blacks, Hispanics, and whites in poor and non-poor neighborhoods, we will be able to assess the relative impact of forces that generate not only poverty, but also affluence.

Household interviews average about 70–90 minutes in length in three of the cities, and 115 minutes in the fourth (Los Angeles). Interviewers and respondents are matched by race/ethnicity and language in as many cases as possible. This is essential to minimize what is known in survey research as race-of-interviewer effects. Previous research has shown that whites will often give more liberal responses to black interviewers and that for some

Table 15.1 The MCSUI sample

City	*Whites*	*Blacks*	*Hispanics*	*Asians*	*Total*
Atlanta	800	800	–	–	1,600
Boston	600	600	600	–	1,800
Detroit	600	600	–	–	1,200
Los Angeles	1,000	1,000	1,000	1,000	4,000
Total	3,000	3,000	1,600	1,000	8,600

racial questions (i.e., those that might involve expression of an anti-white attitude) blacks will respond more positively to white than to black interviewers. Given the ethnic diversity of our sample in Los Angeles, the Los Angeles household instrument was translated into Spanish, Korean, and two dialects of Chinese (Mandarin and Cantonese). And to prevent the exclusion of monolingual Spanish, Chinese, and Korean speaking respondents, native speaking interviewers are used when needed.

KEY THEORETICAL ISSUES

The MCSUI will afford researchers the opportunity to move beyond single factor to more complex explanations of contemporary urban inequality. To illustrate how the data can be used in this way, Figure 15.1 shows a heuristic model, developed by the MCSUI research team, which delineates a set of macro- and micro-level causal agents and specifies how these forces, through a fairly complex web of interactions, influence employment outcomes for various racial or ethnic, gender, and demographic groups in the restructured American economy.

The heuristic model is comprised of five exogenous variables (labor market context, neighborhood context, school context, family background, and individual and human capital attributes) and five endogenous variables (social resources, cultural capital attributes, group-specific employer attitudes, job search behavior, and employment outcomes). Embedded in the structure of the model are a number of competing theoretical perspectives and hypotheses that the linked household–employer survey design of the MCSUI will enable us to test.

Four of these competing hypotheses are highlighted here: the Wilson hypothesis, the Kirschenman/Neckerman hypothesis, the Mead hypothesis, and the Social Resources hypothesis (Figure 15.2).

The Wilson hypothesis

Wilson's theory of the underclass (1987) attributes the high rates of male joblessness in urban America to the decline of high wage, highly unionized manufacturing employment (i.e., deindustrialization) and to the increasing social (and spatial) isolation of inner city neighborhoods from mainstream economic opportunities. In our heuristic model, as Figure 15.2a shows, Wilson's thesis can be reduced to five specific, testable hypotheses which can be summarized as follows:

Hypothesis 1: Employment outcomes are directly influenced by local labor market conditions. Individuals who find themselves in local labor markets that have experienced deindustrialization are more likely to be unemployed or outside the normal workings of the labor market than their counterparts

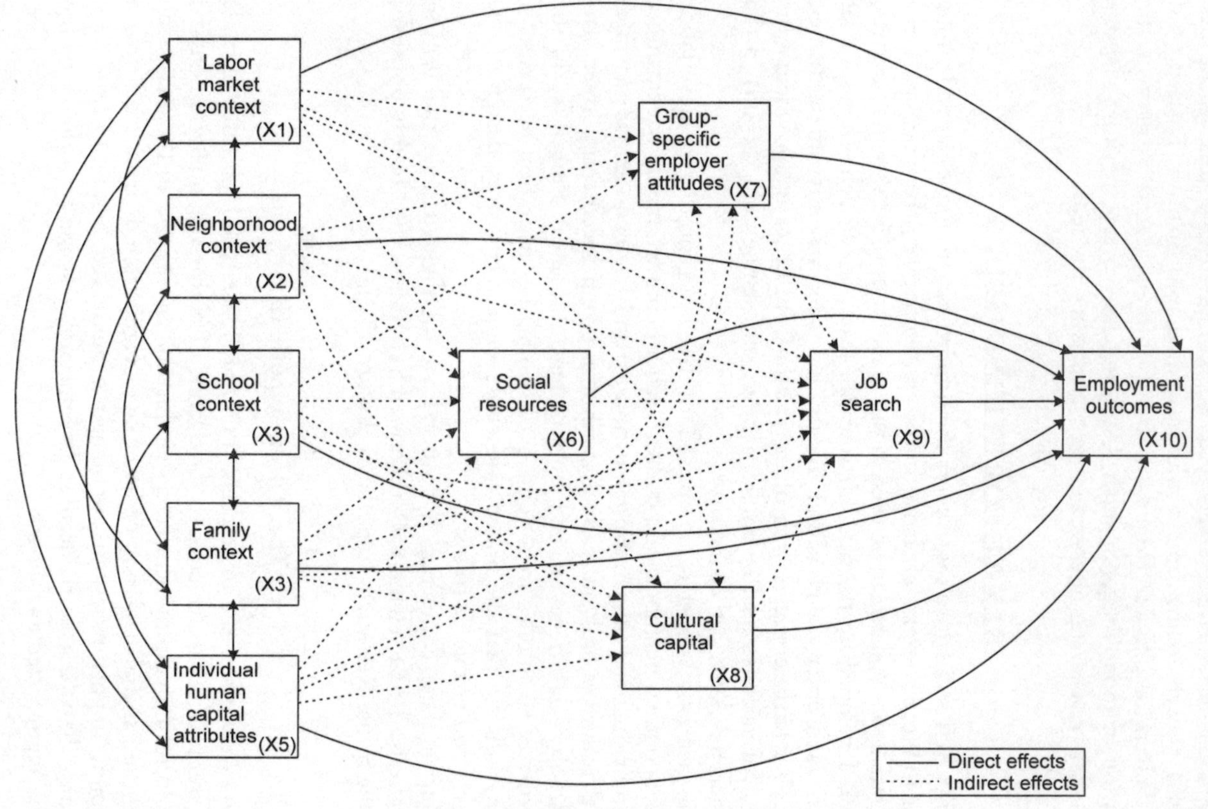

Figure 15.1 A heuristic model of employment outcomes

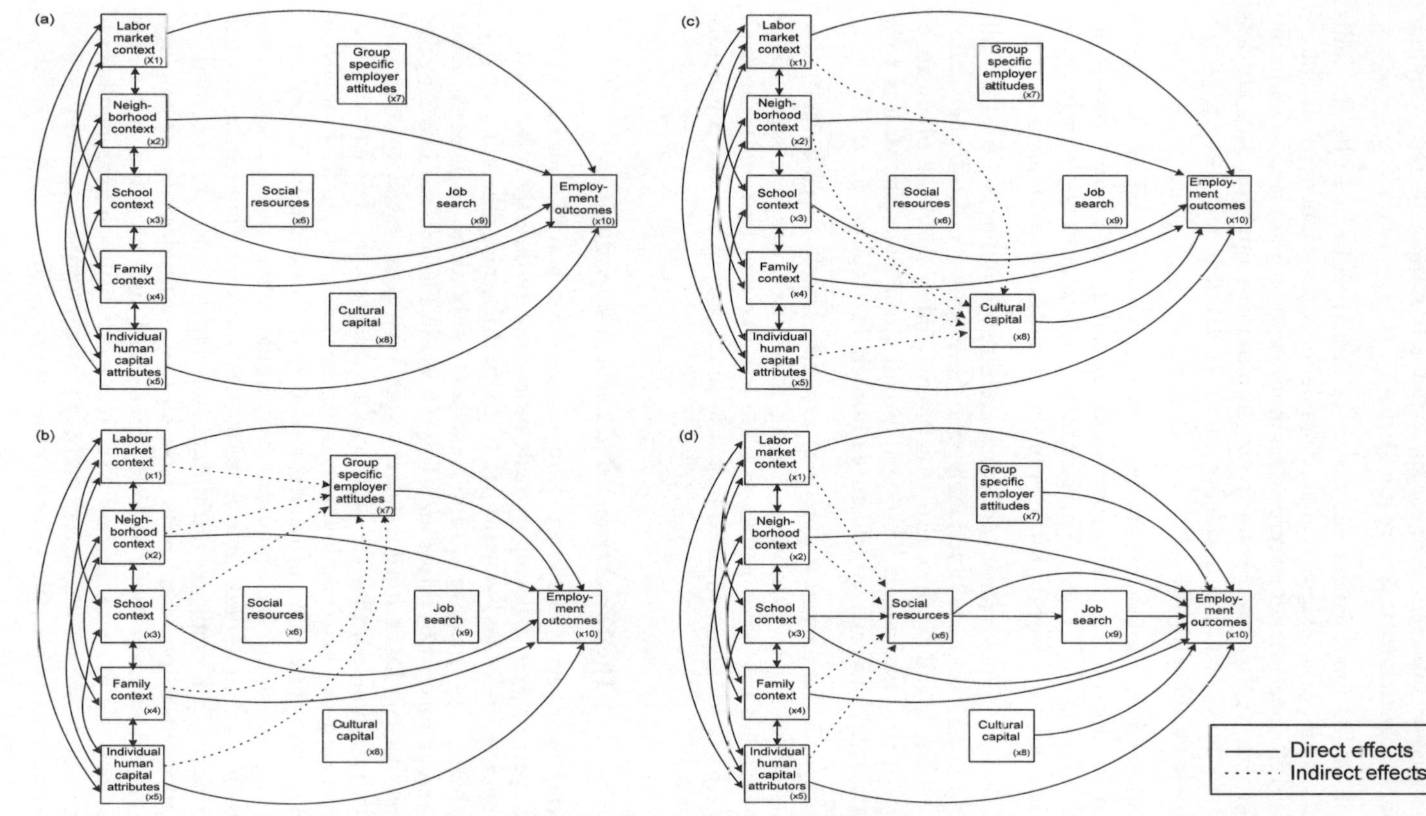

Figure 15.2 Competing theoretical perspectives: (a) Wilson hypothesis; (b) Kirschenman/Neckerman hypothesis; (c) Mead hypothesis; (d) Social Resources hypothesis

in local labor markets experiencing rapid job growth in the economic sectors that match local skill requirements.

Hypothesis 2: Employment outcomes are directly influenced by the individual's neighborhood environment. Residents of poor inner city neighborhoods (i.e., concentrated poverty communities) which are isolated, socially and geographically, from mainstream employment opportunities are less likely to find jobs than residents of more affluent and geographically accessible neighborhoods.

Hypothesis 3: Employment outcomes are directly influenced by the type of school an individual attends. Individuals attending inner city schools are less likely than their counterparts attending suburban schools to have the requisite skills to compete for jobs in the restructured economy.

Hypothesis 4: Employment outcomes are directly influenced by the individual's family context. Individuals who have grown up in higher status, well-educated, and traditionally structured families are more likely to be employed than individuals who have grown up in lower status, less well-educated, and alternatively structured households.

Hypothesis 5: Employment outcomes are directly influenced by an individual's human capital attributes. Young individuals who are high school drop-outs and have criminal records are less likely to find jobs than their counterparts who have finished high school and have not had a brush with the law.

The Kirschenman/Neckerman hypothesis

The employer surveys conducted by Kirschenman and Neckerman (1991) in Chicago suggest that employment outcomes are directly influenced by employer attitudes and stereotypes of the work ethic, reliability, and dependability of prospective job applicants and job holders. Their work, along with recent surveys by Moss and Tilly (1991) in Detroit and Los Angeles, suggest that employer attitudes/stereotypes vary along racial or ethnic and gender lines, and that they are often applied categorically. For Kirschenman and Neckerman, then, employment outcomes are not a direct function of the exogenous forces in our heuristic model, as postulated by Wilson.

Rather, as Figure 15.2b shows, they would argue that the exogenous forces in the model influence employment outcomes indirectly through interaction with employer attitudes. Individuals who are members of groups about whom employers have negative attitudes/stereotypes (e.g., black males) are more likely to have experienced discrimination in the labor market and less likely to be employed than individuals who are members of groups about whom employers have positive attitudes/stereotypes (e.g., Latino men and white, black, and Latino women). We hypothesize further that employer attitudes are likely to exert the strongest influence on employment outcomes in labor surplus environments and a much weaker influence in tight labor markets (Freeman 1991).

The Mead hypothesis

Mead (1992) argues that the high rates of joblessness and poverty in urban America are due neither to structural constraints in the labor market, as posited by Wilson (1987), nor to employer discrimination, as postulated by Kirschenman and Neckerman (1991). Rather, Mead contends that the existence of these problems reflects character deficiencies and deviant values of inner city residents. He argues that inner city residents actually choose not to work regularly and that this unwillingness to work is embedded in the nature and culture of the inner city. Negative attitudes toward work, he asserts, are rooted in

> *ghetto life* (the breakdown of authority and lack of disapproval of antisocial behavior); *ethnicity* (the lack of value placed on getting ahead by some ethnic groups); *culture* (a history of slavery and dependence on Whites created a world view among Blacks that makes them uniquely prone to anti-hero attitudes); and the *Third World origins of immigrants* (less industrious work attitudes shaped by African and Latin rather than the European origins of today's poor).
>
> (Abramovitz 1992, emphasis added)

For Mead, then, employment outcomes are directly influenced by the individual's cultural capital attributes. Individuals who do not possess the appropriate attitude toward work (i.e., willingness to work at any job even if it is part-time, pays poverty level wages, and does not provide benefits) and other cultural capital attributes valued in the workplace (e.g., adherence to appropriate norms of work attire, punctuality, etc.) are less likely to be employed than their counterparts who do possess the appropriate cultural capital package.

The social resources hypothesis

In contrast to Wilson (1987), Kirschenman and Neckerman (1991), and Mead (1992) who emphasize the role of structural changes in the economy, employer discrimination, and individual attitudes and values, respectively, an emerging school of thought posits the centrality of access to social resources as a key determinant of employment outcomes (Johnson and Oliver 1990; Putnam 1993; Fernandez-Kelly 1994). Social resources can be broadly defined as contacts through which the individual maintains his/her social identity and receives emotional supports, material aid and services, information and new social contacts. Such support can be obtained from individuals (e.g., immediate and extended family members, friends, co-ethnics, etc.) and/or institutions (e.g., churches, community-based organizations, schools, etc.) (Granovetter 1985; Coleman 1988; Fernandez-Kelly 1994).

The ability to find and maintain a job, some studies suggest, depends on access to these types of social resources (Kasnick 1993). Results of a Bureau of Labor Statistics survey revealed, for example, that a majority of employed persons found their jobs not through employment agencies, newspaper ads, and the like, but, rather, through an acquaintance, friend, or relative. But access to valuable social resources varies by the individual's race, ethnicity, gender, neighborhood context, and human capital attributes. Thus, as Figure 15.2d shows, we hypothesize that access to valuable social resources is a critical mediating variable in determining employment outcomes.

Taken together these four competing perspectives specify a number of the direct and indirect linkages in our heuristic model (Figure 15.1). The MCSUI data will enable us to test the relative weight of these competing perspectives in explaining contemporary urban inequality.

EXPLORATORY ANALYSES OF THE MCSUI DATA

In my initial explorations of the MCSUI data, I have focused principally on the cultural capital hypothesis. The reasons for this are twofold.

First, the cultural capital hypothesis has garnered far greater public policy attention than any of the other explanations outlined above. But the policies enacted and/or advocated by proponents of this view appear to be driven by political ideology rather than solid empirical evidence acquired through careful social science research.

Second, the concept of "cultural capital" (Bordieu 1979) poses a unique methodological challenge in terms of operationalization and measurement. It is clear from the recent writings of its proponents that cultural capital is a multi-dimensional concept not easily captured in a single variable or indicator (Sowell 1994; Harrison 1992). The issues of measurement and operationalization, therefore, must be resolved before the hypothesis can be subjected to rigorous empirical testing – both independent of and relative to alternative explanations of growing inequality in urban America.

Thus, in the remainder of this chapter, I present the preliminary results of my initial efforts – first, to operationalize the cultural capital concept and second, to assess the statistical effects of the empirically derived dimensions of this theoretical construct on the labor market experiences of able-bodied, working age men in the MCSUI sample. I have limited these exploratory analyses to data from the Los Angeles component of the MCSUI for two reasons.

The first pertains to the demand side and the supply side features of the Los Angeles labor market. On the one hand, the Los Angeles labor pool is large and extremely diverse – nearly 60 per cent of the population is non-white (blacks, Asian, or Hispanic); on the other, while there was substantial job growth during the 1980s – 732,000 jobs were added to the Los Angeles economy – labor demand was insufficient to accommodate the burgeoning supply of labor. Moreover, the demand that did exist during the 1980s was highly concentrated in two economic sectors, producer services (high wage jobs) and personal services (mainly low-wage jobs) (Table 15.2), which contributed to the growing gap between the haves and the have-nots in Los Angeles (Johnson and Farrell 1993).

Further, since 1990, the demand for labor in all sectors of the Los Angeles economy has been on a downward trajectory. This is due, in part, to major federal cuts in defense spending, and partly to a more general trend in corporate America toward downsizing, re-engineering, and capital flight, especially from the state of California, in an effort to facilitate efficiency and competitiveness in the global marketplace. Unfortunately, on the supply side, the number of job-seekers arriving in Los Angeles, primarily from abroad, has not declined accordingly.

When the foregoing demand side and supply side realities are juxtaposed, Los Angeles emerges as a labor surplus environment, a community in which there are far more job seekers than there are available jobs. This type of labor market context, where there is enormous competition for available positions (Oliver and Johnson 1984; Johnson and Oliver 1989; Johnson, *et al.* 1995), is ideal for an empirical test of the cultural capital hypothesis.

The second reason relates to the unique features of the Los Angeles component of the MCSUI dataset. It is a very large sample which is highly representative not only of the dominant ethnic groups – Asians, blacks, Hispanics, non-Hispanic whites – in the local labor market but also of population residing in both poor and non-poor neighborhoods in Los Angeles (Table 15.3).

I limit the analysis to males in the Los Angeles sample in part for reasons of manageability in this early phase of exploratory data analysis. But, also, this decision reflects my research interest in the steadily declining economic status of young black males nationally, and in urban America in particular. As I have argued elsewhere (Johnson and Oliver 1992), the black male jobless problem must be critically evaluated within the context of the broader changes occurring on both the demand side and the supply side of the labor market (Holzer 1994), and MCSUI data are ideal for such analyses.

Unpacking the cultural capital box

Cultural capital theorists have specific cultural explanations for the relative success or failure of the various ethnic minority groups – Chinese

Table 15.2 Employment change by industry, 1980–90

Place of employment and employment change between 1980 and 1990		*Industry*				
	Total employment	*Transformative*	*Distributive*	*Producer services*	*Personal services*	*Social services*
Los Angeles County						
1980	3,471,764	1,038,751	948,524	492,278	254,320	694,150
1990	4,203,792	1,107,917	1,150,053	709,066	365,534	810,096
Change 1980–90	732,028	69,166	201,529	216,788	111,214	115,946
%	21	16.6	21.0	44.0	44.0	16.7
Los Angeles City						
1980	1,394,855	376,656	365,858	229,350	129,901	275,733
1990	1,670,488	405,447	437,548	315,409	184,850	302,367
Change 1980–90	275,633	28,791	71,690	86,059	54,949	26,634
%	19.7	7.6	19.6	37.5	42.3	9.7
Balance of County						
1980	2,076,909	662,095	582,666	262,928	124,419	418,417
1990	2,533,304	702,470	712,505	393,657	180,684	507,729
change 1980–90	456,395	40,375	129,839	130,729	56,265	89,312
%	21.9	6.1	22.3	49.7	45.2	21.3

Source: Census of Population, 1980 and 1990

Table 15.3a Comparison of LASUI data with 1990 Census of Population and Housing data – neighborhood poverty status (%)

Neighborhood poverty level	*LASRUI Raw sample*	*LASUI weighted sample*	*LA County eligibles*[1]	*LA County total*
< 20	52.7	75.2	72.6	70
20–40	31.5	22.2	24.7	27
40+	15.8	2.6	2.6	3
Sample and population totals	4,025	4,025	6,108,478	8,863,164

Table 15.3b Comparison of LASUI data with 1990 Census of Population and Housing data – race and ethnicity (%)

Group	*LASRUI raw*	*LASUI weighted*	*LA County eligibles*[1]	*LA County*
White	21.4	43.2	49.4	47.0
Black	27.8	11.0	10.9	10.3
Asian	26.2	7.7	6.5	6.2
Latino	24.5	38.1	33.2	31.5
Other	–	–	–	5.0
Sample and population totals	4,025	4,025	5,787,991	6,090,712

Source: US Bureau of the Census, 1990 Census of Population and Housing, STF3A
Note: 1 Population 21 years of age or older

Americans, Koreans, Japanese Americans, Hispanics and blacks – captured in the Los Angeles component of the MCSUI. In trying to unpack this concept, it might be useful to review, briefly, these explanations.

Proponents argue that the poor performance of blacks in the labor market is due in large measure to the debilitating effects of slavery and subsequently of the southern share-cropper system. Writing about the effects of slavery, Sowell states, for example, that "As workers, Blacks had little sense of personal responsibility under slavery. Lack of initiative, evasion of work, half done work, unpredictable absenteeism, and abuse of tools and equipment were pervasive under slavery, and these patterns did not suddenly disappear with emancipation" (Sowell 1981, p. 200). The slavery experience, cultural capital theorists argue, inculcated in blacks "values that are impediments to work, savings, education, and upward mobility, impediments that operated with stultifying effects..." (Harrison 1992, p. 194).

Further, Harrison (1992) contends that these values and behaviors persisted under Jim Crowism in the South, and Lemann (1991) argues that blacks who migrated from the South brought these behavioral traits with them to the urban North, where they were once again reinforced by the liberal social welfare policies of the 1960s.

In a similar vein, Harrison argues that immigrants from Latin America lag behind in economic performance as a consequence of their traditional Iberian culture and values. He states further that the "Mexicans who migrated to the United States bring with them a repressive culture that is disconcertingly persistent" (1992, p. 223). Sowell (1981, 1994) contends that the goals and values of Mexican Americans have never been centered on education, and Mead (1992) argues that they have less industrious work attitudes.

Unlike blacks and Hispanics, who are perceived to possess the wrong set of cultural capital attributes, Harrison argues that "the Chinese, Japanese, and the Koreans who have migrated to the United States have injected a dose of the work ethic, excellence, and merit at a time when those values appear particularly beleaguered in the broader society" (Harrison 1992, p. 223). The success of these three groups, he contends, is rooted in a set of "culturally derived" characteristics flowing from their Confucian value system, which emphasizes education, hard work, excellence, risk taking, and frugality. Further, in contrast to blacks and Hispanics, these groups are perceived as having a strong future orientation and a sense of self as part of a collectivity that extends the radius of trust outside the family to the community (Harrison 1992).

Based on the foregoing descriptions of "culturally derived" characteristics which purportedly explain who prospers and who does not in American society, I selected fifteen questions from the MCSUI which, based on my reading of the recent works of the cultural capital theorists, I believe capture the forces that shape one's morals, values, and work orientation. I have grouped these questions into five categories in Table 15.4, which also indicates how the responses to each question are coded.

The categories are: *geographical influences*, including the respondent's place of birth and place of residence most of the time up to age 16; *family background influences*, whether the respondent lived with both parents most of the time until age 16, the employment status of respondent's father and mother during his formative years (i.e., until age 16), and whether the respondent's family ever received welfare or lived in public housing during his formative years; *educational influences*, years of school completed by respondent's father and mother, and years of school completed by respondent prior to coming to the US; *religious influences*, church affiliation and frequency of church attendance; *political influences*, party affiliation, political leaning, citizenship status, whether the respondent was a green card-holder, and whether the respondent was registered to vote. I also included, as Table 15.4 shows, indicators of *ethnic identity* and *language skills*.

To identify the underlying structures in these data, I first transformed the responses to each of the items/questions in Table 15.4 to dummy variables. I then subjected this re-coded dataset to a principal component analysis which reduced the individual variables to a smaller, more manageable

Table 15.4 Cultural capital indicators

Concept	*Variables*	*Specific measures*
Geographic influences	Where was your mother living when you were born?	Recoded: (1) Third World country; (2) Other foreign country; (3) Southern US; (4) Elsewhere
	In what city and state did you live most of the time before you were age 16?	Recoded: (1) Third World country; (2) Other foreign country; (3) Southern US; (4) Elsewhere
Family background influences	Did you live with both of your parents most of the time until you were 16 years old?	Coded: (1) yes; (2) no
	What is the highest grade of school or year of schooling your father completed?	Coded: absolute years
	Did he usually work during the year when you were age 16?	Coded: (1) yes; (0) no; (B) DK
	What is the highest grade of school or year of schooling your mother completed?	Coded: absolute years
	Did she usually work during the year when you were age 16?	Coded: (1) yes; (0) (a) DK
	Most of the time when you were 16 years old, did you and (selected sib) grow up together in same household?	Coded: (1) yes; (0) no
	Does (selected sib) work?	Recoded: (1) yes; (0) no
	Was there ever a time up to when you were 16 years of age when your family received AFDC, public assistance, or welfare?	Coded: (1) yes; (0) no
Religious influences	Are you:	Coded: (1) Protestant; (2) Catholic; (3) Jewish; (4) Other; (5) No preference
	Which category best describes how often you attend religious services?	Coded: (1) if attends church at least once a month or more; (0) else.
Political influences	Generally speaking, do you think of yourself as:	Coded: (1) Republican; (2) Democrat; (3) Independent; (4) Some other; (5) No preference; (6) No preference for religious reasons

Table 15.4 (contd.)

Concept	*Variables*	*Specific measures*
	We hear a lot of talk about liberals and conservatives... Where would you place yourself on this scale?	Recoded: (1) liberal; (2) moderate; (3) Conservative; (4) Haven't thought about it
	Are you a US citizen?	Recoded: (1) yes; (0) no
	Are you registered to vote?	Coded: (1) yes; (0) no
Race/Ethnic identity	Please choose from this page the number that best describes your race:	(1) White; (2) Black/African American; (3) Asian American; (4) American Indian; (5) Other
	Are you of Spanish or Hispanic origin?	(1) yes; (0) no
	Please look at the card and tell me which group you belong to:	(1) Mexican; (2) Mexican American; (3) Puerto Rican; (4) Cuban; (5) Salvadorian; (6) Dominican; (7) Guatemalan; (8) Nicaraguan; (9) Other
Language skills	How would you rate the respondent's ability to understand English?	Coded: (1) Excellent; (2) Very Good; (3) Good; (4) Fair; (5) Poor
	How would you rate the respondent's ability to speak clearly in English?	Coded: (1) Excellent; (2) Very Good; (3) Good; (4) Fair; (5) Poor

number of "principal components" representing the underlying structure of the original responses.

Those principal components with eigenvalues greater than one – a total of fifteen – were considered to be significant and thus were rotated using the varimax solution to identify more clearly the cluster of variables loading on each component. Together these fifteen components accounted for 69 per cent of the total variance in the original set of cultural capital indicators.

I shall describe only seven of the principal components here – those which proved, as I discuss below, to be statistically significant predictors of the employment status of males in the Los Angeles labor market (Table 15.5). The full set of principal components is available from the author upon request.

The first component, accounting for 16.1 per cent of the variance, distinguishes US citizens (−0.869) who vote (−0.769) and speak standard English (−0.765) from individuals who were born in a Third World Country (0.861), who lived in a Third World Country most of the time before they

Table 15.5 Principal components of cultural capital

Variable	*Loading*	*Communality*
Component 1		
(16.1% of total variance)		
Citizenship		
Born in Third World	0.861	0.899
Lived in Third World	0.852	0.885
Educated outside of US	0.867	0.857
Green Card	0.753	0.637
US Citizen	−0.869	0.829
Voter	−0.769	0.679
Speaks Standard English	−0.765	0.789
Component 2		
(6.4% of total variance)		
Mexican immigrants		
Mexican	0.525	0.864
Spanish speaking	0.559	0.801
Component 3		
(5.8% of total variance)		
Non-Third World immigrants		
Born in foreign country	0.915	0.857
Lived in foreign country	0.920	0.885
Component 4		
(4.8% of total variance)		
Southern roots		
Born in South	0.905	0.862
Lived in South	0.905	0.847
Component 5		
(3.4% of total variance)		
English proficiency		
Understands English well	0.898	0.906
Speaks English well	0.883	0.888
Component 6		
(3.1% of total variance)		
Parental education influences		
Mother's education	0.792	0.705
Father's education	0.772	0.650
Component 7		
(3.0% of total variance)		
Family dependency		
Lived in Public Housing as a child	0.563	0.931
Family received AFDC when respondent was a child	0.619	0.505

were 16 years old (0.852), and who have a green card (0.753). Individuals with positive scores on this component are documented aliens from the

Third World while those with negative scores are US citizens. Given this pattern of loadings, I labeled this component *Citizenship*.

The next two components tap into other dimensions of immigrant cultural influences in Los Angeles. One (Component 2) captures Mexicans (0.864) whose primary language is Spanish (0.801) and the other (Component 3) captures individuals who were born in a foreign country outside the Third World (0.857) and who lived in that country most of the time before they were 16 years old (0.885). Component 2, labeled *Mexican Immigrants*, accounts for 6.4 per cent of the total variance, and Component 3, labeled *Non-Third World Immigrants*, accounts for 5.8 per cent of the total variance.

Component 4, labeled *Southern Roots*, captures individuals who were born in the southern US (0.857) and who lived in that region most of the time before they were 16 years old (0.885). This factor taps those individuals who, according to cultural capital theorists, are supposed to have poor attitudes toward work, especially if they are black.

Whereas Components 1 through 4 tap geographic influences, Component 5 is a measure or indicator of *English Proficiency*. Accounting for 3.4 per cent of the total variance, this component identifies individuals who, according to ratings by the interviewer, understand English well (0.898) and are able to speak English clearly (0.883).

Components 6 and 7 appear to capture household and family influences. Years of school completed by the survey respondent's mother (0.792) and the years of school completed by his father (0.772) loaded on Component 6. Two indicators of growing up in a household that received government assistance loaded on Component 7: whether the survey respondent lived in public housing as a child (0.431) and whether the family received AFDC when the respondent was a child (0.505). Component 6, labeled *Parental Educational Influences*, accounted for 3.1 per cent of the variance in the original set of variables, and Component 7, labeled *Family Dependency*, accounted for 3.0 per cent.

Together this subset of principal components appears to capture several specific types of influences, including geographic, historical, and family background effects, that cultural capital theorists contend shape one's morals and values and attitudes toward family, community, and work. The crucial empirical question here is: to what degree do these factors influence statistically one's employment status – that is, whether able-bodied men work or not?

Cultural capital and employment: is there a link?

To answer this question, I recoded the male responses to a question in the MCSUI regarding present work status as a dichotomous variable: after excluding individuals who were in school, disabled, or retired, those who were employed part-time or full time were classified as *working* and those who were unemployed, temporarily laid off, or not attached to the labor market were classified *not working*. Using logistic regression analysis, I then tested the statistical effects of four sets of independent variables.

In addition to the empirically derived principal components of cultural capital, I also included in the logistic regression analyses several human capital, contextual, and social status variables, which are defined in Tables 15.6 and 15.7. The goal here was to determine the effects of cultural capital

Table 15.6 Variables used in logistic regression analysis

Type of variable	*Attributes*	*Specific variables*
Independent	Cultural capital	Mexican immigrants Southern roots English proficiency Parental educational Family dependency Citizenship Non-Third World immigrants
Control	Human capital	Age Marital status (married) Job training (yes) Highest grade completed
	Contextual	Neighborhood poverty rate
	Social status	Criminal record (yes) Black (yes) Skin tone (dark)
Dependent	Employment status	Working (yes)

Table 15.7 Descriptive statistics – control variables used in logistic regression analyses

Concept/ attribute	*Variable*	*N*	*Working (%)*	*Not working (%)*
Human capital	Age (mean in years)	1363	37.0	37.0
	Marital status (married)	1364	91.7	8.3
	Job training (yes)	365	85.8	14.2
	Years of school completed	1184	14.0	12.0
Contextual	High poverty area (> 40 %)	223	88.3	11.7
	Medium poverty area (20–39%)	457	86.4	13.6
Social status	Criminal record (yes)	168	66.0	33.0
	Non-Hispanic white	306	88.6	11.4
	African American	255	76.9	23.1
	Asian American	365	93.4	6.6
	Latino/Hispanic	438	85.8	14.2

independent of and controlling for other factors that have been posited as determinants of employment status in urban labor markets (Holzer, 1994).

I entered the variables into the logit model in blocks beginning with the empirically derived cultural capital indicators followed by the human capital variables, the contextual variables, and the social status variables. Within each block, I used the backward stepwise selection procedure to identify the statistically significant predictor variables. The results of the logistic regression analyses are summarized in Tables 15.8 through 15.12.

As Table 15.8 shows, three of the seven empirically derived components of cultural capital – Mexican Immigrants, Southern Roots, and Family Dependency – emerged as statistically significant predictors of the employ-

Table 15.8 Logistic regression results – cultural capital variables

Variables	*B*	*S.B.*	*Wald*	*df*	*Sig*	*R*	*Exp (B)*
Mexican immigrants	−0.1471	0.0861	2.9176	1	0.0876	−0.0353	0.8632
Southern roots	−0.2106	0.0849	6.1491	1	0.0131	−0.0750	0.8101
Family dependency	−0.1749	0.0846	4.2769	1	0.0386	−0.0656	0.8396
Constant	2.0338	0.0999	414.4295	1	0.0000	–	–

Table 15.9 Logistic regression results – cultural capital and human capital attributes

Variables	*B*	*S.B.*	*Wald*	*df*	*Sig*	*R*	*Exp (B)*
Mexican immigrants	0.1190	0.1127	1.1163	1	0.2907	0.0000	1.1264
Southern roots	−0.1579	0.0866	3.3211	1	0.0684	−0.0427	0.8539
Family dependency	−0.1110	0.0869	1.6320	1	0.2014	0.0000	0.8949
Marital status	0.6720	0.2066	10.5744	1	0.0011	0.1087	1.9581
Years of school completed	0.1384	0.0322	18.5201	1	0.0000	0.1509	1.1485
Constant	−0.1165	0.4351	0.0717	1	0.7889	–	–

Table 15.10 Logistic regression results – cultural capital, human capital attributes, context

Variables	*B*	*S.B.*	*Wald*	*df*	*Sig*	*R*	*Exp (B)*
Mexican immigrants	0.0579	0.1146	0.2552	1	0.6133	0.0000	1.0596
Southern roots	−0.0880	0.0902	0.9515	1	0.3293	0.0000	0.9158
Family dependency	−0.0650	0.0893	0.5296	1	0.4668	0.0000	0.9371
Marital status	0.5462	0.2120	6.6401	1	0.0100	0.0817	1.7267
Years of school completed	0.1316	0.0330	15.9320	1	0.0001	0.1415	1.1407
Criminal record	−1.2398	0.2498	24.6246	1	0.0000	−0.1803	0.2894
Constant	0.2528	0.4532	0.3111	1	0.5770	–	–

Table 15.11 Logistic regression results – cultural capital, human capital attributes, context, and social status

Variables	*B*	*S.B.*	*Wald*	*df*	*Sig*	*R*	*Exp (B)*
Mexican immigrants	0.0320	0.1154	0.0770	1	0.7814	0.0000	1.0325
Southern roots	−0.0360	0.0951	0.1433	1	0.7050	0.0000	0.9646
Family dependency	−0.0182	0.0943	0.0371	1	0.8473	0.0000	0.9820
Marital status	0.5294	0.2121	6.2315	1	0.0126	0.0758	1.6979
Years of school completed	0.1228	0.0264	21.6538	1	0.0000	0.1633	1.1307
Criminal record	−1.2304	0.2458	25.0484	1	0.0000	−0.1769	0.2922
Black and dark skinned	−0.7307	0.2963	6.0829	1	0.0136	−0.0744	0.4816
Constant	0.4598	0.3617	1.6165	1	0.2036		

Table 15.12 Summary results of logistic regression analysis

	Working	*B*	*Exp (B) (percentage)*	*Not working*	*B*	*Exp (B) (percentage)*
Statistically significant	Marital status	0.529	70	Criminal record	−1.23	71
	Years of school completed	0.123	13	Black and dark skinned	−0.731	52
Not statistically significant	Non Third World Immigrant	0.152	16	Parental educational Influence	−0.01	1
	English proficiency	0.160	17	Age	−0.01	2
	Citizenship	0.146	15	High poverty Tract	−0.02	3
	Medium poverty	0.182	20	Skin Tone	−0.114	11
	Black	0.063	6	Southern roots	−0.037	4
	Mexican immigrant	0.034	3	Family dependency	−0.018	2

ment status of our sample of Los Angeles men. Moreover, the signs of the corresponding beta values on each of these variables are consistent with the cultural capital hypothesis.

Being a Spanish-speaking Mexican immigrant (b = −0.147), being born in the South and spending most of your formative years in this region (b = −0.211), and having lived as a child either in publicly subsidized housing and/or in a family that received welfare as a child (b = −0.175) all have negative effects on the likelihood of working. Translating the exponential betas in Table 15.8 into odds or probabilities, the findings indicate that Mexican immigrants are 14 per cent less likely to be working, males with Southern Roots are 19 per cent less likely to be working, and those in the Los Angeles sample who grew up in publicly subsidized family situations are 17 per cent less likely to be working.

Do these findings hold up when statistical controls for individual human capital attributes such as age, martial status, years of school completed, and job training are introduced into the model? Table 15.9 provides an answer to this question.

Two of the human capital variables, marital status (b = 0.672) and years of school completed (b = 0.138), emerged as statistically significant predictors of the employment status of men in our sample. Every additional year of school completed increased the odds or likelihood of working by 14 per cent and married men in our sample were 95 per cent more likely to be working.

What impact did these two variables have on the cultural capital components of the model? When these two human capital variables were introduced, two of the cultural capital variables, Mexican Immigrants and Family Dependency, were rendered statistically insignificant. Only one of the empirically derived cultural capital attributes, Southern Roots (b = −0.158, p = 0.07), maintained its statistical significance; however, its effect was less than it was before the human capital variables were introduced.

The next block of variables that I entered into the model consisted of one social status variable (i.e., whether the respondent had a criminal record) and two contextual variables (neighborhood poverty status) (Table 15.10). Neither one of the poverty indices was significant, but the crime variable was highly significant (b = −1.24); in fact, the effects of this variable were so strong that it rendered the influence of Southern Roots statistically insignificant. The results indicate that a criminal record reduces the likelihood or odds of working by 72 per cent.

Given the enormous racial disparity in joblessness in our urban centers, I entered into the model, as the final block of independent variables, a measure of race (Black) and skin tone (Dark), both of which might be viewed as indicators of social status. As Table 15.11 shows, neither variable was statistically significant independent of the other, but the interaction effect between these two variables was statistically significant. Being dark in skin tone *and* black (b = −0.731) has a negative impact on the likelihood or odds of working.

Table 15.12 summarizes the findings of the logistic regression analyses. None of the empirically derived principal components of cultural capital, in the final analysis, were statistically significant predictor variables. The most influential variables in distinguishing who was working and who was not working in our Los Angeles sample included whether or not the individual had a criminal record, years of school completed, and marital status. However, it is noteworthy that, after controlling for these and other cultural capital and contextual variables, being a dark skinned black male reduced the odds of working by 52 per cent.

DISCUSSION AND CONCLUSIONS

Interest in urban inequality in the late 1980s and early 1990s has intensified among both scholars and policy makers as the gulf between the rich and the poor has widened. The MCSUI has generated data that will enable scholars and policy analysts to address important research and policy issues in the urban inequality debate by drawing upon the unique economic, social, and demographic contexts of four case-study communities: Atlanta, Boston, Detroit, and Los Angeles. While much of the debate has been hopelessly mired in biracial conceptions of urban inequality, this study's significance lies in its multi-ethnic focus, which will shed light on the future racial and ethnic composition of America's largest urban centers, rather than on their previous black–white history.

Another weakness of previous research has been its preoccupation with single focus explanations of urban inequality. This research will transcend such conceptions by exploring how the complex interplay of three major forces – racial residential segregation, inter-ethnic attitudes and polarization, and labor market dynamics – contribute to the maintenance and growth of inequality in the late twentieth century. It is only with a multicultural and multivariate framework that explores how various forces, singularly and in concert, influence the placement of individuals and groups within the urban hierarchy that we can begin to understand, and eventually develop sound policy to ameliorate, the worst features of urban inequality.

Despite the fact that there are multiple and competing explanations, with varying degrees of plausibility, for the growing schisms between the haves and the haves-not in urban America, what I have characterized in this paper as the cultural capital hypothesis appears to be the most popular among both the broader public and political and civic leaders: *that the trend toward continued inequality in American society is due not to structural changes in the economy, employer discrimination, or increasing social isolation and economic marginalization of the most disadvantaged elements from the mainstream of the society, but, rather, to a deterioration in values, morals, and personal responsibility.*

It was this view that undergirded the sweeping changes in the US Congress in the mid-term elections, which enabled the new Republican majority to forge its *Contract With America* (Gillespie and Schellhaus 1994). And it was this view that served, throughout the 1980s, as the basis for the enactment, at both the federal and state levels of government, of a wide range of what some consider, paternalistic and punitive public policies to deal with the seemingly intractable problems of drugs, crime, and long-term welfare dependency in our cities (Farrell and Johnson 1994).

Yet my admittedly very preliminary and exploratory analyses of the MCSUI data, based on the ethnically diverse Los Angeles sample, do not support the cultural capital hypothesis, and they question the attention that this school of thought has been receiving in the public policy arena. The types of cultural influences – geographical (e.g., being born in the South or in the Third World), historical (e.g. slavery and share-cropper system), and family (e.g., growing up in a household dependent on government assistance) – cited by proponents of this thesis clearly have negative effects on employment *when viewed in isolation of other factors*. But the negative effects of the cultural capital variables disappeared once statistical controls for a range of human capital (education and marital status) and social status (race, skin tone, and criminal record) variables were incorporated into the model.

That the likelihood of working is positively influenced by years of school completed and marital status (i.e., being married) is unsurprising. The crucial question is what are the policy implications of these findings?

If, as Wilson (1987) and others (Testa *et al.* 1989) suggest, the key to marriage is having a good job which, in turn, enables one to form and maintain a stable family, and if the odds of securing employment, as this and many other studies have shown (Holzer 1994), increases with years of school completed, then the policy implications are fairly straightforward: we need to invest far more resources in improving the public education system, especially school-to-work transition programs, for non-college bound youth.

On the other hand, it is also clear from my preliminary explorations of the MCSUI data that a criminal record is a major impediment to employment. And it also is clear from this research that having a criminal record is not necessarily a function of one's package of cultural capital attributes, as some conservative policy analysts would lead us to believe.

Rather, it reflects, I believe, this nation's obsession with punishment, as opposed to prevention and rehabilitation, not just for major crimes but most minor offenses as well, especially if the offenses occur in economically distressed inner city communities (Petersilia 1992). The crime epidemic is related, in part, to the fact, I believe, that the kinds of personal resources and so-called mediating institutions that once encouraged young men to pursue mainstream avenues of economic and social mobility, and that discouraged them from engaging in dysfunctional behavior are no longer effective or available in inner city communities. Previous research indicates that such community-based institutions as the Boy's and Girl's Club and the YMCA lost much of their financial support during the 1980s, and thus became less effective precisely at the time that the problems confronting disadvantaged youth were worsening (Grant and Johnson 1995).

There is also emerging evidence which suggests that programs designed to mend the social fabric of economically distressed communities will go a long way toward resolving the urban crime problem. Recently, for example, I was a member of a research team that conducted an evaluation of a Midnight Basketball league in Milwaukee, Wisconsin (Farrell *et al.* 1995).

The results revealed that the program: 1 created a safe haven in which the participants and the fans could engage in positive social activities; 2 channeled the energy of gang members in a positive direction; and 3 significantly improved the educational and career aspirations of program participants. In addition, according to Milwaukee Police Department statistics, crime rates in the target area decreased by 30 per cent during the program's first year of operation (Farrell *et al.* 1995).

Moreover, the program achieved these highly desirable outcomes with a modest investment of $70,000 – roughly the same amount required to maintain two inner-city males in prison for one year. One does not have to be an investment banker to realize that programs like Midnight Basketball will contribute far more to the revival of economically distressed inner city communities than any or all of the enormously popular punitive and/or paternalistic policies currently advocated at all levels of government.

Finally, the preliminary results of this study suggest that discrimination is still alive and well in the Los Angeles labor market. Even after controlling for a range of cultural capital attributes, human capital attributes, and contextual variables, the results indicate that a dark-skinned black is 52 per cent less likely to be employed.

This finding is consistent with the results of a recent study by Bluestone *et al.* (1992) which documents the disparity in employment for black and white males controlling for age and education. During the mid 1980s, according to their study, the jobless rate for 20 year-old black men (21.6 per cent) was almost five times higher than the rate for their white counterparts (4.8 per cent). And for 20 year-old men with less than a high school education, the racial disparity in the jobless rate was even greater: 10.3 per cent for white men and 36.1 per cent for black men.

Moreover, their findings suggest that, over the last twenty years, race-based discrimination has been increasing rather than decreasing in the US labor market. Their data indicate that the disparity in jobless rates of young black and white men, with and without a high school diploma, were not nearly as stark in the 1960s as in the 1980s (Bluestone *et al.* 1992).

My findings with respect to the effect of race (black) and skin-tone (dark) on the odds of working in Los Angeles are also consistent with the results of recent public opinion surveys (Bobo *et al.* 1995a), face-to-face interviews with employers (Kirschenman and Neckerman 1991), and focus group discussions held with black, white, Latino, Korean, and Chinese residents of Los Angeles County (Bobo *et al.* 1995b). These studies indicate that black males in particular are viewed negatively not only by whites but also by other non-white minority groups (especially Asians) – as being less intelligent, more violence prone, and more likely to prefer to rely on the government dole than on work. The evidence indicates that black men are substantially disadvantaged in the labor market because these negative stereotypes are often applied categorically (Kirschenman and Neckerman 1991; Moss and Tilly 1991).

These findings should give pause to those who, in the current debate about affirmative action, advocate class-based (Kaus 1995) as opposed to race-based (Cohen 1995) remedies for past discrimination, especially in the labor market. The Los Angeles data suggest that even if you have played by the rules – gone to school, avoided trouble with the law, and gotten married, etc – race still matters a great deal if you are a dark-skinned black male.

REFERENCES

Abramovitz, Mimi, 1992, "The new paternalism," *The Nation*, vol. 255, 368–71.

Bluestone, Barry and Harrison, Bennett, 1982. *The Deindustrialization of America*. New York: Basic Books.

Bluestone, Barry, Stevenson, Mary Huff, and Tilly, Chris, 1992, "An Assessment of the Impact of 'Deindustrialization' and Spatial Mismatch on the Labor Market Outcomes of Young White, Black, and Latino Men and Women Who Have Limited Schooling," University of Massachusetts at Boston, The John McCormick Institute of Public Affairs.

Bobo, Lawrence and Kluegel, James R., 1991. "Modern American Prejudice: Stereotypes, Social Distance, and Perceptions of Discrimination Towards Blacks, Hispanics, and Asians." Presented at Meetings of the American Sociological Association, Cincinnati, OH, August 23–27.

Bobo, Lawrence D., Zubrinsky, Camille L., Johnson, James H., Jr., and Oliver, Melvin L., 1995a, "Work Orientation, Job Discrimination, and Ethnicity: A Focus Group Perspective," in R. L. Simpson and I. H. Simpson (eds) *Research in the Sociology of Work, volume 5, The Meaning of Work*, Greenwich, CT: JAI Press, pp. 45–85.

Bobo, Lawrence D., Zubrinsky, Camille L., Johnson, James H., Jr., and Oliver, Melvin L., 1995b, "Public Opinion Before and After the Spring of Discontent," in M. Baldassare (ed.) *The Los Angeles Riots: Lessons for the Urban Future*, Boulder: Westview Press, pp. 103–33.

Bordieu, P, 1979, "Les trois États du Capital Culturel," *Actes de la Recherche en Sciences Sociales*, vol. 30, 3–5.

Cohen, Richard, 1995, "The Right Pick in Piscataway," *Washington Post National Weekly*, 13–19 March, p. 29.

Coleman, J. S. 1988, "Social Capital in the Creation of Human Capital," *American Journal of Sociology* (Supplement), 95–121.

Cross, H., Kenney, Genevieve, Mell, Jane, and Zimmerman, Wendy, 1990, *Employer Hiring Practices: Differential Treatment of Hispanic and Anglo Job Seekers*, Report No.90–4, Washington, DC: The Urban Institute Press.

Danziger, Sheldon H., Sandefur, Gary D., and Weinberg, Daniel H. (eds), 1994, *Confronting Poverty: Prescriptions for Change*, New York: Russell Sage Foundation.

Ellwood, David T., and Summers, Lawrence M., 1988, "Poverty in America: is welfare the answer or the problem?" In S. H. Danizger and D. H. Weinberg (eds) *Fighting Poverty: What Works and What Doesn't* Cambridge: Harvard University Press.

Farley, Reynolds, *et al.*, 1978, "Chocolate city, vanilla suburbs," *Social Science Research*, vol. 7, 319–44.

Farley, Reynolds, *et al.*, 1994, "The causes of continuing residential segregation: chocolate city, vanilla suburbs revisited," *Housing Policy Research*, vol. 4, 1–38.

Farrell, Walter C., Jr., Johnson, James H. Jr., (Sapp, Marty, Pumphrey, Roger M., and Freeman, Shirley), 1995, "Redirecting the Lives of Inner City Black Males:

An Assessment of Milwaukee's Midnight Basketball League," *Journal of Community Practice*, vol. 2, 91–107.

Farrell, Walter C., Jr. and Johnson, James H. Jr., 1994, "Access to local resources is key to problems in the inner city," *Wisconsin Review*, vol. 2, 23.

Feagin, Joe E., 1991, "The continuing significance of race: anti-Black discrimination in public places," *American Sociological Review*, vol. 56, 101–16.

Fernandez-Kelly, M. P., 1994, "Towandas Triumph: Social and Cultural Capital in the Urban Ghetto," in A. Portes (ed.) *Economic Sociology of Immigration*, New York: Russell Sage Foundation.

Freeman, Richard, B., 1991, "Employment and earnings of disadvantaged young men in a labor shortage economy," in C. Jencks and P. Peterson (eds), *The Urban Underclass*, Washington, DC: The Brookings Institution.

Gillespie, Ed and Schellhaus, Bob (eds), 1994, *Contract With America: The Bold Plan by Rep. Newt Gingrich, Rep. Dick Armey, and the House Republican to Change the Nation*, New York: Random House.

Granovetter, M., 1985, "Economic Actors and Social Structure: The Problem of Embeddedness," *American Journal of Sociology*, vol. 93, 481–510.

Grant, David and Johnson, James H. Jr., 1995, "Conservative policy-making and growing urban inequality in the 1980s," in R. Ratcliff, M. Oliver, and T. Shapiro (eds) *Research in Politics and Society*, JAI Press, 127–59.

Hacker, Andrew, 1992, *Two Nations: Black and White, Separate, Hostile, and Unequal*, New York: Scribners.

Harrison, Bennett and Bluestone, Barry, 1988, *The Great U-Turn*, New York: Basic Books.

Harrison, Lawrence E., 1992, *Who Prospers? How Cultural Values Shape Economic and Political Success*, New York: Basic Books.

Holzer, Harry J., 1994, "Black Employment Problems: New Evidence, Old Questions," *Journal of Policy Analysis and Management*, vol. 13, 699–722.

Jargowsky, Paul and Bane, Mary Jo, 1991, "Ghetto poverty in the United States, 1970–1980," in C. Jencks and P. Peterson (eds) *The Urban Underclass*, Washington, DC: Brookings Institution.

Jaynes, Gerald D., and Williams, Robin M., Jr. (eds), 1989, *A Common Destiny: Blacks and American Society*, Washington, DC: National Academy Press.

Johnson, James H. Jr., 1995, "The Real Issues for Reducing Poverty," in M. Darby (ed.), *Reducing Poverty in America*, Washington, DC: American Enterprise Institute, 337–63.

Johnson, James H., Jr., and Farrell, Walter C., Jr., 1993, "The fire this time: the genesis of the Los Angeles rebellion of 1992," *North Carolina Law Review*, vol. 71, 1403–20.

Johnson, James H., Jr., and Oliver, Melvin L., 1989, "Interethnic minority conflict in urban America: the effects of economic and social dislocations," *Urban Geography*, vol. 10, 449–63.

Johnson, James H., Jr., and Oliver, Melvin L., 1990, "Modeling urban underclass behaviors: theoretical considerations," *CSUP Occasional Paper Series*, vol. 1, no. 2.

Johnson, James H., Jr., and Oliver, Melvin L., 1992, "Structural changes in the economy and black male joblessness: a reassessment," in G. Peterson and W. Vrohman (eds) *Urban Labor Markets and Job Opportunity*, Washington, DC: The Urban Institute Press, pp. 113–47.

Johnson, James H., Jr., Jones, Cloyzelle K., Farrell, Walter C. Jr., and Oliver, Melvin L. 1995, "The Los Angeles Rebellion of 1992: A Retrospective View," in J. M. Stein (ed.) *Classic Readings in Urban Planning*: New York: McGraw Hill.

Kasarda, John D., 1992, "The severely distressed in economically transforming cities," Center for Competitiveness and Employment Growth, Kenan Institute of Private Enterprise, University of North Carolina, Chapel Hill, March.

Kasnick, Phillip, 1993, "The real jobs problem," *Wall Street Journal*, 26 November, p. A8.

Kaus, Mickey, 1995, "Class Is In," *The New Republic*, Issue 4, 184, 27 March, p. 6.

Kirschenman, Joleen and Neckerman, Kathyrn, 1991, "We'd love to hire them... but: the meaning of race for employers," in C. Jencks and P. Peterson (eds) *The Urban Underclass*, Washington, DC: The Brookings Institution.

Lemann, Nicholas, 1991, *The Promised Land*, New York: Alfred Knopf.

Levy, Frank, 1987, *Dollars and Dreams: The Changing American Income Distribution*, New York: Russell Sage.

Loury, Glen C., 1985, "The moral quandary of the Black community," *The Public Interest*, vol. 79, 9–22.

Marsden, Peter V., Kalleberg, Arne L., and Cook, Cynthia R., 1993, "Gender differences in organizational commitment: influences of work positions and family roles," *Work and Occupations*, vol. 20, 368–90.

Massey, Douglas and Denton, Nancy, 1992, *American Apartheid*, Cambridge, MA: Harvard University Press.

Mead, Lawrence, 1992, *The New Politics of Poverty*, New York: Basic Books.

Michel, Richard, 1991, "Economic growth and income inequality since the 1982 recession," *Journal of Policy Analysis and Management*, vol. 10, 181–203.

Mincy, Ronald and Ricketts, Erol, 1990, "Growth of the underclass, 1970–1980," *Journal of Human Resources*, vol. 25, 13145.

Moss, Philip and Tilly, Chris, 1991, *Why Black Men Are Doing Worse in the Labor Market*, New York: Social Science Research Council.

Murray, Charles, 1984, *Losing Ground*, New York: Basic Books.

Oliver, Melvin L., and Shapiro, Thomas M., 1990, "Race and wealth," *The Review of Black Political Economy*, vol. 17, 5–25.

Oliver, Melvin L., and Johnson, James H., Jr., 1984, "Interethnic minority conflict in an urban ghetto: the case of Blacks and Latinos in Los Angeles," *Research in Social Movements, Conflict, and Change*, vol. 6, 57–94.

Orfield, Gary and Ashkinaze, Carol, 1991. *The Closing Door: Conservative Policy and Black Opportunity*, Chicago: University of Chicago Press.

Osterman, Paul, 1991, "Gains from growth? the impact of full employment on poverty in Boston," in C. Jencks and P. Peterson (eds), *The Urban Underclass*, Washington, DC: Brookings Institution.

Petersilia, Joan, 1992, "Crime and Punishment in California: Full Cells, Empty Pockets and Questionable Benefits," in J. B. Steinberg *et al.* (eds), *Urban America: Policy Choices for Los Angeles and the Nation*, Santa Monica: Rand Corporation.

Phillips, Kevin, 1990, *The Politics of Rich and Poor: Wealth and the American Electorate in the Reagan Aftermath*, New York: Random House.

Putnam, R. D., 1993, "The Prosperous Community: Social Capital and Public Life," *The American Prospect*, vol. 13, 37.

Ricketts, Erol and Sawhill, Isabel, 1988, "Defining and measuring the underclass," *Journal of Policy Analysis and Management*, vol. 7, 316–25.

Schuman, Howard, Steeh, Charlotte G., and Bobo, Lawrence, 1988, *Racial Attitudes in America: Trends and Interpretations*, Cambridge: Harvard University Press.

Smith, Tom W., 1991, *Ethnic Images*, General Social Survey Technical Report, NORC: University of Chicago.

Sowell, Thomas, 1981, *Ethnic America*, New York: Basic Books.

Sowell, Thomas, 1994, *Race and Culture: A World View*, New York: Basic Books.
Testa, Mark, Astone, Nan Marie, Krough, Marilyn, and Neckerman, Kathryn M., 1989, "Employment and Marriage Among Inner City Fathers," *Annals of the American Academy of Political and Social Sciences*, vol. 501, 79–91.
Turner, Margery A., Fix, Michael, and Struyk, Raymond J., 1991, *Opportunities Denied, Opportunities Diminished: Racial Discrimination in Hiring*, Urban Institute Report 91–9, Washington, DC: The Urban Institute Press.
Wilson, William Julius, 1987, *The Truly Disadvantaged*, Chicago: University of Chicago Press.

16

SOME HETERODOX MODELS OF INEQUALITY IN THE MARKET FOR LABOR POWER

Patrick L. Mason

INTRODUCTION

The economics of discrimination attempts to reconcile persistent (noncompensating) income differentials with the competitive process. In addition to logical and empirical consistency, theories of discrimination must explain why various forms of discrimination persist over time, as opposed to why a particular form of discrimination may exist at any one point in time. A theory of racial or gender discrimination has to recognize that discrimination in the market for labor power is a multi-dimensional process; there are intergroup differences in the probability of obtaining stable employment, in occupational and sectoral mobility, in remuneration for labor services, and in access to on-the-job training.

The Marxian and radical contribution to racial inequality focuses on the theoretical and empirical analysis of persistent discrimination in the market for labor power, racial conflict and worker organization, and (more recently) the social construction of race, i.e., the nature and development of alternative racial formations. The primary focus of this chapter is on the economics of racial discrimination in the market for labor power. Clearly, this is a narrow subset of the issues that are generally subsumed under the rubric of "the political economy of race and class." The advantage of such a narrow focus is that one is able to clearly distinguish the nature of alternative hypotheses and analyses regarding the interaction of race, labor market phenomena, pricing, and the competitive process. The disadvantage of such a narrow focus is that some political and social issues regarding race and class (Boston 1985; Gorman 1989), as well as some historical issues regarding racial formations (Omi and Winant 1994; Roediger 1991) are dealt with in a tangential manner.[1]

There is no generally accepted heterodox theory of racial discrimination under actually existing competitive capitalism. In broad terms, there are at least four Marxian and radical economic models of discrimination: 1 divide-and-conquer (DC); 2 segmented labor market dual economy

(SLM-DE); 3 race relations (RR); and 4 classical Marxian (CM). Often, these models overlap. However, in the analysis below I will treat each approach separately.

MICHAEL REICH AND THE ECONOMICS OF DIVIDE AND CONQUER

In many quarters, Michael Reich's (1981, 1988) analysis of racial discrimination is the radical theory of racial discrimination in the market for labor power. Reich (1981) uses an effort extraction model to explore the interrelationships among racial inequality, worker bargaining power, and the distribution of income. This relationship is formalized in equations 16.1–16.3, where p = the price of output, w_A and w_w are the wage rates for African American and white workers, respectively, L_A and L_w are similarly defined employment levels, and Q = f(LD) is a short run production function.

$$\pi = p^{*}f(LD) - w_A L_A - w_w L_w \qquad 16.1$$

$$LD = g(L, BP), \quad \text{where} \quad L = L_A + L_w \qquad 16.2$$

$$BP = h(R_w, R_q), \quad \text{where} \quad R_w = w_w/w_A, R_q = L_w/L_A \qquad 16.3$$

The amount of "labor done" (LD) depends on the amount of labor power purchased (L) and the bargaining power (BP) of workers; further, the bargaining power of workers depends on the extent of interracial wage and employment inequality, R_w and R_q, respectively.[2]

$$\pi = p^{*}f(g(L, h(R_w, R_q))) - (R_w R_q + 1)w_B L_B \qquad 16.4$$

Given $w_A > 0$, maximization of equation 16.4 with respect to R_w, R_q and L_A reveals that employers are willing to pay white workers a premium until the benefits (lower bargaining power) are just matched by increased wage costs. Atomistic and profit maximizing behavior then leads to stable interracial inequality in a neoclassically competitive economy. Reich concludes that discrimination harms all workers by lowering the average wage rate and increasing profit; hence, workers have a strategic interest to unite across racial lines as capital continually seeks to divide-and-conquer workers in order to increase profit.

Reich (1988) extends the divide-and-conquer (DC) model from its microeconomic focus on power and conflict within the firm to a dynamic macroeconomic focus on power and conflict "that stresses the rise and fall of socio-political movements pressing for institutional change (p. 145)." This approach grounds Reich's macroeconomic explanation of discrimination in the social structure of accumulation (SSA) model (Gordon, Edwards, and Reich 1982).

SSA theorists argue that private investment decisions, the motor force of capital accumulation, take place within the context of a political and social structure whose institutions and social norms are external to the individual firm but which are endogenous to dynamics of macroeconomic development. Phases in the pattern of capitalist development are defined by changes in the SSA. There are long swings, periods of boom and bust, within each SSA, and when each secular boom meets its demise, social and political forces are rearranged to establish a new SSA which will lead to renewed economic development.

Social change then does not automatically occur because of economic development or political freedom *per se*, "but because socio-political movements arise that undermine and then restructure the existing institutions and norms of economic and political relations (Reich 1988: 147)."

The capital–labor accord was a central component of the postwar SSA, and racial relations were an element in that accord.

> This accord involved an explicit and implicit *quid pro quo*, assuring management control over enterprise decision-making (with union submission and cooperation) in exchange for the promise to workers of real compensation rising along with labor productivity, improved working conditions, and greater job security – in short, a share in capitalist prosperity.
>
> (Gordon, Weisskopf, and Bowles 1987: 48)

Both African American and white workers *within industrial unions* gained enormously from the Congress of Industrial Organizations (CIO) organizing efforts. However, the year 1948 was a turning point. The labor movement's failure to challenge race relations in the South lead to the failure of "operation dixie," labor's attempt to organize the South.

Most African Americans lived in the South and labored *outside of the (organized) industrial sector* and, hence, outside of the capital–labor accord. The exclusion of African Americans generated pressure on the capital–labor accord, especially from 1957–74, as the African American liberation movement transformed expectations among African American workers.

Indeed, Reich argues that the strength of the labor and social movements (African American, feminist, environmentalist) was so great that by the 1974–5 recession "labor, minorities, and women were able to maintain their relative position while capital . . . proved surprisingly weak (Reich 1988: 162)."

The very success of these movements generated a counter-offensive by capital. The essence of this counter-offensive was to employ a DC strategy with respect to the establishment, organization, and maintenance of all multiracial social and political organizations. Moreover, because capital no longer perceived African Americans as a supply of cheap docile laborers, new groups of workers (Caribbean, Asian, Mexican) were imported to fulfill roles traditionally assigned to African Americans.

Empirical evaluation

Empirical evaluation of the DC model has yielded mixed results. Reich (1981: 109–63, 268–304) and Syzmanski (1976) provide favorable evaluations. On the other hand, Shulman (1990), Beck (1980), and Cloutier (1987) claim to disaffirm the central hypotheses of Reich's model. Both sets of empirical investigations are only partially convincing.

Reich uses data from the 1960 and 1970 decennial census to provide robust statistical evidence that the extent of income inequality among whites tends to increase with the extent of racial income inequality between African Americans and whites. In particular, increases in racial inequality are "associated with a substantial improvement in the share of the richest 1 per cent of white families, with a lesser increase in white inequality overall and smaller decreases in the share of middle- and lower-income whites." The ratio of African American to white family income (B/W) is used as the proxy for racial inequality within a Standard Metropolitan Statistical Area (SMSA), while a gini coefficient was constructed to measure the extent of inequality in the white distribution of income. Reich's results remained fairly intact when he controlled for a number of characteristics that might reasonably be expected to influence the (white) distribution of income across SMSAs, i.e., industry structure, occupational structure, the extent of public sector employment, median income, African Americans as a share of the local labor market, and region of the country.

Syzmanski restricts his sample to full-time, full-year male employees and thereby does not conflate the possible effects of gender discrimination with racial discrimination. Also, Syzmanski uses earnings to measure racial inequality within a particular state (as opposed to SMSAs in Reich's analysis). Syzmanski is able to replicate Reich's results: white male median earnings increase with declines in racial inequality (increases in B/W) and the white male gini index declines as the level of racial inequality declines. The qualitative nature of Syzmanski's results does not change when he controls for percent urban, "third world people"[3] as a fraction of the state's population, per capita income, industrial composition, and national region (South versus non-South).

Contradicting Reich and Syzmanski, Cloutier finds that 1980 census data shows no statistically significant relationship between racial inequality and the distribution of white income. However, Cloutier has no regional controls in his model, nor does he separate public from private sector employment. There are well known regional differences in the history of racial conflict, in regional inter-racial earnings and employment-to-population ratios, and in regional earnings and employment-to-population levels. Presumably, also, the not-for-profit sector has less incentive to engage in DC strategies than the profit maximizing private sector. Without regional or sectoral controls, a downward bias occurs with respect to the impact of racial inequality on the white distribution of income.

Beck provides the only time series analysis of the relationship between inequality in the distribution of white income and racial inequality. After adjusting for autocorrelation, Beck was unable to affirm a statistically significant relationship between racial inequality and the distribution of white income. This study is suggestive but not conclusive. At a minimum, if the passage of the 1964 Civil Rights Act represented a structural change in the economy, a dummy variable (and possibly an interaction term) should have been included in the equation. Beck mentions but does not provide data on regressions that included the aggregate unemployment rate; the claim is that the addition of the aggregate unemployment does not alter the character of the results. The inclusion of an extent of joblessness variable however may have significantly altered his results if Beck had also controlled for regional differences in his statistical model. Beck's data, compiled from *Current Population Reports*, *Directory of National Unions and Employees Associations*, and *Statistics of Income – 1971, Corporate Income Tax Returns*, covers 1947–75 – a rather small sample size for robust hypothesis testing.

Shulman claims that the DC model has drawn the bargaining power hypothesis too narrowly. He argues that Reich merely concentrates on the "solidarity effect" of bargaining power while ignoring the "isolation effect." The solidarity effect is the previously discussed notion that worker solidarity rises as inter-racial wage rates approach equality. The isolation effect implies that worker solidarity may increase as dominant group workers exclude subordinant group workers. If the isolation effect is operative, racial inequality in earnings is indicative of reduced job competition for whites and hence white employment should rise.

Shulman uses cross sectional census data on SMSAs to fit the following model.

$$\mathrm{UR_i/UR_t} = \alpha_1 + \alpha_2(\mathrm{B/W}) + \alpha_3(LS_i) + \alpha_4(LD) \qquad 16.5$$

$\mathrm{UR_i}$ is the unemployment rate for racial/gender group "i," $\mathrm{UR_t}$ is the unemployment rate for the SMSA, B/W is the interracial ratio of family income for black and white families within a SMSA, *LD* is a vector of labor demand variables for the SMSA, and $\mathrm{LS_i}$ is a vector of labor supply variables for racial/gender group "i" within the SMSA.

The expectation is that α_2 will be positive for whites and negative for African Americans. For 1970 census data, the results weakly affirm Shulman's expectations on α_2: the coefficient is negative and strongly significant for African American women, insignificant for African American males, and positive and nearly significant for both white gender groups. For 1980 census data, the results strongly affirm Shulman's expectations on α_2: the coefficient is negative and strongly significant for African American women, insignificant for African males, and positive and strongly significant for both white gender groups.

Although Shulman's discussion of the insulation effect is a welcomed level of complexity to the discussion of worker bargaining power, the interpretation of his empirical results is not a settled issue. Consider a rather simple bargaining power equation:

$$BP = R_q^{\beta} R_w^{\sigma} Z^{-1} \qquad 16.6$$

where Z is a vector of nonracial variables that influence bargaining power and $0 \leqslant \sigma \leqslant 1$ and $0 \geqslant \beta \geqslant -1$. A logarithmic transformation of this equation and a rearrangement of its terms yields the following:

$$Ln(R_q) = (1/\beta)Ln(BP) + (1/\beta)Ln(Z) - (\sigma/\beta)Ln(R_w) \qquad 16.7$$

This equation implies that for *a given level of bargaining power* and given levels of nonracial variables that influence bargaining power, the inter-racial elasticity of employment with respect to the interracial wage rate must be positive, i.e., $-(\sigma/\beta) > 0$.

In Shulman's specification, α_2 is the empirical proxy for $-(\sigma/\beta)$, but equation 16.5 does not control for the level of bargaining power and therefore has an omitted variable. One cannot rule out an intrepretation of Shulman's results that is consistent with Reich's model. Portions of both the $BP - R_q$ and $BP - R_w$ loci are upward sloping and therefore R_w and R_q may be positively correlated in a manner entirely consistent with Reich's model. The core of Shulman's "isolation effect" critique is that movements along the $BP - R_w$ locus produce a rightward shift in the $BP - R_q$ locus. Equation 16.5 does not allow us to evaluate the validity of this claim.

Shulman's results are also suggestive of a more complex intrepretation of the DC model. If white workers utilize their collective strength to exclude African American workers, capital may switch to a gender-based DC strategy rather than a strictly race-based DC strategy. This is an issue open to further research.

There are other (minor) problems assoicated with the empirical evaluations of Reich's model. First, the empirical specifications have been completely linear and therefore have not attempted to account for the nonlinearities in Reich's theoretical model. Second, Reich's theoretical model is developed at the level of the firm but the empirical evaluations have attempted to affirm the model at the level of geographical units. Third, each of the empirical models uses family income as the measure of interracial inequality in earnings not the wage rates of Reich's theoretical model. Although individual empirical studies have been highly suggestive, none is definitive.

Theoretical evaluation[4]

This section presents three important results: 1 the logic of Reich's DC model is inconsistent with the primary conclusion of the model and with empirical reality; however, Reich's results are quite consistent with Arrow's (1972) neoclassical model of employer discrimination where the employer's utility function is quasi-concave in profits and the inter-racial employment ratio; 2 within the context of the model's choice theoretic analysis, there are no incentives for inter-racial coalitions (once a DC strategy is in place); and 3 a state (or union) imposed uniform wage rate will encourage capital to attempt to integrate the labor force and labor to attempt to exclude members of the opposite race.

Arrow argued that employer utility is an increasing function of profit and the inter-racial employment ratio. Assuming that employer utility is quasi-concave with respect to the inter-racial employment ratio produces the DC model. The quasi-concavity condition implies that increases in the inter-racial employment ratio lower worker bargaining power (and thus increase employer utility) at a decreasing rate. Since Reich's model is a special case of Arrow's model, the well known Becker–Arrow result that long-run (neoclassical) competition is incompatible with the persistence of employer discrimination is immediately applicable to Reich's model.

Additionally, Mason (1992) shows that the equilibrium employment ratio,

$$R_q^e = -[\{w_A - p(\delta f/\delta g)(\delta g/\delta L)\}/\{R_w w_A - p(\delta f/\delta g)(\delta g/\delta L)\}] \qquad 16.8$$

$$= \frac{-\{\text{African American wage} - \text{value of marginal product of labor}\}}{\{\text{white wage} - \text{value of marginal product of labor}\}}$$

Since $R_q^e \geqslant 0$ and $w_w > w_A$, the numerator of this expression must be negative and the denominator must be positive. Moreover, whether R_q^e is greater than, less than, or equal to one is theoretically indeterminate – despite its centrality to the political and empirical implications of Reich's model.

Since $w_A - \text{VMPL} < 0$ African Americans are unambiguously exploited. But $R_w w_A - \text{VMPL} > 0$ indicates that white workers are not exploited – they receive a pure wage premium. Let $w_A = \text{VMPL} - \delta$, $w_w = \text{VMPL} + \delta_w$, where $\delta_A, \delta_w > 0$, then $R_q = -(\text{VMPL} - \delta_A - \text{VMPL})/(\text{VMPL} + \delta_w - \text{VMPL}) = \delta_A/\delta_w$. Profit maximizing capitalists will employ a DC strategy if and only if $\delta_A > \delta_w$, then $w_A + w_w = 2\text{VMPL} + (\delta_w - \delta_A) < 2\text{VMPL}$ and $R_q > 1$. The divide-and-conquer strategy reduces the total wage bill and increases profit. Further, under neoclassical competition, the successful adoption of a DC strategy by any one firm in the industry will force all other firms to adopt the same strategy.

But this condition raises questions related to the incentives of workers to form inter-racial coalitions. A criterion for successful coalition building between African American and white workers requires that an increase in w_A does not have any adverse effects on L_w, given L_A and w_w, that is $dL_w/dw_A \geqslant 0$. Otherwise, there may exist sufficiently negative incentives to inhibit inter-racial unity: if w_A cannot be increased unless L_A declines, then African American workers have substituted wage discrimination for employment discrimination; if L_w or w_w declines when w_A increases white workers are required to behave irrationally, joining a coalition that makes them worse off.

The sign of dL_w/dW_A can be derived by taking a total derivative of the first order conditions. Specifically,

$$dL_w/dw_A = [2(\delta BP/\delta R_q)w_A - (\delta^2 BP/\delta R_w^2)(R_w/w_A)(w_w - VMPL)^2]/$$
$$2(\delta BP/\delta R_w)(w_w - VMPL)(\delta VMPL/\delta L) + (\delta^2 BP/\delta R_q^2)(VMPL/L_A)$$
$$(\delta^2 BP/\delta R_q^2)(w_A^2/L_A) \qquad 16.9$$

If the second partial derivatives for both arguments of the bargaining power function are positive (at the equilibrium values), the numerator is negative and the denominator is positive. Therefore, a *ceteris paribus* increase in w_A will lead to a decline in L_w; an inter-racial coalition to raise wage rates cannot be formed.

Given the dependence of this model on the variability of worker effort, that is, the distinction between the hours of labor time purchased and the amount of labor performed, one is forced to ask, "Why is a divide-and-conquer labor elicitation strategy necessary?" Indeed, why is any form of discrimination necessary? Capitalists in this model are not Beckerian "Archie Bunkers" with a taste for discrimination, they are Marxian "Mr. Moneybags" interested in making a profit and expanding the size of their capital. Surely, such capitalists will experiment with a variety of labor elicitation regimes, for example, efficiency wages.[5]

There are no obvious reasons why an efficiency wage regime is any less profit maximizing than a divide-and-conquer regime. Moreover, if we consider an economy where (blatantly) differential pay for the same work is illegal and where firms are subjected to publicly scrutinized affirmative action hiring plans, then the efficiency wage regime dominates the divide-and-conquer regime as a labor elicitation strategy and Mr. Moneybags (who, in all likelihood, is Archie Bunker's father) is no worse off. But an efficiency wage regime in an economy of perfectly substitutable workers will not produce persistent discrimination in pay or probability of employment (Darity 1991; Mason 1993).

Interestingly, if the state (or a union) imposes a uniform wage rate capitalists will become the racially progressive agents in Reich's DC model. With a uniform wage rate[6] the objective function becomes:

$$\pi = p^* f(g(L, h(1, R_q))) - w_u L \qquad 16.10$$

Standard reasoning implies that workers will be hired up to the point where $p^*(\delta f/\delta g)(\delta g/\delta L) = w_u$. But the value of the marginal product of labor is not strictly determined by the output price and the technology of production because $\delta g/\delta L = \phi(L, h(R_q))$ and Reich assumes that $h(R_q)$ is a "cup-shaped" function where bargaining power reaches its minimum value at

$R_q = \Theta$. Accordingly, once the firm has determined the optimal quantity of labor power (L) to purchase at w_u it has every incentive to reduce worker bargaining power by *integrating* its workforce up to $R_q = \Theta$; on the other hand, workers have every incentive to *exclude members of the opposite race* up to the point of a perfectly segregated labor force. Under these conditions, it is still the case that the extent of segregation at the workplace depends on the balance of power between labor and capital, but there are no material incentives for working class unity.

SEGMENTED LABOR MARKET–DUAL ECONOMY[7]

The segmented labor market–dual economy (SLM–DE) theory of discrimination implies that racial inequality persists because of inter-racial differences in labor mobility between competitive and monopoly sectors of the economy and between secondary and primary jobs. SLM–DE theory, best represented in Gordon *et al.* (1982), posits that the economy is divided into competitive and monopoly sectors. Firms within the monopoly sector are characterized by market power in the output market and highly structured input markets. In particular, monopoly sector firms are said to have internal labor markets governed by custom and bureaucratic procedures (Doeringer and Piore 1971). Firms in the competitive sector are said to face competitive output markets and nonstructured input markets.

The basic unit of analysis for SLM–DE theory is the job. Jobs are segmented into secondary and primary jobs, with the latter consisting of subordinate primary jobs and independent primary jobs. Independent primary jobs are the most desirable. Generally, they require high levels of education, pay well, provide secure employment, and structured patterns of advancement with minimal supervision. Subordinate primary jobs require skilled labor; they are high paying but heavily supervised positions.

Secondary jobs are the major type of jobs offered in the economic periphery. These jobs are distinctly undesirable. They provide low pay, few (if any) benefits, little opportunity for advancement, very insecure employment tenure, and rigid supervision.

Given the core–periphery industrial structure and the independent primary, subordinate primary, secondary job segments, it is easy to deduce that the market for labor power is segmented into good and bad jobs (Jeffries and Standback 1984: 121). Good jobs are (independent) primary jobs in core firms, while bad jobs are secondary jobs in peripheral firms. Good jobs are characterized by employment with large corporations with relatively higher wages and salaries than bad jobs in the economic periphery. Additionally, jobs in the primary sector provide: 1 greater job security; and 2 greater opportunities for promotion than jobs in the secondary sector of the economy.

The crux of the SLE–DE explanation of racially differential outcomes in the market for labor power is that African Americans occupy a disproportionate share of jobs in the secondary market. However, *within the secondary sector African Americans and whites are treated in a similar manner* (Gordon *et al.* 1982: 206–10; Jeffrics and Standback 1984: 121; Albelda 1985). Since African American upward (downward) mobility between sectors is less (greater) than whites, racially differential outcomes in the market for labor power persist over time. Interindustry and interoccupational movement can alter a worker's income without the worker having made any changes in human capital acquisition.[8]

In its bare essentials the SLM–DE theory of discrimination is an elaborate restatement of the orthodox market power hypothesis: discrimination will arise and persist only in those areas of the economy least protected from the competitive forces of the market. SLM–DE theorists argue that core sector firms are able to discriminate in their market for inputs because barriers to entry in their output markets provide protection from competition; hence, the monopoly profits earned by these firms allow them to discriminate without being penalized by the forces of competition.

Segmentation theory has no uniquely defined theory of competition. Its operational utilization of competition is the choice theoretic world of neoclassical competition. Any large firm with market power is considered to be a member of the core sector, that is, a monopolistic firm. By establishing barriers to entry these firms are able to restrict output, raise prices above marginal costs and earn monopoly profit, that is, profit above and beyond the normal rate of profit. In short, the bedrock of SLM–DE theory is the "market concentration doctrine" (Demsetz 1973) of neoclassical industrial organization theory. On the other hand, Marx's theory of competition demonstrates that corporate power (Semmler 1984) and large firm size are not necessarily conditions of monopoly, but may in fact be prerequisites for competitive existence (Shaikh 1977, 1980, 1982, 1984a–b, ; Mandel 1983; Weeks 1981).

SLM–DE theory does not provide an explanation of racially differential patterns of mobility and racially differential returns to labor quality *within* secondary markets (Rosenberg 1989; Heywood 1987). A segmentation based theory of discrimination has to explain these phenomena; otherwise, it is indistinguishable from the orthodox market power hypothesis (Arrow 1972). But given the equivalence of SLM–DE's secondary labor market and the perfectly competitive market structure of neoclassical economics, SLM–DE may have considerable difficulty explaining racially differential outcomes in secondary markets for labor power.

SHULMAN'S RACE RELATIONS MODEL OF DISCRIMINATION

Shulman (1991, 1984) suggests that both competition and discrimination are practiced in a variety of ways. It is possible then that an observed decrease in wage discrimination may be associated with an increase in occupational and employment discrimination.

Orthodox models of discrimination focus solely on the cost of discrimination, arguing that in a full employment economy, firms that discriminate will be driven out of the market. Shulman, however, provides a series of reasons why ceasing discrimination may also be costly, especially in a labor surplus economy.[9] The core element of the race relations model is that both continuing and ceasing discrimination may be costly. Therefore, the extent of discrimination will depend on the balance of these costs. The extent of discrimination is a positive function of the net benefits of discrimination. Hence, discrimination may be endogenous, but its intensity and form are historically contingent.

Figure 16.1 represents Shulman's model. The cost associated with continuing discrimination falls with an increase in the unemployment rate while the cost of ceasing discrimination rises with an increase in the unemployment rate.

The firm will engage in employment discrimination if and only if the aggregate unemployment rate is greater than the critical unemployment rate (U_C), otherwise profit maximizing firms have no incentive to discriminate. Shulman (1991) uses this model to explain the "last hired – first fired" phenomenon that has been a hallmark of the demand for African American

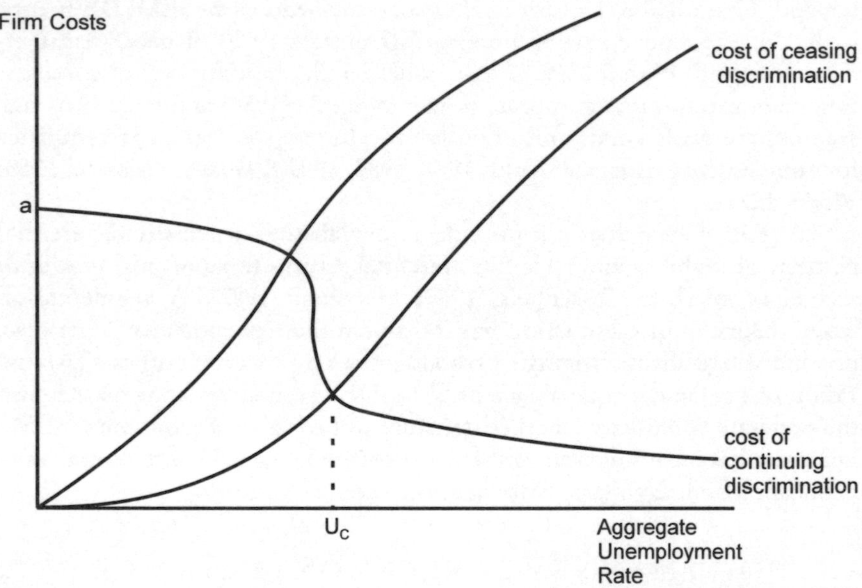

Figure 16.1 Shulman model of microeconomics of employment discrimination
Source: Adapted from Shulman's model

labor. During booms, the aggregate rate of unemployment (U) declines towards U_c thereby the incentives to discriminate are reduced and the relative demand for African American labor is increased. Similarly, during a recession U increases relative to U_c; accordingly, the incentives to discriminate increase and the relative demand for African American labor declines.

Shulman's discussion regarding the complexity of the discriminatory process may also be illustrated. A reduction in wage discrimination, which is relatively easy to detect, may increase employment discrimination. The reduction in wage discrimination increases the cost of ceasing discrimination, as managers seek to use alternative forms of discrimination to create disunity among workers and to maintain managerial control; hence, the "cost of ceasing discrimination" function will rotate upward and thereby lead to a reduction in U_c.

Shulman's focus on the composition of labor market discrimination and his attempt to show the connection between the firm's microeconomic decision to engage in discrimination and the state of the macroeconomy, via the aggregate unemployment rate, are imaginative innovations that must surely be a part of any model of discrimination in the market for labor power.

Currently, there is no empirical information on inter- and intra-industry critical unemployment levels. Such information would provide the basis for a more definitive evaluation of the race relations model.

CLASSICAL MARXIAN

Marxian economics has combined the reserve army hypothesis (RAH) with recent developments in its analysis of the distribution of wages and a social-historical-political analysis of household reproduction and state action to explain the persistence of racial inequality in the market for labor power.

The reserve army hypothesis

The RAH contains three core elements:[10] 1 The reserve army is an endogenous outcome of capitalist competition and capital accumulation. Technological change and the accumulation of capital, combined with the inter- and intra-industry competition of capitals, alternatively aborb and release squadrons of workers from the reserve army of unemployed and under-employed. Over time, the continual process of capital accumulation (and the social deepening of capitalist relations) increases the absolute size of the reserve army; 2 The reserve army ratio[11] regulates wages, benefits, and working conditions over the course of the business cycle. When the reserve army rate rises (falls), these variables tend to worsen (improve); 3 The reserve army rate regulates labor intensity. As the reserve army ratio increases (declines), greater (less) pressure is exerted on workers to increase the speed of work; employed workers become increasingly subjected to managerial attempts to get them to work harder and faster – or else become members of the reserve army with severely diminished opportunities for finding an alternative job.[12]

The RAH implies that the possibility of employment discrimination, the most basic form of exclusion, arises because of the reproduction of the reserve army of unemployed.

The supply of labor power[13]

The market for labor power is mediated by a vast array of historically determined social conventions, political institutions, and worker organizations that operate within an economic environment.[14] Workers have group and individual characteristics that shape their terms of participation in economic activity. The confluence of individual and group characteristics, social conventions, and political-historical institutions that shape the labor market are continually reformed and reproduced within the limits given by the process of accumulation. These considerations have led modern scholars to expand on Marx's insight that "social and historical elements" enter into the determination of the value of labor power.[15]

The reproduction of the reserve army and the limited level of nonlabor resources among workers reveals that labor is inherently weak relative to capital. Workers must sell their labor power in order to continue to exist as human beings; capitalists have the assets to continue to exist as human beings even if they are unsuccessful in their aspirations as capitalists. Individual workers can redress this power imbalance if they have access to domestic resources, informal market resources, or state resources. As a rule, these areas provide insufficient resources for workers to maintain their standard of living independently of the market for labor power.

Groups of workers can utilize collective action to partially redress the labor–capital power imbalance experienced by individual workers. These labor organizations reflect, and also contribute to, the development of workers' political, social, cultural, and economic norms. Collective action may be organized at the domestic, community, market, or state level. Organization at the level of the family and the community facilitates the interaction between market and market-related processes, e.g., household production, the organization of educational institutions, rules governing child labor, etc., and provides alternative sources of subsistence and mutual support which strengthens the bargaining power of individual workers. The household also provides a portion of the resources required for skill acquisition, which enhances the market value of individuals.

Organization within the market, via unions, professional associations, or informal worker social networks, provides a measure of protection against the reserve army and the arbitrariness of "managerial prerogatives."

State actions are designed to reproduce a disciplined, trained, healthy labor force for capital, as well as the maintenance of the reserve army of labor by the provision of social welfare expenditures. State policies then, like shop floor policies, become an arena of struggle between labor and capital, as well as the various groups among labor and capital.

The dialectical nature of worker organizations is clear. On the one hand, domestic, community, state, and market organizations are sources of strength for those within the organization. On the other hand, these same institutions become sources of exclusionary pressure for those outside the organization. Indeed, Darity (1989) warns that racial/ethnic culture can function as a coalescing agent in the monopolization of jobs by racial/ethnic groups to the exclusion of "others."[16]

Worker segmentation within organizations may also develop as a result of the institutional framework of worker organizations. For example, patriarchy, which forms the basis of family organization, inherently weakens the position of women in domestic production. Moreover, market, domestic, informal market, and state outcomes are mutually reinforcing.

The demand for labor power

The distribution of employment is determined by the technical requirements of production and by power relationships between and among the contending classes of society. In turn, technological design is governed by the structure and certainty of product demand, the ownership and control of productive resources, availability, quality, and relative strength of alternative groups of workers, and the nature, quality, and capability of labor organization (across and within groups).

The relations of production, i.e., the manner in which the actual labor process is organized or the quality, level, and type of effort extracted from workers, is not simply a technical matter but involves an exercise of power as well.

The demand for and supply of labor power are inter-dependent. Managers who hire workers are subject to the same socially constructed identities as workers engaged in supply side structuring, i.e., family and community, state, and market organizations that on the one hand increase the competitive strength of those included in the organization but on the other hand facilitate the exclusion of non-organization members.

Hence, just as racism and sexism influence worker segmentation on the supply side, those same phenomena influence the demand for alternative laborers because managers are not immune to the values, norms, habits, traditions, etc. of their family and neighborhood, political leadership, or traditional practices in their market segment. Similar arguments can be advanced regarding the role of the educational system, professional training, and skilled trade unions in the allocation of apprenticeships.

On the nonlabor side of the production process, firms do not have equal access to financial capital nor do they utilize machinery of equal efficiency. Firms utilize different vintages of technology because they enter (or exit) industries at different dates and because they develop different strategies regarding the timing of fixed capital investments; fixed capital investments "lock in" technological commitments for the time period that the capital is depreciating. The greater the fixed capital investment the longer the period of depreciation and therefore the more likely it is that one will observe firms using machinery of differing efficiency. Firms, like labor, have intra-industry hierarchies regarding profitability and efficiency of production. The rate of profit within and between industries tends towards equality only for regulating capitals (those firms using the best reproducible means of production).

Botwinick (1993) provides a detailed analysis of the relationship between the competitive structure of firms and the distribution of wages. Botwinick's theory of wage differentials demonstrates that the inter- and intra-industry competitive structure of capitals – capital intensity, size of the firm, location of regulating capitals, special conditions of production, value of fixed capital investment, and cost differentials between regulating and subdominant capitals – yields differential technical limits (sources of downward pressure) to wage differences between and within industries. Inter-capital differences in the nature and extent of worker organization affect the capacity of workers to push wages towards these limits.

The concentration and centralization of capital in product markets leads to the concentration and centralization of laborers in resource markets. Similarly, the specialization and product differentiation associated with the agglomeration of capital is mirrored by the segmentation and deskilling of the labor process associated with the development of labor power (Marx 1906: 405–556; Braverman 1974). There is a rough consensus that the employed labor force is segmented by skill requirements, remuneration schemes, and degree of protection from the reserve army of unemployed (Knights and Wilmott 1990).

Some employment positions carry greater strategic significance than others.[17] Hence, the segmentation of the collective worker and the deskilling of individual occupations establishes job positions with varying degrees of protection from reserve army competition. Jobs will be reproduced along a skill–worker control continuum. Within the ongoing processes of accumulation and segmentation, the competitive significance of occupations, and hence also the level of strategic protection of workers from the reserve army, varies across occupations.

Summing up, the distribution of jobs is characterized by the potential wage rate and wage differential of an occupation and the associated degree of worker control over the labor process. Jobs at the top of the queue tend to pay higher than average wage differentials and are associated with an above average level of worker control over the labor process. Jobs at the end of the queue tend to pay low wages, have unpleasant working conditions, and are associated with little effective worker control over the labor process.

Persistent inequality

On the one hand, there is a queue of workers, arrayed according to a vector of characteristics: for example, skill, ability, marital and family status, non-capitalist employment opportunities, potential labor intensity, organizational or group affiliations, etc. On the other hand, there is a queue of jobs, arrayed according to potential income, wage differential, protection from the reserve army, and degree of job control. However, the job allocation process is mediated by two rather important constraints: the continuous reproduction of both involuntary unemployment and underemployment and the hierarchical organization of work.

Combining the notion of continuously scarce employment opportunities with the hierarchical organization of work, and the fact that workers may compete across several layers of the occupational pyramid and among several positions on the same layer, implies that *for any given layer of the occupational pyramid the supply of potential workers generally exceeds the number of available jobs*. Every layer of the occupational hierarchy then has its own particular queue, with the longest queues established for jobs at the top of the hierarchy.

Micro-queues operate in a manner analogous to the aggregate reserve army. If the quantity of laborers demanded for an occupation grows rapidly, the queue will become exhausted. Relative wages and working conditions for the occupation will improve, while labor intensity declines. Over time, a reaction sets in: workers from other occupations, regions, and nations enter the rising wage occupation. Eventually, the queue is replenished; but, this may take a long time if the occupational category requires large amounts of training. As such, the improved wages and working conditions, ushered in by the draining of the labor queue, may persist for a substantial period of time. Indeed, this persistence is likely to lead to an over-reaction in the replenishment of the labor queue.

At any rate, labor migration is not the only method available to capital to restock its labor queues. Fractionalization of skill content and increased mechanization, automation, and computerization as job tasks are fragmented can be potent methods for increasing control over the labor process, undercutting wages, and releasing labor stocks. Or, if necessary, jobs may be exported to areas with the available supply of labor.

The reproduction of the aggregate reserve army, the excess demand for the more desirable jobs and the lack of desire to accept or remain in low wage positions forces capital and labor to develop a series of social institutions, customs, and conventions to allocate the supply of workers among the scarce employment opportunities. And the jobs allocation process also requires a means for demarcating a potential supply of workers for the jobs with the shortest queues, that is low wage jobs.

A detailed discussion of wage discrimination allows one to move from a possibility to an actuality theory of discrimination (Mason 1994a, 1995; Williams 1987, 1991). The inclusion of intra-and inter-industry wage differentials into the analysis also creates another dimension of complexity into the discriminatory process. Since it is now possible for economically identical workers to receive persistently unequal pay for equivalent occupations, exclusion can be actualized through employment, occupational training, and wage discrimination.

Wage discrimination occurs because socially constructed racial and gender identities function as job allocation mechanisms for "high" wage positions and markers of "low" wage laborers for capital. Measured intergroup earnings differentials are a persistent outcome of the interaction of two phenomena. One, the adverse effect of racial conflict on the organizational strength of workers which, in turn, affects the formation of intercapital wage differentials. I refer to this as the class struggle effect. Two, the interracial employment ratio for a unit of capital has a negative correlation with the wage differential associated with that capital, across all occupations. I refer to this as the racial exclusion effect. The interaction of the class struggle and racial exclusion effects implies persistent discrimination.

Botwinick's analysis suggests that for a given occupation the upper bound on the wage rate of regulating capitals (w_R) is related to: the competitive structure of capitals (CS), labor quality (LQ), job desirability (JD), market stability (MS), and the nature and extent of worker organization (BP). This relationship is expressed in equation 16.11.

$$w_R = f(CS, LQ, JD, MS, BP) \qquad 16.11$$

The job desirability vector (JD) represents working conditions. Under Marxian competition, wage differentials are paid for undesirable jobs only if labor has forced capital to increase the pecuniary returns to work. Disagreeable working conditions will not lead to higher monetary wages but do provide proxies for the relative dominance of capital over labor: *ceteris paribus*, poor working conditions are associated with low pay,[18] (especially when the reserve army rate is high).

The wage rate is regulated by the amount of socially necessary labor required to produce a family's consumption bundle. Therefore, increases (decreases) in the quality of labor power (LQ) required to produce the output of regulating capitals will raise (lower) the wage rate. Similarly, demand pressures (MS) will tend to raise (lower) the wage rate at capitals growing above (below) their long term planned rate of growth.

Finally, the distribution of wages is nondecreasing with respect to the collective strength of workers (BP). As the levels of worker organization and unity increase, labor has greater power to extract favorable terms of trade for the exchange of labor power.

The relationship between class struggle, racial conflict, and the distribution of wages is straightforward. At a minimum, racial conflict lowers the quality of worker organization. In turn, workers are less able to attain (or maintain) higher wages. Formalizing this relationship is somewhat problematic. Let equation 16.12 represent a generalization of the relationship between bargaining power and racial inequality.

$$BP = h(\text{Nature of Worker Organization, Racial Inequality}) \qquad 16.12$$

Labor–labor conflict lowers the quality of worker organization. One option available to individual capitals to sustain such conflict is racial segmentation of the workforce. Such segmentation may occur along several dimensions: differential hiring into alternative job ladders, different wages for comparable work, racially differential layoff policies, or even differential legitimation tactics in racially segregated communities. There is then no a priori theoretically "best" method of modelling the inverse relationship between racial conflict and wage attainment; any specific model is, at best, an initial working hypothesis that attempts to formalize a historically contingent relationship.

Accordingly, one can apply the Reich hypotheses regarding bargaining power and racial inequality to equation 16.12 to obtain (16.12′), where NU represents the extent of worker organization, R_q, R_w are proxies for the quality of labor organization, and Z_1 is a vector of variables designed to capture the nature of worker organization, e.g., formal versus informal worker organization, business versus social union, industrial versus craft union, etc.

$$BP = h(Z_1, NU, R_q, R_w) \qquad 16.12'$$

Mason (1993) has formalized the idea of racial domination by focusing on the consistency between racially differential access to income positions and the segmentary nature of the accumulation process. *The principle of exclusion*, the utilization of ascriptive characteristics, for example, race and gender, as labor allocation mechanisms, *provides the operative framework for formalizing racial domination*. It implies that African Americans are more likely to be excluded from high wage positions and are more likely to be forced into low wage positions.[19] A natural extension of this line of argument is that *racial dominance, in the first instance, is actualized via a negative correlation between the extent of African American employment and the size of wage differentials*.

The focus on exclusion as the expression for racial domination in economic activity was popularized first in the works of internal colony theorists (Harris 1972). The internal colony model sought to connect the specific issue of racial discrimination in the market for labor power with the broader issues of racial conflict in American society and the historical development of these issues. It recognized that racial domination and class exploitation are the twin pillars of a racist-capitalist state.

Internal colony theorists extended Marx's analysis of a labor surplus economy. They developed at least two unique hypotheses regarding the market for labor power that are directly associated with the internal colony model. One, *minority workers can be restricted to or concentrated in lower status jobs and industries*. The implication here is that the exclusion of minority workers from "better" jobs or industries raises the labor intensity (work effort) of white workers. Hence, employers gain because the average level of work effort increases and white workers gain (at least in the short run) because they are spared undesirable employment positions.

Bonacich's (1979) split labor market theory also examines the relationship between exclusion and labor market discrimination (or labor–labor conflict more broadly defined). A split labor market occurs when racial or ethnic differentiation is inaugurated as an economic synonym for labor groups with historically differentiated conditions of proletarianization (labor supply). "Cheap labor" becomes a mark of identification for workers with the most disadvantaged entry into capitalist society, for example "blacks" in the US, and "high priced" labor becomes the mark of distinction for workers with the most advantageous entry into capitalist society, for example "whites" in the US. Bonacich argues that this historically determined differentiation "sets into motion a pressure for employers (capital) to displace high-priced with cheap labor." In turn, high-priced labor attempts to protect itself from the actuality or threat of displacement by trying to reduce capital's access to cheap labor. Hence, the class struggle between capital and high-priced labor, as the former attempts to the displace the latter, leads to a persistent victimization of cheap labor groups "since their exclusion from full participation in the capitalist economy hinders their development and escape" from the bottom of the economic ladder. Accordingly, the split labor market is continually reproduced as accumulation reproduces the reserve army of unemployed.

Finally, both Darity (1989) and Williams (1987) recognize that workers can use racial/ethnic culture to exclude others from the more desirable occupations.

The exclusionary process, however, is mediated by the nature and extent of worker organization. For example, there is widespread evidence that craft unions tend to be more discriminatory towards African Americans than industrial unions (Freeman and Medoff 1984; Spero and Harris 1968; Hill 1989). Accordingly, worker organization is also an important determinant of the inter-racial allocation of labor.

Equation 16.13 states that the wage differential (μ) is captured by the differential between the potential wage rate of regulating capitals and the minimum wage (w_{min}) rate for labor power of the occupation.

$$\mu = w_R - w_{min}, \tag{16.13}$$

$$R_q = g(\mu, NU, JD, R_w, MS, Z_2) \tag{16.14}$$

Equation 16.14 summarizes the principle of exclusion. White employment relative to African American employment (R_q) has a positive correlation with the wage differential (μ) and a negative correlation with the relative wage rate (R_w). But R_q decreases as the extent of (industrial) worker organization (NU) increases (and as the level of racism within the worker organization declines). Similarly, the working conditions vector (JD) captures the terms associated with the dirty worker hypothesis; as working conditions worsen, African American exclusion decreases. African American employment has a positive correlation with fluctuations in capital's demand for labor (MS) and Z_2 captures state policy and community pressures.

Figure 16.2 represents the classical Marxian theory of discrimination. Equations 16.11 to 16.13 yield the class struggle curve for regulating capitals (CS_3), while equations 16.13 and 16.14 yield the racial exclusion curve. The distribution of wages and employment is a joint outcome of the class struggle between labor and capital over the production and appropriation of surplus value and the racial struggle among workers over the scarce employment opportunities. For example, between industries or within an

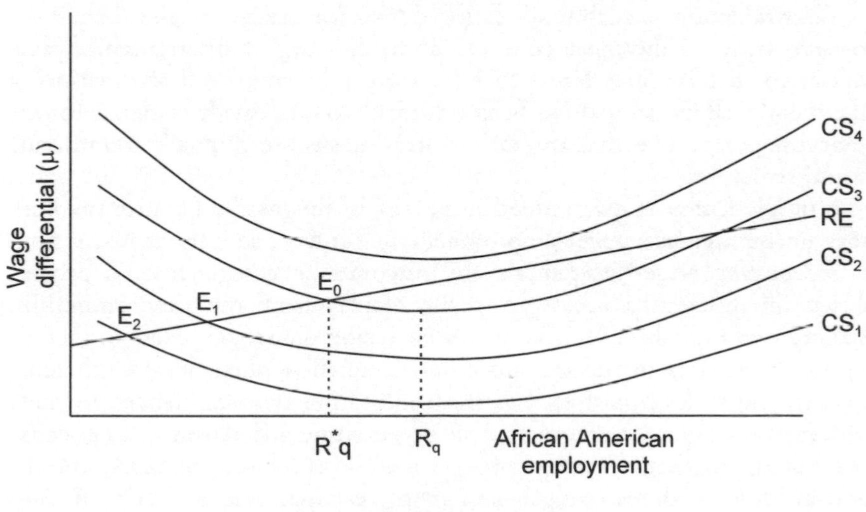

Figure 16.2 Wage differentials and the inter-racial distribution of employment
Source: Mason (1995)

industry, for a given occupation, regulating capitals would imply R_q^* workers, while the next most efficient firms would employ relatively more African Americans at E_1 and the least efficient firms would employ the most African Americans at E_2. On the other hand, if there are firms operating with nonreproducible conditions of production, and thereby able to pay higher wage differentials, these firms may not hire any African Americans.

The race–class dynamics are revealing. Suppose regulating capitals currently have "too many" African Americans, i.e., employment is at $R_h < R_q^*$. Under this scenario, the potential wage differential (μ_{CS}) exceeds the wage differential consistent with the inter-racial allocation of employment opportunities (μ_{RE}). Also, capital will note that it can lower its labor costs by hiring more whites since $R_h < R_q^* < \Theta$. Hence, a strategic coalition can be formed between white labor and white capital to limit African American employment opportunities; this coalition begins to break down when the interracial employment ratio is in the vicinity of R_q^* and white workers perceive relatively more desirable jobs elsewhere. A similar set of dynamics can be worked out when $R_q > R_q^*$. Additionally, the construction of this model yields a wealth of hypotheses regarding the relationship between the model's endogenous and exogenous variables.

Unique contribution

The classical Marxian model moves from the most abstract understanding of discrimination as a labor allocation device for determining service in the reserve army to the most concrete understanding of discrimination as a device for determining access to high wage jobs. Statistical affirmation of the theoretical model that has been outlined would provide evidence for the Marxian perspective that capitalism and racism are mutually reinforcing social structures.

Multiple forms of discrimination persist in this model because involuntary unemployment, under-employment, and inter- and intra-industry noncompensating wage differentials are outcomes of a segmentation process based on differential access to stable employment and the competitive structure of capitals. The principle of exclusion – unequal access to income opportunities – is an endogenous outcome of the model, as race, ethnicity, gender, and so forth, are used as labor allocation criteria. Hence, not only will capital seize upon and reproduce pre-existing differences among workers, but the market allocation process itself is conducive to race-, ethnic-, and gender- invidious comparisons in the competition for scarce income procurement opportunities.

The results imply that it is untenable to assume that individual wage income is solely, or even predominently, a function of individual specific characteristics and that the wage–productivity connection is somewhat "loose." Labor market remuneration then is not solely a function of individual-specific productivity enhancing characteristics, but is also determined by the nature of the firm, industry, and labor organization.

Exclusion is an endogenous allocation mechanism that is not solely limited to race. The principle of exclusion can easily be used as an explanation of gender based differences in earnings. Granted, the historically specific conditions of the latter form of discrimination and the (empirically related) proxy variables which capture these may be very different from the historically specific conditions of racial discrimination. But, this does obviate the operation of the principle of exclusion with respect to the role of women in a capitalist labor market; on the contrary, the principle of exclusion is operative for many groups, but its specific impact and operational processes will differ across groups.

If one views intergroup differences in labor remuneration that are dissassociated with intergroup differences in productive ability as inequitable, then there is justification in this model for aggressive and permanent social involvement in the determination of labor market outcomes. In this light, we may be forced to view comparable worth, affirmative action, or socially aggressive, imaginative, and non-traditional strategies as permanent aspects of social policy rather than temporary measures to alter past historical wrongs.

To the extent that libertarian preconceptions govern social policy, these policy prescriptions will appear to advocate "reverse discrimination" or appear to provide benefits to individuals who were not specifically injured and harm to individuals who did not specifically discriminate. The libertarian perspective ignores the fact that the principle of exclusion is a group based phenomenon: individuals are hurt or harmed (or, conversely helped or benefited) according to whether they belong to different groups, not solely according to the specific characteristics of individuals *per se*.

SUMMARY

This paper has made an attempt to evaluate the contributions of recent radical and Marxian economics to the understanding of the color line and market competition. Toward that end, four models of discrimination in the market for labor power were critically appraised. In each case, the central element of the critique was the relationship between the model's theoretical and empirical implications and the conceptualization of competition embedded in the model.

The divide-and-conquer model represents an important theoretical innovation with its discussion of bargaining power and multiple forms of racial inequality. But this model is weakened by its theoretical adherence to neoclassical competition. The empirical status of the model remains contentious.

The segmented labor market–dual economy model gained significance for alerting analysts to the importance of inter-racial differences in occupational mobility and access to on-the-job training. The insights from this model, however, are limited because of its fatal attraction to neoclassical competition in the secondary/peripheral sectors of the economy.

The race relations model provides an impressive attempt to incorporate the strengths of earlier models (by revealing that the aggregate state of the labor market is a mediating influence on the microeconomic decision making of firms). This model also requires further empirical evaluation before one can assess its lasting impact on the economics of racial discrimination.

The classical Marxian model is theoretically encompassing with respect to prior economic models, and its theoretical development is clearly connected to the Marxian analysis of prices, crises and the business cycle, segmentation and so forth. Specifically, racial discrimination in the market for labor power is a reflection of the inter-racial competition for scarce employment opportunities. Discrimination persists over time as an endogenous outcome of the reproduction of the reserve army, the hierarchical structure of employment opportunities, and the reproduction of non-compensating wage differentials. Yet, even more than the previous models, the Marxian competition model has not been fully subjected to the fire of intense empirical investigation.

Also, the classical Marxian model can be credited with incorporating the major insights of internal colony theory, which provides the stylized facts of racism and discrimination in the market for labor power within a racist–capitalist state. By alerting analysts to the fact that discrimination is a reflection of both racial domination and class exploitation, the latter model has made a lasting imprint on the economics of discrimination. Proponents of this perspective warned that the highly abstract notion that discrimination injures all workers as a class (and hence all workers have a material interest in its elimination) is a conclusion that is constantly challenged by the immediate material incentives for individual workers to acquire racially invidious perspectives regarding outcomes in the market for labor power.

Marxian and radical economists have provided a wealth of insights into the economics of discrimination. Moreover, the continuous attempt to provide a validated theory of discrimination has yielded insights into theories of involuntary unemployment, wage differentials, and labor market segmentation as concrete expressions of outcomes associated with the Marxian vision of the competitive process.

NOTES

1 Phenotypical differences and sexual variation are biological facts. However, the manner in which physical differences are transformed into racial, ethnic, and gender categories is neither time, space, nor culture invariant. The set of pro-

cesses by which physical differences are transformed into racial, ethnic, and gender categories is known as the social construction of identity. Further, a historical materialistic methodology asks, "What is the relationship between socially constructed identities and the material reproduction of society?" For modern Marxists, within and across time, space, and cultures, neither the presence nor the absence of the black skin pigment, melanin, is sufficient to define racial categories; similarly, genital variation is not sufficient to define gender – social theorists must seek to understand race and gender as economic institutions.

2 The model's convexity assumptions include: (i) $\delta(LD)/\delta(BP) < 0$; (ii) $\delta(BP)/\delta(R_w) = 0$ at $R_w = 1, \delta(BP)/\delta(R_w) > 0$ at $R_w < 1, \delta(BP)/\delta(R_w) < 0$ at $R_w > 1$; (iii) bargaining power reaches a minimum when the employment ratio is near equality but reaches a maximum as the labor force becomes more homogeneous, $\delta(BP)/\delta(R_q) = 0$ at $R_q = 1, \delta(BP)/\delta(R_q) < 0$ at $R_q < 1, \delta(BP)/\delta(R_q) > 0$ at $R_q > 1$.

I say "near equality" in order to be consistent with the effect of wage inequality on bargaining power. Reich does not explicitly make this assumption; however, his graphical presentation of the relationship between bargaining power and employment inequality does tend to indicate, *ceteris paribus*, a monotonicly decreasing relationship between BP and $0 < R_q \leqslant \Theta$ and a monotonicly increasing relationship between BP and employment inequality whenever $\Theta \leqslant R_q$.

The assumption captures the idea that a racially homogeneous labor force is a stronger bargaining unit than a racially heterogeneous labor force. If this is true workers have a strong incentive to insulate themselves from the competition of "outsiders." Shulman (1990) presents empirical evidence that the existence of an "insulate effect" on bargaining power may contradict the results of Reich's model.

3 Third world people refers to African Americans, Asian Americans, Native Americans, and Latinos.

4 Reich (1981: 209) provides the following limitations of his divide-and-conquer model.

> (a) Worker coalitions may be able to prevent employers from reaching the profit-maximizing point. The three instruments are not entirely under employer control. (b) It is important to consider the case when some workers occupy skilled jobs. (c) The relationship between racial inequality within firms to that produced outside firms must be specified. (d) Microeconomic competitive models must be extended to incorporate macroeconomic variables and imperfect competition.

These straightforward comments indicate that Reich is well aware that there are important limitations to abstract models of discrimination. Hence, I do not dwell on these limitations in the body of text. Rather, I attempt to analyze Reich's presentation at its own level of abstraction.

5 Efficiency wage models assume that worker effort (LD/L) is an increasing function of the wage rate.

6 The uniform wage is one such that Robinsonian exploitation no longer exists, that is $w_u \geqslant$ VMPL, but that "radical exploitation" does exists, that is $w_u <$ the value of the average product of labor.

7 Rosenberg (1989) provides a detailed review of the current status and empirical content of segmentation theory. Accordingly, it is not necessary to repeat his insights here. Instead, I will simply highlight the relationship between segmentation theory and racial inequality.

8 Albelda (1985) seizes this point to explain the convergence of earnings for African American and white women. First, she demonstrates that from 1958 to 1982 both groups of women have almost identical labor force participation rates outside of private household employment. Second, occupational convergence has occurred. From 1940 to 1980, the fraction of employed African American women who were private household workers declined from 60 to 6 per cent. Similarly, the fraction of African American women employed as farm workers, another low wage occupation, fell from 16 to 1 per cent. At the same time, the fraction of African American women employed as professionals rose from 4 to 15 per cent. On the other hand, during the postwar era white women have never been employed significantly as farmworkers: 1 per cent in 1940 and even less than that in 1980. The fraction of white women employed as professionals showed little increase over this time period, rising from 15 to 17 per cent. Hence, gender discrimination tends to keep both African American and white women in secondary jobs.

If one adds to Albelda's observations that African American women tend to suffer higher unemployment rates than white women then one can explain the convergence in wage rates but the higher earnings of white women.

The changing occupational status of African American women cannot be divorced from the tremendous internal migration of all African Americans out of the South and from rural areas to urban areas. As Heckman (1989) demonstrates, African American–white wage ratios differ across regions, with the lowest ratios in the South; however, among women, the South and the Northeast are the only two regions to exhibit sustained growth in wage ratios (from 1953 to 1979).

9 One, a "decline in discrimination can disrupt traditional patterns of authority and association," thereby creating discontinuity in terms of the relationship between the firm and its operational environment. Two, diminishing discrimination leads to Reich-style class struggle effects. Three, lessening discrimination entails (costly) changes in the rules of internal labor markets; especially, if these rules were originally designed to exclude particular groups of workers due to the hegemonic control achieved by capital as a result of the capital–labor accord. Four, "a reduction in discrimination can increase training costs and/or lower output if white workers resist the integration of the work force, the diminution of their prerogatives and the alteration of an accepted wage and occupational structure." Finally, lessening discrimination may impair team efficiency. If white males prefer not to work with women and African Americans, especially in positions with non-standardized decision making requiring cooperation and trust, it is not cost effective to hire African Americans or women.

10 See Keysar (1989) and Green (1991b) for a detailed evaluation of the historical and empirical relevance of the Reserve Army Hypothesis.

11 The reserve army of unemployed consists of all workers at least 16 years of age who are either involuntarily employed part time, have no employment at all but are actively pursuing work during some recent time period, or would participate in the labor force if there were available jobs. The reserve army concept clearly recognizes that the distinction between being unemployed and being out of the labor force is more academic than real. The reserve army ratio (RAR) is defined as follows: $RAR \equiv 1 - FE/PLF$, where $FE \equiv$ all fully employed persons aged 16–64, and $PLF \equiv$ the potential labor force = all individuals aged 16–64, except those with health conditions which prevent market participation and nonmarket social reproduction activities.

12 Bowles and Gintis (1990), Green and Weisskopf (1990), Weisskopf, Bowles, and Gordon (1983) summarize this as saying the cost of job loss rises with the

unemployment rate and since the intensity of labor is positively correlated with the costs of job loss, the intensity of labor also rises with the unemployment rate.

13 Much of this subsection and the first half of the next subsection is taken from Craig *et al.* (1985).

14 There is no way to "aggregate up" from atomistic maximizing behavior regarding allegedly voluntary tradeoffs between paid market time and nonmarket time to obtain market supply curves.

15 Factors (Marx 1906: 612) which determine the supply of labor power and the supply of laborers include: 1 the price and composition of labor's consumption bundle as historically developed; 2 the nature and cost of training; 3 the role of women and children in the labor market; 4 the speed of work (intensity of labor) and the length of workday; and 5 noncapitalist employment opportunities outside of the formal economy.

16 Shulman's isolation effect can be viewed as empirical affirmation of Darity's analysis of culture.

17 For a more detailed discussion on the strategic significance of occupations see Botwinick (1993), Mason (1995), Ferber *et al.* (1986), Ferber and Spaeth (1984), Kluegel (1978) and Perrone (1984).

18 In Marx's (1906: 526–52; 1967: 87–96) own work, poor working conditions hold down the unit cost of operation for individual capitals. Specifically, poor working conditions effectively transfer part of the cost of factory maintenance from constant capital outlays to workers via higher health and insurance costs associated with the greater disease, illness, and injury rates that are the typical result of poor working conditions. The clear implication is that working conditions are endogenous; however, for the purposes at hand (clearly demarcating the neoclassical and Classical Marxian analysis), it is permissible to view working conditions as exogenous.

19 Indeed, the notion of exclusion is often central to the work of African American authors (Du Bois 1968; Harris 1989; Lewis 1985; Work 1984; Swinton 1978). In addition, one should also see Foner (1982) and Hill (1989) on the role of unions and African American exclusion, Milkman (1980) and Hartmann (1976) on gender divisions and the American labor movement, and Williams and Smith (1990) and Glenn (1985) on exclusion (from high paying occupations) and racial–gender devaluation (of occupational positions not occupied by white males) as central elements of the race, gender, and class interaction and the historically contingent role of white males in that interaction. See also Takaki (1990) for an enlightening comparative analysis of the accumulation of capital, technological change, and the historical-cultural origins of Latino, African, Native, and Asian American exclusion.

REFERENCE

Albelda, R. (1985) "'Nice Work If You Can Get It:' Segmentation of White and Black Women Workers in the Post-War Period," *Review of Radical Political Economics*, 17(3) (Fall): 72–85.

Arrow, K. (1972) "Some Mathematical Models of Race Discrimination in the Labor Market," in A. Pascal (ed.), *Racial Discrimination in Economic Life*, Lexington, MA: Lexington Books.

Beck, E. M. (1980) "Discrimination and White Economic Loss: A Time Series Examination of the Radical Model," *Social Forces*, 59(1) (September): 148-159.

Bonacich, E. (1979) "The Past, Present, and Future of Split Labor Market Theory," in C. Marrett and C. Leggon, *Research in Race and Ethnic Relations*, Volume 1, Greenwich, CT: JAI Press Inc., pp. 17–64.

Boston, T. (1985) "Racial Inequality and Class Stratification: A Contribution to a Critique of Black Conservatism," *Review of Radical Political Economics*, 17(3) (Fall): 46–71.

Botwinick, H. (1993) *Persistent Inequalities: Wage Disparity under Capitalist Competition*, Princeton: Princeton University Press.

Bowles, S. and H. Gintis. (1990) "Contested Exchange: New Microfoundations for the Political Economy of Capitalism," *Politics and Society*, 18(2) (June): 165–222.

Braverman, H. (1974) *Labor and Monopoly*, New York: Monthly Review Press.

Cloutier, N. R. (1987) "Who Gains From Racism?: The Impact of Racial Inequality on White Income Distribution," *Review of Social Economy*, 45: 152–62.

Craig, C., J. Rubery, R. Tarling, and F. Wilkinson. (1985) "Economic, Social and Political Factors in the Operation of the Labour Market," in B. Roberts, R. Finnegan, and D. Gallie (eds), *New Approaches to Economic Life, Economic Restructuring: Unemployment and the Social Division of Labour*, Manchester: Manchester University Press, pp. 105–23.

Darity, W. (1989) "What is Left of the Theory of Discrimination," in S. Shulman and W. Darity (eds), *The Question of Discrimination: Racial Inequality in the US Labor Market*, Middletown, CT: Wesleyan University Press.

——(1991) "Critical Reflections on the NeoKeynesian Theory of Discrimination," in R. Cornwall and P. Wunnava (eds), *New Approaches to the Economic and Social Analysis of Discrimination*, New York: Praeger.

Demsetz, H. (1973) "Market Concentration Doctrine," Washington, DC: American Enterprise Institute.

Doeringer, P. and M. Piore (1971) *Internal Labor Markets and Manpower Analysis*, Boston: D. C. Heath.

Du Bois, W. (1968) *Dusk of Dawn: An Essay Toward An Autobiography of A Race Concept*, New York: Schocken Books.

Edwards, R. (1979) *Contested Terrain: The Transformation of the Workplace in the Twentieth Century*, New York: Basic Books, Inc.

Ferber, M., C. Green, and J. Spaeth (1986) "Worker Power and Earnings of Women and Men." Paper and Proceedings of American Economic Association, 76(2) (May): 53–6.

Ferber, M. and J. Spaeth (1984) "Work Characteristics and the Male–Female Earnings Gap." Paper and Proceedings of American Economic Association, 74(2) (May): 260–4.

Foner, P. (1982) *Organized Labor and the Black Worker: 1619–1981*, New York: International Publishers.

Freeman, R. B. and J. L. Medoff (1984) *What do Unions do?*, New York: Basic Books.

Gordon, D., T. Weisskopf, and S. Bowles (1987) "Power, Accumulation, and Crisis: The Rise and Demise of the Postwar Social Structure of Accumulation," in R. Cherry, *et al.* (eds), *The Imperiled Economy: Book I, Through the Safety Net*, New York: The Union for Radical Political Economics.

Gordon, D., R. Edwards, and M. Reich (1982) *Segmented Work, Divided Workers: The Historical Transformation of Labor in the United States*, New York: Cambridge University Press.

Gorman, R. (1989) "Black Neo-Marxism in Liberal American," *Rethinking Marxism*, 2(4) (Winter): 118–40.

Green, F. (1991a) "The Relationship of Wages to the Value of Labour-Power in Marx's Labour Market," *Cambridge Journal of Economics*, 15: 199–213.

——(1991b) "The 'Reserve Army': A Survey of Empirical Applications," in *Quantitative Marxism*.

Green, F. and Weisskopf, T. (1990) "The Worker Discipline Effect: A Disaggregative Analysis," *Review of Economics and Statistics*.

Harris, A. (1989) *Race, Radicalism, and Reform: Selected Papers*, ed. by William Darity, Jr., New Brunswick, NJ: Transactions Publishers.

Harris, D. (1972) "The Black Ghetto as 'Internal Colony': A Theoretical Critique and Alternative Formulation," *The Review of Black Political Economy*, (Summer): 3–33.

Hartmann, H. (1976) "Capitalism, Patriarchy, and Job Segmentation by Sex," *Signs: Journal of Women in Culture and Society* 1(2): 137–69.

Heckman, J. (1989) "The Impact of Government on the Economic Status of Black Americans," in S. Schulman and W. Darity (eds), *The Question of Discrimination: Racial Inequality in the US Labor Market*, Middletown, CT: WesleyanUniversity Press.

Heywood, J. (1987) "Wage Discrimination and Market Structure," *Journal of Post Keynesian Economics*, IX(4) (Summer): 617– 28.

Hill, H. (1989) "Black Labor and Affirmative Action: An Historical Perspective," in S. Shulman and W. Darity (eds), *The Question of Discrimination*, Wesleyan, CT: Wesleyan University Press, pp. 190–267.

Hill, M. (1980) "Authority at Work: How Men and Women Differ," in Greg J. Duncan and James N. Morgan (eds), *Five Thousand American Families: Patterns and Progress*, Ann Arbor: Institute for Social Research.

Jeffries, J. and H. Standback (1984) "The Employment and Training Policy for Black America: Beyond Placebo to Progressive Public Policy," *The Review of Black Political Economy*, vol. 13.

Keysar, A. (1989) "History and the Problem of Unemployment", *Socialist Review*, 19(4) (October – December): 15–34.

Kluegel, J. (1978) "The Causes and Cost of Racial Exclusion From Job Authority," *American Sociological Review*, 43 (June): 285–301.

Knights, D. and H. Willmott (eds) (1990) *Labour Process Theory*, London: Macmillan.

Lewis, W.A. (1985) *Racial Conflict and Economic Development*, Cambridge, MA: Harvard University Press.

Mandel, E. (1983) *Late Capitalism*, London: Verso Editions.

Marx, K. (1906) *Capital*, Volume I, Clark H. Kerr & Co.

——(1955) *The Poverty of Philosophy*, Moscow: Progress Publishers.

——(1977) "Wages, Prices, and Profit," in K. Marx and F. Engels, *Selected Works, Volume 2*, Moscow: Progress Publishers, 31–76.

——(1992) "The Divide-and-Conquer and Employer/Employee Models of Discrimination: Neoclassical Competition as a Familial Defect," *The Review of Black Political Economy* 20(4) (Spring): 73–89.

——(1993a) "Accumulation, The Segmentation of Labor, and Racial Discrimination in Employment," *Review of Radical Political Economics* 25(2) (June): 1–25.

——(1993b) "Variable Labor Effort, Involuntary Unemployment, and Effective Demand: Irreconcilable Concepts?," *Journal of Post Keynesian Economics*, 15(3) (Spring).

——(1994a) "Discrimination," in P. Arestis and M. Sawyer (eds), *The Handbook of Radical Political Economy*, Cheltenham, UK: Edward Elgar Publishing, 91–7.

——(1994b) "An Empirical Derivation of the Industry Wage Equation," *Journal of Quantitative Economics*, 10(1) (January): 155–170.

——(1995) "Race, Competition, and Differential Wages," *Cambridge Journal of Economics*, 19(4) (August): 545–68.

Milkman, R. (1980) "Organizing the Sexual Division of Labor: Historical Perspectives on 'Women's Work' and the American Labor Movement," *Socialist Review.*

Omi, M. and H. Winant (1994) *Racial Formation in the United States: From the 1960s to the 1990s,* 2nd edition, New York: Routledge.

Perrone, L. (1984) "Postwar Power, Strikes and Wages," *American Sociological Review*, 49: 412–26.

Reich, M. (1981) *Racial Inequality: A Political Economic Analysis*, Princeton: Princeton University Press.

——(1988) "Postwar Racial Income Differences: Theories and Trends," in G. Magnum and P. Philips (eds), *Three Worlds of Labor Economics*, Armonk, NY: M.E. Sharpe, Inc.

Roediger, D. (1991) *The Wages of Whiteness*, New York: Verso.

Rosenberg, S. (1989) "From Segmentation to Flexibility," *Labor and Society*, June.

Semmler, W. (1984) *Competition, Monopoly, and Differential Profit Rates: On the Relevance of the Classical and Marxian Theories of Production Prices for Modern Industrial and Corporate Pricing*, New York: Columbia University Press.

Shaikh, A. (1977) "Marx's Theory of Value and Transformation Problem," in J. Schwartz (ed.), *The Subtle Anatomy of Capital*, Santa Monica, CA: Goodyear Publishing.

——(1980). "Foreign Trade and the Law of Value: Part II," *Science and Society*, XLIV(1) (Spring): 27–57.

——(1982) "Neo-Ricardian Economics: A Wealth of Algebra, A Poverty of Theory," *Review of Radical Political Economics*, 14(2) (Summer): 67–83.

——(1984a) "Marxian Competition versus Perfect Competition: Further Comments on the So-Called Choice of Technique," *Cambridge Journal of Economics*, 4: 75–83.

——(1984b) "Political Economy and Capitalism: Notes on Dobb's Theory of Crisis," *Cambridge Journal of Economics*, 2: 233–51.

Shulman, S. (1984) "Competition and Racial Discrimination: The Employment Effects of Reagan's Labor Market Policies," *Review of Radical Political Economics*, 16(4) (Winter): 111–28.

——(1990) "Racial Inequality and White Employment: An Interpretation and Test of the Bargaining Power Hypothesis," *The Review of Black Political Economy*, 18(3) (Winter): 5–20.

——(1991) "Why is the Black Unemployment Rate Always Twice as High as the White Unemployment Rate?," in R. Cornwall and P. Wunnava (eds), *New Approaches to the Economic and Social Analysis of Discrimination*, New York: Praeger.

Spaeth, J. (1985) "Job Power and Earnings," *American Sociological Review*, 50: 603–17.

Spero, S.D. and A.L. Harris (1931) *The Black Worker: the Negro and the Labor Movement*, New York: Columbia University Press.

Swinton, D. (1978) "A Labor Force Competition Model of Racial Discrimination in the Labor Market," *The Review of Black Political Economy*, 9(1) (Fall): 5–42.

Szymanski, A. (1976) "Racial Discrimination and White Gain," *American Sociological Review*, 41 (June): 403–14.

Takaki, R. (1990) *Iron Cages: Race and Culture in 19th-Century America*, Oxford: Oxford University Press.

Weeks, J. (1981) *Capital and Exploitation*, Princeton: Princeton University Press.

Weisskopf, T., S. Bowles, and D. Gordon. (1983) "Hearts and Minds: A Social Model of US Productivity Growth," Brookings Papers on Economic Activity, 2: 381–450.

Williams, E. (1964) *Capitalism and Slavery*, London: Andre Deutsch.

Williams, R. (1991) "Competition, Discrimination and Differential Wage Rates: On the Continued Relevance of Marxian Theory to the Analysis of Earnings and Employment Inequality," in R. Cornwall and P. Wunnava (eds), *New Approaches to the Economic and Social Analysis of Discrimination*, New York: Praeger.

——(1987) "Capital, Competition, and Discrimination: A Reconsideration of Racial Earnings Inequality," *Review of Radical Political Economics*, 19(2) (Summer) 1–15.

Williams, R. and P. Smith. (1990) "What Else Do Unions Do?: Race and Gender in Local 35," *The Review of Black Political Economy*, 18(3) (Winter): 59–77.

Work, J. (1984) *Race, Economics, and Corporate America*, Scholarly Resources Inc., Wilmington, DE.

17

A THEORY ON THE EVOLUTION OF BLACK BUSINESS DEVELOPMENT

John W. Handy

INTRODUCTION

A useful theory of black business development should perform two functions: it should identify the underlying causes of complex observable phenomena regarding the interaction of race and commerce, thus forming a basis of organizing the multitudinous detail of actual black business experience; and, second, it should yield testable predictions and conclusions that provide a basis for comparison to alternative explanations of black business development. While a theory generalizing the evolution of black business development in the United States should not be contoured to simply fit facts in order to fulfill these two requirements, it should, nonetheless, be convincing in explaining the observable industry skewness of black-owned firms toward small retail and personal service establishments, the low sales-to-black population ratio compared to other groups, the widespread under-capitalization of black-owned firms, the sparsity of employment generating firms and relatively low number of black entrepreneurial mentors and role models.

A central contention of this chapter is that a correct theory of black business development is fundamentally a theory of the evolution of black entrepreneurship. This emphasis recasts entrepreneurship from a vague factor of production to the centerpiece of the evolution of black business development. Just as Schumpeter stressed the role of the entrepreneur, above all other factors, as the key to economic growth and change in capitalism, the role of black entrepreneurs and the constraints placed upon them are sufficient in explaining the evolution and low growth of black business enterprise.

The successful entrepreneur must display special aptitudes for bearing risk and uncertainty which permit him to act as a catalytic agent and promoter for new investment and product opportunities. This role in black business development seems especially critical since black entrepreneurs must not only shift and expand the opportunity set available to the community, but must also often overcome unique problems of discrimination in capital markets and racial stereotypical attitudes of consumers in the product market. Entrepreneurship as an alternative career choice for African Americans, therefore, must be understood in its historical context as evolving from and, in large measure, being conditioned by decades of severely constrained market demand for black business enterprise goods and services. Consequently, the employment of other productive factors, such as the hiring of labor and the acquisition and deployment of capital, must be seen as largely emanating from the African American entrepreneur's ability to successfully acquire and organize such productive resources within a set of parameters largely predetermined by a lack of effective demand for their goods and services.

The theory posits that black business's access to capital, managerial skills, business acumen and business-specific human capital has been endogenously determined by the historical evolution of purposeful withholding of effective market demand for African American goods and services. A careful consideration of the lack of effective demand for black produced goods and services for over 100 years demonstrates why this factor constitutes a sufficient condition for the observable outcomes of capital shortage, inefficiency, paucity of entrepreneurial models, skewness toward small size firms with few or no employees, and lower business formation rates compared to other ethnic groups. This essay seeks to show that the full implications of this apparently simple theory are in fact remarkably comprehensive and highly predictive in explaining causal relationships and observable impacts.

Several authors have long maintained that the purposeful withholding of economic demand for the goods and services of black producers over time by the predominantly white US society has itself inevitably led to a shortage not only of black entrepreneurs, but also black accountants, bankers, engineers, and managers.[1] Theodore Cross has cited this factor as a simple fulfillment of classical economics – the result of a history of sustained withdrawal of serious economic demand for black people in these larger economic roles. By never furnishing adequate wants or demands for goods that might be made, sold and serviced by African Americans, predictably the supply of entrepreneurs and producers has been curtailed.

> If conventional wisdom about black people missing a tradition of entrepreneurship, ownership, and "need for achievement" holds even a grain of truth, it is a statement – not of original condition – but of an assured economic result of the solid and sustained preference of white people not to trade or exchange commercial promises with black people.... I find it strange that this [increasing the visible supply of black people who are trained entrepreneurs and professionals] should be the total strategy in a *market* economy where the best way to increase the supply of something has always been to make sure there was a very solid demand for it.[2]

This purposeful curtailment of demand amounts to a system of tariff premiums on black products and capital.[3] The concept that black businesses have been, in effect, isolated by a system of tariffs on capital, retail sales, rents, and consumer and business credit can be effectively shown as a barrier-to-entry model.

DISCRIMINATION AS A BARRIER-TO-ENTRY AND CONTINUATION

Barriers-to-entry as an expression of demand discrimination can either deter potential entrants at the outset or lower the likelihood of success of those who do enter into business ownership.

Protracted economic and social discrimination actualized through market demand has not only prevented black businessmen from importing white capital, but it has forced the export of scarce black capital away from their communities to where effective tariffs do not exist and returns are greater. Thurow has noted that this type of discrimination forces the black community to export its productive factors and import its consumption goods.[4]

A straight-forward barriers to entry model as a reflection of effective tariffs can be constructed. Under any given state of nature, barriers to entry consist of those obstacles outside the control of the entrepreneur which raise the cost curves of affected firms to such an extent that it prevents or constrains new firms from producing a particular category of good or service profitably. In our model, then, market demand discrimination impacting both production possibilities and access to capital clearly imposes a discrimination coefficient (tariff) on the cost of doing business by black entrepreneurs. This tariff is reflected not only in higher capital premiums and other restrictions to capital, but also in socially restricted access to all business resources including: 1 information and knowledge available to the majority business sector; 2 supplies and materials at preferred customer rates; 3 equitable insurance rates; and 4 bonding availability, all of which significantly increase the cost of business.

General impact of discrimination tariff on price and quantity

A total cost function *without* discrimination barriers can be expressed as,

$$C = cq + k \qquad 17.1$$

where q = output; k = fixed costs; and c = variable costs. We specify a linear demand curve,

$$P = a - bq \qquad 17.2$$

The profit maximizing entrepreneur would therefore seek to maximize

$$\pi = TR - TC = PQ - TC = (aq - bq^2) - (cq + k)$$

Solving for $d\pi/dQ = 0$, we obtain profit maximizing output as $q = (a - c)/2b$ at profit maximizing price, $p = (a + c)/2$. Thus, in a non-discriminatory world profit maximization depends solely on "C" the marginal cost of production and "a" the y intercept level of demand.

Discrimination, however, as a barrier to entry changes the profit maximizing output level (q^*) and price (p^*). Holding the demand curve constant, we investigate its impact on the cost structure. The total cost function is now subject to a tariff (d):

$$C(1 + d) = (cq^* + k)(1 + d) \tag{17.3}$$

Profit maximizing conditions now give us,

$$q^* = (a - c - dc)/2b \quad \text{and} \quad p^* = (a + c + dc)/2 \tag{17.4}$$

Consequently, in a world of discrimination, output is lower ($q^* < q$) and prices are higher ($p^* > p$) for the discriminated entrepreneur. This is reflected in an upward shift of the marginal cost curve by the vertical distance "dC" in Figure 17.1

Impact of discrimination premium on entry and continuation

We can reasonably assume the Sylos postulate (see Sylos-Labini; and Needham[5]) that potential entrants behave as though they expect existing producers in an industry to maintain their output at the pre-entry level in the face

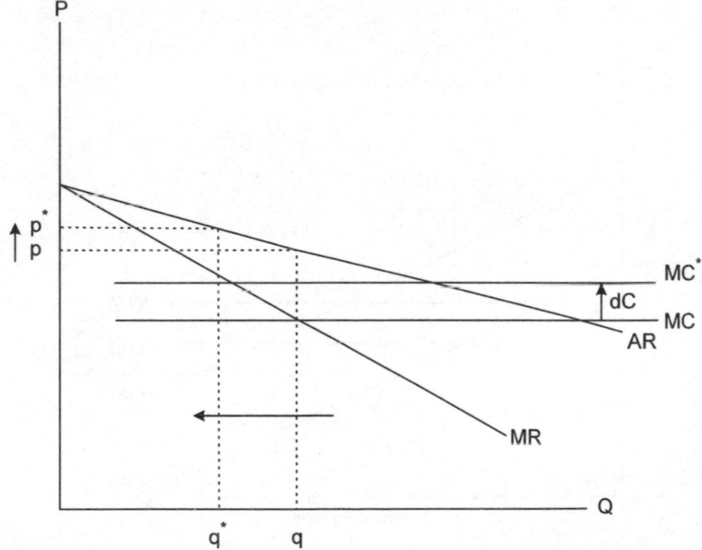

Figure 17.1 Impact of discrimination on pricing and output

of entry, and that established firms do, in fact, behave in this manner if entry occurs. Since the output from black-owned businesses is so small a fraction of total output in every industry, this is an eminently reasonable assumption for our model.

Given the Sylos postulate, black entrepreneurs are confronted by a sloping demand curve which is the segment of the industry demand curve to the right of the pre-entry quantity produced by existing firms. Entrepreneurs must decide whether to enter or remain in business by comparing this demand curve to their own cost conditions, which must include the opportunity costs of being self-employed and any discrimination premiums.

While market discrimination premiums increase inefficiency and lower the probability of success, entry and continuation can still occur in the presence of discrimination *if the entrepreneur's anticipated or actual demand conditions* result in a situation where market price can be generated over the full average cost (inclusive of the discrimination tariff and opportunity costs of self-employment). This cost difference between black-owned and majority established firms is measured by the XY distance in Figure 17.2. In Figure 17.2, entry and continuation can occur if black-owned firms can set their price within the WX range, which is above the XY difference.

Entry and continuance will not occur if the black entrepreneur's price exceeds cost of established firms by less than the difference between the full average cost of the black entrepreneur and that of established firms. For

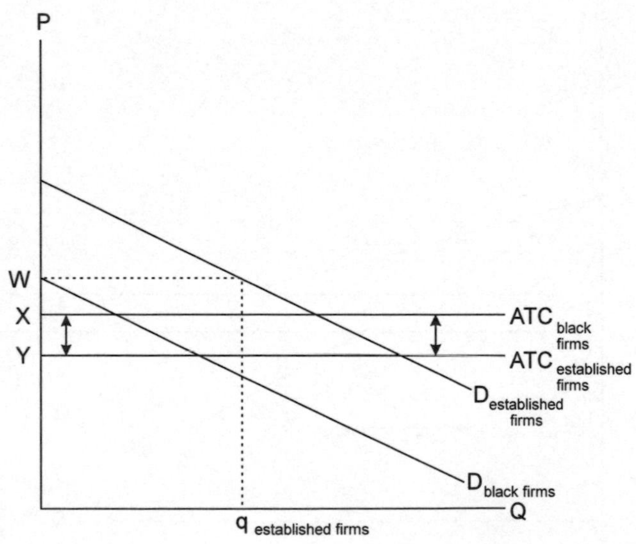

Figure 17.2 Entry and continuation under discrimination as a non-operative barrier

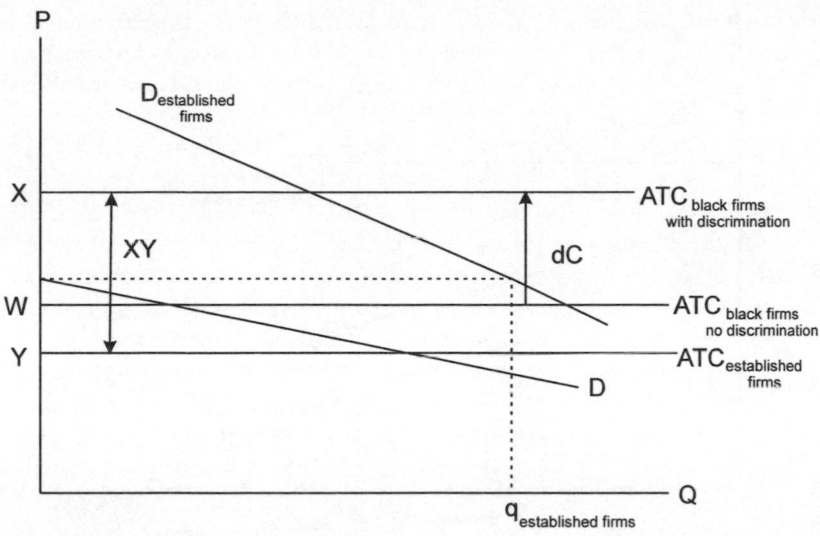

Figure 17.3 Entry and continuation under discrimination

under this circumstance, the black entrepreneur's anticipated demand curve will be below his full cost curve. If the discrimination tariff (d) raises the full average total cost curve for black firms too much (distance dC) relative to their price-setting ability, entrepreneurs will be unsuccessful either as new entrants or as business continuations. Consequently, African American entrepreneurs who labor under social and economic discrimination will have inefficient production (lower output at higher prices), and lower likelihood of successful start-ups and continuations.

In this case, no entry or continuation is feasible since dC is too great and black firms' prices can only be established within the WY range, at best, which is less than the XY difference (Figure 17.3).

Withholding of demand for black entrepreneurial output: the full model

Discriminatory withholding of market demand not only affects the cost structure of black-owned firms, but also most directly affects the market for goods and services produced by such firms. Its effect on any given entrepreneurial demand curve is to shift the demand curve down in the southwest direction. Black entrepreneurs' product price will be even further below their full cost curve than was true previously. Thus, the effect of discrimination on *both* the supply and demand functions of black-owned firms tends to reinforce lower probability of successful entry and continuation. In Figure 17.4, the amount of market unavailable to black firms due to market discrimination is shown by the difference between Q^*_{est} and Q_{est}.

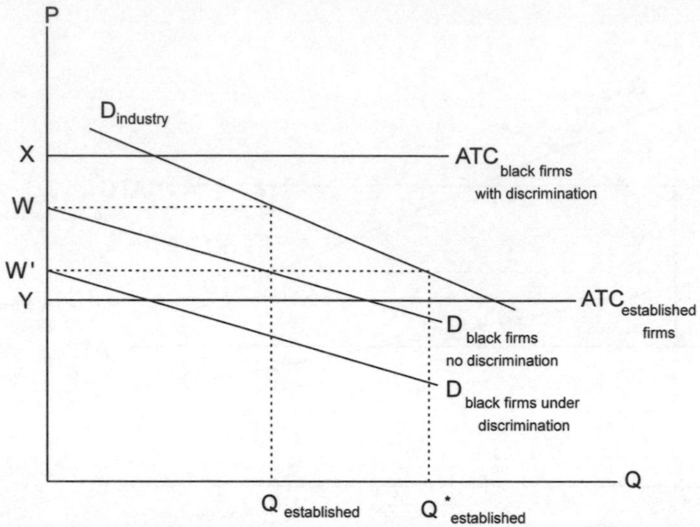

Figure 17.4 Discrimination for black entrepreneurial products and services: the full model

The full model shows that dC is now increasingly too large such that black firms' prices can only be set within an even lower W′Y range which is yet lower than the XY difference (Figure 17.4).

Impact of barrier to entry on learning by doing

This lower rate of output and higher cost structure of black business enterprise over any period under a given state of technology (often referred to as a period of cumulative gross investment of a given serial number G) has also had important implications for the learning experience, or learning by doing curve, of black enterprises compared to the general business sector. A general experience-learning curve that has a wide range of applications in operations management and economics is of the form[6]

$$Y_m(t) = Y_c + Y_f(1 - e^{t/T}) \qquad 17.5$$

where,

$Y_m(t)$ = Output rate at time t, measured as units of output per unit of time

T = Model time period, which measures the rate of performance improvement. $t = T$, for instance, reflects the length of time required to obtain a rate of output 63 per cent greater than the initial rate of output

Y_c = Initial rate of output

Y_f = Maximum possible gain in the output rate over an asymptotic time value

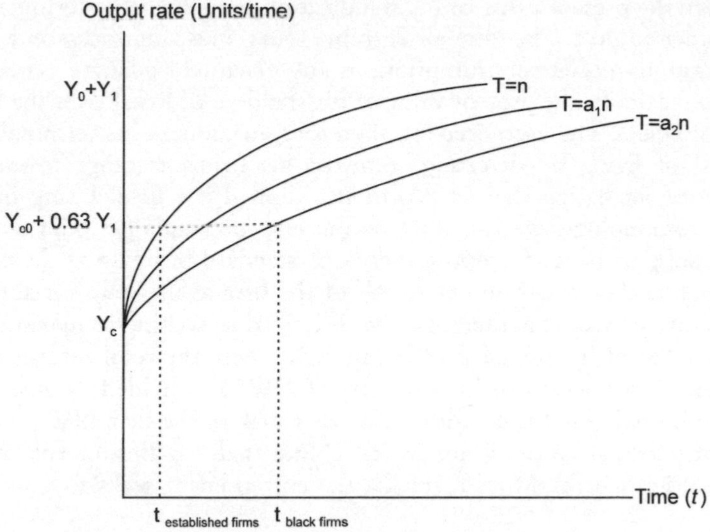

Figure 17.5 Impact of barrier to entry on learning by doing

From our tariff-coefficient of discrimination model, we know that the persistence of lower effective demand, higher costs and lower access to capital must result in black business enterprises having a persistently lower potential maximum rate of output gain (Y_f) compared to the general business sector in any given industry under a given technology of serial number G. Moreover, given the *cumulative* effects of learning by doing over time, which are so important in developing a skilled work force and improved management performance over ensuing decades, these factors have also resulted in black businesses requiring longer model time periods (T) before they can obtain a certain level of proficiency more customarily obtained by established firms not subject to tariff premium barriers and market constraints.

In Figure 17.5, established firms obtain a 63 per cent increase over their initial output rate by time t = T = n, whereas black-owned firms require $t = T = a_{2n}$ or a_1n to obtain this rate increase.

ENTREPRENEURIAL CHOICE

Self-employment under conditions of certainty: optimal control model

In the next two sections we fully explore the choice for entrepreneurship, first, under conditions of certain market demand and, subsequently, under conditions of risk and uncertainty. We assume that the African American entrepreneur's objective is similar to all other business owners. He seeks to maximize the present value of his standard of living by some terminal time T. In order to do so, he, like all entrepreneurs, must sacrifice some of his short-term, immediate consumption, in any given intermediate period t, in order to maximize the present value of his standard of living over the longer time horizon T. The entrepreneur, therefore, maximizes his terminal point standard of living by diverting some of his firm's earnings toward the purpose of increasing the net worth position of the firm. Using optimal control terminology, we can refer to the entrepreneur's periodic withdrawals to support his consumption needs or standard of living as the control variable, and the growth in net worth of the firm as the state variable.

The entrepreneur can, therefore, be described as seeking to maximize the present value of his standard of living (C), where the total returns to the accumulated net worth in his own firm ($\hat{\imath}$NW) are divided in any period between investing in future additional net worth of the firm NW′(t) and in his own personal consumption, C(t). (Note that $\hat{\imath}$ is the internal rate of return on net worth). More formally, the entrepreneur seeks to,

$$\text{Max} \int_0^T e^{-rt} U\{C(t)\} dt \qquad 17.6$$

subject to,

$$\hat{\imath}NW(t) = NW'(t) + c(t)$$

or

$$NW'(t) = \hat{\imath}NW(t) - C(t) \qquad 17.7$$

This can also be shown to be identical to choosing the path which produces the maximum utility stream (W) of personal consumption and net worth through time, and where consumption over any time $t + 1$ is a function of business savings and consumption decisions in period t. More formally, Eqns. 17.6 and 17.7 can be shown to amount to,[7]

$$\begin{aligned} &\text{Max} W[C(t), W(t)]dt \\ &= \text{Max}\{W[C(1), NW(1)] + W[C(2), NW(2)], \ldots + W[C(T), NW(T)]\} \end{aligned} \qquad 17.8$$

subject to, $C(t + 1) = f[C(t), NW(t)]$, and given C(0).

By expanding (17.6), subject to its constraints, we get

$$\int_0^T e^{-rt} U[C(t)] dt = \int_0^T e^{-rt} U[\hat{\imath}NW(t) - NW'(t)] dt \qquad 17.9$$

The Euler equation for this formulation is,[8]

$$dF_{NW'}/dt = F_{NW} \qquad 17.10$$

where,

$$F_{NW} = e^{-rt}U'(C)\hat{\imath} \quad 17.11$$

and,

$$F_{NW'} = -e^{-rt}U'(C) \quad 17.12$$

By substituting Eqns 17.11 and 17.12 into Eqn. 17.10, we get

$$d[-e^{-rt}U'(C)]/dt = e^{-rt}U'(C)\hat{\imath}$$

Thus,

$$-e^{-rt}U''(C)C' + re^{-rt}U'(C) = e^{-rt}U'(C)\hat{\imath}$$

Solving, we obtain

$$-U''(C)C'/U'(C) = \hat{\imath} - r \quad 17.13$$

Since $-U''(C)C'/U'(C) > 0$ by standard assumptions (i.e., $U' > 0$, $U'' < 0$), the optimal solution is characterized by increasing consumption over time, $C' = dc/dt > 0$, if and only if $\hat{\imath} > r$. That is, the optimal standard of living path rises if the rate of return on the entrepreneur's personal net worth in the firm ($\hat{\imath}$) exceeds the entrepreneur's rate of impatience or rate of time preference (r). Moreover, if the standard of living path is greater, the greater the difference between ($\hat{\imath}$) and (r). In other words, a relatively patient entrepreneur, with low rate of time preference, forgoes some current personal withdrawals from the firm to allow the value of the firm to improve so that higher level of consumption and living standard may be obtained later.

The optimal solution satisfies both the basic equation $NW'(t) = \hat{\imath}NW(t) - C(t)$ and the Euler equation (17.10). To develop qualitative properties of the optimal solution, we construct a diagram in the non-negative C–NW plane. From (17.13), it is clear that $C' = 0$ when $\hat{\imath} = r$, which also characterizes the net worth steady state solution NW_s. It immediately follows from (17.13) that to the right of NW_s, where $\hat{\imath} < r$, C must fall (i.e., $C' < 0$), and to the left of NW_s, where $\hat{\imath} > r$, C must rise (i.e., $C' > 0$).

It can be shown utilizing equation 17.7 that the NW' curve, where $C = \hat{\imath}NW$, is increasing and concave, passes through the origin and cuts the NW–C plane into two regions. Using the standard analysis for phase diagrams analysis, it follows that NW is falling at every point above the $NW' = 0$ locus. Similarly, for any point below the $NW' = 0$ locus NW must be rising. The directional arrows in Figure 17.6 reflect these conclusions, and indicate the general direction of movement that (NW, C) would take from any location.

There is a steady-state level of firm net worth (NW_s) and standard of living (C_s) that is sustainable. A steady-state position has $C' = 0$ and

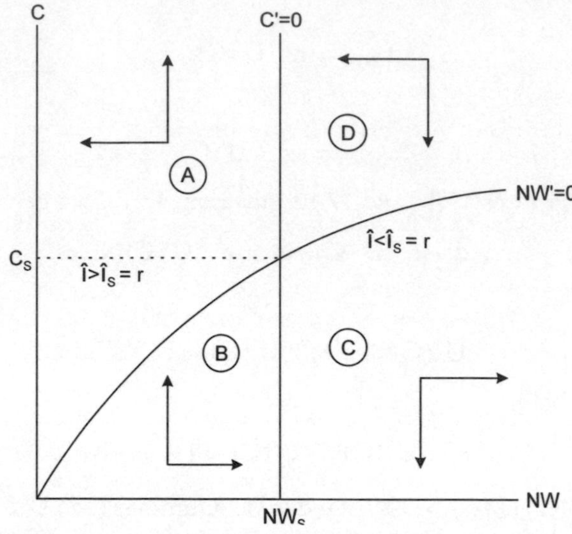

Figure 17.6 Directional arrows for change in consumption and net worth

$NW' = 0$, where the optimal values of C and NW can be maintained indefinitely. This position occurs at (NW_s, C_s) where $C_s = f(NW_s)$. From the theory regarding the existence of a solution to a differential equation, there is at most one path from the starting position NW_0, to the point (NW_s, C_s) coming from the left of NW_s, and, at most, only one optimal path approaching the sustainable steady-state solution (NW_s, C_s) from the right of NW_s.

The exact nature of optimal paths and paths that are either infeasible or inferior is determined both by the rate of return on net worth ($\hat{\imath}$) relative to the entrepreneur's given rate of time preference (r), and by the rate of return on net worth that can be sustained over the steady-state ($\hat{\imath}_s$). Thus, the nature of the paths describing the outcomes of entrepreneurial choice depends both on his willingness to reinvest in the firm, and the long-run sustainable rate of return dictated by the nature and extent of the market for his product or service. As long as the rate of return on net worth is greater than that required in the steady-state and simultaneously greater than the entrepreneurial's rate of time preference ($\hat{\imath} > \hat{\imath}_s = r$), then personal consumption increases over time ($C' > 0$). Likewise, net worth can be either increasing or decreasing ($NW' \gtrless 0$), depending on whether consumption withdrawals are sufficiently moderate or too large. The case where $\hat{\imath} > \hat{\imath}_s = r$ and $C > \hat{\imath}NW$ is shown in Figure 17.6 as area Ⓐ where C is increasing and NW is falling. The case where $\hat{\imath} > \hat{\imath}_s = r$, and $C < \hat{\imath}NW$ is shown as area Ⓑ in Figure 17.6, where both C and NW are increasing continuously over time.

All paths in area Ⓐ are inferior to those in Ⓑ since ever-increasing levels of consumption withdrawals are too large, relative to market demand, and cannot be sustained indefinitely with net worth continuously falling and ultimately crossing into $NW < 0$, an infeasible region. All paths in Ⓑ are superior to all paths in Ⓐ since both consumption withdrawals and firm net worth are increasing in region Ⓑ in every period. However, only one such path in Ⓑ will be optimal.

All paths in Ⓒ are also inferior to those in Ⓑ since the discounted utility stream of the sum of consumption and net worth cannot be maximized at the terminal point since the entrepreneur's standard of living (consumption) is falling continuously over time. Here, even though withdrawals are less than the returns to the firm, resulting in some growth in net worth, the rate of return on net worth, determined by the extent of the market, is continuously falling below that required for steady-state equilibrium. Consequently, in this case the business-owner is heedlessly trying to expand the firm's net worth in the face of continuously declining rates of return and declining living standards.

All paths in area Ⓓ also have net worth levels in excess of that which is market-sustainable at the steady-state level of net worth (NW_s). Likewise, consumption levels in Ⓓ exceed that which is sustainable at the steady-state consumption level (C_s). The discounted utility stream of higher net worth and higher consumption levels in Ⓓ would be preferable, but all such paths are unstable since the market rate of return is both less than the entrepreneur's rate of time preference and less than that, therefore, required in the steady-state. In addition, consumption withdrawals continuously exceed the declining returns, thereby further depressing net worth in future periods, such that $NW' < 0$. Consequently, both total net worth and total consumption must fall continuously over time. Only one such path in Ⓓ can optimally approach the steady-state solution from above. All other paths veer off either into inferior region Ⓐ or into inferior region Ⓒ.

Thus, the nature of the paths describing the outcomes of entrepreneurial choice depends both on his willingness to reinvest in the firm, and the long-run sustainable rate of return dictated by the nature and extent of demand for his product or service.

It follows that if initial firm net worth NW_0 is less than the steady-state solution, then the approach to (NW_s, C_s) must be from below with NW and C both increasing monotonically from their initial values to their stationary values along unique path ① (see Figure 17.7)

If the initial amount of withdrawals for personal consumption is too large (as in path ②), then net worth could only be accumulated for a short while and would eventually diminish to the point where net worth could ultimately cross into $NW < 0$, an infeasible solution. If, on the other hand, initial consumption withdrawals were chosen too low, then consumption would increase in later periods and peak, and then decline as shown in path

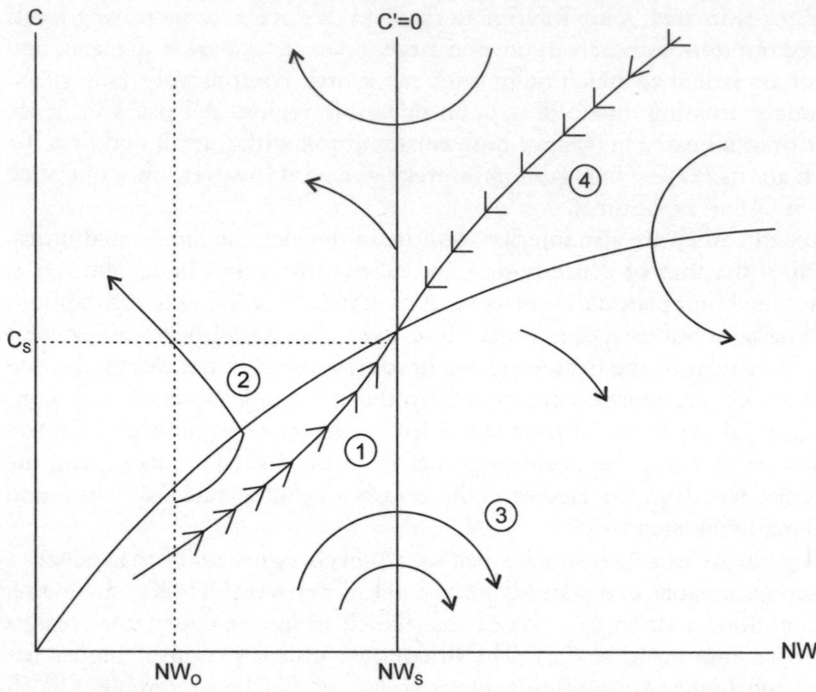

Figure 17.7 Optimal paths of living standard and net worth

③. This case would occur if the entrepreneur were trying to increase the value of the firm beyond what was warranted by the extent of the market for his final product or service. Path ①is, therefore, the only optimal plan for $NW_0 < NW_s$. This path is the most feasible for black entrepreneurs.

If $NW_0 > NW_s$, then the optimal path to the steady state would have both the net worth and personal consumption path to the steady state declining monotonically along path ④. Other paths in the neighborhood of path ④can, again, be ruled out as infeasible or inferior by arguments similar to those cited above. Path ④in Ⓓ, again, reflects a situation of both excessive net worth and high standard of living beyond what is market-sustainable. Moreover, this problem of over-capitalization is certainly an anomaly for black entrepreneurs and is ruled out of our discussion.

We are, therefore, primarily concerned with the necessary conditions describing optimal path ①, and their implications for black entrepreneurs.

The results of the optimal control model allow us to conclude:

1 For any starting position below the sustainable steady-state standard of living/net worth position, the only optimal path for black entrepreneurs is the path of both increasing net worth to the firm and increasing standard of living.

2 This optimal path rises if and only if the rate of return on net worth ($\hat{\imath}$) exceeds the entrepreneur's rate of time preference (r). Consequently, the more impatient (patient) the entrepreneur, the lower (higher) the likelihood of continuing in business, and under a rational choice model, the less (more) desirable it is for him to start a business.

3 A necessary condition for movement along the optimal standard of living/net worth path is that the market demand for the entrepreneur's product must be large enough to obtain a rate of return on net worth ($\hat{\imath}$) greater than the long run sustainable rate of return in the steady state ($\hat{\imath}_s$) over T – 1 periods.

4 The standard of living path and the value of the entrepreneur's income stream are both greater the larger the difference between $\hat{\imath}$ and r. The size of this difference is fundamentally determined by two factors. First, for any given level of business-saving behavior (reflected in the entrepreneur's rate of time preference (r)), higher levels of market demand increase the difference between $\hat{\imath}$ and r. Second, the greater the previous investment in business human capital, the greater the gap between $\hat{\imath}$ and r since returns to investment in the firm are higher the greater past accumulation of knowledge and experience of the entrepreneur. However, the learning by experience model described above pp. 385–6 clearly shows that the required gap between $\hat{\imath}$ and r must ordinarily be significantly smaller for black entrepreneurs since past accumulation of business knowledge and experience has been heavily constrained over time.

Self-employment under risk and uncertainty

While a largely riskless alternative wage can be reasonably estimated with some certainty, even under conditions where it is not fixed and allowed to fluctuate, remuneration for self-employment is a purely stochastic payment derived essentially from owning and operating a risky firm. In fact, the role of the entrepreneur and his claim to the net returns of the business is largely based on his being rewarded for accepting the risk and uncertainty of personal reward. According to Schumpeter this reward is the payment for the entrepreneur's undertaking the role of being an innovator, of organizing and coordinating factors of production in combination with previously unutilized or under-utilized inventions.[9]

Consistent with the choice theoretic framework discussed previously, individuals are assumed to have a choice between owning and operating a risky firm or working for a riskless wage. Consequently, it is reasonable to conjecture that individuals who are willing to assume more risk, *ceteris paribus*, are more likely to become entrepreneurs, while more risk averse individuals work for entrepreneurs who tend to assume such risks. We now, therefore, define the opportunity costs of self-employment as the *certainty utility foregone* by being an entrepreneur instead of working as an employee. Conversely, the opportunity cost of being a worker is the *expected utility* foregone by being an employee instead of an entrepreneur.

In developing the properties of this stage of the theory, we follow very closely the model of Kihlstrom and Laffont regarding their entrepreneurial theory of the firm formation based on risk aversion.[10] Our model, however, differs from theirs in several important respects:

1 In our model, individuals differ in their ability to perform entrepreneurial functions and outside labor. Consistent with our previous discussion, we assume individuals do differ in ability and aptitude. The model, however, is consistent with our assumption that the distribution of individual abilities is identical among all ethnic and racial groups.
2 We assume that wealth differs among individuals, whereas Kihlstrom and Laffont assume everyone has an identical amount of wealth. This assumption seems to be particularly restrictive in generating implications for black entrepreneurs who have significantly lower endowments of personal wealth.
3 We explicitly include nonpecuniary income in our model.

General equilibrium conditions

Following Kihlstrom and Laffont, we define a set of agents whereby any individual α has the Von Neumann–Morgenstern utility function $U(I, \alpha)$, where "I" represents total money income from self-employment (π) and nonpecuniary income (S), and where $I \in (0, \infty)$. That is, the entrepreneur seeks to maximize the present value of I such that,

$$\int_0^T e^{-rt} I(t) = \int_0^T e^{-rt}(\pi(t) + S(t)), \quad \text{where,} \quad \pi = \hat{\imath}NW \qquad 17.14$$

For all $I(t) \geqslant 0$, the first and second derivatives U' and U'' exist and are continuous. The marginal utility U' is positive and non-increasing, i.e., $U'' \leqslant 0$. Thus, all agents are either risk averse, to varying degrees, or indifferent to risk (risk neutral).

We employ the customary Arrow–Pratt absolute risk aversion measure which is non-decreasing in α. If α is more risk averse than agent β then by definition,

$$r(I, \alpha) > r(I, \beta) \qquad 17.15$$

or,

$$-U''(I, \alpha)/U'(I, \alpha) > -U''(I, \beta)/U'(I, \beta)$$

for all $I \in (0, \infty)$

If an individual α becomes an entrepreneur and employs L workers, he will receive profits equal to,

$$\pi(w, \alpha) = g(L, e, n) - wL(w, \alpha) \qquad 17.16$$

where $g(L, e, n)$ is a continuous production function whose arguments are labor (L), entrepreneurial skill (e), and a random parameter n representing deviations from the normal state of market demand (state of nature), with $E(n) = 0$.

Each individual α has a given amount of accumulated savings and wealth, $H(\alpha)$, which varies across individuals, such that certain agents are unable to hire workers if $H(\alpha) = 0$. We are, therefore, employing a type of wage-fund theory where labor-hiring must be less than or equal to $H(\alpha)/w$:

$$L(w, \alpha) < H(\alpha)/w \qquad 17.17$$

Consequently, possession of wealth constitutes a necessary condition for generating firms with paid employees. However, we learned from pp. 386–92 that this requirement constitutes a stringent constraint on the ability of black business enterprise to generate firms with paid employees since business wealth is largely a function of the historical stream of past accumulations to the value of the firm (NW) and entrepreneurial standard of living (C), both of which rise over time only if intertemporal market demand and learning by experience are sufficiently strong.

An individual α who becomes an entrepreneur, therefore, will employ $L(w, \alpha)$ workers where $L(w, \alpha)$ is the L value in $\{0, H(\alpha)/w\}$ which maximizes the expected utility function,

$$EU\{H(\alpha) + g(L, e, n) - wL(w, \alpha), S(\alpha)\} \qquad 17.18$$

If either $U'' < 0$, or $g'' < 0$ which is customarily assumed, then L is unique. By 17.16 we know that $\pi(w, \alpha) = g(L, e, n) - wL$. It follows, then, that individual α will choose to be an entrepreneur when the expected utility of entrepreneurial choice exceeds the certain utility of outside employment:

$$EU\{H(\alpha) + \pi(w, \alpha), S(\alpha)\} > U\{H(\alpha) + w\} \qquad 17.19$$

And he will choose to be an employee and work at wage w if

$$EU\{H(\alpha) + \pi(w, \alpha), S(\alpha)\} < U\{H(\alpha) + w\} \qquad 17.20$$

He will be indifferent if the equality in 17.19 and 17.20 holds. In the case where the equality holds, a *certainty equivalent wage* $w(\alpha)$ exists which is the market wage that makes agent α indifferent between the two activities – work and entrepreneurship – and is defined by

$$EU\{H(\alpha) + \pi(w, \alpha), S(\alpha)\} = U\{H(\alpha) + w\} \qquad 17.21$$

Given the standard assumptions, $g'' < 0$ and $U'' < 0$, the following results clearly emerge from the general equilibrium model,

1 For each α, $EU\{H(\alpha) + \pi(w, \alpha), S(\alpha)\} - [U\{H(\alpha) + w\}]$ is a continuous monotonically decreasing function of w.
2 If $w > (<) w(\alpha)$, then $EU\{H(\alpha) + \pi(w, \alpha), S(\alpha)\} < (>) U\{H(\alpha) + w\}$
3 If $r(I, \alpha) > r(I, \beta)$, then $w(\alpha) < w(\beta)$.
4 If $r(I, \beta) > (<) r(I, \alpha)$, then $EU\{H(\beta) + \pi[w(\alpha)], S(\beta), \beta\} < (>) U\{H(\beta) + w(\alpha), \beta\}$.

These results show that the higher the riskless wage and the more it exceeds the certainty equivalent wage, the lower the expected utility from entrepreneurship as compared to the certain utility of working for others (results 1 and 2). Moreover, more risk averse individuals are induced to become workers at lower certainty equivalent wages than greater risk taking individuals (result 3). At any given certainty equivalent wage $W(\alpha)$, there are marginal entrepreneurs α; and all individuals who are more risk averse than the marginal entrepreneur will choose to work for others, while those who are greater risk takers than the marginal entrepreneur will choose entrepreneurship (result 4).

Comparative statics

We now extend the model to investigate the impact of exogenous factors on the choice for entrepreneurship over any two points in time. In the following section, therefore, we utilize the general equilibrium results of the previous section to compare an initial equilibrium position with subsequent equilibrium positions resulting from exogenous changes in economy-wide or area-wide risk (changes in the state of nature). Such exogenous changes in the state of nature is reflected in such things as substantial swings in local market demand and employment, shifts in population, and the influx or outflight of substantial number of industries and sources of capital in the area.

The following two propositions immediately follow from the previous section (for formal proofs of two lemmas similar to these see Kihlstrom and Laffont; and Baron[11]).

Proposition 1

If $r\{H(\alpha), I(\alpha)\}_t > (<) \; r\{H(\alpha), I(\alpha)\}_0$ for all I, then $EU\{H(\alpha) + \pi(w, \alpha), S(\alpha)\}_t > (<) \; EU\{H(\alpha) + \pi(w, \alpha), S(\alpha)\}_0$.

This means that increasing area-wide risk reduces the expected utility from entrepreneurship, and that decreasing area-wide risk increases the expected utility from entrepreneurship.

Since increases in economy-wide risk decrease the expected utility from entrepreneurship, it follows that increased risk in the African American

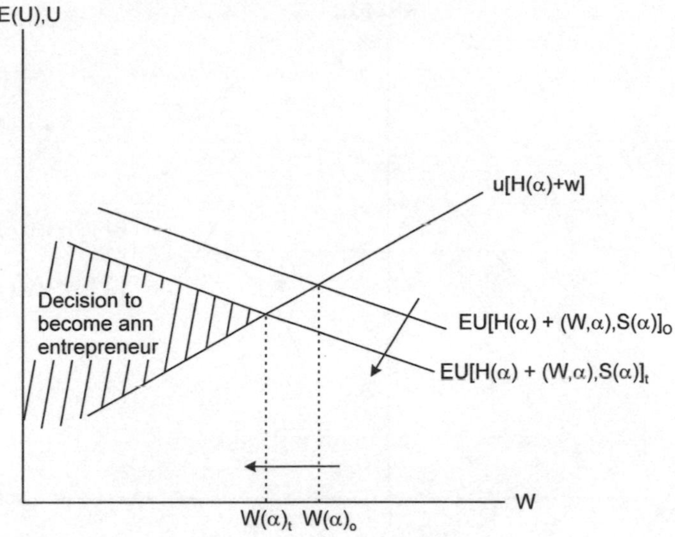

Figure 17.8 Change in area-wide risk and the decision to become an entrepreneur

business environment is associated with a decrease in the number of individuals deciding to become entrepreneurs. It will also, equivalently, lower the certainty equivalent wage at which African Americans will choose employee status in alternative employment (see Figure 17.8).

Proposition 2

If $r\{H(\alpha), I(\alpha)\}_t > (<)\ r\{H(\alpha), I(\alpha)\}_0$ for every I, then $L_t(w, \alpha)$ is lower (higher) at every w then was $L_0(w, \alpha)$.

This means that increases in economy-wide risk reduce the number of workers hired, and decreases in economy-wide risk increase the number of workers hired. By proposition 2, it follows that state-of-nature factors, which increase risk and uncertainty, induce firms to use less labor (i.e., smaller sized firms). This implies fewer firms with paid employees and greater number of firms with no paid employees as r(I) rises for all I. (Note this is not a change in the shape of the risk averse schedule but a *shift* in the schedule due to the impact of external factors for each and every entrepreneurial income I (see Figure 17.9).

CONCLUSION

This paper has sought to demonstrate an inclusive theory of the evolution of black business development. The theory essentially states that the cumu-

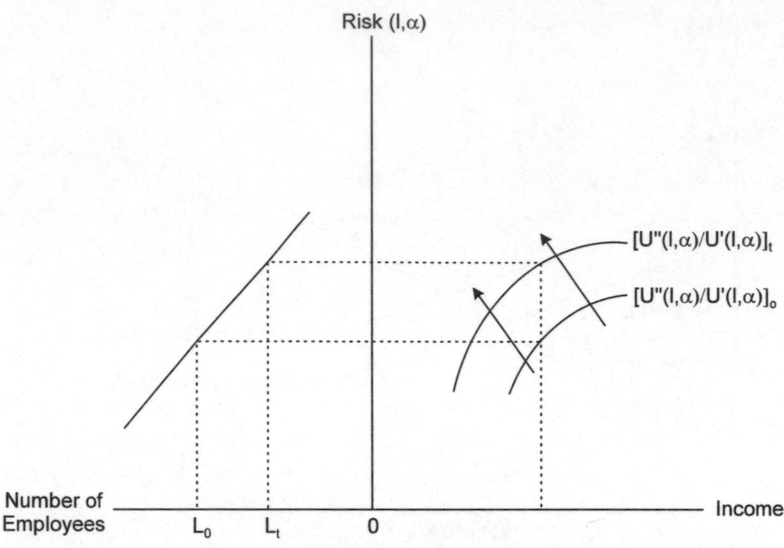

Figure 17.9 Change in area-wide risk and size of firm

lative effects of protracted, intertemporal withholding of demand for black entrepreneurial goods and services constitutes a sufficient condition for obtaining observed outcomes of low-level equilibrium states of low capital formation, low scale of operations, limited learning by doing opportunities, low business formation rates, and high proportion of firms with few or no paid employees. While conventional explanations citing limited capital resources, low operating scale, and competitive disadvantage in managerial experience are clearly correct in explaining contemporaneous low performance of the black business sector, historically these other factors are redundant explanations since permanent states of low demand levels replicated decade after decade must inevitably result in such additional constraints to business development. Thus, these other important ensuing factors are endogenously determined once a relative racial operating scale has been predetermined. The theory emphasizes the finding that the protracted recurrence of insufficient or deliberate withdrawal of demand is itself sufficient in deriving these other co-requisite causes of poor performance. Fundamentally, then, the theory relates the evolution of black business performance to its most essential, antecedent cause.

In the Schumpeterian sense, the historical denial of a meaningful place for the African American entrepreneur has effectively curtailed the central role of the essential catalytic agent and promoter of capital formation, technology adaptation and acquisition. Explorers of new business opportunities crucial to expanding the black-owned business sector will continue to be deterred by the fundamental, low level of demand.

By showing the impact of prolonged demand-withholding as both a barrier to entry issue and an effective tariff on resources, the unavoidable result of higher capital premiums, higher cost structure and lower operating scale were immediately derived. The resulting low operating scale in each succeeding period has replicated in each ensuing period a lower potential maximum rate of output gain compared to the general business sector and therefore comparatively longer operating periods to obtain a given rate of increase in actual output compared to the general business sector. With this diminished access and exposure to technological change and indigenous low operating scale, learning by doing was mitigated, and the diffusion of wide-scale professional development abbreviated.

With the inevitable low revenue stream, higher cost structure, competitive disadvantage to technology enhancement and impaired learning by doing all following on the heels of protracted, limited demand, entrepreneurship as a career choice for African Americans was severely abridged. Even with employment and wage discrimination in the general economy, the opportunity cost of self-employment even for the best prepared individuals was still too high since foregone stochastic, high risk returns to business ownership were viewed as too low compared to the nonstochastic, riskless wage level in the labor market. Until recently, this was especially true for a black middle class buttressed by public-sector employment, unionized manufacturing jobs and teaching.

An optimal control model was also investigated. The model's objective was to maximize the present value of business owners' standard of living while linked to the growth in the value of the firm. Results showed that the optimal growth path for living standard and firm valuation critically depend on a revenue stream and market demand which allows a long-run rate of return greater than that required for terminal point steady-state equilibrium and personal rate of time preference. For all the reasons already discussed, clearly this required rate of return could not be generally sustained across much of the black business sector throughout the periods of the late nineteenth century and most of the twentieth century.

In further considering an environment of risk and uncertainty, within which entrepreneurial choice must be made, the theory consistently predicts that the more risk averse African American will choose to work for majority firms that have not been confined by similar long-term market and resource constraints. With the low, foregone business earnings of the black business sector, the certainty equivalent wage where individuals begin to choose outside employment is lower than it ordinarily would be within a less risky black business environment. Moreover, the overall business climate for black-owned enterprises, which has already factored in the complete effects of weak markets, was shown to result in prohibitive state of nature risks that simultaneously reduce the utility of entrepreneurship and induce existing black-owned firms to hire few or no workers.

NOTES

1 This view has been most notable in Roy F. Lee, *The Setting for Black Business Development* (Ithaca, New York: School of Industrial and Labor Relations, Cornell University, 1973, ch. IV); Lester Thurow, *Poverty and Discrimination*, (Washington, DC: The Brookings Institution, 1969, pp. 117–22); Theodore Cross, *Black Capitalism* (New York: Atheneum, 1969); Theodore Cross, *A White Paper on Black Capitalism* (Boston: Warren, Gorham and Lamont, 1971); Henry Wallich, "The Negro Economy," *Newsweek*, 70, 1967; Carter G. Woodson, *The Story of the Negro Retold*, (Washington, DC: The Associated Press, 1935, pp. 257–71).

2 Cross, *White Paper on Black Capitalism*, p. 27.

3 This use of the tariff concept differs from that of Gary Becker's discrimination coefficient. Becker's use of a discrimination coefficient constitutes a tariff or premium on money wages paid by white employers to compensate white workers to work with black workers; thereby discouraging the hiring of black workers. Here we are investigating tariffs as a premium charged on capital which reduces the real purchasing power of black entrepreneurial capital through the increased cost and difficulty of securing capital funds.

4 Lester Thurow, *Poverty and Discrimination*, p. 123.

5 Paolo Sylos-Labini, *Oligopoly and Technical Progress*, (Cambridge MA: Harvard University Press, 1962); Douglas Needham, *Economic Analysis and Industrial Structure*, (New York: Holt, Rinehart and Winston, 1969, pp. 99–110).

6 Richard Chase and Nicholas Aquilano, *Production and Operations Management* (Homewood, IL: Irwin, 1989, pp. 529–35); Kenneth Arrow, "The Economic Implications of Learning by Doing" *Review of Economic Studies*, 29, 1962: 155–73.

7 Hywel Jones, *An Introduction to Modern Theories of Economic Growth* (New York: McGraw-Hill, 1972, pp. 204–26).

8 M. Kamien and N. Schwartz, *Dynamic Optimization: The Calculus of Variations and Optimal Control in Management and Economics* (New York: North Holland, 1981).

9 Joseph Schumpeter, *The Theory of Economic Development* (Cambridge, MA: Harvard University Press, 1934).

10 Richard Kihlstrom and Jean Laffont. "A General Equilibrium Entrepreneurial Theory of Firm Formation Based on Risk Aversion," *Journal of Political Economy*, 87, 1979: 714–48.

11 Kihlstrom and Laffont, pp. 725–30; David Baron, "Price Uncertainty, Utility and Industry Equilibrium in Pure Competition," *International Economic Review*, 11, October, 1970: 463–80.

18

INSTABILITIES AND ECONOMIC GROWTH IN CONTEMPORARY AFRICA

The role of export price instability

Augustin K. Fosu

I INTRODUCTION

Recent attention has focused on the role of instabilities in the economic performance of contemporary Africa (e.g., Fosu (1992a, 1992b), Fosu (1991), Gyimah-Brempong (1991)). The present study attempts to advance the existing literature by examining the extent to which export price instability might influence economic growth in sub-Saharan Africa.

The above studies have revealed that instabilities have generally been deleterious to economic growth in Africa. These include capital and political instabilities (Fosu (1991), Fosu (1992b)). There have been conflicting findings as to the role of export instability (EI), however. For example, Gyimah-Brempong (1991) reveals an adverse influence of EI on GDP growth for sub-Saharan African countries over the 1960–86 period. In contrast, Fosu (1992a) uncovers little evidence in support of this conclusion over the 1970–86 period for either sub-Saharan Africa or Africa at large, although the study reveals a substantial negative impact for non-African countries over the same period.

Fosu (1991) observes that it is the path of capital formation that ultimately matters. That is, EI is consequential for economic growth only if it is transmitted into capital instability (CI). There is no guarantee that such a transmission is automatic, however, "since substantial portions of export proceeds may be channelled into consumption rather than investment" (p. 82). Indeed, for the 1967–86 period, the author observes a substantial negative influence of CI on GDP growth in Sub-Saharan Africa but finds little evidence in support of EI.

Since export price is generally outside the control of an individual country, it is important to examine the degree to which its fluctuations may influence economic performance. Might these fluctuations be translated into CI, and hence into economic growth, for example? Or, is there an independent transmission mechanism? Such an examination should provide useful information for the ongoing debate regarding the external implications for economic development in (African) less developed countries (LDCs).

We begin by presenting in section II a set of theoretical propositions regarding the consequences of export price instability. In section III, the empirical model is specified and the data used in the analysis described. The model is then estimated and the results presented in section IV. Section V concludes the paper.

II THEORETICAL PROPOSITIONS

Export price instability (XPI) may influence economic growth directly, independently of the levels of the arguments of the production function, or indirectly via its effects on the functional arguments themselves. The latter can be categorized into two mechanisms. The first is that instability in the export price would reduce overall investment in the economy by increasing the uncertainty in export proceeds as potential sources for investment. To demonstrate this route, we note that

$$r = p + x \tag{18.1}$$

where r, p, and x are the revenue, price, and quantity of exports, respectively, expressed in logarithms. Then

$$\mathrm{Var}(r) = \mathrm{Var}(p) + \mathrm{Var}(x) + 2\mathrm{Cov}(p, x) \tag{18.2}$$

where Var and Cov are variance and covariance, respectively, of the variables indicated. Thus, unless the covariance between p and x is negative with a sufficiently large magnitude, we should expect an increase in XPI (higher Var(p)) to raise the overall export proceeds instability (higher Var(r)). Hence, a higher XPI should reduce the reliability of export proceeds as potential investment funds. That is, by decreasing the reliability of export proceeds as investment funds, XPI might encourage the use of export proceeds for consumption rather than investment. This would be an indirect effect, with the impact of XPI channelled through the level of investment. To facilitate the exposition, we label this proposition as:

Proposition 1

XPI reduces economic growth by decreasing overall investment in the economy.

The second "indirect" mechanism is via exports. Suppose export price constitutes a significant part of the returns to investment in exports. Then an increase in XPI should lower the level of investment in the export sector and, therefore, the level of exports, assuming investors are risk-averse. Thus, overall output growth would be reduced partly because exports are a subset of output and partly because there may be additional positive differential effects of exports as advocated by many (Fosu 1990, Balassa 1985, Ram 1985, Feder 1982, Tyler 1981, Balassa 1978, Michaeli 1977, Maizels 1968, Emery 1967). We term this as:

Proposition 2

XPI reduces economic growth by decreasing the volume of exports.

Alternatively, XPI can "directly" influence output, given the levels of the production inputs. That is, XPI may be translated into CI,[1] which affects output "directly" through its negative impacts on the efficiency of the production process (Fosu 1991). We label this as:

Proposition 3

XPI reduces economic growth by increasing CI.

Whether the above propositions hold empirically or not will depend on the validity of the critical assumptions underlying them. For example, Proposition 1 assumes that XPI increases consumption rather than investment. To evaluate the implication of this assumption, consider a two-period model where all consumption in the second period results from investment in the first. Then, the above proposition implies that in the face of sufficiently high XPI, the given economy is willing to suffer a decrease in consumption during the second period, or that sources other than export proceeds exist for providing investment funds for the first period. Whether either or both conditions hold, however, is an empirical question.

Proposition 2 critically depends on the assumption that economic agents are risk-averse. This may not be the case, however, since agents could be expected-income maximizers and hence risk-neutral. If so, then exports and XPI would not be inversely related.

Proposition 3 suggests that CI increases with XPI. For this to be the case, first, export proceeds must constitute a significant portion of investment funds; and second, XPI must significantly increase the instability in the portion of capital derivable from exports. This CI–XPI relationship would therefore be weakened if either of these conditions fails.

III MODEL SPECIFICATION AND DATA DESCRIPTION

To test the above propositions, we postulate for a given country the following augmented production function, with XPI entering both directly and indrectly, consistent with the above propositions:

$$Q = Q[L, K(I); X(I), I] \qquad 18.3$$

where Q is real aggregate output; L and K are the respective traditional production functional arguments of labor and capital; X denotes exports, and I is the export price instability. Equation 18.3 is a version of the production function used in Fosu (1991). Whereas L and K are the traditional arguments of the production function, X is intended to capture international forces influencing Q but not reflected in L or K. These include economies of scale and the need to adopt relatively efficient technologies due to the larger international market (Emery 1967: 471).

Propositions 1 and 2 are represented by expressing K and X in equation 18.3 as partial functions of I, respectively, with the partial derivatives $K'(I)$ and $X'(I)$ expected to be negative. Expressing Q as a direct function of I is intended to reflect Proposition 3, which postulates a negative effect of XPI on Q independent of L, K, or X, but through CI.

We assume XPI, defined as the perturbation of export price about its trend, is generated by demand and supply shocks outside the control of a given country. That is, each nation is assumed to be sufficiently small such that its actions have little influence on the movement in export prices; thus export perturbations are externally induced.[2] Hence, it seems appropriate to consider XPI as exogenous.

Based on equation 18.1, the following “growth-form” equation can be estimated:[3]

$$Q^* = a + bL^* + cK^* + dX^* + eI + u \qquad 18.4$$

where a variable with an asterisk denotes the respective growth rate; a, b, c, d, and e are coefficients to be estimated, and u is the respective stochastic perturbation term. Under Propositions 1 and 2, K^* and X^* are endogenous with respect to I. We shall first estimate equation 18.4 directly on the assumption that K^* and X^* are exogenous and then directly test these two propositions separately. Proposition 3 implies that e is negative.

Except for data for L, which derive from World Bank (1988), all data for estimating equation 18.4 are drawn from World Bank (1989). All variables are measured over the 1967–86 period for each country in the sample. Q^*, L^*, and X^* are measured as the mean annual growth rates of real GDP, the labor force, and real exports (goods and non-factor services), respectively. To appropriately account for unit differences across countries and over time, and consistent with standard practice (e.g., Fosu (1990: fn. 11) and Ram (1985: fn. 6), K^* is measured as the gross domestic investment as a proportion of GDP.

Instability variables employed in the present analysis are calculated as:

$$I = \mathrm{Min}(I_1, I_2, I_3) \qquad 18.5$$

where $I_s (s = 1, 2, 3)$ is the prediction standard error of the estimated trend based on the linear, quadratic, and exponential specification, respectively. That is,

$$I_s = \left[\left\{ \sum_{t=1}^{T} (Z_t - Z_{st})^2 \right\} / df \right]^{1/2} \quad s = 1, 2, 3 \qquad 18.6$$

where z_t is the value of the respective variable for the tth period; Z_{st} is the predicted value of z_t based on the linear ($s = 1$), quadratic ($s = 2$), or exponential ($s = 3$) specification.; T is the sample period; and df is the degrees of freedom, which equal ($T - 2$) for the lincar and exponential, and ($T - 3$) for the quadratic. The choice of the minimum prediction error is intended to insure that the underlying trend is appropriately eliminated, since otherwise a country with a more rapid growth in a given variable would be shown to spuriously exhibit greater instability (Massell, 1970).

The main instability variable of interest here is the export price instability (XPI), which is calculated for each country in the sample over the 1967–86 period using the World Bank's annual export price index. We briefly describe the behavior of XPI across countries. The minimum (7.60) and maximum (21.77) values of XPI are exhibited by Botswana and the Sudan, respectively. Botswana's XPI value is more than one standard deviation below the mean of the sample, whereas Sudan's exceeds the mean by over two standard deviations. Hence XPI is rather well dispersed, with a standard deviation of 4.07. XPI is also positively skewed, with extreme values to the right of the distribution displayed by Mauritius and Burundi in addition to the Sudan.

Export instability (EI) and capital instability (CI) are additionally computed in order to observe any relationship of XPI with these other forms of instability. In particular, a direct test of Proposition 3 would involve observing if a positive correlation exists between CI and XPI. EI and CI are computed similarly as XPI but using real exports (goods and nonfactor services) and gross domestic investment respectively, both expressed as proportions of GDP in order to neutralize unit differences across countries and over time (Fosu 1991).

IV ESTIMATION AND RESULTS

Due to data availability constraints and the need for comparison with the above instability studies on Africa, equation 18.4 was estimated over the 1967–86 period for a sample of thirty-one Sub-Saharan African countries, listed in the appendix, for which complete data existed. The estimation was performed separately using OLS on the assumption that the error term u was i.i.d. To provide some support for this assumption, and considering the cross-section nature of the analysis, tests for heteroscedasticity using the Bartlett likelihood ratio statistic were performed. Results from estimating the entire and constrained versions of the equation are reported in Table 18.1.

Table 18.1 Export price instability and economic growth in Sub-Saharan Africa, 1967–86. Regression results: estimated coefficients and summary statistics (absolute value of the t ratio in parentheses)

	(1)	*(2)*	*(3)*	*(4)*
L*	0.040	−0.078	0.581	0.466
	(0.06)	(0.11)	(1.14)	(0.91)
K*	0.263[a]	0.280[a]	0.078	0.095
	(4.39)	(4.46)	(1.37)	(1.63)
X*	–	–	0.360[a]	0.359[a]
			(5.02)	(5.05)
XPI	–	0.094	–	0.090
		(0.92)		(1.22)
C	−1.70	−2.95	−.384	−1.58
R^2	.422	.440	.701	.717
Adj.R^2	.381	.378	.668	.673
SEE	2.15	2.15	1.57	1.56
B	0.516	0.615	0.125	0.377

Notes: The dependent variable is Q*, GDP growth, measured as the mean annual percentage GDP growth rate; L* is the mean annual percentage growth rate of the labor force; K* denotes the growth of capital, measured as the mean annual gross domestic investment as a percentage of GDP; X* is the annual percentage growth rate of real exports (goods plus non-factor services). XPI is the export price instability, measured as the standard error of the export price index from trend (see the text for details). Data for L* are from World Bank (1988); all other data are from World Bank (1989). C is the constant (intercept) term. R^2, Adj.R^2, and SEE are the usual regression statistics. The sample size (number of countries) is 31. B is the likelihood ratio statistic to test for heteroscedasticity, and it is distributed as chi-square with 2 degrees of freedom for all equations

[a] Significant at the 0.01 level (two-tailed)

With reference to Table 18.1, we first note from the Bartlett likelihood ratio test statistic (B) that there is no evidence to support the existence of heteroscedasticity in any of the specifications,[4] thus lending some credence to the assumption of u in equation 18.4 as i.i.d. Column (1) of Table 18.1 contains estimates of the traditional neoclassical model, and column (2) augments this specification with XPI. We note that the coefficient of XPI is insignificant, so that XPI is independently inconsequential for GDP growth. Using the usual augmented model with exports in the production function, as in equations 18.3 and 18.4, similarly reveals little independent influence of XPI on economic growth (column 4). Indeed, the coefficient of XPI is positive in both specifications, though statistically insignificant. Thus, there appears to be no empirical support for Proposition 3 advocating a "direct" adverse effect of XPI on economic growth.

Table 18.2 reports summary statistics of the regression variables as well as the measures of EI and CI. It additionally presents zero-order correlations of XPI with respect to these variables, in order to shed additional light on the impact of XPI on economic growth.

Table 18.2 Export price instability and economic growth in Sub-Saharan Africa, 1967–86. Summary statistics of variables and zero-order correlation coefficients of export price instability vs other variables

	Mean	*Standard deviation*	*Correlation Coefficient (with XPI)*
Q*	3.47	2.73	−0.041
L*	2.29	0.59	0.114
K*	19.29	6.72	−0.260
X*	2.79	5.22	−0.184
XPI	12.60	4.07	1.000
EI	3.56	1.65	0.192
CI	4.16	2.21	−0.078

Notes: EI = Export (volume) instability; CI = Capital instability; all other variables are defined in Table 18.1

First, we note that the correlation coefficient of XPI with respect to GDP growth Q*, although negative, is rather insignificant (t = −0.22), so that there appears to be little correlation between XPI and economic growth overall, that is, without controlling for production inputs. Furthermore, the correlation coefficient of XPI with CI is negative and rather insignificant (t = −0.42). Thus, there is no evidence in support of Proposition 3 that XPI would adversely influence economic growth via augmenting CI. This result then is in concert with our finding reported in Table 18.1 that XPI does not exercise an independent influence on GDP growth.

Second, the correlation coefficient is negative with respect to both K* and X*, suggesting that Propositions 1 and 2 might be supportable. Nevertheless, with respective ratios of 1.45 and 1.01, the present evidence is rather weak. Research is currently underway to estimate the XPI effect on K* and X* in a multiple regression framework, in order to better assess the "indirect effect" of XPI on economic growth.[5]

V CONCLUDING REMARKS

The present paper has attempted to investigate the possible effects of export price instability (XPI), defined as the variance of export price around trend, on economic growth in sub-Saharan Africa. Both "direct" and "indirect" impacts of XPI were examined in the form of three theoretical propositions. Results from analyzing 1967–1986 data for a sample of 31 countries in an augmented production function framework did not confirm the proposition of a negative direct effect. While evidence supporting the propositions of the adverse indirect effects of XPI is weak, this result is rather preliminary, and additional empirical investigation is in order.

NOTES

1 For this to be the case we must assume that XPI is translated into export revenue instability as in Proposition 1 and then into CI.

2 Except for very few countries which may exercise some monopoly power in some commodities, this assumption is generally reasonable; see, for example, Svedberg (1991).

3 A model similar to equation 18.4 is estimated in Fosu (1991).

4 With three groupings of the sample, B is distributed as chi-square with two degrees of freedom under the null hypothesis of homoscedasticity, which we fail to reject even at the relatively large risk of type one error of 0.30 with an associated critical value of 2.41. (For details see, for example, Kmenta (1986: pp. 297–8).)

5 Other measures of XPI: the minimum standard error deflated by the mean export price and the minimum mean absolute percentage error, similarly measured as above, yielded results similar to the ones reported here.

REFERENCES

Balassa, Bela, "Exports and Economic Growth: Further Evidence," *Journal of Development Economics* 5 (1978), 181–9.

——,"Exports, Policy Choices, and Economic Growth in Developing Countries after the 1973 Oil Shock," *Journal of Development Economics* 18 (1985), 23–35.

Bhagwati, Jagdish, *Foreign Trade Regimes and Economic Development: Anatomy and Consequences of Exchange Control regimes* (Cambridge, MA: Ballinger, 1978).

Emery, Robert F., "The Relation of Exports and Economic Growth," *Kyklos* 20, no. 2 (1967), 470–86.

Feder, Gershon. "On Exports and Economic Growth," *Journal of Development Economics* 12 (1982), 59–73.

Fosu, A.K., "Exports and Economic Growth: The African Case," *World Development* vol. 18, no. 6 (June, 1990), 831–5.

——,"Capital Instability and Economic Growth in Sub-Saharan Africa," *Journal of Development Studies* vol. 28, no. 1 (October, 1991), 74–85.

——, "Effect of Export Instability on Economic Growth in Africa," *Journal of Developing Areas* vol. 26, no. 3 (April, 1992a), 323–32.

——,"Political Instability and Economic Growth: Evidence from Sub-Saharan Africa," *Economic Development and Cultural Change* vol. 40, no. 4 (July, 1992b), 829–41.

Gyimah-Brempong, K., "Export Instability and Economic Growth in Sub-Saharan Africa," *Economic Development and Cultural Change* vol. 39, no. 4 (July, 1991), 815–28.

Kmenta, Jan, *Elements of Econometrics* (New York, Macmillan, 2nd. ed, 1986).

Maizels, Alfred, *Exports and Economic Growth in Developing Countries* (London: Cambridge University Press, 1968).

Massell, Benton E., "Export Instability and Economic Structure," *American Economic Review* vol. 32 (September, 1970), 618–30.

Michaeli, Michael, "Exports and Growth: An Empirical Investigation," *Journal of Development Economics* 4 (1977), 49–53.

Ram, Rati, "Exports and economic Growth: Some Additional Evidence," *Economic Development and Cultural Change* vol. 33, no. 2 (1985), 415–42.

Svedberg, Peter, "The Export Performance of Sub-Saharan Africa," *Economic Development and Cultural Change* vol. 39, no. 3 (April, 1991), 548–66.

Tyler, William G. "Growth and Export Expansion in Developing Countries," *Journal of Development Economics* 9 (1981), 121–30.

World Bank, *World Development Report, 1988* (New York: Oxford University Press), 1988.

World Bank, *World Tables, 1988–89* (Baltimore, MD: Johns Hopkins University Press), 1989.

APPENDIX: SAMPLE OF SUB-SAHARAN AFRICAN COUNTRIES

Benin
Botswana
Burundi
Cameroon
Central African Republic
Congo
Cote d'Ivoire
Ethiopia
Ghana
Guinea
Kenya
Lesotho
Liberia
Madagascar
Malawi
Mali
Mauritania
Mauritius
Niger
Nigeria
Rwanda
Senegal
Sierra Leone
Somalia
Sudan
Tanzania
Togo
Uganda
Zaire
Zambia
Zimbabwe

19

MACROECONOMIC POLICY, CYCLICAL FLUCTUATION, AND INCOME INEQUALITY

Some cointegration results

Willie J. Belton, Jr.

INTRODUCTION

Since the late 1950s, there has been significant concern over the impact of income inequality on the American economic landscape. Among other things this concern manifested itself in the Kennedy–Johnson Great Society programs of the 1960s and their objective to reduce poverty in the United States. In retrospect, many modern economists argue that these programs failed to have much impact on the economic conditions of the poor and unskilled in the United States. Moreover, many politicians, economists, and other public figures of the Reagan–Bush era argue that the Great Society programs were directly responsible for increasing the number of Americans who have become dependent on government. They argue that the programs created reverse incentives and encouraged behavior which has reduced upward mobility.

The two opposing views of the Great Society programs have not gone unnoticed by the academic profession. However, the research in this area has taken on a more general focus in that the impact of general federal governmental policy on income inequality has usually been examined. For example, Danziger, Haveman, and Plotnick (1981) and Burtless (1990) have studied the impact of fiscal policy on the size distribution of income. Given that government policy is clearly related to the cyclical behavior of the economy, other economists such as Metcalf (1972), Beach (1976), Blinder and Esaki (1978), and Haslag and Slottje (1994) have examined the impact of business cycle fluctuations on the distribution of income.

This research represents an extension of the Beach and Blinder and Esaki work and provides somewhat more structure to the work of Haslag and Slottje. It is different from previous research in that it examines the long-term relationship among economic variables which are alleged to explain variations in inequality. To estimate this long-term relationship, the *method of cointegration* is employed. This relatively recent statistical method was initially developed by Granger and Weiss (1983) and was later extended by Engle and Granger (1987), Granger (1986), Johansen (1988), Johansen and Juselius (1990), and Stock and Watson (1988).

THE MODEL

The income distribution literature, unlike most other areas of research in economics, is not filled with a large number of models that have been tested and established as the "conventional wisdom" in the field. The scarcity of econometric research in this area stems very likely from the fact that, from about 1950 through 1970 the income distribution was stable, and the growth in output per worker was so large this era has become known as the "golden age" (Maddison 1987). The studies that were undertaken over this period, for the most part, were primarily focused on income inequality at a given point in time and consequently employed cross-section econometric methodologies. It was not until the middle 1960s and the work of Miller (1966) and Schultz (1969) that some trend analysis of inequality was attempted. The reason for such slow progress along the time series dimension was the absence of data sets that would support such analysis.

The variables which have been included in most studies of income distribution fall into three categories: demographic, economic conditions, and public policy. The inclusion of demographic variables such as age, educational composition of the potential labor force, and female share of labor force have been extensively justified on theoretical grounds by Welch (1969) and Mincer (1970) and are included in most models. Blinder and Esaki (1978) reveal that measures of business conditions such as inflation and unemployment help to explain variations in income inequality. Haslag and Talyor (1993), Haslag and Slottje (1994), Danziger, Haveman, and Plotnick (1981) and Burtless (1990) have all argued that macroeconomic policy in general, and fiscal policy in particular, should have a significant impact on income inequality.

There are several available measures of income inequality; however for this study the Theil entropy measure is used.[1] This measure is employed because of the need, when estimating by cointegration, for a time series of significant length.[2] The Theil entropy index is derived as follows:

$$T(y,n) = (1/n)\sum_{j=1}^{n}(y_j/\mu)\ln(y_j/\mu) \qquad 19.1$$

where n is the number of equal-sized population groups, y denotes income for population group j, and μ is average income (that is $\mu = \sum_{j=1}^{n} y_j/n$).[3] The Theil index is defined to take on values greater than or equal to zero and as the index increase in value income inequality increases. Figure 19.1 reveals that the Theil index has generally increased across the 1952–89

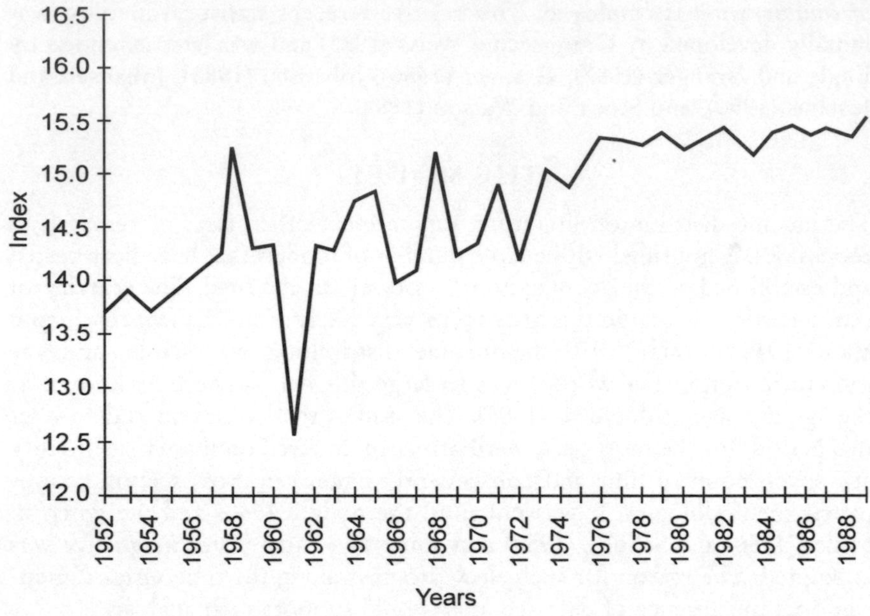

Figure 19.1 Theil index for adjusted gross income, 1952–89

period. Haslag and Taylor (1993) argue that Bluestone and Harrison's (1988) argument regarding workers falling into the low wage stratum following a U-turn may be incorrect. They suggest that income inequality has steadily increased since the 1950s, and no evidence of a U-turn can be found in the data.[4]

Given the discussion above, the following model generally captures the essence of most of the discussion in the literature:

$$T_t = b_0 + b_1(Age_t) + b_2(ED_t) + b_3(FMS_t) + b_4(Tax_t) + b_5(GDP_t) + b_6(P_t) + b_7(Trans_t) + b_8(D_t) + b_9(MP_t) + v_t \qquad 19.2$$

where T_t is the Theil index, Age_t is the population between 15 and 25 divided by population over 16, less those over 65, ED_t is the percentage of population over 25 with four or more years of college completed, FMS_t is the total number of employed women as a percentage of the total labor force, Tax_t is the marginal personal income tax rate, GDP_t is real gross domestic product, P_t is the inflation rate, $Trans_t$ is real transfer payment paid to individuals by federal, state, and local governments, D_t is the real federal deficit as measured by the National Income and Product Accounts, and MP_t is a monetary policy proxy.

The age variable included in equation 19.2 provides the only proxy for labor market experience. O'Neill (1985) provides evidence of the importance of experience premiums in that workers with more experience tend to demand and garner higher salaries. Given this fact, one would expect an increase in the average age, i.e., average labor market experience of the work force should lead to lower income inequality.

Freeman (1976), Levy and Michel (1987), and others have examined the impact of education on income inequality. Most of this research suggests that the education premium garnered by college graduates is indeed an important determinant of income inequality. However, as the average education level of the labor force increases across time, the premium paid for education should have less of an impact on inequality.

Traditionally women have been employed in lower-end jobs which pay less. O'Neill (1985) and others have examined the gender difference and found that as women have become more educated and are a larger part of the work force, the difference in earnings between males and females has started to narrow. However, in a time series setting, the increase in the number of women in the labor force could have an unclear impact on inequality. For example, if women are entering the labor force in large numbers in low-end jobs, then this may increase inequality. Conversely, if the women entering the labor force are more highly educated than the average labor force participant, then this may tend to lower income inequality.

The income tax system of the US is progressive, implying that those with higher incomes pay higher taxes. The net impact of an increase in taxes under such a system should be a reduction in inequality. However, the extent of progressivity of the US tax system is open to question.

Blinder and Esaki (1978) argue that some measure of business conditions should be included in the model to explain variations in inequality. Clearly, GDP represents one such measure in that, as national income increases, one might expect inequality to decrease since increases in output increase the demand for labor. Conversely, economic downturns hurt low-end workers more since they are more likely to experience unemployment. Inflation is also included in the model as a measure of business conditions because higher inflation rates tend to benefit borrowers at the expense of lenders. Hence, inflation would tend to have redistribution effects, i.e., inflation should affect the income distribution over time.

Haslag and Slottje (1994) suggest that policy variables should be included in the model to examine the redistributive power of government action. They argue that fiscal policy actions may affect inequality in a "program specific" manner in the sense that some programs of the fiscal type may affect the size distribution of income while other programs may not. Following Haslag and Slottje (1994), two measures of fiscal policy are employed in this study. First, the federal deficit measure as the most comprehensive measure of fiscal policy is employed. Secondly, Danziger, Haveman and Plotnik (1981) show that transfer payments affect the level of inequality, and in effect the size distribution of income should also be included. Blanchard and Fisher (1989) argue that monetary policy can also affect the size distribution of income because some economic agents cannot immediately respond to monetary shocks. Given the Blanchard and Fisher argument, narrowly defined money, M_1, is used as a monetary policy variable.[5]

In what follows, the method of cointegration is described in detail, and the model above is employed to examine the long-term impact of each variable on the Theil index. Given that public policy variables are clearly under the control of government, following Haslag and Slottje (1994), special attention is given to the impact of public policy on income inequality.

THE METHOD OF COINTEGRATION

Traditional time series methods require variables to be stationary. Because macroeconomics time series display some trend, researchers are often forced to first-difference variables before they can be used to test models. Such differencing removes much of the long-term trend characteristics of the data. If a variable becomes stationary only after first-differencing, then the variable is said to be integrated of order one and is denoted by "1(1)." However, if two variables are non-stationary in levels individually, but a linear combination of the variables is actually stationary in levels, then the variables are said to be cointegrated.

Tests for cointegration, such as those proposed by Engle and Granger (1987), Johansen and Juselius (1990) and Stock and Watson (1988), are all multivariate extensions of the unit root test developed by Dickey and Fuller (1979). The Dickey–Fuller test entails estimating the following regression:

$$\Delta x_t = b_0 + b_1 x_{t-1} + b_2 t + \sum_{j=1}^{p} g_j \Delta x_{t-j} + e_t \qquad 19.3$$

where x_t is the time series variable in question, t is a deterministic time trend variable, and p is large enough to ensure that the e_t is white noise. The test statistic examines the significance of b_1. The null hypothesis is that x_t is l(1). The null hypothesis is rejected if the estimated b_1 is negative and significantly different from zero.

After determining the order of integration of each variable, the cointegration test can be performed. The Engle–Granger test relies on a super convergence result and uses OLS to obtain estimates of the cointegrating vector. The problem with this approach is that the estimate will differ with the arbitrary selection of the dependent variable in the regression equation. In effect, different normalization schemes can alter the Engle–Granger result. By contrast, the Johansen–Juselius procedure yields maximum likelihood estimates of the cointegrating relationship and allows one to test for more than one cointegrating vector. Moreover, the Johansen–Juselius procedure does not rely on arbitrary normalization.

To implement the Johansen–Juselius procedure, consider the following model:

$$\mathbf{X}_t = \mathbf{\Omega}_1\mathbf{X}_{t-1} + \ldots + \mathbf{\Omega}_k\mathbf{X}_{t-k} + \mathbf{e}_t \quad (t = 1 \ldots T) \qquad 19.4$$

where $\mathbf{X}_t$ is a sequence of random vectors with components $(X_{1t} \ldots, X_{pt})$. The innovations $\mathbf{e}_1 \ldots \mathbf{e}_T$ are drawn from a p-dimensional i.i.d Gaussian distribution with covariance Λ, and $X_{k+1}, \ldots X_0$ fixed. Given that most macroeconomic time series are non-stationary in levels, VAR models such as equation 19.4 must be estimated in first-differences. This approach satisfies fundamental times series requirements but not without the cost of losing valuable information about the potential long-term relationship among the series.

Allowing Δ to represent the first difference operator, Johansen and Juselius (1990) suggest writing equation 19.4 in the following form:

$$\Delta\mathbf{X}_t = \mathbf{\Gamma}_1\Delta\mathbf{X}_{t-1} + \cdots + \mathbf{\Gamma}_{k-1}\Delta\mathbf{X}_{t-k+1} - \mathbf{\Omega}\mathbf{X}_{t-k} + \mathbf{e}_t \qquad 19.5$$

where

$$\mathbf{\Gamma}_i = -\mathbf{I} + \mathbf{\Omega}_1 + \cdots + \mathbf{\Omega}_i \quad (i = 1, \ldots, k-1) \qquad 19.6$$

and

$$\mathbf{\Omega} = \mathbf{I} - \mathbf{\Omega}_1 - \ldots - \mathbf{\Omega}_k \qquad 19.7$$

Equation 19.5 is essentially a standard first-difference VAR model. The major innovation of cointegration is the addition to equation 19.5 of the term $\mathbf{\Omega}\mathbf{X}_{t-k}$, which is the multivariate representation of b_1 of the Dickey-Fuller unit root test. The $\mathbf{\Omega}$ matrix conveys information about the long-term relationship among the X variables. The eigenvalues of $\mathbf{\Omega}$ are computed to determine the number of linearly independent columns and rows. If the rank of $\mathbf{\Omega}$ is full, p, then any linear combinations of the X variables will be stationary. Conversely, if the elements in $\mathbf{\Omega}$ are all zeros, then any combination of the X variables will be a unit root and, therefore, non-stationary. In most cases, $\mathbf{\Omega}$ is neither full rank nor a matrix of zeros, i.e., $0 < rank(\mathbf{\Omega}) = r < p$, where r is the number of cointegrating relationships. It is this intermediate case that provides the most interesting results. If the $\mathbf{\Omega}$ matrix is not full rank but greater than zero, then $\mathbf{\Omega} = \boldsymbol{\alpha\beta}$, where $\boldsymbol{\alpha}$ is a matrix of error correction parameters and $\boldsymbol{\beta}$ is the matrix of cointegrating vectors.

In what follows, the Johansen–Juselius procedure and the two recommended tests for cointegration, the *maximum eigenvalue* and *trace* tests, are used to examine the relationship among: the Theil index, T_t, the working population between the ages of 15 to 25 as a percentage of the total labor force, Age_t; the percentage of population over 25 with four or more years of college, ED_t; total number of employed women divided by the total labor force, FMS_t; the marginal personal income tax rate, Tax_t; the real gross domestic product, GDP_t; the inflation rate, P_t; real transfer payment paid to individuals by federal, state, and local governments, $Trans_t$; the federal deficit as measured by the National Income and Product Accounts, D_t; and the monetary policy proxy, M_{1t}.

EMPIRICAL ESTIMATION

To proceed with the estimation, the Dickey–Fuller unit root test is applied to each of the time series. Equation 19.3 is estimated using each of the ten variables. The results of the test can be found in Table 19.1. For nine of the ten variables in the analysis, the Dickey–Fuller test indicates stationarity in first differences.[6] This result is not surprising since most economic time series are differenced-stationary. However, the age variable, Age_t, proved to be stationary in levels and had to be dropped from the analysis.

To implement the Johansen–Juselius cointegration test, the order of a VAR system of nine equations must be identified. To determine the lag length necessary to provide a reasonable specification, an F-test is per-

Table 19.1 Augmented Dickey–Fuller test for a unit root, estimation interval: 1952–89 (annual data)

Variables	t_μ *2 lags*	t_τ *2 lags*	*First Difference*	t_μ
T_t	−2.06	−3.40	ΔT_t	−5.68*
Age_t	−2.47		ΔAge_t	
ED_t	−1.65	−1.85	ΔED_t	−8.27*
FMS_t	−1.98	−2.60	ΔFMS_t	−6.46*
Tax_t	−1.68	−2.30	ΔTax_t	−4.31*
GDP_t	−0.95	−1.91	ΔGDP_t	−4.56*
P_t	−1.67	−1.73	ΔP_t	−2.40*
D_t	−1.98	−2.27	ΔD_t	−4.02*
$Trans_t$	−2.06	−2.37	$\Delta Trans_t$	−3.40*
$M1t$	−1.79	−2.07	ΔM_{1t}	−2.40*

Notes:
T_t = Theil index
Age_t = The working age population between 15 and 25 as a percentage of the total labor force minus 65 and over
ED_t = Percentage of population over 25 with four or more years of college.
FMS_t = Number of women in the labor force divided by the total labor force
Tax_t = Marginal federal income tax rate
GDP_t = Real Gross Domestic Product
P_t = Inflation Calculated from the CPI for urban consumers.
D_t = Real Federal Deficit
$Trans_t$ = Transfer payments from the Federal, State, and Local Governments
M_{1t}^* Indicates rejection of the null hypothesis at the 95% confidence level.
Critical values: $t_\mu(t = 100) = -2.89$, $t_\tau\ (t = 100) = -3.45$

formed.[7] Two sets of residuals are computed for the nine variable system. The first set arises from nine OLS regressions of the first differences of each variable on two lagged differences of each series and a constant. The second series of residuals arises from nine OLS regressions of lagged levels of the nine series and a column of ones on the same lagged differences. The following equation systems are estimated:

$$\Delta \boldsymbol{X}_t = \boldsymbol{B}_0 + \boldsymbol{B}_1 \Delta \boldsymbol{X}_{t-1} + \boldsymbol{B}_2 \Delta \boldsymbol{X}_{t-2} + \varepsilon_{it} \quad 19.8$$

$$\boldsymbol{X}_{t-1} = \boldsymbol{B}_0 + \boldsymbol{B}_1 \Delta \boldsymbol{X}_{t-1} + \boldsymbol{B}_2 \Delta \boldsymbol{X}_{t-2} + \zeta_{it} \quad 19.9$$

where $\boldsymbol{X}_t$ is a sequence of random vectors with components $T_t, ED_t, FMS_t, Tax_t, GDP_t, P_t, Trans_t, D_t, M_{1t}$ and $VONE_t$.[8] The canonical correlations of the two sets of residuals, (ϵ_{it}) and (ζ_{it}), are calculated. Eigenvalues generated from this process, which are squared canonical correlations, are employed in the *maximum eigenvalue* and *trace* tests developed by Johansen and Juselius (1990).

The calculation of the *maximum eigenvalue* and *trace* tests are straightforward once eigenvalues are derived. If the number of co-integrating vectors is denoted by r, the *trace* test for Ho: $r = 0$ is computed from $(-n)\sum_{i=1}^{r}\ln(1-\lambda_i)$, where n is the sample size and λ_i refers to the eigenvalues described above. Dropping the largest eigenvalue from this calculation permits a test of $r \leqslant 1$. To test Ho: $r = 0$ in the *maximum eigenvalue* test, we compute $(-n)\ln(1-\lambda_1)$, where λ_1 is the largest eigenvalue. To compute $r = 1$, the second largest eigenvalue is used.

Table II reports the results of the cointegration test. The *maximum eigenvalue* and *trace* test statistics are reported to determine the number of cointegrating vectors. The *trace* test allows evaluation of the null hypothesis that there are r or fewer co-integrating vectors against a general alternative. The *maximum eigenvalue* test evaluates the null hypothesis $r = 0$ against the alternative $r \leqslant 1$. Turning first to the results from the *trace* test, in Table 19.2, it is clear that the nulls $r = 0$, $r \leqslant 1$, $r \leqslant 2$, $r \leqslant 3$, $r \leqslant 4$, $r \leqslant 5$, $r \leqslant 6$, and $r \leqslant 7$ are rejected at the 99% confidence level.

The *maximum eigenvalue* test provides an alternative check to the *trace* test for the number of cointegrated variables. Johansen and Juselius (1990) note that the maximum eigenvalue test is more reliable than the trace test in identifying the number of co-integrated variables. The result of the *maximum eigenvalue* test in Table 19.2 reveals that the null of $r = 0$, and $r \leqslant 1$, $r \leqslant 2$, $r \leqslant 3$, $r \leqslant 4$, $r \leqslant 5$, $r \leqslant 6$, and $r \leqslant 7$ are rejected at the 99% level. These test results strongly suggest that a reliable long-term relationship exists (excluding Age_t) among the variables in equation 19.2.

To provide economic meaning to the estimated vectors, the cointegrated vectors are normalized by dividing each vector by its value of the reported Thiel index coefficient. This normalization yields the following long-run model:

Table 19.2 Maximum eigenvalue and trace test for the inequality model, estimation interval: 1952–89 (annual data)

	Max eigenvalue		*Trace*	
	λ_{max}	λ_{max}	*trace*	*trace*
		(0.99)		(0.99)
$r \leqslant 7$	24.26*	20.20	25.15**	24.60
$r \leqslant 6$	33.86*	26.81	62.65*	41.06
$r \leqslant 5$	44.55*	33.24	106.05*	60.159
$r = 4$	56.85*	39.78	162.4*	84.44
$r \leqslant 3$	100.29*	46.82	260.75*	111.01
$r \leqslant 2$	156.90*	51.91	422.1*	143.08
$r \leqslant 1$	161.18*	57.95	744.45*	177.20
$r = 0$	322.36*	63.75	1066.80*	215.74

Notes: * Indicates rejection of the null hypothesis at the 99.0% confidence level

** Indicates rejection of the null hypothesis at the 95.0% confidence level

$$T_t = 24.74 + 0.186(M_{1t}) + 1.05(ED_t) + 0.3012(FMS_t) - 0.2254(Tax_t) - 2.14(GDP_t) - 0.60(P_t) + 0.225(Trans_t) + 0.0001(D_t) + v_t \qquad 19.10$$

All of the coefficients in equation 19.10 are actually long-run elasticities. The policy variables of equation 19.10 provide unclear signals as to the impact of policy on income inequality. Even though monetary policy and transfer payments both reveal an inelastic impact on income inequality, the model indicates that each tends to be associated with increased inequality across time. This evidence is consistent with evidence provided by Haslag and Slottje (1994) in that transfer payments and money do affect the income distribution; however, the evidence calls into question the Danziger, Haveman and Plotnick (1981) argument that transfer payment have been sucessful in reducing inequality. The tax variable also has an inelastic impact and has the expected negative sign, which is somewhat surprising given the questionable progressivity of the federal income tax system.

The business conditions variables, real GDP, inflation, and the deficit all have the expected impact on inequality. However it should be noted that real GDP is the lone variable of the model that has an elastic impact on inequality. This result suggests that "a rising tide does indeed sail all ships." This result also helps to make sense of the Haslag and Slottje (1994) argument that identifies business cycle fluctuations or macroeconomic policy actions as a primary source of shocks affecting the income distribution.

The demographic variables education and female participation both have an inelastic impact on inequality, but both have unexpected positive signs suggesting that, as the work force becomes more educated and experienced, increased female participation inequality should rise. Both results may be implicitly capturing the impact of the between group labor supply effects on income inequality see O'Neill 1985.

The α coefficients, which can be thought of as the average speed of adjustment toward the equilibrium state, are given in equation 19.11. Large α values indicate rapid adjustment, and smaller α values reveal slow adjustment.

$$\alpha = (-0.45, -0.06, -3.52, -0.35, -0.05, -0.04, +0.23, +38.5) \qquad 19.11$$

The α coefficients suggest that the convergence to equilibrium is much faster for policy and business condition variables than for the demographic variables.

To further test the basic model, the likelihood ratio test recommended by Johansen and Juselius (1990) is used to examine the impact of each variable in the model. The likelihood ratio test has a X^2 distribution and compares the eigenvalues associated with a restricted model to those of the unrestricted model. The restricted model is derived by dropping one variable from the model and then re-estimating the cointegrating relationship. For example, $Trans_t$ is dropped from the model and eigenvalues are derived. The eigenvalues from this model are compared to those of the complete model. The test statistic is derived from the following equation:

$$(-2)\ln(Q) = T\sum_{i=1}^{r} \ln\{(1-\lambda_i^*)/(1-\lambda_i)\} \qquad 19.12$$

where λ_i^* are the r largest eigenvalues from the restricted model, and λ_i are the r largest eigenvalues from the complete model.

Table 19.3 reveals that for each variable in the model the null hypothesis of no significant difference between the restricted and unrestricted models is clearly rejected at beyond the 99.0% confidence level. These results imply that all variables employed in the model do indeed make a significant contribution. Thus, to eliminate any of the variables in the system would introduce omitted-variable bias.

CONCLUSIONS

One of the goals of this research was to examine the question of income inequality in a time series context using the latest technology available. The model contained demographic, business conditions, and policy variables. This research finds that most of the variables that have been hypothesized to influence inequality do indeed play a role in explaining variation in inequality across time. However, conventional wisdom as to the direction of influence of these variables is still open to question. Policy variables such as transfer payments, tax rates, and monetary growth affect inequality, but as Haslag and Slottje (1994) suggest, it is very difficult to separate the policy

Table 19.3 Likelihood ratio test for inequality model, estimation interval: 1952–89 (annual data)

	Test statistic value (0.95)	*Critical*
ED_t	234.5*	104.22
FMS_t	227.5*	104.22
Tax_t	224.7*	104.22
GDP_t	230.58*	104.22
P_t	235.2*	104.22
$Trans_t$	212.4*	104.22
D_t	245.9*	104.22
$M1t$	235.16*	104.22

Notes:
T_t = Theil index
Age_t = The working age population between 15 and 25 as a percentage of the total labor force minus 65 and over
ED_t = Percentage of population over 25 with four or more years of college
FMS_t = Number of women in the labor force divided by the total labor force
Tax_t = Marginal federal income tax rate
GDP_t = Real Gross Domestic Product
P_t = Inflation calculated from the CPI for urban consumers
D_t = Transfer payment from the Federal, State, and Local Governments
$Trans_t$ = Real Federal Deficit
*Indicates rejection of the null hypothesis at the 99% confidence level

variable impact from closely related impacts of business cycle conditions. The only clear signal emanating from the model results is that economic conditions as measured by real GDP do indeed have a significant impact on inequality. This result appears to suggest that economic growth may be the best medicine for the ills of the income distribution in the United States.

NOTES

1 The Gini coefficient is also used but the results are not significantly different for those obtained when the Theil measure is employed.
2 The method of cointegration examines long-term trends among economic variables across time. As the number of available observations increases the reliability of the results is enhanced.
3 Shorrock (1980), Bishop, Formby and Thistle (1989) and Slottje (1989) all discuss the set of qualities embodied in an income inequality measure.
4 Haslag and Taylor argue that the comparison between the Theil index and the Bluestone–Harrison result may be unfair given that the Theil index uses the IRS adjusted gross income data and Bluestone and Harrison used CPS data.
5 The literature on the impact of monetary policy on the distribution of income is less developed than the fiscal policy literature on this subject. However, two measures of monetary policy are employed in this study: narrowly defined M_1; and the federal funds rate. The results of the model which use M_1 are present in

the text because results were not appreciably different when the federal funds rate was substituted for M_1.

6 The time trend variable proved to be non-significant for all variables individually, i.e., b_2 is set equal to zero.

7 Not more than two lags were necessary to produce white noise in the residuals.

8 "VONE" is a vector of one which appears as a dependent variable in equation 19.8. This variable does not appear in equation 19.9 for obvious reasons.

REFERENCES

Beach, C. (1976) 'Cyclical Impact on the Personal Distribution of Income,' *Annals of Economic and Social Measurement* 5: p. 29–54.

Bishop, John, John Formby, and Paul Thistle (1989) 'Statistical Inference Income Distributions and Social Welfare,' in *Research on Income Inequality*, vol. 1, Daniel J. Slottje (ed.), Greenwich, CN: JAI Press, Inc., pp. 49–81.

Blanchard, Olivier Jean and Stanley Fisher (1989) *Lectures on Macroeconomics*, Cambridge MA: MIT Press.

Blinder, Alan S. and Howard Y. Esaki (1978) 'Macroeconomic Activity and Income Distribution in the Postwar United States,' *Review of Economics and Statistics* 60 (April): 604–7.

Bluestone, Barry and Bennett Harrison (1988) 'The Growth of Low-wage Employment, 1963–1986,' *American Economic Review* 78 (May): 124–8.

Burtless, Gary, (ed.) (1990) *A Future of Lousy Jobs*?, Washington DC: The Brookings Institution.

Danziger, Sheldon, Robert Haveman, and Plotnick, R. (1981) 'How Income Transfer Programs Affect Work, Savings, and the Income Distribution: A Critical Review,' *Journal of Economic Literature* 29 (September): 975–1028.

Dickey, D. A. and W. A. Fuller (1979) 'Distribution of the Estimators Autoregressive Time Series with a Unit Root,' *Journal of the American Statistical Association*: 427–31.

Dickey, David A., Dennis W. Jansen, and Daniel L. Thornton (1991) 'A Primer on Cointegration with an Application to Money and Income,' Federal Reserve Bank of St. Louis, *Review*, (March/April), vol. 73, no. 2, pp. 58–78.

Engle, R. F. and C. W. J. Granger (1987) 'Co-integration and Error-Correction: Representation, Estimation and Testing,' *Econometrica*: 176–255.

Freeman, Richard B. (1976) *The Overeducated American*, New York: Academic Press.

Granger, C. W. J. (1986) 'Developments in the Study of Co-integrated Economic Variables,' *Oxford Bulletin of Economics and Statistics*: 213–28.

Granger, C. W. J. and P. Newbold (1974) 'Spurious Regressions in Econometrics,' *Journal of Econometrics*: 111–20.

Granger, C. W. J. and A. A. Weiss (1983) 'Time Series Analysis of Error-Correcting Models,' in *Studies in Econometrics. Time Series Multivariate Statistics*, New York: Academic Press, pp. 255–78.

Haslag, Joseph H. and Daniel J. Slottje (1994) 'Cyclical Fluctuations, Macroeconomic Policy and the Size Distribution of Income: Some Preliminary Evidence,' *Journal of Income Distribution* 4 (1): 3–23.

Haslag, Joseph H. and Lori Taylor (1993) 'A Look at Long-term Developments in the Distribution of Income,' *Economic Review* Federal Reserve Bank of Dallas, (January): 19–30.

Johansen, Soren, (1988) 'Statistical Analysis of Cointegration Vectors,' *Journal of Economic Dynamics and Control*: 231–54.

Johansen, Soren and K. Juselius (1990) 'Maximum Likelihood Estimation and Inference on Cointegration – With Applications to the Demand for Money,' *Oxford Bulletin of Economics and Statistics*: 169–210.

Levy, Frank and Michel, Richard C. (1987) 'Understanding the Low Wage Jobs Debate,' Urban Institute, Mimeo, (September).

Maddison, Angus, (1987) 'Growth and Slowdown in Advanced Capitalist Economies: Techniques of Quantitative Assessment,' *Journal of Economic Literature*, (June): 649–98.

Metcalf, Charles E. (1972) *An Econometric Model of Income Distribution*, Chicago: Markham.

Miller, Herman P. (1966) *Income Distribution in the United States*, Washington, DC Bureau of the Census, US GPO.

Mincer, Jacob, (1970) 'The Distribution of Labor Incomes: A Survey with Special Reference to the Human Capital Approach,' *Journal of Economic Literature*, (March) 8(1): 1–26.

O'Neill, June (1985) 'The Trend in the Male–Female Wage Gap in the United States,' *Journal of Labor Economics* (January): 3(1, part 2) S91–S116.

Schultz, T. Paul (1969) 'Secular Trends and Cyclical Behavior of Income Distributions in US 1944–1965,' in L. Solow (ed.), *Six Papers on the Size Distribution of Income*.

Shorrock, Anthony (1980) 'The Class of Additive Decomposable Inequality Measures,' *Econometrica* 48 (April): 613–16, 26.

Slottje, Daniel J. (1989) *The Structure of Earnings and the Measurement of Income Inequality in the US*, Amsterdam: North Holland.

Stock, J. H. and Watson, Mark W. (1988) 'Testing Common Trends,' *Journal of American Statistical Association*, 83: 1097–107.

Welch, Finis (1969) 'Linear Synthesis of Skill Distribution,' *Journal of Human Resources*, (Summer): 4(3) 311–27.

INDEX

Note: numbers in *italic* refer to data in tables